ARGENTINA

3RD EDITION

Where to Stay and Eat
for All Budgets

Must-See Sights
and Local Secrets

Ratings You Can Trust

Portions of this book appear in *Fodor's South America*

Fodor's Travel Publications   New York, Toronto, London, Sydney, Auckland
www.fodors.com

FODOR'S ARGENTINA
Editor: Carissa Bluestone

Editorial Production: Ira-Neil Dittersdorf, Kristin Milavec
Editorial Contributors: Eddy Ancinas, Diego Bigongiari, Brian Byrnes, Michael de Zayas, Robin S. Goldstein, Satu Hummasti, Victoria Patience
Maps: David Lindroth *cartographer;* Bob Blake and Rebecca Baer, *map editors*
Design: Fabrizio La Rocca, *creative director;* Guido Caroti, *art director;* Melanie Marin, *senior picture editor*
Production/Manufacturing: Robert B. Shields
Cover Photo (Andes Mountains, Patagonia): John Warden/Superstock

SPECIAL SALES
This book is available for special discounts for bulk purchases for sales promotions or premiums. Special editions, including personalized covers, excerpts of existing books, and corporate imprints, can be created in large quantities for special needs. For more information, write to Special Markets/Premium Sales, 1745 Broadway, MD 6-2, New York, New York 10019, or e-mail specialmarkets@randomhouse.com

AN IMPORTANT TIP & AN INVITATION
Although all prices, opening times, and other details in this book are based on information supplied to us at press time, changes occur all the time in the travel world, and Fodor's cannot accept responsibility for facts that become outdated or for inadvertent errors or omissions. So **always confirm information when it matters,** especially if you're making a detour to visit a specific place. Your experiences—positive and negative—matter to us. If we have missed or misstated something, **please write to us.** We follow up on all suggestions. Contact the Argentina editor at editors@fodors.com or c/o Fodor's at 1745 Broadway, New York, New York 10019.

PRINTED IN THE UNITED STATES OF AMERICA

10 9 8 7 6 5 4 3 2 1

DESTINATION ARGENTINA

Think of Argentina as South America's Big Sky Country. Here, gauchos work ranches that sprawl over every horizon, and the windswept reaches of Patagonia roll on forever and a few miles more. But think of it also as electric Buenos Aires, a city of Paris-inspired boulevards, bustling plazas, and a patchwork of historical neighborhoods that offer vibrant nightlife and an intense spirit found in few other places. And the country's treasures extend far beyond the bustling capital: the southern coast has carnaval-like beach resorts, while the remote Northwest has adobe hamlets nestled among vibrantly colored mountains. Nature takes a dramatic turn at the Cataratas de Iguazú in the Northeast, where water meets gravity symphonically in the form of more than 270 waterfalls. In the Mendoza and San Juan Provinces, the Andes tower above vineyards. Shopping, dining, skiing, culture, history—name your pleasure. You'll probably find it in Argentina, against some of the most beautiful natural backdrops on Earth. Have a fabulous trip!

Karen Cure, Editorial Director

CONTENTS

Maps

CloseUps

ABOUT THIS BOOK

There's no doubt that the best source for travel advice is a like-minded friend who's just been where you're headed. But with or without that friend, you'll have a better trip with a Fodor's guide in hand. Once you've learned to find your way around its pages, you'll be in great shape to find your way around your destination.

SELECTION — Our goal is to cover the best properties, sights, and activities in their category, as well as the most interesting communities to visit. We make a point of including local food-lovers' hot spots as well as neighborhood options, and we avoid all that's touristy unless it's really worth your time. You can go on the assumption that everything you read about in this book is recommended wholeheartedly by our writers and editors. Flip to On the Road with Fodor's to learn more about who they are. It goes without saying that no property mentioned in the book has paid to be included.

RATINGS — Orange stars ★ denote sights and properties that our editors and writers consider the very best in the area covered by the entire book. These, the best of the best, are listed in the Fodor's Choice section in the front of the book. Black stars ★ highlight the sights and properties we deem Highly Recommended, the don't-miss sights within any region. Fodor's Choice and Highly Recommended options in each region are usually listed on the title page of the chapter covering that region. Use the index to find complete descriptions. In cities, sights pinpointed with numbered map bullets ❶ in the margins tend to be more important than those without bullets.

SPECIAL SPOTS — Pleasures & Pastimes focuses on types of experiences that reveal the spirit of the destination. Watch for Off the Beaten Path sights. Some are out of the way, some are quirky, and all are worth your while. If the munchies hit while you're exploring, look for Need a Break? suggestions.

TIME IT RIGHT — Wondering when to go? Check On the Calendar up front and chapters' Timing sections for weather and crowd overviews and best days and times to visit.

SEE IT ALL — Use Fodor's exclusive Great Itineraries as a model for your trip. (For a good overview of the entire destination, follow those that begin the book, or mix regional itineraries from several chapters.) In cities, Good Walks guide you to important sights in each neighborhood; ☛ indicates the starting points of walks and itineraries in the text and on the map.

BUDGET WELL — Hotel and restaurant price categories from ¢ to $$$$ are defined in the opening pages of each chapter—expect to find a balanced selection for every budget. For attractions, we always give standard adult admission fees; reductions are usually available for children, students, and senior citizens. Look in Discounts & Deals in Smart Travel Tips for information on destination-wide ticket schemes. Want to pay with plastic? AE, D, DC, MC, V following restaurant and hotel listings indicate whether American Express, Discover, Diners Club, MasterCard, or Visa are accepted.

BASIC INFO	Smart Travel Tips lists travel essentials for the entire area covered by the book; city- and region-specific basics end each chapter. To find the best way to get around, *see* the transportation section; *see* individual modes of travel ("Car Travel," "Train Travel") for details. We assume you'll check Web sites or call for particulars.
ON THE MAPS	Maps throughout the book show you what's where and help you find your way around. Black and orange numbered bullets ❶ ① in the text correlate to bullets on maps.
BACKGROUND	In general, we give background information within the chapters in the course of explaining sights as well as in CloseUp boxes.
FIND IT FAST	Within the book, chapters are arranged in a roughly clockwise direction starting with Buenos Aires. Chapters are divided into small regions, within which towns are covered in logical geographical order; attractive routes and interesting places between towns are flagged as En Route. Heads at the top of each page help you find what you need within a chapter.
DON'T FORGET	Restaurants are open for lunch and dinner daily unless we state otherwise; we mention dress only when there's a specific requirement and reservations only when they're essential or not accepted— it's always best to book ahead. Hotels have private baths, phone, TVs, and air-conditioning and operate on the European Plan (a.k.a. EP, meaning without meals). We always list facilities but not whether you'll be charged extra to use them, so when pricing accommodations, find out what's included.
SYMBOLS	

Many Listings

★ Fodor's Choice
★ Highly recommended
⊠ Physical address
✢ Directions
🏚 Mailing address
☎ Telephone
🖷 Fax
⊕ On the Web
🖎 E-mail
🎫 Admission fee
☉ Open/closed times
► Start of walk/itinerary
Ⓜ Metro stations
☵ Credit cards

Outdoors

🏌 Golf
⚠ Camping

Hotels & Restaurants

🏨 Hotel
🛏 Number of rooms
♨ Facilities
🍴 Meal plans
✕ Restaurant
🍽 Reservations
🏛 Dress code
🚬 Smoking
🍷 BYOB
✕🏨 Hotel with restaurant that warrants a visit

Other

🅒 Family-friendly
🛈 Contact information
⇨ See also
⊠ Branch address
☞ Take note

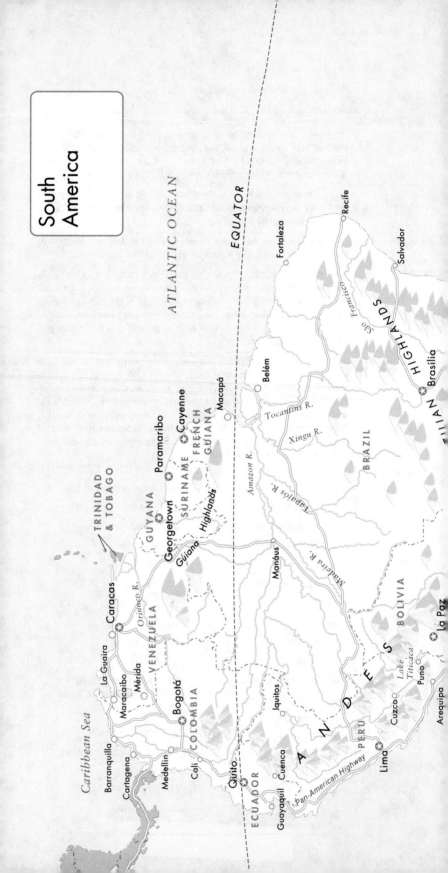

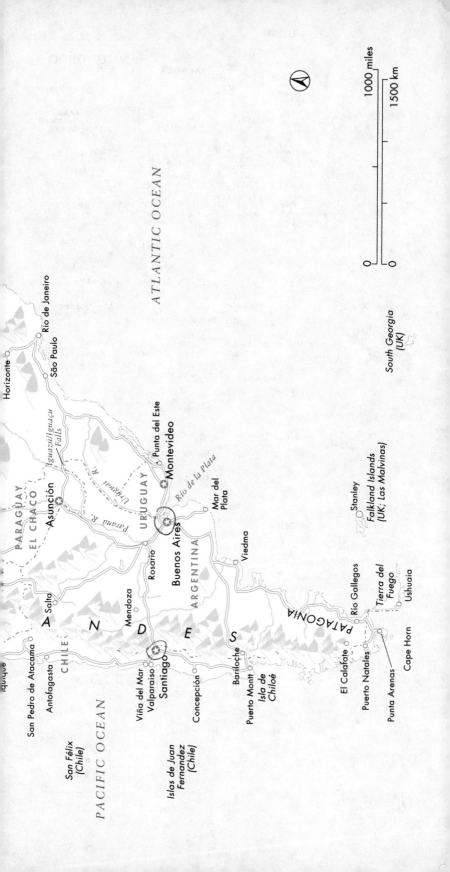

ON THE ROAD WITH FODOR'S

A trip takes you out of yourself. Concerns of life at home completely disappear, driven away by more immediate thoughts—about, say, what marvels await the next day, or where you'll have dinner. That's where Fodor's comes in. We make sure that you know all your options, so that you don't miss something that's around the next bend just because you didn't know it was there. Because the best memories of your trip might well have nothing to do with what you came to Argentina to see, we guide you to sights large and small all over the region. You might set out to learn to tango or tour the wine country, but back at home you find yourself unable to forget watching glaciers shed icicles in Patagonia or taking a train ride into the clouds in the Northwest. With Fodor's at your side, serendipitous discoveries are never far away.

Our success in showing you every corner of Argentina is a credit to our extraordinary writers. Although there's no substitute for travel advice from a good friend who knows your style, our contributors are the next best thing—the kind of people you would poll for travel advice if you knew them.

Eddy Ancinas was one of the authors of the first edition of *Fodor's Argentina*; she updated Destination: Argentina, the Cuyo, and Andean Patagonia for this edition. Eddy met an Argentine ski racer at the 1960 Winter Olympics; after they were married in 1962, they traveled and lived in Argentina. Since then, she has led ski and horseback trips in Peru, Argentina, and Chile, and has written about skiing and adventure travel in these countries.

After living in Europe and spending several years as deck officer on Swiss cargo ships, **Diego Bigongiari** settled near Buenos Aires, where he now works as a freelance writer and translator. In the 1990s he wrote best-selling Spanish-language travel guides to Buenos Aires, Argentina, and Uruguay. He updated the Northeast chapter.

Brian Byrnes has worked as a freelance journalist in Buenos Aires since 2001. His radio reports can be heard on CBS Radio News, National Public Radio (NPR), Australian Broadcasting Corp. (ABC), and Voice of America. He has also written for the *Washington Post, Christian Science Monitor, Baltimore Sun,* and others. Brian updated Exploring Buenos Aires and Smart Travel Tips for this book.

Michael de Zayas, a Cuban-American writer and poet, updated Atlantic Patagonia for this book. A frequent traveler to South America, he covered the Pampas and Buenos Aires nightlife for the previous edition of Argentina; he's also worked on Fodor's guides to Uruguay, Chile, Cuba, Mexico, the Caribbean, Central America, the Bahamas, and New York City, among others. His travel experiences inspired him to create a successful clothing company, Neighborhoodies.com, which he runs from his home base in Brooklyn.

Although **Robin S. Goldstein** trained in philosophy at Harvard and law at Yale, his heart has always been in travel and food writing. His credits include many editions of *Fodor's Italy* and stints in Spain, Mexico, Ecuador, and the Galapagos Islands. He is also the author of *The Menu,* the first restaurant guide to New Haven, Connecticut. He updated the Northwest and the Buenos Aires Province & Córdoba chapters.

Victoria Patience, who updated the Where to Eat, Where to Stay, Nightlife & the Arts, Sports & the Outdoors, and Shopping sections of the Buenos Aires chapter, has been hooked on the city since she first laid eyes on it. She studied Spanish and Latin American literature at the University of London and traveled throughout Mexico, Colombia, Peru, Bolivia, and Chile before going to Argentina to spend a year at the University of Buenos Aires. Three years later, she's still in the city—and has no plans to leave.

(1) Buenos Aires

The gateway to all the splendors of Argentina is the sophisticated and cosmopolitan capital city of Buenos Aires, on the banks of the Río de la Plata. Here in the Capital Federal, as this sprawling metropolis is known, 10 million people (one-third the population of Argentina) live in the city's 46 *barrios* (neighborhoods), each with its own soccer team and its own identity. Fashionably dressed *Porteños* make their way across wide boulevards, down crowded streets, and through leafy parks. This is the place to shop in chic boutiques, dine in eclectic restaurants, revel in first-class museums and theaters, and learn the tango.

(2) Buenos Aires Province & Córdoba

Beaches along the coast are crowded with Buenos Aires locals on week-ends; some are casual and family-friendly and others attract jet-setters the world over. Surrounding Buenos Aires, though worlds apart, are the flat, expansive grasslands of Las Pampas, which radiate to the Atlantic Ocean in the east and the mountains to the west. This is the home of the horses and cattle that make up the mainstay of the region's—and Argentina's—economy. Signs of active ranch life are everywhere, from the cattle grazing to the gauchos working the wide-open landscape. Alfalfa, sunflowers, wheat, and corn are grown in the rich topsoil. Córdoba is the nation's historic second city, and the countryside surrounding it is marked by mountains and is dotted with Jesuit estates.

(3) The Northeast

The northeast region of the country is dominated by two rivers: the Uruguay and the Paraná. Across the Río Paraná to the north lies Paraguay, and across the Río Uruguay to the east are Brazil and Uruguay. The two great rivers finally meet at the southernmost point of the region, right above Buenos Aires, where they form the famous Río de la Plata. The topography of the region varies considerably: flat, fertile plains extend through the south; lagoons and marshlands are found near the center; dry, desolate land covers much of the west; and subtropical forest fills the northeastern corner, also home to the Cataratas del Iguazú, the impressive system of waterfalls that straddle Argentina and Brazil.

(4) The Northwest

The Northwest is where Argentine history began, yet few have ventured beyond its cities—Catamarca, Jujuy, Salta, and Tucumán—to its high-mountain passes, deep red gorges, peaceful valleys, and sub-tropical jungles. In the northernmost province of Jujuy, a polychromatic palette of reds, greens, and yellows washes across the mountain slopes of the Quebrada Humahuaca (Humahuaca Gorge) as it follows the Río Grande north. The great high plateau of the Puna stretches along the borders with Bolivia and Chile. A mixture of pre-Columbian and Spanish culture is apparent throughout in the architecture, costumes, festivals, music, and handicrafts. In the sunny Calchaquí Valley, between Tucumán and Salta, former colonial settlements dot the landscape amidst *Torrontés* (a white-wine grape) vineyards, and in the cities, the plazas and churches recall the Spanish influence. Even pre-Inca civilizations have left their marks on ghostly menhirs.

5 The Cuyo

Nestled in the shadow of the soaring Andes, the Cuyo was once a desert before irrigation transformed it into the fourth-largest wine-producing region in the world, Mendoza being the province with the greatest reputation. North of Mendoza, the slow-paced capital city of San Juan is the birthplace of Argentina's great educator, writer, and past president, Domingo Faustino Sarmiento. It's also the gateway to the curious paleontological treasures of the Parque Provincial Ischigualasto (Valley of the Moon). San Luís Province is home to the giant Parque Nacional las Quijadas. The Pan-American highway passes through Mendoza, heading west over spectacular Uspallata Pass to Chile: Along the way are hot springs, Inca ruins, Los Penitentes ski area, and an incomparable view of Aconcagua Mountain. Farther south near the city of San Rafael, you can raft down the Atuel or Diamante rivers, ride horseback over the Andes, or ski at the super resort of Las Leñas near Malargüe.

6 Patagonia

Argentine Patagonia extends 1,920 km (1,200 mi) along the spine of the Andes from Río Colorado in the north to Cape Horn—the southernmost land mass on the continent. Marine life on the Atlantic coast is abundant, exotic, and entertaining from Península Valdéz to Tierra del Fuego. On the eastern slopes of the Andes, high peaks rise above thousands of lakes, streams, glaciers, waterfalls, and ancient forests—most of them protected within five national parks in the area known as Andean Patagonia, or the Patagonian lake district. Bariloche, San Martín, and Esquel all have airports served by major airlines, and there are good bus connections to points in between. The main attraction of the southern lake district is the Parque Nacional los Glaciares near Calafate, and the Fitzroy mountains, which lie 230 km (142 mi) north. It's possible to link the two lake districts in one long adventurous drive on R40, known as "the loneliest road in the world."

GREAT ITINERARIES

Highlights of Argentina
18 days

From jungle falls to vineyards, mountain lakes to glaciers, and miles of air travel in between, you will see a lot of Argentina with this itinerary.

BUENOS AIRES 2 days. Every trip begins and ends in Buenos Aires, and should include a Sunday for a visit to the San Telmo market. After two days in the city, fly north to the country's border with Brazil and Paraguay.

IGUAZÚ FALLS 2 days. You can take a direct flight from Buenos Aires to Iguazú on either the Argentine or Brazilian side of the falls. You'll need two full days to fully appreciate of the world's largest—and most beautiful—waterfalls. Vapor spraying above the tree tops and a thunderous roar beckon you down a jungle path to discover a wall of water spilling over a wide horseshoe-shape ledge.

MENDOZA 3 days. After returning to Buenos Aires, catch a connecting flight to the wine country. Check into a downtown hotel and explore the city—on the city tour bus (you can hop on and off) or on foot. The tourist office provides maps. Spend the next day touring nearby wineries, and on your final day, rise early and drive up to the border with Chile and a view of the highest mountain in the western hemisphere.

BARILOCHE 6 days. On arrival and the first full day, enjoy the town, buy chocolate, visit the Civic Center, tourist office, and Patagonian museum. Leave time for an afternoon excursion to Llao Llao, stopping along the way for tea and cakes. The following day, catch a boat to Isla Victoria and the forest of Arrayanes trees, then enjoy Day 3 on land—either visiting Villa Angostura across the lake, or signing up for a horseback ride to Tronodor, a mountain bike ride from the ski area to Mascardi Lake, a float trip, fishing, or a hike. Crossing to Chile is a two-day trip by boat and bus to Puerto Montt, Chile, with a return by bus to Bariloche.

CALAFATE 3 days. On the first day, shop the main street for Patagonian souvenirs and sign up for trips to the glaciers (⇨ El Calafate, Chapter 6), visiting Upsala one day and Perito Moreno the next.

PENINSULA VALDÉZ 2 days. Fly to Trelew and experience the phenomenal variety of marine life, or continue north to Buenos Aires for your final two days.

By Public Transportation The great distances covered in this itinerary require air travel to all destinations. Check with travel and tour agents for direct flights from Iguazú to Mendoza and Mendoza to Bariloche, and which days you can fly Bariloche to Calafate, Calafate to Trelew.

Outdoor Adventures in the Andean Lake District
14 days

From November through March, rivers are full, wildflowers are in bloom and trails to pristine lakes, past waterfalls to high mountain glaciers await adventurous travelers of all ages. Cottages, cabins, hostals, mountain huts, or luxury resorts welcome weary hikers, and campsites are plentiful. Whether with family, friends, or on your own, you'll find many novel ways to explore three areas near Bariloche.

BARILOCHE 5 days. If you haven't planned your itinerary before arriving, on the first day visit the tourist office and tour companies that offer activities that interest you. Rafting the Río Manso can be an eight-hour outing with easy rapids through a unique ecosystem—or it can be a 13-hour excursion to the Chilean border or even a three-day trip, where you'll barrel down a deep canyon and camp on sandy beaches. Hikes and mountain bike tours come in all distances and degrees of difficulty. Serious hikers can boat across Masacardi Lake to Pampa Linda, then hike to the black glaciers of Tronodor, continuing up above timberline to Otto Meiling hut, spend the night, walk along the crest of the Andes with glacier views, then return to Pampa Linda. Day hikes to the foot of Tronodor leave more time for a mountain bike or horseback ride in the same area.

ESQUEL **3 days.** After driving south through Bolsón, take the detour to Los Alerces National Park, where you can camp or stay at an inn. Here you can rent a kayak or catch the boat across Lake Futalaufquen and hike through ancient redwood forests to the hanging Torrecillos glacier. On the third day, continue on to Esquel, making that your headquarters for rafting either the Corcovado River (easy) or the Futaleufú (more challenging) to Chile.

SAN MARTÍN DE LOS ANDES **5 days.** After an overnight in Bariloche, drive the seven lake route to San Martín de Los Andes, stopping for lunch or a picnic on Lago Trafú. A three-day mountain bike trip starts at the Hua Hum pass on the Chilean border, where you ride down to the lake, cross in a ferry, and continue on to another pass. On Day 4, it's into the hot-springs—both in Chile and Argentina, then back through the forests and around the lakes to San Martín. Combination bike–canoe trips and horseback–rafting trips lead to lakes and lagoons, through silent forests and lofty mountain tops.

By Public Transportation Buses leave Bariloche for El Bolsón, Esquel, and San Martín daily, and tour buses can be arranged from Esquel or El Bolsón to Los Alerces National Park. Renting a car gives you the freedom to take detours and stop for picnics and photos. Guided tours are recommended for most activities, as they will get you to and from trailheads, lakes, and river put-ins; provide equipment; prepare meals (often an asado); and share their love of the land with you.

Scenic Wine Routes of Mendoza
10 days

You can begin your wine tour in either Mendoza or San Rafael, depending on airline schedules, and take a bus or rental car in between the two cities. Harvest time is around the end of February or early March. Trucks loaded with grapes crowd the highways, and pickers arrive by bus from Chile, Ecuador, and Peru. *Vendimia,* the local wine festival, takes place the first week of March. Hotel rooms in Mendoza are scarce at this time, as parades clog the otherwise peaceful streets, and open stalls in the city parks sell homemade food and craft items. You may want to avoid this week for the crowds or embrace it for its local color.

SAN RAFAEL **2 days.** Quiet tree-lined streets and a slow pace make this country town seem like a mini-Mendoza, although there is no doubt the town and its friendly inhabitants have their own identity. Family-run vineyards (mostly Italian descent, some Swiss) bask in the warm sun of this southern wine-growing region. There are plenty of attractions nearby to augment wine tours. Valentín Bianchi, one of Argentina's largest wine producers, exports Malbec, cabernet, chardonnay, and sparkling wines to the United States and Europe, but it's the impressive champagne operation that draws wine enthusiasts to its modern facility with landscaped plazas, gardens, and fountains. Suter, a Swiss pioneer family, probably planted the first vineyards in South America. Now in their fourth generation, three brothers maintain its spotless bodega and six vineyards. Balbi, Lavaque, and Simonassi Lyon are other bodegas you can visit.

TUPUNGATO & THE UCO VALLEY **3 days.** After crossing the desert, the foothills of the Andes rise up to the often snow-covered pre-cordillera, culminating in the white dome of Tupungato volcano, which reigns serene above a sea of vineyards. Names like Catena, Chandon, La Rural, and Trapiche testify to the fact that you are in one of the great grape-growing areas of the world. The ultra-modern dutch-owned Salentein Bodega has a nearby inn, or you can stay at the grand old Chateau d'Ancon. Both these places will help plan your wine tours. More independent types can stay in town and use the tourist office.

MENDOZA **5 days.** Enjoy one day exploring the tree-lined streets and plazas of this lovely city, taking time out for an afternoon siesta. Most tours arranged through tour offices begin with a program on wine production and a wine-tasting class at the *Centro de Bodequeros* (Bodega owners center), followed by dinner and wine-pairing. Wine tours from two to five days will take you to two or three wineries a day in seven regions around Mendoza, with lavish lunches, dinners, music, and other diversions. The tourist office has a booklet with a map of the different areas, and which bodegas are open for tourists.

By Public Transportation San Rafael and Mendoza have airports with flights to Buenos Aires. You can take a bus to Tupungato and use local tours in all three locations. Local buses in Mendoza are confusing, but taxis are cheap. A remise can be hired for the day for a private (or shared) tour. Renting a car in Mendoza and driving to the Uco Valley to San Rafael gives you the freedom to linger at the bodegas or take sight-seeing trips off the beaten path.

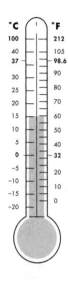

If you're heading to the Lake District or Patagonia and want good weather without the crowds, the shoulder seasons of December and March are the months to visit.

Climate

Because of the great variety of latitudes, altitudes, and climatic zones in Argentina, you're likely to encounter many different climates during any given month. The most important thing to remember is the most obvious—when it's summer in the northern hemisphere, it's winter in Argentina, and vice versa. Winter in Argentina stretches from July to October, and summer settles in from December to March.

The sea moderates temperatures in the coastal region of Argentina, while the mountains do so for the hinterland. Winter can be chilly and rainy, although average winter temperatures are usually above freezing in the coastal cities (it hasn't snowed in Buenos Aires in more than 100 years).

If you can handle the heat (January–February temperatures usually range in the high 90s to low 100s [35°C–40°C]), Buenos Aires can be wonderful in summer, which peaks in January. At this time, the traditional vacation period, Argentines are crowding inland resorts and Atlantic beaches, but Buenos Aires has no traffic, and a host of city-sponsored events and concerts takes place, bringing city dwellers out into the sun and moonlight.

In January a few businesses shut down and others may have reduced hours in the provinces, though this does not apply for major cities. Government offices close for January, but this should not affect your vacation.

If you have an aversion to large crowds, avoid visiting popular resort areas in January and February and in July, when they become overcrowded again due to school holidays.

Spring and fall—the most temperate seasons—are excellent times to visit Argentina. It's usually warm enough (over 50°F) for just a light jacket, and it's right before or after the peak (and expensive) tourist season.

The best time to visit the Iguazú Falls is August–October, when temperatures are lower and the spring coloring is at its brightest. Rain falls all year, dropping about 80 inches annually. Bring a lightweight waterproof jacket for this reason.

Resort towns such as Bariloche and San Martín de los Andes are packed during the peak winter season. Summer temperatures can get up into the high 70s (about 25°C), but most of the year, the range is from the 30s to the 60s (0°C–20°C).

The Patagonia coast is on the infamous latitude that sailors call the "Roaring Forties," with southern seas that batter Patagonia throughout the year. Thirty-mile-per-hour winds are common, and 100-mile-per-hour gales are not unusual. Summer daytime temperatures reach the low 80s (about 28°C) but can drop suddenly to the 50s (10°C–15°C). Winters hover near the freezing mark.

Most travelers visit Tierra del Fuego in summer, when temperatures range from the 40s to the 60s (5°C–20°C). Fragments of glaciers cave into southern lakes with a rumble throughout the thaw from October to the end of April, which is the best time to enjoy the show.

🗂 Forecasts **Servicio Meteorológico Nacional** (National Weather Service for Argentina) ☎ 11/4514-4248 automated information ⊕ www.meteofa.mil.ar has information in Spanish. **Weather Channel Connection** ☎ 900/932-8437, 95¢ per minute from a Touch-Tone phone ⊕ www.weather.com.

BUENOS AIRES

Jan.	85F	29C	May	64F	18C	Sept.	64F	18C
	63	17		47	8		46	8
Feb.	83F	28C	June	57F	14C	Oct.	69F	21C
	63	17		41	5		50	10
Mar.	79F	26C	July	57F	14C	Nov.	76F	24C
	60	16		42	6		56	13
Apr.	72F	22C	Aug.	60F	16C	Dec.	82F	28C
	53	12		43	6		61	16

BARILOCHE

Jan.	70F	21C	May	50F	10C	Sept.	50F	10C
	46	6		36	2		34	1
Feb.	70F	21C	June	45F	7C	Oct.	52F	11C
	46	8		34	1		37	3
Mar.	64F	18C	July	43F	6C	Nov.	61F	16C
	43	6		32	0		41	5
Apr.	57F	14C	Aug.	46F	8C	Dec.	64F	18C
	39	4		32	0		45	7

ON THE CALENDAR

Argentina's top seasonal events are listed below, and any one of them could provide the stuff of lasting memories. If you want your visit to coincide with one of these occasions, be sure to plan well in advance. Remember that Argentina's seasons are the reverse of those in North America.

SUMMER

December

Trelew, in Patagonia, celebrates the Fiesta Provincial del Pinguino (Provincial Festival of the Penguin).

January

Cosquín, near Córdoba, is the home of the Festival Nacional de Folklore (National Festival of Folklore), held the last week of January in the Plaza Próspero Molina. At the same time, the town hosts the Festival Provincial de las Artesanias (Provincial Festival of Artisans), during which craftspeople from all over the province come to sell their wares. During the second week in January, Viedma and Carmen de Patagones host the Regata del Río Negro, a race of boats from around the region.

February

Every year during the second week of February, Camarones, in Patagonia, hosts the Fiesta Nacional de Salmon (National Salmon Festival), with festivities and a fishing contest.

FALL

March

In Viedma and Carmen de Patagones, March 7 begins the annual, weeklong Fiesta de Soberania y la Tradición, during which the towns celebrate their defeat of Brazil in an 1827 incursion, with music, food, crafts, and cultural exhibits. Mendoza celebrates the Festival de La Vendimia, the grape-harvest festival, during the first week of March. Parades, folk dancing, and fireworks take place, and the crowning of a queen marks the grand finale in the huge amphitheater in Parque General San Martín.

WINTER

June

In the Northwest, Inti Raymi (Festival of the Sun) is celebrated on June 20, the night before winter solstice, when the sun is thanked for last year's harvest. On June 17, when the Salta Gaucho Parade takes place, hundreds of gauchos *Salteños* ride into Salta in full gaucho regalia: big, wide wraparound leather chaps (for the thorny bushes that grow in the region); black boots; *bombachas* (baggy pants); knife tucked into their belts; and their signature red-and-black ponchos. The nation's best folk artists hold forth in outdoor *peñas*.

July

The Fiesta del Poncho (Gaucho Festival) takes place in Catamarca for a week in July: artisans from all over the province exhibit and sell their best weavings, baskets, ceramics, and wood carvings, and folk singers perform in the evening. In Tucumán, Día de Independencia (Independence Day) is celebrated with much fervor on July 9. In July, Bariloche hosts the Fiesta de las Colectividades (Party of Different Communities), a celebration of the town's diversity; dancing, music, handicrafts, and food from Europe, Scandinavia, the Middle East, Central Europe, and South America are represented.

August	Pachamama (Mother Earth) is celebrated August 1 in Humahuaca, in Jujuy Province. On August 22, Jujuy celebrates the Semana de Jujuy (Jujuy Week) with a reenactment of the great 1812 exodus: citizens dress in period costumes and ride their horses or carts through town; hotels are usually booked up during this week. The Fiesta Nacional de la Nieve (National Snow Festival) is a monthlong winter carnival that takes place in August all over Bariloche and at the Catedrál ski area.

SPRING

September	On September 24, Tucumán celebrates the Battle of Tucumán, commemorating Belgrano's victory over the Spanish during the War of Independence. One of Trelew's major cultural events is the Eisteddfod de la Juventud in early September, which celebrates the music, food, and dance of Welsh tradition. During Bariloche's Semana Musical Llao Llao (Llao Llao Musical Week) in September, international soloists and orchestras perform classical, jazz, and tango music at the Llao Llao Hotel & Resort.
October	Belen de Escobar (known as the national flower capital) holds a flower exhibition during October. The Festival Nacional de la Cerveza (National Beer Festival, or Oktoberfest) takes place in the town of Villa General Belgrano, which was originally settled by Bavarian and Alsatian immigrants. The second half of October marks Trelew's Eisteddfod de Chubut, a Welsh literary and musical festival, first held in Patagonia in 1875.
November	In mid-November, San Antonio de Areco hosts the weeklong Fiesta de la Tradióon, a celebration of the area's gaucho past. Each year in late November, San Clemente del Tuyu hosts the festival of its patron saint, San Clemente Romano. The entire city comes out to see the procession, which ends in a huge asado.

PLEASURES & PASTIMES

The Distinctive Cuisine

Argentina is basically a steak-and-potatoes country. The beef is so good, most Argentines see little reason to eat anything else, though pork, lamb, and chicken are tasty alternatives, and *civito* (kid), when in season, is outstanding. *Carne asado* (roasted meat) usually means grilled *a la parrilla* (on a grill over hot coals), but it can also be baked in an oven or slowly roasted at an outdoor barbecue (*asado*). Here, the meat is attached to a metal spit (*asador*), which is stuck in the ground aslant on a bed of hot coals. A *tira de asado* (strip of rib roast), skewered on its own spit, often accompanies the asado.

A *parrillada mixta* (mixed grill) is the quintessential Argentine meal for two or more. Families gather for noon *parrilladas* (grills) in restaurants and backyards across the country. They choose from different cuts of beef, which come sizzling on a portable grill delivered to your table along with french fries cooked on a hot skillet (not submerged in oil).

Beyond beef, many Argentine dishes are influenced by other cultures. Pasta, pizza, and Italian specialties are on every menu in almost all restaurants. Fish has not been a favored dish in this meat-loving country, even though trout and salmon from lakes and streams yield both quality and quantity and *centolla* (giant crab) and *mejillones* (mussels) are trapped offshore in Ushuaia.

Argentines tend to ignore vegetables, except for salads, which usually include shredded carrots, tomatoes, onions, cabbage, and cucumbers. Ask for *aceite de olivo* (olive oil) or you'll get corn oil for your salad. Not to be missed, when available, is the white asparagus that grows south of Buenos Aires. Vegetables and fruits are fresh, crisp, and flavorful in their seasons—no need for hothouse assistance in this country.

Ecotourism

In Argentina, where climates range from tropical to subantarctic and altitudes descend from 22,000 feet to below sea-level, every conceivable environment on Earth is represented: high, low, hot, cold, temperate, dry, wet, and frozen. Because the population (about 40 million) is small relative to its land mass (roughly 2,000 mi long and 900 mi wide), plants, birds, and animals thrive undisturbed in their habitats.

Along the South Atlantic coast, sea mammals mate and give birth on empty beaches and in protected bays. Guanaco, rhea, and native deer travel miles over isolated Andean trails and across windswept plains. Birds are everywhere—passing above in clouds of thousands, descending on a lagoon like a blanket of feathers, or rising in a flutter of pink flamingos.

Iguazú Falls National Park protects 2,000 species of vascular plants, thousands of butterflies and moths, more than 400 bird species, 100 mammals, and countless amphibia and insects—many of which have not been identified. Nature trails disappear into a greenhouse of intertwined lianas, creepers, epiphytes, bamboo, and hanging gardens of orchids and bromeliads.

An organic carpet of decaying branches, leaves, and bushes nourish mushrooms, mosses, and countless plants struggling for light.

In the north central region, the Gran Chaco encompasses hundreds of miles of marshes and jungle teeming with monkeys, reptiles, land mammals, waterfowl, birds, and fish. Farther east in Corrientes Province, the Esteros de Iberá (Ibera marshlands) create a green labyrinth of swamps, lagoons, islets, and seas of grass, where endangered species of swamp deer, maned wolves, and golden alligators live with other exotic creatures: caiman, boa constrictors, anaconda, piranhas, capybara, tapir, and coati, to name a few.

Local guides in each region can explain the importance of every plant, spider, and insect (except, perhaps, the mosquito) and its particular ecodependency on the millions of plants and animals, seen and unseen, around you.

Love of the Game

River Plate, Boca Juniors, Maradona, Bautistuta—these names are as familiar to Argentines as the Dodgers, Yankees, and Red Sox are to Americans. They are the subject of fiery dispute, suicidal despair, love, hate, pride, and all the emotions that soccer arouses in this nation whose blue-and-white striped jerseys have flashed across TV screens since it won the 1978 and 1986 World Championships. Nothing can lift the spirits of the nation like a soccer victory. (Rugby, too, attracts thousands of fans to stadiums and practice fields across the country.)

Polo, like soccer, was introduced by the British. Natural riding skills and an abundance of good horses quickly produced the world's top players, who, like soccer players, are paid enormous sums to compete for foreign teams. Argentine polo ponies, known for their quickness, intelligence, and strength, are sold the world over, as are race, show-jumping, and dressage horses. The best polo matches occur in Buenos Aires (in November), as do other equestrian events such as horse racing, show jumping, and dressage, which attract dedicated devotees both local and international.

Sports & the Outdoors

Fishing in the the national parks of Patagonia's northern lake district (especially around Bariloche) is legendary. Either hire a local guide or stay a week in a rustic fishing lodge and enjoy the pristine lakes and streams jumping with trout and salmon. Hiking and mountain biking in Argentina's national and provincial parks—over mountain trails, and through forests to lakes, villages, and campgrounds—provide unique memories of an abundant and vast wilderness. If you're a serious mountaineer, you know the challenges of Aconcagua (in Mendoza Province) and Cerro Fitzroy, Mt. Tronadór, and Lanín Volcano in Patagonia. The Club 'Andinos (Andean Mountaineering Clubs) in Bariloche, Mendoza, Ushuaia, and other towns organize national and international excursions.

Since Argentina's seasons are the opposite of North America's, you can ski or snowboard from June to September. Las Leñas near Mendoza (in the Cuyo), Catedral near Bariloche, and Chapelco near San Martín de los Andes (in Patagonia) are some of the best ski areas. These areas offer groomed runs, open bowls, and trails that follow the fall line to cozy inns or luxurious hotels. Smaller areas near Bariloche, Esquel, and Mendoza have good day facilities and lodgings in the towns. Tierra Mayor, a family-run Nordic center near Ushuaia has such novelties as dogsled rides, snowcat trips, and wind skiing.

Wine

Given the high consumption of beef rather than fish, Argentines understandably drink a lot of *vino tinto* (red wine); Malbec and Cabernet are the most popular. If you prefer *vino blanco* (white wine), try a sauvignon blanc or chardonnay from Mendoza, or lesser-known wineries from farther north, such as La Rioja and Salta, where the Torrontés grape thrives. This varietal produces a dry white with a lovely floral bouquet. A popular summer cooler is *clericot,* a white version of sangría (available in some restaurants), made with strawberries, peaches, oranges, or whatever fruits are in season.

FODOR'S CHOICE

The sights, restaurants, hotels, and other travel experiences on these pages are our editors' top picks—our Fodor's Choices. They're the best of their type in the area covered by the book—not to be missed and always worth your time. In the destination chapters that follow, you can find all the details.

LODGING

$$$$	**Hostería Los Notros, Patagonia.** Eat, sleep, and wake in plain view of Glaciar Moreno while you stay in rustic luxury near El Calafate.
$$$$	**Llao Llao Hotel & Resort, near Bariloche.** This first-class resort in Patagonia sits on a hill between two lakes and is surrounded by snow-clad peaks.
$$$$	**Marriott Plaza Hotel, Buenos Aires.** The capital's first grand hotel draws illustrious guests.
$$$$	**Posada Aguapé, Colonia Carlos Pellegrini.** This small inn by a lake in the Northeast takes a creative approach to the traditional guest house.
$$$$	**Sheraton Internacional Cataratas de Iguazú.** Have breakfast or a drink on a balcony overlooking the falls—and be sure to ask for a room with a view.
$$$–$$$$	**Hotel Correntoso, Villa La Angostura.** From its perch overlooking Nahuel Huapi Lake, you can watch the fish jump at this hotel steeped in Patagonian tradition.
$$$–$$$$	**Posada San Eduardo, Barreal.** After a day of active outdoor adventures, the yellow adobe is an oasis of peace, where evenings are shared with new friends and good wine.
$$$	**Estancia Cerro de la Cruz, The Pampas.** This quiet ranch near Sierra de la Ventana has its own private mountain and a jeep to cover its vast property.
$$$	**Hotel y Resort Las Hayas, Ushuaia.** Pampering amenities abound at this Patagonian hotel and spa nestled in the foothills of the Andes.
$$$	**NH Jousten, Buenos Aires.** The latest in boutique chic is in a restored 1930s building.
$$	**El Manantial del Silencio, Purmamarca.** Tranquility and tasteful luxury are surrounded here by cactus-studded red rock cliffs.

BUDGET LODGING

$	**Hotel El Lagar, Salta.** Plush amenities and colonial art await inside this cozy bed-and-breakfast.

RESTAURANTS

$$$	**Cabaña las Lilas, Buenos Aires.** Robust wines complement succulent steaks from this handsome restaurant's own cattle ranch.
$$$	**Tomo Uno, Buenos Aires.** Three decades of imaginative interpretations of classic Argentine dishes have made this restaurant the best known in Buenos Aires.

$$-$$$	1884 Restaurante, Mendoza. The gracious stone halls of a century-old bodega provide the backdrop for sensational Argentine haute cuisine.
$-$$	El Trapiche, Buenos Aires. This friendly neighborhood grill serves up huge portions of traditional Argentine fare.
$-$$	La Nietáe La Pancha, Córdoba. This intimate little restaurant is a temple to creative Córdoban food—even the menu is in the local dialect.

BUDGET RESTAURANTS

¢–$	Almacen de Ramos Generales, Buenos Aires Province. You won't find a better *bife de chorizo* (sirloin steak) than at this elegant restaurant, which remembers its country-store roots.
¢–$	El Viejo Molino, Trelew. This converted 1886 mill defines fun, sophisticated dining in a city where you'd never expect to find it.
¢–$	Manos Jujeñas, San Salvador de Jujuy. Perhaps the best place in the entire region to sample locro, the typical Andean stew, this restaurant in the center of Jujuy is warm, atmospheric, and even inexpensive.

HISTORIC SIGHTS & MUSEUMS

Calle Museo Caminito, Buenos Aires. Vibrant scenes of colorful buildings, tango dancers, and artisans at work fill this pedestrian-only street.

Cementerio de La Recoleta, Buenos Aires. A veritable who's who of Argentine history, this city of the dead is filled with elaborate mausoleums.

Museo Marítimo, Ushuaia. A museum in part of Tierra del Fuego's original penal colony sheds light on Patagonia's and Argentina's past.

Museo Paleontológico, Trelew. You can marvel at dinosaur bones and other fossils, and watch archaeologists at work at this impressive paleontology museum.

San Ignacio Miní, Northeast. These are the most stunning and well-preserved remains of the many Jesuit missions that thrived in Argentina more than 200 years ago.

San Telmo, Buenos Aires. Cobblestone streets and colonial buildings keep a sense of history alive in this neighborhood.

NATURAL WONDERS

Bosque Petrificado José Ormaechea, Patagonia. The wood is 65 million years old in this eerie, wind-swept petrified forest.

Cataratas de Iguazú, Northeast. This set of 275 waterfalls ranks as one of the world's greatest wonders.

Cruce a Chile por Los Lagos, Patagonia. Blue lakes, volcanoes, waterfalls, and forests are all part of this Andean-lake odyssey from Bariloche to Chile.

Glaciar Moreno, Patagonia. One of the few advancing glaciers in the world is also a noisy one—tons of ice peel off and crash into Lago Argentino on a regular basis.

Parque Provincial Aconcagua. As you follow the Mendoza River up to the top of the Andes, the dramatic scenery along the way makes getting there every bit as spectacular as the final destination.

Península Valdés, Patagonia. This is the best place to view southern right whales as they feed, mate, give birth, and nurse their off-spring. Seals and penguins will keep you company, too.

Quebrada de Humahuaca. Vibrant pinks, yellows, and greens color the walls of this canyon like giant swaths of paint.

Reserva Faunistica Punta Tombo, Patagonia. Visit the largest colony of Magellanic penguins in the world at this nature reserve.

Tren a las Nubes, Salta. The "train into the clouds" takes you on a winding 14-hour trip into the mountains.

SMART TRAVEL TIPS

Finding out about your destination before you leave home means you won't squander time organizing everyday minutiae once you've arrived. You'll be more street-wise when you hit the ground as well, better prepared to explore the aspects of Argentina that drew you here in the first place. The organizations in this section can provide information to supplement this guide; contact them for up-to-the-minute details, and consult the A to Z sections that end each chapter for facts on the various topics as they relate to Argentina's many regions. Happy landings!

AIR TRAVEL

If your national airline does not fly directly into Buenos Aires, it's often possible to fly into Brazil and take a two- to three-hour flight on Aerolíneas Argentinas into Ezeiza. Miami and New York are the primary departure points for flights to Argentina from the United States. Regular flights also depart from Los Angeles, but these usually have at least one stopover.

Major sights within Argentina are often far apart, and although transportation over land can be more economical, it is slower, so it's best to save time and travel the country by plane.

BOOKING

When you book, look for nonstop flights and remember that "direct" flights stop at least once. Try to avoid connecting flights, which require a change of plane. Two airlines may operate a connecting flight jointly, so ask whether your airline operates every segment of the trip; you may find that the carrier you prefer flies you only part of the way. To find more booking tips and to check prices and make on-line flight reservations, log on to ⊕ www.fodors.com.

CARRIERS

🛪 To & from the U.S. **Aerolíneas Argentinas** ☎ 800/333-0276 in U.S., 0/810-2228-6527 in Buenos Aires ⊕ www.aerolineas.com.ar. **Air Canada** ☎ 888/247-2262 in U.S. and Canada, 11/4327-3640 in Buenos Aires ⊕ www.aircanada.com. **American Airlines** ☎ 800/433-7300 in U.S., 11/4318-1111 in Buenos Aires ⊕ www.aa.com. **LanChile** ☎ 800/735-5526 in U.S., 11/4378-2200 in Buenos Aires ⊕ www.lanchile.com to Buenos Aires via Santiago. **Lloyd Aéro Boliviano** ☎ 800/327-7407 in U.S., 11/4323-1900 in Buenos Aires ⊕ www.labairlines.com to Buenos Aires via Santa Cruz.

Southern Winds ☎ 800/379-9179 in U.S., 0/810-777-7979 in Argentina ⊕ www.sw.com.ar. **United Airlines** ☎ 800/538-2929 in U.S., 11/4316-0777 in Buenos Aires ⊕ www.united.com. **Varig Brasil** ☎ 800/468-2744 in U.S. and Canada, 11/4329-9211 in Buenos Aires ⊕ www.varig.com to Buenos Aires via Rio de Janeiro and São Paulo.

7 To & from the U.K. **American Airlines** ☎ 0345/789789 ⊕ www.aa.com from London Heathrow via Miami or New York. **British Airways** ☎ 0345/222111 in the U.K., 11/4320-6600 in Buenos Aires ⊕ www.britishairways.com from London Gatwick. **Iberia** ☎ 0171/830-0011 in the U.K., 11/4327-2739 or 11/4131-1000 in Buenos Aires ⊕ www.iberia.com via Madrid.

7 Within Argentina **Aerolíneas Argentinas** ☎ 800/333-0276 in U.S., 0/810-2228-6527 in Buenos Aires ⊕ www.aerolineas.com.ar. **Austral** ☎ 11/4340-7800 in Buenos Aires. **Dinar** ☎ 11/5371-1111 in Buenos Aires ⊕ www.dinar.com.ar. **LADE** ☎ 11/5129-9000 ⊕ www.lade.com.ar. **Laer** ☎ 343/436-2177 in Argentina. **LAPA** ☎ 0810/777-5272 in Buenos Aires ⊕ www.lapa.com.ar. **Southern Winds** ☎ 800/379-9179 in U.S., 0810/777-7979 in Argentina ⊕ www.sw.com.ar.

CHECK-IN & BOARDING

Always **find out your carrier's check-in policy.** Plan to arrive at the airport about two hours before your scheduled departure time for domestic flights and 2½ to 3 hours before international flights. You may need to arrive earlier if you're flying from one of the busier airports or during peak air-traffic times. To avoid delays at airport-security checkpoints, try not to wear any metal. Jewelry, belt and other buckles, steel-toe shoes, barrettes, and underwire bras are among the items that can set off detectors.

Assuming that not everyone with a ticket will show up, airlines routinely overbook planes. When everyone does, airlines ask for volunteers to give up their seats. In return, these volunteers usually get a several-hundred-dollar flight voucher, which can be used toward the purchase of another ticket, and are rebooked on the next flight out. If there are not enough volunteers, the airline must choose who will be denied boarding. The first to get bumped are passengers who checked in late and those flying on discounted tickets, so get to the gate and check in as early as possible, especially during peak periods.

Always **bring a government-issued photo ID** to the airport; even when it's not required, a passport is best.

CUTTING COSTS

The least expensive airfares to Argentina are priced for round-trip travel and must usually be purchased in advance. Airlines generally allow you to change your return date for a fee; most low-fare tickets, however, are nonrefundable. It's smart to call a number of airlines and check the Internet; when you are quoted a good price, book it on the spot—the same fare may not be available the next day, or even the next hour. Always check different routings and look into using alternate airports. Also, price off-peak flights, which may be significantly less expensive than others. Travel agents, especially low-fare specialists (⇨ Discounts & Deals), are helpful.

Consolidators are another good source. They buy tickets for scheduled flights at reduced rates from the airlines, then sell them at prices that beat the best fare available directly from the airlines. Sometimes you can even get your money back if you need to return the ticket. Carefully read the fine print detailing penalties for changes and cancellations, purchase the ticket with a credit card, and confirm your consolidator reservation with the airline.

7 Consolidators **AirlineConsolidator.com** ☎ 888/468-5385 ⊕ www.airlineconsolidator.com, for international tickets. **Best Fares** ☎ 800/576-8255 or 800/576-1600 ⊕ www.bestfares.com, $59.90 annual membership. **Cheap Tickets** ☎ 800/377-1000 or 888/922-8849 ⊕ www.cheaptickets.com. **Expedia** ☎ 800/397-3342 or 404/728-8787 ⊕ www.expedia.com. **Hotwire** ☎ 866/468-9473 or 920/330-9418 ⊕ www.hotwire.com. **Now Voyager Travel** ✉ 45 W. 21st St., 5th fl., New York, NY 10010 ☎ 212/459-1616 🖷 212/243-2711 ⊕ www.nowvoyagertravel.com. **Onetravel.com** ⊕ www.onetravel.com. **Orbitz** ☎ 888/656-4546 ⊕ www.orbitz.com. **Priceline.com** ⊕ www.priceline.com. **Travelocity** ☎ 888/709-5983, 877/282-2925 in Canada, 0870/111-7060 in the U.K. ⊕ www.travelocity.com.

ENJOYING THE FLIGHT

Traveling between the Americas is a bit less tiring than to Europe or Asia, as there's less of a time difference and thus less jet lag. Buenos Aires is only one hour ahead of New York and four hours ahead of Los Angeles, for instance, in summer (Argentina does not observe daylight saving time, which means an additional hour difference during winter). Flights to Buenos Aires are generally overnight, so you can sleep during the trip.

If you happen to be taking LanChile from the United States, you must change planes in Santiago, which means you'll probably get a lovely view of the Andes on your connecting flight to Buenos Aires. Southbound, the best views are usually out the windows on the left side of the plane.

State your seat preference when purchasing your ticket, and then repeat it when you confirm and when you check in. For more legroom, you can request one of the few emergency-aisle seats at check-in, if you are capable of lifting at least 50 pounds—a Federal Aviation Administration requirement of passengers in these seats. Seats behind a bulkhead also offer more legroom, but they don't have underseat storage. Don't sit in the row in front of the emergency aisle or in front of a bulkhead, where seats may not recline.

Ask the airline whether a snack or meal is served on the flight. If you have dietary concerns, request special meals when booking. These can be vegetarian, low-cholesterol, or kosher, for example. It's a good idea to pack some healthful snacks and a small (plastic) bottle of water in your carry-on bag. On long flights, try to maintain a normal routine, to help fight jet lag. At night, get some sleep. By day, eat light meals, drink water (not alcohol), and **move around the cabin** to stretch your legs. For additional jet-lag tips consult *Fodor's FYI: Travel Fit & Healthy* (available at bookstores everywhere).

Most carriers follow international standards and prohibit smoking on both international and domestic flights.

FLYING TIMES

Flying times to Buenos Aires are 11–12 hours from New York and 8½ hours from Miami. Flights from Los Angeles are often routed through either Lima, Bogotá, or Miami.

HOW TO COMPLAIN

If your baggage goes astray or your flight goes awry, complain right away. Most carriers require that you **file a claim immediately.** The Aviation Consumer Protection Division of the Department of Transporta-

tion publishes *Fly-Rights,* which discusses airlines and consumer issues and is available on-line. You can also find articles and information on mytravelrights.com, the Web site of the nonprofit Consumer Travel Rights Center.

🎵 Airline Complaints **Aviation Consumer Protection Division** ✉ U.S. Department of Transportation, C-75, Room 4107, 400 7th St. SW, Washington, DC 20590 ☎ 202/366-2220 ⊕ airconsumer.ost.dot.gov. **Federal Aviation Administration Consumer Hotline** ✉ For inquiries: FAA, 800 Independence Ave. SW, Washington, DC 20591 ☎ 800/322-7873 ⊕ www.faa.gov.

RECONFIRMING

Check the status of your flight before you leave for the airport. You can do this on your carrier's Web site, by linking to a flight-status checker (many Web booking services offer these), or by calling your carrier or travel agent. Always confirm international flights at least 72 hours ahead of the scheduled departure time. On the majority of routes to Argentina, flights are fully booked—usually with returning passengers checking a lot of baggage. Airlines request that passengers **arrive at the airport two hours before takeoff.** When leaving Argentina, you'll need to show your passport and pay a departure tax of about $30.50 dollars.

AIRPORTS & TRANSFERS

The major gateway to Argentina is Buenos Aires's Ezeiza International Airport, 47 km (29 mi) and a 45-minute drive from the city center. Ezeiza, also known as Aeropuerto Internacional Ministro Pistarini, is served by a variety of foreign airlines, along with domestic airlines running international routes. Though Argentina has other international airports, they generally only serve flights from other South American countries.

Flights from Buenos Aires to other points within Argentina depart from the Aeroparque Jorge Newbery, a 15-minute cab ride from downtown.

🎵 **Aeroparque Jorge Newbery** ☎ 11/5480-6111. **Ezeiza Airport** ☎ 11/5480-6111 ⊕ www.aa2000. com.ar.

AIRPORT TRANSFERS

Bus, van, taxi, and *remis* (car service charging a fixed, prearranged price) service is available at Buenos Aires's Ezeiza

International Airport. There are several round-the-clock private bus and remis services run by licensed companies; buses depart from the airport at scheduled intervals while taxis and remises are readily available.

Transportation tickets can be purchased from the well-marked service counters right outside the customs area. Taxis and remises from the airport to downtown cost around 35 pesos; vans 11–16 pesos, per person. Taxis and remises can transport up to four people; if your party does not exceed this limit, a remis is the cheaper option. Prices do not include tolls. City buses (2 pesos) operate on a regular schedule, but it's a two-hour ride and there's a limit of two bags. Beware of unsolicited chauffeurs who accost you with offers to drive you to your destination; they may not be a licensed service.

APTA provides licensed, metered taxi service to and from Ezeiza International Airport. Manuel Tienda León vans run from 4 AM to 8:30 PM between the airport and Buenos Aires. If you speak Spanish, call Remis Le Coq upon your arrival. They offer the best rate, around 20 pesos, plus tolls. They pick up passengers in front of the Banco Nacion outside Terminal A on the outdoor walkway.

🚖 Taxis & Shuttles **APTA** 🚕🚕 11/4480-9383 ⊕ www.taxiaeropuerto.com.ar. **Manuel Tienda León** 📞 11/4383-4454 or 0810/888-5366 ⊕ www. tiendaleon.com.ar. **Remis Le Coq** 📞 11/4964-2000.

BIKE TRAVEL

If you want to travel Argentina by bike, check with specialized agencies for tour packages. The roads and highways are filled with long-distance bikers, though pavement conditions are not optimum. Bike rentals are available in cities and most resort towns. Refer to individual chapters for more information.

BIKES IN FLIGHT

Most airlines accommodate bikes as luggage, provided they are dismantled and boxed; check with individual airlines about packing requirements. Some airlines sell bike boxes, which are often free at bike shops, for about $15 (bike bags can be considerably more expensive). International travelers often can substitute a bike for a piece of checked luggage at no

charge; otherwise, the cost is about $100. U.S. and Canadian airlines charge $40–$80 each way.

BOAT & FERRY TRAVEL

Buquebus provides frequent ferry service between Argentina and Uruguay and has several packages and promotions. Round-trip rates for economy travel range 100–300 pesos from Buenos Aires to the cities of Colonia, La Paloma, Montevideo, Piriápolis, and Punta del Este, all in Uruguay. All destinations, except Colonia, include bus transfers; the duration of the trip varies from 45 minutes to around 3 hours. You can order tickets by phone or on the Web site.

The more modest Ferry Lineas Argentina also serves the Buenos Aires–Uruguay route on a smaller scale with fewer boats per day; they sometimes work in conjunction with Buquebus.

🚢 **Buquebus** ✉ Antártida Argentina 821, at Av. Córdoba, Buenos Aires ✉ Patio Bullrich in Unicenter [Martínez] shopping mall, Buenos Aires 📞 11/4316-6550 ⊕ www.buquebus.com. **Ferry Lineas** ✉ Maipú 866, Buenos Aires 📞 11/4311-2300 ⊕ www.ferrylineas.com.uy.

BUS TRAVEL

Frequent and dependable bus service links Buenos Aires with all the provinces of the country and with neighboring countries. Keep in mind when crossing the border that you will need to present your passport and visa at customs and immigration checkpoints.

Buenos Aires's Estación Terminal de Omnibus is the gateway for bus travel to bordering countries and within Argentina. Around 200 bus companies are housed in the station, with their stands arranged in order by destinations served, allowing for easy price comparison. *See* individual chapters' A to Z sections for information about local bus stations.

When traveling by bus, it's a good idea to **bring your own food and beverages,** though *paradas* (food stops) are made en route. Travel light, dress comfortably, and **keep an eye on your belongings.**

CLASSES

There are generally two types of buses: *común* and *diferencial*. On común buses, the cheaper option, you'll usually get a seat, but it may not be that comfortable and there may not be air-conditioning or heating. Diferencial, only marginally more expensive, usually have reclining seats (some even have *coche-camas,* bedlike seats), an attendant, snacks, and videos. To get between neighboring towns, you can generally get a local city bus.

FARES & SCHEDULES

Tickets can be purchased at bus terminals right up until departure time. Note that in larger cities there may be different terminals for buses to different destinations. Arrive early to get a ticket, and **be prepared to pay cash.** On holidays, buy your ticket as far in advance as possible and arrive at the station extra early.

Ticket prices depend on the bus company and destination. For longer trips, **compare bus prices with airfares** as it may cost the same price to fly.

RESERVATIONS

Buses generally do not accept reservations, although you can buy over the phone with a credit card. You can purchase your tickets in advance at the terminal; usually there are no assigned seats, so arrive well in advance of boarding time, especially on weekends and holidays.

🚌 **Estación Terminal de Omnibus** ✉ Antártida Argentina and Calle 10, Buenos Aires ☎ 11/ 4310-0700 ⊕ www.microbus.com.ar.

BUSINESS HOURS

BANKS & OFFICES

Official business hours are weekdays 9–noon and 2–7 for offices and 9–3 for banks; some currency exchange offices remain open until 7 PM. Offices in larger cities remain open all day.

GAS STATIONS

Most gas stations in cities are open 24 hours.

MUSEUMS & SIGHTS

Museums are usually closed on Tuesday. Many close for one month during the summer. In small towns and more rural areas, museums may close for lunch.

POST OFFICES & TELEPHONE CENTERS

Post offices are open weekdays from around 9 to 8 and Saturday 9–1. Telephone centers generally stay open daily 8–8.

SHOPS

In Buenos Aires street shops are open weekdays 10–8 to compete with the malls, which remain open until 10 daily. On Saturday, street shops remain open until 1 PM, and almost all are closed Sunday. In the provinces, store hours are weekdays 9–noon and 2–7. The larger, more modern supermarket chains are open daily until 9.

CAMERAS & PHOTOGRAPHY

The higher the altitude, the greater the ultraviolet rays. Light meters do not read these rays, so except for close-ups or full-frame portraits where the reading is taken directly off the subject, photos may be overexposed. A skylight (81B or 81C) or polarizing filter can minimize haze and light problems; these filters may also reduce glare caused by white adobe buildings, sandy beaches, and snow.

Taking pictures in the rain forest poses problems with low light, so it's a good idea to **use high-speed film** to compensate.

The *Kodak Guide to Shooting Great Travel Pictures* (available at bookstores everywhere) is loaded with tips.

🚌 Photo Help **Kodak Information Center** ☎ 800/ 242-2424 ⊕ www.kodak.com.

EQUIPMENT PRECAUTIONS

Before departing you should **register your foreign-made camera with U.S. Customs** to avoid possible duties upon entering Argentina (⇨ Customs & Duties). At the very least, if you plan to use your equipment in Argentina, it's a good idea to register it at customs upon entering the country.

Don't pack film or equipment in checked luggage, where it is much more susceptible to damage. X-ray machines used to view checked luggage are extremely powerful and therefore are likely to ruin your film. Try to ask for hand inspection of film, which becomes clouded after repeated exposure to airport X-ray machines, and keep videotapes and computer disks away from metal detectors. Always keep film, tape, and computer disks out of the sun. Carry an extra supply of batteries, and be prepared to turn on your camera, camcorder, or laptop to prove to airport security personnel that the device is real.

Keep in mind that dampness and sand pose a problem when you travel in humid areas such as the rain forest or beaches; **keep all equipment in resealable plastic bags and use lens filters for extra protection.**

FILM & DEVELOPING

All major cities as well as most smaller towns provide complete camera services, including one-hour photo shops. The quality of processing is equal to that of the United States, though a bit more expensive. Always check the expiration date for film, and specify any color adjustments for processing beforehand.

VIDEOS

Note that though the N-PAL video system used in Argentina differs from the NTSC system used in the United States, all video recorders in Argentina are *binorma*, allowing for both types.

CAR RENTAL

Renting a car in Argentina is expensive (around 150 pesos per day plus tax for a midsize car). Extras such as car seats and air-conditioning drive the fee even higher. Ask about special rates; generally a better price can be negotiated. Keep in mind that almost all cars have manual transmission rather than automatic.

All cities and most areas that attract tourists have car-rental agencies. You can also rent cars from airports and some hotels. If the rental agency has a branch in another town, arrangements can usually be made for a one-way drop off. Offices in Buenos Aires can make reservations in other locations; provincial government tourist offices also have information on car-rental agencies.

An alternative to renting a car is to hire a *remis*, a car with a driver, especially for day outings. Hotels can arrange this service for you. Remises are more comfortable and cheaper than taxis for long rides. They're also usually less expensive for rides within cities, especially on round-trip journeys because there's no return fare.

You have to pay cash—but you'll often spend less than you would for a rental car. In cities, remises cost about 25–30 pesos per hour; sometimes there's a three-hour minimum and an additional charge per kilometer when you go outside city limits. In smaller towns, the rate is often much less (perhaps 20–25 pesos for the entire day). Some local car agencies offer chauffeur-driven rentals as well. Refer to individual chapters for more information on hiring remises.

🚗 Major Agencies **Avis** ☎ 800/331-1084, 800/879-2847 in Canada, 0870/606-0100 in the U.K., 02/9353-9000 in Australia, 09/526-2847 in New Zealand, 11/4130-0130 in Buenos Aires ⊕ www.avis.com. **Dollar** ☎ 800/800-6000, 0124/622-0111 in the U.K., where it's affiliated with Sixt, 02/9223-1444 in Australia, 11/4315-8800 in Buenos Aires ⊕ www.dollar.com. **Hertz** ☎ 800/654-3001, 800/263-0600 in Canada, 0870/844-8844 in the U.K., 02/9669-2444 in Australia, 09/256-8690 in New Zealand, 11/4129-7777 in Buenos Aires ⊕ www.hertz.com. **National Car Rental** ☎ 800/227-7368, 0870/600-6666 in the U.K. ⊕ www.nationalcar.com.

CUTTING COSTS

For a good deal, book through a travel agent who will shop around. Also, price local car-rental companies—whose prices may be lower still, although their service and maintenance may not be as good as those of major rental agencies—and research rates on the Internet. Remember to ask about required deposits, cancellation penalties, and drop-off charges if you're planning to pick up the car in one city and leave it in another. If you're traveling during a holiday period, also make sure that a confirmed reservation guarantees you a car.

🚗 Local Agencies **ABC Rent a Car** ✉ Embassy Gallery, Marcelo T. de Alvear 628, Buenos Aires ☎🖶 11/4315-0313 ⊕ www.abc-car.com.ar. **AI International** ✉ Marcelo T. de Alvear 678 ☎ 11/4311-1000 or 11/4313-1515 ⊕ www.airentacar.com.ar.

INSURANCE

When driving a rented car you are generally responsible for any damage to or loss of the vehicle. You also may be liable for any property damage or personal injury that you may cause while driving. Before you rent, see what coverage you already have under the terms of your personal auto-insurance policy and credit cards. Argentine rental-car insurance is often higher than in the United States.

REQUIREMENTS & RESTRICTIONS

Your own driver's license may be valid in Argentina, though you may want to take out an International Driver's Permit; contact your local automobile association (⇨ Auto Clubs *in* Car Travel). The minimum driving age is 18. You'll need to present a major credit card at the agency counter in order to rent a car.

SURCHARGES

Before you pick up a car in one city and leave it in another, ask about drop-off charges or one-way service fees, which can be substantial. Note, too, that some rental agencies charge extra if you return the car before the time specified in your contract. To avoid a hefty refueling fee, fill the tank just before you turn in the car, but be aware that gas stations near the rental outlet may overcharge. It's almost never a deal to buy the tank of gas that's in the car when you rent it; the understanding is that you'll return it empty, but some fuel usually remains. Note that airport rental agencies may charge an airport concession recovery fee of 10%.

CAR TRAVEL

Your driver's license may not be recognized outside your home country. International driving permits (IDPs) are available from the American and Canadian automobile associations and, in the United Kingdom, from the Automobile Association and Royal Automobile Club. These international permits, valid only in conjunction with your regular driver's license, are universally recognized; having one may save you a problem with local authorities.

AUTO CLUBS

The Automóvil Club Argentino (ACA) provides complete mechanical assistance, including towing, detailed maps and driver's manuals, and expert advice (often in English). The ACA can help chart your itinerary, give you gas coupons, and even set you up with discounted accommodations in affiliated hotels and campgrounds. Present your own auto-club membership card to enjoy these benefits.

Note that ACA service is also available at many of the YPF service stations throughout Argentina.

In Argentina **Automóvil Club Argentino (ACA)** ✉ Av. del Libertador 1850 ☎ 11/4802-6061 ⊕ www.aca.org.ar.
In Australia **Australian Automobile Association (AAA)** ☎ 02/6247-7311 ⊕ www.aaa.asn.au.
In Canada **Canadian Automobile Association (CAA)** ☎ 613/247-0117 ⊕ www.caa.ca.
In New Zealand **New Zealand Automobile Association** ☎ 09/377-4660 ⊕ www.aa.co.nz.
In the U.K. **Automobile Association (AA)** ☎ 0870/550-0600. **Royal Automobile Club (RAC)** ☎ 0870/572-2722 ⊕ www.rac.co.uk.
In the U.S. **American Automobile Association (AAA)** ☎ 800/564-6222 ⊕ www.aaa.com.

EMERGENCY SERVICES

The ACA will provide emergency mechanical assistance, as will your rental-car agency (included in the rate).

You can get your tires filled at gas stations, but if you have a flat you'll have to find a *gomería* (tire repair), many of which are open 24 hours.

GASOLINE

You'll find Esso, Shell, and national YPF service stations throughout Buenos Aires, in the provinces, and along major highways. The stations usually include full service, convenience stores, snack bars, and ATMs. In rural areas, gas stations are few and far between and have reduced hours; when traveling in the countryside, it's a good idea to **start looking for a station when your tank is half empty.**

Gas is expensive (around 1.50 pesos per liter, or about 6 pesos per gallon) and may run you 80 pesos to fill a midsize car. There are several grades of unleaded fuels, as well as diesel and gas oil.

INTERNATIONAL TRAVEL

Paved highways run from Argentina to the Chilean, Bolivian, Paraguayan, and Brazilian borders. If you do cross the border by land you'll be required to present your passport, visa, and documentation of car ownership at immigration and customs checkpoints. It's also common for cars and bags to be searched for contraband, such as food, livestock, and drugs.

ROAD CONDITIONS

Ultramodern multilane highways exist in Argentina, usually connecting the major cities. Gradually these highways become narrower routes, and then county roads. Many of these rural roads are not divided and are not in particularly good condition.

You must pay tolls on many highways, and even on some unpaved roads. Tolls come frequently and can be steep (one toll, for instance, on the five-hour drive between Buenos Aires and Mar del Plata is around 13 pesos).

Night driving can be hazardous: some highways and routes are poorly lit, routes sometimes cut through the center of towns, cattle often get onto the roads, and in rural areas *rastreros* (old farm trucks) seldom have all their lights working.

City streets throughout Argentina are notorious for potholes, and lanes are generally poorly marked.

For highway-condition reports, updated daily, and basic routes in Spanish, contact La Dirección Nacional de Vialidad.
🚩 **La Dirección Nacional de Vialidad** ☎ 0800/333-0073 ⊕ www.vialidad.gov.ar.

RULES OF THE ROAD

Don't drive after dark. Obey speed limits (marked in kilometers per hour) and traffic regulations. If you do get a traffic ticket, don't argue. Although you'll see Argentines offering cash on the spot to avoid getting a written ticket, this isn't a good idea.

Seat belts are required by law, as are car lights at daytime on highways. The use of cellular phones while driving is forbidden, and turning left on two-way avenues is prohibited unless there's a left-turn signal; likewise, there are no right turns on red. Traffic lights turn yellow before they turn red, but also before turning green, which is interpreted by drivers as an extra margin to get through the intersection, so take precautions.

In Buenos Aires, drivers in general, and buses and taxis (which cruise slowly on the right-hand side), often drive as though they have priority, so it's a good idea to defer to them for safety. If you experience a small accident, jot down the other driver's information and supply your own.

A police officer will not assist you; you must go down to the police station in the area to file a report. Contact your rental agency immediately.

In towns and cities, a 40-kph (25-mph) speed limit applies on streets, and a 60-kph (37-mph) limit is in effect on avenues. On expressways the limit is 100 kph (62 mph), and on other roads and highways out of town it's 80 kph (50 mph). These limits are enforced by strategically placed cameras triggered by excessive speed.

CHILDREN IN ARGENTINA

Having your children along may prove to be your ticket to meeting locals, as Argentines generally adore children. Many Argentines prefer to take their children along for a late evening out rather than leave them behind. As a result, children are welcome at restaurants, and it's not uncommon to see kids eating midnight dinners with their parents. Waiters are especially attentive to any dietary requirements for your child; they will often even warm your infant's bottle.

Children should have had all their inoculations before leaving home.

If you are renting a car, don't forget to arrange for a car seat when you reserve. For general advice about traveling with children, consult *Fodor's FYI: Travel with Your Baby* (available in bookstores everywhere).

FLYING

If your children are two or older, ask about children's airfares. As a general rule, infants under two not occupying a seat fly at greatly reduced fares or even for free. But if you want to guarantee a seat for an infant, you have to pay full fare. Consider flying during off-peak days and times; most airlines will grant an infant a seat without a ticket if there are available seats. When booking, confirm carry-on allowances if you're traveling with infants. In general, for babies charged 10% to 50% of the adult fare you are allowed one carry-on bag and a collapsible stroller; if the flight is full, the stroller may have to be checked or you may be limited to less.

Experts agree that it's a good idea to use safety seats aloft for children weighing less than 40 pounds. Airlines set their own policies: if you use a safety seat, U.S. carriers usually require that the child be ticketed, even if he or she is young enough to ride free, because the seats must be strapped into regular seats. And even if you pay the full adult fare for the seat, it may be worth it, especially on longer trips. Do **check your airline's policy about using safety seats during takeoff and landing.** Safety seats are not allowed everywhere in the plane, so get your seat assignments as early as possible.

When reserving, request children's meals or a freestanding bassinet (not available at all airlines) if you need them. But note that bulkhead seats, where you must sit to use the bassinet, may lack an overhead bin or storage space on the floor.

LODGING

Most hotels in Argentina allow children under a certain age to stay in their parents' room at no extra charge, but others charge for them as extra adults; be sure to **find out the cutoff age for children's discounts.**

SIGHTS & ATTRACTIONS

On weekends and holidays Argentine families can be found in droves on daylong outings to the mall, parks, zoos, and other kid-friendly sights. Places that are especially appealing to children are indicated by a rubber-duckie icon (☺) in the margin.

SUPPLIES & EQUIPMENT

Major supermarkets and pharmacies sell diapers and sometimes baby food, though you may want to stock up beforehand on items that your child favors.

TRANSPORTATION

If you're traveling with an infant, chances are someone will give up his or her seat for you on public transportation.

COMPUTERS ON THE ROAD

Declare your computer upon arrival for duty fees, though you can sometimes avoid paying a fee if you explain your need for the computer. To avoid any inconveniences register your computer when you leave your country, and declare your computer at customs when you enter Argentina— you'll need to produce either a document from U.S. customs or its receipt, and be sure to declare it on the way out (keep your receipts for this purpose).

CONSUMER PROTECTION

Whether you're shopping for gifts or purchasing travel services, **pay with a major credit card** whenever possible, so you can cancel payment or get reimbursed if there's a problem (and you can provide documentation). If you're doing business with a particular company for the first time, contact your local Better Business Bureau and the attorney general's offices in your state and (for U.S. businesses) the company's home state as well. Have any complaints been filed? Finally, if you're buying a package or tour, always consider travel insurance that includes default coverage (⇨ Insurance).

CUSTOMS & DUTIES

When shopping abroad, keep receipts for all purchases. Upon reentering the country, **be ready to show customs officials what you've bought.** Pack purchases together in an easily accessible place. If you think a duty is incorrect, appeal the assessment. If you object to the way your clearance was handled, note the inspector's badge number. In either case, first ask to see a supervisor. If the problem isn't resolved, write to the appropriate authorities, beginning with the port director at your point of entry.

IN ARGENTINA

Upon arriving to Buenos Aires by air or ship, you'll find that customs officials usually wave you through without close inspection. International airports have introduced a customs system for those with "nothing to declare," which has streamlined the arrival process.

If you enter the country by bus, take the time to have the border officials do a proper inspection of your belongings and documents. This could prevent problems later when you are trying to leave the country.

Personal clothing and effects are admitted free of duty, provided they have been used, as are personal jewelry and professional equipment. Fishing gear presents no problems. Up to 2 liters of alcoholic beverages, 400 cigarettes, and 50 cigars are admitted duty-free.

Note that you must pay $30.50 dollars in departure tax upon leaving through Ezeiza International Airport.

IN AUSTRALIA

Australian residents who are 18 or older may bring home A$400 worth of souvenirs and gifts (including jewelry), 250 cigarettes or 250 grams of cigars or other tobacco products, and 1,125 ml of alcohol (including wine, beer, and spirits). Residents under 18 may bring back A$200 worth of goods. Members of the same family traveling together may pool their allowances. Prohibited items include meat products. Seeds, plants, and fruits need to be declared upon arrival.

Australian Customs Service Regional Director, Box 8, Sydney, NSW 2001 02/9213-2000 or 1300/363263, 02/9364-7222 or 1800/803-006 quarantine-inquiry line 02/9213-4043 www.customs.gov.au.

IN CANADA

Canadian residents who have been out of Canada for at least seven days may bring in C$750 worth of goods duty-free. If you've been away fewer than seven days but more than 48 hours, the duty-free allowance drops to C$200. If your trip lasts 24 to 48 hours, the allowance is C$50. You may not pool allowances with family members. Goods claimed under the C$750 exemption may follow you by mail; those claimed under the lesser exemptions must accompany you. Alcohol and tobacco products may be included in the seven-day and 48-hour exemptions but not in the 24-hour exemption. If you meet the age requirements of the province or territory through which you reenter Canada, you may bring in, duty-free, 1.5 liters of wine *or* 1.14 liters (40 imperial ounces) of liquor *or* 24 12-ounce cans or bottles of beer or ale. Also, if you meet the local age requirement for tobacco products, you may bring in, duty-free, 200 cigarettes and 50 cigars. Check ahead of time with the Canada Customs and Revenue Agency or the Department of Agriculture for policies regarding meat products, seeds, plants, and fruits.

You may send an unlimited number of gifts (only one gift per recipient, however) worth up to C$60 each duty-free to Canada. Label the package UNSOLICITED GIFT—VALUE UNDER $60. Alcohol and tobacco are excluded.

Canada Customs and Revenue Agency 2265 St. Laurent Blvd., Ottawa, Ontario K1G 4K3 800/461-9999, 204/983-3500, or 506/636-5064 www.ccra.gc.ca.

IN NEW ZEALAND

All homeward-bound residents may bring back NZ$700 worth of souvenirs and gifts; passengers may not pool their allowances, and children can claim only the concession on goods intended for their own use. For those 17 or older, the duty-free allowance also includes 4.5 liters of wine or beer; one 1,125-ml bottle of spirits; and either 200 cigarettes, 250 grams of tobacco, 50 cigars, *or* a combination of the three up to 250 grams. Meat products, seeds, plants, and fruits must be declared upon arrival to the Agricultural Services Department.

New Zealand Customs Head office: The Customhouse, 17–21 Whitmore St., Box 2218, Wellington 09/300-5399 or 0800/428-786 www.customs.govt.nz.

IN THE U.K.

From countries outside the European Union, including Argentina, you may bring home, duty-free, 200 cigarettes or 50 cigars; 1 liter of spirits or 2 liters of fortified or sparkling wine or liqueurs; 2 liters of still table wine; 60 ml of perfume; 250 ml of toilet water; plus £145 worth of other goods, including gifts and souvenirs. Prohibited items include meat products, seeds, plants, and fruits.

HM Customs and Excise Portcullis House, 21 Cowbridge Rd. E, Cardiff CF11 9SS 0845/010-9000 or 0208/929-0152, 0208/929-6731 or 0208/910-3602 complaints www.hmce.gov.uk.

IN THE U.S.

U.S. residents who have been out of the country for at least 48 hours may bring home, for personal use, $800 worth of foreign goods duty-free, as long as they haven't used the $800 allowance or any part of it in the past 30 days. This exemption may include 1 liter of alcohol (for travelers 21 and older), 200 cigarettes, and 100 non-Cuban cigars. Family members from the same household who are traveling together may pool their $800 personal exemptions. For fewer than 48 hours, the duty-free allowance drops to $200, which may include 50 cigarettes, 10 non-Cuban cigars, and 150 ml of alcohol (or 150 ml of perfume containing alcohol). The $200 allowance cannot be combined with other individuals' exemptions, and if you exceed it, the full value of all the goods will be taxed. Antiques, which the U.S. Bureau of

Customs and Border Protection defines as objects more than 100 years old, enter duty-free, as do original works of art done entirely by hand, including paintings, drawings, and sculptures. This doesn't apply to folk art or handicrafts, which are in general dutiable.

You may also send packages home duty-free, with a limit of one parcel per addressee per day (except alcohol or tobacco products or perfume worth more than $5). You can mail up to $200 worth of goods for personal use; label the package PERSONAL USE and attach a list of its contents and their retail value. If the package contains your used personal belongings, mark it AMERICAN GOODS RETURNED to avoid paying duties. You may send up to $100 worth of goods as a gift; mark the package UNSOLICITED GIFT. Mailed items do not affect your duty-free allowance on your return.

To avoid paying duty on foreign-made high-ticket items you already own and will take on your trip, register them with Customs before you leave the country. Consider filing a Certificate of Registration for laptops, cameras, watches, and other digital devices identified with serial numbers or other permanent markings; you can keep the certificate for other trips. Otherwise, bring a sales receipt or insurance form to show that you owned the item before you left the United States.

DISABILITIES & ACCESSIBILITY

Although international chain hotels in large cities have some suitable rooms, and it's easy to hire private cars with drivers for excursions, Argentina is not well equipped to handle travelers with disabilities. On only a few streets in Buenos Aires, for instance, are there ramps and curb cuts. Beware of potholes and various obstructions on streets and sidewalks. It takes effort and planning to negotiate museums and other buildings (many have steps that are unfortunately almost entirely unnegotiable with a wheelchair) and to explore the countryside.

Several *telecentros* and *locutorios* (telephone centers) provide facilities for people with hearing impairments.

Contact Argentina's Fundación FUARPE for special tours and additional information.

🚹 **Local Resources Fundación FUARPE** ☎ 11/4393-7210 ⊕ www.fuarpe.org.ar.

RESERVATIONS

When discussing accessibility with an operator or reservations agent, ask hard questions. Are there any stairs, inside *or* out? Are there grab bars next to the toilet *and* in the shower/tub? How wide is the doorway to the room? To the bathroom? For the most extensive facilities meeting the latest legal specifications, opt for newer accommodations. If you reserve through a toll-free number, consider also calling the hotel's local number to confirm the information from the central reservations office. Get confirmation in writing when you can.

TRAVEL AGENCIES

In the United States, the Americans with Disabilities Act requires that travel firms serve the needs of all travelers. Some agencies specialize in working with people with disabilities.

🚹 **Access Adventures/B. Roberts Travel** ✉ 206 Chestnut Ridge Rd., Scottsville, NY 14624 ☎ 585/889-9096 ⊕ www.brobertstravel.com ✎ dltravel@prodigy.net, run by a former physical-rehabilitation counselor. **CareVacations** ✉ No. 5, 5110-50 Ave., Leduc, Alberta, Canada, T9E 6V4 ☎ 780/986-6404 or 877/478-7827 🖷 780/986-8332 ⊕ www.carevacations.com, for group tours and cruise vacations. **Flying Wheels Travel** ✉ 143 W. Bridge St., Box 382, Owatonna, MN 55060 ☎ 507/451-5005 🖷 507/451-1685 ⊕ www.flyingwheelstravel.com.

DISCOUNTS & DEALS

Be a smart shopper and compare all your options before making decisions. A plane ticket bought with a promotional coupon from travel clubs, coupon books, and direct-mail offers or purchased on the Internet may not be cheaper than the least expensive fare from a discount ticket agency. And always keep in mind that what you get is just as important as what you save.

Note that most museums are free one morning or afternoon per week and movies are half price on Wednesday and for matinees.

DISCOUNT RESERVATIONS

To save money, look into discount reservations services with Web sites and toll-free numbers, which use their buying power to get a better price on hotels, airline tickets (⇨ Air Travel), even car rentals. When booking a room, always **call the hotel's local toll-free number** (if one is available) rather than the central reservations number—you'll often get a better price. Always ask about special packages or corporate rates.

When shopping for the best deal on hotels and car rentals, look for guaranteed exchange rates, which protect you against a falling dollar. With your rate locked in, you won't pay more, even if the price goes up in the local currency.

The Automóvil Club Argentino (ACA) recognizes your auto-club card for discounts on gas within Argentina (⇨ Auto Clubs *in* Car Travel).

✈ Airline Tickets **Air 4 Less** ☎ 800/AIR4LESS; low-fare specialist.

🏨 Hotel Rooms **Accommodations Express** ☎ 800/444-7666 or 800/277-1064 ⊕ www.accommodationsexpress.com. **Steigenberger Reservation Service** ☎ 800/223-5652 ⊕ www.srs-worldhotels.com. **Turbotrip.com** ☎ 800/473-7829 ⊕ www.turbotrip.com.

PACKAGE DEALS

Don't confuse packages and guided tours. When you buy a package, you travel on your own, just as though you had planned the trip yourself. Fly–drive packages, which combine airfare and car rental, are often a good deal. In cities, ask the local visitor's bureau about hotel packages that include tickets to major museum exhibits or other special events.

EATING & DRINKING

The restaurants we list are the cream of the crop in each price category. Properties indicated by a ✕▥ are lodging establishments whose restaurant warrants a special trip.

CATEGORY	COST
$$$$	over 35 pesos
$$$	25-35 pesos
$$	15-25 pesos
$	8-15 pesos
¢	under 8 pesos

Prices are for one main course at dinner.

MEALS & SPECIALTIES

Argentina is known for its quality beef, which has always been a big part of its cuisine and culture. The *asado* (barbecue) refers both to the grilling of meat and the event itself. If you are invited to an asado at an *estancia* (ranch) or restaurant, be prepared for abundant servings of various beef cuts, tripe, sweetbreads, kidney, and chorizo. A *parrilla* is not only the grill upon which meats are cooked but also those restaurants serving beef as a main attraction. Robust Argentine *tintos* (red wines) are excellent accompaniments, as are the white varietals; smaller ¾ bottles can be ordered.

Argentina's strong Italian heritage manifests itself in the cuisine; you'll find delicious pastas smothered in hearty sauces, crusty pizzas, polenta, and creamy *helados* (ice cream).

Mate is a strong tealike beverage drunk in Argentina as well as Uruguay, Paraguay, and southern Brazil. The word mate derives from the native Quechua for "drinking vessel"; the tea is served in a carved-out gourd and is sipped through a metal *bombilla* (filter-straw).

MEALTIMES

Breakfast is usually served until 11 AM; lunch runs from 12:30 to 3:30; dinner is from 8 to around midnight. Several restaurants in Buenos Aires and other large cities stay open all night, or at least well into the morning, catering to the after-theater and nightclub crowd.

Unless otherwise noted, the restaurants listed in this guide are open daily for lunch and dinner.

RESERVATIONS & DRESS

Reservations are always a good idea; we mention them only when they're essential or not accepted. Book as far ahead as you can, and reconfirm as soon as you arrive. (Large parties should always call ahead to check the reservations policy.) We mention dress only when men are required to wear a jacket or a jacket and tie. Even when it's not required, you may want to wear a jacket and tie or dress for evening dining at more formal restaurants in the top price category; casual chic or informal dress is fine for most other restaurants.

ELECTRICITY

The electrical current in Argentina is 220 volts, 50 cycles alternating current (AC); wall outlets usually take Continental-type plugs, with two round prongs or three flat, angled prongs.

To use electric-powered equipment purchased in the United States or Canada, **bring a converter and adapter;** some high-end accommodations provide these, but you're better off bringing them if you're unsure.

If your appliances are dual-voltage, you'll need only an adapter. Don't use 110-volt outlets marked FOR SHAVERS ONLY for high-wattage appliances such as blow-dryers. Most laptops operate equally well on 110 and 220 volts and so require only an adapter.

EMBASSIES

In addition to providing assistance, some embassies host evening parties, usually once a month; call to find out when and where.

Australia embassy ✉ Villanueva 1400, Buenos Aires ☎ 11/4779-3500 ⊕ www.argentina.embassy. gov.au. **Canada embassy** ✉ Tagle 2828 ☎ 11/4808-1000 ⊕ www.dfait-maeci.gc.ca/argentina. **Ireland embassy** ✉ Suipacha 1280, fl. 2, Buenos Aires ☎ 11/4325-8588. **New Zealand embassy** ✉ Carlos Pellegrini 1427, fl. 5, Buenos Aires ☎ 11/4328-0747, 15/4148-7633 for an emergency. **South Africa embassy** ✉ Marcelo T. de Alvear 590, fl. 8, Buenos Aires ☎ 11/4317-2900, 15/4446-8978 for an emergency. **United Kingdom embassy** ✉ Luis Agote 2412 ☎ 11/4803-7799 or 11/4576-2222, 15/5331-7129 for an emergency ⊕ www.britain.org.ar. **United States embassy** ✉ Colombia 4300, Buenos Aires ☎ 11/5777-4533 ⊕ www.usembassy.state.gov.

EMERGENCIES

Emergency numbers are the same nationwide, so wherever you find yourself you can call the numbers below to be connected to a local emergency unit.

Emergency Services Ambulance & Medical ☎ 107. **Fire** ☎ 100. **Police** ☎ 111 or 4346-5770.

ENGLISH-LANGUAGE MEDIA

The best source of information in English is the *Buenos Aires Herald.* You'll find a complete listing of what's going on around town—the weekend supplement is especially helpful—as well as airline information and concise articles. It can be purchased at any kiosk throughout the city, for 1.40 pesos on weekdays and for 1.80 pesos on Sunday.

ETIQUETTE & BEHAVIOR

Argentines are very warm and affectionate people, and they greet each other as such. The customary greeting between both friends and strangers is one kiss on the right cheek. This is done by both men and women. If you don't feel comfortable kissing a stranger, a simple hand shake will suffice, but don't be surprised when you see men kissing men and women kissing women.

When arriving at parties, Argentines will often have something in hand to offer the hosts: a bottle of wine, a cake or other goodies, but there is certainly no rule about giving gifts.

When you leave a party or restaurant it's normal to say good-bye to everyone in the room or in your party, which means kissing everyone once again. Argentines are never in a hurry to get anywhere, so a formal good-bye can certainly take awhile.

Smoking is very common in Argentina, so be prepared for some smoke with your steak. Most restaurants offer nonsmoking sections, but make sure to ask before you are seated. If you are at a dinner party, don't be surprised if the room fills up with smoke right after the main course; if it bothers you, you should excuse yourself—don't ask others to smoke outside.

GAY & LESBIAN TRAVEL

In Buenos Aires, local attitudes towards same-sex couples are tolerant, and there are numerous gay bars, organizations, and publications. In the rural areas and small towns of Argentina, people are less accepting; still, though you may find people staring at public displays of affection, you shouldn't encounter any hostility.

Gay- & Lesbian-Friendly Travel Agencies Different Roads Travel ✉ 8383 Wilshire Blvd., Suite 520, Beverly Hills, CA 90211 ☎ 323/651-5557 or 800/429-8747 (Ext. 14 for both) 🖷 323/651-3678 ✎ lgernert@tzell.com. **Kennedy Travel** ✉ 130 W. 42nd St., Suite 401, New York, NY 10036 ☎ 212/840-8659 or 800/237-7433 🖷 212/730-2269 ⊕ www. kennedytravel.com. **Now, Voyager** ✉ 4406 18th St., San Francisco, CA 94114 ☎ 415/626-1169 or 800/255-6951 🖷 415/626-8626 ⊕ www.nowvoyager.

com. **Skylink Travel and Tour** ✉ 1455 N. Dutton Ave., Suite A, Santa Rosa, CA 95401 ☎ 707/546–9888 or 800/225–5759 🖷 707/636–0951, serving lesbian travelers.

HEALTH

ALTITUDE SICKNESS

Soroche, or altitude sickness, which results in shortness of breath and headaches, may be a problem when you visit the Andes. To remedy any discomfort, walk slowly, eat lightly, and drink plenty of fluids (avoid alcohol). If you have high blood pressure and a history of heart trouble, **check with your doctor before traveling to high Andean elevations.** If you experience an extended period of nausea, dehydration, dizziness, severe headache or weakness while in a high-altitude area, seek medical attention.

FOOD & DRINK

Buenos Aires residents drink tap water and eat uncooked fruits and vegetables. However, if you've got just two weeks, you don't want to waste a minute of it in your hotel room; exercise caution when choosing what you eat and drink—on as well as off the beaten path. It's best to drink bottled water, which can be found throughout Argentina for about 1.50 pesos for a half liter.

Each year there are cases of cholera in the northern part of Argentina, mostly in the indigenous communities near the Bolivian border; your best protection is to avoid eating raw seafood.

MEDICAL PLANS

No one plans to get sick while traveling, but it happens, so consider signing up with a medical-assistance company. Members get doctor referrals, emergency evacuation or repatriation, hot lines for medical consultation, cash for emergencies, and other assistance.
🚩 Medical-Assistance Companies **International SOS Assistance** ⊕ www.internationalsos.com ✉ 8 Neshaminy Interplex, Suite 207, Trevose, PA 19053 ☎ 215/245–4707 or 800/523–6586 🖷 215/244–9617 ✉ Landmark House, Hammersmith Bridge Rd., 6th fl., London, W6 9DP ☎ 20/8762–8008 🖷 20/8748–7744 ✉ 12 Chemin Riant-bosson, 1217 Meyrin 1, Geneva, Switzerland ☎ 22/785–6464 🖷 22/785–6424 ✉ 331 N. Bridge Rd., 17-00, Odeon Towers, Singapore 188720 ☎ 6338–7800 🖷 6338–7611.

SHOTS & MEDICATIONS

No specific vaccinations are required for travel to Argentina. According to the Centers for Disease Control (CDC), however, there's a limited risk of cholera, hepatitis B, and dengue. The local malady of Chagas' disease is present in remote areas. If you plan to visit remote regions or stay for more than six weeks, **check with the CDC's International Travelers Hot Line.** In areas with malaria (in Argentina, you are at risk for malaria only in northern rural areas bordering Bolivia and Paraguay) and dengue, which are both carried by mosquitoes, take mosquito nets, wear clothing that covers the body, apply repellent containing DEET, and use a spray against flying insects in living and sleeping areas. The hot line recommends chloroquine (analen) as an antimalarial agent; no vaccine exists against dengue or Chagas.

Children traveling to Argentina should have current inoculations against measles, mumps, rubella, and polio.

A major health risk is traveler's diarrhea, caused by eating unfamiliar foods or contaminated fruit or vegetables or drinking contaminated water. Mild cases may respond to Imodium (known generically as loperamide) or Pepto-Bismol (not as strong), both of which can be purchased over the counter; paregoric, another antidiarrheal agent, does not require a doctor's prescription in Argentina. Drink plenty of purified water or tea—chamomile is a good folk remedy. In severe cases, rehydrate yourself with a salt-sugar solution (½ teaspoon salt and 4 tablespoons sugar per quart of water).

Note that many medications that require a prescription in the United States and elsewhere, including some antibiotics, are available over the counter in Argentina.
🚩 Health Warnings **National Centers for Disease Control and Prevention (CDC)** ✉ National Center for Infectious Diseases, Division of Quarantine, Travelers' Health, 1600 Clifton Rd. NE, Atlanta, GA 30333 ☎ 877/394–8747 international travelers health line, 404/498–1600 Division of Quarantine, 800/311–3435 other inquiries 🖷 888/232–3299 ⊕ www.cdc.gov/travel.

HOLIDAYS

New Year's Day; Day of the Epiphany (January 6); Veteran's Day (April 2); Labor Day (May 1); Anniversary of the

1810 Revolution (May 25); *Semana Santa* (Holy Week; 4 days in April leading up to Easter Sunday); National Sovereignty Day (June 10); Flag Day (June 20); Independence Day (July 9); Anniversary of San Martín's Death (August 17); *Día de la Raza* (Race Recognition Day) (October 12); Day of the Immaculate Conception (December 8); and Christmas. Some holidays that fall on weekdays may be moved to Monday to create a three-day holiday weekend. Note that all banks and most commercial and entertainment centers are closed on these days.

INSURANCE

The most useful travel-insurance plan is a comprehensive policy that includes coverage for trip cancellation and interruption, default, trip delay, and medical expenses (with a waiver for preexisting conditions).

Without insurance you'll lose all or most of your money if you cancel your trip, regardless of the reason. Default insurance covers you if your tour operator, airline, or cruise line goes out of business. Trip-delay covers expenses that arise because of bad weather or mechanical delays. Study the fine print when comparing policies.

If you're traveling internationally, a key component of travel insurance is coverage for medical bills incurred if you get sick on the road. Such expenses aren't generally covered by Medicare or private policies. U.K. residents can buy a travel-insurance policy valid for most vacations taken during the year in which it's purchased (but check preexisting-condition coverage). British and Australian citizens need extra medical coverage when traveling overseas.

Always **buy travel policies directly from the insurance company**; if you buy them from a cruise line, airline, or tour operator that goes out of business you probably won't be covered for the agency or operator's default, a major risk. Before making any purchase, review your existing health and home-owner's policies to find what they cover away from home.

⨻ Travel Insurers In the U.S.: **Access America** ⊠ 6600 W. Broad St., Richmond, VA 23230 ☎ 800/284-8300 🖷 804/673-1491 or 800/346-9265 ⊕ www.accessamerica.com. **Travel Guard International** ⊠ 1145 Clark St., Stevens Point, WI 54481 ☎ 715/345-0505 or 800/826-1300 🖷 800/955-8785 ⊕ www.travelguard.com.

⨻ In the U.K.: **Association of British Insurers** ⊠ 51 Gresham St., London EC2V 7HQ ☎ 020/7600-3333 🖷 020/7696-8999 ⊕ www.abi.org.uk. In Canada: **RBC Insurance** ⊠ 6880 Financial Dr., Mississauga, Ontario L5N 7Y5 ☎ 800/565-3129 🖷 905/813-4704 ⊕ www.rbcinsurance.com. In Australia: **Insurance Council of Australia** ⊠ Insurance Enquiries and Complaints, Level 3, 56 Pitt St., Sydney, NSW 2000 ☎ 1300/363683 or 02/9251-4456 🖷 02/9251-4453 ⊕ www.iecltd.com.au. In New Zealand: **Insurance Council of New Zealand** ⊠ Level 7, 111–115 Customhouse Quay, Box 474, Wellington ☎ 04/472-5230 🖷 04/473-3011 ⊕ www.icnz.org.nz.

LANGUAGE

Argentines speak *Castellano,* Castilian Spanish, which differs slightly from the Spanish of most other Latin American countries. For example, the informal *vos* (you) is used instead of *tu,* in conjunction with the verb *sos* (are) instead of *eres.* The double "L" found in words like *pollo* phonetically translates to the ZH-sound, rather than a Y-sound. English is considered the second most widely used language. Services geared toward tourism generally employ an English-speaking staff. It's also common to find English-speaking staff at commercial and entertainment centers.

LANGUAGE SCHOOLS

A wide selection of language courses can be found in the classifieds of Argentina's English-language daily newspaper, the *Buenos Aires Herald.* The list includes schools as well as private tutors.

If you prefer to arrange for Spanish classes prior to your arrival in Argentina, try Berlitz International School of Languages or the local Instituto de Lengua Española para Extranjeros (ILEE), both of which specialize in teaching Spanish to foreigners and have classes beginning every week. The ILEE can also help you find a place to stay.

⨻ **Berlitz International School of Languages** ⊠ Av. de Mayo 847, fl. 1, Buenos Aires ☎🖷 11/4342-0202 ⊕ www.berlitz.com. **Instituto de Lengua Española para Extranjeros** ⊠ Av. Callao 339, fl. 3, Buenos Aires ☎🖷 11/4372-0223 ⊕ www.argentinailee.com.

LANGUAGES FOR TRAVELERS

A phrase book and language-tape set can help get you started. *Fodor's Spanish for*

Travelers (available at bookstores everywhere) is excellent.

LODGING

The lodgings we list are the cream of the crop in each price category. We always list the facilities that are available—but we don't specify whether they cost extra: when pricing accommodations, always ask what's included and what costs extra. Properties marked ✕⊞ are lodging establishments whose restaurants warrant a special trip.

CATEGORY	COST
$$$$	over 300 pesos
$$$	220–300 pesos
$$	140–220 pesos
$	80–140 pesos
¢	under 80 pesos

Prices are for two people in a standard double room in high season.

Assume that hotels operate on the **European Plan** (EP, with no meals) unless we specify that they use the **Continental Plan** (CP, with a Continental breakfast), **Breakfast Plan** (BP, with a full breakfast), or **Full American Plan** (FAP, with all meals).

APARTMENT & VILLA RENTALS

If you want a home base that's roomy enough for a family and comes with cooking facilities, consider a furnished rental. Called *apart-hotels* in Argentina, these can save you money, especially if you're traveling with a group.
🚩 Local Agents **B&T Travel & Housing** ☎ 11/4804-1783 🖷 11/4809-0129 ⊕ www.bytargentina.com. **Suevia** ☎ 11/4327-2626 ⊕ www.suevia.com.ar.

CAMPING

Campgrounds can be found in popular tourist destinations, including some beach areas. They usually have running water, electricity, and bathroom facilities with toilets and showers; some even provide tent rentals for spur-of-the-moment camping. Rates generally range 10–15 pesos per tent. The **Automóvil Club Argentino** (⇨ Auto Clubs *in* Car Travel) can provide a list of campgrounds nationwide. Provincial tourist offices in Buenos Aires have lists of campgrounds in their regions. Some have telephones so that you can make reservations.

ESTANCIAS

In the Pampas, the Northeast, and the Northwest you can stay at *estancias* (working ranches). Unique activities include horseback riding and *asados* (barbecues). They range from rustic structures to mansions, and provide a memorable experience.

HOME EXCHANGES

If you would like to exchange your home for someone else's, join a home-exchange organization, which will send you its updated listings of available exchanges for a year and will include your own listing in at least one of them. It's up to you to make specific arrangements.
🚩 Exchange Clubs **HomeLink International** ☎ Box 47747, Tampa, FL 33647 ☎ 813/975-9825 or 800/638-3841 🖷 813/910-8144 ⊕ www.homelink. org; $110 yearly for a listing, on-line access, and catalog; $70 without catalog. **Intervac U.S.** ☎ 30 Corte San Fernando, Tiburon, CA 94920 ☎ 800/756-4663 🖷 415/435-7440 ⊕ www.intervacus.com; $105 yearly for a listing, on-line access, and a catalog; $50 without catalog.

HOSTELS

No matter what your age, you can save on lodging costs by staying at hostels. In some 4,500 locations in more than 70 countries around the world, Hostelling International (HI), the umbrella group for a number of national youth-hostel associations, offers single-sex, dorm-style beds and, at many hostels, rooms for couples and family accommodations. Membership in any HI national hostel association, open to travelers of all ages, allows you to stay in HI-affiliated hostels at member rates; one-year membership is about $28 for adults (C$35 for a two-year minimum membership in Canada, £13.50 in the U.K., A$52 in Australia, and NZ$40 in New Zealand). Members have priority if the hostel is full; they're also eligible for discounts around the world, even on rail and bus travel in some countries. Hostels in Argentina charge about 10–25 pesos per night.
🚩 Best Options **Asatej** ✉ Calle Florida 835, Buenos Aires, 1005 ☎ 11/4511-8700 or 11/4114-7595 ⊕ www.almundo.com. **Buenos Aires Hostel** ✉ Av. Brasil 675, Buenos Aires, 1154 ⊕ www.ba-h.com.ar. **Hostelling International–Argentina (RAAJ)** ✉ Calle Florida 835, 319B, Buenos Aires, 1005 ☎ 11/4511-8712 ⊕ www.hostels.org.ar.

F Organizations **Hostelling International–
Canada** ✉ 205 Catherine St., Suite 400, Ottawa,
Ontario K2P 1C3 ☎ 613/237-7884 or 800/663-5777
🖷 613/237-7868 ⊕ www.hihostels.ca. **Hostelling
International–USA** ✉ 8401 Colesville Rd., Suite
600, Silver Spring, MD 20910 ☎ 301/495-1240
🖷 301/495-6697 ⊕ www.hiayh.org. **YHA Australia**
✉ 422 Kent St., Sydney, NSW 2001 ☎ 02/9261-1111
🖷 02/9261-1969 ⊕ www.yha.com.au. **YHA England
& Wales** ✉ Trevelyan House, Dimple Rd., Matlock,
Derbyshire DE4 3YH, U.K. ☎ 0870/870-8808, 0870/
770-8868, or 0162/959-2700 🖷 0870/770-6127
⊕ www.yha.org.uk. **YHA New Zealand** ✉ Level 4,
Torrens House, 195 Hereford St., Box 436,
Christchurch ☎ 03/379-9970 or 0800/278-299
🖷 03/365-4476 ⊕ www.yha.org.nz.

HOTELS

Amenities in most nice hotels—private
baths, 24-hour room service, heating and
air-conditioning, cable TV, dry cleaning,
minibars, and restaurants—are above average. The less expensive the hotel, the
fewer amenities available, though you can
still find charm, cleanliness, and hospital-
ity. You may or may not have a television
and a phone in your room, though they
are usually provided somewhere in the
hotel. Rooms that have a private bath
may only have a shower, or in some
cases, you'll share a bath in the hall. In
all but the most upscale hotels, you may
be asked to leave your key at the reception desk whenever you leave. Many
small hotels have a curfew, so if you arrive after the reception desk closes, you
may have to ring to get in. Most hotels in
all categories include a Continental
breakfast in the room rate, whether or
not there is a full restaurant in the hotel;
the pricier hotels offer buffet-style breakfasts, some at an extra charge.
F Toll-Free Numbers **Best Western** ☎ 800/528-
1234 ⊕ www.bestwestern.com. **Choice** ☎ 800/424-
6423 ⊕ www.choicehotels.com. **Four Seasons**
☎ 800/332-3442 ⊕ www.fourseasons.com. **Hilton**
☎ 800/445-8667 ⊕ www.hilton.com. **Holiday
Inn** ☎ 800/465-4329 ⊕ www.sixcontinentshotels.
com. **Howard Johnson** ☎ 800/446-4656 ⊕ www.
hojo.com. **Hyatt Hotels & Resorts** ☎ 800/233-1234
⊕ www.hyatt.com. **Inter-Continental** ☎ 800/327-
0200 ⊕ www.intercontinental.com. **Marriott**
☎ 800/228-9290 ⊕ www.marriott.com. **Ramada**
☎ 800/228-2828, 800/854-7854 international
reservations ⊕ www.ramada.com or www.
ramadahotels.com. **Sheraton** ☎ 800/325-3535
⊕ www.starwood.com/sheraton.

MOTELS

Family-oriented motels can be found
through the Automóvil Club Argentino
(⇨ Auto Clubs *in* Car Travel). Generally
these motels are inexpensive (40–50 pesos
a night) and more than adequate.

You may want to avoid *albergues transito-
rios* (temporary lodgings), the euphemistic
term for drive-in motels used for romantic
trysts. They're also known as *telos*. Very
common in this country where people
often live with their parents until mar-
riage, they are easily recognizable by their
pink or purple neon exterior lights. Room
rates are by the hour.

RESIDENCIALES

Residenciales can be either family-run pensions or bed-and-breakfasts. These are
generally found in smaller towns.

MAIL & SHIPPING

Mail delivery is quite dependable and
should take around 6–15 days from
Buenos Aires to the United States and
10–15 days to the United Kingdom, but
like many things in Argentina, this is not
guaranteed. Put postcards in envelopes
and they will arrive more quickly.

There are mail drops located around the
city, and you can usually buy stamps from
your hotel.

EXPRESS MAIL

Express mail takes three–five days for all
international destinations, and the cost
can be steep (for instance, a letter to the
United States via FedEx costs $27).
F Major Services **Correo Argentino** ✉ Sarmiento
151, Buenos Aires ☎ 11/4316-3000 ⊕ www.
correoargentino.com.ar. **DHL** ✉ Moreno 927,
Buenos Aires ☎ 0800/2222-345 ⊕ www.dhl.com.
ar. **Federal Express** ✉ Maipú 753, Buenos Aires
☎ 11/4630-0300 ⊕ www.fedex.com. **UPS**
✉ Bernardo de Yrigoyen 974, Buenos Aires ☎ 11/
4307-2174 or 0800/2222-877 ⊕ www.ups.com.

POSTAL RATES

An international airmail letter costs 3
pesos (up to 20 grams).

RECEIVING MAIL

You can receive mail in Buenos Aires at the
Correo Central (Central Post Office). Let-
ters should be addressed to your name, A/C
Lista/Poste Restante, Correo Central, 1000

Capital Federal, Argentina. You will be asked to present ID and pay 1.50 pesos for handling when recovering your mail. American Express cardholders can have mail sent to American Express. Some embassies allow your mail to be delivered to their consulate address; inquire beforehand.

🔢 Locations **American Express** ✉ c/o American Express, Arenales 707, 1061 Buenos Aires ☎ 11/4310-3000. **Buenos Aires Correo Central** ✉ Sarmiento 151, fl. 1, Buenos Aires ☎ 11/4316-3000.

MONEY MATTERS

If you're traveling from a country with a strong currency like the U.S. dollar or the euro, Argentina is very inexpensive. Bargains are everywhere to be found. Sumptuous dinners, particularly in finer restaurants, can run as high as 100 pesos per person with wine, dessert, and tip—the equivalent of around $35. A large wood-grilled sirloin with salad, potatoes, a house wine, and an espresso will run around 30 pesos at steak houses in Buenos Aires and much less in the hinterlands.

In Buenos Aires you're likely to pay 1.50–2 pesos for a *cafecito* (small cup of coffee) in a café. A soda costs 1.50 pesos. A taxi ride will run you 4–8 pesos in the larger cities. A tango show dinner with a couple of drinks costs about 100 pesos. A double room in a moderately priced, well-situated hotel costs $100–$130 dollars, including taxes. Many hotels are now in the habit of charging all their prices in dollars. **Make sure that the rate you are paying is valid for both tourists and Argentines**; some hotels have been known to take advantage of foreigners who are unaware of the favorable exchange rate by charging them an increased price.

When ordering alcoholic drinks, ask for Argentine liquors or suffer the import fees. A bottle of Chivas Regal costs 80 pesos in shops, for instance. When ordering drinks, specify your preference for whiskey or vodka *nacional*, for example. Happy hours, with half-price drinks and a party ambience, have become standard in the trendier city areas.

Prices throughout this guide are given for adults. Substantially reduced fees are almost always available for children, students, and senior citizens. For information on taxes, *see* Taxes.

ATMS

ATMs are easy to find, especially in major cities and resort towns; you'll find them in banks, services stations, and shopping malls, and all airports have at least one. The Banelco ATM system is the most widely used, indicated by a burgundy-color sign with white lettering. During the height of Argentina's recent economic crisis, banks were allowing only limited withdraws from ATMs. This problem is effectively over; you should have no trouble withdrawing large amounts.

Before leaving home, **make sure that your credit cards have been programmed for ATM use in Argentina.** Your local bank card may not work overseas; ask your bank about a MasterCard–Cirrus or Visa–Plus debit card, which works like a bank card but can be used at any of the ATMs displaying their logo.

Although fees charged for ATM transactions may be higher, Cirrus and Plus exchange rates are excellent because they are based on wholesale rates offered only by major banks.

🔢 **ATM Locations Banelco** ✉ Mexico 444, Buenos Aires ☎ 11/4334-5466. **Cirrus** ☎ 800/424-7787 ⊕ www.mastercard.com. **Plus** ⊕ www.visa.com/pd/atm.

CREDIT CARDS

If you choose to bring just one card, Visa is recommended, as it is the most readily accepted. American Express, Diners Club, and MasterCard are the most commonly accepted after Visa. It may be easiest to use your credit card whenever possible—the exchange rate only varies by a fraction of a cent, so you won't need to worry whether your purchase is charged on the day of purchase or at some point in the future. Note, however that you may get a better deal if you pay with cash. Because of the recent economic instability in Argentina, some restaurants have temporarily suspended the use of credit cards. It's best to **inquire before you dine whether credit cards are accepted.**

Throughout this guide, the following abbreviations are used: **AE**, American Express; **DC**, Diners Club; **MC**, MasterCard; and **V**, Visa.

🔢 **Reporting Lost Cards American Express** ☎ 11/4310-3000 ⊕ www.americanexpress.com. **Diners Club** ☎ 0810/444-2484 toll free ⊕ www.dinersclub.

com.ar. **MasterCard** ☎ 0800/555-0507 toll free ⊕ www.mastercard.com. **Visa** ☎ 114379-3333 ⊕ www.visa.com.

CURRENCY

Throughout its history, Argentina has had one of the most volatile economies in the world, and that tradition continues today. After a decade of relative calm, the Argentine economy crashed in 2001, when the country defaulted on billions of dollars in foreign debt. The economic uncertainty sent citizens scurrying to the banks to withdraw their savings, only to be denied access because of government-imposed banking restrictions known as *el corralito*. Angry, and sometimes bloody, protests followed, as many middle-class Argentines joined the lower-class in a revolt against the government and the banks. The banking sanctions have since been lifted and most Argentines once again have access to their money, but the value of their savings has been slashed by two-thirds.

One peso equals 100 centavos. Peso notes are in denominations of 100, 50, 20, 10, 5, and 2. Coins are in denominations of 1 peso, and 50, 25, 10, 5, and 1 centavos. When giving change, the cashier may round your purchase to the nearest 5 or even 10 centavos. Always check your change.

CURRENCY EXCHANGE

During the 1990s the Argentine peso was pegged to the U.S. dollar. This policy provided Argentina with a decade of unparalleled prosperity, when foreign products were available and affordable for the first time. This 1:1 peg eventually proved fatal for Argentina, and in 2002 the peso was unhinged on the open market. It has since lost around 60 percent of its value. This currency meltdown wiped out many Argentines' life savings, but has proved to be advantageous for tourists. Once one of the most expensive countries on the planet, Argentina is now a bargain for travelers.

If possible, exchange your local currency for pesos before you travel, but check to make sure you are getting a good rate. Once you arrive in Buenos Aires, there are many places where you can get pesos. Ask in your hotel or visit a *casa de cambio* (money changers) in El Centro, where you

should be prepared to show your passport to complete the transaction.

There are two exchange desks at Buenos Aires's Ezeiza Airport, on the upper level in Terminal A, and a desk at the city's domestic Jorge Newbery Airport. Keep in mind that banks charge exchange fees, as do some hotels. Plan ahead, since it's often hard to change large amounts of money at hotels on weekends, even in cities.

For the most favorable rates, change money through banks. Although ATM transaction fees may be higher abroad than at home, ATM rates are excellent because they are based on wholesale rates offered only by major banks. To avoid lines at airport exchange booths, get a bit of local currency before you leave home.

You may not be able to change currency in rural areas at all, so **don't leave major cities without adequate amounts of pesos** in small denominations.

At this writing, the rate of exchange was 2.9 pesos to the U.S. dollar, 2.2 pesos to the Canadian dollar, 5.48 pesos to the pound sterling, 3.66 pesos to the euro, 2.26 pesos to the Australian dollar, 2 pesos to the New Zealand dollar, and 0.44 pesos to the South African rand.

🖪 **Exchange Services International Currency Express** ✉ 427 N. Camden Dr., Suite F, Beverly Hills, CA 90210 ☎ 888/278-6628 orders 🖷 310/278-6410 ⊕ www.foreignmoney.com. **Thomas Cook International Money Services** ☎ 800/287-7362 orders and retail locations ⊕ www.us.thomascook.com.

TRAVELER'S CHECKS

Most larger stores in Buenos Aires accept traveler's checks, but smaller shops and restaurants are leery of them. When using traveler's checks, remember to carry a valid ID with you for any purchases or when changing them at a bank or the American Express office. You'll have trouble changing traveler's checks outside of Buenos Aires, so if you want to bring them plan on changing them before you leave the city.

PACKING

Argentines are very fashion and appearance conscious. If you're doing business in Argentina, bring the same attire you would wear in U.S. and European cities: for men, suits and ties; for women, suits for day wear and cocktail dresses or other suitable dinner clothes.

For sightseeing and leisure, casual clothing and good walking shoes are desirable and appropriate. In smaller towns and villages, dress is more conservative.

In Buenos Aires, people dress stylishly, whether casual or elegant, for dinner, depending on the restaurant. If you walk around the city in shorts, a T-shirt, sneakers, and a baseball hat, you will definitely be spotted as a tourist and may draw some unwanted attention.

For beach vacations, bring lightweight sportswear, and sweaters, a windbreaker, or a jacket for evenings when the temperatures drop. You can purchase all of these items here, but they are more expensive than they are in the United States.

Travel in the tropical rain forest requires long-sleeve shirts, long pants, socks, sneakers, a hat, a light waterproof jacket, a bathing suit, and plenty of insect repellent with DEET.

If you're visiting high altitudes or southern Patagonia, bring a fleece jacket, thermal underwear, and thick sweaters—you'll need even heavier clothing in winter months. Local markets often carry hand-knit sweaters, ponchos, and Andean headgear.

Depending on where you go, you may also want to pack a screw-top water bottle, a money pouch, a travel flashlight, extra batteries, a pocketknife with a bottle opener, a medical kit, and binoculars. Don't forget to check camera batteries and bring along your favorite film; though these items are readily available in major cities, they may be harder to find elsewhere.

In your carry-on luggage, pack an extra pair of eyeglasses or contact lenses and enough of any medication you take to last a few days longer than the entire trip. You may also ask your doctor to write a spare prescription using the drug's generic name, as brand names may vary from country to country. In luggage to be checked, **never pack prescription drugs, valuables, or film.** Check *Fodor's How to Pack* (available at on-line retailers and bookstores everywhere) for more tips.

To avoid customs and security delays, carry medications in their original packaging. Don't pack any sharp objects in your carry-on luggage, including knives of any size or material, scissors, and corkscrews, or anything else that might arouse suspicion.

To avoid having your checked luggage chosen for hand inspection, don't cram bags full. The U.S. Transportation Security Administration suggests packing shoes on top and placing personal items you don't want touched in clear plastic bags.

CHECKING LUGGAGE

You're allowed to carry aboard one bag and one personal article, such as a purse or a laptop computer. Make sure what you carry on fits under your seat or in the overhead bin. Get to the gate early, so you can board as soon as possible, before the overhead bins fill up.

Baggage allowances vary by carrier, destination, and ticket class. On international flights, you're usually allowed to check two bags weighing up to 70 pounds (32 kilograms) each, although a few airlines allow checked bags of up to 88 pounds (40 kilograms) in first class. Some international carriers don't allow more than 66 pounds (30 kilograms) per bag in business class and 44 pounds (20 kilograms) in economy. On domestic flights, the limit is usually 50 to 70 pounds (23 to 32 kilograms) per bag. In general, carry-on bags shouldn't exceed 40 pounds (18 kilograms). Most airlines won't accept bags that weigh more than 100 pounds (45 kilograms) on domestic or international flights. Check baggage restrictions with your carrier before you pack.

Airline liability for baggage is limited to $2,500 per person on flights within the United States. On international flights it amounts to $9.07 per pound or $20 per kilogram for checked baggage (roughly $640 per 70-pound bag), with a maximum of $634.90 per piece, and $400 per passenger for unchecked baggage. You can buy additional coverage at check-in for about $10 per $1,000 of coverage, but it often excludes a rather extensive list of items, shown on your airline ticket.

Before departure, itemize your bags' contents and their worth, and label the bags with your name, address, and phone number. (If you use your home address, cover it so potential thieves can't see it readily.)

Include a label inside each bag and pack a copy of your itinerary. At check-in, make sure each bag is correctly tagged with the destination airport's three-letter code. Because some checked bags will be opened for hand inspection, the U.S. Transportation Security Administration recommends that you leave luggage unlocked or use the plastic locks offered at check-in. TSA screeners place an inspection notice inside searched bags, which are re-sealed with a special lock.

If your bag has been searched and contents are missing or damaged, file a claim with the TSA Consumer Response Center as soon as possible. If your bags arrive damaged or fail to arrive at all, file a written report with the airline before leaving the airport.

🔊 Complaints **U.S. Transportation Security Administration Consumer Response Center** ☎ 866/289-9673 ⊕ www.tsa.gov.

PASSPORTS & VISAS

When traveling internationally, carry your passport even if you don't need one (it's always the best form of ID) and **make two photocopies of the data page** (one for someone at home and another for you, carried separately from your passport). If you lose your passport, promptly call the nearest embassy or consulate and the local police.

U.S. passport applications for children under age 14 require consent from both parents or legal guardians; both parents must appear together to sign the application. If only one parent appears, he or she must submit a written statement from the other parent authorizing passport issuance for the child. A parent with sole authority must present evidence of it when applying; acceptable documentation includes the child's certified birth certificate listing only the applying parent, a court order specifically permitting this parent's travel with the child, or a death certificate for the non-applying parent. Application forms and instructions are available on the Web site of the U.S. State Department's Bureau of Consular Affairs (⊕ www.travel.state.gov).

ENTERING ARGENTINA

U.S., Canadian, and British citizens do not need a visa for visits of up to 90 days, though they must carry a passport. Upon entering Argentina, you'll receive a tourist visa stamp on your passport valid for 90 days. If you need to stay longer, exit the country for one night; upon reentering Argentina, your passport will be stamped allowing an additional 90 days. The fine for overstaying your tourist visa is $50 dollars, payable upon departure at the airport. If you do overstay your visa, plan to arrive at the airport several hours in advance of your flight so that you have ample time to take care of the fine.

PASSPORT OFFICES

The best time to apply for a passport or to renew is in fall and winter. Before any trip, check your passport's expiration date, and, if necessary, renew it as soon as possible.

🔊 Australian Citizens **Passports Australia** ☎ 131-232 ⊕ www.passports.gov.au.

🔊 Canadian Citizens **Passport Office** ✉ To mail in applications: 200 Promenade du Portage, Hull, Québec J8X 4B7 ☎ 819/994-3500 or 800/567-6868 ⊕ www.ppt.gc.ca.

🔊 New Zealand Citizens **New Zealand Passports Office** ☎ 0800/22-5050 or 04/474-8100 ⊕ www.passports.govt.nz.

🔊 U.K. Citizens **U.K. Passport Service** ☎ 0870/521-0410 ⊕ www.passport.gov.uk.

🔊 U.S. Citizens **National Passport Information Center** ☎ 900/225-5674 or 900/225-7778 TTY (calls are 55¢ per minute for automated service or $1.50 per minute for operator service), 888/362-8668 or 888/498-3648 TTY (calls are $5.50 each) ⊕ www.travel.state.gov.

SAFETY

Buenos Aires is one of the safer cities in the world; however, recent political and economic stability has produced an increase in crime. Most of these crimes are limited to robberies and petty theft, but you should be aware of your surroundings at all times and don't take any unnecessary chances. Do your best to blend in with the locals and you will not attract attention. Police constantly patrol any areas where tourists are likely to be, and violent crime is rare. Smaller towns and villages in Argentina are even safer.

If you're hailing a taxi, make sure it says "radio taxi"; this means that the driver works for a licensed company and is required to call in every new fare over the radio. Also look for the driver's photo ID, which should be well displayed inside the car. Better yet, call a licensed *remis,* which is always safer and usually cheaper, as you agree on a fixed-price beforehand.

Argentines like to speak their minds, and there has been a huge increase in street protests in recent years. Most of these have to do with government policies, but there has been an increase in anti-U.S. and anti-British sentiment, stemming primarily from Argentina's strained relationship with the International Monetary Fund (IMF) and the war in Iraq. If you do see a demonstration, don't panic—as the overwhelming majority of them are peaceful—just be aware of the atmosphere.

Don't wear a money belt or a waist pack, both of which peg you as a tourist. Distribute your cash and any valuables (including your credit cards and passport) between a deep front pocket, an inside jacket or vest pocket, and a hidden money pouch. Do not reach for the money pouch once you're in public. Don't carry valuables swinging from your shoulder or hanging around your neck. Always remain alert for pickpockets. Tickets and other valuables are best left in hotel safes.

Don't wear any jewelry you're not willing to lose—there have been incidents of chains and even earrings being yanked off of unsuspecting tourists. Keep cameras in a secure camera bag, preferably one with a chain or wire embedded in the strap.

Generally you'll find that people are friendly and helpful and that the biggest crime you're likely to encounter is the exorbitant price of a gaucho poncho.

WOMEN IN ARGENTINA

If you carry a purse, choose one with a zipper and a thick strap that you can drape across your body; adjust the length so that the purse sits in front of you at or above hip level. (Don't wear a money belt or a waist pack.) Store only enough money in the purse to cover casual spending. Distribute the rest of your cash and any valuables between deep front pockets, inside jacket or vest pockets, and a concealed money pouch.

Women are safer in Buenos Aires than in many other major cities in the world, but crimes still occur. It's best not to over- or underdress, or wear flashy jewelry on the street.

Women can expect pointed looks, the occasional catcall, and some advances. Act confident, and ignore the men.

SENIOR-CITIZEN TRAVEL

Senior citizens are highly revered in Argentina and are generally treated with respect. There's no reason that active, well-traveled senior citizens should not visit Argentina, whether on an independent vacation, an escorted tour, or adventure vacation. Argentina has plenty of good hotels and competent ground operators who can meet your flights and organize your sightseeing.

To qualify for age-related discounts, **mention your senior-citizen status up front** when booking hotel reservations (not when checking out) and before you're seated in restaurants (not when paying the bill). Note that discounts may be limited to certain menus, days, or hours. When renting a car, ask about promotional car-rental discounts, which can be cheaper than senior-citizen rates.

Before you leave home, **determine what medical services your health insurance will cover.** Note that Medicare does not provide for payment of hospital and medical services outside the United States. If you need additional travel insurance, buy it (⇨ Insurance).

🔀 **Educational Programs Elderhostel** ✉ 11 Ave. de Lafayette, Boston, MA 02111-1746 ☎ 877/426-8056, 978/323-4141 international callers, 877/426-2167 TTY 📠 877/426-2166 ⊕ www.elderhostel.org. **Folkways Institute** ✉ 14600 S.E. Aldridge Rd., Portland, OR 97236-6518 ☎ 503/658-6600 📠 503/658-8672 ⊕ www.folkwaysinstitute.org. **Interhostel** ✉ University of New Hampshire, 6 Garrison Ave., Durham, NH 03824 ☎ 603/862-1147 or 800/733-9753 📠 603/862-1113 ⊕ www.learn.unh.edu.

SHOPPING

Buenos Aires is a great place to buy clothing, leather goods, and furs, especially because of the favorable exchange rate for those with dollars and euros. Paintings, engravings, antiques, fine local wine, and handicrafts are excellent items to bring back home. Just looking at the displays—of Tierra del Fuego fox in the latest Yves St-Laurent styles, butter-soft leathers, evening gowns with snakeskin appliqués, cashmere sweaters, loafers, boots, briefcases, and bags—can be a window-shopper's delight.

Look for seasonal *liquidación* (sale) signs in the windows, as well as duty-free signs (⇨ Taxes).

Argentine shops have fixed prices but often give discounts for cash (in the smaller shops, you can often begin a bargaining session by asking, *Cuanto en efectivo?* ["How much is the cash price?"]).

STUDENTS IN ARGENTINA

To save money on everything from transportation, hostels, movies, and pubs to phone calls, CDs, and hamburgers, check out student-oriented travel agencies and Council Travel's Web site. To qualify you'll need a student ID card. Members of international student groups are also eligible.

🖪 IDs & Services **STA Travel** ✉ 10 Downing St., New York, NY 10014 ☎ 212/627-3111, 800/777-0112 24-hr service center 🖷 212/627-3387 ⊕ www.sta. com. **Travel Cuts** ✉ 187 College St., Toronto, Ontario M5T 1P7, Canada ☎ 800/592-2887 in U.S., 416/979-2406 or 866/246-9762 in Canada 🖷 416/979-8167 ⊕ www.travelcuts.com.

TAXES

Sales tax (IVA) in Argentina is 21%. The tax is usually included in the price on your receipt. Keep your receipts: the IVA tax is entirely refundable for purchases exceeding $200 dollars at stores displaying a duty-free sign. When you depart, plan enough time to visit the return desk at the airport to obtain your refund.

TELEPHONES

With the deregulation in telecommunications, new phone numbers and additional prefixes have been added, and telephoning can be confusing. Your hotel operator can assist you, or call for information.

Telecom's *telecentros* and Telefónica's *locutorios* offer a variety of services, including metered phone calls, faxes, telegrams, and access to the Internet; some even provide wire transfers. They are convenient to use and abound throughout all cities; some are specially equipped for people with hearing impairments.

🖪 **Telecom** ☎ 0800/555-0112 ⊕ www.telecom. com.ar. **Telefónica** ☎ 0800/222-4262 ⊕ www. telefonica.com.ar.

AREA & COUNTRY CODES

The country code for Argentina is 54. To call Argentina from overseas, dial 00 + country code (54) + area code (omitting the first 0, which is for long-distance calls within Argentina). The area code for Buenos Aires is 11.

DIRECTORY & OPERATOR ASSISTANCE

For information, dial 110. For the time, dial 113. For information about international calls, dial 19 or 000.

INTERNATIONAL CALLS

Hotels have *DDI*, international direct dialing, but may charge up to 3 pesos for a long-distance call. You're best off calling from telecentros or locutorios, where your call is metered and will run around 95 centavos for the first minute, and 68 centavos each additional minute, during peak hours to the United States. Rates are much higher for England (starting at 1.40 pesos for the first minute and 1.25 pesos for each additional minute) and Australia (2.85 pesos for the first minute and 2.30 pesos for each additional minute).

The country code is 1 for the United States and Canada, 61 for Australia, 64 for New Zealand, and 44 for the United Kingdom. To call out from Argentina, dial 00 + country code + area code + number.

LOCAL CALLS

Hotels charge steep rates for local calls; before dialing, ask at the front desk about phone charges.

Local calls can be made from public phones booths and telephone centers with coins or phone cards sold at kiosks. A local call will cost you 23 centavos for two minutes during peak hours (weekdays 8 AM–8 PM, Saturday 8 AM–1 PM).

LONG-DISTANCE CALLS

When calling from one area code to another in Argentina, add a 0 before the area code, then 1 for Capital Federal and Greater Buenos Aires, 2 for the Southern region, and 3 for provinces in the North. Charges increase with distances, beginning at 30 km (18½ mi) outside of the city.

Many hotels charge up to 4 pesos per call on top of the regular rate. It's best to call from a public phone or telephone center.

LONG-DISTANCE SERVICES

AT&T, MCI, and Sprint access codes make calling long-distance relatively convenient, but you may find the local access number blocked in many hotel rooms. First ask the hotel operator to connect you. If the hotel operator balks, ask for an international operator, or dial the international operator yourself. One way to improve your odds of getting connected to your long-distance carrier is to travel with more than one company's calling card (a hotel may block Sprint, for example, but not MCI). If all else fails, call from a pay phone.

Access Codes For local access numbers abroad, contact **AT&T Direct** ☎ 0800/555-4288, **MCI WorldPhone** ☎ 0800/222-6249 or 0800/ 555-1002, or **Sprint International Access** ☎ 0800/222-1003.

MOBILE PHONES

To call the cell phone number of a Buenos Aires resident, dial 15 before the number (unless you're also calling from a cell phone with a Buenos Aires number). Local cell phone charges vary depending on certain factors, such as the company and time of day, and can cost up to 2 pesos per call; the fee is charged to the caller, not the recipient, unless on a pay phone.

Cellular phone rentals are available, though pricey. Some hotels even rent phones.

Mobile Phone Rental **Unifon** ⊠ Av. Corrientes 645, Buenos Aires ☎ 0800/333-6868 ⊕ www.unifon.com.ar.

PHONE CARDS

Phone cards, called *tarjetas chip,* are available at kiosks, pharmacies, and telephone centers. Prices range 4–10 pesos, at 23¢ for every two minutes during peak hours (weekdays and Sunday 8–8, Saturday 8 AM–1 PM), and half rate off-peak. You can use them for local, long-distance, and international calls.

PUBLIC PHONES

Public phones in Argentina are reliable and can be found on nearly every block. You can make your call using coins or a phone card. Simply slide the card in, wait for the reading of how many minutes you have remaining, then dial.

To make a long-distance call from a public phone, you're better off finding a telephone center.

TIME

New York is one time zone behind Buenos Aires from April to October (it's two hours behind the rest of the year, as Argentina does not observe daylight savings time). There's a four-hour difference between Los Angeles and Buenos Aires.

TIPPING

Propinas (tips) range 10%–15% in bars and restaurants (10% is enough in a casual café or if the bill runs high). Note that some restaurants charge a *cubierto,* covering table service, not waiter's tip. Argentines round off a taxi fare, though some cabbies who frequent hotels popular with tourists seem to expect more. Hotel porters should be tipped at least 1 peso. Also give doormen and ushers about 1 peso. Beauty- and barbershop personnel generally get around 10%.

TOURS & PACKAGES

Because everything is prearranged on a prepackaged tour or independent vacation, you spend less time planning—and often get it all at a good price.

BOOKING WITH AN AGENT

Travel agents are excellent resources. But it's a good idea to collect brochures from several agencies, as some agents' suggestions may be influenced by relationships with tour and package firms that reward them for volume sales. If you have a special interest, find an agent with expertise in that area; the American Society of Travel Agents (ASTA; ⇨ Travel Agencies) has a database of specialists worldwide. You can log on to the group's Web site to find an ASTA travel agent in your neighborhood.

Make sure your travel agent knows the accommodations and other services of the place being recommended. Ask about the hotel's location, room size, beds, and whether it has a pool, room service, or programs for children, if you care about these. Has your agent been there in person or sent others whom you can contact?

Do some homework on your own, too: local tourism boards can provide information about lesser-known and small-niche operators, some of which may sell only direct.

BUYER BEWARE

Each year consumers are stranded or lose their money when tour operators—even large ones with excellent reputations—go out of business. So check out the operator. Ask several travel agents about its reputation, and try to **book with a company that has a consumer-protection program.** (Look for information in the company's brochure.) In the United States, members of the National Tour Association and the U.S. Tour Operators Association are required to set aside funds to cover payments and travel arrangements in the event that the company defaults. It's also a good idea to choose a company that participates in the American Society of Travel Agents' Tour Operator Program; ASTA will act as mediator in any disputes between you and your tour operator.

Remember that the more your package or tour includes, the better you can predict the ultimate cost of your vacation. Make sure you know exactly what is covered, and beware of hidden costs. Are taxes, tips, and transfers included? Entertainment and excursions? These can add up.

⚑ Tour-Operator Recommendations American Society of Travel Agents (⇨ Travel Agencies). **National Tour Association (NTA)** ✉ 546 E. Main St., Lexington, KY 40508 ☎ 859/226-4444 or 800/682-8886 📠 859/226-4404 ⊕ www.ntaonline.com. **United States Tour Operators Association (USTOA)** ✉ 275 Madison Ave., Suite 2014, New York, NY 10016 ☎ 212/599-6599 📠 212/599-6744 ⊕ www.ustoa.com.

TRAIN TRAVEL

Argentina's rail system, which was built by the British, no longer plays an important role in the national transportation system. Most lines lead out of Buenos Aires to various destinations and are often not as comfortable as luxury buses. The most popular routes are from Buenos Aires to Mar del Plata and Bariloche. There are also two special tourist-oriented trains: the Tren a las Nubes (Train of the Clouds), which goes through the Andes (⇨ Chapter 4), and the Tren de la Costa (Coast Train), which runs from Buenos Aires to the river delta area of Tigre (⇨ Chapters 1 and 2).

FARES & SCHEDULES

Train tickets are inexpensive. Usually there are two classes. Plan to **buy your train tickets a few days ahead of your trip** (two weeks in summer months), and arrive at the station well before departure time. Reservations must be made in person at the local train station. Refer to individual chapters for more information about train service.

TRAVEL AGENCIES

A good travel agent puts your needs first. Look for an agency that has been in business at least five years, emphasizes customer service, and has someone on staff who specializes in your destination. In addition, **make sure the agency belongs to a professional trade organization.** The American Society of Travel Agents (ASTA)—the largest and most influential in the field with more than 20,000 members in some 140 countries—maintains and enforces a strict code of ethics and will step in to help mediate any agent-client disputes involving ASTA members if necessary. ASTA (whose motto is "Without a travel agent, you're on your own") also maintains a Web site that includes a directory of agents. (If a travel agency is also acting as your tour operator, *see* Buyer Beware *in* Tours & Packages.)

⚑ Local Agent Referrals American Society of Travel Agents (ASTA) ✉ 1101 King St., Suite 200, Alexandria, VA 22314 ☎ 703/739-2782 or 800/965-2782 24-hr hot line 📠 703/739-3268 ⊕ www.astanet.com. **Association of British Travel Agents** ✉ 68-71 Newman St., London W1T 3AH ☎ 020/7637-2444 📠 020/7637-0713 ⊕ www.abta.com. **Association of Canadian Travel Agencies** ✉ 130 Albert St., Suite 1705, Ottawa, Ontario K1P 5G4 ☎ 613/237-3657 📠 613/237-7052 ⊕ www.acta.ca. **Australian Federation of Travel Agents** ✉ Level 3, 309 Pitt St., Sydney, NSW 2000 ☎ 02/9264-3299 📠 02/9264-1085 ⊕ www.afta.com.au. **Travel Agents' Association of New Zealand** ✉ Level 5, Tourism and Travel House, 79 Boulcott St., Box 1888, Wellington 6001 ☎ 04/499-0104 📠 04/499-0786 ⊕ www.taanz.org.nz.

VISITOR INFORMATION

The city of Buenos Aires has a tourist office representing each province of Argentina. These offices can provide you with maps and regional information. Ask at your hotel for their locations throughout the city. Check out the Argentine Government Tourist Offices.

F Argentina Government Tourist Offices **Miami** ✉ 2655 Le Jeune Rd., Miami, FL 33134 📠 305/442–1366. **New York** ✉ 12 W. 56th St., New York, NY 10019 📠 212/603–0443.

F Government Advisories **Australian Department of Foreign Affairs and Trade** 📠 02/6261–1299 Consular Travel Advice Faxback Service ⊕ www.dfat.gov.au. **Consular Affairs Bureau of Canada** 📠 800/267–6788 or 613/944–6788 ⊕ www.voyage.gc.ca. **U.K. Foreign and Commonwealth Office** ✉ Travel Advice Unit, Consular Division, Old Admiralty Building, London SW1A 2PA 📠 020/7008–0232 or 020/7008–0233 ⊕ www.fco.gov.uk/travel. **U.S. Department of State** ✉ Overseas Citizens Services Office, Room 4811, 2201 C St. NW, Washington, DC 20520 📠 202/647–5225 interactive hot line, 888/407–4747 ⊕ www.travel.state.gov; enclose a cover letter with your request and a business-size SASE. **New Zealand Ministry of Foreign Affairs and Trade** 📠 04/439–8000 ⊕ www.mft.govt.nz.

WEB SITES

Do check out the World Wide Web when planning your trip. You'll find everything from weather forecasts to virtual tours of famous cities. Be sure to visit Fodors.com (⊕ www.fodors.com), a complete travel-planning site. You can research prices and book plane tickets, hotel rooms, rental cars, vacation packages, and more. In addition, you can post your pressing questions in the Travel Talk section. Other planning tools include a currency converter and weather reports, and there are loads of links to travel resources.

Don't rule out foreign-language sites; some have links to sites that present information in more than one language, including English.

F Web Sites **Argentina phone book** ⊕ www.guiatelefonica.com. **Argentina Secretary of Tourism** ⊕ www.turismo.gov.ar. **Buenos Aires Herald** ⊕ www.buenosairesherald.com. **Embassy of Argentina** ⊕ www.embajadaargentinaeeuu.org. **Tango** ⊕ www.abctango.com.

BUENOS AIRES

1

FODOR'S CHOICE

Cabaña las Lilas, *restaurant in Puerto Madero*

Calle Museo Caminito, *La Boca*

Cementerio de La Recoleta

El Trapiche, *restaurant in Palermo*

Marriott Plaza Hotel, *El Centro*

NH Jousten, *hotel in El Centro*

San Telmo neighborhood

Tomo Uno, *restaurant in El Centro*

HIGHLY RECOMMENDED

Jardín Japonés, *Palermo*

Museo de Arte Español Enrique Larreta, *Belgrano*

Museo Histórico Nacional, *San Telmo*

Museo MALBA, *Palermo*

Museo Nacional de Arte Decorativo, *La Recoleta*

Paseo del Rosedal, *Palermo*

Plaza Dorrego, *San Telmo*

Plaza de Mayo

Teatro Colon, *El Centro*

Many other great restaurants, hotels, and experiences enliven this city.
For other favorites, look for the black stars as you read this chapter.

Updated by
Brian Byrnes
and Victoria
Patience

BUENOS AIRES, THE NINTH LARGEST CITY in the world and the hub of the southern cone, is a sprawling metropolis rising from the Río de la Plata and stretching more than 200 square km (75 square mi) to the surrounding pampas, the fertile Argentine plains. With more than one-third of the country's 39 million inhabitants living in or around Buenos Aires, the city is the political, economic, and cultural center of Argentina and the gateway to the rest of the country.

Unlike most other Latin American cities, where the architecture reveals a strong Spanish colonial influence, Buenos Aires has a mix of styles. Modern high-rises sit side by side with ornate buildings from days long gone. At every turn you'll be reminded of the city's European heritage: with their boulevards lined with palatial mansions and spacious parks, the neighborhoods of El Centro, La Recoleta, and Belgrano evoke Rome, Madrid, Paris, and Budapest. The plazas of Palermo and Belgrano mirror those in Paris; Rome's Pantheon inspired the Parroquia de Nuestra Señora; the Avenida de Mayo has been compared to both Madrid and Budapest; and the Vatican Embassy on Avenida Alvear replicates the Jacquemart-André Museum in Paris. San Telmo and La Boca have a distinctly working-class Italian feel, in contrast to the stately aplomb of Plaza de Mayo and Avenida de Mayo.

Buenos Aires locals refer to themselves as *Porteños* because many of them originally arrived by boat from Europe and settled in the port area. Known as thinkers, Porteños delve into philosophical discussions and psychoanalysis (as proven by the large number of psychoanalysts per capita—in fact, the most of any city in the world). With 85% of the Argentine population of European origin, there's a blurred sense of national identity in Buenos Aires—South American or European?—and residents are often concerned with how outsiders perceive them. People here look at one another closely, whether it be a casual, appreciative glance or a curious stare, making many of them deeply image-conscious.

Buenos Aires has no Eiffel Tower, no internationally renowned museums, no must-see sights that clearly identify it as a world-class city. Rather, the essence of Buenos Aires resides in singular encounters imbued with intense Latin spirit—a flirtatious glance, a heartfelt chat, a juicy steak, an impassioned tango—to create a vibrant and unforgettable urban experience.

EXPLORING BUENOS AIRES

Buenos Aires is a sprawling city, best explored one neighborhood at a time on foot and by public transportation—*colectivo* (bus), *subte* (subway), or relatively inexpensive taxis. Streets are basically laid out in a grid, though a few streets transverse the grid diagonally; these are helpfully called *diagonales. Avenidas* are two-way streets, while *calles* are generally one-way. Streets and avenues running north–south change names at Avenida Rivadavía. Each city block is 100 meters (328 feet) long, and addresses are based on the building's measured position from the corner (for instance, 180 Calle Florida is 80 meters from the corner, and 100 meters, or one block, from 80 Calle Florida).

About the Restaurants

Dining in Buenos Aires is an art, a passion, and a pastime. Whether at home or in a restaurant, meals are events. *Sobremesa* (chatting at the table after the meal) is just as important as the dining ritual itself, and people linger over wine or coffee long after the dishes have been cleared away. World-renowned beef is a staple, cooked on a *parrilla* (grill), or

If you have 3 days

With three days in Buenos Aires, you'll have time to appreciate the city— but at breakneck speed. Plan to spend a half day around Plaza de Mayo, El Centro, San Telmo, La Boca, Palermo, and La Recoleta. If you're in town on a weekend, visit La Recoleta on Saturday and San Telmo and La Boca on Sunday in order to visit the neighborhoods' outdoor arts-and-crafts markets. If you're in town on weekdays, stick to Palermo on Monday or Tuesday; its outdoor offerings will be open, whereas most museums are closed one of those two days. Schedule time for a siesta to allow you a lengthy night out at a club, bar, or performance, or an evening of tango.

1

If you have 5 days

With five days you can enjoy all the sights listed in the three-day itinerary above at a more leisurely pace. You'll also have more time to tour the riverside promenade of Puerto Madero or head north to the neighborhood of Belgrano.

If you have 7–10 days

With more than a week in Buenos Aires, you can fully enjoy all the sights suggested in the three- and five-day itineraries above and venture off the beaten path. Consider a day trip to the picturesque and historic city of Colonia, Uruguay, 45 minutes away by river ferry. Include a visit to the northern suburbs and ride the Tren de la Costa for a scenic journey along the Río de la Plata to Tigre and the Puerto de Frutos market. Daylong excursions to the nearby cities of Luján or La Plata are also a good option.

---

sometimes over quebracho wood for a savory *asado* (barbecue). A typical meal consists of steak, fries, salad, and a robust *tinto* (red wine), followed by *flan* (creme caramel) with *dulce de leche* (a gooey caramel-like spread).

About the Hotels

Buenos Aires has an array of hotels, inns, *apart-hotels* (short-term rental apartments), and hostels. World-class facilities include the majestic Alvear Palace Hotel, the elegant Marriott Plaza, and the ultramodern Hilton Hotel Buenos Aires. Intimate hotels dot the city on and off the beaten path, providing charm at affordable prices. High season in Argentina includes the summer months of mid-December through February, and the winter holidays that fall in July. As a rule, hotel prices in Buenos Aires do not vary between high and low seasons; however, it is advisable to book ahead during high season, especially at more upmarket establishments, which may fill up months in advance.

WHAT IT COSTS In Argentina Pesos					
	$$$$	$$$	$$	$	¢
RESTAURANTS	over 35	25–35	15–25	8–15	under 8
HOTELS	over 300	220–300	140–220	80–140	under 80

Restaurant prices are for one main course at dinner. Hotel prices are for two people in a standard double room in high season.

Timing

When planning your trip to Buenos Aires, remember that the seasons are in exact opposition to those in the northern hemisphere. When it's summer in the United States, it's winter in Argentina, and vice versa. Winters (July–September) are chilly and rainy, though temperatures never drop below freezing. Summer's muggy heat (December–March) can be taxing at midday but makes for wonderful, warm nights. Spring (September–December) and autumn (April–June), with their mild temperatures, blossoms, and changing leaves, are ideal for urban trekking.

San Telmo

The bohemian San Telmo neighborhood, named after the patron saint of seafarers, sits midway between bustling El Centro and the quiet port area of La Boca. Its cobblestone streets teem with early-19th-century colonial buildings, once inhabited by affluent Spaniards. Upon the outbreak of yellow fever in the late 1800s, the wealthy moved northward, leaving behind opulent mansions that were converted into tenements and occupied by immigrant families in the late 19th century. Thanks to renewed urban planning and government subsidies, the worn sidewalks and formerly crumbling structures have been transformed into quaint streets lined with antiques shops, galleries, chic restaurants, and traditional tango halls. The neighborhood is a cradle of the city's historic and cultural traditions, and all its landmarks have been declared National Historic Monuments.

a good walk

To reach San Telmo by subway, take Line E to the Independencia station, and be prepared to walk nine blocks east along Avenida Independencia to Calle Defensa, the oldest street in the city. The sights in this walk are all grouped around this street. Head south down Calle Defensa until you reach **Plaza Dorrego** ❶ ▶, framed by bars, restaurants, and antiques shops. On Calle Humberto Primero, which borders the south side of Plaza Dorrego, visit the **Museo Penitenciario Antonio Ballvé** ❷ and its adjoining chapel, Nuestra Señora del Carmen. Next door, a mix of colonial, baroque, neoclassical, and Italianate architecture can be seen in the **Parroquia de San Pedro González Telmo** ❸. Head back to Plaza Dorrego and south again on Defensa toward **Pasaje de la Defensa** ❹, with its hodgepodge of tiny shops selling antiques and curios. Continue down Calle Defensa to the southern edge of San Telmo to reach **Parque Lezama** ❺, home to the **Museo Histórico Nacional** ❻. Overlooking the park, the onion-shape domes of the **Catedral Santísima Trinidad Iglesia Ortodoxa Rusa** ❼ rise above the treetops lining Avenida Brasíl. From here head north again along Calle Defensa to reach Avenida San Juan and the **Museo de Arte Moderno de Buenos Aires** ❽. Remains of the colonial period are found just off Calle Defensa on Calle Carlos Calvo, where you'll see **La Casa de Esteban de Luca** ❾, and down **Pasaje Giuffra** ❿, also off Calle Defensa. The legendary **Viejo Almacén** ⓫, open only for dinner and shows, is on Avenida Independencia. **Calle Balcarce** ⓬, which runs parallel to Calle Defensa, and the intersecting **Pasaje San Lorenzo** ⓭ lead you past unique period architecture.

TIMING & PRECAUTIONS

San Telmo thrives on Sunday, when the art and antiques market in Plaza Dorrego bustles with activity and street performers. A few hours will give you plenty of time to see the sights, but you could easily spend a full day exploring the neighborhood. San Telmo is one of the city's seedier districts, and you should exercise caution when walking here—especially at night. Violent crime is rare, but unemployment in the area, combined with the knowledge that tourists flock here, has led to instances of petty crime.

What to See

❶ **Calle Balcarce** (Balcarce Street). Although a stretch of this street is known for its touristy tango dinner shows, it nevertheless leads you past some

Barrios

Buenos Aires's identity lies in its 48 *barrios* (neighborhoods)—each with its own character and history. Many residents have lived in the same barrio for generations and feel more of an affinity to their neighborhood than to the city as a whole. As its name implies, El Centro is the heart of the city, and in it are theaters, bars, cafés, bookstores, and the crowded streets you'd expect to find in any major city center. In keeping with the traditions of Spain, the city's central institutions, both governmental and religious, frame Plaza de Mayo, which is in the first established barrio of the city (1769), Monserrat, and unofficially linked to El Centro. Highlights of Bohemian San Telmo, to the west of Plaza de Mayo, include Sunday strolls, antiques shopping at Feria de San Pedro and surrounding antiques stores, and the tango halls that come to life nightly. La Boca, south of San Telmo, retains much of its Italian heritage and you can still enjoy inexpensive authentic Italian fare in a cantina along Avenida Patricios. Upscale and European in style, La Recoleta, to the east of El Centro, comprises a four-block area, semifree of transit, where people-watching, at sidewalk bars and cafés, is a highly developed art form. Next to La Recoleta, Palermo not only has the honor of being the barrio with the most green space, but also the one with the most New York-style sub-neighborhoods—with names such as Palermo Hollywood and Palermo SoHo. Buenos Aires's Chinatown can be found within Belgrano, a neighborhood of both narrow cobblestone streets and wide European boulevards. The newest barrio, Puerto Madero, consists mostly of a chic riverside promenade, perfect for an evening stroll.

Nightlife

When a date at 7 PM is considered an afternoon coffee break, you know you're in a city that likes to party. Porteños never go early to discos—they wouldn't want to be seen before 2 AM. Tango, too, gets going after midnight and never seems to stop. The best neighborhoods are La Recoleta, Costanera Norte, and Palermo, which is the focal point of Buenos Aires's night-time scene. You can hit the clubs and tango, dine on grilled meats at a late-night *parrilla,* and then relax in a tony café or continue the revelry at one of Costanera Norte's after-hours clubs. In addition to enthusiastic club-hopping, Buenos Aires has serious jazz musicians and appreciative audiences to go along with them. And if you're looking for something a little tamer, there's plenty going on in the arts—film, dance, and opera especially—to make for a classy and classic evening out.

Shopping

High-quality Argentine silver, gold, leather goods, as well as fashionable clothing and accessories are available at first-rate shopping malls and in specialty shops and boutiques. Open-air markets carry regional and European antiques, objets d'art, curios, and provincial handicrafts, such as dried gourds designed for drinking *mate* (a strong green tea that is the national beverage), or gaucho ponchos.

---

unique Spanish colonial architecture, such as the Viejo Hotel at No. 1053, and No. 1016, the former home of artist Juan Carlos Castagnino (it now houses his son's art gallery). Stroll down this street to reach one of the first of the quickly vanishing *conventillos* (tenements) of the past, on the corner of Humberto Primero. ⊠ *San Telmo.*

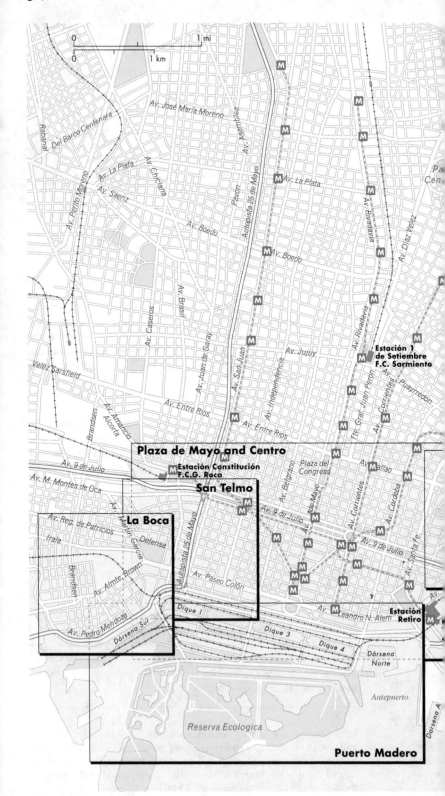

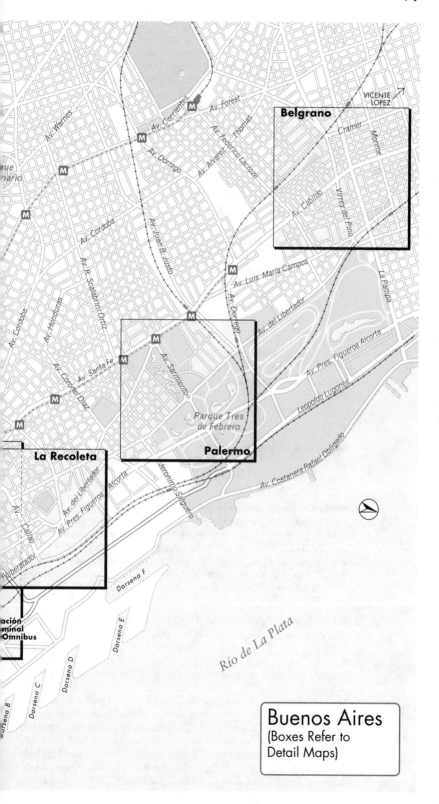

Belgrano

VICENTE LOPEZ

La Recoleta

Palermo

Parque Tres de Febrero

Río de La Plata

Buenos Aires
(Boxes Refer to
Detail Maps)

⑨ La Casa de Esteban de Luca (Esteban de Luca's House). Distinguished poet and soldier Esteban de Luca, who wrote the country's first national anthem and was a hero of the May Revolution of 1810, once lived in this house, where he entertained the local literati. It now operates as a quaint, if somewhat touristy, restaurant serving international and local cuisine; Antonio Banderas dined here during the filming of *Evita*. ✉ *Calle Defensa 1000, San Telmo* ☎ *11/4361–4338.*

❼ Catedral Santísima Trinidad Iglesia Ortodoxa Rusa (Holy Trinity Russian Orthodox Church). Five towering sky-blue domes characterize the first Orthodox church built in Latin America, in 1904. Venetian mosaics, stained glass, and icons sent from St. Petersburg by Czar Nicholas II and Czarina Alexandra adorn the church. ✉ *Av. Brasíl 315, San Telmo* ☎ *11/4361–4274* 🎫 *Free* ☽ *Sat. 5 PM–8:30 PM, Sun. 10 AM–12:30 PM.*

❽ Museo de Arte Moderno de Buenos Aires (Museum of Modern Art of Buenos Aires). Once the site of a tobacco company, MAMBA retains the original exposed-brick facade and fabulous wooden door with wrought-iron fixtures. Local and international contemporary artists, both prominent and up-and-coming, display their paintings, sculptures, and media arts here. And you can often see the exhibiting artists, either giving lectures or just hanging out. Note that the museum closes one month in summer, usually in February, so it's best to call ahead to confirm. ✉ *Av. San Juan 350, San Telmo* ☎ *11/4361–1121* 🎫 *1 peso, free Wed.* ☽ *Tues.–Sat. 10–8, Sun. 11–8.*

★ ❻ Museo Histórico Nacional (National History Museum). The Lezama family's stately mansion now houses artifacts and paintings illustrating Argentine history, spanning the 16th through 20th centuries. Ask to see the extensive collection of paintings by Cándido López, who learned to paint with his left hand after losing his right arm in the War of the Triple Alliance of the 1870s. López's panoramic paintings depicting battlefield scenes spearheaded contemporary primitive painting. Also among the displays are articles from General José de San Martín's campaigns during the 1810 War of Independence against Spain. ✉ *Calle Defensa 1600, San Telmo* ☎ *11/4307–4457* 🎫 *1 peso* ☽ *Feb.–Dec., weekdays 11–5, Sat. 3–6, Sun. 2–6.*

❷ Museo Penitenciario Antonio Ballvé (Antonio Ballvé Penitentiary Museum). Exhibiting artifacts from early-20th-century prison life, this modest museum, once a women's hospice, includes a genuine striped uniform and jail cell. Behind its large courtyard stands **Nuestra Señora del Carmen** chapel, named after the patron saint of the federal penitentiary service. The chapel dates from the Jesuit period. ✉ *Humberto Primero 378, San Telmo* ☎ *11/4362–0099* 🎫 *1 peso* ☽ *Wed.–Fri. 2–6, Sun. noon–7.*

❺ Parque Lezama (Lezama Park). Enormous magnolia, palm, cedar, and elm trees shade the sloping hillside and winding paths of this park, where families and couples gather. Immortalized by Argentine writer Ernesto Sabato in his novel *Sobre Heroes y Tumbas* (*Of Heroes and Tombs*), the park is steeped in history and is said to be the site on which the city was first founded by Pedro de Mendoza. In the 1700s the Company of Guinea operated its slave trade here. Entrepreneur Gregorio Lezama eventually purchased the large tract of land in 1858, forging his expansive estate. Exotic flora, bronze statues of Greek heroes, enormous urns, and an imposing fountain shipped from Paris decorate the land. Lezama's widow donated the property to the city, enabling the ⇨ **Museo Histórico Nacional** to be housed here. The weekend artisan fair attracts large crowds. ✉ *Brasíl and Paseo Colón, San Telmo* 🎫 *Free* ☽ *Daily dawn–dusk.*

❸ **Parroquia de San Pedro González Telmo** (San Pedro González Telmo Parish Church). Abandoned halfway through its construction by the Jesuits in 1767, when the order was expelled from Argentina, this church was finally completed in 1858. The cloisters and domed chapel, designed by Father Andrés Blanqui in 1738, are the only remnants of the original structure. ⊠ *Humberto Primero 340, San Telmo* ☎ *11/4361–1168* 💲 *Free* ⊘ *Weekdays 10–noon, Sat. 6–8:30, Sun. 9–12:30.*

❹ **Pasaje de la Defensa** (Defense Alley). The long, internal, Roman-style courtyards of this colonial building, known as a *casa chorizo* (sausage home) because of its narrowness, give the structure the feel of a passageway. Centuries ago this was a home for people with hearing impairments. It eventually became a conventillo but is now a picturesque spot for antiques and curio shopping. ⊠ *Calle Defensa 1179, San Telmo* ⊘ *Shops daily 10–6.*

❿ **Pasaje Giuffra** (Giuffra Alley). A glimpse down this short alley gives you a sense of what the city looked like two centuries ago. ⊠ *Off Calle Defensa, San Telmo.*

⓭ **Pasaje San Lorenzo** (San Lorenzo Alley). A typical colonial-era alleyway, Pasaje San Lorenzo still retains the charm of its past. At No. 380 stand the ruins of the thinnest building—about 8 feet wide—in the city; it once belonged to a freed slave. ⊠ *Off Calle Balcarce, San Telmo.*

★ ▶ ❶ **Plaza Dorrego** (Dorrego Plaza). Stately old trees shade outdoor tables at this square, the second oldest in the city and a peaceful haven on weekdays. On Sunday from 10 to 5 the plaza comes alive with the bustling **Feria de San Pedro Telmo** (San Pedro Telmo Fair), with its street vendors, performers, and tango dancers. Here you'll find tango memorabilia, leather goods, antique silver, brass, jewelry, crystal, and a wide variety of Argentine and European turn-of-the-20th-century curios. The architecture surrounding the plaza provides an overview of the influences—Spanish colonial, French classical, and ornate Italian masonry—that shaped the city in the 19th and 20th centuries. ⊠ *San Telmo.*

⑪ **Viejo Almacén** (Old General Store). This popular spot for tango is a fine example of colonial architecture. Built in 1798 as a general store, it also served as the British Hospital in the 1840s, and then as a customhouse. Tango artist Edmundo Rivero purchased the building in 1969 and turned it into a hot spot for tango. It's only open for dinner and shows. ⊠ *Av. Independencia 1064, at Calle Balcarce, San Telmo* ☎ *11/ 4307–6689 or 11/4300–3388* ⊕ *www.viejo-almacen.com.ar.*

La Boca

The vibrant working-class neighborhood of La Boca, just south of San Telmo, served as the first port of Buenos Aires, on the now polluted waters of the Riachuelo River. The imposing Avellaneda Bridge towers over the sunken, decaying ships; humble corrugated-metal dwellings; and brightly painted conventillos (the use of bright colors originated from the custom of using paint left over from the boatyards). Waves of immigrants passed through this area; the most significant and lasting group were Italian immigrants from Genoa, who arrived between 1880 and 1930. Cafés, pubs, and general stores that once catered to passing sailors now dot the renovated port. Note that the subte does not go to La Boca, and the surrounding neighborhoods can be a bit rough, so your safest and easiest option is to take a taxi.

a good walk

The highlight of La Boca is the **Calle Museo Caminito** ⑭ ▶, an open-air art market and museum on a pedestrians-only street off Avenida Pedro de Mendoza. Once you reach the end of Caminito, turn right on Calle Garibaldi. Along the railway, two blocks up, you'll find the **Estadio Boca Juniors** ⑮, home to one of Argentina's most popular soccer teams. Make a right onto Calle Brandsen and another onto Calle del Valle Iberlucea; this will lead you back to Caminito. To your left, on La Vuelta de Rocha, is the **Museo de Bellas Artes de La Boca de Artistas Argentinos** ⑯, a noteworthy neighborhood museum; to your right, the **Fundación Proa** ⑰ houses modern art and design.

TIMING & PRECAUTIONS A couple of hours should give you enough time to explore La Boca. Visit the area during the weekend daylight hours; although the nightlife here is singular, it's best not to wander about after dark. Stay in the area of the Caminito, which is patrolled by local police, and avoid straying into surrounding areas.

What to See

▶ ⑭ **Calle Museo Caminito** (Little Path Museum Street). Since 1959, the pedestrian-only Caminito has been an open-air art museum and market, flanked by colorful, haphazardly constructed dwellings. The two-block walk along the street takes you past local artists, many of whom create their work on-site against a backdrop of tango music and dancers. You may find the perfect souvenir here. ⊠ *Av. Pedro de Mendoza (La Vuelta de Rocha promenade), La Boca* ⊠ *Free* ☉ *Daily 10–6.*

FodorśChoice ★

⑮ **Estadio Boca Juniors** (Boca Juniors Stadium). The Boca Juniors, one of Argentina's most popular soccer teams, are the proud owners of this distinctive stadium, with vibrant murals by artists Pérez Celis and Romulo Macció. Should you chance a game, be prepared for throngs, pandemonium, and street revelry—and never wear red and white, the

colors of the rival River Plate team. The bordering street shops sell Boca paraphernalia. ✉ *Brandsen 805, corner of Calle del Valle Iberlucea, La Boca* ☎ *11/4309–4700* ⊕ *www.bocasistemas.com.ar.*

need a break? With an excellent view of the port activity, the century-old, wood-paneled **La Perla** café is a traditional spot for a *licuado* (milk shake), an inexpensive *cortado* (coffee "cut" with a drop of milk), or a tostada. ✉ *Av. Pedro de Mendoza 1899, La Boca* ☎ *11/4301–2985.*

🛈 **Fundación Proa** (Prow Foundation). This thoroughly modern art museum is a refreshing addition to the traditional neighborhood—the building fuses classic Italianate architecture with modern elements to represent the prow of a ship. Choice international exhibits, concerts, and events take place year-round. After you're done looking at the artwork, you can watch the sun set over the river from the terrace. There's also a reading room. ✉ *Av. Pedro de Mendoza 1929, La Boca* ☎ *11/4303–0909* ⊕ *www.proa.org* 🎫 *3 pesos* 🕐 *Tues.–Sun. 11–7.*

🛈 **Museo de Bellas Artes de La Boca de Artistas Argentinos** (La Boca Fine Arts Museum of Argentine Artists). Artist and philanthropist Benito Quinquela Martín donated this building to the state to create a cultural center in 1933. Then he personally set out to fill it from top to bottom with an extensive collection of works by Argentine artists. You'll also find some 800 works by Martín, who was known for his vibrant depictions of the port area. The view from the terrace alone makes the museum worth a visit. ✉ *Av. Pedro de Mendoza 1835, La Boca* ☎ *11/4301–1080* 🎫 *1 peso* 🕐 *Tues.–Fri. 9–6:30, weekends 10–6.*

...za de Mayo

Many of the country's most significant historical events transpired around the axis of Plaza de Mayo (May Plaza), though outsiders perhaps best know the square from the balcony scene in the 1996 film *Evita*. Named for the May Revolution of 1810, Plaza de Mayo has witnessed both sociopolitical upheaval and national triumphs and continues to be an emblem of the nation. Its attractions are principally architectural. Government workers and businesspeople crowd the area on weekdays; on weekends it becomes a haven for homing pigeons and migrating swallows, as well as the children who delight in feeding them.

a good walk

All subway lines lead to **Plaza de Mayo** ⑱ ⏵. The architecturally eclectic Casa de Gobierno, better known as the **Casa Rosada** ⑲, stands at the eastern end of the square, with its back to the river. Two examples of stately neoclassical architecture sit along the northern side of the plaza: the **Banco de la Nación Argentina** ⑳ and the **Catedral Metropolitana** ㉑. Directly opposite the Casa Rosada, on the western side of the plaza, the historic town council is housed in the colonial **Cabildo** ㉒. At this point you have two options. Walk west along Avenida de Mayo to admire the architectural wonders of yesteryear—lots of French-inspired domes and towers with Iberian accents—and to stop in at one of the numerous sidewalk cafés. The avenue was built to connect the Casa Rosada to the legislative **Palacio del Congreso** ㉓. Alternatively, you can walk from Plaza de Mayo southwest along Avenida Julio A. Roca (also known as Diagonal Sur) to the Jesuit-constructed cluster of buildings known as **La Manzana de las Luces** ㉔, including catacomblike tunnels and the **Parroquia de San Ignacio de Loyola** ㉕. Walk east on Calle Alsina to the **Museo de la Ciudad** ㉖, exhibiting the city's historic artifacts. Continue east on Calle Alsina; across Calle Defensa are the colonial **Basílica y Convento de San Francisco** ㉗ and the smaller San Roque Chapel, to its left. Another of the city's oldest churches, **Convento Santo Domingo** ㉘, is two blocks south on Calle Defensa.

TIMING & PRECAUTIONS

This walk can take the better part of the day if you thoroughly explore each sight. Taxis are best hailed far from financial institutions, as robbers, assuming tourists have extracted money from bank machines, have been known to pose as taxi drivers to search for potential victims in these areas. On weekends this area, aside from the square, is deserted, so take precautions.

What to See

⑳ **Banco de la Nación Argentina** (National Bank of Argentina). The state bank's imposing neoclassic building was designed in 1940 by Alejandro Bustillo, architect of numerous government buildings in the 1930s and 1940s. Its vaulted ceiling is the world's third largest, after those of St. Peter's in Rome and the U.S. Capitol. You can visit its **Museo Numismática** (Coin Museum) at Bartolome Mitre 326. ⊠ *At Reconquista and Rivadavía, Plaza de Mayo* ☎ *11/4347–6277* 🎟 *Free* ☾ *Weekdays 10–3.*

㉗ **Basílica y Convento de San Francisco** (Convent and Basilica of St. Francis). A 1911 Bavarian baroque facade now fronts this structure, which was originally built in 1754 in a neo–Italian Renaissance style. Its interior was lavishly refurbished after being vandalized in 1955, during the turmoil surrounding the siege of Perón's government. The basilica houses the second-largest tapestry in the world, depicting the Glorification of St. Francis, and a 20,000-volume archive—one of the city's oldest and most treasured, though not always open to the casual bit...

liophile. ✉ *Defensa and Alsina, Plaza de Mayo* ☎ *11/4331–0625* 🎟 *Free* ☉ *Weekdays 8 AM–7 PM, Sat. 6:30 PM–8 PM, Sun. 9:30 AM–11 AM and 5:30 PM–7 PM.*

㉒ Cabildo (Town Hall). The epicenter of the May Revolution of 1810, where patriotic citizens gathered to vote against Spanish rule, the hall is one of Argentina's national shrines. The original building dates from 1765 but has undergone successive renovations, mostly to its detriment. Inside, a small museum exhibits artifacts and documents pertaining to the events of the May Revolution as well as a jail cell. Thursdays and Fridays from 11 to 6, an artisan fair takes place on the **Patio del Cabildo.** You can participate in glassblowing and other crafts; musical performances are held from 1 to 3. ✉ *Bolívar 65, Plaza de Mayo* ☎ *11/4334–1782* 🎟 *1 peso* ☉ *Tues.–Fri. 11:30–6, Sun. 1–6; tours at 3 and 5.*

⑲ Casa Rosada (Pink House). The Casa de Gobierno (Government House), dubbed the Casa Rosada by President Domingo Fausto Sarmiento in 1873 for its pink color, houses the executive branch of the government. The building was originally constructed in the late 19th century over the foundations of an earlier customhouse and fortress. Swedish, Italian, and French architects have since modified the structure, which accounts for the odd mix of styles. The balcony facing Plaza de Mayo has served as a presidential podium for addressing crowds. Evita rallied the *descamisados* (shirtless working class), the Pope blessed the crowd during a visit in 1998, and Madonna sang her filmed rendition of "Don't Cry for Me Argentina" from this lofty stage. Check for a small banner hoisted alongside the nation's flag, indicating "the president is in." Behind the structure, you can find the brick-wall remains of the 1845 **Taylor Customs House,** discovered after being buried for almost a century. Enter Casa Rosada through the basement level of the **Museo de la Casa Rosada,** the only area open to the public, which exhibits presidential memorabilia along with objects from the original customhouse and fortress. Call ahead to arrange an English-language tour. ✉ *Hipólito Yrigoyen 219, Plaza de Mayo* ☎ *11/4344–3802 or 11/4344–3600* 🎟 *Free* ☉ *Museum weekdays 10–6, Sun. 2–6; tours at 11 and 4.*

㉑ Catedral Metropolitana (Metropolitan Cathedral). Keep an eye out for eclectic details on the cathedral—from the neoclassic facade and neo-Renaissance vessels to the 12 Corinthian columns representing the apostles. The first building on this site was a 16th-century adobe ranch house; the current structure dates to 1827. The embalmed remains of General José de San Martín, known as the Argentine Liberator for his role in the War of Independence, rest here in a marble mausoleum carved by the French sculptor Carrière Belleuse. Soldiers of the Grenadier Regiment, an elite troop created and trained by San Martín in 1811, permanently guard the tomb. Group tours in English are available, but you need to call ahead. ✉ *At Rivadavía and San Martín, Plaza de Mayo* ☎ *11/4331–2845* 🎟 *Free* ☉ *Weekdays 8–7, weekends 9–7:30; guided tours in Spanish weekdays at 11:30 and 4 and weekends at 4.*

㉘ Convento Santo Domingo (St. Dominick Convent). Here, at this historic convent from the 1750s, Spanish troops thwarted British attempts to invade the then-Spanish colony in 1807. Bullet holes on the left-hand bell tower and captured British flags testify to the battle. General Manuel Belgrano, a hero from the War of Independence, lies buried in the courtyard's mausoleum. ✉ *Defensa 422, Plaza de Mayo* ☎ *11/4331–1668* 🎟 *Free* ☉ *Weekdays 10–7, Sat. 9–noon and 2:30–6:30, Sun. 10:30–12:30 and 2:30–6:30.*

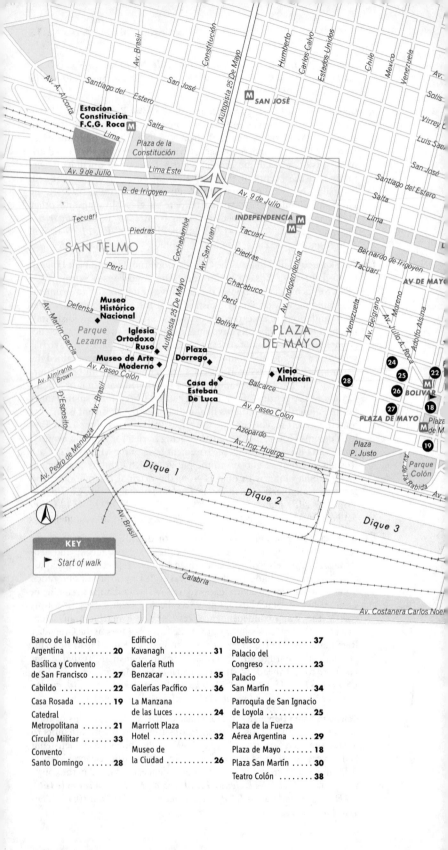

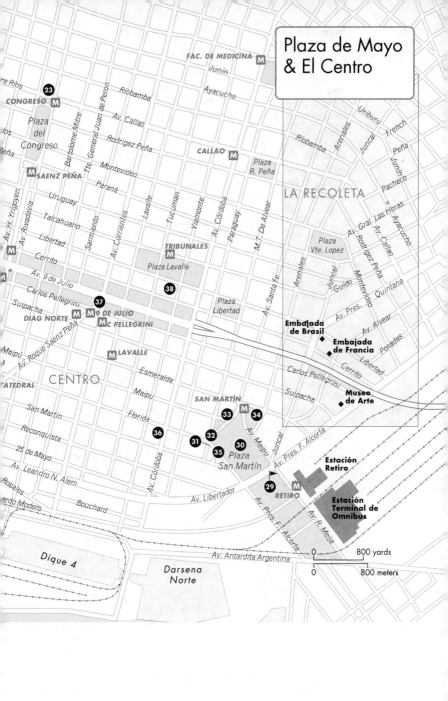

Plaza de Mayo
& El Centro

FAC. DE MEDICINA Ⓜ

re Rios
Junín
Ayacucho

23
CONGRESO Ⓜ
Riobamba
Uriburu
French

Plaza
del
Congreso
Av. Callao
Riobamba
Arenales
Juncal
Peña

Battolome Mitre
Rodriguez Peña
CALLAO Ⓜ
Junín
Pacheco

Tte. General Juan de Perón
Montevideo
Plaza
R. Peña

Ⓜ SAENZ PEÑA
Paraná
LA RECOLETA

Av. H. Yrigoyen
Uruguay
Av. Córdoba
Av. Gral. Las Heras
Ayacucho

Av. Rivadavia
Talcahuano
Lavalle
Tucuman
Viamonte
Paraguay
Plaza
Vte. Lopez
Av. Callao

Libertad
Sarmiento
TRIBUNALES
Ⓜ
Arenales
Juncal
Rodriguez Peña
Quintana

Ⓜ
Cerrito
Av. Corrientes
Plaza Lavalle
Guido
Montevideo

Ⓜ
Av. 9 de Julio
38
M.T. De Alvear
Av. Pres.
Alvear

Carlos Pellegrini
Plaza
Libertad
Av. Santa Fe
Embajada
de Brasil
Posadas

Suipacha
37
9 DE JULIO
Carlos Pellegrini
Embajada
de Francia
Libertad

DIAG NORTE Ⓜ Ⓜ C PELLEGRINI
Suipacha
Cerrito

Maipú
Ⓜ LAVALLE
Esmeralda
Museo
de Arte

Av. Roque Sáenz Peña
CENTRO
Maipu

ATEDRAL
San Martin
Florida
SAN MARTÍN

San Martin
33 Ⓜ 34
Av. Maipu
Juncal

Reconquista
36
32
Estación
Retiro

25 de Mayo
31
35 30
Av. Pres. F. Alcorta

Av. Leandro N. Alem
Plaza
San Martín
Av. Córdoba
Estación
Terminal de
Omnibus

Rosales
29 RETIRO Ⓜ

ardo Modero
Bouchard
Av. Libertador
Av. R. Mejia

Dique 4
Av. Pres. F. Alcorta

Darsena
Norte
Av. Antardita Argentina
0   800 yards

0   800 meters

㉔ La Manzana de las Luces (Block of Bright Lights). Constructed by the Jesuits in the early 1800s, prior to their expulsion, La Manzana de las Luces was an enclave meant for higher learning. This was the former colonial administrative headquarters for the Jesuits' vast land holdings in northeastern Argentina and Paraguay. In 1780 the city's first School of Medicine was established here, and this eventually became home to the University of Buenos Aires early in the 19th century. Among the historic buildings still standing are the ⇨ **Parroquia de San Ignacio de Loyola** and the neoclassic Colegio Nacional, traditionally the top-notch public school for society's future leaders. You can tour parts of the historic tunnels, still undergoing archaeological excavation, which linked the area to the Cabildo and the port. The original purpose of these tunnels is a source of speculation—were they used for defense or smuggling? ✉ *Perú 272, Plaza de Mayo* ☎ *11/4342–6973* 💲 *3 pesos guided tours; free Tues. and Fri.* ⊙ *Guided tours weekdays at 3; weekends at 3, 4:30, and 6.*

㉖ Museo de la Ciudad (City Museum). This museum houses temporary exhibits both whimsical and probing on aspects of domestic and public life in Buenos Aires in times past. The **Farmacia La Estrella** (Star Pharmacy) is a quaint survivor from the 19th century. ✉ *Calle Alsina 412, Plaza de Mayo* ☎ *11/4331–9855 or 11/4343–2123* 💲 *1 peso* ⊙ *Weekdays 11–7, Sun. 3–7.*

㉓ Palacio del Congreso (Palace of the Congress). The facade of the congressional building, constructed in 1906, resembles that of the U.S. Congress—except for the trumpet-wielding angels of revelation. The monumental structure stands on the west end of the expansive **Plaza del Congreso.** This spot marks Km 0 for routes leading out of the city. ✉ *Plaza del Congreso, Plaza de Mayo* ☎ *11/4959–3000* 💲 *Free* ⊙ *Guided tours in English Mon., Tues., and Fri. at 4; in Spanish at 11 and 5.*

㉕ Parroquia de San Ignacio de Loyola (St. Ignatius of Loyola Parish Church). Dating from 1713, this church is the only one from that era to have a baroque facade. It's part of ⇨ **La Manzana de las Luces.** ✉ *Bolívar 225, Plaza de Mayo* ☎ *11/4331–2458* 💲 *Free* ⊙ *Daily 9–2 and 5–8:30.*

★ ⮞ **⑱ Plaza de Mayo** (May Square). Dating to 1580, this central square has been the stage for many important events throughout the nation's history, including the uprising against Spain on May 25, 1810—hence its name. The central obelisk, **Pirámide de Mayo,** was erected in 1811 on the anniversary of the Revolution of May; the crowning small bronze statue of liberty was added later. The bronze equestrian statue of General Manuel Belgrano, designer of Argentina's flag, dates from 1873 and stands at the east end of the plaza. The plaza remains the traditional site for ceremonies as well as mass protests, most recently the bloody clashes in December 2001 that led to the resignation of then-President Fernando de la Rua. It's here that the Madres de la Plaza de Mayo (Mothers of May Square) have marched silently for more than two decades, every Thursday at 3:30; they demand justice for *los desaparecidos,* the young people who "disappeared" during the military government's reign from 1976 to 1983. Here, too, you can witness the changing of the Grenadier Regiment guards; it takes place weekdays every two hours from 9 until 7, Saturday at 9 and 11, and Sunday at 9, 11, and 1. ✉ *Plaza de Mayo.*

El Centro

El Centro is the Porteño's mecca; if you have not visited its urban flux, you have not visited Buenos Aires. Illuminated by flashing billboards, the Obelisk, at the intersection of bustling Avenida Corrientes and

Avenida 9 de Julio, rises above this commercial and social hub. If all the activity is too much for you, don't despair: just steps away from the bustling pedestrian Calles Florida and Lavalle are serene, shaded plazas with fountains, monuments, and statues.

a good walk

El Centro can be reached by subte; lines run beneath the main avenues and are worth taking to admire the tiled murals within the stations. Begin your walk at the **Plaza de la Fuerza Aérea Argentina** ㉙ ►, across from the Retiro train station. Cross Avenida Libertador to admire the **Plaza San Martín** ㉚, with its statues and fountains. Walking the square's perimeter, you'll see the surrounding grandiose architecture along the eastern end. The neorationalist **Edificio Kavanagh** ㉛ stands in stark contrast to the opulent **Marriott Plaza Hotel** ㉜. Crowning the plaza's southern tip is the **Círculo Militar** ㉝. At Calle Maipú 994, near the intersection with Calle Marcelo T. de Alvear, Jorge Luis Borges wrote some of his short stories and poems in the sixth-floor corner apartment. Nearby, on Calle Arenales, you'll find the Ministry of Foreign Affairs, housed in the **Palacio San Martín** ㉞. Walk back to Avenida Santa Fe and follow it east around the plaza; the basement-level **Galería Ruth Benzacar** ㉟ stands at the entrance to Calle Florida. Take this pedestrian street, crowded with shops and people, south to the magnificent **Galerías Pacífico** ㊱. Next door, on the corner of Calle Florida and Avenida Córdoba, stop and admire the magnificent facade of the 1914 Versailles-inspired Centro Naval; its intricate iron door was fashioned from the metal and bronze of cannons fired during the War of Independence. Continue south along Calle Florida until you reach bustling Avenida Corrientes, the traditional theater district. Head west on Corrientes, toward Avenida 9 de Julio, to reach the **Obelisco** ㊲. Walk two blocks toward the river along Avenida 9 de Julio, the widest avenue in the world, to the **Teatro Colón** ㊳ for a backstage tour.

TIMING &
PRECAUTIONS

Set aside a full day to explore El Centro. It's easy to navigate the area on foot. Avenida Corrientes is jammed during the evening with restaurant- and theatergoers. Weekends, historic areas are relatively deserted, and some stores and restaurants have limited hours. Calle Lavalle, although a shopping and commerce center, is also peppered with adult entertainment and a mega–bingo hall, so take proper precautions at night.

What to See

㉝ **Círculo Militar** (Military Circle). A monument to the nobler historic pursuits of the Argentine armed forces, the Officers' Club was built in 1902 by French architect Louis Sortais in the heavily ornate French style of the period. The **Museo Nacional de Armas** (National Arms Museum), in the basement, is packed with military memorabilia. You can only visit inside the Círculo Militar with a guided tour. ✉ *Av. Santa Fe 750, El Centro* ☎ *11/4311–1071* 💰 *3.50 pesos* ☉ *Guided tours Mar.–Dec., Wed. and Thurs. at 3.*

㉛ **Edificio Kavanagh** (Kavanagh Building). The monolithic 1930s-era Kavanagh apartment building, inaugurated in the same year as Avenida 9 de Julio, was constructed in an imposing neorationalist style, with art deco touches. For a time this was the tallest high-rise in South America, with 31 floors. ✉ *Florida 1065, El Centro.*

㉟ **Galería Ruth Benzacar** (Ruth Benzacar Gallery). Monthly exhibits showcase the works of modern Argentine artists. Ask to see the vast collection of paintings in the basement. ✉ *Florida 1000, El Centro* ☎ *11/4313–8480* 💰 *Free* ☉ *Weekdays 11:30–8, Sat. 10:30–1:30.*

㊱ **Galerías Pacífico** (Pacific Gallery). Milan's Galleria Vittorio Emanuele served as the architectural model for this former headquarters of the

Buenos Aires–Pacific Railway, designed during Buenos Aires's turn-of-the-20th-century golden age. It's now an upscale shopping mall and cultural center. Noteworthy features include the facade, skylighted dome, and murals. The **Centro Cultural Borges** (⊕ www.ccborges.org.ar), a showcase for young talent, is on the mezzanine level. ⊠ *Florida 753, El Centro* ☎ *11/5555–5100.*

need a break?

More than just a coffeehouse, **Florida Garden** (⊠ Florida 899, at Paraguay, El Centro ☎ 11/4312–7902), a unique '60s-style bordering-on-kitsch café, is a landmark because of its association with the intelligentsia of yesteryear. Among other cultural icons, writer Jorge Luis Borges sat here. Sit elbow to elbow along the 20-foot bar or in the sitting room upstairs and enjoy afternoon tea or some of the richest hot chocolate in the city.

㉜ Marriott Plaza Hotel. In 1908 local financier Ernesto Tornquist commissioned German architect Alfred Zucker to build the city's first luxury hotel. The Plaza, like its namesake in New York City, continues a tradition of old-world elegance and is famous for the illustrious guests who have stayed here. ⊠ *Calle Florida at Plaza San Martín, El Centro.*

off the beaten path

MUSEO DE ARTE HISPANOAMERICANO ISAAC FERNÁNDEZ BLANCO – The distinctive Peruvian neocolonial style serves as the perfect backdrop for the Isaac Fernández Blanco Hispanic-American Art Museum, originally built as the residence of architect Martín Noel in the late 18th century. Noel and Blanco donated the majority of the collection—the most extensive in the region of silver, wood carvings, furnishings, and paintings from the Spanish colonial period. Concerts are held in the lush, Spanish-style garden, and there's a library. Guided tours in English can be arranged with prior notice. ⊠ *Suipacha 1422, El Centro* ☎ *11/4327–0228* ⊉ *1 peso, free Thurs.* ⊙ *Tues.–Sun. 2–7.*

㉛ Obelisco (Obelisk). Towering over the city at 221½ feet, the Obelisk is one of Buenos Aires's most prominent landmarks, built in 1936 on the site where the nation's flag was first raised. Open-air concerts are frequently staged in the area surrounding the Obelisk, and during elections or major soccer matches, crowds of Porteños converge here, rejoicing in the outcome of the day's events. ⊠ *Av. 9 de Julio and Corrientes, El Centro.*

㉞ Palacio San Martín (San Martín Palace). Originally the home of the Anchorena family, the palace has housed the Ministry of Foreign Affairs since 1936. The ornate building, designed in 1909 by Alejandro Cristophersen in grandiose French neoclassical style, exemplifies the turn-of-the-20th-century opulence of Buenos Aires. ⊠ *Arenales 761, El Centro* ☎ *11/4819–7000 Ext. 7985* ⊙ *Guided tours in English and Spanish Fri. at 3, 4, and 5.*

▶ **㉙ Plaza de la Fuerza Aérea Argentina** (Argentine Air Force Square). England donated the central brick clock tower in this square, **Torre Monumental,** on the occasion of the 1910 centennial celebration of the May Revolution. Originally known as Plaza Británica (British Square), the plaza was defiantly renamed by the city in 1982 as a result of the Falkland Islands War. ⊠ *Av. Libertador and Calle San Martín, El Centro.*

㉚ Plaza San Martín (San Martín Square). Once a muddy riverbank suburb at the northern end of the city, this plaza gradually evolved, taking its place as the second most important in the city. At one time populated by marginal members of colonial society, the area was transformed in the late 1800s when the aristocratic families of San Telmo fled here to escape yellow fever. Today it's one of the most sumptuous neighborhoods in Buenos Aires. French landscape architect Charles Thays designed the square in the 1800s, juxtaposing local and exotic trees. The imposing bronze equestrian monument to General José de San Martín, designed in 1862 by French artist Louis Daumas, dominates the park, as does the Monumento a los Caídos en las Malvinas. Guarded by a Grenadier, the 25 black marble slabs of the monument are engraved with the names of those who died in the 1982 Falkland Islands War. ⊠ *Av. Libertador and Calle Florida, El Centro.*

★ ③ **Teatro Colón** (Colón Theater). Its magnitude, magnificent acoustics, and opulence (grander than Milan's La Scala) position the Colón among the top five opera houses worldwide. Inaugurated in 1908 with Verdi's *Aida,* it has hosted the likes of Maria Callas, Richard Strauss, Arturo Toscanini, Igor Stravinsky, Enrico Caruso, and Luciano Pavarotti. The Italianate building with French interiors is the result of successive modifications by various architects. The seven-tier theater has a grand central chandelier, with 700 lights to illuminate the 2,490 mere mortals in the audience. Many seats are reserved for season-ticket holders, so tickets are hard to come by for choice performances. However, don't forego the opportunity to sit in the lofty upper-tier *paraíso,* which is more economical and an experience in itself (side entrance on Calle Tucuman; no reservation required). Check availability for guided tours in Spanish of the theater, museum, workshops, and rehearsal halls. The season runs from March to December. ⊠ *Toscanini 1180, El Centro* ☎ *11/4378–7100 tickets, 11/4378–7133 tours* ⊕ *www.teatrocolon.org.ar* ✉ *10 pesos* ⊗ *Guided tours Mon.–Sat. hourly 10–5, Sun. 11–3.*

Puerto Madero

With a view of the sprouting skyline on one side and the exclusive yacht club on the other, this riverside promenade has become *the* place to go for a casual stroll, nightlife activity, and elegant dining. The port was originally constructed in 1890 as the European gateway to Argentina but spent most of the 20th century abandoned because of the creation of a new port, Puerto Nuevo. In an ambitious undertaking, the city revived the area, transforming its redbrick warehouses and grain mills into chic office and living spaces, university buildings, a cinema complex, a luxury hotel, and a string of restaurants. It was recently designated as the 47th and newest barrio of Buenos Aires, a tribute to its significant overhaul.

a good walk

You can reach the port, five blocks east of Calle Florida, from the Leandro Alem subte station; once you leave the station, walk down Avenida Corrientes toward the river. On your right you'll see the majestic Correo Central (Central Post Office); on your left is Luna Park, where many sporting events and concerts are held. Crossing Avenida Eduardo Madero, you'll reach Avenida Alicia M. de Justo, which runs the length of the port area. Docked here are the **Buque Museo Fragata A.R.A. Presidente Sarmiento** ③ ► and, farther south, the **Buque Museo Corbeta Uruguay** ④, two impressive Argentine battleships–cum–floating museums.

TIMING & PRECAUTIONS

Walking the 15-block boardwalk should take you no more than a few hours. In the morning the port area is a nice place to jog or to sip coffee at a waterfront café. Business commotion reigns during the day; in the evenings a fashionable crowd gathers for dinner. Although tony Puerto Madero is well patrolled by private security and police, you should avoid strolling far from the boardwalk at night.

What toSee

40 **Buque Museo Corbeta Uruguay** (Uruguay Corvette Ship Museum). The oldest of the Argentine fleet, bought from England in 1874, the ship was used in the nation's Antarctic campaigns at the turn of the 20th century. ⊠ *Dique 1, at Av. Garay and Alicia M. de Justo, El Centro* ☎ *11/ 4314–1090* 🎫 *1 peso* ☉ *Daily 9–9.*

⊳ **39** **Buque Museo Fragata A.R.A. Presidente Sarmiento** (President Sarmiento Frigate Museum). The navy commissioned this frigate from England in 1898 to be used as an open-sea training vessel. It has completed 39 voyages across the world's oceans. ⊠ *Dique 3, at Pte. Perón and Alicia M. de Justo, El Centro* ☎ *11/4334–9386* 🎫 *2 pesos* ☉ *Daily 9–10.*

> off the
> beaten
> path

RESERVA ECOLÓGICA (Ecological Reserve) – If you find yourself feeling out of touch with nature, head to this paradise built over a landfill and home to more than 500 species of bird and a variety of flora and fauna. It's ideal for nature treks. A monthly guided "Walking under the Full Moon" tour begins at 8:30 PM. Threatened by pollution as well as developers who lust after its prime location, the reserve suffers occasional scorching by "spontaneous" fires, only to rise again defiantly from its ashes. It's just a short walk across any bridge from Puerto Madero. ⊠ *Av. Tristán Achával Rodríguez 1550, El Centro* ☎ *11/4315–1320, 11/4893–1588 tours* 🎫 *Donation suggested* ☉ *Apr.–Nov., Tues.–Sun. 8–6; Dec.–Mar., Tues.–Sun. 8–7.*

La Recoleta

Open green spaces border this elegant residential and shopping district, replete with boutiques, cafés, handsome old apartment buildings, mansions, plazas, and cultural centers. Named for the barefoot Franciscan Recoleto friars who settled here in the early 1700s, the neighborhood later became home to brothels and seedier activities, including the then-ruffian's tango. The outbreak of yellow fever in 1871 in the south of the city caused the elite to swarm to this area, laying the foundations for a concentration of intellectual and cultural activity.

> a good
> walk

Though a number of buses run through here, a taxi ride is your best bet. No subway route directly serves La Recoleta; the closest station is eight blocks away at Estación Pueyrredón.

Begin at **Plazoleta Carlos Pellegrini** **41** ⊳ on Avenida Alvear. Flanking the square are the imposing embassies of France and Brazil and the Jockey Club. Head west on the elegant Avenida Alvear, lined with French-style

architecture and haute couture boutiques, to reach the exquisite **Alvear Palace Hotel** ㊷. Continue two blocks along Alvear; the staired sidewalk on the left, called R. M. Ortiz, leads past a gargantuan rubber tree and a string of Parisian-style cafés, pubs, and eateries. Continue in the same direction until you encounter the final resting ground for some of Argentina's most illustrious citizens at the **Cementerio de La Recoleta** ㊸. Next door are the **Basílica de Nuestra Señora del Pilar** ㊹ and the cultural playground, **Centro Cultural La Recoleta** ㊺. Finally, at the end of the *veredita* (little sidewalk), you'll find the Paseo del Pilar lined with places to eat and the Buenos Aires Design Center. The grassy Plaza Intendente Alvear surrounds the area and on weekends hosts the city's largest artisan fair. At the foot of the slope, across Alvear, is the ocher-color **Palais de Glace–Salas Nacionales de Cultura** ㊻. From here walk west along Avenida del Libertador to reach the **Museo Nacional de Bellas Artes** ㊼, the city's fine-arts museum. The enigmatic public library **Biblioteca Nacional** ㊽ towers over the Plaza Ruben Darío. A few blocks farther west, bordering the neighborhood of Palermo, is the opulent **Museo Nacional de Arte Decorativo** ㊾, a decorative arts museum.

TIMING &   You can explore La Recoleta in half a day, though you could easily spend
PRECAUTIONS a full morning or afternoon in the cemetery or cultural centers alone. This area is relatively safe day and night, but always stay aware of your surroundings.

What to See

㊷ **Alvear Palace Hotel.** Old-world elegance characterizes this hotel, opened in 1932. The Porteño elite gather in the lobby piano bar, which is ideal for high tea or cocktails. Visiting presidents, dignitaries, and celebrities often stay here when they are in town. ⊠ *Av. Alvear 1891, La Recoleta* ☎ *11/4808–2100* ⊕ *www.alvearpalace.com.*

⓬ ㊹ Basílica de Nuestra Señora del Pilar (Basilica of Our Lady of Pilar). In 1732 the Franciscan Recoleto friars built this colonial-style basilica and adjoining cloister. The church is considered a national treasure for its six German baroque–style altars, the central one overlaid with Peruvian engraved silver, and relics sent by Spain's King Carlos III. Buenos Aires's elite families take pride in celebrating weddings and other religious events here. ⊠ *Junín 1904, La Recoleta* ☎ *11/4803–6793* ✆ *Free* ☉ *Daily 8 AM–9 PM.*

㊽ Biblioteca Nacional (National Library). Conceived by its director, writer Jorge Luis Borges, and possibly stemming from the infinite labyrinth of books depicted in his novel *El Aleph,* this monolithic structure took three decades to complete. It opened in 1992 after much red tape and now towers over Plaza Ruben Darío. The work of Le Corbusier inspired the modernist structure, which was designed by Clorinda Testa. Check for scheduled cultural activities. You'll need to show an official document like a passport or driver's license to enter. ⊠ *Agüero 2502, La Recoleta* ☎ *11/4808–6000* ⊕ *www.bibnal.edu.ar* ✆ *Free* ☉ *Weekdays 9 AM–8 PM, weekends noon–7.*

㊸ Cementerio de La Recoleta (La Recoleta Cemetery). The ominous gates, Doric-columned portico, and labyrinthine pathways of the oldest cemetery in Buenos Aires (1822) lend a sense of foreboding to this virtual city of the dead. The cemetery covers 13½ acres of prime property and has more than 6,400 elaborate vaulted tombs and majestic mausoleums, 70 of which have been declared historic monuments. The mausoleums resemble chapels, Greek temples, pyramids, and miniature mansions. The cemetery is a veritable who's who of Argentine history: this is the final resting place for the nation's most illustrious figures. The administrative offices at the entrance provide a free map, and caretakers throughout the grounds can help you locate the more intriguing tombs, such as the embalmed remains of Eva Perón and her family; Napoléon Bonaparte's granddaughter; the brutal *caudillo* (dictator) Facundo Quiroga, buried standing, at his request; and prominent landowner Dorrego Ortiz Basualdo, in the most monumental sepulchre, complete with chandelier. ⊠ *Junín 1760, La Recoleta* ☎ *11/4803–1594* ☉ *Daily 8–5:30; free guided tours in Spanish last Sun. of month at 2:45.*

Fodor'sChoice
★

㊺ Centro Cultural La Recoleta (La Recoleta Cultural Center). The former cloisters and internal patios of the Franciscan monks have been converted into a dynamic cultural center with exhibits, performances, and workshops. Weekends the entire area teems with artisans and street performers in the city's largest arts-and-crafts market. ⊠ *Junín 1930, La Recoleta* ☎ *11/4803–1041 or 11/4803–9744* ⊕ *www.centroculturalrecoleta.org* ✆ *1 peso* ☉ *Tues.–Fri. 2–9, weekends 10–9.*

★ **㊾ Museo Nacional de Arte Decorativo** (National Museum of Decorative Art). This dignified, harmonious French neoclassic landmark houses a fascinating collection of period furnishings, silver, and objets d'art—but it's worth the price of admission just to enter this breathtaking structure. The museum also contains Asian art as well as the Zubov collection of miniatures from Imperial Russia. Stop in for tea or lunch at the elegant museum café, **Errázuriz.** ⊠ *Av. del Libertador 1902, La Recoleta* ☎ *11/4801–8248* ✆ *4 pesos* ☉ *Daily 2–7; free guided tours (in English) weekends at 4:30.*

㊼ Museo Nacional de Bellas Artes (National Museum of Fine Arts). Some 11,000 works of art—from drawings and paintings to statues and tapestries—are displayed in a building that used to be the city's waterworks. The museum's exhibits of significant international and local masters range from medieval times to the postmodern era, and the collection of 19th- and 20th-century Argentine art is its crowning achievement. Check out Cándido López's first-hand renderings of soldier life during the War of the Triple Alliance. His work can also be found in the National History Museum. The temporary-exhibit pavilion showcases modern international and Argentine art and photography. You'll also find a gift shop, library, and cafeteria here. ⊠ *Av. del Libertador 1473, La Recoleta* ☎ *11/4803–0802 tours* ⊕ *www.mnba.org.ar* ⊠ *Free* ☉ *Tues.–Fri. 12:30–7:30, weekends 9:30–7:30.*

🟢 **Palais de Glace–Salas Nacionales de Cultura** (Ice Palace–National Cultural Exhibition Halls). Always worth checking out are the changing exhibits, ranging from fine art to ponchos to national foods to African art, at this exhibition hall, formerly an ice-skating rink. The banner outside will tell you what's going on. ⊠ *Posadas 1725, La Recoleta* ☎ *11/ 4805–4354* ⊠ *Free* ☉ *Tues.–Sun. 2–8.*

🏃 🔵 **Plazoleta Carlos Pellegrini** (Carlos Pellegrini Square). Stately mansions, the highbrow Jockey Club, private apartments, and the embassies of France and Brazil frame this square, now primarily used for parking. The Brazilian Embassy has a stately neoclassic facade; the early-20th-century building of the French Embassy was of such importance that the city decided to loop the continuation of Avenida 9 de Julio around the back of it rather than raze the structure. ⊠ *La Recoleta.*

Palermo

With nearly 350 acres of parks, wooded areas, and lakes, Palermo provides a peaceful escape from the rush of downtown. Families flock here on weekends to picnic, suntan, bicycle, in-line skate, and jog. The polo field and hippodrome make this the city's nerve center for equestrian activities. One of the largest barrios, Palermo is also one of the most dynamic, with several distinct subneighborhoods: Palermo Viejo has classic Spanish-style architecture; Las Cañitas, Palermo Hollywood, and SoHo have trendy shopping, nightlife, and dining. Some of the most exclusive and expensive real estate in Buenos Aires can be found here, in opulent Palermo Chico, an elegant residential area, and in the prime properties lining the Avenida del Libertador and overlooking the parks.

a good walk

The Estación Plaza Italia, on subte Line D, takes you to the entrance of the zoo and botanical gardens in Palermo. Some of the city's biggest parks are found in this neighborhood around the **Plaza Italia** 🟢 🏃, at the intersection of Avenidas Sarmiento, Santa Fe, and Las Heras: the **Jardín Botánico Carlos Thais** 🔵, the **Jardín Zoológico** 🔵, and the historic **Sociedad Rural Argentina** 🔵, the city's most extensive fairgrounds and exhibition center. **Parque Tres de Febrero** 🔵 is at the far end of the zoo, along Avenida Sarmiento, past the U.S. Consulate on the left and across Avenida del Libertador. Here you will find the **Paseo del Rosedal** 🔵, abloom with more than 1,000 species of roses in season. Head southeast on Avenida del Libertador to the **Jardín Japonés** 🔵, a tranquil Japanese garden, or continue north along Sarmiento to the **Planetario Galileo Galilei** 🔵, for astronomy buffs. After staring at the stars, head southeast on Avenida Presidente Figueroa Alcorta to reach the superb **Museo MALBA** 🔵, for an impressive display of Latin American artwork.

TIMING   An even-pace ramble through Palermo should take no more than two hours, though you could easily spend an entire afternoon at the zoo, Japanese Garden, and the Botanical Garden. If you're up for shopping, visit the Alto Palermo shopping center (at the Bulnes stop on Line D) or the entire length of shops and boutiques along Avenida Santa Fe.

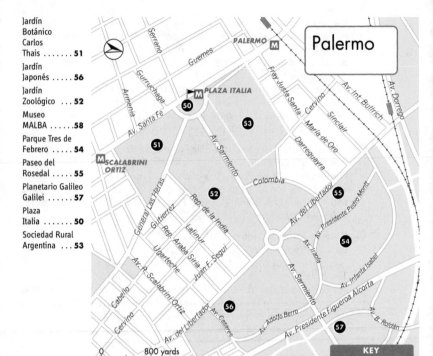

What to See

⑤ Jardín Botánico Carlos Thais (Charles Thays Botanical Garden). With 20 acres of gardens and 8,000 varieties of exotic and local flora, the Botanical Garden is a welcome, unexpected oasis in the city. Different sections of the park re-create the environments of Asia, Africa, Oceania, Europe, and the Americas. Among the garden's treasures is the Chinese "tree of gold," purportedly the only one of its kind. Winding paths lead you to hidden statues, a brook, and past the resident cats and dragonflies. The central area contains a greenhouse and the exposed-brick botanical school and library. ✉ *Av. Santa Fe 3951, Palermo* ☎ *11/4832–1552* 🎫 *Free* ☉ *Daily 8–6.*

> **need a break?** Near the Botanical Garden and steps away from the Palermo Polo field is **La Cátedra** (✉ Cerviño and Sinclair, Palermo ☎ 11/4777–4601), a perfect spot for lunch or a drink outdoors.

★ ⑤ Jardín Japonés (Japanese Garden). Arched wooden bridges and walkways traverse still waters in this Japanese oasis. A variety of shrubs and flowers frame the ponds, which brim with golden carp. The traditional teahouse, where you can enjoy adzuki-bean sweets and tea, overlooks the Zen garden. ✉ *Avs. Casares and Adolfo Berro, Palermo* ☎ *11/4804–4922* ⊕ *www.jardinjapones.com.ar* 🎫 *3 pesos* ☉ *Daily 10–6.*

☾ ⑤ Jardín Zoológico (Zoological Garden). You enter through the quasi-Roman triumphal arch into this architecturally eclectic, 45-acre city zoo dating from 1874. The pens, mews, statuary, and fountains themselves are well worth the visit. Among the expected zoo community are a few surprises: a rare albino tiger; indigenous monkeys, known to perform lewd acts for their audiences; and llamas (watch out—they spit). Some smaller animals roam freely, and there are play areas for children, a petting farm, and a seal show. *Mateos* (traditional, decorated horse-drawn carriages) stand poised at the entrance to whisk you around the greens. ⊠ *Avs. General Las Heras and Sarmiento, Palermo* ☎ *11/4806–7412* 🎟 *8 pesos* ☉ *Tues.–Sun. 10–5.*

★ ⑤⑧ **Museo MALBA** (Museo de Arte de Latinoamericano de Buenos Aires). This fabulous museum has more than 220 works from the private collection of businessman and founder Eduardo Constantini. The sleek, modern structure is home to one of the largest collections of Latin American art in the world, including original works by Frida Kahlo, Fernando Botero, and a slew of Argentine artists. The museum also features seasonal exhibitions, lectures, movies, and live music. The adjoining café is a fashionable place to end your day with a cup of coffee and a piece of cake. ⊠ *Av. Presidente Figueroa Alcorta 3415, Palermo* ☎ *11/4808–6500* ⊕ *www.malba.org.ar* 🎟 *4 pesos, free on Wed.* ☉ *Thurs.–Mon. noon–8, Wed. noon–9.*

☙ ⑤④ **Parque Tres de Febrero** (February 3 Park). With 1,000 acres of woods, lakes, and trails, Parque Tres de Febrero is the city's playground. Here you can take part in organized tai chi and gym classes and impromptu soccer matches or jog, bike, in-line skate, or take a boat out on the lake. If you're looking for something less active, try the park's **Museo de Artes Plásticas Eduardo Sívori** (Eduardo Sívori Art Museum; ⊠ *Av. Infanta Isabel 555, Palermo* ☎ *11/4774–9452* 🎟 *1 peso*), exhibiting 19th- and 20th-century Argentine art; it's open Tuesday–Friday noon–7 and weekends 10–7. Street vendors sell refreshments within the park, as do the many cafés lining the Paseo de la Infanta (running from Libertador toward Sarmiento in the park). ⊠ *Bounded by Avs. del Libertador, Sarmiento, Leopoldo Lugones, and Dorrego, Palermo.*

★ ⑤⑤ **Paseo del Rosedal** (Rose Garden). Approximately 15,000 rosebushes, representing more than 1,000 different species, bloom seasonally in this garden. A stroll along the clay paths takes you through the Jardín de los Poetas (Poets' Garden), dotted with statues of literary figures, and to the enchanting Patio Andaluz (Andalusian Patio), covered in vines and ideal for picture-taking. ⊠ *Avs. Infanta Isabel and Iraola, Palermo.*

☙ ⑤⑦ **Planetario Galileo Galilei** (Galileo Galilei Planetarium). The sci-fi exterior of this landmark holds more appeal than its flimsy content. This great orb positioned on a massive concrete tripod looks like something out of *Close Encounters of the Third Kind,* and it seems as though small green men in foil suits could descend from its central staircase at any moment. A highlight is the authentic asteroid at the entrance; the pond with swans, geese, and ducks is a favorite with children. ⊠ *Avs. Sarmiento and Belisario Roldán, Palermo* ☎ *11/4771–6629* ⊕ *www.earg.gov.ar/planetario* 🎟 *4 pesos* ☉ *Weekdays 9–6, weekends 2–8.*

⚑ ⑤⓪ **Plaza Italia** (Italian Square). A monument to the Italian general Giuseppe Garibaldi towers over this square at the intersection of avenidas Santa Fe, Las Heras, and Sarmiento. Here you'll also see a fragment of a 2,000-year-old Roman column, donated by Italy to the city in 1955. A landmark in the area, the square is an ideal meeting spot. ⊠ *Palermo.*

☙ ⑤③ **Sociedad Rural Argentina** (Rural Society of Argentina). Exhibitions relating to agriculture and cattle raising are often held at the fairgrounds here. The biggest is the annual monthlong summer **Exposición Rural** (Rural Exposition), where you can see livestock such as cows and horses, gaucho shows, and expert horse performances. ⊠ *Off Plaza Italia, Palermo* ☎ *11/4324–4700* ⊕ *www.ruralarg.org.ar.*

Belgrano

European-style parks and plazas, Paris-inspired boulevards, shopping strips, residential areas, a fashionable district of mansions and luxury high-rises, and cobblestone streets characterize historic Belgrano. It's also home to the expanding Barrio Chino (China Town).

To reach Belgrano by subte, take Line D to Estación Juramento, the next-to-last stop. You can also take the Mitre Line commuter train from Retiro station to Belgrano station.

Head first to the **Museo de Arte Español Enrique Larreta** ⑤⑨ ▶, on Calle Juramento, for a taste of Spanish colonial art. Across Juramento, on the west side of the plaza, is the **Museo Histórico Sarmiento** ⑥⓪, which commemorates Argentina's independence from Spain. From here, walk across the romantic **Plaza Manuel Belgrano** ⑥① to reach the **Parroquia de Nuestra Señora de la Inmaculada Concepción** ⑥②. After visiting the church, head two blocks west along Calle Juramento, across busy Avenida Cabildo, to the **Mercado** ⑥③, a traditional open-air food market.

TIMING & PRECAUTIONS This walk can be done in two to three hours, though you may want to spend more time wandering around this beautiful barrio. If you want to see all the museums, it's best to visit in the afternoon, when they're all open. The atmospheric cafés are open 24 hours. Patrolled around the clock by private security and city police, Belgrano is relatively safe, though you should still watch your belongings.

What to See

off the beaten path

BARRANCAS DE BELGRANO (Slopes of Belgrano) – Meandering brick pathways lead you to historic—and sometimes unusual—sights in this park. The **Glorieta Antonio Malvagni** arbor, named after the founder-conductor of the Municipal Band of Buenos Aires, was the site of many a political oratory. The bust of General San Martín, one of many tucked away in the greenery, stands near the pine tree under which the national independence hero wrote his victory speech in 1813. Also here are a massive native ombu tree, declared a monument; wondrous sculptures and fountains; and an exact miniature replica of the Statue of Liberty. Historic architecture lines the hill of the park. ⊠ *Bounded by Avs. Virrey Vertiz, 11 de Septiembre, La Pampa, and Juramento, Belgrano.*

⑥③ **Mercado.** This open-air local market is a trove of cheeses, fruits, vegetables, sausages, and beef cuts, plus a few surprises. ⊠ *Juramento and Ciudad de la Paz, Belgrano* ⊘ *Daily 5 PM–11 PM.*

★ ▶ ⑤⑨ **Museo de Arte Español Enrique Larreta** (Enrique Larreta Museum of Spanish Art). Once the beautiful home of a Spanish governor, the building now houses poet and novelist Enrique Larreta's vast collection of Spanish 13th- through 20th-century art and artifacts. ⊠ *Juramento 2291, Belgrano* ☎ *11/4783–2640* 💲 *1 peso* ⊘ *Mon., Wed.–Fri. 12:30–7:45, weekends 3–7:45.*

⑥⓪ **Museo Histórico Sarmiento** (Sarmiento Museum of History). This 1873 Italianate building showcases historical documents and artifacts relating to the nation's founders. ⊠ *Cuba 2079, Belgrano* ☎ *11/4783–7555* 💲 *1 peso* ⊘ *Tues.–Fri. 2–6:45, Sun. 3–6:45; guided tours in Spanish Sun. at 4.*

⑥② **Parroquia de Nuestra Señora de la Inmaculada Concepción** (Our Lady of the Immaculate Conception Parish Church). Nicknamed *La Redonda* (The Round One), this beautiful church, modeled after Rome's Pantheon,

has a relief replica of Da Vinci's *Last Supper*. ⊠ *Vuelta de Obligado 2042, Belgrano* ☎ *11/4783–8008* ⊘ *Daily 7 AM–9 PM.*

🖲 **Plaza Manuel Belgrano** (Manuel Belgrano Square). The square, named after General Belgrano, the War of Independence hero, is the site of a bustling artisan fair on weekends. ⊠ *Juramento and Av. Cuba, Belgrano.*

WHERE TO EAT

Although international cuisine can be found throughout Buenos Aires, it's the traditional *parrilla*—a restaurant serving grilled meat—that Argentines (and most visitors) flock to. These restaurants vary from upscale eateries to local spots. The meal often starts off with *chorizo* (a large, spicy sausage), *morcilla* (blood sausage), and *chinchulines* (tripe), before moving on to the myriad cuts of beef that make Argentina famous. Don't pass up the rich *provoleta* (grilled provolone cheese sprinkled with olive oil and oregano) and garlic-soaked grilled red peppers as garnish. Beef dishes are traditionally accompanied by a salad and/or French fries.

Most Porteños have Italian ancestry, which is evident in the *other* national dishes: pizza, fresh pastas, and homemade ice cream. Argentine pizzas are slightly different than their Italian and American cousins, but equally delicious: don't miss the chance to try a classic *muzzarella* (cheese and tomato pizza) or the local invention known as the *fugazza* (tomato-less pizza covered with onion and cheese). You will be overwhelmed by choice in the *heladerías* (ice-cream shops), but dulce de leche and *sambayon* (an alcohol-infused custard ice cream) are both national classics and must-tries.

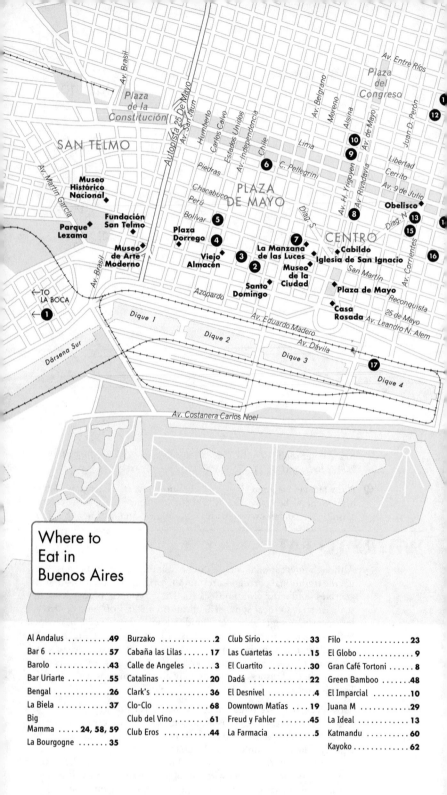

Where to
Eat in
Buenos Aires

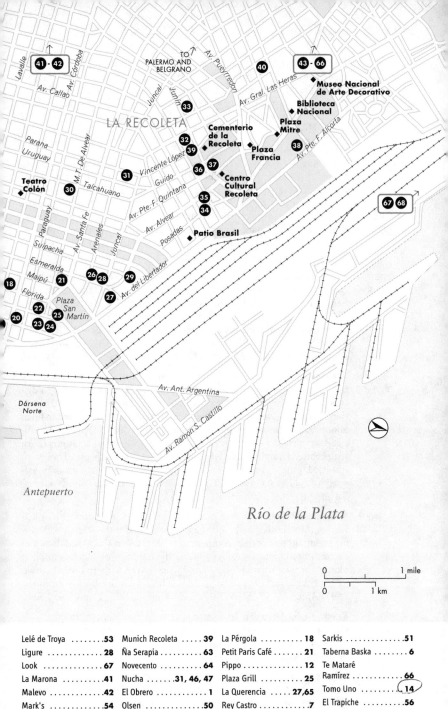

La Recoleta

Cafés are a big part of Buenos Aires culture: open long hours, they constantly brim with locals knocking back a quick *cafecito* (espresso) or taking their time over a *café con leche* (coffee with milk) served with *medialunas* (croissants) or *facturas* (small pastries). Many places have bilingual menus or someone on hand who is eager to practice his or her English.

Almagro

Immediately west of the city center and south of La Recoleta, Almagro is one of Buenos Aires's traditional tango neighborhoods. At its center is the Abasto district, which surrounds the Abasto Shopping Mall, one of the city's best malls. The Mall's opening in 1998 has caused many changes in this formerly run-down neighborhood: it's now increasingly trendy, with many bars, nightclubs, restaurants, and fringe theatres complementing the long-established tango spots. Almagro is easily accessible by the subte (Line B); taxis to the neighborhood are also very cheap.

ARGENTINE ✕ **La Maroma.** The specials in this chaotic *bodegón* (tavern-style restau-
¢–$ rant) are erratically scrawled on bits of paper stuck on the walls under hams hanging from the ceiling, strings of garlic, and demijohns of wine. The homemade pastas are excellent, especially the lasagna, and so are the *milanesas* (breaded meat cutlets). Portions are large—don't be surprised if you can't finish your order. ⊠ *Mario Bravo 598 at Humahuaca, Almagro* ☎ *11/4862–9308* ⊟ *AE, V* Ⓜ *Line B, Estación Carlos Gardel.*

ECLECTIC ✕ **Malevo.** Named for the villain of the tango, Malevo was the first eatery
★ $–$$ to bring sleek modern dining to Almagro, the city's classic tango district. The old corner building has large plate-glass windows and an intimate slate and aubergine interior where lights are low and white linen abounds. The house's excellent wine selection is on display behind a polished wooden bar—savor a bottle with your *Rebelión en la Granja* (pork with braised fennel and tapenade) or homemade goat-cheese ravioli with sundried tomatoes and almonds. ⊠ *Mario Bravo 908 at Tucumán, Almagro* ☎ *11/4861–1008* ⊟ *AE, D, MC, V* ✆ *Closed Sun. No lunch Sat.* Ⓜ *Line B, Estación Carlos Gardel.*

INDIAN ✕ **Katmandu.** Step over rose petals into an Indian oasis of sensory plea-
$–$$ sures—Katmandu may be off the beaten path, but the serene, welcoming hospitality more than compensates. Chefs create spicy vindaloos and curries in full view. Consider sharing the tandoori or Indian sampling platter for two; then indulge in milky desserts. An international crowd gathers here. Upstairs you can purchase Indian furnishings. ⊠ *Córdoba 3547, Almagro* ☎ *11/4963–1122* ⊟ *AE, DC, MC, V* ✆ *Closed Sun.*

Costanera (Río de la Plata)

Having started out as little carts, these established restaurants, known as *carritos,* still have no numbered addresses. Located near the Jorge Newbery Airport, Costanera has no subway access.

ARGENTINE ✕ **Look.** This restaurant, which has been here for 16 years, attempts a
$–$$ more sophisticated look than the other carritos in the area. Try the parrilla for two (or more), served sizzling at your table. The waiters, some of whom have been around since the place opened, are efficient and friendly. ⊠ *Rafael Obligado, on the Costanera, Costanera* ☎ *11/4783–1375 or 11/4788–4995* ⊟ *AE, DC, MC, V.*

ITALIAN ✕ **Clo Clo.** Garden-enclosed Clo Clo may be directly under the path of
$$–$$$ incoming domestic flights, but the dining is nonetheless elegant, and the service and cuisine are impeccable. Breads, hors d'oeuvres, and champagne are served before the meal, but be sure to leave room for your entrée, which could be an excellent cut of beef, *trucha capri* (trout in

cream sauce with prawns), or eggplant cappelletti. ✉ *Costanera Norte and La Pampa, Costanera* ☎ *11/4788–0488* 🖃 *AE, DC, MC, V.*

El Centro

Expect crowds of office workers at lunchtime in El Centro. Some restaurants are quite busy in the evening as well, so reserve ahead or else catch an early or late supper.

ARGENTINE ✕ **Tomo Uno.** For the last 35 years the famed Concaro sisters have made
$$$ Tomo Uno a household name with such dishes as spicy squid and quail
Fodor'sChoice egg salad or perfectly cooked lamb *en croute* (baked in a pastry shell)
★ with wild mushrooms and garnished with crispy eggplant and spinach. For dessert, try the grapefruit in Riesling with pear ice cream or the chocolate tart that oozes warm, dark *ganache* (semisweet chocolate and whipped cream heated and stirred together). White linen–covered tables are set far apart, making quiet conversation easy, and the service is excellent. The restaurant, on the mezzanine of the Hotel Panamericano, has views over the Obelisco. ✉ *Carlos Pellegrini 521, El Centro* ☎ *11/4326–6698* ⏦ *Reservations essential* 🖃 *AE, DC, MC, V* ☺ *Closed Sun. No lunch Sat.* Ⓜ *Line B, Estación Carlos Pellegrini; Line D, Estación 9 de Julio.*

¢–$ ✕ **El Palacio de la Papa Frita.** This old standby is popular for its hearty traditional meals—succulent steaks, homemade pastas, and fresh salads. The *papas soufflé* (inflated french fries) reign supreme; try them *a la provençal* (sprinkled with garlic and parsley) along with the classic *bife a medio caballo* (steak topped with a fried egg). ✉ *Lavalle 735, El Centro* ☎ *11/4393–5849* Ⓜ *Line C, Estación Lavalle* ✉ *Av. Corrientes 1612, El Centro* ☎ *11/4374–8063* Ⓜ *Line B, Estación Callao* 🖃 *AE, DC, MC, V.*

¢–$ ✕ **Juana M.** The minimalist chic decor of this basement restaurant is in stark contrast to what's on the menu: traditional down-to-earth *parilla* fare at prices that are hard to beat. Catch a glimpse of meats sizzling on the grill behind the salmon-colored bar—the only swath of color in the restaurant—then head to your table to devour your steak and *chorizo* (fat, spicy sausage). The staff is young and friendly. ✉ *Carlos Pellegrini 1535, La Recoleta* ☎ *11/4326–0462* ☺ *No lunch Sat.* Ⓜ *Line C, Estación San Martín.*

¢–$ ✕ **Pippo.** Pippo is known for its simplicity and down-to-earth cooking. Try the *estofado* (beef stew), filled pastas, or *lomo* (sirloin) with fries. For dessert, flan is topped off with cream or dulce de leche. It's in the heart of the Corrientes theater district. ✉ *Paraná 356, El Centro* ☎ *11/4374–6365* Ⓜ *Line B, Estación Uruguay* ✉ *Av. Callao 1077, La Recoleta* ☎ *11/4812–4323* 🖃 *No credit cards.*

¢ ✕ **La Querencia.** Northern Argentinian fare is dished up fast-food style in a rustic setting. Choose from combos that include empanadas and tamales as well as rich local stews such as *locro* (hard corn cooked slowly with meat and vegetables). The *humitas* (ground corn wrapped in a corn husk) are excellent. You can eat in at basic wooden tables, or carry out. ✉ *Esmeralda 1392, El Centro* ☎ *11/4393–3202* Ⓜ *Line C, Estación San Martín* ✉ *Junín 1308, La Recoleta* ☎ *11/4393–3202* Ⓜ *Line D, Estación Facultad de Medicina* 🖃 *No credit cards* ☺ *No lunch Sun.*

CAFÉS ✕ **La Ideal.** Part of the charm of this spacious 1918 confitería is its sense
¢–$ of nostalgia: a fleur-de-lis motif prevails, and the timeworn European furnishings and stained glass create an atmosphere of bygone days, which set the tone for scenes filmed here for the 1998 film *The Tango Lesson.* La Ideal is famous for its *palmeritas* (glazed cookies) and tea service. Tango lessons are offered Monday through Thursday from noon to 3, with a full-blown *milonga* (tango dance ball) Wednesday and

Saturday from 3 to 8. The waitstaff seem to be caught up in their own dreams—service is listless. ⊠ *Suipacha 384, at Av. Corrientes, El Centro* ☎ *11/4326–0521* ▤ *No credit cards* ⊘ *No breakfast weekends* Ⓜ *Line C, Estación C. Pellegrini; Line D, Estación 9 de Julio.*

¢–$ ✕ **Petit Paris Café.** The crystal chandeliers and marble tabletops are reminiscent of a Parisian café. Choose from a variety of coffees, cakes, sandwiches, and salads, or more filling pastas and *milanesas.* ⊠ *Av. Santa Fe 774, El Centro* ☎ *11/4312–5885* ▤ *AE, MC, V* Ⓜ *Line C, Estación San Martín.*

CONTINENTAL ✕ **Plaza Grill.** Wrought-iron lamps and fans hang from the high ceilings,
$$–$$$$ and original Dutch delft porcelain tiles decorate the walls at this favorite spot of executives and politicians. The wine list is extensive, and the Continental menu includes excellent steak, salmon with basil and red wine, and pheasant with with foie gras. ⊠ *Marriott Plaza Hotel, Florida 1005, El Centro* ☎ *11/4590–8974* ⌂ *Reservations essential* ▤ *AE, DC, MC, V* Ⓜ *Line C, Estación San Martín.*

$$ ✕ **La Pérgola.** On the third floor of the Sheraton Libertador hotel, this restaurant serves mouthwatering appetizers such as salmon bisque. Among the flavorful entrées are pasta; grilled steak; and sole with shrimp, artichoke hearts, shallots, capers, and asparagus, served in a white wine sauce. ⊠ *Sheraton Libertador, Av. Córdoba 680, El Centro* ☎ *11/ 4322–8800 or 11/4322–6622* ⌂ *Reservations essential* ⋔ *Jacket and tie* ▤ *AE, DC, MC, V* Ⓜ *Line C, Estación Lavalle.*

ECLECTIC ✕ **Bengal.** Bengal serves a mixture of Italian and Indian fare in quiet wood-
$$ panelled surroundings. If you're anxious for some heat, try the *jhing masala* (prawn curry). Those with tender tastebuds should go for one of the delicious homemade pasta dishes. ⊠ *Arenales 837, El Centro* ☎ *11/ 4394–8557* ▤ *AE* ⊘ *Closed Sun. No lunch Sat.* Ⓜ *Line C, Estación San Martín.*

★ $ ✕ **Dadá.** Eclectic Porteño '60s pop culture characterizes one of the city's best-kept secrets, where murals inspired by Dalí, Miró, Lichtenstein, and Mondrian are splashed across the walls and smoky jazz fills the small, intimate space. Seasonal specials are chalked up behind the cluttered bar. The short but inventive menu showcases the best of local produce. ⊠ *San Martín 941, El Centro* ☎ *11/4314–4787* ▤ *AE, MC, V* ⊘ *Closed Sun.* Ⓜ *Line C, Estación San Martín.*

FRENCH ✕ **Catalinas.** Chef Ramiro Pardo's exclusive recipes lend a strong Iberian
★ $$$$ touch to the superb French seafood and game served in this century-old building. Savor the lobster tail with caviar and cream or the *pejerrey* (a kind of mackerel) with king-crab mousse filling. Businesspeople lunch here, and a varied crowd gathers for dinner. Several fixed-price menus make this delight easier on the pocket, but wines and desserts can double the price of your meal. ⊠ *Reconquista 850, El Centro* ☎ *11/ 4313–0182* ⌂ *Reservations essential* ⋔ *Jacket and tie* ▤ *AE, DC, MC, V* ⊘ *Closed Sun. No lunch Sat.* Ⓜ *Line C, Estación Florida.*

$–$$ ✕ **Ligure.** French cuisine adapted to Argentine tastes is the specialty here. Try thistles *al parmesano* with your steak *au poivre* with brandy sauce and the *panqueques* (crepes) de dulce de leche. Despite the busy downtown location, the inside is very quiet. ⊠ *Juncal 855, El Centro* ☎ *11/ 4394–8226* ▤ *AE, MC, V* Ⓜ *Line C, Estación San Martín.*

IRISH ✕ **Downtown Matías.** Wash down a savory lamb stew or a chicken pie
$–$$ with a brew at this cheery Irish pub. The steaks are excellent—try the *lomo relleno* (wrapped in bacon and served with plums) or the *lomo al bosque* (in a wild mushroom sauce). ⊠ *Reconquista 701, El Centro* ☎ *11/ 4311–0327* ▤ *AE, DC, MC, V* ⊘ *Closed Sun.* Ⓜ *Line C, Estación San Martín.*

PIZZA **✕ Filo.** Come here for the lively, arty atmosphere, but be prepared for
$–$$ crowds at all hours. The excellent flat-bread pizza is not the only spe-
cialty; try the pasta or the spinach salad tossed with mushrooms and
bathed in balsamic vinegar. On your way to the rest room, check out
the arts space in the basement. ⊠ *San Martín 975, El Centro* ☎ *11/
4311–0312* 🖃 *AE, MC, V* Ⓜ *Line C, Estación San Martín.*

★ **$** **✕ Las Cuartetas.** Probably the most famous pizzeria in town, Las Cuar-
tetas specializes in huge deep-dish pizzas that are packed with flavor and
quite a challenge to finish. The restaurant extends back through three
retro-tiled rooms adorned with plastic plants—the Formica-topped tables are usually all full. ⊠ *Corrientes 838, El Centro* ☎ *11/4326–0171*
🖃 *No credit cards* ☺ *No lunch Sun.* Ⓜ *Line B, Estación C. Pellegrini;
Line C, Estación Diagonal Norte; Line D, Estación 9 de Julio.*

¢–**$** **✕ El Cuartito.** A true porteño classic, El Cuartito has been doing some
of the best pizza in town since 1934 and the surroundings have changed
little in the last 40 years. Drop in for a quick couple of slices at the
mostrador (counter) or make yourself comfortable under the portraits
of Argentine sporting greats for fantastic, no-nonsense pizzas and empanadas. Try a slice of *fainá* (chickpea-flour bread), the typical local ac-
companiment to pizza, and don't miss out on their flan with dulce de
leche. ⊠ *Talcahuano 937, El Centro* ☎ *No phone* 🖃 *No credit cards*
Ⓜ *Line D, Estación Tribunales.*

La Boca

ARGENTINE **✕ El Obrero.** When the rock band U2 played Buenos Aires they asked
$–$$ to be taken to a traditional Argentine restaurant and were brought to
this legendary hole-in-the-wall. For 50 years El Obrero has served abundant portions of consistently good juicy grilled steaks, sweetbreads,
sausages, and chicken. The extensive menu is chalked up on a black-
board and includes *rabas* (breaded squid) and *puchero* (meat and vegetables in a broth). Try the traditional *budín de pan* (Argentine version
of bread pudding). This spot is popular with tourists and local work-
men alike, so expect a short wait for a table. Note that this area is not
served by public transportation and is sketchy at night, so you may want
to make taxi arrangements. ⊠ *Augustín R. Caffarena 64, La Boca*
☎ *11/4363–9912* 🖃 *No credit cards* ☺ *Closed Sun.*

Palermo

Palermo is the focal point of the Buenos Aires food scene. Restaurants
are especially thick on the ground in the areas known as Palermo Hollywood (on the other side of Avenida Juan B. Justo) and Palermo Viejo
(around Plaza Serrano) and range from long-running local classics to
the latest trendy eateries. Quiet cobbled streets mean you can often enjoy
eating outside.

ARGENTINE **✕ Club del Vino.** A wine lover's paradise, this multidimensional eatery
$–$$ has a wine cellar, museum, and shop, along with live entertainment in
the downstairs theatre–café. Past the fountain and tall, stained-glass ceiling of the entrance hall is an intimate yellow dining room and a large
patio filled with candelit tables. The fixed-price *catador* (wine taster)
menu includes *milanesa* (breaded veal cutlet) with sweet potatoes and
flan, accompanied by a merlot, malbec, and cabernet. The restaurant is
not always open for lunch, so call ahead. ⊠ *Cabrera 4737, Palermo* ☎ *11/
4833–0048* 🖃 *AE, DC, MC, V* ☺ *Closed Sun.*

$–$$ **✕ El Trapiche.** The menu is endless and so are the portions at this busy
Fodor'sChoice parrilla on the edge of trendy Palermo Hollywood. High ceilings hung
★ with hams, walls stacked with wine, contain a pleasant racket—Trapiche
is always packed with locals who keep coming back for what's ar-
guably the best classic Argentine food in town, with a wine list to

match. Share a selection of barbecued meats or have the *sorrentinos de calabaza al scarparo* (squash-filled fresh pasta in a spicy cream sauce) all to yourself. If you have room, finish off with a fruit-filled crepe, flambéed for you at your table. ⊠ *Paraguay 5099, Palermo* ☎ *11/4772–7343* ⊟ *AE, DC, MC, V* Ⓜ *Line D, Estación Palermo.*

$–$$ ✕ **Freud y Fahler.** Red walls, colored pane-glass screens, and vintage chandeliers give warmth to this quiet corner restaurant on a peaceful cobbled street in Palermo Viejo. The menu is short but imaginative; try the *pollo dos cocciones* (chicken cooked in two different ways) with sweet-potato pasta, and follow it with spiced white-chocolate cake with plum ice cream and orange sauce. The well-informed young staff give friendly advice on food and wine. The lunch menus are an excellent value. ⊠ *Gurruchaga 1750, Palermo* ☎ *11/4833–2153* ⊟ *V* ⊙ *Closed Sun.*

¢ ✕ **Club Eros.** A basic dining room at the back of an old sports club in the heart of Palermo Viejo, Club Eros is a long-kept secret that is beginning to get out. The excellent renditions of classic *criolla* fare at rock-bottom prices have begun to draw young Palermo trendies as well as older customers who have been loyal to the club for decades. There's no menu, but you can confidently order a *bife de chorizo* (steak) and fries, a *milanesa*, or a huge plate of *ravioles de ricotta*; alternatively, ask one of the waiters for advice. The flan con dulce de leche is one of the best (and biggest) in town. ⊠ *Uriarte 1609, Palermo* ☎ *11/4832–1313* ⊟ *No credit cards.*

¢ ✕ **Ña Serapia.** Diners come to Ña Serapia for the authentic country food— tamales, locro, empanadas—and inexpensive wines. This is strictly no-frills, but the food is consistently good. ⊠ *Av. Las Heras 3357, Palermo* ☎ *11/4801–5307* ⊟ *No credit cards* Ⓜ *Line D, Estación Bulnes.*

CONTINENTAL **$$** ✕ **Bar 6.** The seasonally changing menu at Bar 6 may include risotto, stir-fry, shellfish, salads, *pappardelle* (extra-thick pasta ribbons) served with grilled vegetables and succulent prawns, and duck. If it's available, start with the grilled polenta topped with goat cheese; move on to marinated salmon with dill and cilantro; and finish off with goat-cheese ice cream and candied tomatoes. The waiters are usually too busy being beautiful to attend to you in a hurry, but the food makes up for their indifference. Stone, wood, and glass create a thoroughly modern yet inviting and down-to-earth spot. ⊠ *Armenia 1676, Palermo* ☎ *11/4833–6807* ⊟ *AE, MC, V* ⊙ *Closed Sun.*

$$ ✕ **Bar Uriarte.** Don't be fooled by Bar Uriarte's minimalist front: the exposed kitchen gives way to the low lights of a sophisticated bar with two intimate dining spaces. You can simply lounge on the cozy sofas with a drink or have a longer meal at one of the airy dining room's oiled-wood tables. Chef Paula de Felipe's dishes are as sleek as the surroundings: try the martini-lemon chicken and be sure to leave room for a piece of pear-and-almond cake with cinnamon ice cream. Pass by in the afternoon—Uriarte's modern afternoon tea snacks will tide you over until dinner. Discrete live DJs warm things up on the weekend. ⊠ *Uriarte 1572, Palermo* ☎ *11/4834–6004* ⊟ *AE, DC, MC, V* ⊙ *Closed Sun.*

$$ ✕ **Barolo.** An old town house done up in bright green and mauve, Barolo offers modern bistro dining on a quiet street in Palermo Hollywood. The lamb in mascarpone is unmissable, as are the sweet potato gnocchi with hazelnut cream sauce. Wines of the month are chalked up on a blackboard over the bar. ⊠ *Bonpland 1612, Palermo* ☎ *11/4772–0841* ⊟ *AE, V* ⊙ *Closed Sun. No lunch Sat.*

DELICATESSEN **¢–$** ✕ **Big Mamma.** This Porteño version of a New York deli has everything you'd expect (except pickles): made-to-order sandwiches, hot pastrami, bagels and lox, and even knishes. Breakfast combos are great value, and there's an eat-everything-on-the-menu deal if you're really hungry.

✉ *Cabello 3760, Palermo* ☎ *11/4806–6822* ✉ *Matienzo 1599, Belgrano* ☎ *11/4772–0926* ✉ *Reconquista 1080, El Centro* ☎ *11/ 4894–1232* ▤ *AE, DC, MC, V.*

¢–$ ✗ **Mark's.** The first deli to arrive in Palermo Viejo, Mark's big sandwiches and salads have been steadily drawing crowds for all-day munching (it's open 10:30 AM–8:30 PM). Ingredients are top quality, combinations inventive, and the large variety of breads—the house specialty—are all baked on premise. Tastefully mismatched tables, chairs, and sofas are available if you want to eat in; there's also a small patio if you want some sun. The cheesecake in itself is an excuse for a visit. ✉ *El Salvador 4701, Palermo* ☎ *11/4832–6244* ▤ *No credit cards* ◷ *Closed Mon.*

ECLECTIC ✗ **Te Mataré Ramírez.** Te Mataré Ramírez, which translates as "I Will
$$–$$$ Kill You, Ramirez," is as unusual as it sounds. A self-styled aphrodisiac haven, the restaurant seduces with such dishes as "With Two Women" (caramelized chicken in a sherry, ginger, and grapefruit sauce) and desserts such as "Premature Palpitations of Pleasure" (warm white-chocolate cake). Thursday the temperature rises with a tastefully done "erotic theater" show and Wednesday night brings live jazz. From behind the red velvet bar comes all variety of cocktails to sip as you peruse the illustrated menu or gaze at the restaurant's erotic art collection. ✉ *Paraguay 4062, Palermo* ☎ *11/4831–9156* Ⓜ *Line D, Estación Scalabrini Ortíz* ✉ *Primera Junta 702, San Isidro* ☎ *11/4747–8618* ▤ *AE, DC, MC, V* ◷ *No lunch Sat.*

$–$$ ✗ **Lelé de Troya.** Each room of this converted old house is drenched in a different color—from the walls to the chairs and plates—and the food is just as bold. The kitchen is on view from the covered lemon-yellow patio, and you can watch as loaf after loaf of the restaurant's homemade breads is drawn from the clay oven. Follow dishes like salmon ravioli or *mollejas* (a cut of beef) in cognac with one of Lelé's many Middle Eastern and Italian desserts. The restaurant holds tango classes on Monday nights and has a changing art space. ✉ *Costa Rica 4901, Palermo* ☎ *11/4832–2726* ▤ *AE, MC, V.*

ITALIAN ✗ **Novecento.** With the feel of a Little Italy eatery, this bistro, which has
$$–$$$ branches in New York and Miami Beach, is a magnet for young, highbrow Porteños. Snug, candlelit tables offer intimacy. Try the pyramid of green salad, steak, and fries, or shrimp with bacon. Crème brûlée and "Chocolate Delight" are tempting desserts. In summer you can dine outdoors. ✉ *Báez 199, Palermo* ☎ *11/4778–1900* ▤ *AE, MC* ◷ *No lunch Mon.* Ⓜ *Line D, Estación Ministro Carranza.*

JAPANESE ✗ **Kayoko.** Misao Sekiguchi had 20 years of restaurant experience in Tokyo
$–$$ under her sash before she opened this bit of Japan in the heart of Palermo. Authentic tempura, sashimi, sushi, and *oyako* (pork stir-fry with seaweed and spring onion) are among the choices here. Exquisite silk kimonos and the owner's own handmade carvings decorate the dining area. You can dine outdoors, weather permitting, on a wooden deck framed by a Japanese garden. Early evenings, there are great value happy hour sushi and drinks combos. ✉ *Gurruchaga 1650, Palermo* ☎ *11/4832–6158* ▤ *AE, MC, V* ◷ *Closed Sun. No lunch.*

MEXICAN ✗ **Xalapa.** This kitschtastic tangerine-color corner restaurant serves up
¢–$ reasonably authentic tacos, burritos, and enchiladas, as well as more complicated dishes such as chicken *con mole* (a rich, spicey, chocolatey sauce), all at excellent prices. Dishes can be spiced up on request. Things get chaotic on weekends when Xalapa fills up with returning local diners, but the wait for a table is worth it. ✉ *El Salvador 4800, Palermo* ☎ *11/4833–6102* ▤ *No credit cards* ◷ *No lunch.*

MIDDLE EASTERN
¢–$

✕ **Sarkis.** Full to bursting with cane tables and chairs, this chaotic family-style restaurant does some of the best Middle Eastern food in town. The house specialties are *keppes* and *shawarmas*, but you could easily fill yourself up on several dishes from the large selection of *mezzes*. Nevertheless, be sure to leave room for a few *baklava* and other dripping, nut-filled pastries on offer. ⌂ *Thames 1101 at Jufré, Palermo* ☎ *11/ 4772–4911* ⊟ *No credit cards.*

SCANDINAVIAN
★ $$

✕ **Ølsen.** Ølsen is a showcase for Nordic flavors and contemporary Scandinavian design. Past the rectangular, walled garden filled with scattered sculptures and white lounge chairs is a cavernous space with walls of painted-white exposed bricks. Lime-green tables and chairs give a '70s feel to the place, as do the cowhide barstools and veneer bar, behind which lurks the restaurant's impressive vodka selection. Snack on *smørrebrød* (open sandwiches) with different vodka shots, or try the *bifes gravlax* (beef with specially cured salmon) and *rösti* (sauteed on both sides until crisp) potatoes. The prix fixe menu is an excellent value, and this is *the* place for Sunday brunch. ⌂ *Gorriti 5870, Palermo* ☎ *11/ 4776–7677* ⊟ *AE, V* ☉ *Closed Mon.*

SPANISH
★ $–$$

✕ **Al Andalus.** The food at this Andalusian restaurant is truly spectacular. You'll have trouble choosing between the lamb *tagine* (a rich, dark stew cooked with plums and almonds), the *Pastel Andalusí* (a sweet-and-sour filo packed with lamb and chicken), or the goat cheese, saffron, and wild mushroom risotto. The *torta antigua* (chocolate cake) is a not to be missed. You can eat in a tented dining room, under the ceramic lights of the quieter rust-red bar, or stretch out on sofas draped with Moroccan rugs beside a tiled fountain in the plant-filled courtyard. ⌂ *Godoy Cruz 1823, Palermo* ☎ *11/4832–9286* ⊟ *AE, MC, V* ☉ *Closed Sun. and Mon.*

VIETNAMESE
$$

✕ **Green Bamboo.** At Buenos Aires's only Vietnamese restaurant the walls are black, the waiters slick, and the olive-green vinyl chairs usually occupied by trendy thirtysomething actors and producers from nearby Palermo Hollywood. The food is reasonably authentic; take your time over it and then move on to one of the fantastic *maracuyá* (passionfruit) daiquiris once Green Bamboo's bar begins to warm up. ⌂ *Costa Rica 5802, Palermo* ☎ *11/4775–7050* ⊟ *AE, V* ☉ *Closed Sun. No lunch.*

Plaza de Mayo

CAFÉ
★ ¢–$

✕ **Gran Café Tortoni.** The art nouveau decor and high ceilings transport you to the faded, glorious past of the city's first confitería, established in 1858. Carlos Gardel, one of Argentina's most famous tango stars; writer Jorge Luis Borges; local and visiting dignitaries; and intellectuals have all eaten and sipped coffee here. Don't miss the *chocolate con churros* (thick hot chocolate with baton-shaped donuts for dipping). You must reserve ahead of time for the nightly tango shows. ⌂ *Av. de Mayo 829, Plaza de Mayo* ☎ *11/4342–4328* ⊟ *AE, MC, V* Ⓜ *Line A, Estación Perú.*

CUBAN
$

✕ **Rey Castro.** A high, stained-glass ceiling and exposed brick walls hung with black-and-white photos of old Havana are the backdrop for this tasteful tribute to all things Cuban. The efficient service and fixed-price menus attract businesspeople at lunchtime, but things relax at night when DJs or live musicians often perform. As well as the usual rice-and-beans classics are dishes such as *cazuela de mariscos* (a rich seafood caserole); follow it with a flambéed lime crepe or coconut rice pudding. Alternatively, go straight to the cigar bar for a rum. ⌂ *Perú 342, Plaza de Mayo* ☎ *11/4342–9998* ⊟ *No credit cards* ☉ *Closed Sun. No lunch Sat.* Ⓜ *Line A, Estación Perú; Line E, Estación Bolívar.*

SPANISH
$$

✕ **El Globo.** Hearty pucheros, suckling pig, squid, and other Spanish-Argentine fare are served in a large dining area in a century-old building. ⊠ *Hipólito Yrigoyen 1199, Plaza de Mayo* ☎ *11/4381–3926* ⊟ *AE, DC, MC, V* Ⓜ *Line C, Estación Av. de Mayo; Line A, Estación Lima.*

$–$$

✕ **El Imparcial.** Founded in 1860, the oldest restaurant in town owes its name (meaning impartial) to its neutrality in the face of the warring political factions of Buenos Aires's Spanish immigrants. Hand-painted tiles, heavy wooden furniture and paintings of Spain are all strong reminders of the restaurant's origins, as are the elderly waiters, many of whom are from the old country. Talking politics is no longer banned within, good news for today's Argentines, who keep coming to El Imparcial for the renowned *paellas* and *mariscos* (seafood dishes). ⊠ *Hipólito Irigoyen 1201, Plaza de Mayo* ☎ *11/4383–2919* ⊟ *AE, DC, MC, V* Ⓜ *Line A, Estación Lima.*

Puerto Madero

ARGENTINE
$$$
Fodor'sChoice
★

✕ **Cabaña las Lilas.** Corporate credit cards allow Porteño executives to afford the juicy steaks and impeccable service in this handsome eatery. The restaurant has its own *estancia* (ranch), where it raises cattle for its dishes. The *lomo* (loin) and *cuadril* (rump), accompanied by a robust Catena Zapata from the well-stocked wine cellar, make for a memorable, albeit costly, evening. You can sip a glass of champagne at the cigar bar while waiting to be seated. ⊠ *Av. Alicia Moreau de Justo 516, Puerto Madero* ☎ *11/4313–1336* ⊟ *AE, DC, V* Ⓜ *Line B, Estación L. N. Alem.*

La Recoleta

ARGENTINE
¢–$

✕ **El Sanjuanino.** Authentic Andean fare is served at this long-established spot. El Sanjuanino is especially known for its *pollo a la piedra* (chicken pressed flat by stones), venison, and antelope stew, but you can also take out piping-hot empanadas or tamales or *humita* (steamed corn cakes wrapped in husks) for a picnic in the park. ⊠ *Posadas 1515, La Recoleta* ☎ *11/4804–2909* ⊟ *AE, MC, V.*

¢–$

✕ **Melo.** This popular café in Barrio Norte, a neighborhood bordering La Recoleta, serves up large portions of juicy steaks, crepes, salads, and pastas. The friendly service makes up for the spartan decor. Try the beef brochettes with vegetables or the spinach crepes with cream sauce. ⊠ *Pacheco de Melo 1829, La Recoleta* ☎ *11/4801–4251* ⊟ *AE, DC, MC, V.*

CAFÉS
$–$$

✕ **La Biela.** Porteños linger at this quintessential sidewalk café opposite the Recoleta cemetery, sipping espressos, discussing politics, and people-watching—all of which are best done at an outdoor table beneath the shade of an ancient rubber tree. ⊠ *Quintana 596, at Junín, La Recoleta* ☎ *11/4804–0449* ⊟ *V.*

$

✕ **Modena Design.** This spacious Internet café has an ultramodern techno feel and showcases Ferraris—not surprisingly, it attracts Porteño trendsetters. Log on while snacking on sushi, or nurse a *lagrima* (milk with a teardrop of coffee) while you sit back in an oversize chair. It's behind the Museo Nacional de Bellas Artes in La Recoleta. ⊠ *Av. Figueroa Alcorta 2270, La Recoleta* ☎ *11/4809–0122* ⊟ *AE, V.*

¢–$

✕ **Nucha.** Choosing from the mouthwatering selection of handmade cakes and pastries on display at this chic but cosy Recoleta café can be difficult. Take your time over cake and fantastic coffee at polished dark-wood tables looking out onto Plaza Vicente López. Service is very friendly. ⊠ *Paraná 1343, La Recoleta* ☎ *11/4813–9507* ⊠ *Salguero 2587, Palermo* ☎ *11/4802–1615* ⊠ *O'Higgins 1400, Belgrano* ☎ *11/4783–6120* ⊟ *No credit cards.*

CONTINENTAL
$–$$

✕ **Clark's.** Deer heads stare out blankly from the dark-wood-paneled walls over red-checkered tables at this restaurant reminiscent of a British pub in the pre–World War II era. The elaborate meals sometimes miss their mark, so stick with the traditional specialties, such as the pastas and grilled meats. (The steak with goat cheese, shrimp, and wild mushroom sauce is the exception to this rule.) Profiteroles with ice cream and chocolate sauce is the dessert of choice. Daily fixed-price menus include four courses and wine, making a satisfying dinner quite affordable. ⊠ *Junín 1777, La Recoleta* ☎ *11/4801–9502* ▤ *AE, DC, MC, V.*

FRENCH ✕ **La Bourgogne.** This French restaurant is generally considered one of the
★ **$$$$** best—and most expensive—restaurants in town. White tablecloths and fresh roses emphasize the restaurant's innate elegance. A sophisticated waitstaff brings you complimentary hors d'oeuvres as you choose from chef Jean-Paul Bondoux's creations, which include foie gras, rabbit, escargots, chateaubriand, *côte de veau* (veal steak), and wild boar cooked in *cassis* (black-currant liqueur). The fixed-price menu is more affordable than à la carte selections. ⊠ *Alvear Palace Hotel, Ayacucho 2027, La Recoleta* ☎ *11/4805–3857* ⌂ *Reservations essential* ⌂ *Jacket and tie* ▤ *AE, DC, MC, V* Ⓜ *Line C, Estación San Martín.*

GERMAN ✕ **Munich Recoleta.** Jam-packed Munich Recoleta has been a favorite gath-
$–$$ ering spot for more than 40 years. Premium cuts of meat, creamed spinach, shoestring potatoes, and *chucrut* (cabbage) are served quickly and in generous portions. The reasonably priced wine list is enormous but well-chosen. The lively atmosphere attracts young and old alike, despite the often cantankerous waiters. Arrive early to avoid a wait. ⊠ *R. M. Ortíz 1879, La Recoleta* ☎ *11/4804–3981* ⌂ *Reservations not accepted* ▤ *AE, V.*

ITALIAN ✕ **San Babila.** This trattoria is known for its excellent handmade pastas
$$$ and classic Italian dishes, created from the century-old recipes of the chef's grandmother. *Cappelletti di formaggio* (cheese-filled round pasta) and *risotto de funghi porcini* (wild mushroom and saffron risotto) are good bets. There are fixed-price menus to choose from, and a friendly English-speaking staff. ⊠ *R. M. Ortíz 1815, La Recoleta* ☎ *11/4801–9444* ▤ *AE, DC, MC, V.*

MIDDLE EASTERN ✕ **Club Sirio.** A walk up a curved double staircase leads you to the wel-
$–$$ coming lobby bar of this breathtaking second-floor Syrian restaurant. You'll find hummus, stuffed grape leaves, and lamb in the superb Middle Eastern buffet. Belly dancers entertain Wednesday through Saturday, and coffee-ground readers predict fortunes. You can order a *narguilah* (large water-filtered tobacco pipe) to finish off dinner in true Syrian style. ⊠ *Pacheco de Melo 1902, La Recoleta* ☎ *11/4806–5764* ▤ *AE, V* ☺ *Closed Sun. No lunch.*

San Telmo

ARGENTINE ✕ **Calle de Ángeles.** Colón Theater's set designers have created a San Telmo
$–$$ alfresco with tree branches overhead and winged angels peering over balconies, justifying the restaurant's name—"Street of Angels." A cobblestone path runs down the middle, dimly lit by street lamps. Chefs prepare Argentine dishes with a Mediterranean slant. Garnish your parrilla with grilled eggplant or bell peppers, or try the juicy lamb. The coffee mousse on almond rings is a perfect ending. Locals gather at the bar to play the Spanish card game *truco*. ⊠ *Chile 318, San Telmo* ☎ *11/4361–8822* ▤ *AE, MC, V* ☺ *Closed Sun. No lunch Sat.*

$ ✕ **La Farmacia.** Mismatched tables and chairs, comfy leather sofas, and poptastic colors fill this century-old corner house that used to be a traditional pharmacy. Generous breakfasts and afternoon teas are served on the cozy ground floor, lunch and dinner are in the first-floor dining room, and you can have late-night drinks on the bright-yellow roof terrace, which has a view over San Telmo. Arts and dance workshops are run upstairs, and the building has two boutiques selling local designers' work. The modern Argentine dishes are simple but well done, and the fixed-price lunch and dinner menus get you a lot for a little. ⊠ *Bolívar 898, San Telmo* ☎ *11/4300–6151* ⊟ *No credit cards* ⊗ *Closed Mon.* Ⓜ *Lines C and E, Estación Independencia.*

¢ ✕ **El Desnivel.** Chaotic and always packed with both locals and tourists, this tavernlike San Telmo parrilla does huge portions of steaks and pastas at excellent prices—you can watch your meat being cooked on the huge barbecue at the front. The surly waiters are renowned for their rudeness, but it's all part of the experience. ⊠ *Defensa 855, San Telmo* ☎ *11/4300–9081* ⊟ *No credit cards* ⊗ *Closed Mon.* Ⓜ *Lines C and E, Estación Independencia.*

SPANISH ✕ **Taberna Baska.** Old-world decor and efficient service are hallmarks
$–$$ of this busy, no-nonsense Spanish restaurant. Try such typical dishes as *chiripones en su tinta* (a variety of squid in ink) or *fideua gandiense* (a seafood-packed pasta paella with a saffron-and-pepper sauce). ⊠ *Chile 980, San Telmo* ☎ *11/4334–0903* ⊟ *AE, DC, MC, V* ⊗ *Closed Mon.* Ⓜ *Line C, Estación Independencia.*

★ $ ✕ **Burzako.** Classic Basque dishes reinvented for a young Argentine public are what keep Burzako's tables busy. Dishes such as *rabo de buey* (a rich oxtail-and-wine stew) and seasonally changing fish use only the best and freshest local ingredients, and the huge portions leave you loathe to move. Recover from the meal over another bottle from their savvy, well-priced wine list. Despite the rustic tavern furnishings, Burzako draws a funky crowd, and weekends the basement becomes a bar where local bands often play. ⊠ *México 345, San Telmo* ☎ *11/4334–0721* ⊟ *AE, DC, MC, V* ⊗ *Closed Sun.*

WHERE TO STAY

In general, hotels are not standardized, and although major chains are appearing, they adapt their services and decor to match the personality of the city: most have bidets but not ice makers or vending machines. Smaller hotels have a family-run feel, with all the charming quirks that entails. The rooms in medium-price hotels may be smaller than expected, but the facilities and service are usually of high quality. And posh, exclusive hotels afford world-class comfort and conveniences. Most lodging establishments have Internet and/or e-mail access.

Since the devaluation of the peso, hotel prices have changed unpredictably. Many hotels charge the same as before but in pesos, others charge in dollars but at a much lower rate, and a few (mainly major International chains) have maintained the same dollar price as before. As a result, it's quite easy to find locally run hotels with four- or five-star service at a fraction of the cost of their international competitors. To avoid confusion, always confirm which currency is being used in price quotes. The lodging tax is 21%; note that this may or may not be included in the rate quoted. As a general rule, check-in is after 3 PM, checkout before noon; smaller hotels tend to be more flexible.

Almagro

★ $$$$ ⌂ **Abasto Plaza Hotel.** In the spirit of the surrounding traditional tango neighborhood and the Abasto Shopping Center, this is Latin-America's first international theme hotel, showcasing all things tango. Rooms are decorated with navy, hunter green, and burgundy and feature local artwork depicting surrealist tango scenes; public areas are scattered with original art deco furniture. Though a bit removed from the city's nerve

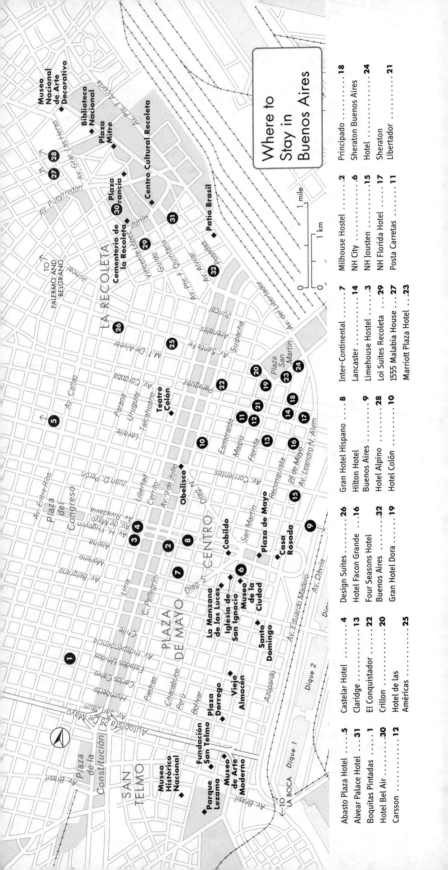

Where to Stay in Buenos Aires

center, the hotel has convenient access to sights and shopping. On Friday there are free tango classes and a tango show with dinner for guests. Ask for a room with a balcony, or for one with a view over the beautiful Abasto building, which is stunningly lit at night. ⊠ *Av. Corrientes 3190, El Centro, 1193* ☏ *11/6311–4466* 📠 *11/6311–4465* ⊕ *www. abastoplaza.com* 🛏 *120 rooms, 6 suites* ⚲ *Restaurant, snack bar, room service, IDD phones, in-room data ports, minibars, cable TV, pool, gym, health club, bar, lobby lounge, Internet, business services, 7 meeting rooms* 🖃 *AE, DC, MC, V* ⋓ *BP* Ⓜ *Line B, Estación Carlos Gardel.*

El Centro

$$$$ 🏨 **Claridge.** Stylish wood paneling and high ceilings lend a distinctly British feel to this hotel with a traditionally Anglo-Argentine clientele. Rooms are done in shades of blue, with dark-wood furnishings and bronze fittings. The hotel is in the hectic business district, and it's nice to wind down in the spa or heated outdoor pool after a busy day. ⊠ *Tucumán 535, El Centro, 1049* ☏ *11/4314–7700, 800/223–5652 in U.S.* 📠 *11/4314–8022* ⊕ *www.claridge.com.ar* 🛏 *155 rooms, 6 suites* ⚲ *Restaurant, room service, IDD phones, in-room data ports, in-room safes, minibars, cable TV, pool, gym, health club, massage, spa, bar, laundry service, concierge, Internet, business services, meeting room, airport shuttle, no-smoking floors* 🖃 *AE, DC, MC, V* ⋓ *BP* Ⓜ *Line C, Estación San Martín.*

$$$$ 🏨 **Inter-Continental.** This luxury hotel may be a modern construction, but it was designed with the elegance of the 1930s in mind. The handsome lobby—in marble, leather, bronze, and wood—leads to an outdoor courtyard with a fountain. Rooms are adorned with large black armoires, marble-top nightstands, sleeper chairs, and black-and-white photos of Buenos Aires. The hotel has convenient access to the bordering city nerve center but is itself in a tranquil area. There's a transit lounge for early arrival and late departure. ⊠ *Moreno 809, El Centro, 1091* ☏ *11/4340–7100* 📠 *11/4340–7199* ⊕ *www.buenos-aires.interconti. com* 🛏 *315 rooms, 15 suites* ⚲ *2 restaurants, café, room service, IDD phones, in-room data ports, in-room safes, cable TV, indoor pool, gym, hot tub, massage, sauna, Turkish bath, bar, baby-sitting, laundry service, concierge, business services, meeting room, parking (fee), no-smoking floors* 🖃 *AE, DC, MC, V* ⋓ *BP* Ⓜ *Line E, Estación Belgrano.*

$$$$ 🏨 **Marriott Plaza Hotel.** Crystal chandeliers and Persian carpets decorate
Fodor'sChoice the sumptuous public spaces at the city's first grand hotel. The rooms
★ are spacious and elegantly appointed, and some have bay windows overlooking the park. The pool affords views of the park at the health club, a modern oasis. ⊠ *Florida 1005, El Centro, 1005* ☏ *11/4318–3000, 800/228–9290 in U.S.* 📠 *11/4318–3008* ⊕ *www.marriott.com* 🛏 *325 rooms, 12 suites* ⚲ *2 restaurants, coffee shop, room service, IDD phones, in-room data ports, in-room safes, minibars, cable TV with movies, pool, gym, health club, hair salon, hot tub, sauna, bar, laundry service, concierge, Internet, business services, meeting rooms* 🖃 *AE, DC, MC, V* ⋓ *BP* Ⓜ *Line C, Estación San Martín.*

$$$$ 🏨 **Sheraton Buenos Aires Hotel.** The Sheraton is popular with American businesspeople and tour groups seeking familiar comforts. The rooms are standard but afford views of the Río de la Plata, Plaza de la Fuerzas Aérea Argentina and its clock tower, or the glass skyscrapers of the Catalinas area. The separate Park Tower next door, part of Sheraton's Luxury Group, has spacious, expensive rooms with cellular phones, entertainment centers, and 24-hour butler service. ⊠ *San Martín 1225, El Centro, 1104* ☏ *11/4318–9000, 800/325–3535 in U.S.* 📠 *11/4318–9353* 🛏 *713 rooms, 29 suites* ⚲ *2 restaurants, coffee shop, room service, IDD phones, in-room data ports, in-room fax, in-room safes, minibars, cable*

TV with movies, 2 tennis courts, 2 pools, fitness classes, gym, health club, hair salon, massage, sauna, bar, lobby lounge, baby-sitting, laundry service, concierge, Internet, business services, convention center, meeting rooms, car rental, travel services, parking (fee), no-smoking rooms ▤ *AE, DC, MC, V* ❿ *BP* Ⓜ *Line C, Estación Retiro.*

$$$$ ▥ **Sheraton Libertador.** The central Sheraton Libertador is a functional hotel with small, standard rooms in subdued tones and the usual amenities. Deluxe rooms offer more luxuries; the ample Presidential Suite, for example, comes equipped with a sauna. The fine La Pergola restaurant serves Continental cuisine. ✉ *Av. Córdoba 690, El Centro, 1054* ☎ *11/4322–0000* 🖷 *11/4322–9703* ⊕ *www.sheraton.com* ✍ *193 rooms, 6 suites* ⚊ *Restaurant, room service, IDD phones, in-room data ports, in-room fax, in-room safes, some kitchenettes, minibars, cable TV with movies, indoor-outdoor pool, gym, health club, hot tub, massage, sauna, bar, baby-sitting, laundry service, concierge, Internet, business services, meeting rooms, no-smoking rooms* ▤ *AE, DC, MC, V* ❿ *BP* Ⓜ *Line C, Estación Lavalle.*

$$$ ▥ **El Conquistador.** Businesspeople flock to this efficient hotel, near Plaza San Martín. Wood paneling, a small art gallery in the lobby, and a cheerful restaurant serving breakfast and snacks create an inviting atmosphere. Simple rooms in neutral tones have large windows; ask for an upper floor for a view. ✉ *Suipacha 948, El Centro, 1008* ☎ *11/4328–3012* 🖷 *11/4328–3252* ⊕ *www.elconquistador.com.ar* ✍ *140 rooms, 14 suites* ⚊ *Restaurant, room service, IDD phones, some in-room data ports, minibars, cable TV, gym, massage, sauna, piano bar, concierge, Internet, business services* ▤ *AE, DC, MC, V* ❿ *BP* Ⓜ *Line C, Estación San Martín.*

$$$ ▥ **Gran Hotel Dorá.** A cozy lobby with a small '50s-style bar greets you at this old-fashioned hotel, located just off Plaza San Martín. Public areas are filled with original Latin American paintings and sculpture, including a mural by Argentine artist Castagnino in the lobby lounge. Simple elegance permeates the comfortable rooms, which are decorated in Louis XVI style. It caters primarily to Europeans and Argentines who prefer a Continental atmosphere. Ask for one of the front-facing rooms, which are larger. ✉ *Maipú 963, El Centro, 1006* ☎ *11/4312–7391* 🖷 *11/4313–8134* ⊕ *www.dorahotel.com.ar* ✍ *96 rooms, 1 suite* ⚊ *Snack bar, room service, IDD phones, in-room data ports, in-room safes, minibars, cable TV, bar, laundry service, Internet, business center, meeting rooms, free parking* ▤ *AE, DC, MC, V* ❿ *CP* Ⓜ *Line C, Estación San Martín.*

★ $$$ ▥ **NH City.** The clean art deco lines of the NH City's facade are mirrored within: in the spacious lobby, moulded pillars support an original stained-glass ceiling, which filters sunlight onto the white marble floors. Warm wood paneling and comfy boutique furniture in mocha, russet, and slate invite you to relax from the first step through the door. In the rooms, indulgence takes the form of huge beds made up with masses of white cotton linen, and NH even provides *à la carte* pillows, to make sure you really sleep well. The roof-top pool has spectacular views over the cupolas of nearby historic neighborhood San Telmo. ✉ *Bolívar 160, El Centro, 1066* ☎ *11/4121–6464* 🖷 *11/4121–6450* ⊕ *www.nh-hotels.com* ✍ *297 rooms, 6 suites* ⚊ *Restaurant, café, room service, IDD phones, in-room data ports, in-room safes, minibars, cable TV, pool, gym, sauna, bar, laundry service, concierge, Internet, business services, meeting rooms* ▤ *AE, DC, MC, V* ❿ *BP* Ⓜ *Line A, Estación Perú, Line E, Estación Bolívar.*

$$$ ▥ **NH Jousten.** From the 1930s on, the Jousten was one of the best-known
Fodor'sChoice luxury hotels in town—guests included local deities Perón and Evita—
★ before the building fell into disrepair and eventual abandonment. Thanks to the massive renovation carried out by Spanish hotel group NH, the

latest in contemporary boutique design rubs shoulders with the hotel's stunning original architectural features, such as an ornate moulded ceiling in the lobby and hand-painted tiles in the Spanish-style bar. The well-appointed rooms are filled with warm grays and deep reds, and furnished with sleek hardwood furniture and big, inviting beds. Suites have private terraces overlooking the River Plate. ⊠ *Corrientes 280, El Centro, 1043* ☎ *11/4321–6750* 🖷 *11/4321–6775* ⊕ *www.nh-hoteles.com* ⇔ *80 rooms, 5 suites* ⌂ *Restaurant, room service, IDD phones, in-room data ports, in-room safes, minibars, cable TV, lobby lounge, baby-sitting, concierge, dry-cleaning, laundry service, Internet, business services, travel services* ▭ *AE, DC, MC, V* ⎮⎮ *BP* Ⓜ *Line B, Estación L. N. Alem.*

$$$ 🏨 **Posta Carretas.** This comfortable *hostería* (inn) has the atmosphere of a mountain lodge. Wood paneling creates a cozy atmosphere, a nice contrast to the bustle outside. Suites are brightly decorated and have whirlpools. The lobby bar overlooks the indoor pool, and there's a small garden where you can relax. ⊠ *Esmeralda 726, El Centro, 1007* ☎ *11/4322–8567* 🖷 *11/4322–8606* ⊕ *www.postacarretas.com.ar* ⇔ *90 rooms, 26 suites* ⌂ *Coffee shop, room service, IDD phones, in-room data ports, in-room safes, some in-room hot tubs, minibars, cable TV, indoor pool, gym, sauna, bar, dry cleaning, laundry service, Internet, business services, meeting room, parking (fee)* ▭ *AE, DC, MC, V* ⎮⎮ *BP* Ⓜ *Line C, Estación San Martín.*

$$ 🏨 **Crillon.** Spacious, luminous front guest rooms overlook Plaza San Martín in this classic French-style hotel, built in 1948. The lobby is stately and sedate, which may explain why this establishment appeals to provincial governors and high society. Service, however, is indifferent. Inquire about special summer rates. ⊠ *Av. Santa Fe 796, El Centro, 1059* ☎ *11/4310–2040 or 0800/888–4448* 🖷 *11/4310–2020* ⊕ *www.hotelcrillon.com.ar* ⇔ *84 rooms, 12 suites* ⌂ *Restaurant, room service, IDD phones, in-room safes, tennis court, gym, sauna, squash, bar, laundry service, concierge, business services, meeting room* ▭ *AE, DC, MC, V* ⎮⎮ *CP* Ⓜ *Line C, Estación San Martín.*

$$ 🏨 **Design Suites.** With its harmonious minimalist aura, and chrome and pine fittings complemented by tones of beige and gray, this central hotel has been designed to feng shui perfection. Rooms overlook the Plaza Pizurno and are flooded with sunlight. A nightcap is included in the rate, and you can count on professional and friendly service. ⊠ *M. T. de Alvear 1683, El Centro, 1060* ☎🖷 *11/4814–8700* ⊕ *www.designsuites.com* ⇔ *40 rooms* ⌂ *Restaurant, room service, in-room data ports, some in-room hot tubs, in-room safes, some kitchenettes, cable TV, pool, gym, bar, laundry service, Internet, meeting room* ▭ *AE, DC, MC, V* Ⓜ *Line D, Estación Callao.*

$$ 🏨 **Hotel Colón.** Right off busy Avenida 9 de Julio, the shiny, modern Colón faces the Obelisk. The suites have private patios; standard rooms, however, are shoe-box size. The open-air roof pool is spectacular, with great views over the city. Airport buses are available at the door. ⊠ *Av. Carlos Pellegrini 507, El Centro, 1009* ☎ *11/4320–3500 or 800/666–2526* 🖷 *11/4320–3507* ⊕ *www.colon-hotel.com.ar* ⇔ *147 rooms, 23 suites* ⌂ *Restaurant, room service, IDD phones, in-room data ports, in-room safes, minibars, cable TV, pool, bar, Internet, business services, meeting rooms, airport shuttle, parking (fee)* ▭ *AE, DC, MC, V* ⎮⎮ *CP* Ⓜ *Lines B, C, and D, Estación 9 de Julio.*

$$ 🏨 **NH Florida.** Although hotel group NH bills this as their no-frills option in Buenos Aires, the boutique chic of this downtown hotel suggests otherwise. The low, '70s-style lobby has a long wood-lined reception area filled with sculpted-looking armchairs in warm neutrals and arresting modern flower arrangements. Upstairs, rooms go easy on the eye with beige, gold, and russet furnishings, fluffy white linen, pale parquet flooring, and white marble bathrooms. The friendly young staff deals quickly with the requests. A few blocks away, the NH Latino has similar decor and services. ⊠ *San Martín 839, El Centro, 1004* ☎ *11/4321–9850* 🖷 *11/4321–9875* ⊕ *www.nh-hoteles.com* 🛏 *148 rooms* ⚬ *Restaurant, IDD phones, in-room data ports, in-room safes, minibars, cable TV, bar, laundry service, Internet, business services, free parking* ▭ *AE, DC, MC, V* ⛾ *BP* Ⓜ *Line C, Estación San Martín.*

$ 🏨 **Carsson.** A walk down the long, red-carpeted foyer takes you away from the bustle of the city and into a welcoming English-style hotel with first-rate service. The spacious rooms vary in color schemes, but all have Louis XIV–style furniture; request one *contra frente* (room not facing the street) to avoid street noise. ⊠ *Viamonte 650, El Centro, 1053* ☎ *11/4322–3601* 🖷 *11/4322–3551* 🛏 *108 rooms, 9 suites* ⚬ *Restaurant, coffee shop, room service, IDD phones, in-room data ports, in-room safes, minibars, cable TV, bar, baby-sitting, laundry service, Internet, business services, meeting room, parking (fee)* ▭ *AE, DC, MC, V* ⛾ *CP* Ⓜ *Line C, Estación Lavalle.*

$ 🏨 **Castelar Hotel.** Classic Spanish lines define the exterior of this 1928 hotel; the French classical interior has Italian marble and handsome furnishings. Though small, rooms are well equipped, and the service is very good. Breakfast is included in the rate, as is partial access to the spa, with its Turkish baths and Finnish saunas, massage, and beauty treatments. ⊠ *Av. de Mayo 1152, El Centro, 1085* ☎ *11/4383–5000* 🖷 *11/4383–8388* ⊕ *www.castelarhotel.com.ar* 🛏 *153 rooms, 7 suites* ⚬ *Coffee shop, restaurant, room service, IDD phones, minibars, health club, hair salon, massage, sauna, spa, Turkish bath, laundry service, business services, meeting room, Internet, parking (fee)* ▭ *AE, MC, V* ⛾ *BP* Ⓜ *Line A, Estación Lima.*

$ 🏨 **Hotel de las Américas.** Though the lobby is drab, rooms are comfortable and spacious at this residential hotel just off the shopping stretch of Avenida Santa Fe. The clientele consists mainly of South American groups and visitors from the provinces. ⊠ *Libertad 1020, El Centro, 1012* ☎ *11/4816–3432* 🖷 *11/4816–0418* ⊕ *www.americas-bue.com.ar* 🛏 *150 rooms, 14 suites* ⚬ *Restaurant, room service, IDD phones, in-room data ports, cable TV, minibars, bar, Internet, business services, meeting rooms, free parking, no-smoking rooms* ▭ *AE, DC, MC, V* ⛾ *BP* Ⓜ *Line D, Estación Tribunales.*

$ 🏨 **Hotel Facon Grande.** A lobby filled with Argentine handicrafts and rustic wood and leather furniture remind you that this hotel was named for a Gaucho hero. The Argentine countryside is further invoked in the muted greens and browns of the room furnishings. Guests are mainly from other Latin American countries or the provinces. ⊠ *Reconquista 645, El Centro, 1003* ☎🖷 *11/4312–6360* ⊕ *www.hotelfacongrande.com* 🛏 *98 rooms, 3 suites* ⚬ *Restaurant, room service, IDD phones, minibars, cable TV, bar, laundry service, Internet, meeting room, parking (fee)* ▭ *AE, DC, MC, V* ⛾ *CP* Ⓜ *Line B, Estación Alem.*

★ $ 🏨 **Lancaster.** The countess who decorated this traditional and central hotel made good use of her family heirlooms—old family portraits, marble pillars, and a 200-year-old clock grace the lobby. All rooms have antique mahogany furniture, and some have views of the port of Buenos Aires. You can dine on French cuisine with Iberian accents at the hotel's excellent Catalinas restaurant. ⊠ *Av. Córdoba 405, El Centro, 1054* ☎ *11/4311–3201* 🖷 *11/4312–4068* ⊕ *www.lancasterhotel-page.com* 🛏 *72 rooms, 18 suites* ⚬ *Restaurant, room service, IDD phones, in-room data ports, in-room safes, minibars, cable TV, pool, gym, hair salon, sauna, spa, squash, pub, dry cleaning, laundry service, concierge, Internet, business services, meeting room, travel services* ▭ *AE, DC, MC, V* ⛾ *CP* Ⓜ *Line C, Estación San Martín.*

$ 🏨 **Principado.** Rooms are modern and comfortable at this central hotel, built for the World Cup in 1978. Sunlight floods through the large windows in the reception area. The decor is cozy Spanish colonial, with comfortable leather couches in the split-level lobby. The highlight is the friendly coffee shop. ⊠ *Paraguay 481, El Centro, 1057* ☎ *11/4313–3022* 🖷 *11/4313–3952* ⊕ *www.principado.com.ar* ⤵ *88 rooms* ♨ *Restaurant, coffee shop, room service, IDD phones, in-room data ports, in-room safes, minibars, cable TV, bar, dry cleaning, laundry service, Internet, business services, parking (fee)* ☰ *AE, DC, MC, V* ⦿⎮ *CP* Ⓜ *Line C, Estación San Martín.*

★ ¢   🏨 **Gran Hotel Hispano.** The Spanish colonial architecture and small but charming rooms bordering the central patio of an old-style casa chorizo give this hotel a traditional and friendly feel. Outside, walls are pink, plants abound, and the patio's glass ceiling is opened up on sunny days. Inside, the well-appointed rooms are high-ceilinged yet cozy. The hotel has been owned by the Perreira family for the last 50 years, and the service is efficient and personal. ⊠ *Av. de Mayo 861, El Centro, 1084* ☎ *11/4345–2020* 🖷 *11/4345–2020* ⊕ *www.hhispano.com.ar* ⤵ *60 rooms* ♨ *Café, room service, IDD phones, minibars, cable TV, laundry service, Internet, airport shuttle, parking (fee)* ☰ *AE, DC, MC, V* ⦿⎮ *CP* Ⓜ *Line A, Estación Piedras.*

¢   🏨 **Limehouse Hostel.** High ceilings, wooden floors, and exposed brick are part of the charm of this turn-of-the-20th-century corner building that has been completely recycled into a hostel for laid-back young travelers. Dorm rooms are spacious, and communal areas include a pool room, two eating areas, a fully equipped kitchen, and a sofa-filled lounge where beers and home-made pizza are served up at night while guests swap tales. There's also a room with a library of maps, guidebooks, and travel information to help you plan the rest of your trip, and the hip, young staff are always on hand to help. There are a few private rooms, some of which can be rented by the month. The hostel is right on 9 de Julio Avenue, so things can get noisy at night. ⊠ *Lima 11, El Centro, 1073* ☎ *11/4383–4561* ⊕ *www.limehouseargentina.com* ⤵ *10 private rooms, 50 dorm beds* ♨ *Snack bar, fans, bar, library, laundry facilities, Internet, travel services; no a/c, no room phones, no room TVs* ☰ *No credit cards* ⦿⎮ *CP* Ⓜ *Line A, Estación Lima.*

¢   🏨 **Milhouse Hostel.** Backpackers flock to Milhouse for the low prices and slick service. The cozy private rooms open out on to a terraced walkway overlooking the central plant-filled patio. Dorm rooms are large, with brightly colored walls that offset the high, white ceilings. In addition to a restaurant serving no-frills Argentine fare, there are cooking facilities for guests, and an all-night café-bar to keep you going through marathon pool and Ping-Pong sessions. Milhouse's ultra-efficient staff organize all kinds of social activities, from *asados* (barbecues), visits to the football stadium, and tango lessons to all-night clubbing marathons. ⊠ *Hipólito Irigoyen 959, El Centro, 1086* ☎ *11/4345–9605 or 11/4343–5038* ⊕ *www.milhousehostel.com* ⤵ *13 private rooms, 42 dorm beds* ♨ *Restaurant, fans, Ping-Pong, bar, library, laundry facilities, Internet, travel services, parking (fee); no a/c, no room phones, no room TVs* ☰ *MC* ⦿⎮ *CP* Ⓜ *Line A, Estación Piedras; Line C, Estación Av. de Mayo.*

La Recoleta

★ $$$$ 🏨 **Alvear Palace Hotel.** Built in 1932 as a luxury apartment building, the Alvear retains its old-world opulence and is a preferred reception venue for visiting dignitaries. Decorated in French Empire style, with regal burgundy and deep blue, the rooms have large windows draped in silk, and feather beds with Egyptian cotton linen. Fine shops, museums, and restaurants are all nearby. ☒ *Av. Alvear 1891, La Recoleta, 1129* ☏ *11/4808–2100 or 11/4804–7777, 800/448–8355 in U.S.* ☐ *11/4804–9246* ⊕ *www.alvearpalace.com* ☞ *100 rooms, 100 suites* ♢ *2 restaurants, coffee shop, room service, IDD phones, in-room data ports, in-room safes, some in-room hot tubs, minibars, indoor pool, health club, gym, sauna, lobby bar, laundry service, concierge, Internet, business services, meeting room, no-smoking rooms* ☐ *AE, DC, MC, V* ⦿ *BP.*

★ **$$$$** ▦ **Four Seasons Hotel Buenos Aires.** The luxurious Four Seasons Hotel has a 13-floor marble tower and an adjacent late-19th-century mansion, with private butler service for its handsome suites. In addition to its priceless art collection, the hotel houses a beautiful Roman-style pool, health club, and landscaped garden. Guest rooms are spacious, and outstanding service ensures many repeat visitors. ☒ *Posadas 1086, La Recoleta, 1011* ☏ *11/4321–1200* ☐ *11/4321–1201* ⊕ *www.fourseasons.com* ☞ *138 rooms, 27 suites* ♢ *Restaurant, room service, IDD phones, in-room data ports, in-room fax, in-room safes, minibars, cable TV, pool, fitness classes, health club, gym, massage, sauna, bar, lobby lounge, babysitting, dry cleaning, laundry service, concierge, Internet, business services, meeting rooms, airport shuttle, travel services, parking (fee), no-smoking rooms* ☐ *AE, DC, MC, V* ⦿ *BP.*

$$$$ ▦ **Loi Suites Recoleta.** The spacious rooms here are decorated with tasteful beiges and creams. In addition to the usual amenities, all rooms have large-screen TVs, stereo systems, and microwaves. Breakfast and a nightly happy hour take place at the elegant white-stone pool area. Nearby are restaurants, bars, cafés, shopping, cultural centers, and a cinema. Loi Suites also operate two smaller apart-hotels downtown. ☒ *Vicente López 1955, La Recoleta, 1128* ☏ *11/5777–8950* ☐ *11/5777–8999* ⊕ *www.loisuites.com.ar* ☞ *88 rooms, 24 suites* ♢ *Restaurant, room service, IDD phones, in-room data ports, in-room safes, minibars, microwaves, cable TV, indoor-outdoor pool, gym, sauna, bar, dry cleaning, laundry service, Internet, business services, meeting rooms, parking (fee)* ☐ *AE, DC, MC, V* ⦿ *CP.*

★ **$$** ▦ **Hotel Bel Air.** The classic facade of the Bel Air belies the smooth modern lines within. The small lobby has a curving pale-wood bar and a café where trendy Recoleta-ites meet for coffee. The spacious rooms have parquet flooring and simple modern furnishings in beige and cream—you can upgrade at little extra cost to a superior room, which have small terraces. On a quiet street in the heart of Recoleta, the Bel Air is within a few blocks of shops and eateries and the Recoleta cemetery. ☒ *Arenales 1462, La Recoleta, 1062* ☏ *11/4021–4000* ☐ *11/4816–0016* ⊕ *www.hahoteles.com* ☞ *67 rooms, 15 suites* ♢ *Restaurant, café, room service, IDD phones, in-room data ports, in-room safes, minibars, cable TV, gym, bar, dry cleaning, laundry service, Internet, business services, meeting rooms, airport shuttle, travel services, no-smoking rooms* ☐ *AE, DC, MC, V* ⦿ *BP.*

Palermo

★ **$** ▦ **1555 Malabia House.** A classic turn-of-the-20th-century town house, 1555 Malabia House is a tranquil home-away-from-home in the heart of trendy Palermo SoHo. Pale wood fittings and harmonious white-and-beige furnishings are interrupted by splashes of color from Oriental rugs, original paintings, and bold flower arrangements. You can curl up with a drink on the sofas in the common living room or sit amongst the rich greens of three plant-filled inner patios. Service is highly personalized and the young staff are knowledgeable about the nearby eateries, clubs, and fashionable shops. ☒ *Malabia 1555, Palermo, 1414* ☏ *11/4832–3345 or 11/4833–2410* ⊕ *www.malabiahouse.com.ar* ☞ *11 rooms, 4 suites* ♢ *Room service, IDD phones, fans, in-room safes, mini-*

bars, cable TV, bar, laundry service, concierge, Internet, meeting room, airport shuttle, parking (fee) ☰ *AE, DC, MC, V* ⍥ *CP* Ⓜ *Line D, Estación Scalabrini Ortiz.*

¢ 🏨 **Hotel Alpino.** Decorated with leather sofas in the lobby, dark browns, and wood paneling, this hotel has functional, though somber, rooms. It's close to the Parque Zoológico and the Jardín Botánico. ⊠ *Cabello 3318, Palermo, 1425* ☎ *11/4802–5151* ⊕ *www.geocities.com/ alpinohotel* ⤳ *35 rooms* ⚴ *Room service, IDD phones, in-room data ports, in-room safes, minibars, cable TV, laundry service, meeting rooms, parking (fee)* ☰ *AE, DC, MC, V* ⍥ *CP* Ⓜ *Line D, Estación Plaza Italia.*

Puerto Madero

$$$$ 🏨 **Hilton Hotel Buenos Aires.** The futuristic glass-and-steel building with a seven-floor atrium lobby provides spacious, comfortable rooms with unobstructed panoramic skyline or river views. It was the setting for the 2001 Argentine hit film *Nine Queens*. Butlers attend to your every whim on the two executive floors, and the executive lounge provides a private recreation area and a host of extras such as a free happy hour. For those with simpler needs, an impressive health club and rooftop pool offer breathtaking views. Even the hotel's location is superb: at the docks, overlooking the Ecological Reserve. ⊠ *Macacha Guemes 351, Puerto Madero, 1106* ☎ *11/4891–0000, 800/774–1500 in U.S.* ☎ *11/ 4891–0001* ⊕ *www.hilton.com* ⤳ *418 rooms, 13 suites* ⚴ *Restaurant, room service, IDD phones, in-room data ports, in-room safes, mini-bars, cable TV, pool, gym, health club, hair salon, massage, 2 bars, lounge, baby-sitting, laundry service, concierge, business services, meeting rooms, parking (fee), no-smoking rooms* ☰ *AE, DC, MC, V* ⍥ *BP.*

San Telmo

★ ¢–$ ✕🏨 **Boquitas Pintadas.** This petite, self-proclaimed pop hotel—whimsically called "Little Painted Mouths" as a tribute to Manuel Puig's novel of the same name—is as intimate as it is extraordinary. Rooms have names like "Gilda" and "The Chamber of Roses," and the kitschy decor changes every three months. A library features Puig's works, and the hotel hosts ongoing film screenings and art exhibits. A modern restaurant serves unique, eclectic dishes and funky cocktails; weekends there's an all-night party with DJs. Though it's slightly outside the city center, bordering San Telmo, Boquitas Pintadas nevertheless has easy access to the city center. ⊠ *Estados Unidos 1393, San Telmo, 1101* ☎ *11/ 4381–6064* ⊕ *www.boquitas-pintadas.com.ar* ⤳ *6 rooms, 1 suite* ⚴ *Restaurant, room service, cable TV, library, bar, nightclub, dry cleaning, laundry service, Internet, business services, travel services* ☰ *No credit cards* Ⓜ *Line E, Estación San José.*

NIGHTLIFE & THE ARTS

Listings of events can be found daily in the English-language *Buenos Aires Herald* as well as in the more comprehensive Friday edition. The tourist office distributes free copies of a helpful guide called "Buenos Aires Day and Night." If you read Spanish, check out the major papers's Friday supplements: Via Libre in *La Nación* and Sí in *Clarín*. The latter's daily "Espectáculos" section also has listings. Trendier spots can be found in *Wipe*, a pocket-sized magazine distributed in bars, restaurants, and boutiques. On-line, check out www.dondevamos.com for general nightlife suggestions and www.buenosaliens.com for clubbing and electronic music information.

Nightlife

It's good to begin with a basic understanding of the Argentine idea of nightlife: theater performances start at 9 PM or 9:30 PM; the last movie begins after midnight; and nightclubs don't begin filling up until 2 or 3 AM. In fact, even if you wanted to go clubbing early, you might not be allowed in: "early evening" hours (meaning before midnight) are often reserved for teenagers, and no one over 18 may be permitted to enter until after that time. For the most part, Buenos Aires's dance clubs attract young crowds (in the 18–30 age range). Note that the subte closes at 10 PM, so if you go out late, either count on taking a taxi home or waiting until 5 AM for the subte to start running again.

Bars & Clubs

ALMAGRO The young and beautiful groove to hip-hop and R&B at **El Codo** (⊠ Guardia Vieja 4085, Almagro ☎ 11/4862–1381). For a quiet drink, head for the wooden tables and exposed brick of **El Imaginario** (⊠ Bulnes 905, Almagro ☎ 11/4866–0672), a converted old corner building in the heart of Almagro. Live bands play the basement on weekends.

COSTANERA NORTE There are several popular bars, dance clubs, and after-hours clubs clustered in this area.

Twenty- to thirtysomethings let off steam at relaxed bar **La Diosa** (⊠ Rafael Obligado 3731 at Salguero, Costanera ☎ 11/4806–1079), where anything from live bands to strippers fills the stage. The best international house, trance, and techno DJs play to crowds of thousands at Buenos Aires's biggest nightclub, **Pachá Clubland** (⊠ Costanera Norte and La Pampa, Costanera ☎ 11/4788–4280), which looks out over the river.

EL CENTRO The best place downtown for electronic music is **Big One** (⊠ Alsina 940, El Centro ☎ 11/4775–4804), where a cool set gathers to listen to local and imported DJs. Trendy thirtysomethings order wine and sushi at fashionable **Gran Bar Danzón** (⊠ Libertad 1161, 1st fl., El Centro ☎ 11/4811–1108). For a little rowdy Irish-bar action and some (canned) Guinness, check out **The Kilkenny** (⊠ Marcelo T. De Alvear 399, El Centro ☎ 11/4312–7291). **La Cigale** (⊠ 25 de Mayo 722, El Centro ☎ 11/4312–8275) has a large turquoise bar where you can sip cocktails while smooth sounds spin. Classic café **La Ideal** (⊠ Suipacha 384, El Centro ☎ 11/4326–0521) hosts an electronica club night every Saturday. At converted old mansion **Milín** (⊠ Paraná 1048, El Centro ☎ 11/4815–9925) you can sip drinks at the bar or out in the garden while quiet sophisticates chat around you. An older, more refined crowd gathers for drinks and cigars at the Marriott's elegant **Plaza Bar** (⊠ Florida 1005, El Centro ☎ 11/4318–3000). An English-speaking expat crowd often gathers at **Shamrock** (⊠ Rodríguez Peña 1220, El Centro ☎ 11/4812–3584), an Irish-style bar; late nights head downstairs to the Shamrock Basement where local DJs spin house and techno.

LA RECOLETA A mixed crowd gathers for beer and rock at the only microbrewery in town, **Buller** (⊠ R. M. Ortíz 1827, La Recoleta ☎ 11/4808–9061), which has seven house beers. Buenos Aires has its own **Hard Rock Cafe** (⊠ in La Recoleta Design Center, Av. Pueyrredón 2501, La Recoleta ☎ 11/4807–7625), serving typical American drinks and snacks; on weekends an irritatingly high cover is charged.

PALERMO At former toy store **Acabar** (⊠ Honduras 5733, Palermo ☎ 11/4772–0845) you can enjoy board games with your cocktails. You may see a model or rock star at **Buenos Aires News** (⊠ Av. Libertador 3883, Palermo ☎ 11/4778–1500), one of the city's hottest nightspots. **El Living** (⊠ M.

T. de Alvear 1540, Palermo ☎ 11/4811–4730) is a trendy disco and bar with lounge chairs and great drinks. A Palermo classic, **Malas Artes** (✉ Honduras 4999 on Plaza Serrano, Palermo ☎ 11/4831–0743) draws a mixed crowd for Quilmes beer and peanuts at wooden tables. A hip crowd gathers at **Mundo Bizarro** (✉ Guatemala 4802, Palermo ☎ 11/4773–1967), a shrine to '50s bizarre that serves the best cocktails in town.

A varied menu of live music is on offer at laid-back bar **Niceto** (✉ Cnel. Niceto Vega 5510 at Humboldt, Palermo ☎ 11/4779–9396), which also hosts raunchy club night '69 on Thursdays. Classic rock and indie fill the ground floor of Palermo mainstay **El Podestá** (✉ Armenia 1742, Palermo ☎ 11/4832–2776): upstairs a more trendy crowd grooves to electronic beats. The cream of the Argentine rock scene hang out at **The Roxy** (✉ Arcos del Sol, between Casares and Sarmiento, Palermo ☎ 11/4899–0313), a large club with several different theme nights. Palermo Hollywood darlings gather for drinks at **Único** (✉ Honduras 5604, Palermo ☎ 11/4775–6693), a large corner bar that's usually packed.

SAN TELMO Students, bohemians, old men, and young trendies all gather to down a beer or a coffee at **Bar El Británico** (✉ Brazil 399 at Defensa, San Telmo ☎ 11/4300–6894), a vintage classic that's open all night. The ground floor of pop hotel **Boquitas Pintadas** (✉ Estados Unidos 1393, San Telmo ☎ 11/4381–6064) starts off the night as a retro-kitsch cocktail bar and segues into all-night weekend dance parties and cool after-hours sessions, finishing with breakfast at dawn.

Gay & Lesbian Clubs

Angels (✉ Viamonte 2168, El Centro) has several dance floors and attracts a primarily gay and transvestite clientele. The most popular gay dance club (men only) is **Contramano** (✉ Rodríguez Peña 1082, El Centro ☎ No phone); it's open from midnight Wednesday–Saturday and Sunday from 8 PM. The young and hip head to **Glam** (✉ Cabrera 3046, Palermo ☎ 11/4963–2521) for smooth cruising in a classy setting. Utter excess is the idea at **Oxen** (✉ Sarmiento 1662, El Centro ☎ 11/4375–0366), where a mainly male crowd gets down to pumping club anthems. On Friday, the dance club **Palacio** (✉ Alsina 940, near Plaza de Mayo) is the place to be.

Jazz Clubs

There are particularly good jazz listings in newspaper *Página 12*'s Thursday supplement, *No*.

An older, arty crowd gathers for drinks, philosophy, and live jazz at **Clásica y Moderna** (✉ Callao 892, El Centro ☎ 11/4812–8707). Wine and choice live jazz come together at **Club Del Vino** (✉ Cabrera 4737, Palermo ☎ 11/4833–0050), which has a classic smoky theater–café packed with tables. The 1858 classic **Gran Café Tortoni** (✉ Av. de Mayo 829, near Plaza de Mayo ☎ 11/4342–4328) hosts jazz on weekends. **Notorious** (✉ Av. Callao 966, El Centro ☎ 11/4815–8473) stages jazz shows several times per week, and when there isn't live music, CD players at each table provide the background music. **La Revuelta** (✉ Alvarez Thomas 1368, Chacarita ☎ 11/4553–5530 Ⓜ Line B, Estación F. Lacroze) is a quiet, sophisticated bar that has a varied program of live jazz and blues several times a week. The best of Porteño jazz bands (and occasional imports) play at intimate **Thelonious Bar** (✉ Salguero 1884, La Recoleta ☎ 11/4829–1562).

The Arts

Buenos Aires has a busy schedule of world-class cultural events. Except for some international short-run performances, tickets to most events are surprisingly easy to get. Note that, like most other businesses in Argentina, theaters take a summer vacation (January–February). Men usually wear jackets and ties to theater performances, and women also dress accordingly.

Tickets can be purchased at the box office of the venue or at various ticket outlets. **Entrada Plus** (☎ 11/4324–1010) sells tickets for theater, dance performances, and concerts; tickets can be sent to your hotel or picked up at the box office. **Ticketmaster** (☎ 11/4321–9700) sells tickets for events at the Colón, Luna Park, Teatro Globo, and the Teatro Municipal San Martín and accepts MasterCard and Visa for phone purchases. **Ticketek** (☎ 11/4323–7200) has tickets for concerts, local theaters, and music halls. Tickets for international gigs are often available at branches of **Tower Records** (⊠ Florida 770, El Centro ☎ 11/4327–5151).

You can purchase discount tickets for music-hall revues, plays, concerts, and movies through **Cartelera Baires** (⊠ Av. Corrientes 1382, Local 24, El Centro ☎ 11/4372–5058). **Cartelera Vea Más** (⊠ Av. Corrientes 1660, Paseo La Plaza, Local 26 El Centro ☎ 11/4370–5319) sells discount movie and theater tickets.

Classical Music & Opera

By any standard, the **Teatro Colón** (⊠ Ticket office, Tucumán 1111, El Centro ☎ 11/4378–7100 or 11/4370–7132) is one of the world's finest opera houses. Tiered like a wedding cake, the gilt and red-velvet auditorium has unsurpassed acoustics. Pavarotti has said that the Colón has only one flaw: the acoustics are so good, every mistake can be heard. An ever-changing stream of imported talent bolsters the well-regarded local company. The opera and symphony seasons run from March to December. The **Teatro San Martín** (⊠ Av. Corrientes 1530, El Centro ☎ 11/4374–9680) holds year-round classical music performances by top Argentine performers: many concerts are free.

Dance

When you think dance in Buenos Aires, you think of the tango—and this is the capital of that most passionate of dances. But dance is not only about the tango: Porteños also gather in droves on weekends to dance to the pulsating beats of samba and salsa.

Dance all night to fantastic salsa at relaxed **Calle 24** (⊠ Aráoz 2424, Palermo ☎ 11/4943–7736); some nights feature other Latin rhythms, so call ahead to check what's on. The best salsa dancers in town show off their moves (and their outfits) at **Caribean Salsa** (⊠ Rivadavia 2217, Once ☎ 11/4326–4546). Get into Brazilian rhythms at **Maluco Beleza** (⊠ Sarmiento 1728 Capital Federal, Palermo ☎ 11/4372–1737), where you can learn to samba, lambada, and even *capoeira*. Cuban rhythms fill the floor at **Ron y Son** (⊠ Salta 508, San Telmo ☎ 11/4382–3427)—Friday and Saturday there's a dinner orchestra playing *son* and *boleros,* then things heat up when owner Ibrahim Ferrer Junior (son of the Buena Vista Social Club star) and his band take to the stage. **La Trastienda** (⊠ Balcarce 460, at Belgrano, San Telmo ☎ 11/4342–7650) is a large dance hall hosting salsa classes and energetic crowds; it also occasionally doubles as a performance space for tango shows. The oldest and most important club in the Buenos Aires salsa scene is undoubtedly **La Salsera** (⊠ Yatay 961, Almagro ☎ 11/4866–1829), which has great music in a casual setting.

The **Ballet del Colón** is headquartered at the Teatro Colón but gives open-air performances in Palermo in summer. When world-famous Argentine dancer **Julio Bocca and the Ballet Argentino** perform in Buenos Aires, it's often at unconventional locations such as the rock and sports sta-

THE ART OF TANGO

THE TANGO IS MACHO, *the tango is strong. It smells of wine and tastes like death."*

So goes the famous tango "Why I sing like this," whose mix of nostalgia, violence, and sensuality sum up what is truly the dance of Buenos Aires. The tango was born at the end of the 19th century in the conventillos (tenement houses) of the port neighborhood of La Boca, although its roots are not known for sure: different theories place its origins in Spain, Italy, and even Africa. Nevertheless, the tango swept quickly from the immigrant quarter to the brothels and cabarets of the whole city, and by the 1920s had become respectable enough to fill the salons and drawing rooms of the upper class. In the 1930s, with the advent of Carlos Gardel, tango's great hero, the tango became known outside Argentina. Since then, tango has had its ups and downs in Buenos Aires, but remains a key part of the city's culture.

Today, you can experience tango culture all over Buenos Aires: from street performers on Calle Florida and Plaza Dorrego to glitzy shows at expensive clubs. Opening days and times of tango halls vary greatly, so call ahead to check. Be sure to visit the Chacarita cemetery grave of Carlos Gardel, who died in a plane crash in 1935 at the age of 40.

Both musicians and dancers perform at **Bar Sur** (✉ Estados Unidos 299, San Telmo ☎ 11/4362–6086), a small, traditional bar in San Telmo. In Boedo, **La Esquina de Homero Manzi** (✉ San Juan 3601, Boedo ☎ 11/4957–8488) has reasonably priced shows in an opulent café. Consistently excellent, well-attended performances are held at the classic tango café **El Querandí** (✉ Perú 302, at Moreno, San Telmo ☎ 11/4342–1760 ⊕ www.querandi.com.ar). Perhaps the glitziest spot in town is **Señor Tango** (✉ Vieytes 1655, Barracas ☎ 11/4303–0231), whose daily shows are aimed at tourists. The fancy show at **Taconeando** (✉ Balcarce 725, San Telmo ☎ 11/4307–6696) is also very popular with tourists. A traditional show takes place in a colonial-style house at **Viejo Almacén** (✉ Balcarce 786, at Independencia, San Telmo ☎ 11/4307–6689).

Celebrated old-guard tango musicians Salgán and De Lío frequently perform at **Club del Vino** (✉ Cabrera 4737, Palermo ☎ 11/4833–0050). The classic **Gran Café Tortoni** (✉ Av. de Mayo 829, Plaza de Mayo ☎ 11/4342–4328) is one of the best places to listen to tango music. Small, recycled theater **ND Ateneo** (✉ Paraguay 918, El Centro ☎ 11/4328–2888) has become a showcase for live music performances.

Akarense (✉ Donado 1355 at Av. Los Incas, Villa Ortúzar ☎ 11/4651–2121) draws the best dancers to its beautiful hall. Behind the unmarked doors of **La Catedral** (✉ Sarmiento 4006, Almagro ☎ No phone) is a contemporary club where you can eat, drink, and hit the floor. Milongas are danced weekends at **Centro Cultural Torcuato Tasso** (✉ Defensa 1575, San Telmo ☎ 11/4307–6506). Crowds of local regulars gather on Friday night at **Club Gricel** (✉ La Rioja 1180, San Cristóbal ☎ 11/4957–7517), which sometimes has classes. All ages come to practice at **La Ideal** (✉ Suipacha 384, Plaza de Mayo ☎ 11/4601–8234). The very special **Sin Rumbo** (✉ Tamborini 6157, Villa Urquiza ☎ 11/4571–9577 or 11/4574–0972) attracts old milonga dancers and also has some classes. A young crowd gathers at informal club **La Viruta-La Estrella** (✉ Armenia 1366, Palermo ☎ 11/4774–6357).

For more information contact **Academia Nacional de Tango** (✉ Av. de Mayo 833, Plaza de Mayo ☎ 11/4345–6968).

dium **Luna Park** (⊠ Bouchard 465, El Centro ☎ 11/4311–1990). Avant-garde contemporary Argentine dance troupes often perform at **Centro Cultural Recoleta** (⊠ Junín 1930, La Recoleta ☎ 11/4803–1040). World-class contemporary dance is performed several times a year at the **Teatro San Martín** (⊠ Av. Corrientes 1530, El Centro ☎ 11/4374–9680).

Film

Buenos Aires is a great city for film lovers, with about 50 movie theaters in the downtown area offering everything from standard Hollywood flicks to Argentine films to world art-house fare. The names of films are generally given in Spanish, but English-language films are shown undubbed, with Spanish subtitles. The stretch of Calle Lavalle between Florida and 9 de Julio is lined with old one- or two-screen cinemas, which, with their plush bucket seats and classic theater architecture, make up in charm for what they lack in audio-visual finesse. The Lavalle theaters charge 4 to 5 pesos for all screenings. There are several art-house theaters on Avenida Corrientes, but be aware that foreign-language films are only subtitled in Spanish. Many museums and cultural centers also have screening rooms for off-beat movies. All of the major shopping malls have large state-of-the-art cinema complexes that charge 8 or 9 pesos, with half-price tickets available for the first show of the day and all day Wednesday. Weekends, there are *trasnoche* show times starting after midnight. Check the *Herald, Clarín,* or *La Nación* for daily listings. Every April, Buenos Aires hosts the *Festival de Cine Independiente,* which showcases the choicest independent films from all over the world.

Cine Lorca (⊠ Corrientes 1428, El Centro ☎ 11/4371–5017) has two screens showing the best of independent and art-house films in classic surroundings. At the 10-screen multiplex **Cinemark Palermo** (⊠ Beruti 3399, Palermo ☎ 11/4827–9500) you can catch the latest from Hollywood in comfort. **Cinemark Puerto Madero** (⊠ Av. M. de Justo 1960, Puerto Madero ☎ 11/4315–3008) has comfortable seating and eight screens. If you know Spanish, check out the **Complejo Cultural Tita Merello** (⊠ Suipacha 442, El Centro ☎ 11/4322–1195), which screens only Argentine cinema. The **Hoyts General Cinema** (⊠ Av. Corrientes 3200, El Centro ☎ 11/4866–4800) complex is inside the Abasto shopping mall and is the main location for films shown in the *Festival de Cine Independiente* (Independent Film Festival). The largest and most luxurious theater in the city is the **Village Recoleta** (⊠ Vicente Lópes and Junín, La Recoleta ☎ 0810–444–66843), inside the entertainment complex next to the Recoleta cemetery.

Theater

Buenos Aires has some 40 theaters, ranging from those presenting Argentine dramatic works to those showing foreign plays in translation, musicals, and *revistas* (revues) with comedians and dancers known for the brevity of their costumes. **La Plaza** (⊠ Av. Corrientes 1660, El Centro ☎ 11/4382–4177) is an open-air shopping center with a small outdoor amphitheater and two theaters, along with shops and small restaurants. The traditional **Maipo** (⊠ Esmeralda 443, El Centro ☎ 11/4322–8238) stages revistas showcasing sassy comedians and dancers scantily adorned in sequins and feathers. The state-run **Teatro Nacional Cervantes** (⊠ Libertad 815, El Centro ☎ 11/4816–4224) lives up to its namesake with its quixotic Spanish architecture and passionate drama. Publicly supported theater, mime, puppet shows, and dance are performed on the three stages of the municipal theater complex, **Teatro San Martín** (⊠ Av. Corrientes 1530, El Centro ☎ 11/4374–9680).

SPORTS & THE OUTDOORS

Athletic Clubs & Health Clubs

Athletic clubs in Buenos Aires are not only gyms with weightlifting equipment, aerobics classes, and pools, but they're also places to participate in organized sports. As part of the services, all pools require a simple medical exam, performed on the premises, to detect such transmittable diseases as head lice and athlete's foot. The following clubs all offer pickup soccer games, volleyball, tennis, paddle tennis, running tracks, aerobic classes, weight rooms, swimming pools (sometimes only in summer), and lots of people-watching.

At **Club de Amigos** (⊠ Av. Figueroa Alcorta 3885, El Centro ☎ 11/4807–3811), the indoor pool is open year-round. **Parque Norte** (⊠ Intendente Cantilo and Av. Costanera Norte, Costanera ☎ 11/4787–1382) has four Olympic-size pools and water slides. **Punta Carrasco** (⊠ Costanera Norte and Av. Sarmiento, Costanera ☎ 11/4807–1010) is a lovely sports complex overlooking the river: the three pools, including one for kids, are open November through March. You can also rent Jet Skis here.

Many hotels have their own fitness facilities or have arrangements for their guest to use nearby gyms. The following fitness chains have a range of fitness classes, a good range of exercise machines, and changing facilities and lockers. Some branches have pools. Membership at each chain allows the use of any of its clubs.

Services at ultrafashionable (and ultrapricey) **LeParc** (⊠ Main branch: San Martín 645, El Centro ☎ 11/4311–9191) include state-of-the-art machinery and an aromatherapy spa. **Megatlon** (⊠ Main branch: Megatlon Center, Reconquista 335 ☎ 11/4322–7884) has a large range of machines, a sauna, and extended opening hours. Daily membership is available at the different branches of **Sport Club** (⊠ Main branch: Sport Club Obras, Paraguay 2060, La Recoleta ☎ 11/4961–4422), all of which have pools and varied fitness activities.

Bicycling, In-Line Skating & Running

You can cover a lot of Buenos Aires on wheels and heels, but cyclists should beware, as Porteño drivers are not known for their tolerance of two-wheelers: expect to be cut off frequently, and to find even marked bicycle routes full of parked cars. Twenty-three kilometers (14 mi) of well-marked bike trails, known as *bicisendas* (⊠ Trailhead: Av. Lugones at General Paz, Núñez, at the edge of Capital Federal), connect the major green spaces within the city. You can rent bikes and in-line skates at the **Circuito KDT** (⊠ Salguero 3450, El Centro ☎ 11/4802–2619). The **Reserva Ecológica** (⊠ Av. Tristán Achával Rodríguez 1550, Puerto Madero ☎ 11/4315–1320) is ideal for running, skating, and cycling, but it's wise to do so with a partner, for safety's sake.

Chess

Pursuing a hobby, especially one with such a universal language as chess, is a good way to meet Argentines. You can pick up a game at the following places. In Palermo Hollywood, funky **Acabar** (⊠ Honduras 5733, Palermo ☎ 11/4772–0845) is dedicated to all things ludic—shelves are stacked with all kinds of board games that diners and drinkers can use. **Gran Café Tortoni** (⊠ Av. de Mayo 829, Plaza de Mayo ☎ 11/4342–4328) offers old-world elegance. Play under chandeliers and to the sounds of tango at the classic *confitería* **La Ideal** (⊠ Suipacha 384, El Centro ☎ 11/4326–1081). If you prefer a game in the sun, **Parque Rivadavia** (⊠ Rivadavia between Acoyte and Doblas, Caballito) has dozens of outdoor tables, which fill up afternoons and weekends with local chess and checkers players.

Cricket

Cricket is played at the Anglo-Argentine enclave of the **Hurlingham Club** (✉ Av. J. A. Roca 1411, Hurlingham, Buenos Aires Province ☎ 11/4662–5510), in the northeastern suburbs. Check the *Herald* for information.

Golf

Equipment rental and caddy hire are available at all courses. Call for tournament reservations, though you can usually just sign up at the tee. For more information on golfing in the area, contact the **Asociación Argentina de Golf** (Argentine Golf Association; ☎ 11/4394–2743).

The 18-hole **Club Lagos de Palermo** (✉ Tornquist and Olleros, Palermo ☎ 11/4774–9158), in the Parque de Febrero in Palermo, is open to nonmembers Thursday through Sunday for a 20 peso greens fee on weekdays, and 30 pesos on weekends. **Costa Salguero** (✉ Rafael Obligado and Salguero, El Centro ☎ 11/4804–2444) is a complete sports complex with a driving range. The 27-hole **Olivos Golf Club** (✉ Ruta Panamericana, Ramal Ruta 8, Km 32.4, Buenos Aires Province ☎☎ 11/4463–0035 for reservations), in the suburb of Olivos is open to nonmembers on Wednesdays and charges 40 pesos.

Horse Racing

It is said that the mighty Argentine Thoroughbreds were one of the contributing factors for the British victory in the South African Boer War. Argentines import select stock for breeding swift horses, prized throughout the world. Although the past 40 years of rough economic instability has handicapped the Thoroughbred industry, Argentine horses still win their share of races worldwide. There are two main tracks in Buenos Aires; check the *Buenos Aires Herald* for schedules.

The **Hipódromo Argentino de Palermo** (✉ Av. del Libertador 4101, Palermo ☎ 11/4777–9009), across from the polo fields in Palermo, is 10 minutes from downtown. The 1878 belle epoque architecture of the Tattersall (grandstand) and gardens add an elegant touch to the sport.

Generally, two races per week take place at the **Hipódromo de San Isidro** (✉ Av. Márquez 504, Buenos Aires Province ☎ 11/4743–4010).

Polo

The major Argentine Polo tournaments are played in November. Stunning athletic showmanship is displayed on the two excellent fields of the Palermo **Campo Argentino de Polo** (Argentine Polo Field; ✉ Av. del Libertador 4000 at Dorrego, Palermo), a source of national pride. Admission to autumn (March–May) and spring (September–December) matches is free. The much-heralded Campeonato Argentino Abierto (Argentine Open Championship) takes place in November; admission runs 15–120 pesos. Tickets can be purchased in advance by phone through Ticketek (☎ 11/4323–7200) or at the polo field on the day of the event. For match information contact the **Asociación Argentina de Polo** (✉ H. Yrigoyen 636, fl. 1, Apt. A, Plaza de Mayo ☎ 11/4331–4646 ⊕ www.aapolo.com).

Soccer

For most Porteños, *fútbol* (soccer) is a fervent passion. The national team is one of the top five of 203 teams in the FIFA–Coca-Cola World Ranking. The World Cup can bring the country to a standstill. Matches are held year-round and are as exciting as they are dangerous. You're safest in the *platea* (preferred seating area), which cost around 20–60 pesos, rather than in the chaotic 10 pesos *popular* (standing room) section. Passions run especially high when the Boca Juniors take on their arch rivals, the River Plate in the match known as the *superclásico. Hinchas* (fans) paint their faces accordingly: blue and yellow for Boca Juniors or red and white for the River Plate.

Tickets can be purchased at long lines at the stadiums, through **Ticketek** (☎ 11/4323–7200), or through the teams' official Web sites. The River Plate play at **Estadio Antonio Vespucio Liberti** (✉ Av. Pte. Figueroa Alcorta 7597, Núñez ☎ 11/4788–1200 ⊕ www.cariverplate.com.ar), better known as the Monumental, for its size. Argentina's international football matches also take place here. **Estadio Boca Juniors** (✉ Brandsen 805, La Boca ☎ 11/4362–2152 ⊕ www.bocajuniors.com.ar), also known as *La Bombonera* (meaning candy box, supposedly because the sound of fans' singing reverberates as it would inside a candy box), is the Boca Juniors' home stadium.

Spas
Many of the luxury hotels listed in the lodging section offer spa and health facilities. With more than a century of experience, **Colmegna Spa** (✉ Av. Sarmiento 839, El Centro ☎ 11/4326–1257) is a standout in urban spas. For 150 pesos you can luxuriate for a day with a Turkish bath, body peel, massage, hair treatment, and a healthy light lunch. Reservations are essential. It's open Monday–Saturday 11–8. French-run **Evian Agua Club & Spa** (✉ Cerviño 3626, Palermo ☎ 11/4807–4688) has a variety of day-spa programs, which include massages and hydrotherapy as well as access to their other facilities, with prices ranging 140–240 pesos. Reservations are essential.

Tennis, Squash & Racquetball
Many athletic clubs have tennis and squash courts that you can use for a fee. Paddle tennis, a typical Argentine game that is a cross between tennis and squash, is popular with all ages. There are public tennis courts at the **Buenos Aires Lawn Tennis Club** (✉ Av. Olleros 1510, Palermo ☎ 11/4772–9227). There are tennis, squash, and paddle courts at the friendly **Bulnes Squash Tenis** club (✉ Bulnes 2552, Palermo ☎ 11/4807–4754). Try **Circuito KDT** (✉ Salguero 3450, El Centro ☎ 11/4807–7700) for paddle tennis. A good place to play squash is at the central **Olimpia Cancillería** (✉ Esmeralda 1042, El Centro ☎ 11/4313–7375), which also has racquetball courts. **Salguero Tenis** (✉ Salguero 3350, Palermo ☎ 11/4805–5144) has a variety of tennis and squash courts. Arrangements can be made through the **Sheraton Buenos Aires Hotel** (✉ San Martín 1225, El Centro ☎ 11/4318–9000 Ext. 2834) to play on the hotel's courts for 20 pesos an hour (25 pesos an hour at night). Reservations are essential.

ON THE SIDELINES Most professional tennis matches are played at the **Buenos Aires Lawn Tennis Club** (✉ Av. Olleros 1510, Palermo ☎ 11/4772–9227). Check the local calendar in the *Herald,* or contact the **Asociación Argentina de Tenis** (☎ 11/4304–2470 ⊕ www.aat.com.ar) for more information on professional matches.

SHOPPING

Porteños are known for their obsession with fashion. As a result, Buenos Aires has a wide range of options for buying clothing and footwear, from shopping malls and commercial strips to cobbled streets with designer boutiques. Open-air markets are a great source for souvenir handicrafts.

Many shops in traditional tourist areas (such as Calle Florida) are taking advantage of the confusion caused by currency devaluation, and may try to charge tourists in dollars for what they charge Argentines for in pesos, so always confirm which currency you're dealing with up front.

When shopping in Buenos Aires, keep your receipts: the 21% VAT tax, included in the sales price, is entirely refundable for purchases exceeding $200 at stores displaying a duty-free sign. When you depart, allow plenty of time to visit the return desk at the airport to obtain your refund.

Markets

The array of open-air markets throughout Buenos Aires testifies to the esteem in which Argentina holds its artists. You'll find unique items while enjoying wonderful street performances. The selections include crafts, art, antiques, and curios. Opening times vary, though most take place on weekends from 10 to 5. Feel free to bargain, but don't expect it always to work. Traditional handicrafts, steak sandwiches, and folkloric dance displays are what makes the **Feria de Mataderos** (⊠ Lisandro de la Torre and Av. de los Corrales, Mataderos ☎ 11/4372–4836) famous. The market is open on Sunday only. **Feria de San Pedro Telmo** (⊠ Plaza Dorrego, Humberto I y Defensa, San Telmo ☎ 11/4331–9855), open Sunday only, packs a small San Telmo square with all kinds of antiques and curios, to the sound of tango, which is danced on the surrounding cobbled streets. Local artisans sell handmade clothes, jewelry, and homeware as well as more traditional crafts at the large **Feria Recoleta** (⊠ Avs. Libertador and Pueyrredón, La Recoleta ☎ 11/4343–0309), open weekends only. In the heart of colorful La Boca, **Vuelta de Rocha handicraft market (Caminito)** (⊠ Av. Pedro de Mendoza and Caminito, La Boca) has a good selection of work from local artists, as well as handicrafts and souvenirs.

Shopping Districts

Avenida Santa Fe
Hundreds of small boutiques line downtown Avenida Santa Fe. Some of these are chains, which can be found in the shopping malls as well, but some shops in arcades such as *Bond Street* (Santa Fe at Rodríguez Peña) and *La Quinta Avenida* (Santa Fe at Talcahuano) sell unique, non-brand name clothing.

Calle Florida & the Microcentro
Pedestrians-only Calle Florida is a riot of fast-food chains, boutiques, and persistent vendors selling (and haggling over) leather goods. You'll also find souvenirs, food shops, and bookstores. The closer you get to Plaza San Martín, the better the offerings.

La Recoleta
Exquisite antiques and haute-couture shops—including Kenzo, Ermengildo Zegna, Louis Vuitton, Hermes, Escada, Christian Dior, and Versace—are concentrated on Avenida Alvear and Calle Quintana. The traditional Feria Artesanal de Recoleta, the largest open-air market for arts and crafts in the city, takes place weekends from 10 to 5 near the Centro Cultural Recoleta, at Junín and Libertador. Inside the Buenos Aires Design complex are funky interior design shops Morph and Puro Diseño Argentino.

Palermo

Palermo is the center of the Buenos Aires fashion scene: the quiet neighborhoods of Palermo Viejo (surrounding Plaza Serrano at Borge and Serrano) and Palermo Hollywood (on the other side of Juan B. Justo) are *the* places to go for cutting-edge design. You'll have to wander the streets, but it's worth it to discover the vanguard clothing at Trosman Churba, Cat Balou, Juana de Arco, Salsipuedes, Rapsodia, Jazmin Chebar, and los Hermanos Estebecorena.

The many furniture and interiors boutiques mean Palermo is also the place to dress your house: contemporary Argentine designers are showcased at Calma Chicha, Amo Mi Living, and Spoon. In most Palermo boutiques you can pick up the free *Mapa Naranja* to school you in the latest Porteño trends.

San Telmo

Head to San Telmo to purchase antiques and curios while enjoying the area's colonial architecture. Tucked behind the historic buildings are dozens of small shopping galleries dealing entirely in antiques or forgetabilia, such as the Pasaje de la Defensa and El Solar de French, both on Calle Defensa near Plaza Dorrego. The plaza itself hosts the open-air Feria de San Pedro Telmo, with street vendors, performers, and antiques, every Sunday from 10 to 5.

Shopping Malls

Abasto (✉ Av. Corrientes 3247, El Centro, ☎ 11/4959–3400 Ⓜ Line B, Estación Carlos Gardel), in a renovated marketplace, has clothing stores, restaurants, cinemas, a children's museum, and several interesting tango spots housed in a huge historic building that used to be the city's main market.

Busy **Alto Palermo** (✉ Av. Santa Fe 3251, at Av. Colonel Díaz, Palermo ☎ 11/5777–8000 Ⓜ Line D, Estación Bulnes) has three floors with about 130 shops, an extensive food hall, a cinema, and an entertainment center.

Galerías Pacífico (✉ Calle Florida 753, at Av. Córdoba, El Centro ☎ 11/4319–5100 Ⓜ Line B, Estación Florida) is in a building designed during Buenos Aires's turn-of-the-20th-century golden age in the style of Milan's Galleria Vittorio Emanuele, and features original murals by several Argentine greats. Now a polished, split-level, multipurpose center, it includes refined shops and boutiques, a food court, a cinema, and the Centro Cultural Borges, a showcase for young talent.

Argentine designers show their new lines of ready-to-wear clothing for men and women at **Paseo Alcorta** (✉ Salguero 3172, at Av. F. Alcorta, Palermo ☎ 11/5777–6500). You'll find international labels, such as Christian Dior, Kenzo, Ralph Lauren, Mozel, and Yves St-Laurent. Also here are an entertainment center, a movie theater, and a food court.

Patio Bullrich (✉ Enter at Posadas 1245 or Av. del Libertador 750, La Recoleta ☎ 11/4815–3501) has some of the finest and priciest shops in town, as well as a movie theater. The multilevel mall was once the headquarters for the Bullrich family's renowned auction house.

Solar de la Abadía (✉ Marie Luis Campos at Arcos, Belgrano ☎ 11/4778–5005) has an upbeat feeling and is a great place to pick up souvenirs, buy trendy clothing, or enjoy a snack in the food court or at one of the surrounding bistros and bars.

Specialty Shops

Art & Antiques

Most antiques shops are grouped together in San Telmo near Plaza Dorrego. One of the city's largest auction houses, **Posadas** (⊠ Posadas 1227, La Recoleta ☎ 11/4815–3573), has furnishings and artwork from local estates. Check the *Herald* and *La Nación* for scheduled estate auctions.

Bookstores

Most malls have at least one bookstore with a few English titles; however, since devaluation these have become costly and increasingly harder to find. Avenida Corrientes is the strip for used bookstores, and the San Telmo neighborhood is an excellent source for antique books and posters. One of the best bookstores in the city is **El Ateneo** (⊠ Av. Santa Fe 1860, La Recoleta ☎ 11/4813–4154 ⊠ Florida 340, El Centro ☎ 11/4325–6801). For a highbrow selection of books, music, and magazines in Spanish, try **Gandhi** (⊠ Av. Corrientes 1743, El Centro ☎ 11/4374–7501), which also has an upstairs café. **Kel** (⊠ M. T. de Alvear 1369, Palermo ☎ 11/4814–3788) carries a wide selection of English-language books.

Clothing

Head to Avenida Alvear and Calle Quintana for haute couture; ready-to-wear clothing can be found along the shopping strips at Avenida Santa Fe 800–1500, on Calle Florida from Plaza San Martín to Corrientes, and at Belgrano's Avenida Cabildo 1600–2200, with discount and seconds stores on Avenida Córdoba 4400–5000. The following chain stores appear in nearly every mall and shopping strip: **Voss** (funky baby clothes), **Cheeky** (colorful, smart clothing for children from infants to preteens), **Chocolate** (good-quality clothing for women in their twenties), **Cristóbal Colón** (rugged outdoorsy clothes), **Mancini** (clothes for the modern professional man). A wide range of trendy young menswear is available at **Bensimon. Ona Saez** and **Kosiuko** sell edgy women's and men's clothes. **Paula Cahen D'Anvers** has a modern, clean line for women and an adorable selection for very young children. **Port Said** does stylish clothes for older women. For young designers, head to Palermo Viejo, and check out the arcades on Santa Fe for vintage and club wear.

Handicrafts

Among the unique crafts you'll come across are traditional ponchos, mates, *boleadoras* (gaucho lassos), wood carvings, leather goods, silver, and alpaca products. With wide selections and good prices, open-air markets are the best places for purchasing crafts, but you can also find them throughout the city in specialty shops. For authentic, top-quality furniture and textiles, try **Arte Étnico Argentino** (⊠ El Salvador 4900, Palermo ☎ 11/4833–6661 ☾ Closed mornings). **Kelly's** (⊠ Paraguay 431, El Centro ☎☎ 11/4311–5712 Ⓜ Line C, Estación San Martín) sells high-quality crafts from all over Argentina. The best silverware in town, including *mates*, gaucho belt buckles, and jewelry, is at **Platería Parodi** (⊠ Av. de Mayo 720, El Centro ☎ 11/4342–2207 Ⓜ Line A, Estación Piedras). The cream of Argentine designers show off unusual contemporary handicrafts, as well as cutting-edge jewelry, clothing, accessories, furniture, and items for the home at **Puro Diseño Argentino** (⊠ Buenos Aires Design Center Shop 1004, Av. Pueyrredón 2501, La Recoleta ⊕ www.purodiseno.com.ar).

Jewelry

You'll find 18- and 20-karat gold and silver in Argentina at competitive prices. The inexpensive gold district is on **Calle Libertad,** between avenidas Corrientes and Rivadavía. Bargaining is expected. Be sure to ask if the stone is real, or you may take home a surprise. You'll find Brazilian emeralds and the semiprecious *rodocrosita,* "rose of the Inca," ranging in color from pink to red and native only to Argentina. **Antonio Belgiorno** (✉ Av. Santa Fe 1347, La Recoleta ☎ 11/4811–1117), an excellent silversmith, crafts singular quality pieces. Decorated sculptures of birds in flight from **Cousiño** (✉ in Sheraton Buenos Aires Hotel, San Martín 1225, El Centro ☎ 11/4318–9000 ⊕ www.cousinojewels.com) are exhibited in the National Museum of Decorative Arts. **Guthman** (✉ Viamonte 597, El Centro ☎ 11/4312–2471) has an acclaimed selection of jewelry. For high-quality classic silver jewelry, and silverware in general, try **Juan Carlos Pallarols Orfebre** (✉ Defensa 1039, San Telmo ☎ 11/4362–0641), famous locally for having crafted pieces for Máxima, Argentina's export to the Dutch royal family. For unusual handmade contemporary designs, call to visit the workshop of designer **Paula Levy** (☎ 11/4553–9885 or 11/155–607–6135).

Leather

Anything that can be worn is available in leather in Buenos Aires. Items are cut from cowhide, antelope, kidskin, pigskin, sheepskin, lizard, snake, and porcupine in an array of colors and styles. You can often find prices that are cheaper than those abroad, but be sure to check the quality and stitching. The hub of Buenos Aires's leather industry are the dozens of specialist and wholesale stores on Murillo at Scalabrini Ortíz in Villa Crespo (accessible by subway), where some great bargains can be had, but shop carefully as quality and price vary wildly. Leather stores and shopping galleries line Calle Florida, where bargaining is commonplace.

For sheepskin jackets, head to **Arandú** (✉ Paraguay 1259, El Centro ☎ 11/4816–6191), which also sells fur-lined saddles, boots, and other leather goods for that Marlboro-man look, Argentine-style. For well-designed jackets and other clothing in high-quality leather, try **Breeders** (✉ Patio Bullrich Posadas 1245, La Recoleta ☎ 11/4814–7495). **Casa López** (✉ M. T. de Alvear 640, Palermo ☎ 11/4311–3044) is known for classic designs with a modern twist, and is particularly good for jackets and bags. **La Martina** (✉ Paraguay 661, El Centro ☎ 11/4311–5963) carries items for the discriminating equestrian. **Murillo 666** (✉ Murillo 666, Villa Crespo ☎ 11/4855–2024 Ⓜ Line B, Estación Malabia), though out of the way, has a selection of women's bags and jackets at bargain prices. Check out **Prune** (✉ Florida 963, El Centro) for chic, contemporary shoes and handbags. **Rossi y Caruso** (✉ Av. Santa Fe 1601, La Recoleta ☎ 11/4811–1538) has quality riding equipment and classic handbags, clothing, shoes, and boots; King Juan Carlos of Spain and many other celebrities are customers here.

Shoes

Guido (✉ Florida 704, El Centro ☎ 11/4322–7548 ✉ Av. Quintana 333, La Recoleta ☎ 11/4811–4567) carries men's shoes and loafers in traditional styles. Since 1897 **López Taibo** (✉ Av. Corrientes 350, El Centro ☎ 11/4328–2132 ✉ Av. Alvear 1902, La Recoleta ☎ 11/4804–8585) has made refined, durable men's and women's shoes and accessories. **Paruolo** (✉ Alto Palermo Mall Av. Santa Fe 3251, Palermo ☎ 11/5777–8000 Ext. 8216) does hip, affordable shoes for young women. The weird and wonderful designs of **Ricky Sarcany** (✉ Paseo Alcorta, Salguero 3172, La Recoleta ☎ 11/4806–5439) are must-haves for local celebrities. For original designs and beautiful finishes, try well-priced **Zapatos de María** (✉ Showroom: Libertad 1661, La Recoleta ☎ 11/4815–5001); all shoes are handmade.

Wool

Argentina has traditionally been the world's largest exporter of wool. Shopping malls sell quality wool items in a variety of styles. Unusual hand-made knitwear and woven clothing is sold at some Palermo fashion boutiques as well as in the open-air markets. For classic, well-made knitwear try **Alessia** (⊠ Galerías Pacífico, Calle Florida 753, El Centro ☎ 11/5555–5321). High-quality contemporary woolen clothing for men, women, and children is made by **María Aversa** (⊠ El Salvador 4580, Palermo ☎ 11/4833–0073). **Silvia y Mario** (⊠ M. T. de Alvear 550, Palermo) stocks a huge selection of elegant cashmere ensembles.

BUENOS AIRES A TO Z

To research prices, get advice from other travelers, and book travel arrangements, visit www.fodors.com.

AIRPORTS & TRANSFERS

All international flights arrive and depart from Aeropuerto Internacional Ministro Pistarini, more widely known as Ezeiza International Airport, 47 km (29 mi) outside of downtown Buenos Aires. Ezeiza is served by a variety of foreign airlines, as well as domestic airlines with international routes. Departure tax is $30.50, or the equivalent in pesos.

Domestic flights within Argentina and flights from Uruguay generally depart from Aeroparque Jorge Newbery, about 15 or 20 minutes from downtown. The airport tax is about $15 for domestic flights and $10 for flights to Uruguay.

🛈 **Aeroparque Jorge Newbery** ☎ 11/5480-6111. **Ezeiza International Airport** ☎ 11/5480-6111.

AIRPORT TRANSFERS   There are several means of transportation between the airports and Buenos Aires. Information counters within the airports can help you choose among the various licensed transport services; you can also check with the airport's Secretary of Tourism office for additional assistance. Generally, the cheapest transportation is by colectivo (2 pesos), but the trip can take a while—up to two hours from Ezeiza International Airport—and you're only allowed two bags. Privately owned bus or van service is about 15 pesos per passenger to downtown from Ezeiza, with scheduled departures. *Remises* (unmarked taxis with prearranged fixed prices) run 35–45 pesos from Ezeiza and 8–12 pesos from Jorge Newbery Airport; they're limited to four passengers. Metered taxi service, available at the sidewalk, can be a bit steeper depending on traffic.

🛈 **Manuel Tienda León** ☎ 11/4383-4454 or 0810/888-5366 ⊕ www.tiendaleon.com.

BOAT & FERRY TRAVEL

Hydrofoils and ferries cross the Río de la Plata between Buenos Aires and Uruguay several times a day. Boats often sell out quickly, particularly on summer weekends, so it's important to book tickets at least a few days in advance. This can be done by going to the dock or ticket sales office, or by reserving tickets with a credit card via phone. The most popular company, with the most frequent service, is Buquebus. Buquebus provides service for passengers and their vehicles between Buenos Aires and Colonia, Montevideo, Piriápolis, and Punta del Este Uruguay. There's also a cheaper and slower (and less environmentally sound) ferry between Buenos Aires and Colonia.

Ferry Lineas Argentina also serves the Buenos Aires–Uruguay route on a smaller scale with fewer boats per day.

🚢 Buquebus ✉ Av. Antartida Argentina 821, Puerto Madero ✉ Patio Bullrich Shopping Mall, Av. Libertador 750, La Recoleta ☎ 11/4316-6550 ⊕ www.buquebus.com. **Ferry Lineas Argentina** ✉ Florida 780, El Centro ☎ 11/4314-2300.

BUS TRAVEL

Most long-distance and international buses arrive at and depart from the Estación Terminal de Omnibus. The terminal houses more than 60 bus companies, arranged in order of destinations served, not by name. Rates vary according to distance, services, and season; compare prices before purchasing. For more information, *see* Bus Travel *in* Smart Travel Tips.

Colectivos (city buses) connect the city's barrios and the Greater Buenos Aires area. You're assured a seat on a *diferencial* bus (indicated by a sign on the front of the bus); they run less frequently than colectivos and are more expensive. Bus stops are on every other block (200 meters [656 feet] apart) and are marked by an easy-to-miss small metal sign with the number of the bus line. Hail your bus and let the driver know your destination; then insert your coins in the machine (exact change is not necessary, but coins are), which will print your ticket. Fares within the perimeter of the city are 65¢ to 80¢; diferencials cost 2 pesos for any destination in the city. Once on board, head for the back, where you'll disembark. A small bell on the grab bar lets you indicate where you'd like to get off to the driver. Don't depend on the drivers for much assistance; they're busy trying to navigate traffic. You can purchase "Lumi Guía de Transporte," a handy guide to the routes, at any news kiosk, or visit the Spanish-language colectivo Web site.

🚌 Colectivo ⊕ www.loscolectivos.com.ar. **Estación Terminal de Omnibus** ✉ Av. Ramos Mejía 1680, El Centro ☎ 11/4310-0700.

CAR RENTAL

Note that some reputable local agencies tend to be more affordable than international companies and offer the same quality service.

Hiring a remis—car with driver—is a comfortable and convenient way to tour the city. This service costs about 25–35 pesos per hour, sometimes with a three-hour minimum and an additional charge per kilometer (½ mi) if you drive outside the city limits.

🚗 Local Agencies Annie Millet ✉ Av. Santa Fe 883, 1st fl., El Centro ☎ 11/6777-7777 ⊕ www.amillet.com.ar. **GVS** ✉ Leandro N. Alem 699, El Centro ☎ 11/4315-0777. **Localiza** ✉ Maipu 924, El Centro ☎ 0800/999-2999 or 11/4315-8483 ⊕ www.localiza.com.ar. **Rent-a-Sol** ✉ Av. Libertador 6553, Belgrano ☎ 11/4787-2140 or 11/4787-1414. **🚗 Major Agencies Avis** ✉ Ezeiza International Airport, Ezeiza ☎ 11/4480-9387 ✉ Jorge Newbery Airport, Costanera ☎ 11/4776-3003 ✉ Cerrito 1527, El Centro ☎ 11/4326-5542 ⊕ www.avis.com.ar. **Dollar** ✉ M. T. de Alvear 449, El Centro ☎ 11/4315-8800 ⊕ www.dollar.com.ar.

🚗 Remises Annie Millet Transfers ✉ Santa Fe 883, fl. 1, El Centro ☎ 11/6777-7777. **Remises REB** ✉ Billinghurst 68, Palermo ☎ 11/4863-1226 or 11/4862-6271. **Remises Rioja** ✉ Rioja 3023, Olivos ☎ 11/4794-4677. **Remises Universal** ✉ 25 de Mayo 611, fl. 4, El Centro ☎ 11/4315-6555.

CAR TRAVEL

Avenida General Paz completely encircles Buenos Aires. If you're driving into the city from the exterior, you'll know you're in Buenos Aires proper once you've crossed this road. If you're entering the city from the north, chances are you will be on the Ruta Panamericana, which has wide lanes and good lighting. Autopista 25 de Mayo is the quickest way to the airport from downtown. The R2 (Ruta 2) takes you to the Atlantic coastal beach resorts in and around Mar del Plata.

Porteños drive with verve, independence, and a general disdain for traffic rules. A more convenient and comfortable option is to have your travel agent or hotel arrange for a remis, especially for a day's tour of the suburbs or nearby pampas. This service costs about 25–35 pesos per hour, sometimes with a three-hour minimum and an additional charge per kilometer if you drive outside the city limits. Remises usually end up being cheaper than cabs, especially during peak hours.

If you prefer to take the wheel and try your hand at dealing with Buenos Aires road rage, you can rent a car at any agency in the city. Drive defensively and use caution when approaching overpasses and upon exiting, as there have been incidences of *ladrillazos* (brick throwing) for the purpose of theft.

PARKING Parking can be a problem in the city, but there are several underground municipal parking garages and numerous private garages. Look for a blue sign with an E (for *estacionamiento* [parking]). The cost is about 3–4 pesos for the first hour, and 1–1.50 pesos for each additional half hour. Most shopping malls have parking garages, which are usually free or give you a reduced rate with a purchase.

RULES OF THE ROAD Most driving rules in the United States apply here, but keep in mind the following: right turns on red are not allowed; never park on the left side of the street, where there is a yellow line on the curb, or near a bus stop; and left turns are seldom allowed, unless indicated. Where there are no traffic lights, intersections are a free-for-all; vehicles coming from your right have the right-of-way. During the week, Microcentro, the bustling commercial and financial district bounded by Carlos Pellegrini, Avenida Córdoba, Avenida Leandro Alem, and Avenida de Mayo, is off-limits to vehicles other than public transportation. *See* Car Travel *in* Smart Travel Tips for more information.

COMMUTER TRAIN TRAVEL

Commuter rail lines provide extensive service throughout the city proper and the suburbs for a great price. A network of lines operated by six different companies—Ferrobaires, Ferrovías, Metropolitano, Metrovías, Trenes de Buenos Aires, Tren de la Costa—spreads out from five central stations in Buenos Aires.

Most trains leave at regular 7- to 20-minute intervals, though there may be less frequent service for trains traveling long distances. Fares range from 35¢ to 1.50 pesos. Purchase tickets before boarding the train at ticket windows or through coin-operated machines at the stations. Hold on to your ticket until you reach the end of the line, where it will be collected by an official. If you do not have your ticket, you will be asked to pay a 3.50–6.50 pesos on-the-spot fine.

Estación Buenos Aires, in the city of Temperley, connects lines in the southern part of Greater Buenos Aires; Metropolitano operates out of here.

Two rail companies operate out of Estación Constitución. The Metropolitano rail line serves the southern part of Greater Buenos Aires and extends to the city of La Plata. Ferrobaires serves the Atlantic coastal resorts, such as Mar del Plata, Pinamar, and Miramar.

Estación Federico Lacroze, in the Belgrano neighborhood, provides train service to the northeastern part of the city and Greater Buenos Aires through the Metrovías rail company.

Estación Once, in the city center, serves the western part of the city and Greater Buenos Aires through Trenes de Buenos Aires. Ferrobaires provides train service to some cities in the provinces of Buenos Aires and La Pampa.

Trains running out of Estación Retiro, across from Plaza San Martín, serve the northern part of the city and Greater Buenos Aires. Several rail companies operate from here: Ferrovías, Metropolitano, Trenes de Buenos Aires, and Tren de la Costa.

🚆 Commuter Lines **Ferrobaires** ☎ 11/4553-1295. **Ferrovías** ☎ 11/4511-8833. **Metropolitano** ☎ 0800/666-358-736 ⊕ www.tms.com.ar. **Metrovías** ☎ 11/4959-6800 or 0800/555-1616 ⊕ www.metrovias.com.ar. **Tren de la Costa** ☎ 11/4002-6000 ⊕ www.trendelacosta.com.ar. **Trenes de Buenos Aires** (TBA) ☎ 11/4317-4409 or 11/4317-4400 ⊕ www.tbanet.com.ar.

🚆 Commuter Stations **Estación Buenos Aires** ✉ Padre Mugica 426, Temperley ☎ 11/4244-2668. **Estación Constitución** ✉ Av. General Hornos 11, near San Telmo, San Telmo ☎ 11/4304-0028. **Estación Federico Lacroze** ✉ Federico Lacroze 4181, Belgrano ☎ 11/4553-1916. **Estación Once** ✉ Av. Pueyrredón and Bartolomé Mitre, Balvanera ☎ 11/4861-0043. **Estación Retiro** ✉ Av. Ramos Mejía 1430, El Centro ☎ 11/4317-4400.

EMBASSIES

In addition to providing assistance, many embassies also host cocktail parties, where both foreigners and locals mingle. There's usually a small entrance fee; call any embassy to find out the location of the next event.

🏛 **Australia** ✉ Villanueva 1400, Belgrano ☎ 11/4779-3500 ⊕ www.argentina.embassy.gov.au. **Canada** ✉ Tagle 2828, Palermo ☎ 11/4808-1000 ⊕ www.dfait-maeci.gc.ca/argentina. **Ireland** ✉ Suipacha 1280, fl. 2, El Centro ☎ 11/4325-8588. **New Zealand** ✉ Carlos Pelligrini 1427, 5th fl., El Centro ☎ 11/4328-0747, 15/4148-7633 emergencies. **South Africa** ✉ M. T. de Alvear 590, fl. 8, El Centro ☎ 11/4317-2900. **United Kingdom** ✉ Luis Agote 2412, La Recoleta ☎ 11/4803-7799 or 11/4576-2222, 15/5331-7129 emergencies ⊕ www.britain.org.ar. **United States** ✉ Av. Colombia 4300, Palermo ☎ 11/5777-4533 ⊕ www.usembassy.state.gov.

EMERGENCIES

There's a pharmacy on nearly every block in Buenos Aires, indicated by a green cross. Your hotel will be able to guide you to the nearest one. *Farmacias de turno* rotate 24-hour shifts or remain open 24 hours and will deliver to your hotel, if in the area.

🆘 Emergency Services **Ambulance** ☎ 107. **Fire** ☎ 100. **Police** ☎ 111 or 114346-5770. 🆘 Hospital **British Hospital** ✉ Pedriel 74, Barracas ☎ 11/4304-2052, 11/4334-9000 emergencies.

🆘 24-hour Pharmacies **Farmacia Cabildo** ✉ Cabildo 1971, Belgrano ☎ 11/4781-8788. **Farmacia DeMaria** ✉ F. J. Sta. Maria de Oro 2927, Palermo ☎ 11/4778-7311. **Farmacia Luciani** ✉ Las Heras 2002, La Recoleta ☎ 11/4803-6111.

HEALTH

Some travelers experience slight discomfort due to the changes in water and diet, as well as seasonal differences. The city water and sanitation services are optimum, though you may prefer to purchase bottled water for drinking: many find the chlorine in the city's water supply unpleasant.

MAIL & SHIPPING

You can mail cards and packages from various convenience-type stores located throughout the city; pharmacies, telephone centers, and malls even provide mail services, in addition to the post offices throughout the city.

Several local and international private couriers compete with the national Correo Argentino (Argentine Post) to complete mail services, including packaging, money wires, telegrams, and on-line and phone tracking for certified letters.

🏢 Overnight Services **Correo Argentino** ☒ Sarmiento 151, El Centro ☎ 11/4316-3000. **DHL** ☒ Moreno 927, El Centro ☎ 0800/2222-345. **Federal Express** ☒ Maipú 753, El Centro ☎ 11/4630-0300. **UPS** ☒ Bernardo de Yrigoyen 974, El Centro ☎ 11/4307-2174 or 0800/222-2877.

MONEY MATTERS

Ever since the Argentine peso was devalued in 2002, U.S. dollars have not been as widely accepted. If you arrive in Buenos Aires with dollars or euros, it's best to get them changed at one of the many "casa de cambios" or change houses located in El Centro. Use caution though, as would-be thieves are known to canvas the area. Another option is to ask your hotel to change your money into pesos, although you will likely get a less favorable exchange rate.

ATMS You can find ATMs throughout the city. The most widely used is the Banelco network, identified by a burgundy sign and located in banks, service stations, and shopping malls.

CURRENCY EXCHANGE At Ezeiza International Airport you can exchange currency at Casa Piano and Banco Nación, in Terminal A, on the ground level. You may want to use an ATM, also found in Terminal A, to extract local currency for a better rate. You can exchange currency at any of the locations below.

🏢 Exchange Services **American Express** ☒ Arenales 707, El Centro ☎ 11/4310-3000. **Banco Piano** ☒ San Martín 345, El Centro ☎ 11/4394-2463. **BankBoston** ☒ Florida 99, El Centro ☎ 11/4820-2000. **Cambio America** ☒ Sarmiento 501, El Centro ☎ 11/4393-0054. **Citibank** ☒ Bartolomé Mitre 530, El Centro ☎ 11/4329-1000. **Forex Cambio** ☒ M. T. de Alvear 540, El Centro ☎ 11/4312-7729 or 11/4311-5543. **HSBC Republic** ☒ Florida 201, El Centro ☎ 11/4320-2800. **Western Union** ☒ J. L. Borges 2472, Palermo ☎ 11/4777-1940.

SAFETY

Buenos Aires is generally a safe city. Violent crime is rare, and at any time of night, you'll see young children and old ladies strolling about, apparently unconcerned about the hour or the darkness. Police consistently patrol areas where tourists are likely to be. That said, keep in mind that Buenos Aires is a big city and take precautions: pickpocketing and robberies are not uncommon. Go out at night in pairs or, better yet, in groups.

Though there are still sporadic protests, they have taken on a much calmer and more subdued tone compared to the height of the economic crisis in 2001 and 2002. If you happen upon a demonstration, exercise caution, but don't be overly concerned—there have not been any violent protests in the city for a while.

SIGHTSEEING TOURS

Buenos Aires Tur organizes extensive bus tours of the city and can help you plan travel all over the country. Grin Tours can arrange bus and private car tours of the city, travel to neighboring provinces and countries.

Gobierno de la Ciudad (city government) offers free, bilingual guided walking tours; contact the tourist information centers (⇨ Visitor Information) for more information.

🏢 **Buenos Aires Tur** ☒ Lavalle 1444, El Centro ☎ 11/4371-2304 or 11/4371-2390 ⊕ www.buenosairestur.com. **Grin Tours** ☒ Av. Tte. Dellepiane 4294, Villa Lugano ☎ 11/4602-4378.

SUBWAY TRAVEL

The *subte,* the oldest subway system in Latin America, dating to 1913, has five underground lines and the *premetro,* which runs above ground in the General Savio barrio. All begin in El Centro and fan out in different directions. Though not as extensive as the bus system, subte service is efficient and inexpensive. Trains marked with R (for *Rapido*) run express.

Line A travels beneath Avenida Rivadavía from Plaza de Mayo to Primera Junta and is serviced by handsome antique wooden cars. Line B begins at Leandro Alem Station, in the financial district, and runs under Avenida Corrientes to Federico Lacroze Station. Line C, under Avenida 9 de Julio, connects the two major train stations, Retiro and Constitución, making stops along the way in El Centro. Line D runs from Catedral Station on Plaza de Mayo to Congreso de Túcuman in Belgrano. Line E takes you from Bolívar Station, at Plaza de Mayo, to Plaza de los Virreyes, in the neighborhood of Chacabuco.

Cospeles (tokens) and subway passes cost 70¢ and will take you anywhere in the subway system. The subte shuts down around 10 PM and reopens at 5 AM.

🚇 **Metrovías** ☎ 11/4553-9214 or 0800/555-1616 ⊕ www.metrovias.com.ar.

TAXIS

Taxis are easy to identify: they're black and have yellow tops. An unoccupied one will indicate LIBRE on the left-hand side of the windshield. Hail it, or call for a radio taxi and wait a few minutes. There's always a slight risk of coming across a thief posing as a taxi driver, and there's no way of identifying one until it's too late. If you telephone for a taxi, you'll have to wait a few minutes, but you can be sure of its origin.

Meters start at 1.12 pesos and charge 14¢ per ¼ km (⅛ mi); you'll also end up paying for standing time spent at a light or in a traffic jam. In the central downtown area, fares average 2–4 pesos out to Recoleta will cost you 5–6 pesos, San Telmo 4–6 pesos, and Belgrano 8 pesos.

🚖 Taxi Companies **Blue Way Taxi** ☎ 11/4777-8888. **City Taxi** ☎ 11/4585-5544. **Cirtax Taxi** ☎ 11/4504-8440. **Su Taxi** ☎ 11/4635-2500.

TELEPHONES & INTERNET ACCESS

INTERNET ACCESS Many hotels have Internet access, or you can try the Telefónica or Telecom phone offices located throughout the city. Every neighborhood has at least one Internet café—in some neighborhoods there are Internet cafés on nearly every corner. Prices average about 2 pesos an hour.

TELEPHONES Public phones are found on nearly every block and usually operate with a telephone card, which can be purchased at any kiosk. Simply slide the card in, check your card's remaining minutes, then dial. Some public phones are coin operated. To make a long-distance call from a pay phone, go to a *telecentro* or *locutorio*—found throughout the city—providing private booths and fax service, as well as Internet and e-mail services for about 3 pesos per hour. (Note that you may still need a local phone card to make a long-distance call, even if you have your own calling card.)

When calling cellular phone numbers in Buenos Aires, dial 15 before the number (unless calling from another cellular phone with a Buenos Aires number). Local cellular phone charges vary and are charged to the caller, unless made from a public phone. Cellular-phone rentals are available, though pricey; some hotels even rent phones.

VISITOR INFORMATION

Tourist information centers at the airports and in six locations around the city provide maps, though few brochures, and have English-speaking personnel. You'll find the centers on the Caminito; Calle Florida; Centro Cultural General San Martín, at Avenida Sarmiento 1551; at the Obelisk; in Puerto Madero; and at the Retiro Bus Terminal, at the corner of Avenida Antártida Argentina and Calle 10. For friendly guidance and brochures, maps, and even vacation-planning tips, try the information counter on the second floor of the Galerías Pacífico shopping center at Calle Florida 753.

You can get information over the phone, on weekdays from 9 to 5, from the Dirección de Turismo del Gobierno de la Ciudad de Buenos Aires. The Secretaría de Turismo de la Nación runs a telephone information service, which is toll-free from any point in Argentina, 24 hours a day. **🚩 Dirección de Turismo del Gobierno de la Ciudad de Buenos Aires** ☎ 11/4313–0187 ⊕ www.buenosaires.gov.ar. **Secretaría de Turismo de la Nación** ✉ Av. Santa Fe 883, El Centro ☎ 11/4312–2232 or 0800/555–0016 ⊕ www.turismo.gov.ar.

BUENOS AIRES PROVINCE & CÓRDOBA

THE PAMPAS, THE ATLANTIC COAST & CÓRDOBA

2

FODOR'S CHOICE

Almacen de Ramos Generales, *San Antonio de Areco*

Estancia Cerro de la Cruz, *hotel in Sierra de la Ventana*

La Nieta'e La Pancha, *restaurant in Córdoba*

HIGHLY RECOMMENDED

Alcorta Carnes y Vinos, *restaurant in Córdoba*

Casa de Marqués de Sobremonte, *Córdoba*

Catedral de Córdoba

Cervecería Modelo, *restaurant in La Plata*

Compañia de Jesus

Córdoba Subterranea, *Córdoba*

El Hostal de Alem, *hotel in Mar del Plata*

El Mirador, *hotel in Sierra de la Ventana*

La Imprenta Café, *restaurant in Córdoba*

Sheraton Mar del Plata

Updated by
Robin S.
Goldstein

THE MOST FAMOUS AREA OF BUENOS AIRES PROVINCE is the Pampas—an unending sea of grass, occasionally interrupted by winding streams and low hills. The region comprises nearly one-quarter of Argentina (including the provinces of La Pampa and southern Córdoba and Santa Fé, in addition to Buenos Aires Province) and it is deeply infused in the Argentine identity. The name derives from the native Quéchua word for "flat field"—the Pampas's famous fertile grasslands are home to the horses and cattle that make up the mainstay of Argentina's economy. All over are signs of active ranch life, from the cattle grazing to the modern-day gauchos working the wide-open spaces. The region is also noted for its crops; throughout are extensive farms dotted with alfalfa, sunflowers, wheat, corn, and soy.

In 1880, during the Campaign of the Desert undertaken by General Julio A. Roca, the Pampas were "cleared" of indigenous tribes, making extensive agriculture and cattle breeding possible. The percentage of Argentine agricultural exports originating in the Pampas rose from 0 to 55 in the latter half of the 19th century. The region became known as the grain supplier for the world. From 1850 to 1950 more than 400 important estancias were built in Buenos Aires Province alone. Some of these have been modified for use as guest ranches and provide the best glimpse of the fabled Pampean lifestyle.

During the last few decades, increased tourism has transformed the Atlantic coastal towns of Buenos Aires province into summer vacation retreats. Argentines flood the shore (most notably Mar del Plata) in January and February. Although it's not exactly the Caribbean, Argentina's exchange rate (along with its southern hemisphere seasons) has brought an increasing number foreign tourists to its resorts.

Córdoba province adds mountains to the mix, which are dotted with Jesuit estates. The city of Córdoba, Argentina's second-largest, is a chaotic, cosmopolitan hub filled with students and businesspeople. Although tourists often overlook its charms, the city has a beautifully preserved colonial downtown, a great restaurant scene, and a hopping nightlife—and the surrounding hill towns make the area even more attractive.

Exploring Buenos Aires Province & Córdoba

It's possible to travel from town to town by train and bus in the Pampas. However, deserted beaches in between towns can only be reached by car. Auto travel is also rewarding in the mountain ranges around Córdoba and Sierra La Ventana, and the highways in the Pampas are generally easy to negotiate. The best way to get from the Pampas or the Atlantic Coast to Córdoba is to fly.

About the Restaurants

Cuisine in the Pampas, not surprisingly, revolves around beef. A typical meal consists of a plethora of grilled meats accompanied by a tossed salad and lots of red wine. Larger towns like Rosario, Mar del Plata, and Córdoba have some restaurants serving international fare, and all towns have plenty of low- to mid-quality pizzerias and burger joints.

About the Hotels

Pampas lodgings are best known for their sprawling, secluded, all-inclusive estancias—country mansions complete with an on-site staff of gauchos to lead guests through the grasslands. A visit to the Pampas region isn't complete without a stay at one of these memorable old-world estates.

Numbers in the text correspond to numbers in the margin and on the Buenos Aires Province and Córdoba map.

If you have 3 days Three days doesn't leave much time to get very far. If your aim is sun and noisy fun, head directly south to 🖼 **Mar del Plata** ⑩, and don't leave, unless you seek secluded beaches and smaller towns—in which case travel west along the coast to 🖼 **Miramar** ⑪ and 🖼 **Necochea** ⑫. Alternatively, if you seek a taste of the culture and history of the Pampas, start your first morning with a cruise on the Paraná River delta near the town of 🖼 **Tigre** ③. Then travel inland to an estancia near 🖼 **San Antonio de Areco** ⑤. Spend two days at the estancia and be sure to visit the gaucho museum in town.

If you have 7 days Combine the two three-day tours outlined above, or if the beach scene doesn't interest you, start the northern portion of the tour as above, and head west for a three-day visit to 🖼 **Córdoba** ⑮ and its mountain towns. It's easiest to fly from Buenos Aires to Córdoba. If you decide to travel by car, budget in a full day's driving time—in both directions—to cross the Pampas.

If you have 10 days Tour the region counterclockwise: start with a half-day in 🖼 **La Plata** ①, checking out that city's urban architecture and monumental edifices. The rest of the day will be spent driving down the Atlantic coast. Spend the night in 🖼 **Mar del Plata** ⑩, and wake to the frolic of its surf, casino, and various attractions. Spend your second night in Mar del Plata as well; for your third night, move on to 🖼 **Miramar** ⑪ or 🖼 **Necochea** ⑫. Spend Day 4 at 🖼 **Sierra de la Ventana** ⑭, hiking along the mountain range and sleeping in an estancia. On the fifth day, fly or drive to 🖼 **Córdoba** ⑮ and visit the Jesuit relics of this city's proud past. Then spend time exploring the Córdoban mountain range, with its old Jesuit estates and mountain towns. Head south into Buenos Aires Province on the ninth day 🖼 **San Antonio de Areco** ⑤, visiting the gaucho museum and sleeping at an estancia. On the 10th day explore the Paraná River with a stop in 🖼 **Tigre** ③, which is just outside Buenos Aires.

Many hotels in the Pampas require partial payment to secure a reservation during tourist season (December–March). Only the most expensive hotels have air-conditioning.

WHAT IT COSTS in Pesos					
	$$$$	$$$	$$	$	¢
RESTAURANTS	over 35	25–35	15–25	8–15	under 8
HOTELS	over 300	220–300	140–220	80–140	under 80

Restaurant prices are for one main course at dinner. Hotel prices are for two people in a standard double room in high season.

Timing
Peak season is summer (January–March). During this time it can be difficult to get a table at a restaurant or a room in a hotel, so be sure to make reservations well in advance. Winter (June–September) has a different feel, but beaches get cold and windy.

THE PAMPAS

Some of the Pampas's best sights, each with a distinct draw, are within an hour's drive of the nation's capital, Buenos Aires. La Plata is notable as a fully planned city; in fact, what's best about the place is the architecture and thinking set in motion more than a century ago. Inland from the capital are Luján, an important Catholic pilgrimage site, and San Antonio de Areco, the Pampean town that most lives up to the gaucho tradition. Just north of Buenos Aires is Tigre, a great base for exploring the beautiful delta of the Paraná River.

La Plata

❶ *50 km (31 mi) southeast of Buenos Aires via R1 and R14.*

At the famous 1889 Paris Exposition (think Eiffel Tower), Jules Verne honored La Plata with a gold medal, citing the newly built city as a symbol of resplendent modernity. Accepting the medal was Dardo Rocha, the Buenos Aires governor who a few years prior assembled a team of architects and planners and created the provincial capital from the dust of semi-arid desert.

La Plata succeeds today from that creative genesis, a beautiful city of palatial estates on an ordered grid intersected by wide, diagonal boulevards and a rational scheme of parks and plazas every six blocks. The core of the city's planning is the "monumental axis" between 51st and 53rd streets, which contains most of the attractive churches, and government and cultural buildings.

Catedral de La Plata stands at the south end of Plaza Moreno's tiled walkway. This graceful, pinkish brick building is a jewel of late-19th-century architecture. The neo-Gothic structure, inspired by cathedrals in Amiens and Cologne, was originally inaugurated in 1932 but lacked the long double spires. During the past decade of restoration, the monumental stained-glass window was completed and a museum documenting the church's history was added. Construction wasn't complete until November 19, 2000—118 years to the day after the city's foundation stone was laid. A carillon with 25 bronze bells enlivens the western (51st Street) tower; the eastern (53rd Street) tower has an elevator that rises to a lookout with the city's best views. ⊠ *Calle 14 between Calles 51 and 53* ☎ *221/4224–4184, museum 221/424–0112* ⊕ *www.catedral.laplata.net* ☉ *Museum Mon.–Sat. 9–7, Sun. 9–1 and 4:30–8:30.*

At the north end of Plaza Moreno is the 1883 German neoclassical **Palacio Municipal,** which is recognizable by its central clock tower. The sumptuous interior is worthy of exploration, especially the Salón Dorado (Golden Salon), with its marble staircase, painted ceilings, and mosaic tile floors. ⊠ *Plaza Moreno s/n* ☉ *Daily 10–6.*

In the northern portion of the city, the eucalyptus-shaded forest promenade, **Paseo del Bosque,** is a good place to relax. Recreational options include a lake with paddle-boat rentals, an outdoor amphitheater, and an equestrian center.

The **Universidad Nacional de La Plata** (La Plata National University; ⊠ Av. 7 No. 776 ☎ 221/483–3349), in Paseo del Bosque, is one of the most famous universities in Argentina and one of the few with a campus in the style of a North American or European school.

The geographic center of the city is **Plaza Moreno,** where the Piedra Fundacional (La Plata's Founding Stone) was laid in 1882.

2

Beaches All along the region's coastline are *balnearios* (small beach clubs), where you can rent tents and umbrellas and find casual meals. The season begins in December, really springs to life in January and February, and tails off in late March. Some cities, such as Mar del Plata and Pinamar, are known for their nightlife, party attitude, and sophisticated crowds. Others, such as Necochea, are family oriented—a more low-key beach getaway.

Estancias Occasionally, along the never-ending horizon, you encounter an oasis that brings you back in time. *Mate* is sipped at high tea, when the estancia owner sits down with his *peones* (ranch hands) in a gesture of communion. To the uninitiated, the estancia can be a jarringly real experience of old-time feudalism. A day at an estancia is typically spent enjoying an *asado,* barbecue accompanied by empanadas and Argentine red wine, while watching a traditional demonstration of gaucho skill and dexterity. Accommodations vary by estancia, but count on comfortable lodgings with a mixed rusticity and European flair, fitting for country aristocracy. Prices usually include all meals and shows. If there are horses on the premises, estancias, geared toward tourists, usually allow you to ride them. And, no, you won't be asked to do any of the actual ranch work.

The equestrian statue of South American liberator José de San Martín stands in the center of **Plaza San Martín.** On the north side of the square is the black slate roof of the French neoclassic Legislatura (provincial legislature) building. On the west end is the Pasaje Dardo Rocha, a building originally designed as a train station, which was converted into a grand cultural center.

Teatro Argentino—a seven-story concrete behemoth by Le Corbusier— replaced a palace that burned down in 1977. Inside is the country's second-largest theater. ⊠ *Av. 51 s/n* ☎ *221/429–1743.*

Fifteen minutes (7 km/4 mi) outside the city, the Eva Perón–founded **Ciudad de los Niños** (City of Children) is part amusement park, part museum. Children can walk through miniature replicas of historic Argentine buildings. ⊠ *Ruta General Belgrano, Km 7* ☎ *221/484–0194* 🎫 *1 peso* ☉ *Daily 9* AM*–sunset.*

Where to Stay & Eat

★ ¢–$ ✕**Cervecería Modelo.** This alehouse restaurant opened its doors in 1892— just 10 years after the city was founded. The most interesting tradition is tossing peanut shells to the floor. Pigeons, who have cleverly found a way inside, peck at the jettisoned shells. It's part of an established quirkiness that includes what might be the largest menu in the country (which an exceptionally friendly and fast waitstaff guide you through). The homemade pasta is a good bet; you have a choice of 25 sauces. The restaurant stays open late: until 2 AM weekdays and 3 AM weekends. ⊠ *Calle 5 at Calle 54* ☎ *221/421–1321* ▤ *AE, DC, MC, V.*

$$$ ✕▨ **Estancia Juan Gerónimo.** South of La Plata in the tiny village of Veronica, this estancia, which is said to have once belonged to a shipwrecked English bandit, makes a perfect weekend getaway. The early 1920s ranch is set on a mammoth plot of land—more than 10,000 acres—that has been

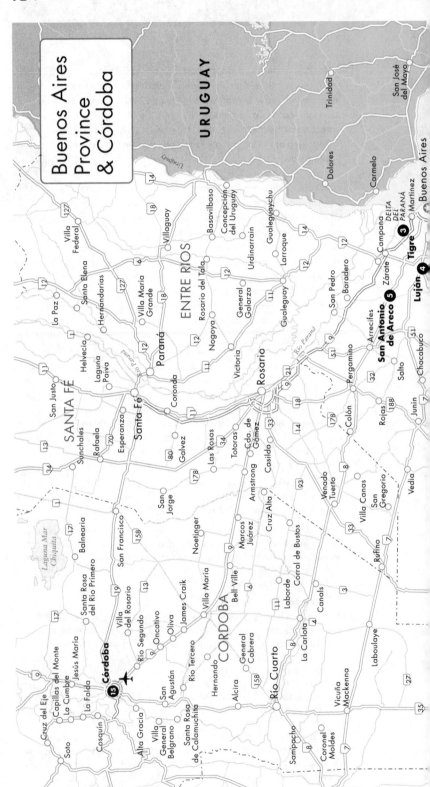

Buenos Aires
Province
& Córdoba

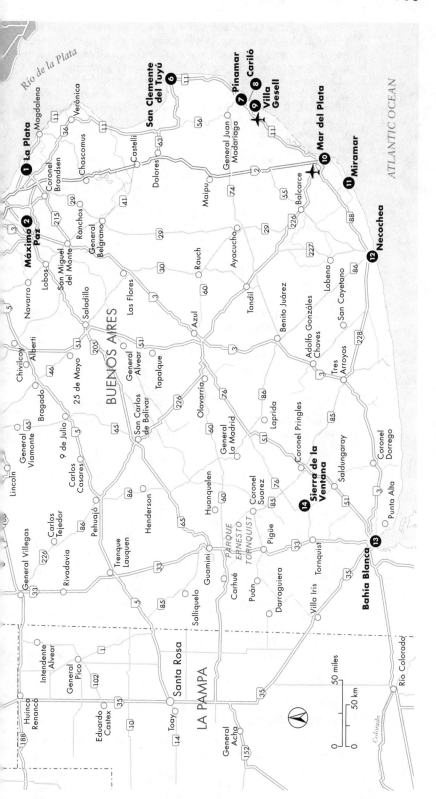

declared a UNESCO World Natural Biosphere Reserve. Day visits can be arranged. Horse enthusiasts love the grounds. It's said that after choosing from among 150 horses, you can ride around the estancia for three days without covering the same terrain. The working farm has a staff of a half-dozen cattle-handling gauchos. ⊠ *In Veronica, 100 km (63 mi) south of La Plata, 165 km (103 mi) south of Buenos Aires* ☏ *Arroyo 873, Buenos Aires, 1007* ☎ *Buenos Aires reservations 11/4937–4326, estancia 222/ 148–1414* 🖷 *11/4327–0105* ⊕ *www.juangeronimo.com.ar* 💭 *11 rooms* ⚲ *Restaurant, fishing, hiking, horseback riding, laundry service* ☱ *AE, MC, V* ᵀᴼᴵ *FAP.*

¢ 🏨 **Benevento Hotel.** This comfortable hotel resulted from the complete restoration of a circa 1890 home, which revealed sumptuous, long-hidden details. The elegant, bright white building has round corner bays on the upper three of its four floors and low, black iron rails on the balconies. Rooms—which have 15-foot ceilings, wood floors, and all-new bathrooms—vary in design, so you might want to look at a few before deciding. The corner rooms are magnificent. ⊠ *Calle 2 645, 1900* ☎🖷 *221/489–1078 or 221/437–7721* ⊕ *www.hotelbenevento.com.ar* 💭 *20 rooms, 1 suite* ⚲ *Restaurant, room service, in-room safes, bar, laundry service* ☱ *AE, MC, V* ᵀᴼᴵ *BP.*

Nightlife & the Arts

Because La Plata is so close to Buenos Aires, most residents head there for a cultural fix. Nightlife in La Plata generally revolves around quiet nights at a coffee shop or at the movies. Try the movie theater **Cine 8** (⊠ Calle 8 between Calles 51 and 53 ☎ 221/483–4001).

Máximo Paz

❷ *50 km (31 mi) southeast of Buenos Aires, past the Ezeiza airport.*

Máximo Paz is nothing more than a little working-class string of provisions stores and tire shops along a dusty strip of dirt—that is, until you reach the sprawling, luxurious Estancia Villa Maria, the town's only draw. It's an easy day trip or overnight from Buenos Aires—van service to the estancia is available if you don't want to drive.

Where to Stay & Eat

$$$$ 🏨 **Estancia Villa Maria.** This incredible Norman-Tudor mansion on 110 acres of countryside is evocative of the estates of English landed gentry. The expansive estate was bought in the 1890s by one of Argentina's wealthiest families. The crops were planted then, but the mansion itself—designed by Argentine architect Alejandro Bustillo—wasn't built until 1923. Whether wandering amidst the grounds, horseback riding, or sitting down to a formal, family-style lunch in the colonial dining room, you can live out your aristocratic Argentine fantasies here. The omnipresent, attentive service will pamper you at every turn, and the deferential staff speaks English and French. At this writing, some of the breathtaking gardens were slated to be converted into a championship golf course. ⊠ *R205, Km 47, Máximo Paz, 1814* ☎ *Estancia 11/02274–450909, Buenos Aires reservations 11/4322–7785* 🖷 *11/4964–2710* ⊕ *www.estanciavmaria.com.ar* 💭 *15 rooms* ⚲ *Restaurant, golf course, tennis court, pool, bicycles, horseback riding, laundry service* ☱ *No credit cards* ᵀᴼᴵ *FAP.*

Tigre & the Paraná Delta

❸ *30 km (19 mi) northwest of Buenos Aires on the Ruta Panamericana, 35 km (22 mi) northwest of Buenos Aires on Avenida Libertador.*

A drive through the shady riverside suburbs of Buenos Aires takes you to the river port town of Tigre, the embarkation point for boats that ply the Delta del Paraná. The delta is a vast maze of canals, tributaries, and river expanding out like the veins of a leaf. A boat trip from Tigre through the delta makes a nice day trip from Buenos Aires. For an especially memorable ride, take a sunset cruise. Along the way you'll travel past colorfully painted houses built on stilts to protect them from floods. The most comfortable way to travel the delta's waterways is aboard a large catamaran. The picturesque **Puerto de Frutos** market, in the central part of the port area, is a good place to find handcrafted items at good prices. The market is particularly busy on weekends.

Aside from the river, the main attraction is the **Tren de la Costa** (Coastal Train), originally built in 1895 as a passenger train and refurbished in 1990. Along its way from Estación Retiro in Buenos Aires to Tigre, the train meanders through some of Buenos Aires's most fashionable northern suburbs, stopping at 11 stations.

At the end of the Tren de la Costa is **Parque de la Costa** (Coastal Park), one of Argentina's largest, most modern amusement parks. If you want to combine a visit here with sightseeing, take the ferryboat trip for a half-hour ride on the river delta. There's also an IMAX theater and restaurants with surprisingly good Argentine fare.

Luján

❹ *60 km (40 mi) west of Buenos Aires via R7.*

In 1630 a mule train, originating in Portugal, made its way out of Buenos Aires. Among the items being carried were two terra-cotta statues of the Virgin Mary. After the caravan stopped for a break along the banks of the Río Luján, one ox pulling the statues refused to budge. Finally, the leaders of the caravan realized that a statue of the Virgin had fallen out and was blocking the way. They took this as a sign that this is where the Virgin wanted to stay and built a basilica on the spot where the caravan stopped.

Every year at least 4 million people make the pilgrimage to Luján to pray to the Virgin at the imposing **Basilica de la Virgen de Luján.** ✉ *Calle San Martín and Calle Padre Salvaire* ☎ *232/342–1070.*

The local **Museo Histórico** (History Museum) provides a history of the Virgin as well as the gauchos and the native peoples of the area. ✉ *Calles Torrezouri and Lezica* ☎ *232/342–0245* 🎫 *1 peso.*

San Antonio de Areco

❺ *110 km (68 mi) west of Buenos Aires.*

If you look around this small town off R8, you can find the most authentic scenes of traditional life in the Pampas. During the early 1700s the town was a regular stop on the route to Peru. Buenos Aires was still a part of the viceroyalty of Peru, and San Antonio de Areco was the last Spanish-populated settlement on the border of the native inhabitants' territory. The town has come to represent cowboy life, most notably at the gaucho museum. Across the street from the museum entrance is a typical *parrilla* (restaurant specializing in grilled meats), run by a local family, where traditional gaucho songs are sung. In summer the Río Areco (Areco River), which runs through town, is teeming with swimmers—especially a short walk from the museum near the center of town, at the Puente Viejo (Old Bridge). The sleepy downtown itself is made up of a couple of shopping streets typical of the small-town life of the Buenos Aires province.

CloseUp

THE LEGEND OF THE GAUCHO

THE GAUCHO—the rugged Argentine cowboy of yesteryear—is, for the most part, just a legend now, a whisper, a mythical figure from the days when cowboys were allowed to wander unhindered across the Pampas. Gauchos would make a living from the cows that they herded, roaming from one dusty watering hole to the next, free—for a time—from the influence of any individual estancia and its wealthy foreign landowners. The visual image is unmistakable: the huge chest, the leathery hands, the bombacha (baggy pants), the small facón (knife), the scarf and trademark narrow-brimmed hat, and the chifle (bull horn, used for drinking water on long trips).

In the late 19th century, the landowners increasingly saw gauchos as an untapped labor source, and set out to co-opt their skills. A law was pushed through by the landowners, barring men without jobs from traveling around the Pampas. This law, which was aimed solely at the gauchos, forced many of them to take jobs at estancias, stripping them of their famous independence—and with it, much of the romantic ideal. It is the free-roaming gaucho, a long-lost phenomenon, rather than the estancia ranch hand, that is most idealized in Argentine lore.

The writer Ricardo Güiraldes (1886–1927) is credited with making that figure of the gaucho a profound part of the collective consciousness of Argentina. His 1926 novel Don Segundo Sombra, inspired by a man Güiraldes had met at La Porteña, his father's estancia in San Antonio de Areco, introduced the gaucho persona to the world. The book was, in the words of Waldo Frank, "the story of a boy who, like boys the world over, learns to become a man by taking life humbly and bravely." Indeed, Güiraldes's protagonist was not just the Marlboro man of the 1800s—a rugged, wandering, romantic hero who was never portrayed without a cigarette in one hand—but rather an Everyman, a symbol of human struggle. Güiraldes writes: "The gaucho, within his limited means, is a complete type of man. He has moral principles. 'A

gaucho of law', he admits that there exists an 'individual law', a sort of destiny that takes every man down a special road. [the gaucho is] someone who has died according to what he was destined for."

Still, the sex appeal of the gaucho was undeniable. "He has dances of extraordinary charm and gallantry," writes Güiraldes, "little love relations," and "a particular style of movement that involves aesthetics, education, and respect of one's own attitude." Certainly this romantic gaucho is the image that might be most associated with the Pampas region, and it continues to be part of the draw of its estancias as tourist destinations. Indeed, if you stay at an estancia, your horseback riding guide will likely be dressed in the full gaucho get-up: narrow-brimmed hat, scarf, and so on. All this might at first seem a bit contrived, and perhaps it is; after all, even if he does herd cattle, he probably makes most of his living leading tourists around on horses. But give your gaucho a chance. He may come closer than you think to conforming to Güiraldes' mythical, romantic stereotype: the independent spirit, the combination of warm generosity, confident yet quiet wisdom, and rugged good looks. He will lead you around with an open smile, and most importantly, he will assure your safety on horseback. But you might well notice him, in deference to his predecessors, with one eye on the distant horizon of the impossibly wide Pampas grasslands.

— By Robin S. Goldstein

The **Museo Gauchesco Ricardo Güiraldes** (Gaucho Museum) conjures up the gaucho life of the past by letting you explore traditional estancia grounds just outside of town, including a 150-year-old *pulpería* (an old country store from gaucho times) tavern with wax figures, a replica of an 18th-century hacienda, and an old chapel. The museum also documents the life and work of Ricardo Güiraldes (1886–1927), whose gaucho novels fired the popular imagination of the Argentine people. Güiraldes is buried in town. ✉ *Camino Ricardo Güiraldes* ☎ *232/645-6201* ☞ *2 pesos* ✆ *Wed.–Mon. 11–5.*

Where to Stay & Eat

Note that you can do a day trip from Buenos Aires to one of the estancias listed below, though you will be asked to pay for a whole "ranch day"—which includes activities along with drinks, lunch, and afternoon empanadas—even if you only want to stop by for lunch.

¢–$ ✗ **Almacen de Ramos Generales.** This old general store is airy and charm-
Fodor's Choice ing, with remnants stowed away in every corner. The food here is sim-
★ ply outstanding, and the small-town setting makes this all the more remarkable. The *picada* begins with salami, pork, cheese, eggplant *en escabeche* (pickled), and wondrous french fries with basil. The *bife de chorizo* (sirloin steak), meanwhile, is one of the best anywhere, perfectly juicy, tender, and flavorful. The atmosphere, too, is just right: it's country-store-meets-elegant-restaurant. Pleasant hues of light pour in from the plate-glass windows while you enjoy the impeccable service and memorable food. ✉ *Zapiola 143, between Lavalle and Sdo. Sombra* ☎ *2326/456376* ⊕ *www.ramosgeneralesareco.com.ar* ⊟ No credit cards.

$$$$ ✗▥ **Estancia El Ombú de Areco.** This fantastic, faded-glory 1890s house on acres of lush land was built by General Richieri. One of the two relaxing swimming pools, where you'll be brought empanadas and drinks in the afternoon, is set on a miniature hill overlooking the fields. A stay here, complete with gaucho and folkloric shows, participation in daily ranch activities, horseback rides, tours of the nearby town, and four full meals, provides a great taste of the ranching lifestyle. ✉ *Ruta 32, Cuartel VI, 1609* ▦ *Buenos Aires reservations 11/4710–2795; estancia 232/649–2080* ⊕ *www.estanciaelombu.com* ☞ *9 rooms* ⚴ *Restaurant, 2 pools, laundry service* ⊟ *AE, V* ⦿ *FAP.*

$$ ✗▥ **Estancia La Bamba.** The main house, owned by the venerable Aldao family, dates from around 1832 and is done in traditional Argentine style with beautiful, roofed verandas and an interior courtyard with a well. The garden is a great place for sunbathing or stargazing. Living and dining rooms ooze aristocratic country splendor. There are lovely views of the surrounding plains and all kinds of ranch activities. Rooms include the full package—four meals per day, eaten family-style with the other guests. Some staff members speak English. ✉ *Reservations in Buenos Aires: Maipú 859, 4th fl., Buenos Aires, 1006* ▦ *Buenos Aires reservations 11/4314–0394; estancia 232/645–6293* ⊕ *www.la-bamba.com. ar* ☞ *8 rooms* ⚴ *Restaurant, horseback riding, laundry service* ⊟ *AE, V* ⦿ *FAP.*

Nightlife & the Arts

One of the coolest watering holes in the entire region, **Las Ganas** (✉ Vietyes and Pellegrini ☎ 2325/1568–5181) has the requisite dim lighting, live music, a boisterous local crowd (including real gauchos), and an unbelievable collection of bottles lining the walls. **La Ochava** (✉ Alsina and Alem ☎ 2326/452–176) is a dim haunt, with old wooden tables and chairs and creatively modern lamps that swing from the ceiling. In addition to being a laid-back place to down a couple of drinks, it makes great empanadas. Pizza and ravioli might figure into the daily lunch special.

Shopping

A terrific wine store is **Vinoteca 45** (⊠ Alsina 295 ☏ 2326/456296), along San Antonio de Areco's main street. It has been selling notable wines from all over the country since the 1970s—it's a surprising apparition in an otherwise rural village. The friendly owner will put you right at ease and guide your selection.

THE ATLANTIC COAST

Southern Buenos Aires Province is synonymous with one thing—*la playa* (the beach). Every summer Argentines flock to the beaches at resort towns along the coast, many of which were originally large estates converted in the same way: with a *peatonal* (a pedestrians-only street) and a central plaza with a church.

San Clemente del Tuyú

❻ *308 km (192 mi) southeast of Buenos Aires.*

Founded in 1935 as a summer resort, San Clemente del Tuyú is the starting point of the string of beach towns that extends down the Atlantic coast. Though it's not quite as beautiful as its neighbors farther south, it's less expensive and has a more down-to-earth feel. Proximity to Buenos Aires (less than four hours) makes it especially popular with Porteño (residents of Buenos Aires) families that are traveling on public transportation. Like most beach towns, San Clemente del Tuyú has a promenade where you can take in the warm summer breezes. There's also a pier that stretches 150 feet over the ocean.

The pride and joy of the town is **Mundo Marino** (Marine World). Sea animal shows, with whales and dolphins, are the main attractions. There are also rides and games for children and laser shows at night. ⊠ *Av. Décima 157* ☏ *225/230–3000* ✉ *18 pesos* ☉ *Jan. and Feb., daily 10–10; Mar., Wed.–Sun. 10–6; Apr.–June, Fri.–Sun. 10–6.*

The small **Museo Histórico y de Ciencias Naturales** (Museum of History and Natural Sciences) has exhibits that display reptile, insect, and fossil remains. Call the tourist office for hours. ⊠ *Calle 3 between Calle 1 and Costanera* ☏ *No phone* ✉ *Free* ☉ *Daily 6 PM–10 PM.*

> **off the beaten path**
>
> **RESERVA DE VIDA SILVESTRE CAMPOS DEL TUYÚ –** Outside town is a 3,000-acre nature reserve established in 1979 to help protect the native deer. Hiking trails crisscross the park. It's a good idea to pack a picnic lunch. ⊠ *Partido Gral. Lavalle, Bahía de Samborombón* ☏ *In Buenos Aires 11/4343–3778, ext. 35.*

Pinamar

❼ *112 km (80 mi) south of San Clemente del Tuyú on Rte. 11, 342 km (214 mi) southeast of Buenos Aires via R2.*

The chic resort town of Pinamar attracts the Argentinian jet set, including film and television stars, models, and politicians (those who haven't gone to the even snootier Punta del Este in Uruguay). It's an idyllic little beach town with family-run shops lining the main avenue.

Where to Stay

$$ 🏨 **Soleado Hotel.** The modern Soleado is a few feet from the beach, and some rooms have ocean views. The decor is tasteful if reminiscent of a hotel chain in the United States. There are discounts for extended stays. ⊠ *Sarmiento and Nuestros Malvinas, 7167* ☏ *225/449–0340* 🖷 *225/*

449–0201 ⊕ *www.pinamar.com.ar/soleado* 🛏 *52 rooms* ♿ *Restaurant, room service, bar* ☰ *AE, MC, V* ◎ *BP.*

$–$$ ⬚ **Los Pájaros.** At Los Pájaros, accommodations are more like apartments than rooms, with separate bedrooms and dining/living rooms. The look is Argentine country, with exposed brick walls and heavy wooden furniture. Prices double in high season, when rooms are rented out by the week. ✉ *Del Tuyú 919, 7167* ☎ *225/449–0618* 🖷 *225/449–0625* ⊕ *www.lospajaros.com.ar* 🛏 *30 units* ♿ *Restaurant, kitchenettes, pool, gym, bar* ☰ *AE, DC, MC, V.*

Nightlife
Most of Pinamar's nightlife centers on the cafés and ice cream parlors on Avenida Bunge and the streets branching off it. At the **Casino del Bosque** (✉ Avs. Júpiter and Bunge) you can try your luck with roulette, blackjack, and other games. As in other beach towns, going to the movies is an immensely popular nighttime activity; buy your tickets early at **Cine Bahía** (✉ Av. Bunge 74 ☎ 225/448–1012).

Cariló

❽ *8 km (5 mi) south of Pinamar.*

Cariló, the new darling of summer resorters, represents an entirely new concept in Argentine beach tourism. Rather than a built-up town with a central square, a business center, and a bustling beach scene, Cariló is more like a seaside forest, a protected community with bungalows, hotels, and condos hidden in strategic places along a network of winding dirt roads. As a result, the beaches are pristine, the air is clean and quiet, and the beach experience is more intimate, but the cultural experience is not steeped in Argentine history or culture. It's especially good for a group or family looking for a bucolic getaway. The resort was developed in the late 1980s, when the Guerrero family decided to convert what was once a war retreat into a vacation spot by planting trees and stimulating development. That development is still in full bloom, as evidenced by the numerous houses still under construction, especially along the inland areas of the long dirt road that leads into Cariló from the highway to the coast.

Where to Stay
If you don't want to stay in a hotel, there are tons of apartment rentals in the area. The Web site ⊕ www.parquecarilo.com is a clearing house of sorts for links to rental agencies and also has its own listings.

$$–$$$ ⬚ **Hotel Talara.** The second-oldest hotel in Cariló, this fresh, airy establishment a few steps from the beach has comfortable rooms with pleasant balconies, some with spectacular water views. The lobby and upstairs lounge brim with plant life, and the bar and restaurant downstairs are equally stylish. There's a big breakfast spread and a helpful staff. The hotel combines the familiarity and charm of a smaller hotel with the comfort level of a bigger one. ✉ *Laurel and Costanera, 7167* ☎ *2254/470304* ⊕ *http://talara.parquecarilo.com* 🛏 *30 rooms* ♿ *Restaurant, minibars, pool, bar* ☰ *MC, V* ◎ *BP.*

Shopping
There's not much of the way of a commercial district in Cariló—just one little **Centro Comercial** (shopping center)—a couple of square blocks of stores and restaurants. The complex is on the block formed by Cerezo, Avellano, and Divisadero, on the right off the main road as you're driving coastward from the highway. There you'll find a smattering of cute little restaurants, a couple of bars and cafés, clothing stores, a pharmacy, a general store, and most importantly, a good supermarket and

liquor store where you can stock up for picnics or (if you're renting an apartment) plan the night's cookout.

Villa Gesell

⊙ *16 km (10 mi) south of Pinamar.*

Villa Gesell was settled in 1931 by the German businessman Don Carlos Idaho Gesell, who experimented with forestation techniques to stabilize the vast tracts of dunes. Within a decade, Gesell had created a paradise of pine trees and forest. The town became a nature preserve and vacation spot. Affluent Argentine families visit for the tranquillity, the beaches with dunes, and the alpine architecture. It has also become very popular in recent years with young people. Conservation remains a high priority, and the dunes are thoughtfully maintained.

At the **Casa de la Cultura** (Culture House) you can see displays of local crafts. It's also the site of yearly arts festivals, including the Villa Gesell song festival in February. ⊠ *Av. 3 between Paseos 108 and 109* ☏ *Free* ⊙ *Mon.–Sat. 10–6.*

Picturesque **Faro Querandi** (Querandi Lighthouse), about 15 km (9 mi) south of Villa Gesell, is surrounded by forest and sand dunes and is an ideal spot for a sunset stroll. The lighthouse itself is not open to the public. ⊠ *On Rte. 11* ☏ *No phone.*

off the beaten path

MAR DE LA PAMPA – Just 5 km (3 mi) down the Ruta Interbalnearia from Villa Gesell is the town of Mar de la Pampa, which makes a great day trip. It has quiet—sometimes deserted—beaches.

Nightlife & the Arts

In summer, music and theater productions are held at the **Anfiteatro Natural** (⊠ Paseo 102 and Av. 10). Nightlife centers on strolling down **Avenida 3**, which from January to February is made into a pedestrian walkway.

Mar del Plata

⓿ *123 km (77 mi) southeast of Villa Gesell on Rte. 11, 400 km (248 mi) south of Buenos Aires via R2.*

Come summer, Argentina becomes obsessed with Mar del Plata. The city of 600,000 residents is the most popular beach resort in the country—and at least five times as big as any runners-up. Beaches are almost comically crowded in January and February, when there's a carnival-like atmosphere day and night (no one seems to notice that the sun goes down). When not enjoying the beach—there are 47 km (29 mi) of picturesque coastline—people stroll along it or spend hours sitting at outdoor cafés. The tourist infrastructure hums, with more than 700 hotels, countless eateries, and an array of theme parks, theaters, and specialized museums. It's not the most tranquil location, but it's a definite summertime experience.

The oldest structure in the city is the **Capilla Santa Cecilia**, built in 1873 by city founder Don Patricio Peralta Ramos in memory of his wife, Cecilia. The chapel served as the city's developmental center, with the city's grid plan revolving around it. ⊠ *Av. Córdoba at Av. 3 de Febrero* ☏ *No phone* ☏ *Free.*

All roads now lead to the **Casino** (⊠ Av. Marítimo 2100 ☏ 223/495-7011), in an attractive 1930s brick-and-limestone building with black mansard roof. Next door is an identical building that housed the

TOWNS OF MISERY

ONE SIDE OF THE *highway between Buenos Aires and La Plata reveals mile after sobering mile of some of the worst shantytowns in a country whose inequality can still be shocking. It's an especially jarring sight if you're coming straight from the hip, modern Buenos Aires. These illegal settlements, called* villas emergencias *(emergency towns)—or, as they're known to most Argentines,* villas miserias *(towns of misery)—are little conglomerations of shacks slapped together with corrugated tin and even cardboard, carcasses of old automobiles, and piles of deteriorating rubber tires. The Argentine version of the Brazilian* favelas, *these communities tend to form their own micro-economies, often based on the barter system—you'll see little general stores and take-out eateries of sorts. Some villas miserias have electricity or running water; many don't.*

Cityfolk will warn you not to enter a villa miseria, and you should heed their advice—tourists are immediate targets for muggings and kidnappings. In fact, not even the police deign to go in; the result is an underworld that exists on a shadowy plane, completely off the radar screen of Argentina's government and economy. It's not quite lawlessness, rather a makeshift system of community policing enforces a rather different system of norms—a code of conduct driven by the constant and relentless need merely to survive, whatever it takes. Families support each other and the needs of the community, pooling their resources to provide food and shelter. Often you'll see a makeshift soccer field somewhere in the village, which, when in use, seems a profound visual testament to the sport's power to be a ray of light in an otherwise bleak existence.

— By Robin S. Goldstein

city's first beachfront hotel, the Hotel Provincial. The Casino is the centerpiece of city nightlife, open daily 3–3. It is not, however, properly air-conditioned—which, by getting you out sooner, might save you some money.

The port area, simply called **El Puerto,** is worth a visit for its restaurants, attractive boats, and a colony of *lobos marinos* (sea lions). (The frequently powerful stench along the jetty guides you to them.) Sea lions lounge at your feet, cavort in the water, and sun themselves atop decaying, poetically half-sunken ships in an offshore area called the **Barranco de los Lobos.** From this breakwater you can watch the scores of bright orange fishing boats heading back to the port at sunset. ⊠ *2 km (1 mi) west of the casino on Av. Marítimo.*

Punta Mogotes, a few miles west of Barranco de los Lobos, is a wide area of 24 beach clubs side by side. Each has individually colored beach cabanas, snack shops, restaurants, and activities like volleyball and water sports. ⊠ *Off Av. Martítima, 2 km (1 mi) west past the port.*

More of a sea-theme amusement park than a true aquarium, **Mar del Plata Aquarium** has performing dolphins and sea lions, waterskiing shows, and a 3-D movie. The aquarium also has a beach with beach chairs, umbrellas, and a bar. It's south of Punta Mogotes on R11. ⊠ *Av. Martinez de Hoz 5600* ☎ *223/467–0700* ⊕ *www.mdpaquarium. com.ar* ☒ *20 pesos* ☉ *Jan. and Feb., daily 10 AM–11 PM; last ticket sold at 9.*

Museo del Mar is an attractive, modern showcase for a collection of more than 30,000 seashells. The four-story complex has numerous large fish tanks, a multilevel cyber-café, an art exhibition space, a library, and a gift shop. The rooftop Mirador del Faro (Lighthouse Lookout) provides

panoramic views of the city. ⊠ *Av. Colón 1114* ☎ *223/451–3553*
⊕ *www.museodelmar.com* ☒ *2 pesos* ☉ *Jan.–Feb., daily 8 AM–2 AM;
Mar.–Dec., Mon.–Thurs. 8 AM–9 PM, Fri. and Sat. 8 AM–midnight,
Sun. 9–9.*

Where to Stay & Eat

$–$$$ ✕ **Torreón del Monje.** This multilevel castle structure has some of the best
views in town, overlooking the entire beach, bay, and cityscape of Mar
del Plata. Crowds of beachgoers and local folks spread out over a se-
ries of terraces shaded by scores of umbrellas. The fare is predictable—
an overambitious mix of fish, meat, pasta, and Argentine pizza (which
isn't bad). The fried calamari are a decent choice, and a large bottle of
Quilmes served up in an ice bucket hits the spot on a sunny afternoon.
⊠ *Paseo Jesús de Galíndez* ☎ *223/451–5575* ⊟ *AE, DC, MC, V.*

¢–$$ ✕ **El Ciervo Rojo.** This traditional restaurant is 14 km (9 mi) west of Mar
del Plata on Highway 226 in the Sierra de los Padres Nature Preserve,
which is best known for its tranquil lagoon. The restaurant offers a traditional buffet of *parrilla* (grilled meats), as well as pastas and salads.
On Saturday night there's a show with dinner. ⊠ *Santa Fé 1844* ☎ *No
phone* ⊟ *AE, DC, MC, V.*

¢–$$ ✕ **Piazza Caffe.** In a relaxed outdoor setting facing the beaches of Varese
Bay, Piazza Caffe offers an affordable way to dine with a fair degree of
style. The majority of tables are outside on a half-block-long deck, tak-
ing full advantage of the balmy breezes that blow in summer. Entrées—
seafood, burgers, chicken, salads—are huge; ask for half-servings. The
staff is fast and friendly. ⊠ *Av. Alem 2427, at Av. Marítimo* ☎ *223/451–
9939* ⊟ *AE, V.*

¢–$$ ✕ **Trenque Laquen.** Impostors abound in Mar del Plata, but this place is
the original Trenque Laquen; they've been preparing some of the best
steak in the region since 1956. The heavily local, middle-age clientele
seems to know this well, which is why they routinely make the trek to
this somewhat unlikely residential neighborhood (it's within easy walking distance of downtown, though). To begin with, the plate of *mollejas* (grilled sweetbreads) is a revelation, an impossibly tender, crispy, creamy
delight that melts in your disbelieving mouth. The *bife de chorizo*, a bone-
less sirloin steak served on its own wooden cutting board, is juicy and
flavorful. *Espinacas a la crema* (creamed spinach) is a great accompa-
niment. The dining room is traditional, simple, and a bit too bright, but
it's supremely appropriate for a steak house—wine and dark wood are
the dominant themes. ⊠ *Mitre 2807 at Garay* ☎ *223/493–7149* ⊟ *AE,
DC, MC, V.*

★ $$$ ☒ **Sheraton Mar del Plata.** You'll find peerless comforts within this soar-
ing, modern building that sets the standard for luxury in Mar del Plata.
Inside, the 11-story atrium defines the space, and a wide lobby gives way
to second- and third-floor restaurants and cafés. Though it's rather re-
moved from the city center and the shoreline, a sane distance may be a
sign of wisdom in this party-frenzied city. Half of the rooms have views
over a golf course to a naval base and the sea. Las Barcas restaurant is an
elegant setting for its specialty—parrilla. ⊠ *Av. Alem 4221, 7600* ☎ *223/
499–9000* 🖷*223/499–9009* ⊕*www.sheraton.com* ⬅*160 rooms, 32 suites*
⟡ *Restaurant, room service, in-room data ports, in-room safes, minibars,
golf privileges, 2 pools, gym, hair salon, hot tub, sauna, bar, laundry ser-
vice, convention center, meeting rooms* ⊟ *AE, DC, MC, V* ☉*BP.*

★ $ ☒ **El Hostal de Alem.** This 70-year-old stone house is set on a land-
scaped lawn in the quiet, residential neighborhood of Playa Grande.
Beaches are within walking distance. The home was converted to a guest
house and is politely operated and pristinely kept. Rooms have com-
fortable beds (with box springs—a bragging matter in small Argentine

hotels) and new furnishings. The on-site restaurant is very good, and the overall experience is one of tranquility and comfort. ☒ *Rawson 233 at Av. Alem, 7600* 🕾 *223/486–4008 or 486–2265* ⊕ *www. elhostaldealem.com.ar* ⇆ *28 rooms* ♿ *Restaurant, room service, in-room data ports, minibars, bar, laundry service, meeting rooms* ⊟ *AE, DC, MC, V* ⦿ *BP.*

Nightlife & the Arts

Especially in summer, Mar del Plata offers a dizzying selection. In one month's time there were 78 different plays (nearly all in Spanish, of course) and more than 60 different musical performances. The Hotel Provincial Tourist Office publishes a free monthly activity guide. Cinemas generally screen the same Hollywood films that are playing in Buenos Aires. In March, the city hosts an international film festival.

To get the most out of the town's party scene, it's always wise to ask people you meet on the beach where to go dancing that particular night.

NIGHTLIFE   The most popular gay disco in the city is **Amsterdam** (☒ Castelli 3045). If you crave salsa rhythms (and lessons), head to **Azucar Salsoteca** (☒ Constitución 4478 🕾 223/495–7938). Tango shows are held at **Malena Club de Tango** (☒ Rivadavía 2312 🕾 223/495–8533). Be sure to make reservations for the 11 PM show, which always fills up. For a night out, Argentines in their twenties and thirties head to **Sobremonte** (☒ Constitución 6690 🕾 223/479–2600 ⊕ www.sobremonte.com.ar), a very modern complex of restaurants and dance clubs, the latter generally open after midnight and don't really get going until 3 AM. The 10-peso entrance fee includes a drink at any outlet.

THE ARTS   The **Centro Cultural General Pueyrredón** (☒ 25 de Mayo 3108 🕾 223/493–6767) is the largest theater venue, especially in summer. There are four screens at the movie theater **Cines del Paseo** (☒ Diagonal Pueyrredón 3058 🕾 223/496–1100). **Los Gallegos** (☒ Rivadavía 3050 🕾 223/499–6900) is a mall with the newest movie theater in town. Let the professional, English-speaking staff at the **tourist office** (☒ Hotel Provincial, Av. Marítimo 2400 🕾 223/495–1777) direct you to the hottest cultural events. It's open daily 8 AM–10 PM.

Sports & the Outdoors

BEACHES   Mar del Plata's main beach is a crescent that stretches out just below the entire length of the city center. Packed all summer, it attracts young, old, and families alike until 6 or 7 PM, and it's dotted with places to get food or drink.

BIKING   **Cicloturismo** (☒ Av. Alem 3655 🕾 223/481–0082) organizes various biking tours (starting at 25 pesos, including lunch) that lead you around the city's green areas and incorporate city history.

BOATING &   **Turimar** (☒ Banquina de Pescadores at El Puerto 🕾 223/489–1612) or-
FISHING   ganizes hour-long boat tours of the coast departing from the port daily every 40 minutes 10–6:30. Buy tickets (7 pesos) at the kiosk in the Centro Comercial del Puerto. Turimar also arranges five-hour deep-sea fishing expeditions for 75 pesos and up, including equipment.

Crucero Anamora (☒ Dársena B at El Puerto 🕾 223/489–0310) has a boat with a dance floor and bar. The hour-long port-to-casino trip (10 pesos) departs four times a day.

GOLF   **Los Acantilados Golf Club** (☒ Paseo Costanero Sur 5 🕾 223/467–2500) has a 27-hole course that's among the country's best. **Mar del Plata Golf Club** (☒ Aristóbulo del Valle 3940 🕾 223/486–2323) has two 18-hole courses within the city limits.

Miramar

❶ *45 km (28 mi) south of Mar del Plata.*

Miramar likes to promote itself as the *ciudad de los niños* (city of children), and on weekends the park here is packed with families and kids, which has a certain charm but can take away from the getaway feel. With a year-round population of 20,000, this is one of the quietly residential coastal towns. Summer season is still organized around the beach, but there's a much more subdued atmosphere than in Mar del Plata. As with most coastal towns, two pedestrian streets lead away from the beach and are lined with pizzerias and ice cream shops. **Plaza San Marco,** at the end of the pedestrian streets, is a square lined with crafts vendors.

Where to Stay & Eat

$ ✕ **El Pescador Romano.** Italian owners have operated the Roman Fisherman in Miramar for more than 30 years. The constant hustle-bustle suggests it's never been more popular. There's an energetic central dining room where you can watch the chefs at work, and smaller, more private side rooms. The waitstaff is attentive and professional. *Camarones con salsa de puerros* (baby shrimp in a creamy leek sauce with potatoes) is among the seafood and pasta dishes. ✉ *Calle 22 No. 1022, at Calle 19* ☎ *No phone* ⌂ *Reservations not accepted* ▱ *MC, V.*

¢ ▤ **Hotel Marina.** A Frisbee toss away from the beach, Hotel Marina is a solid, economical choice. Most rooms have balconies with sea views. Like most other hotels in Miramar, this one doesn't have air-conditioning, but the open breezes on the eastern edge of town keep it cool. Some nearby hotels charge a bit less, but rooms here are reliably clean and comfortable. ✉ *Av. 9 No. 744, 7607* ☎☎ *2291/420462* ⊕ *www.miramar–digital. com.ar/hotelmarina* ⇆ *18 rooms* ▱ *AE, DC, MC, V* ❏ *BP.*

Nightlife & the Arts

Nightlife in this quiet town centers on **Calle 9 de Julio,** a *peatonal* (pedestrians-only walkway). The small **Casino** (✉ Calle 9 de Julio between Calles 26 and 28 ☎ 2291/442–0457) is a popular place to stop and try your luck after strolling down Calle 9 de Julio. For movies try **Cine Astral** (✉ Calle 21 between Calles 30 and 32 ☎ 2291/443–0376).

Sports & the Outdoors

Miramar's perfect waves make it ideal for surfing and body-boarding. **El Pomol,** the main beach in town, is supposed to have the best waves in Argentina. **Club Náutico** (✉ R11, Km 4), just north of the city, rents Jet Skis and organizes waterskiing. Bicycles can be rented on major streets and plazas. The **Golf Club Miramar** (✉ R11, Km 4 ☎ 2291/442–0833), 1½ km (1 mi) from the city center, is an 18-hole course with ocean views.

Necochea

❷ *127 km (79 mi) southwest of Mar del Plata.*

A relatively isolated town in the middle of the Atlantic coast, Necochea has the country's largest and finest beaches. The solitude along most of its 65-km-long (41-mi-long) strand—which is 200 yards deep—makes the place all the more alluring. Although it is essentially a calm, seaside village, a summer influx brings families who fill the colorful balnearios along the shore.

Just over the Quequén River, the port for Necochea's twin city, Quequén, is one of the country's most important. Grains are transported from the fertile fields of the surrounding Pampas. The beaches here are quieter than in Necochea, and a drive down Quequén's shore is an adventure. A flood in 1980 dropped river boats along the coast, creating a ship graveyard. You can traverse the landscape on dirt roads, occasionally spotting a white, Mediterranean-style villa beyond the dunes.

Parque Miguel Lillo, parallel to the ocean, is said to contain more than a million pine trees. At **Pinolandia,** or Pineland Avenue, kids can board a train that follows a circuit around the park. Nearby along Avenida 2 is **Lago de los Cisnes,** a small lake where you can rent pedal boats.

Quequén has the third-tallest monument in the country, after the Buenos Aires Obelisk and Rosario's national flag monument. The 112-foot-tall **Monumento Gesta a Malvinas** is a Falkland Islands War memorial with real emotional and political significance for Argentines. ⊠ *Av. Almirante Brown and Calle 511, 3 blocks from the port* ☏ *No phone.*

Climb 163 steps to the top of **El Faro** (lighthouse) for a sweeping view of the Atlantic coast. ⊠ *Calle 516* ☏ *No phone* 🎫 *1 peso.*

The coastal drive south from town is beautiful and quite distinct. Rocky outcrops and cliffs form a sandy, calm beach called **Las Grutas** (The Grottos) 10 km (6 mi) from town. Black sand and rocky coast characterize **Punta Negra** (Black Point), a popular destination 15 km (9 mi) south of Necochea. **Cueva del Tigre** is an enormous sea cave named for a gaucho who hid from the law here in the 19th century. The beach area is 28 km (18 mi) south of town. **Médano Blanco** (White Dune) is 10 km (6 mi) south of Cueva del Tigre. The dunes here reach up to 100 yards in height and are used in recreational motor sports by residents.

Where to Stay & Eat

$–$$ ✕ **Cantina Venezia.** The port is the logical destination for fresh seafood, and this experienced Italian cantina has been here nearly 40 years. The dining rooms—under heavily stuccoed, almost cavernous arches—are filled with photos of famous Argentine clients. Menus are available in English. Try the *langostinos al aceto balsámico* (prawns in balsamic vinegar). ⊠ *Av. 59 No. 259* ☏ *226/242–4014* ▤ *AE, DC, MC, V* ⊘ *No lunch.*

¢–$ ✕ **La Cabaña.** Follow the dirt road that skirts Miguel Lillo Park until you reach this comfortable log-cabin restaurant. Choose from three levels of interior dining, or enjoy the weather at tables on the back or front terrace. The menu is typically Argentine—seafood and domestic barbecued meats—though the setting and service are perhaps the finest in town. ⊠ *Av. 10 No. 5194* ☏ *226/215–630–203 cell* ▤ *AE, DC, MC, V.*

$–$$ 🛏 **Hotel Nikén.** This hotel sets the standard for comfort and service in Necochea. Some of the big rooms come with hot tubs and microwaves. The hotel has direct access to the casino, and at the foot of Miguel Lillo park, it's 800 feet from the beach. ⊠ *Calle 87 No. 335, 7630* ☏ *226/ 243–2323* ⊕ *www.hotelniken.com.ar* ☙ *20 rooms, 2 suites* ♤ *Room service, minibars, pool, laundry service* ▤ *AE, DC, MC, V.*

¢ 🛏 **Hotel Necochea.** For the price, it's hard to beat this hotel 100 feet from the beach. Ask for one of the renovated rooms, which have good air-conditioners, and bathrooms with separate shower and bath. The lobby area, bright and spotless, reflects the professional demeanor of the accommodating staff. Downstairs there's a full spa, unusual in a hotel of this modest size. ⊠ *Av. 79 No. 217, 7630* ☏ *226/243–3255* ☙ *50 rooms* ♤ *Restaurant, massage, sauna, spa, meeting rooms* ▤ *AE, DC, MC, V.*

Nightlife & the Arts

The **Casino** (⊠ Av. 2 and Calle 91 ☏ 226/243–0158), on the beach side of Parque Miguel Lillo, is open daily in summer from 9:30 to 3. The rest of the year, operating hours are Friday–Sunday from 9 PM to 3 AM.

Cine Ocean (⊠ Calle 83 No. 450 ☎ 226/243–5672) has three screens showing American movies in English.

For dancing, people in their twenties head to **La Frontera** (⊠ Calle 75 and Av. 2), identifiable by the large inflated beer bottle. Argentine rock is played at **Yamó** (⊠ Calle 85 between Avs. 6 and 8). The crowd at **Bailables Diez** (⊠ Calle 75 and Av. 10) dance club tends to be 35 and up.

Sports & the Outdoors

The range of activities here is almost unparalleled along the coast. The **Necochea Tourist Office** (⊠ Av. 2 and Calle 79 ☎ 226/243–0158 ⊕ www. necocheanet.com.ar) arranges outdoor adventure tours in addition to offering the usual panoply of maps and brochures daily from 8 AM to 10 PM.

BOATING & **Coastline Tours** (☎ 226/215–56–2160 cell) arranges sailboat tours on the
FISHING river or out into the ocean. **Rafting Río Quequén** (☎ 226/215–464–018 cell) provides kayaking equipment, lessons, guides, and transportation to the site.

Lancha Universal (⊠ Av. 10 No. 3616 ☎ 226/242–6272) has 25 years of deep-sea fishing experience. Anglers gather at the breakwaters at the confluence of the **Quequén River** and the Atlantic Ocean. Fishing here is free. A popular fishing spot is **Las Cascadas,** a small falls area 12 km (8 mi) up the Quequén River.

GOLF The **Necochea Golf Club** (⊠ Av. Armada Argentina s/n ☎ 226/245–0684) has 36 holes.

HORSEBACK Unlike riding in the United States, here you choose your horse, ride alone
RIDING (without an instructor or guide), and go wherever you please—the beach, the park, the town. Prices are substantially cheaper, too—about 5 pesos per hour. Call **Recreo Hípico** (☎ 226/242–7984) for details about renting horses directly from their owners, who line up along Avenida 10 and Calle 115, beyond the main park entrance.

Bahía Blanca

⓭ *331 km (207 mi) west of Necochea on Rte. 228 and R3, 653 km (405 mi) southwest of Buenos Aires via R3.*

Bahía Blanca (population 300,000), at the southern edge of Buenos Aires Province, is a gateway to Patagonia. Founded at the turn of the 20th century primarily as a fishing center, this town had other industries, which grew rapidly as well. The name Bahía Blanca ("white bay") was inspired by the town's salt mines. Don't expect a resort—the nearest beaches are 110 km (69 mi) away, at Monte Hermoso, where you'll find a good percentage of townsfolk on weekends.

Bahía Blanca's two principal avenues, Avenida Alem and Avenida Colón, transect the city and the central square, Plaza Rivadavía. This is the most attractive part of downtown, with tree-lined streets and turn-of-the-20th-century buildings.

The remains of the city's founder, Coronel Ramón Estomba, are buried in the **Catedral Nuestra Señora de la Merced** (⊠ Plaza Rivadavía).

The contemporary arts center **Museo de Arte Contemporáneo** hosts changing exhibitions. ⊠ *Sarmiento 454* ☎ *291/459–4006* 🎟 *2 pesos* 🕐 *Tues.–Sun. 4–8.*

Inside the Palacio Municipal, the town's fine arts museum, the **Museo de Bellas Artes,** houses Argentine art from the 1930s on, with a focus on gauchos. ⊠ *Alsina 65* ☎ *291/456–4157* 🎟 *2 pesos* 🕐 *Tues.–Sun. 4–8.*

At the edge of town is the **Museo del Puerto** (Port Museum), which tells the story of the railway, the port, immigrants, and the community through archive documents. The museum's restaurant is the central attraction, where traditional recipes find new life. ⊠ *Calle Guillermo Torres 4180, at Calle Cárrega* ☎ *291/457–3006* ✉ *Call ahead for admission cost* ☉ *Weekends 3–6.*

Where to Stay & Eat

¢–$ ✗ **Gambrinus Chopería.** This alehouse and restaurant has been around as long as anything in Bahía Blanca (it opened May 2, 1897). To newer eyes, the place might feel like an authentic version of certain American chain restaurants stuffed with antique bric-a-brac. The waiters act as if they've monopolized something gastronomically important—service can be surly (though the place is informal, serving chicken, beef, sandwiches and salads). Still, there's something to the setting. ⊠ *Arribeños 174, off Calle Brown* ☎ *291/452–2380* ▤ *AE, DC, MC, V.*

$ 🏨 **Argos.** Only five blocks from Plaza Rivadavía, Argos is the top luxury choice in town. Rooms have card-key access to brightly colored interiors with big, soundproof windows. You can also individually control the air-conditioning system (smaller hotels are notorious for shutting off the air in the middle of summer nights). ⊠ *España 149, 8000* ☎ *291/455–0404* ⊕ *www.hotelargos.com* ✎ *97 rooms, 7 suites* ⚱ *Restaurant, room service, minibars, gym, bar, meeting room* ▤ *AE, DC, MC, V* 🍴*BP.*

¢ 🏨 **Austral.** Five rooms on each floor of this four-star hotel are in a separate wing and offer more space, with clean, tiled bathrooms, and individually controlled air-conditioning units. A cozy piano bar in the lobby adds to the feeling of comfort and value. A nearby property offers larger, apartment-style suites three blocks from Plaza Rivadavía. ⊠ *Av. Colón 159, 8000* ☎ *291/456–1700* 🖷 *291/455–3737* ⊕ *www.hoteles-austral.com.ar* ✎ *108 rooms, 20 suites* ⚱ *Restaurant, room service, gym, sauna, 2 bars, meeting rooms* ▤ *AE, DC, MC, V.*

Nightlife

Your best bet for current Hollywood showings is at the **Cinemark 6** (⊠ Av. Sarmiento 4114 ☎ 291/486–1899) inside Paseo del Sol, one of the megamalls at the edge of town.

Sierra de la Ventana

⓮ *90 km (56 mi) northeast of Bahía Blanca, 602 km (376 mi) southwest of Buenos Aires.*

Mountains! In summer when the heat rises off the plains, the sloping hills of the region around Sierra de la Ventana are a refreshing change from the monotony of the Pampas. The Sierras are part of the oldest geological strata in South America.

The town is connected by train to Buenos Aires and Bahía Blanca. It's most popular with domestic tourists, who enjoy the wading, picnicking, and fishing in and around the Sauce Grande River.

The jagged mountain peaks can best be appreciated from the R76 lookout, **Mirador Cerro Ventana.** If you notice a small square opening, that's the mountain's *ventana* (window).

The mountains are contained within the **Parque Ernesto Tornquist** (⊠ R76 ☎ 291/491–0039), which was named after the Swiss-Argentine banker who developed—and later donated—the land for park use. You can hike on various trails, the most memorable of which is **Cerro de la Ventana,** an ascent to the window peak itself. Though it looks microscopic from afar, the window measures about 30 feet by 40 feet. The 3,726-foot climb takes about five hours and is steep in places. From the top there's an excellent view of the surrounding Pampas.

Just 1½ km (2 mi) from the Sierra peaks on R76, **Villa Ventana** is a tree-canopied small town set between two creeks. At 1,200 feet above sea level, it enjoys some of the coolest weather in the Pampas and makes a great base camp for excursions into the park and the surrounding country.

Where to Stay & Eat

¢–$ ✕ **Las Golondrinas.** The best restaurant in Villa Ventana is in this large, two-story, A-frame log house on the main road—which functions as a teahouse until dinner (served 9 to midnight). Choose from a large wine list and creative local delicacies such as *ciervo* (deer) and *trucha a la crema de almendras* (trout in an almond sauce). For starters, try the *tabla de fiambres y quesos,* a sampling of cold meats and cheeses served on a wooden board. ⊠ *Villa Ventana* ☎ *291/491–0047* ▭ *No credit cards.*

$$$ 🏨 **Estancia Cerro de la Cruz.** You cross a private bridge and follow a long,
Fodor's Choice winding dirt road through the countryside, past fields of sunflowers and
★ a creek, to get to this unforgettable family-owned estancia. The cozy, gabled, 1940s-era French-style mansion takes the B&B concept to another level. Disconnect from the urban world—there are no TVs (nor air-conditioning for that matter, although the heaters are splendid). The 6,000-acre site does come with a private mountain (Cerro de la Cruz), four full meals a day, access to a 4x4 Jeep to cover the terrain, and a full staff to cook and clean for you. Picnics can be arranged next to the river, where you can also fish. ⊠ *Off R72, 3 km (2 mi) north of Sierra de la Ventana* ✉ *Casilla de Correo #20, Sierra de la Ventana, 8168* ☎ *291/ 156–449–884 cell* ⇆ *5 rooms* ⚬ *Dining room, tennis court, pool, fishing, bicycles, bar, library* ▭ *AE, DC, MC, V.*

★ ¢–$ 🏨 **El Mirador.** The Lookout is nestled directly on the flats of the Sierras and is simply the best base for exploring the park. One- and two-floor cabañas, designed for four to eight people, come with full living rooms and unparalleled views. The main lodge has simple but very comfortable rooms (there's no air-conditioning, but at these heights, it's rarely a problem). The spacious complex has antique tractors displayed on a wide lawn out front. A restaurant by the same name is noteworthy and has a large, central stone fireplace. ⊠ *R76, Km 226, 8160* ☎ *291/ 494–1338* ⊕ *www.complejoelmirador.com* ⇆ *16 rooms, 4 cabanas* ⚬ *Restaurant, 2 pools* ▭ *AE, DC, MC, V* ⧖ *BP.*

Sports & the Outdoors

Horses are available to rent from individual owners at the side of the main road in Villa Ventana. For organized horseback riding tours, **Campo Equino** (⊠ R76, Km 230 ☎ 291/156–431–582 cell) is a professional stable that offers a choice of routes. In summer there are moonlight riding trips.

Club de Golf (⊠ Parque de Golf ☎ 291/491–5113) incorporates the town's two rivers, hills, and other natural obstacles into its 18-hole course.

Some of the land in the Sierras belongs to private ranch owners. **Estancia Funke** incorporates three mountain peaks, which you can access for a 5 peso entrance fee. **Geotur Excursiones** (⊠ Av. San Martín 198 ☎ 291/ 491–5355) arranges trips and tours (hiking and adventure sports) into the surrounding countryside.

Shopping

In summer there are crafts stalls set up beside the tourist office in Sierra de la Ventana, near the railroad tracks. Vendors sell everything from mate gourds (2 to 15 pesos) to wonderful, handmade gaucho knives.

CÓRDOBA & ENVIRONS

The province of Córdoba and its capital city of the same name have played a vital role in Argentine history. Before Buenos Aires became the country's hub, Córdoba served as an essential middle point between the Spanish in Peru and those in Spain. Gradually, Buenos Aires took over and left the province to its rolling hills and quiet lakes.

The city of Córdoba marks the center of the region; from here the hills spill out. A meandering drive through the mountain towns is a lovely way to spend a day or two—or an entire summer.

Córdoba

⓯ *710 km (426 mi) northwest of Buenos Aires.*

Córdoba is a testament to Spanish rule, with the best collection of surviving colonial buildings in Argentina. The Manzana Jesuítica (Jesuit Block), west of Independencia along cobblestone Obispo Trejo, is a block-long conglomeration of 17th-century buildings that was declared a UNESCO World Heritage Site.

Geronimo Luís de Cabrera was the first colonist to set foot in the city, in July 1573. His family was from Córdoba, Spain, and he named the town accordingly. In 1599 Jesuit priests arrived and established this as the center of their missionary work. The city soon became the cultural and intellectual hub of the country. Its national university, established in 1613, earned the city its nickname—La Docta, or the Learned.

Today Córdoba is the country's second-largest city (population 1.3 million) and the provincial capital. The heart of Córdoba is Plaza San Martín. In the middle of the square, an exuberant equestrian statue of General San Martín faces west, toward Pasaje Santa Catalina, which is a passageway between the city cathedral and the Cabildo Historico, or old city hall.

★ Córdoban poet Luís Roberto Altamira called the **Catedral de Córdoba** a "stone flower in the heart of the homeland." Construction began in 1577, though it wasn't until 1784 that the church was completed—which left a trail of disparate styles. Some of the more unusual architectural details are the musical angels on the Baroque front towers, sculpted by indigenous peoples in 1776, which bear the faces of their sculptors. ⊠ *Calle Independencia 64 at Plaza San Martín* ☎ *351/432–3446* ⊙ *Daily 8–noon and 4:30–8.*

On the western side of Plaza San Martín, the **Cabildo Historico** now functions as a cultural center. Construction of the long, two-story structure with arcades was begun in 1588 (excavated cells—including what was probably a prison—date from as early as the 17th century) but wasn't completed until the late 18th century. For more than 300 years, the wealthy residents gathered here to discuss town affairs. The upstairs Salón Rojo (Red Salon) is still used for official reception of dignitaries. The main floor houses an exhibition space, a café, a public library, a tourist office, and a city souvenir shop. A plaque in the Pasaje Santa Catalina alludes to a darker time in the building's history. It reads THE CABILDO FUNCTIONED, BEGINNING IN 1976 DURING THE MILITARY DICTATORSHIP, AS A CLANDESTINE CENTER OF DETENTION, TORTURE, AND DEATH. ⊠ *Calle Independencia at Plaza San Martín* ☎ *351/428–5856* ⊙ *Weekdays 9–9, weekends 9–8.*

★ A block east of Plaza San Martín is the **Casa de Marqués de Sobremonte,** former home of the Marquis de Sobremonte, a Córdoban governor in the mid-18th century. This is the city's oldest home, and the country's best example of colonial civic architecture. Over two floors are distributed 26 rooms, a chapel, and five courtyards. Rooms are furnished with period pieces, oil paintings, costumes, and old photographs. A tour of the home's labyrinthine corridors can lead your imagination back in time. ☒ *Rosario de Santa Fé 218, at Ituzaingó* ☎ *351/433–1661* ☒ *1 peso* ☉ *Jan.–Feb., weekdays 9 AM–1:30 PM; Mar.–Dec., Tues.–Fri. 10–4.*

★ **Compañia de Jesus** (Society of Jesus), the stone facade at the corner of the Manzana Jesuítica, is Argentina's oldest church, begun in 1640 and consecrated in 1671. Inside note the dome made of Paraguayan cedar that resembles an inverted ship's keel: the Jesuit brother Felipe Lemer who oversaw the work was a Belgian ship maker. From the Calle Caseros side of the church, you can enter the Capilla Domestica—a stunning chapel with a wood ceiling and copies of European paintings done in the 17th century by members of the Peruvian painting school. ☒ *Obispo Trejo at Av. Caseros* ☎ *351/423–9196* ☉ *Tues.–Sat. 10–11:30 and 5–7.*

★ **Córdoba Subterranea** (Underground Córdoba) is a fascinating series of spooky subterranean constructions, including old jail cells, dating to 1588. Guided tours leave from the Cabildo (you can purchase tickets at the Cabildo tourist office) and last a couple of hours. ☒ *Obispo Trejo at Av. Caseros* ☎ *351/423–9196* ☒ *5 pesos* ☉ *Daily at 9:30.*

Universidad Nacional de Córdoba (Córdoba National University), known for its production of psychoanalysts, is part of the historic Manzana Jesuítica. This building is the formal center of a sprawling campus—which in its heyday was said to have been as good as any in Europe. Graduates of the school became the doctors and lawyers who would run the fledging nation of Argentina, and some graduates became Catholic saints. Inside is a Jesuit library (closed to the public), which includes such rarities as a 1645 Bible written in seven languages. The interior patio contains a statue of Fray Fernando Trejo, who donated the money to build the university for Jesuit education in 1613. ☒ *Obispo Trejo between Av. Caseros and Av. Duarte Quirós.*

Next door to the Universidad Nacional de Córdoba, **Colegio Nacional de Montserrat** is a humanities school for children ages 10–17 that was first opened in 1687. Tradition reigns: note the small wooden desks the children use, and the photos of previous graduates. Many university professors teach here as well. Guided tours of the Manzana Jesuítica, including the university and the Colegio, are offered by the Compañia de Jesús. ☒ *Obispo Trejo at Duarte Quirós* ☎ *351/423–9196.*

☺ In Nuevo Córdoba, a southern part of the city, is the splendid **Parque Sarmiento.** Designed by French landscape architect Charles Thays, the park comprises a vast green container for a zoo, a lake skirted by palms and cypress where you can rent rowboats, an outdoor swimming complex, an amusement park, vast gardened zones, cafés, and wide lawns. ☒ *Av. Poeta Lugones and Av. Amado Sabattini (Ruta 9 Sur).*

In Parque Sarmiento's western corner, opposite Plaza España, is the city's leading contemporary art space, the **Museo Caraffa.** The austere 1916 neoclassical facade is deceptive: inside, two simple rooms exhibit a spry collection. ☒ *Av. Hipólito Hirigoyen 651* ☎ *351/433–3414* ☒ *Free* ☉ *Tues.–Sun. 11–7.*

Where to Stay & Eat

★ $$ ✕ **Alcorta Carnes y Vinos.** One of the top choices in town for steak, this restaurant along the Cañada canal takes it to another level. The room is elegant and refined with some hip, modern touches like a wide open, airy interior. The meat itself, including the *bife de chorizo* (sirloin), is simply excellent. Ask for it rare and it really comes rare, which is a welcome aberration in Argentina. Perhaps most impressive of all is the voluminous and consistently good wine list, which has offerings from all over Argentina, including some hard-to-find reds. The service is also some of the best in town—attentive and deferential without ever seeming in the way. Alcorta is a great choice for a long, indulgent, and impeccable meal. ⊠ *Alcorta 330 at Cañada and Santa Rosa* ☎ *351/4247916* ⊕ *www.alcortacarnes.com.ar* ▭ *AE, DC, MC, V.*

$–$$ ✕ **La Nieta'e La Pancha.** This relaxing, intimate little restaurant near the
Fodor'sChoice antique markets may just be the best place of all to try creative Cór-
★   doban food. The unassuming exterior gives way to a cozy room that's familial yet subtly upscale. You won't be disappointed by anything on the menu, which is written in the Córdoban dialect rather than Spanish. Local specialties done with flair include *cabrito* (roast kid) in cream sauce, peppers, and sweet potatoes, while *matambre* (roast pork) is served with a "tower" of eggplant, onions, and cheese. Most memorable is the river trout, from the nearby Rio Ceballos, with sauteed peppers and carrots in olive oil. The warm, rustic decor, soothing live guitar music, and friendly service all come together perfectly. ⊠ *Belgrano 783* ☎ *351/468– 1920* ▭ *AE, MC, V.*

¢–$ ✕ **Al Malek.** Tony Raphael, a Lebanese-American, runs this restaurant, which is a block from the Museo Caraffa in Parque Sarmiento. It's stylish with a youthful elegance—the varied color schemes, for instance, exhibit a flair largely absent in Argentine restaurants. *Picada Árabe* for two has hummus, eggplant, tabbouleh, empanadas, and stuffed grape leaves. The 20% discount for take-out orders makes Al Malek an appealing option for Sarmiento Park picnics. ⊠ *Derqui 255* ☎ *351/468– 1279* ▭ *No credit cards* ☉ *No lunch Mon. No dinner Sun.*

¢–$ ✕ **El Ruedo.** Relax on a colorful, tree-shaded outdoor sidewalk while watching the world go by in the Plazuela del Fundador. This traditional *confitería* (cafeteria) is one of the best spots to soak up the social nuances of Córdoban life. The food isn't the main attraction here, but *pizzetas* (individual pizzas) are only 2 or 3 pesos; there are also burgers, *lomitos,* and a full bar. ⊠ *Obispo Trejo at 27 de Abril* ☎ *351/422–4453* ▭ *AE, DC, MC, V.*

★ ¢–$ ✕ **La Imprenta Café, Vino y Letras.** This hip new café in the modern center of Córdoba is a two-floored, glass-and-metal, see-and-be-seen hotspot. Although many people come just to sip Segafredo coffee or Argentine wine (from a prominently displayed towering steel wine rack) and perhaps munch on a *medialuna,* there's also a menu of good Italian appetizers such as nouveau versions of bruschetta, including smoked eggplant and Roquefort. There are also meat and cheese plates, a tasty selection of grilled panini, and a great-value lunch special. Service is a bit aloof, but that's to be expected for a place this cool-conscious. Comfortable red chairs complete the airy atrium scene. ⊠ *Gral. Paz 156* ☎ *No phone* ▭ *AE, MC, V.*

$$ ▥ **Amerian Cordoba Park Hotel.** This business-style top-class hotel is located in the very center of modern Córdoba, across the street from the Patio Olmos, the city's biggest shopping mall, and within arm's length of all of the city's major sights. The amenities are all there, with rooms every bit as comfortable as you'd expect if you're paying these prices. ⊠ *Bv. San Juan 165, 5000* ☎ *351/420–7000* ▯ *351/424–5772* ⊕ *www.*

amerian.com 🛏 *150 rooms, 5 suites* ☄ *Restaurant, room service, in-room safes, minibars, bar, business services, convention center, meeting rooms, parking* ⊟ *AE, DC, MC, V.*

$$ 🏨 **Sheraton Córdoba Hotel.** Córdoba's five-star hotel rockets 16 floors of glass sleekness into Córdoba's skyline. The Sheraton provides the top level of service and amenities in the city, making it popular with business travelers. It's conveniently next to a big shopping mall, but it's a 15-minute walk (or 3-peso taxi) to historical downtown. Views over the city from the plate-glass windows in rooms on the upper floors are stunning. Prices on the Web site and in person can vary, so ask at the front desk about specials. ⊠ *Duarte Quirós 1300, 5000* ☎ *351/526–9000, 0800/888–3535 toll-free* 🖷 *351/526–9150* ⊕ *www.sheraton.com* 🛏 *183 rooms, 5 suites* ☄ *Restaurant, room service, in-room safes, minibars, golf privileges, tennis court, pool, gym, hair salon, 2 saunas, bar, business services, convention center, meeting rooms, free parking* ⊟ *AE, DC, MC, V.*

$–$$ 🏨 **Ducal Suites Hotel.** All rooms at the Ducal include a kitchenette (hence all the rooms are designated "suites"). If the hotel is guilty of overbilling itself, it does supply basic but tasteful rooms, with clean bathrooms. The extras, like a lobby Internet connection, are appreciated. ⊠ *Corrientes 207, 5000* ☎ *351/570–8800* 🖷 *351/570–8840* ⊕ *www.hotelducal. com.ar* 🛏 *82 suites* ☄ *Restaurant, room service, kitchenettes, pool, gym, sauna, bar, laundry service, business services, meeting rooms, free parking* ⊟ *AE, DC, MC, V* ¶⊚¶ *BP.*

¢ 🏨 **Martins Hotel Córdoba.** Although certainly not luxurious, Martins makes a good budget choice; rooms are comfortable and have central air-conditioning. Now, about all those plastic flowers. . . . ⊠ *San Jerónimo 339, 5000* ☎ *351/421–6091* 🖷 *351/421–8024* ✉ *dallas@cordoba.com.ar* 🛏 *20 rooms* ☄ *Bar, laundry service, travel services, free parking* ⊟ *AE, DC, MC, V* ¶⊚¶ *BP.*

Nightlife & the Arts

NIGHTLIFE **Café Novecento** (⊠ Cabildo) is a café and wine bar so cutting edge that it even has a branch in New York City. It's still Argentine, in spite of the Euro–new-age music, gaslights, and greenery in the airy, American-style space. A good daily selection of wines by the glass is scrawled across a chalkboard. The place couldn't be more central. **La Boquería** (⊠ Rondeau 452 ☎ 15/563–7068) is a tapas and wine bar that's one of the best places in town to sit down with the fruits of Argentina's vines. A good menu by the bottle or glass is served in a dim, relaxing environment. **Paris** (⊠ Independencia 417) is a super-cool bar with jazz echoing across the spectacular murals and multicolored walls. It's open Wednesday through Saturday; things don't get going here until about midnight.

Córdoba is known for its discos, where the action doesn't get going until 2 or 3 AM and continues well past dawn. The **Chateau** and **Cerro de las Rosas** (⊠ Rafael Nuñez) neighborhoods are current hotspots. **Shark** (⊠ Laplace 5675 ☎ 03543/444503), in the Villa Belgrano neighborhood, is a trendy place for drinking, relaxed dancing, and music, catering to a largely thirtysomething crowd. It's open Thursday through Saturday only.

Patio Olmos Hoyts (⊠ Av. Velez Sarsfield and Bv. San Juan ☎ 351/446–2444) has eight movie screens in the sleek Patio Olmos mall downtown; it's surrounded by restaurants and bars.

THE ARTS For dinner shows, head to **El Arrabal** (⊠ Belgrano 899 ☎ 351/460–2990 ⊕ www.elarrabal.com.ar), a restaurant and café with tango shows at midnight Thursday–Saturday, salsa (with lessons) Sunday night, and *milonga*—a sensual and risqué tango (with lessons)—weekdays. Built in 1891, the

Teatro Libertador San Martín (✉ Av. Velez Sarsfield 365 ☎ 351/433–2319) is the oldest operating theater in Argentina. Its exquisite five-tiered interior hall is home to performances of opera, music, ballet, and theater.

Sports & the Outdoors

BIKING **Bicitour** (✉ Rosario de Santa Fe 39, opposite Plaza San Martín ☎☎ 351/ 428–5600 Ext. 9159) runs popular bike tours of Córdoba. They leave from the Obispo Mercadillo information center. English-speaking tours run Tuesday–Saturday at 10:30 AM. Make reservations one day in advance (by 6 PM). Tours cost 8 pesos–10 pesos.

WALKING TOURS The **Cabildo Tourist Office** (✉ Cabildo ☎☎ 351/424–6605) sponsors personalized downtown walking tours (5 pesos in Spanish, 15 pesos in English). It also has a good selection of maps and brochures. English-language tours leave at 9:30 AM and 4:30 PM daily. To visit the Jesuit relics and estancias outside of town, ask the staff to recommend a driving tour.

BUENOS AIRES PROVINCE & CÓRDOBA A TO Z

To research prices, get advice from other travelers, and book travel arrangements, visit www.fodors.com.

AIR TRAVEL

The Aeropuerto de Mar del Plata (on R2, about five minutes outside the city) is the beach region's main airport. There are numerous daily flights year-round to and from Buenos Aires on Aerolíneas Argentinas, LADE, and LAPA. Note that this is a coveted route in summer, so make reservations early. LADE and LAPA fly to most major towns within the country, including Mar del Plata, Córdoba, Villa Gesell, and Bahía Blanca. Two companies provide service between Buenos Aires and Villa Gesell: Aerolíneas Argentinas and LAPA.

The city of Córdoba is served by Aeropuerto Internacional Ingeniero Aeronáutico Ambrosio Taravella. Although it's technically an international airport, it primarily provides connecting flights to major airlines in Buenos Aires as well as domestic flights. Aerolíneas Argentinas flies out of Córdoba and can provide a transfer on its own planes out of Buenos Aires to major hubs in the United States and Europe. Varig, a Brazilian airline, also serves the airport and can provide connections to Europe and the United States via its hubs in São Paulo and Rio.

🛫 Airlines & Contacts **Aerolíneas Argentinas** ☎ 11/4961–9361 in Buenos Aires, 223/ 496–0101 in Mar del Plata ⊕ www.aerolineas.com.ar. **LADE** ☎ 11/4361–0853 in Buenos Aires, 223/493–8220 in Mar del Plata. **LAPA** ☎ 11/4912–1008 in Buenos Aires, 223/492–2112 in Córdoba ⊕ www.lapa.com.ar. **Varig** ☎ 11/4342–4420 in Buenos Aires ⊕ www.varig.com.

🛫 Airports **Aeropuerto de Mar del Plata** ✉ Ruta 2, Km 396, Mar del Plata ☎ 223/ 495–1777. **Aeropuerto Internacional Ingeniero Aeronáutico Ambrosio Taravella** ✉ Camino a Pajas Blancas, Km 11, Córdoba ☎ 351/475–0242.

BOAT & FERRY TRAVEL

Boats are a good way to get around in the Tigre River delta. Fishermen may be willing to take you between coastal towns on their boats; arrangements can be made right at the pier, or your hotel can probably point you in the right direction.

BUS TRAVEL

Traveling by bus to the beach from Buenos Aires is very common. Every beach town has at least a bus stop, and many have a bus station or a bus ticket office in the center of town. Cóndor is a recommended service from Buenos Aires to La Plata and Mar del Plata. The bus from Buenos Aires to La Plata costs about 5 pesos one-way and takes 1½ hours. Buenos Aires to Mar del Plata takes about five hours and costs about 30 pesos. Each of the beach towns is connected by a local bus system.

For Pampas towns such as San Antonio de Areco, bus service is available on companies including Pullman General Belgrano and Chevallier.

For Córdoba, take the bus at the Retiro station in Buenos Aires. Urquiza/ Sierras de Córdoba is reliable for travel between Buenos Aires and Córdoba. From Córdoba, local bus companies can connect you with nearly every mountain town in the region. Most towns, however small, have some sort of bus stop or even a bus station. Remember that when traveling to some of the smaller towns, buses may only run once a day.

Chevallier ⊠ Smith and Gral. Paz, San Antonio de Areco ☎ 2326/453904. **Cóndor** ⊠ Terminal de Autobuses, Mar del Plata ☎ 223/451–2110 ⊠ Terminal de Autobuses, La Plata ☎ 221/423–2745. **Córdoba Terminal de Autobuses** ⊠ Bv. Perón 380, Córdoba ☎ 351/434–1694. **Pullman General Belgrano** ⊠ Segundo Sombra and Smith, San Antonio de Areco ☎ 2326/454059. **Urquiza/Sierras de Córdoba** ⊠ Terminal de Autobuses, Window 8, Córdoba ☎ 351/421–0711 ⊠ San Martín 450, Villa Carlos Paz ☎ 3541/427–777.

CAR TRAVEL

Driving is the best and most convenient option for getting to towns in the region. It's possible to rent cars in all the towns covered in this chapter. Localiza is an Argentine agency with branches in all the large towns and cities.

Car Rentals Avis ⊠ Airport, Córdoba ☎ 223/475–0815 ⊠ Airport, Mar del Plata ☎ 223/470–2100 ⊕ www.avis.com. **Dollar** ⊠ Libertad 3229, Mar del Plata ☎ 223/475–1279 ⊕ www.dollar.com.ar. **Hertz** ⊠ Airport, Córdoba ☎ 223/475–0581 ⊕ www.hertz.com. **Localiza** ☎ 0800/999–2999 toll-free ⊠ Av. Colón 194, Bahía Blanca ☎ 291/456–2526 ⊠ Airport, Córdoba ☎ 351/482–7720 ⊠ Córdoba 2270, Mar del Plata ☎ 223/493–3461 ⊠ Plaza Paso 63, La Plata ☎ 221/483–1145.

EMERGENCIES

Emergency phone numbers are nationwide, and most major hospitals have some English-speaking doctors.

Emergency Services Ambulance ☎ 107. **Fire** ☎ 100. **Police** ☎ 101.

Hospitals Hospital Interzonal Mar del Plata ⊠ Juan B. Justo 6800, Mar del Plata ☎ 0223/477–0265. **Hospital Municipal** ⊠ Diagonal José Maria Dupuy 1150, Miramar ☎ 229/142–0837. **Hospital Privado de Córdoba** ⊠ Av. Chacabuco 4545, Córdoba ☎ 223/499–0000.

MONEY MATTERS

ATMS Local banks in all towns have 24-hour ATMs; most banks are on either the NYCE or Cirrus systems.

SAFETY

When hiking, stay on marked trails. There are some rescue services, but they are not nearly as comprehensive as those in other countries. On beaches you should be careful of the unexpected: there's a good chance you'll be sharing the seemingly quiet beaches with off-road vehicles and the occasional wild horse or stray cow.

SIGHTSEEING TOURS

Córdoba City Tour runs a double-decker bus tour that covers a good portion of the city, including Sarmiento Park, La Cañada, and the downtown area; it's a quick way to get perspective on the entire metropolis. The English-language tour departs from in front of the cathedral daily at 11 AM and 5 PM; tours cost 9 pesos. Various day-long package trips to the Sierra de Córdoba are also available.

Nativo Viajes provides regional tours of Córdoba province and Stylo Viajes has van tours that take you out to various Jesuit sights in the area.
◪ **Córdoba City Tour** ☎ 351/446-9796. **Nativo Viajes** ✉ Av. Rafael Nuñez 4624 ☎▭ 351/481-6525. **Stylo Viajes** ✉ Av. Chacabuco 321 ☎▭ 351/424-6605 ⊕ www.stylocordoba.com.ar.

TELEPHONES

For long-distance calls, using a public phone with a phone card (which can be purchased at newspaper and tobacco stands) usually provides the best rates.

TRAIN TRAVEL

Several daily trains run from Buenos Aires to the Pampas, including the towns of Mar del Plata and Sierra de la Ventana. Fares to Mar del Plata range from 24 to 60 pesos round-trip, depending on class. Tickets can be bought at the train station or booked by phone. Within the Pampas, train service is limited. Buses are generally more reliable.
◪ **Estación de Trenes de La Plata** ✉ Corner of Calle 1 and Calle 44 ☎ 221/423-2575. **Estación de Trenes de Sierra de Ventana** ✉ Av. Roca s/n ☎ 291/491-5303. **Train tickets** ☎ 0800/222-8736 or 11/4304-0028.

VISITOR INFORMATION

In most of the beach towns, hotels are the best places to get information. Even if you're not a guest, almost every hotel will give you a map and point you in the right direction. Many tour agencies in Buenos Aires can help you make arrangements.
◪ **Córdoba** ✉ Cabildo, Deán Funes 15 ☎ 351/428-5856 ✉ Centro Obispo Mercadillo, Rosario de Santa Fe 39 ☎ 351/428-5600 Ext. 9159 ✉ Airport ☎ 351/434-8390 Ext. 9159 ✉ Bus Terminal ☎ 351/433-1982. **Mar del Plata** ✉ Bv. Marítimo 2400, Local 60 ☎ 223/495-1777.

THE NORTHEAST

ARGENTINE MESOPOTAMIA,
LITORAL & CHACO

FODOR'S CHOICE

Cataratas de Iguazú

Posada Aguapé, *Colonia Carlos Pellegrini*

San Ignacio Miní

Sheraton Internacional Cataratas de Iguazú

HIGHLY RECOMMENDED

El Charo, *restaurant in Puerto Iguazú*

Hostería del Puerto, *Colón*

Hostería Puesta del Sol, *Soberbio*

Hotel Cataratas, *Puerto Iguazú*

Hotel Internacional Quirinale, *Colón*

Hotel Presidente, *Presidencia Roque Sáenz Peña*

Hotel Puerto Sol, *Gualeguaychú*

La Aventura, *resort in Posadas*

La Plaza, *restaurant in Colón*

La Rueda, *restaurant in Posadas*

Rich, *restaurant in Rosario*

Saltos de Moconá (Moconá Falls)

Tropical das Cataratas, *hotel in Foz do Iguaçu*

Updated by
Diego
Bigongiari

IN THE NORTHEASTERN PART OF THE COUNTRY, between the Paraná River to the west and Brazil and Uruguay to the east, are the provinces of Entre Ríos, Corrientes, and Misiones—collectively known as Mesopotamia because they are framed by the Paraná and Uruguay rivers (Mesopotamia translates into "between the rivers" in Greek). These two enormous rivers start in Brazil and converge near Buenos Aires in the Río de la Plata, which empties into the Atlantic Ocean. The Argentine Litoral refers mainly to the agriculturally rich province of Santa Fe, lying west of the Paraná River. The northern Litoral merges into the Chaco region, which extends through the provinces of Chaco and Formosa westward into the Andean region and northward into the Paraguayan Chaco.

The provinces of the Northeast have little in common. Entre Ríos is a region of rolling hills very similar to neighboring Uruguay, with beaches along the banks of the Paraná and Uruguay rivers. Lagoons and marshland dominate Corrientes. Misiones, carpeted by subtropical jungle, has several minor mountain chains. Southern and central Santa Fe resemble the Pampas region. The provinces of Chaco and Formosa are marked by flatlands often so dry that human existence here is nearly impossible. The Northeast is a rural region with no large cities and with very small provincial towns—most of which seem abandoned during the lengthy siesta period that starts around noon and lasts until 4 or 5. The natural surroundings are the real attraction—in the numerous kinds of plants and animals and the abundance of waterfalls, especially in Misiones. The most famous are the Cataratas del Iguazú, the breathtaking set of 275 falls that plummet more than 200 feet.

Sights of historical significance include the former home and the numerous monuments to General Justo José Urquiza, the first constitutional president of Argentina, in Entre Ríos. Also scattered throughout the region are the ruins of Jesuit missions, remnants of the remarkable society that thrived from 1610 until 1767. San Ignacio Miní, the most frequently visited Jesuit site, is fairly well conserved and has been partially reconstructed; other missions, however, have not been repaired and aren't as easily visited because getting around this region can be difficult. But this means that if you do get to these out-of-the-way sights, you'll most likely have them all to yourself.

Exploring the Northeast

One problem in exploring this region is that the notable sights are generally far apart, often with very little of interest in between them. This is especially true to the west, in the provinces of Chaco and Formosa. If time is an important factor, stick to the province of Misiones, which has the greatest concentration of noteworthy destinations. Buses, the most common form of transport in the region, run regularly and are very comfortable. Some destinations have airports, but flights can be inconsistent. If you're just going to Misiones, it's easiest to take one of the regular flights between Buenos Aires and Posadas or Cataratas del Igauzú.

About the Restaurants

It seems as if every menu in the region has been photocopied from the same source—only the prices differ. Almost every restaurant serves *pastas caseras* (homemade pastas), typical Argentine *asados* (barbecued meats), and grilled river fish, most notably *surubí* (a regional fish) and *merluza* (hake). In this region of famously long siestas, lengthy, leisurely lunches are eaten around noon or 1. Dinner is eaten quite late, often not until 11 or even midnight. Reservations are rarely necessary.

About the Hotels

Lodging tends to be expensive in relation to the quality of service and facilities provided, and there are few decent mid-price accommodations. Unless otherwise specified, all hotels listed have rooms with private bathrooms, telephones, and color television with cable, as well as complimentary breakfasts.

WHAT IT COSTS In Argentina Pesos				
	$$$$	$$$	$$	$	¢
RESTAURANTS	over 35	25–35	15–25	8–15	under 8
HOTELS	over 300	220–300	140–220	80–140	under 80

Restaurant prices are for one main course at dinner. Hotel prices are for two people in a standard double room in high season.

Timing

If you don't like the heat, don't go to Chaco, Corrientes, or Misiones in summer (December–March). Entre Ríos, however, is most popular in January and February, when Carnaval takes place, and it's the best time for the beach. Esteros del Iberá is best June–September when more wildlife is visible, though most species can be seen year-round. The waterfalls of Saltos de Moconá are generally more spectacular December–July, though they could disappear at any time, depending on the weather. The Cataratas del Iguazú are always breathtaking, though you can save considerably by not coming in high season (November, December, July, and Easter). During this time, reservations are recommended all over the region, often up to a month in advance.

ENTRE RÍOS

Straddled by the Río Paraná (Paraná River) to the west and the Río Uruguay to the east, this province has been fairly isolated from the exterior. The lack of significant contact with the rest of the country is apparent in the reserved disposition of the province's population, most of whom are descendants of French, German, Spanish, Polish, Russian, and Italian immigrants. The province's isolation, however, did not prevent many *Entrerrianos,* as its inhabitants are known, from playing decisive roles in the country's fight for liberation from the Spanish in the early 1800s. In fact, native Entrerriano general Justo José de Urquiza (1801–70) became Argentina's first constitutional president in 1853; you'll see monuments to him all over the province.

With the construction in the 1970s of several bridges connecting Entre Ríos to Uruguay and the building of South America's only river tunnel, connecting the region to the province of Santa Fé, the area's physical isolation ended. And with the advent of MERCOSUR (a free-trade agreement signed by Argentina, Brazil, Uruguay, and Paraguay in 1991), Entre Ríos became an important trade crossroads for products going to and coming from Uruguay and Brazil. It also significantly boosted its own exports—most notably beef, poultry, citrus fruits, rice, and lumber. Tourism is also another source of income: in summer (December–March), many *Porteños* (Buenos Aires locals) and other Argentines come to these tranquil towns to spend the weekend on the riverfront beaches and to attend the celebrated carnivals.

Numbers in the text correspond to numbers in the margin and on the North-east map.

If you have 5 days

Make the 🏛 **Cataratas del Iguazú** ㉑, the spectacular falls on the border of Argentina and Brazil, your main focus. Allow at least three days to see the falls from both the Argentine and Brazilian sides, taking advantage of such activities as boat rides past the falls and hikes through the surrounding jungle. You can stay near the falls or in the close-by town of 🏛 **Puerto Iguazú** ⑳. On the fourth day take the three-hour bus ride or drive south to 🏛 **Posadas** ⑫. Spend the night there, using it as a base to explore the ruins of the Jesuit missions **San Ignacio Miní** ⑭, **Nuestra Señora de Loreto** ⑮, and **Santa Ana** ⑯. On the fifth day return to the Cataratas del Iguazú.

If you have 7 days

Spend three days at the 🏛 **Cataratas del Iguazú** ㉑, staying near the falls or in 🏛 **Puerto Iguazú** ⑳. On the fourth day drive or take the bus two hours to see the main Jesuit ruin, **San Ignacio Miní** ⑭. Later that day, take a bus or drive to **Posadas** ⑫; you can arrange to be picked up by one of the *posadas* (inns) in 🏛 **Esteros del Iberá** (most of the inns are in 🏛 **Colonia Carlos Pellegrini** ⑩). Your options are many: take a boat trip through the wildlife-rich marshlands or scuba dive in the crystal-clear waters. On the seventh day head back to the Cataratas del Iguazú.

If you have 10 days

Go to the 🏛 **Cataratas del Iguazú** ㉑ for three days, staying near the falls or in 🏛 **Puerto Iguazú** ⑳. On the morning of the fourth day, take the somewhat long bus or car ride to the tiny town of 🏛 **Soberbio** ⑱. Spend a day and a night in the charming posada there while you arrange your journey by land or sea to the spectacular **Saltos de Moconá** ⑲. Be sure to find out the waterfalls' condition before you go—when the water level is high, the falls disappear completely. On the morning of the sixth day, take the bus or drive to 🏛 **Posadas** ⑫. Here you can arrange (through your posada) to be taken to the **Esteros del Iberá** (most of the inns are in 🏛 **Colonia Carlos Pellegrini** ⑩). On the ninth day head back to Posadas. On the morning of the tenth day, head back to Cataratas del Iguazú, stopping for a few hours on the way at **San Ignacio Miní** ⑭.

Gualeguaychú

❶ *220 km (136 mi) north of Buenos Aires.*

Gualeguaychú, which translates into "river of the large jaguar" in native Guaraní, was founded in 1783 by the Spanish. It's Entre Ríos's most popular summer vacation destination, in part because of its proximity to Buenos Aires. It's also the southernmost and the largest of the Corredor del Uruguay, the chain of riverside towns running along the eastern border of the province.

Most of the town's action centers on the Costanera, the street running along the narrow Río Gualeguaychú. Restaurants, bars, arcades, clothing shops, and artisan stands line the street. It's particularly lively on summer weekends, when the benches fill with young and old alike sipping yerba mates and watching the world go by.

The big draw on weekends from the end of January to the end of February is Carnaval. Though not in the same league as the large Brazilian carnivals, Gualeguaychú's is considered Argentina's best. Twice a weekend, revelers flock to the enormous *corsodromo* (⊠ Avs. Rocamora and Parque Cándido Irazusta), a long strip of pavement with bleachers on both sides, for celebratory performances. The impressive productions, with large casts, music, garish costumes, and elaborate floats, all conform to that year's Carnaval theme.

The large, concrete **Catedral San José** (San José Cathedral), with its two imposing towers, dominates the town's central square, the Plaza San Martín. In 1863 General Urquiza, who was at the time the governor of the province, sponsored the cathedral's construction. Despite some signs of decay, its ornate interior is still an impressive sight; one of its most noteworthy features is an organ made of 2,200 pipes. ⊠ *Plaza San Martín* ☎ *Free* ☉ *Daily 9:30 AM–11 AM and 6 PM–11 PM.*

In 1898 the **Instituto Magnasco** (Magnasco Institute) became the country's first library to be founded by women. In addition to the thousands of old and rare books, the library also contains 16th-century Jesuit statuary, antique furniture, a collection of weapons from World War I, and temporary exhibits by the region's most prominent artists. ⊠ *Camila Nievas 78* ☎ *3446/427287* ☎ *Free* ☉ *Weekdays 10–noon and 4–8, Sat. 10–noon.*

> **need a break?**
>
> Stop in at **Bahillo** (⊠ Costanera 154 ☎ 3446/426240), an ice cream parlor that is very popular among locals.

Where to Stay & Eat

Hotels, campgrounds, bungalows, and cabanas handle the large crowds that descend on the town on summer weekends. You can also go through the tourist office to find families that will put you up in their homes for around 15 pesos per night.

$ ✕ **Pizzeria Piamonte.** This popular spot on the Costanera serves delicious pan pizza with a thick crust and extra cheese. Dining outdoors—on the softly lighted patio with a fountain in the middle—is quite pleasant. ⊠ *San Lorenzo 282* ☎ *3446/428462* ⊟ *MC, V.*

$ ✕ **Restaurant-Parrila Dacal.** This genuine Argentine grill house is unpretentious and friendly. Outdoor tables, which face the Costanera, are better. ⊠ *Andrade 252* ☎ *3446/427602* ⊟ *AE, MC, V.*

$ 🛏 **Hotel Aguay.** Despite some kitschy details, this small hotel has a lot going for it—for starters, it's the most comfortable in town. The hotel overlooks the river and the Costanera—note that rooms in the front get a lot of street noise on weekends. ⊠ *Av. Costanera 130, 2820* ☎ *3446/42209* ⊕ *www.hotelaguay.com.ar* ⇨ *18 rooms, 2 suites* ⚷ *Restaurant, room service, minibars, pool, gym, bar, laundry service, Internet* ⊟ *AE, DC, MC, V.*

★ $ 🛏 **Hotel Puerto Sol.** To go with the name, Hotel Sun Port, this place is decorated entirely in yellow and blue. Right off the Costanera, it has comfortable, attractively decorated rooms, many with river views. The hotel is small, so make reservations up to a month in advance, especially during Carnaval weekends. ⊠ *San Lorenzo 477, 2820* ☎ *3446/434017* ⊕ *www.puerto-sol.com.ar* ⇨ *20 rooms* ⚷ *In-room safes, bar, business service, Internet* ⊟ *AE, DC, MC, V.*

3

Fishing

On nearly every town's *Costanera* (riverside walkway) you find people stationed with fishing poles in hand and fresh catches by their feet. The region's rivers, primarily the Paraná and Uruguay, offer some of the country's most challenging and fruitful fishing. The *manguruyú* (another type of regional fish) caught here can weigh well more than 200 pounds and the surubí as much as 125 pounds. The real prize, however, is the famously feisty *dorado* (golden fish), the subject of a national fishing competition that takes place every August in the town of Paso de la Patria in Corrientes; here you'll find several inns that organize fishing tours. In general, the best time for fishing is between September and March.

Yerba Mate

This herbal infusion has long been an integral component of not only the region's diet but also its culture. The Guaraní introduced the herb to the Jesuit missionaries, who learned to cultivate it. Yerba mate here is much like tea in England; it often serves as the basis of social interaction: people drink it at almost any hour of the day, and it's often extended to strangers as a welcoming gesture. Typically, ground-up yerba mate leaves are placed in a carved-out gourd. Then hot water from a thermos is added, sometimes accompanied by a spoonful of sugar. You drink the infusion through a metal tube with a filter at the bottom. When the drink is finished, the gourd is refilled with hot water and is passed to the next person in line. In the provinces of Corrientes and Misiones, the nation's largest yerba mate–producing regions, it's not uncommon in public places to find an enormous kettle containing hot water with which to fill your thermos to make the drink.

¢ 🏨 **Hotel Alemán.** From the outside this hotel, one of the city's oldest, resembles a Bavarian chalet. Rooms, while simple, are clean and comfortable, and many are centered on a nice, plant-filled patio. It's right near the bus station in the center of town. ⊠ *Bolívar 535, 2820* ☎ *3446/426153* 🛏 *24 rooms* ⚴ *Bar, meeting room* 🚫 *No credit cards.*

Nightlife & the Arts

The popularity of bars and clubs changes seasonally, but many of the best are along the Costanera. **Bikini** (⊠ Costanera and 25 de Mayo ☎ 3446/435610) is generally a happening spot in the evenings. If you don't mind a late night show (starting at 3 AM!) in a very crowded place, reserve table at **El Ángel** (⊠ San Lorenzo 79 ☎ 3446/434927 ⊕ www. elangelgualeguaychu.com.ar) to see a rather nonprovincial burlesque show by drag queens and transvestite performers. The few theater productions and classical music concerts in town usually take place at the **Teatro Gualeguaychú** (⊠ Urquiza 705 ☎ 3446/431757).

Sports & the Outdoors

Gualeguaychú has a number of ***balnearios*** (riverfront beaches with facilities) within walking distance of town, most with a thin strip of sand. The beaches get very crowded on summer weekends and holidays. On the Río Gualeguaychú are two notable and very similar balnearios: **Costa Azul,** on the northern end of town, and **Solar del Este,** slightly farther north. Both have camping facilities, food stands, and all kinds of sports facilities. The largest, most popular, and most developed bal-

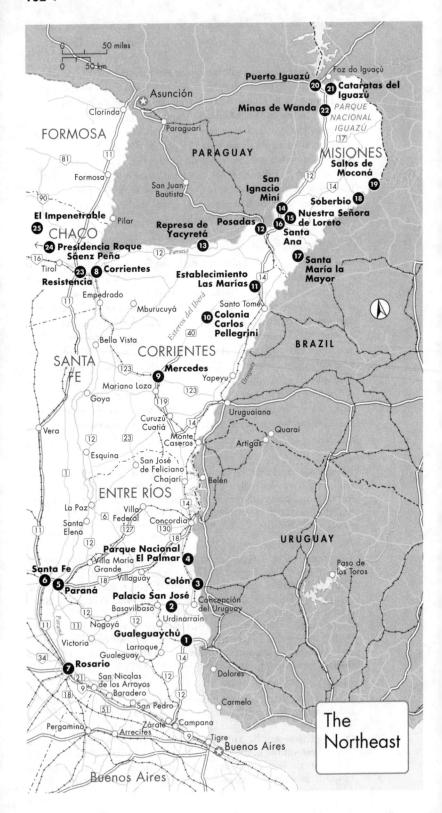

neario is Ñandubaysal, 15 km (9 mi) east of town on the Río Uruguay (you'll need to take a bus from the bus station or a taxi ride for 10 pesos). Here you'll find a campground, horseback riding, a wide variety of water sports, bars, and a supermarket; to organize activities or rent tents, go to the information desk in the main complex. Fishing boats can be rented for about 40 pesos per day per person at **Costa Azul** (☎ 03446/423984). **La Cabaña de Carlitos** (✉ at Ñandubaysal balneario) has sailboats for about 10 pesos per hour. **Solar del Este** (☎ 3446/433303) also rents boats for fishing excursions.

Shopping

Several artisan and souvenir shops along the Costanera carry baskets, leather goods, tapestries, and yerba mate gourds. On summer weekends craftspeople often sell their wares on Plaza Colón, at the southern end of the Costanera. The widest selection of crafts is found at **El Gaucho** (✉ San Lorenzo 346 ☎ No phone). **El Patio del Mate** (✉ Gervasio Méndez and Costanera ☎ 3446/424371) carries a wide selection of mate gourds and other handicrafts.

Palacio San José

❷ *70 km (43 mi) southwest of Colón, 35 km (22 mi) west of Concepción del Uruguay.*

This stately residence, constructed between 1848 and 1857, was once the home of General Urquiza and is now one of the most significant historical monuments for Entrerrianos, though Urquiza was never liked very much by Buenos Aires. The enormous pink palace—with 31 rooms, a chapel, elaborate courtyards, and extensive gardens—brings together colonial and Italian Renaissance styles. It was here that Urquiza and two of his sons were assassinated by political enemies. His assassin was killed years later in the streets of Buenos Aires. Unfortunately most of the valuable coins and silverware were stolen and never recovered. The entrance fee includes an hour-long guided tour; the guides don't speak English, but there are explanatory signs in English. ✉ *Off R39* ☎ *3442/432620* 💰 *3 pesos* ⊘ *Weekdays 8:15–12:45 and 2–6, weekends 9–6.*

Colón

❸ *44 km (27 mi) north of Concepción del Uruguay, 70 km (43 mi) northwest of Colón, 320 km (198 mi) north of Buenos Aires.*

Along this riverside corridor of quaint little towns, Colón outdoes them all. With its pretty beaches a few blocks from the town center, thermal baths, and fully equipped spa, it's one of the best places in the region to spend a few days relaxing. It's also close to the Parque Nacional El Palmar and Palacio San José. The friendly, easygoing residents—most of whom are descendants of Swiss, French, and Italian immigrants who were offered land for agrarian pursuits—also make the town pleasant.

Founded in 1863, Colón served as a port from which farmers could ship products such as rice, oranges, and poultry to the rest of Argentina and other countries. During World War II the town experienced great prosperity as it became a major exporter of grain and meat to Europe. After the war, as demand declined, the economic situation deteriorated, and many residents flocked to Buenos Aires.

Colón's **Aguas Termales** (Thermal Baths) have several pools, an excellent view of the river, and a snack bar. The water, which surges from nearly a mile below the surface, is said to contain many health-enhancing elements; at 93°F, it's warm but not extremely hot. ✉ *La Valle and Savatier* ☎ *No phone* ⊘ *Daily 8–midnight.*

Where to Stay & Eat

Dining is not one of Colón's highlights, and its restaurants' menus differ little from one another; the majority of eateries are found on Urquiza between the central plaza and the river.

Hotels in Colón, however, are rather impressive in terms of quality: though there aren't many to choose from, three are highly recommended (make reservations well in advance for summer weekends). Besides hotels, there are campgrounds, cabanas, and bungalows, which are good for families and groups.

★ ¢–$ ✕ **La Plaza.** This elegantly run-down house, one of the town's oldest, once belonged to Colonel Lezcano, General Urquiza's accountant. These days it's a restaurant—a great spot for lunch or dinner. Opt for one of the tables on the shady sidewalk, overlooking Plaza San Martín. The special "tourist menu" includes an appetizer, entrée, and dessert for about $8. Or you might try the succulent *pollo cristóbal* (chicken in orange sauce served with rice). The restaurant, though always open weekends, closes erratically on weekdays, so call ahead. ⊠ *12 de Abril and Alejo Peyret* ☎ *3447/424037* 🖃 *AE, DC, MC, V.*

¢–$ ✕ **Viejo Almacén.** Come here for a good sampling of river fish, pasta, and steak. There's nothing fancy about this restaurant, though it's nicer than the name "Old Warehouse" suggests. ⊠ *Urquiza and Paso* ☎ *3447/422216* 🖃 *AE, MC, V.*

★ $$–$$$ 🏨 **Hotel Internacional Quirinale.** This enormous riverside hotel offers a level of comfort and number of facilities unparalleled along the rest of the Corredor del Uruguay. Many of the large, modern rooms have spectacular views of the river. Rooms are simply decorated, mostly in beige tones or pastels, but all furnishings are of the highest quality. You must pay to use the hotel's spa, but the pool, gym, and tennis court are free. ⊠ *Av. Quiroz 185, 3280* ☎ *3447/421133* ⊕ *www.hquirinale.com.ar* ➟ *168 rooms, 14 suites* ⌂ *Restaurant, room service, minibars, golf privileges, tennis court, 2 pools, health club, hair salon, massage, sauna, spa, bar, casino, laundry service, meeting room* 🖃 *AE, DC, MC, V.*

$ 🏨 **Hotel Palmar.** You may be reminded of a scene from an old western when you walk into the lobby of this hotel several blocks from the river, with its shiny saloon, deer heads on the walls, dark wood paneling, and classic iron-railed stairs. Rooms have three classifications: "modern" rooms have a basic chain hotel feel and large bathrooms; "special modern" rooms are the largest, most luxurious, and most expensive; and "colonial" rooms have a more classical style, with decorative wrought-iron headboards. Ask to see all three types to decide which suits you best. ⊠ *Bv. Ferrari 295, 3280* ☎ *3447/421952* 🖶 *3447/421948* ⊕ *www.hotelpalmar.com.ar* ➟ *37 rooms* ⌂ *Restaurant, room service, pool, bar, laundry service, Internet* 🖃 *AE, MC, V.*

★ ¢ 🏨 **Hostería del Puerto.** The old-fashioned furnishings and vibrant colors of the colonial patio and lobby of Colón's oldest hotel define charming. All rooms have memorable views of the river and consist of two floors that can easily fit up to five people. Rooms are 20% off from Sunday to Thursday, making this a great weekday bargain. ⊠ *Alejo Peyret 158, 3280* ☎ *3447/422698* 🖶 *3447/421398* ✐ *hosteriadelpuerto@ciudad.com.ar* ➟ *10 rooms* ⌂ *Restaurant, bicycles, bar, laundry service* 🖃 *No credit cards.*

Nightlife

Nightlife in Colón is very limited. **Café del Teatro** (⊠ 12 de Abril 338 ☎ No phone) is an old standby for coffee or drinks. You can always pursue your fortunes at the **Hotel Internacional Quirinale Casino** (⊠ Av. Costanera and Noailles ☎ 3447/421133). The only true dance club is

Kaiman (✉ Evita and Lugones ☎ No phone). **Moment's Music Bar** (✉ 12 de Abril 167 ☎ 3447/422932) is a popular watering hole.

Sports & the Outdoors

Along the banks of the Río Uruguay are five *playas* (free, undeveloped beaches). The beaches' yellow-tinted sand isn't as soft and abundant as ocean sand, but does provide a comfortable spot to lie down and bury your feet. All the beaches have jet-skiing, kayaking, and windsurfing. The largest, **Playa Norte**, is at the north end of town. It has a campground and is the only beach with restaurants; on summer weekends it gets very crowded. Closest to the center, on the south side of town, is **Balneario Piedras Colorados**, named for its reddish-color stones; it also has a camping area. Farther south are three smaller beaches: **Balneario Inkier, Playa Nueva** (the prettiest), and **Playa Honda**. All are either within walking distance or a short taxi ride away.

You can best appreciate Río Uruguay by boat. **Ita i Corá** (☎ 3447/423360 ⊕ www.itaicora.com) has a stand near the entrance to Hotel Internacional Quirinale at Costanera and Noailles, and organizes two different boat trips: one (1½ hours, 15 pesos) goes to an interesting sandbank formation; the second trip (3½ hours, 35 pesos) also includes a stop at a deserted island, on which you take a short hike through the vegetation. Ita i Corá also arranges land safaris by four-wheel-drive vehicles: the three-hour trip (20 pesos) includes visits to an old mill, a semiprecious-stonecutting workshop, and sand dunes. You can also arrange bird-watching tours.

Golf Club Colón (✉ Camino Costera Norte ☎ 3447/421858), next to the hot springs, has nine holes and a nice view of the river. Unlimited play costs 10 pesos, and clubs are available to rent.

Shopping

Alpaca sweaters, baskets, wood statues, semiprecious stone jewelry, ceramics, and other crafts by more than 70 local artisans can be found in the **Centro Artesanal La Casona** (✉ 12 de Abril 106 ☎ No phone), an old colonial building in front of Plaza San Martín. It's open weekdays 7 PM–11 PM and weekends 9–1 and 7–11.

Parque Nacional El Palmar

❹ *50 km (31 mi) north of Colón.*

This 21,000-acre national park was created in 1966, primarily to protect the extraordinary Syagrus yatay palms, which grow up to 50 feet and have been known to live for up to 800 years. At the turn of the last century, these palms covered vast portions of the province as well as Brazil and Uruguay, but agriculture, cattle raising, and forestry in the 20th century rendered them nearly extinct. The visitor center has a small museum detailing the park's flora and fauna. Ask the park ranger for a map of the two short trail walks. One trail starts at the visitor center and ends at the beach, passing ruins of a house built in 1780. The other, a circular path about 1 km (½ mi) long, starts at the campground, which is just down the hill from the visitor center, cuts through the subtropical forest, and passes by Arroyo Los Loros, a tranquil stream along which you are likely to see viscachas and iguanas. You may also spot fox, deer, and capybaras, the world's largest rodent (though they're a less common sight). In the morning and at sunset, a wide variety of birds such as *ñandus* (rheas), egrets, and herons abound. You could easily spend a few hours in the park. There are good paths for bicycles, though no rental shops. Next to the visitor center are a restaurant and campground (reservations aren't necessary). ⊠ *Off R14* ☎ *3447/493049 or 3447/493053* 🎟 *12 pesos* ⊙ *Park 24 hrs; visitor center daily 8–8.*

ALONG THE RÍO PARANÁ

Along the lower part and the southern shores of the enormous Río Paraná, between Buenos Aires and Rosario, lies the heartland of industrial Argentina. North of the traditional Spanish colonial town of Santa Fe, hundreds of miles of lagoons and marshes can be found along the river.

Paraná

❺ *255 km (158 mi) west of Colón, 450 km (279 mi) northwest of Buenos Aires.*

Though it had been the Argentine Confederation capital from 1853 to 1861, Paraná nowadays has the feel of a quintessential provincial town. Small, quiet, clean, and self-contained, the city stands on the heights of impressive hills (up to 250 feet high) above a bend in the Río Paraná. Its provincial temper is due to the insularity of the Entre Ríos Province and its Mesopotamic sisters Corrientes and Misiones. The Túnel Subfluvial (subfluvial tunnel) between the city and Santa Fe has done much to connect Paraná and Entre Ríos Province to the Argentine "mainland," but it has not changed the quiet pace or the locals' accent, much less the proud and long-standing friendly rivalry with Buenos Aires and the Porteños.

Paraná was founded in 1730 by Spanish families from nearby flat and damp Santa Fe, who appreciated the hilly region not only for its climate and views but also as a place to defend themselves against attacks by the indigenous population. Before the nearby city of Rosario was developed, Paraná served as the main inland port of the country, and in the mid-19th century, under the rule of Urquiza, enjoyed prosperity. Urquiza invited American navigators to explore the rivers, German farmers to tend the land, and Italian architects to build the first government buildings, still visible today. Decades later, many Jewish settlers from Poland, Russia, and elsewhere developed agricultural colonies in the province of Entre Ríos, as well as Santa Fe. Though much of this population later emigrated to Buenos Aires, Paraná is still home to an important Jewish community.

Any city visit should start at the **Plaza 1 de Mayo** (May 1 Square), which is surrounded by the Italian-style cathedral, the over-the-top towered town hall, and other late-19th-century buildings. At the southwest corner of the square, the **Café Plaza** is a focal point of city life.

Lining the **Plaza Alvear** are some fine buildings, a church, and two museums—a fine arts museum, with little of interest, and a history museum. The **Museo Histórico de Entre Ríos** (Entre Ríos History Museum; ⊠ Buenos Aires 285 ☎ 343/420–7869) is interesting only for its collection of finely crafted, elaborate silverware. It's open Tuesday–Friday 7:30–12:30 and 3–7, Saturday 5–7, and Sunday 9–noon; admission is 1 peso. To get to Plaza Alvear, walk downhill on the *peatonal* (pedestrian-only) San Martín, which, though very commercial and lively, has little charm.

The large **Casa de Gobierno** (Government House), on Plaza Carbó, just a block away from Plaza Alvear along Avenida Rivadavía, is an eclectic mix of classical Italian and French styles.

In a country of flat squares and parks, the **Parque Urquiza** is all the more beautiful for its hills and curves. Along the river you'll find beaches, nautical clubs, and the old abandoned river port. The elegant **Monumento al General Urquiza,** which is cast in bronze and depicts the general astride his horse, was crafted by Catalonian sculptor Agustín Querol. To get to the park, walk four blocks northwest along Avenida Rivadavía from the Government House.

Where to Stay & Eat

$ ✕ **La Fourchette.** What this hotel restaurant lacks in atmosphere (no windows), it more than makes up for with its refined dishes and haute-cuisine exercises that dress up old-fashioned French cuisine with Argentine touches. Try the surubí with lemon or basil sauce. It's also one of the few places in town where you can order saltwater fish. ⊠ *Gran Hotel Paraná, Urquiza 976* ☎ *343/422–3900* ☐ *AE, DC, MC, V.*

$ ▥ **Gran Hotel Paraná.** This hotel facing the square has three price ranges to match the different quality of the rooms, built at different times. All rooms have standard, uninspired modern-hotel decor, but the rooms facing the square are the best option. ⊠ *Urquiza 976, 3228* ☎ *343/422–3900* ⊕ *www.hotelesparana.com.ar* ⇄ *120 rooms* ⌂ *Restaurant, golf privileges, bar, laundry service, business services* ☐ *AE, DC, MC, V.*

$ ▥ **Hotel Casino Mayorazgo.** All the rooms in this large and modern hotel have great views overlooking the park and the river. Though somewhat run-down, these are still the most luxurious accommodations in town. The casino here lost much of its business when gambling establishments became legal in Buenos Aires and the surrounding area in the 1990s. ⊠ *Avs. Etchevehere and Miranda, 3228* ☎ *343/423–0333* ⊕ *www.mayorazgohotel.com* ⇄ *123 rooms* ⌂ *Restaurant, golf privileges, pool, gym, bar, casino, laundry service, business services* ☐ *AE, DC, MC, V.*

¢ ▥ **Paraná Hotel Plaza Jardín.** Right behind the cathedral, this old hotel has a charming 19th-century Italianate facade, a covered patio, and rooms that turn out to be small, simple, and compressed into a labyrinth of stairs and corridors. All and all this is a good-value, friendly place. ⊠ *9 de Julio 60, 3228* ☎ *343/423–1700* ⊕ *www.hotelesparana.com.ar* ⇄ *63 rooms* ⌂ *Restaurant, meeting room, Internet* ☐ *AE, DC, MC, V.*

Shopping

Leather, mate gourds, ceramics, and formidable caranday-palm baskets from Villaguay can be found at **Centro de Artesanos** (⊠ 9 de Julio y Carbó ☎ 343/422–4493). A must for those interested in the national (and provincial) beverage is the small but unique **Museo del Mate** (⊠ A. Crespo 159 ☎ 343/422–0995), a shop run by Francisco Scutellá, a craftsman who also makes mate gourds and is perhaps the richest living source on the matter.

Santa Fe

❻ *30 km (19 mi) west of Paraná, 475 km (295 mi) northwest of Buenos Aires.*

Founded in 1573 at Cayastá, Santa Fe was moved 80 km (50 mi) south in 1651 to its present location. During the civil wars following Argentina's independence from Spain, the local *caudillo* (provincial dictator) Estanislao López fiercely fought against Buenos Aires for two decades, making this agriculturally rich Litoral province a counterbalance, together with Córdoba, against Porteño power. The first Argentine constitution was drafted in Santa Fe in 1853, and subsequent constitutional amendments, such as the 1994 change that allowed President Menem to run for a second term, traditionally have been ratified here.

Set on flat ground between the huge Lake Setúbal and a tributary of the Río Paraná, Santa Fe, with its low buildings and lack of trees on its older streets, is very much a traditional Spanish colonial town. A pleasant coastal promenade along the lake extends north toward residential neighborhoods. To the south lies the city's **main square**, with a massive, French-style **Palacio de Gobierno** (Government Palace); a rather humble, old **cathedral** (a new cathedral was started 10 blocks away at Plaza San Martín, but was never finished); and the oldest church in town, the late-17th-century **Nuestra Señora de los Milagros** (Our Lady of Miracles).

More interesting than the collection inside the **Museo Histórico Provincial** (Provincial History Museum) is the 17th-century structure itself, a rare colonial adobe house. Inside you'll find the usual old furniture, paintings, and other items of family life in colonial times, plus an exhibit with life-size plaster figures re-creating the 1853 drafting of the constitution. ⊠ *San Martín 1490* ☎ *342/459–3760* 🖅 *1 peso* ⊙ *Tues.–Fri. 8:30–noon and 2:30–7:30, weekends 4–7.*

The sober stone-and-adobe 17th-century **Iglesia y Convento de San Francisco** (Church and Convent of St. Francis) is remarkable for its wooden ceiling and cupola—no nails!—and its religious imagery, also carved from wood. Here you can visit the tomb of the caudillo Estanislao López, with an epitaph by dictator Juan Manuel de Rosas that sounds bizarre inside a church: LONG LIVE THE ARGENTINE FEDERATION! DEATH TO THE SAVAGE UNITARIANS! ⊠ *Amenábar 2557* ☎ *342/459–3303* 🖅 *Free* ⊙ *Mon.–Sat. 8–noon and 4–7:30, Sun. 9–noon and 4–7.*

Inside a neocolonial building, the **Museo Etnográfico y Colonial** (Ethnographic and Colonial Museum) displays archaeological findings from the first foundation of Santa Fe at Cayastá as well as artifacts related to everyday life in colonial times. ⊠ *25 de Mayo 1470* ☎ *342/459–5857* ⊙ *Tues.–Fri. 8:30–noon and 3:30–7, weekends 4–7.*

Where to Stay & Eat

¢–$ ✕ **La Rural.** In a town of many fine parrilla and pasta restaurants, La Rural is the most renowned. The house is proud of its surubí *al paquete* (wrapped and cooked in paper) and grilled pacú. Only available weekends and worth trying are the *cabrito* (goat) and *lechón* (roasted suckling pig). It's on the property of the local Sociedad Rural, where one of the first cattle ranches of the region operated. ⊠ *Bv. Pellegrini 3300* ☎ *342/453–2908* 🖃 *AE, DC, MC, V.*

$ 🏨 **Hotel Río Grande.** This rather characterless hotel is the newest and best choice out of the uninspired business hotels in the city. With meeting rooms and some business services, the hotel attracts many businesspeople and politicians. ⊠ *San Gerónimo 2580, 3000* ☎ *342/450–0700* 🛏 *87 rooms* ⚬ *Restaurant, business services, meeting room, Internet* 🖃 *AE, DC, MC, V.*

Rosario

❼ *320 km (198 mi) northwest of Buenos Aires.*

Rosario enjoys a reputation as a smaller, friendlier, less neurotic version of Buenos Aires. But small it's not: Argentina's second-largest city (on par with Córdoba) is home to more than 1 million people and serves as an important river port and commercial center. And Rosario utilizes the Río Paraná far better than Buenos Aires. Summer weekends, riverside Rosario is pure diversion: its beaches are crowded and the boat station is chock-full of men and women in swimsuits carrying picnic baskets, preparing for a day on the river's islands. This is also an academic town, famous for its university, poets, and writers.

Founded in 1730 by families fleeing attacks by the indigenous population in Santa Fe, Rosario has great cultural and historical significance for Argentina as the first place the nation's flag was raised (a monument stands on the site). A short walk away, the port area, La Fluvial, serves as the departure point for river excursions.

The colossal **Monumento a la Bandera** (Monument to the Flag) commemorates the location (the river's bank used to be here) where, at 6:30 PM February 27, 1812, General Belgrano raised Argentina's flag for the first time. A picture of the monument, which was built between 1936 and 1957, is on the 10 pesos bill. Don't leave the city without taking the elevator to the top; the views are remarkable—a vast, modern city of high-rises cut off by the serpentine Paraná gives way to an expanse of flat, green, uncorrupted land. ⌧ *Av. Belgrano between Calles Córdoba and Santa Fé* ☎ *No phone* ☞ *1 peso* ☉ *Mon. 2–7, Tues.–Fri. 9–12:30 and 2–7, weekends 9–7.*

The narrow greens of the wonderful **Parque Urquiza** begin near La Fluvial boat dock and follow the riverbank. A stream of joggers flows back and forth—on a nice weekend it seems like all the healthy people in Argentina are here exercising. In the center of the park are a carousel and cafés; a planetarium within the park is open weekends at dusk.

The modern **Centro Cultural Parque España** (Spanish Park Cultural Center), designed by Oriol Bohigas, stands out as an uncommon bit of architecture in Rosario. Overlooking the river, the building has impressive brick walls, an imposing outdoor staircase, huge columns, and cypresses in the courtyard. It often exhibits the work of local and Spanish artists. ⌧ *Sarmiento, at the Río Paraná* ☎ *0341/426–0941* ☞ *1 peso donation requested* ☉ *Tues.–Sun. 3–8.*

The beautiful **Parque Independencia** (⌧ Starts at Avs. Carlos Pellegrini and Moreno) houses a soccer stadium, a racetrack, a small theme park, a rose garden, and a museum. A small postmodern square in the downtown area has a large **mural of guerrilla leader Che Guevara** (⌧ Tucumán and Mitre), who was born in Rosario, though he never lived here. The **Museo Municipal de Bellas Artes Juan B. Castagnino** (Juan B. Castagnino Municipal Museum of Fine Arts), within Parque Independencia, displays a small number of European paintings and an interesting collection of renowned Argentine artists. ⌧ *Av. Carlos Pellegrini 2202* ☎ *341/480–2542* ☞ *1* ☉ *Mon. 4–9, Wed.–Sun. 4–9.*

Where to Stay & Eat
Rosario has contributed, however dubiously, to a gastronomic phenomenon: all-you-can-eat restaurants line Avenida Pellegrini shoulder-to-shoulder, trying to outdo each other in gargantuan decor and exuberant amounts of food. These places, especially on weekends, are ever so popular.

\$–\$\$ ✕ **Escauriza.** This simple, riverside parrilla has been around for some 30 years and enjoys a good reputation among Rosarinos. In addition to grilled meats, you can order river fish such as pacú. ⌧ *Bajada Escauriza and Paseo Ribereño* ☎ *341/454–1777* ▭ *AE, DC, MC, V.*

★ **¢–\$** ✕ **Rich.** Homemade pasta, rice-based dishes, poultry, meat, seafood, and memorable breaded frogs make up the most interesting menu in town. Throw in an excellent wine list, efficient table service, and an elegant but unpretentious atmosphere and you can understand the popularity of this traditional restaurant, established in 1932. ⌧ *San Juan 1031* ☎ *341/440–8657* ▭ *AE, DC, MC, V.*

¢–\$ ✕ **Terrasa's Munich.** This relaxed and popular *chopería* (an informal eatery) sits near La Fluvial at the base of Parque Urquiza, where you can enjoy a view of the Flag Monument. It serves mainly homemade pizzas and sandwiches. ⊠ *Avs. Libertad and Colón* ☎ *0341/424–0812* ⊟ *AE, DC, MC, V.*

$$–$$$ ▦ **Holiday Inn.** Glass elevators shoot you up 20 floors from the sleek lobby of this luxury hotel. The exercise room on the top floor almost qualifies as a tourist attraction itself: the views of the city and the river are even better than from atop the Flag Monument. There's also a great pool deck. Rooms—some with whirlpool tubs—are bright and clean. ⊠ *Dorrego 450, 2000* ☎▭ *0341/410–0000 or 0800/222–1010* ⊕ *www.holidayinnrosario.com* ↬ *100 rooms, 12 suites* ⌂ *Restaurant, room service, in-room data ports, in-room safes, minibars, pool, gym, sauna, 2 bars, laundry service, business services, convention center, meeting rooms, Internet* ⊟ *AE, DC, MC, V* �📷 *BP.*

$$ ▦ **Hotel Garden.** Most rooms have views of the garden surrounding the property. Standard rooms, done mostly in white, are somewhat small— there's not much space beyond the beds. Suites, separate from the main building, offer a little more leg room and a few more pieces of furniture, including a more comfortable work station and/or separate sitting area. ⊠ *Callao 45, 2000* ☎ *0341/437–0025* ▭ *0341/437–1413* ⊕ *www.hotelgardensa.com* ↬ *50 rooms, 20 suites* ⌂ *Restaurant, pool, bar, laundry service, meeting room, business services* ⊟ *AE, DC, MC, V.*

$ ▦ **Hotel Libertador.** This hotel is part of small chain, not unlike a standard American motel chain, which means that you expect comfortable, modern, cookie-cutter rooms with small work stations. There's a buffet breakfast. ⊠ *Corrientes 752, 2000* ☎ *341/424–1005* ▭ *341/424–1005* ⊕ *www.solans.com* ↬ *72 rooms, 17 suites* ⌂ *Restaurant, room service, bar, laundry service, meeting room* ⊟ *AE, DC, MC, V* �📷 *BP.*

Boat Trips

La Fluvial (☎ 0341/447–3831) is the departure point for almost all boat trips. Weekdays, boats leave the clean, efficient station for Vladimir and Oasis islands every 20 minutes from 9 AM to dusk (the former, generally speaking, draws a younger crowd and the latter a family crowd). In summer there are nightly dinner catamaran cruises.

The ship **Ciudad de Rosario** (☎ 0341/449–8688) hosts weekend dinner cruises up the river, departing from in front of the Flag Monument weekends 2:30 and 5.

CORRIENTES & MISIONES

The province of Corrientes is dominated by the marshy wetlands of Iberá, which cross the territory and connect the Río Paraná with itself 400 km (248 mi) downstream—thus creating a huge natural cushion for floods. The high plains of the eastern side of the province turn into hills in the north, close to Misiones. The notoriously proud Correntinos, many of whom are descendents of the first Spanish settlers, are said to have more allegiance to their province than to Argentina. Correntinos also tend to be fiercely political: party colors are worn daily and even painted on tombstones, making for colorful cemeteries.

The small, banana-shape province of Misiones juts out from the Argentine mass, surrounded by Paraguay to the east and Brazil to the west. Nowhere else in Argentina is there such a gorgeous subtropical landscape: the lush, green vegetation stunningly contrasts with the rich red tones of the soil, and three minor mountain chains give texture to the forest. The region also has an abundance of waterfalls—the most famous are the Cataratas del Iguazú, but the lesser-known ones such as the Saltos de Moconá are almost as spectacular.

Though nature is the main attraction, Misiones is also known for its Jesuit mission ruins. The Jesuits, who came here in the early 17th century, were the first in a long line of foreigners to make their home in this province. After Misiones split off from Corrientes in the 1880s, the provincial government, in order to promote agricultural production, offered very cheap land to those wanting to immigrate here. The result was that people came in large numbers from all over—Switzerland, Germany, Poland, Lithuania, France, Italy, Spain, and even Japan—giving the province a great ethnic diversity.

Corrientes

8 *858 km (536 mi) north of Buenos Aires, 310 km (192 mi) west of Posadas.*

Corrientes was established in 1588 by Spanish conquistador Juan Torres de Vera y Aragón as a strategic strong point on the river Paraná—near the river's junction with the Paraguay River, the waterway to Asunción del Paraguay, the main conquistador settlement in the region. This is perhaps the least Argentine and most "tropical" of the provincial capitals—its Guaraní influences are strong as is its feeling of autonomy (Correntinos like to speak of an imaginary "República de Corrientes"). Unfortunately, corruption among its politicians has led the town and province into a deep economical crisis, which shows in the ruinous state of the city's streets and the lack of good accommodations. However, there is inexplicably a new and flamboyant casino by the riverside park.

The Costanera or Riverside Drive, lined partly with jacaranda trees, is the town's most attractive side, with a tiny yacht club, half a dozen parrillas, and a couple of trendy bars. The "old town" can be seen by taking a stroll around 25 de Mayo Square; facing the square is the nicest church in town, **Iglesia de la Merced**, built by Italian architect Nicola Grosso. The area surrounding the square is lined by run-down government buildings, a statement on the state of public affairs in "Corrientes Republic."

Carnaval is high time in Corrientes, with a more popular and less produced version of Gualeguaychú's festivities: thousands of Correntinos and Chaqueños crowd the local **Corsódromo** (Avenida Centenario at Reconquista) to watch murgas, the Argentine version of Rio's escolas do samba.

off the beaten path

SAN JUAN PORIAHÚ – This is one of the most remarkable cattle ranches in the region, on 40,000 acres of land near Esteros del Iberá. You can spend the night in the main house, a former Jesuit chapel, which now holds five bedrooms with private baths. Ask for Marie Laure Gall when calling. ☎ *011/4311–0838 or 011/5031–0070 in Buenos Aires.*

Where to Stay & Eat

$ ✕ **Parrilla Restaurant El Mirador.** Dine on the standard Argentine fare, including surubí river fish at this lively and crowded grill. Try to get one of the outdoor tables, which are right by the riverside. ⊠ *Costanera y Edison, Corrientes* ☎ *3783/461806* ▤ *AE, DC, MC, V.*

¢ ✕▥ **Hostal del Río.** This budget hotel has small rooms with small windows, but it's the cheapest way to get a room with the view of the Paraná. ⊠ *Plácido Martínez and Avenida Italia, Corrientes* ☎ *3783/436100* ↴ *70 rooms, 1 suite* ⚬ *Restaurant, pool, gym, business services, meeting room* ▤ *AE, DC, MC, V.*

¢ ✕▥ **Hotel de Turismo.** Facing the Costanera, this old and bit rundown California-style hotel has a popular restaurant and a convenient location. ⊠ *Entre Ríos 650, Corrientes* ☎ *3783/429112 or 3783/433174* ↩ *47 rooms, 3 suites* ⚼ *Restaurant, pool, gym, business services, meeting room* ▤ *AE, DC, MC, V.*

¢ ▥ **Corrientes Plaza Hotel.** The best hotel in town is old and conventional, and its small inner rooms are standard motel-issue with little charm. The hotel faces Cabral Square. ⊠ *Junín 1549* ☎ *3783/421346* 🖷 *3783/ 466500* ⊕ *www.hotelplazactes.com.ar* ↩ *110 rooms, 3 suites* ⚼ *Restaurant, room service, pool, gym, meeting room* ▤ *AE, DC, MC, V.*

Nightlife & the Arts

Beyond a few blocks along the Costanera, where people of all ages dwell until late in places like **Cristóbal Café** (⊠ Edison and Costanera), Corrientes nightlife consists of a few pubs and discos for the very young crowd—or for adult males in search of any sort of paid company.

The most intriguing side of Corrientes's culture is a rather underground and very un-Catholic superstition: San La Muerte (Saint Death) is revered by many locals (they believe he brings good luck in love and other endeavors) and his likeness is carved in different materials, including human bone. Not the easiest souvenir to find, you may start by asking your taxi driver to help you find wooden San La Muertes, which are sometimes carved at the local prison near the bridge.

Sports & the Outdoors

Amazing fly-casting for huge dorado fish can be done with **Guarapo Fly Cast** (☎ 011/4311–0838 or 011/5031–0070 in Buenos Aires ⊕ www. guarapo.com.ar). Organized tours include accommodations on a remote 4,000-acre river island in "luxury" tents, complete with electricity and hot showers. Champagne dinners are served by firelight.

Mercedes

❾ *350 km (217 mi) northwest of Colón.*

Apart from a pleasant square in the center, this tiny town offers nothing in the way of beauty and only one tourist attraction: the colorful cult site of Gaucho Gil, a local version of Robin Hood, by the R123 just west of town (red flags mark the spot where police supposedly killed Gil). You have to pass through the town on the way to Esteros del Iberá and destinations to the north. There are no recommendable hotels, so plan on stopping here for as short a time as possible.

Colonia Carlos Pellegrini & the Esteros del Iberá

❿ *192 km (119 mi) northeast of Mercedes, 870 km (539 mi) northeast of Buenos Aires.*

The 3-million-acre Esteros del Iberá marshland covers nearly 20% of Corrientes Province. It's made up of more than 60 *lagunas* (lagoons), some of which are crystal clear, thus the name Esteros del Iberá ("brilliant waters" in native Guaraní). The lagoons interconnect in a labyrinthine formation, which some consider to be one enormous lake because the lagoons are separated only by masses of floating vegetation. It's in this vegetation that the true beauty of the Esteros del Iberá is found: a spectacular mix of water lilies, hyacinths, red ferns, and irises makes a colorful home for many forms of wildlife and birds. The 368 species of birds that live here include storks, flamingos, blue and purple herons, red cardinals, and several varieties of eagles. On a typical two- or three-hour boat trip (arranged through any posada in the village of Colonia Carlos Pellegrini), you'll also see capybara, alligators, and *ciervo del los pantanos* (marsh deer) and, perhaps, though less likely, *aguará guazú* (maned wolf), *lobito de río* (neotropical otter), and *venado de las pampas* (pampas deer), which are in danger of extinction because they've been heavily hunted for their pelts over the years. In order to protect the wildlife and the fragile ecosystem, the provincial government declared this a natural reserve in 1983.

The capital of the Esteros del Iberá is the tiny village of Colonia Carlos Pellegrini. Here you'll find the park's **information center**—there's no phone or address, but a park ranger is here 24 hours a day. The small museum in the information center has displays on the marshland and its animal and plant life. A short path leads from behind the center into the forest, where you may run across a family of friendly and curious howler monkeys.

Where to Stay & Eat

Most hotel rates include a boat trip on the lake, a hike, and all meals. Note that with the exception of Parrilla Restaurant, there's nowhere to eat other than at the inns and lodges, which serve a mix of local and international cuisine. You must pay extra for English-speaking guides (generally about 50 pesos per day), horseback riding (8 pesos per hour), fishing trips (50 pesos for four hours), and ground transportation to the towns of Mercedes or Posadas (round-trip 150 pesos and 300 pesos, respectively). To preserve the rustic atmosphere, none of the hotels have televisions.

$$$$ ✕🖻 **Posada Aguapé.** The two guest houses of this handsome inn in
Fodor'sChoice Colonia Carlos Pellegrini, next to Laguna Iberá, are built in typical
★ Corrientes style—long one-story buildings with white-plaster walls and metal roofs supported by large wooden posts—with unique touches of eucalyptus branches, palm trunks, and handicrafts incorporated into the design. The original guest house has four medium-size rooms with a direct view of the lake. The eight rooms in the newer guest house are larger and more elaborately furnished. The price includes meals—delicious and plentiful combinations of local and international favorites. ⊠ *For information contact: Coronel Obarrio 1038 (San Isidro), Buenos Aires, 1642* 🕾🖷 *11/4742–3015* ⊕ *www.iberalaguna.8k.com* 🛏 *12 rooms* △ *Restaurant, fans, pool, dock, boating, horseback riding, recreation room, business services, Internet* ▭ *No credit cards* ⊠ *FAP.*

$$$$ ✕🖻 **Posada de la Laguna.** This inn is nearly identical to Posada Aguapé, and it's practically next door, also with direct access to Laguna Iberá. The lovely grounds contain a pool, an indoor restaurant serving international cuisine, and one guest house. The comfortable guest rooms are fashionably rustic. Owner Elsa Güiraldes lives on the premises. Several package deals include transportation to and from Posadas or Mercedes. ⊠ *Colonia Carlos Pellegrini, 3471* 🕾 *3773/499413, 3773/15–629827 cell* 🖃 *posadadelalaguna@ibera.net* 🛏 *6 rooms* △ *Restaurant, fans, pool, dock, boating, horseback riding* ▭ *No credit cards* ⊠ *FAP.*

$$$ ✕🖻 **Estancia Rincón del Diablo.** This extensive cattle ranch with its own landing strip sits on the edge of Laguna Itatí. Guest quarters are reasonably large and comfortable, though blandly decorated. The real draw is the natural surroundings: the crystal-clear lake provides perfect conditions for scuba diving (equipment is provided), sportfishing, and kayaking. You can also go horseback riding or hiking. The room rate includes all of these activities (except scuba diving and more extensive fishing trips), all meals, and transportation to and from Mercedes, 60 km (37 mi) south. ⊠ *Av. Atanasio Aguirre, Km 1, Mercedes, 3470* 🕾 *3773/420103* 🖷 *3773/420247* ⊕ *www.rincondeldiablo.com.ar*

🛏 *7 rooms* ⚒ *Restaurant, golf privileges, pool, dock, boating, fishing, horseback riding, business services, Internet* ▤ *AE, DC, MC, V* ⦿| *FAP.*

$$–$$$ ✕⊡ **Hostería Ñandereta.** Rooms are very comfortable, with simple wooden interiors and checkered curtains and bedspreads, at this large stone-and-log house, which resembles an alpine ski lodge. In the cozy lobby, animal hooves hang from the wooden walls. The friendly, helpful staff speaks English. Note that the hotel, which is in the village of Colonia Carlos Pellegrini, doesn't have direct access to the lagoon, but its private dock is only a short drive away. ⊠ *Colonia Carlos Pellegrini, 3471* ☏ *3773/499411, 3773/420155 in Mercedes* ⦿ *www.nandereta. com* 🛏 *9 rooms* ⚒ *Restaurant, fans, pool, dock, snorkeling, horseback riding* ▤ *MC, V* ⦿| *FAP.*

Establecimiento Las Marías

⓫ *150 km (93) mi northeast of Colonia Carlos Pellegrini via R40, R41, and R14; 135 km (83 mi) south of Posadas via R12 and R38 (R105 and R14 are a shorter distance, but slower because of traffic).*

The yerba tree, from which the popular yerba mate herbal infusion comes, requires a type of soil found only in the northeastern tip of Corrientes, much of Misiones, and vast regions of Brazil and Paraguay. Several *yerbatales* (yerba plantations) and processing plants can be found throughout this region. Establecimiento Las Marías, owned by one Argentine family for four generations, is the largest; it grows and processes popular, high-quality yerba from January to September, and tea year-round. It's also a model enterprise, providing for its workers with on-premise schools and a hospital. A guided tour of the plantation, in Spanish and sometimes in English (reserve ahead), includes a visit to the main house, where yerba leaves are dried and processed, and the vast, lovely park with its lagoons and flowers. As you drive along R14 toward Las Marías, look for the low, green, and neatly trimmed *tesales,* interspersed with the taller, gray, and less beautiful *yerbales* as well as large pine and gumtree forests. ⊠ *R14, Km 739, 15 km (9 mi) south of Gobernador Virasoro* ☏ *3756/493000 Ext. 309 or 222* ⦿ *www.lasmarias.com.ar* ▧ *Free* ◷ *Weekdays 8–5.*

Posadas

⓬ *200 km (124 mi) northeast of Colonia Carlos Pellegrini, 1,060 km (657 mi) northeast of Buenos Aires, 310 km (192 mi) east of Corrientes.*

One of the first Jesuit missions in the area, Reducción Nuestra Señora de la Encarnación de Itapúa was established in 1615 at Posadas, which is now the capital of Misiones Province. The mission later moved across the Río Paraná to present-day Encarnación, Paraguay. The area that is now Posadas was later occupied by Paraguayan troops, who used it as a base for doing commerce with Brazil. During the War of the Triple Alliance (1865–70), Argentina took possession of the land and the valuable stockpile of Brazilian products and christened the town Posadas. Of the wave of immigrants who came to the area in the late 19th century, many settled in Posadas. Today many descendants of these immigrants still live here, giving the town of nearly 250,000 a more cosmopolitan feel than other provincial capitals in the region. The tree-lined streets, plazas, and Costanera make the town very pleasant, though there's actually little to do. It's primarily a base for exploring other sights in the area, most notably the Jesuit mission ruins.

Before you visit the Jesuit mission ruins, it helps to get some background at the **Museo Arqueológico Andres Guacurari** (Andres Guacurari Archaeology Museum). You can learn about the unique society created by the missionaries and see objects found at the missions, such as ceramic tiles, a printing press, clothing, a Bible translated into Guaraní, and wooden statues of Christ. ⊠ *General Páz 1865* 🎫 *Free* ⊙ *Daily 8–11 and 3–6.*

Where to Stay & Eat

★ $ ✕ **La Rueda.** There's no better place in town for a "running spit" and a "free fork." Less literally translated, *espeto corrido* and *tenedor libre* mean all-you-can-eat meat and salad. The enormous 30-year-old restaurant is a true town establishment. As suggested by the name, there's a wheel motif that pervades everything from the shape of the ceiling to the chairs. Although the restaurant is a bit outside town, the excellent quality of the meat and the very reasonable prices make it a good dining option. ⊠ *Juan Manuel de Rosas 6380* ☎ *3752/454111* ▤ *MC, V* ⊙ *No dinner Sun.*

¢–$ ✕ **El Oriental.** Depending on how long you've been in the region, you may be desperate for a change of cuisine: this is as exotic as it gets. The Chinese food here won't knock you off your feet, but it's generally good and quite inexpensive. Beware: in this carnivorous country, even the spring rolls have meat. ⊠ *Junín 2168* ☎ *3752/430586* ▤ *DC, MC, V.*

$ 🏨 **Julio César.** Though the hotel doesn't quite live up to its reputation as the most luxurious accommodation in town (the rooms have shoddy rugs and peeling paint), its location is ideal, and the hotel's facilities are excellent. Note that the superior rooms cost 15 pesos more than standard rooms and are only slightly nicer. ⊠ *Entre Ríos 1951, 3300* ☎ *3752/427930* 🖶 *3752/420599* ⟿ *100 rooms, 5 suites* ⚭ *Restaurant, room service, minibars, pool, gym, bar, laundry service, meeting room, Internet* ▤ *AE, DC, MC, V.*

★ $ 🏨 **La Aventura.** The 30 small cabañas set on stunning grounds have the feel of a far-away weekend resort, yet they're only 15 minutes from town. There's a fantastic view of the Río Paraná, just below. You can sunbathe on the small strip of beach or by the large pool. The cabañas are clean and modern and have kitchenettes. ⊠ *Avs. Urquiza and Zapiola, take Av. A. Guacurari from north end of town due west to Av. Urquiza, 3300* ☎ *3752/465555* ⟿ *30 cabañas* ⚭ *Restaurant, room service, kitchenettes, 2 tennis courts, pool, beach, fishing, volleyball, 2 bars, business services* ▤ *AE, DC, MC, V.*

¢ 🏨 **Le Petit Hotel.** This small hotel, really more of a house, six blocks from the town center, is the best bargain in town. Picasso prints hang in the lobby and halls, and the modest-size guest rooms are cozy and well maintained. ⊠ *Santiago del Estero 1630, 3300* ☎ *3752/436031* ⟿ *10 rooms* ⚭ *Restaurant, Internet* ▤ *No credit cards.*

Nightlife

At the **Casino Club** (⊠ San Lorenzo 1950 ☎ 3752/428686) you can gamble the night away. You can dance to the best of the '60s, '70s, and '80s at **Cesare** (⊠ Entre Ríos 1951 ☎ 3752/427930), in the Hotel Julio César. The hip bar **Mentecato** (⊠ San Lorenzo 1971 ☎ 3752/428380) has live music every Saturday night and Internet access. **Vitrage** (⊠ Bolívar 1887 ☎ 3752/429619) is a classy, upscale bar with outdoor seating in front of the central plaza.

Shopping

Everything from clothes to electronics comes over from cheaper Paraguay and can be found daily at the **Mercado de las Villenas** (⊠ Av. Roque Sáenz Peña between Sarmiento and Santa Fe).

Represa de Yacyretá

⑬ *90 km (56 mi) southwest of Posadas.*

Though it's not especially beautiful, the enormous, modern Represa de Yacyretá (Yacyretá Dam)—one of the world's largest—on the Río Paraná is an impressive sight. The dam stretches 1½ km (1 mi) across the river and measures 67 km (42 mi) in total extension. If the containing wall were to break, it would flood Buenos Aires, roughly 1,100 km (682 mi) away, to the equivalent of eight stories high. Approximately 52,500 cubic feet of water per second pass through 20 gigantic turbines, each 46 feet in diameter. Presently the dam is only working at 50% efficiency. The project has been a study in corruption and inefficiency: construction started in 1983, and projected costs were $1.5 billion; today it's still not completed and has already cost more than $11 billion. Free guided tours, which last about an hour, take place four times daily. Some guides speak English. From Posadas you must take an hour-long bus ride to Ituzaingo, where a taxi can take you to the nearby *relaciones publicas* (public relations) building. Inside are models, posters, and a 20-minute video. Here you meet the guide and catch the minivan to the dam. Tours leave at 9, 11, 3:15, and 4:30. ☎ *3786/420050 information.*

San Ignacio Miní

⑭ *59 km (37 mi) northeast of Posadas.*

Fodor'sChoice
★

San Ignacio Miní is the best-preserved and most frequently visited of the Jesuit missions ruins. The mission was originally established in 1610 in Guayrá, a region of present-day Brazil. Seeking refuge from Portuguese slave traders who were raiding the mission, capturing the native populations living there, and selling them in Brazil, the mission relocated to a spot near the Río Paraná in 1632. In 1695 it moved again, 3½ km (2 mi) away, to where its ruins are today. At its height, in 1733, the mission had more than 3,300 Guaraní inhabitants; there were never more than three Jesuits at any one time.

The mission's layout was typical of others in the region: a school, a cemetery, a church, and living quarters surrounded a central green. Where it stood out was in its dedication to music and the arts. This was one of the first music conservatories in the region, and the precision with which instruments were constructed and played here gained the mission fame throughout the New World and Europe. The facade of the church provides an excellent example of the stellar artwork created here: both the Jesuits and Guaranís sculpted Hellenic columns and traditional Guaraní images into the red sandstone.

Shortly after the expulsion of the Jesuits in 1767, the mission was abandoned and left to the jungle. In the 1940s, however, the National Commission of Historic Monuments began restoring the mission: what you see today is a mixture of the original buildings and new construction. One aspect that cannot be reproduced is the surrounding environment: the jungle was gradually cut down as the town of San Ignacio sprang up, and now ugly brick buildings peek behind the ruins, and a mess of restaurants and artisan shops line the outside walls. It's most likely that you'll just stop in San Ignacio for a few hours. Hour-long guided tours (in Spanish) are available throughout the day and are included in the admission fee. Each day after dusk there's a sound-and-light show. The small museum contains a model of the mission, original tiles, and various metal objects unearthed during the restoration. ⊠ *Off R12, San Ignacio* ☎ *3752/470186* 🎫 *2.50 pesos* ⊙ *Daily 7–7.*

Where to Stay

¢ 🏨 **Hotel San Ignacio.** The only option for an overnight stay in the area is this inexpensive hotel four blocks from the ruins. The majority of lodgers are young backpackers, and the facilities cater to this crowd: a bar, paddleball court, and recreation room with two pool tables and old arcade games. The four simple, clean cabañas all have two rooms and can sleep four to five people. The hotel usually fills up by late afternoon, so it's a good idea to make a reservation. The only phone is the public one in the lobby. ⊠ *San Martín 823, San Ignacio, 3322* 🕾 *3752/470047* 🖷 *3752/470422* ⇆ *4 cabañas* ⚴ *Bar, recreation room* 🚱 *No credit cards.*

Nuestra Señora de Loreto

🕒 *9 km (6 mi) south of San Ignacio Miní, 50 km (31 mi) northeast of Posadas.*

The history of this Jesuit mission is very much intertwined with that of San Ignacio Miní. They were founded near each other in the same year by the same Jesuits, and they migrated together in 1632 from what is now Brazil to the Río Paraná area. The mission moved around several more times before ultimately arriving at its final location in 1686. Because of its great economic productivity, Nuestra Señora de Loreto was one of the most important missions in the region. It was a major supplier of yerba mate and cloth to other parts of the Spanish colony and had extensive cattle-ranch land. When demand for yerba mate declined during the mid-18th century, the mission successfully turned much of its efforts toward rice farming. Nuestra Señora de Loreto also obtained widespread fame around 1700 for its printing press, one of the first in the New World: this enabled the mission to publish numerous books, especially the Bible, in the native Guaraní language.

In 1731 the mission reached its maximum number of inhabitants: close to 7,000 Guaranís. However, most left in the years following the Jesuits' expulsion in 1767. Those who remained were forced to move away in 1817 by the Paraguayans, who were trying to seize large parts of Misiones Province. After evacuating the inhabitants, the Paraguayans set fire to the entire mission, and for this reason little of it exists today. The jungle engulfed the remains, and only within the last decade or so have they been uncovered. No restoration or reconstruction has yet taken place. Nonetheless, a visit to the ruins gives you an idea of the Jesuit missions' original environment. There's also a visitor center with a small museum displaying ceramics and metal objects found during excavations. Spanish-speaking guides are available during high season (November, December, July, and Easter). ⊠ *3 km (2 mi) off R12, look for the sign* 🕾 *3752/470190* 🎫 *1 peso* ☉ *Daily 7–7.*

Santa Ana

🕒 *6 km (4 mi) south of Loreto, 45 km (28 mi) northeast of Posadas.*

The Santa Ana mission was founded in 1633 in the region of Tapé, in southern Brazil. In 1660, to escape invading Portuguese slave traders intent on capturing the native population, the two Jesuit leaders and 2,000 Guaranís relocated to the present location. The mission, which once covered about 1,000 acres, was one of the largest in the region, and its church, the Iglesia de Santa Ana, was considered one of the most beautiful (a few sections of walls are all that remain of the church). It also had highly advanced metal workshops in which iron and copper were used to make a wide range of products, including knives, swords, spears, and

CloseUp

THE JESUIT MISSIONARIES

OVER A SPAN OF more than 150 years, Spanish Jesuit missionaries established 30 missions in the area that now encompasses parts of present-day Argentina, Paraguay, and Brazil. They created an extraordinary society that is still a subject of great interest to scholars, social theorists, and even Hollywood (their story is told in the 1986 film The Mission, starring Robert De Niro and Jeremy Irons).

In 1534 a Catholic priest named San Ignacio de Loyola founded the Jesuits, who were officially approved by Pope Paul III in 1540. With the objective of "seeking the greater glory of God and salvation of souls," they concentrated their efforts on spreading Catholicism throughout the world. In the mid-16th century the first Jesuits arrived in South America, in what is today Peru and Brazil. In 1607 the Jesuit Diego Torres went to Asunción and established the Jesuit province of Paraguay.

The first missions were created in 1610 in the region of Guayrá in present-day Brazil. The Franciscans had previously entered these territories but failed to convert the indigenous Guaraní. The Jesuits were almost immediately successful. Their tactic was to send in a few Jesuits, who bestowed presents on the tribal chiefs and befriended them and then unobtrusively lived among the community, learning the culture and language before spreading their teachings and establishing the missions. The Guaraní, quickly won over, helped the Jesuit missionaries construct the missions. At their apogee, the largest missions had more than 4,000 Guaraní living there, generally along with two or three missionaries.

The greatest problem the missions faced at their outset was the constant raiding by Portuguese slave traders, who found the concentrations of Guaraní to be easy targets. For this reason, the missions of the Guayrá region relocated in 1631 to the banks of the Paraná and Uruguay rivers. Nevertheless, the attacks continued. In 1640 the royal crown of Spain granted the missions the right to use firearms and to raise armies in self-defense. In the

following year Jesuits and Guaranís fought side by side and defeated the slave traders in the Battle of Mbororé.

With the defeat of the slave traders, the missions could now concentrate more on their own development. They became economically self-sufficient through cattle ranching and the cultivation of crops such as corn, manioc, sugar, tobacco, rice, and yerba mate. They also produced honey and made highly detailed metal works, leather goods, and cloth. The missions had an effective communication system, which allowed for the sharing of information and the promotion of uniformity. For instance, nearly all had the same physical layout, with an enormous central plaza, surrounded by living quarters, a church, a school, workshops, and a cemetery.

Culturally, too, the missions were quite advanced. Musical instruments were crafted, and each mission had its own chorus and orchestra. At Nuestra Señora de Loreto, a printing press was built. Works such as the Bible were printed in Guaraní and Spanish. And an architectural and artistic style, Baroque-Guaraní, was developed in the buildings and sculptures.

But in 1767, when the missions were at their economic and cultural peak, King Carlos III of Spain expelled the Jesuits. The prevailing theory as to why this sudden decision was made is that the king feared that the missions had gained too much power and provided too much competition for the region's plantation owners. After the Jesuits departed, the communities they left behind rapidly fell apart. Governmental mismanagement led to large-scale migration of the Guaraní to the large cities or back to the jungle. And most who remained behind at the old missions were killed by Paraguayan troops fighting for territorial expansion.

arrows. Not surprisingly, the mission was the most important center for defense in the region.

When the Jesuits were expelled by King Carlos III of Spain in 1767, the mission was at its apogee, with 4,300 Guaraní inhabitants. Soon after, disease, land conflicts, and poor administration caused a significant reduction in the Guaraní population. By 1784 only 1,800 remained at the mission. In 1821 the Paraguayans, who were looking to seize the land on which the missions sat, sacked and burned the missions. All who did not flee into the forest were killed. The few remains of the mission were taken over by the jungle, and before excavations commenced in 1993, the red-sandstone blocks were covered with moss, split apart by huge roots, and engulfed by mighty trees. In 1997 the visitor center was built with its small museum displaying old ceramics, metal products, and photos from the excavation process. Spanish-speaking guides are available year-round. ⊠ *Just off R12, follow signs* 🎟 *Free* ⊙ *Daily 7–7.*

Santa María la Mayor

⓱ *108 km (67 mi) southeast of Posadas.*

It's worth trying to get to Santa María la Mayor, the least visited of the missions due to its inaccessibility, because the walls of the artisan workshop, school, and church remain almost entirely intact. The mission was founded in 1636 near the site of the Mbororé War, during which the Jesuits and Guaranís defeated the Portuguese slave traders who had been raiding the missions and capturing the Guaranís to sell as slaves. In 1637 the mission moved to its present-day spot. Santa María has a distinct layout: instead of just one central plaza, it has a whole sequence of plazas throughout. It never reached the size or importance of many of the other missions, but construction of a new and grander church was just beginning when the Jesuits were expelled in 1767. There's an information center on the premises, and guided tours are available in Spanish only. ⊠ *Off R2 W* 🎟 *Free* ⊙ *Daily 7–7.*

Soberbio

⓲ *283 km (175 mi) northeast of Posadas.*

As the closest town to Saltos de Moconá (Moconá Falls), tiny Soberbio is the logical base for a trip there, even though the road connecting the town to the falls is horrendous. The town itself has nothing to offer and only two nice hotels. Across the Río Uruguay, which runs alongside Soberbio, you can see the pretty green hills of Brazil. In fact, the only television station that the town gets is Brazilian, so it's no wonder that nearly everyone speaks Portuguese, while few in the Brazilian town across the river speak Spanish.

Where to Stay & Eat

$–$$ ✕🏨 **Posada La Bonita.** Halfway between Soberbio and Saltos de Moconá, set on 125 acres of verdant forest, are the four stone-and-log cabins that make up this rustic-chic jungle spa. In this mosquito-free paradise (the altitude is too high for the insects), there's no need for nets or even window panes, which makes it a bit cold in winter, even with the help of fireplaces. The cabins' verandas are suspended at canopy height among the soothing sounds of tropical birds and a splendid waterfall feeding a private, natural pool. Delicious and simple local cuisine and homemade bread are served in the restaurant. ⊠ *Posada La Bonita, La Bonita, Colonia La Flor, El Soberbio, 3364* ☎ *3755/*

15–680380 cell 🖨 *11/4747–4745* ⊕ *www.posadalabonita.com.ar* 🔄 *4 cabins* ⌂ *Restaurant, boating, fishing, hiking, horseback riding* 🚫 *No credit cards* 🍴 *CP.*

★ $ ✕🖥 **Hostería Puesta del Sol.** From its spot close to the top of a hill, this charming inn has a panoramic view of the town below and the rugged Brazilian countryside just across the Río Uruguay. Banana trees and purple flowers cover the 40-acre grounds, which contain a lovely pool, an open-air restaurant, four bungalows, and a main guest house. Rooms in the main guest house sleep up to three; the bungalows sleep up to six. Trips to Saltos de Moconá are run by the inn: with a group of at least three, a trip costs roughly 60 pesos per person for either a land or boat excursion. In high season (November, December, July, and Easter), you must make a reservation in advance and give a deposit for one night. The restaurant serves simple but tasty local favorites. ✉ *Calle Suipacha, Soberbio* ✉ *San José 124, Buenos Aires, 1076* 🖨 *3755/ 495161* ⊕ *www.hosteriapuestadelsol.8m.com* 🔄 *7 rooms, 4 bungalows* ⌂ *Restaurant, room service, fans, pool, volleyball, laundry service* 🚫 *No credit cards.*

Saltos de Moconá

★ ⑲   *86 km (53 mi) northeast of Soberbio.*

The Saltos de Moconá (Moconá Falls) are a set of waterfalls that run for 3 km (2 mi) along a geological fault that's filled by the Río Uruguay, marking the border between Brazil and Argentina. The falls are fed by the Pepirí, Guazú, and Yabotí rivers, which come from the Argentine side and plunge into the Río Uruguay below. The name Moconá means "that which sucks all" in Guaraní, a reference to the powerful whirlpools created by the falling water. The heights of the falls vary considerably according to the water level—they average 33 feet high and can reach up to 56 feet, but they can disappear altogether with heavy rains. It's very difficult to predict when this will occur, and when it does, it can happen in the span of just a few days. December through July are generally the best months to see the falls, though there are no guarantees that they will be there when you are.

The best way to explore the falls is by motorboat, though you can also explore them by land. Traveling alongside the falls on the Río Uruguay will give you an idea of their amazing length. Most excursions leave from Soberbio and take about 4½ hours round-trip. To explore the falls by land you'll need a Jeep or specially equipped truck because of the horrible road conditions; without having any flat tires or other mechanical problems, which are common, the trip by land takes about three hours each way. The best views are on the Brazilian side (make sure to bring your passport), but note that the border is closed on weekends.

If you really want an adventure, explore the falls on the Argentine side: as long as the water level is not too high, you can walk through the river that feeds into the falls. No climbing is necessary, since the upper level of the waterfall is on the Argentine side. Nevertheless, slippery rocks, often a few feet under the surface, make walking treacherous at times, but the reward is an exhilarating view at the precipice of the falls. The best place to ford the river is in the **Parque Provincial Moconá** (Moconá Provincial Park), just beyond the ranger's station. The approximately 2,500-acre park was created in 1988 in order to protect this natural wonder. For now, the difficult accessibility of the falls keeps the number of visitors low. ☎ *3755/441001 (Grupo Gendarmería) for information about the condition of falls and road.*

Puerto Iguazú

⓴ *308 km (191 mi) northeast of Posadas, 17 km (11 mi) west of the Cataratas del Iguazú.*

This small town of 25,000 is the best base for visiting the stunning Cataratas del Iguazú. The town originated as a port for shipping wood from the region. It was in the early 20th century that Victoria Aguirre, a high-society Porteña, funded the building of a road that extends to Cataratas del Iguazú to make it easier for people to visit the falls. You may find Puerto Iguazú preferable to its Brazilian neighbor, Foz de Iguaçu, because it's considerably more tranquil and safe (when you go to the Brazilian side, leave your valuables in the hotel and be on the alert; crime is more frequent there). But there isn't much to do here, as the falls are the main attraction in the area.

Where to Stay & Eat

Besides staying in town, you can also stay in the Parque Nacional Iguazú at the Sheraton Internacional Iguazú; the Garganta del Diablo, one of the best restaurants in the area, is in the hotel. Competition from hotels in Brazil, which are cheaper, forces hotels in Puerto Iguazú to keep rates down. During low season (late September–early November and February–May, excluding Easter), rooms are discounted up to 50%. The town's restaurants are far from spectacular; generally, the best eating is found in the nicer hotels.

$ ✕ **Jardín Iguazú.** At lunch and at odd hours, when everything else is closed, this restaurant with a wide variety of food serves a good fixed-price meal, which for about $4 provides an empanada, a salad, a main dish with pasta and meat, and a beverage. The place is rather shiny, with highly polished stones on the floor and a stage (used for live music in the evenings) speckled with silver chips. Jardín Iguazú is close to the bus terminal and stays open until 2 AM. ⊠ *Avs. Misiones and Córdoba* ☎ *3757/423200.*

★ ¢ ✕ **El Charo.** This restaurant is in a shabby old house that looks like it could easily be blown down with a huff and a puff: all the paintings are tilted, the roof is sinking, and the cowhide on the seats is faded. Nevertheless, this is one of town's most popular restaurants because of its consistently delicious and inexpensive *parrilladas* (a sampling of grilled meat), as well as its pasta and grilled fish. Note that napkins come only by request. ⊠ *Av. Córdoba 106* ☎ *3757/421529* ▭ *No credit cards.*

★ $$ ✕▥ **Hotel Cataratas.** Though this redbrick hotel with green window sills and white awnings isn't especially attractive from the outside, inside is a different story: the classy lobby and ample guest rooms are tastefully decorated with the finest materials and furnishings. Ask for a master double, which is the same price but slightly nicer than the standard double. The hotel also has beautiful grounds and excellent facilities, including an enormous pool. The high-quality restaurant, serving international cuisine, has an à la carte menu and a fixed-price buffet (dinner only). ⊠ *R12, Km 4, 3370* ☎ *3757/421100* 🖷 *3757/421090* ⬖ *112 rooms, 4 suites ⌕ Restaurant, room service, in-room safes, minibars, tennis court, pool, gym, massage, sauna, volleyball, bar, meeting room, business services* ▭ *AE, DC, MC, V.*

$$$ ▥ **Hotel Esturion.** This slightly aged hotel has gardens and sweeping views of the river, as well as a very helpful staff. Rooms show some signs of wear and tear, though they are spacious and have all the modern amenities you'd expect at a luxury hotel; many have balconies. The restaurant is sometimes the subject of complaints, especially from those whose package deal provides only a few choices at meals. ⊠ *Av. Tres Fron-*

teras 650, 3370 ☎*3757/420100* 🖶*3757/420100* ↩*114 rooms, 4 suites, 4 apartments* ⚐ *Restaurant, coffee shop, in-room safes, minibars, 2 tennis courts, pool, gym, massage, sauna, convention center, business services, Internet* 🗖 *AE, DC, MC, V.*

¢–$ 🏨 **Los Helechos.** It's such a great bargain that this hotel doesn't need to discount its rooms during the off-season. It's also convenient to the center of town and two blocks from the bus terminal. Rooms are simple but clean and comfortable; half have air-conditioning and television (these cost 10 pesos more). ⊠ *Paulino Amarante 76, 3370* ☎🖶 *3757/420338* ↩ *54 rooms* ⚐ *Restaurant, pool, bar; no a/c in some rooms* 🗖 *AE, DC, MC, V.*

Nightlife
Puerto Iguazú is very quiet at night—more happens on the Brazilian side. You can try your luck at the fancy, European-style casino in the **Iguazú Grand Hotel Resort & Casino** (⊠ R12, Km 1, 640 ☎ 3757/498050).

Shopping
Numerous souvenir shops line the main strip, **Avenida Aguirre,** and the surrounding blocks. All carry similar items, such as yerba mate gourds, semiprecious stones, baskets, and weavings.

Cataratas del Iguazú

㉑
Fodor'sChoice *17 km (11 mi) east of Puerto Iguazú, 297 km (184 mi) northeast of Posadas, 1,357 km (841 mi) northeast of Buenos Aires.*
★

The Cataratas del Iguazú (Iguazú Falls) are one of the wildest wonders of the world, with nature on the rampage in a unique show of sound and fury. The grandeur of this cinemascopic sheet of white water cascading in constant cymbal-banging cacophony makes Niagara Falls and Victoria Falls seem sedate. At a bend in the Río Iguazú, on the border with Brazil, the falls extend for almost 3 km (2 mi) in a 270-degree arch. Iguazú consists of some 275 separate waterfalls—in the rainy season there are as many as 350—that send their white cascades plunging more than 200 feet onto the rocks below. Dense, lush jungle surrounds the falls: here the tropical sun and the omnipresent moisture make the jungle grow at a pace that produces a towering pine tree in two decades instead of the seven it takes in, say, Scandinavia. By the falls and along the roadside, rainbows and butterflies are set off against vast walls of red earth, which is so ubiquitous that eventually even peso bills long in circulation in the area turn red from exposure to the stuff.

Allow at least two full days to take in this magnificent sight, and be sure to see it from both the Argentine and Brazilian sides. The Brazilians are blessed with the best panoramic view, an awesome vantage point that suffers only from the sound of the gnatlike helicopters that erupt out of the lawn of the Hotel das Cataratas right in front of the falls. (Unfortunately, most indigenous macaws and toucans have abandoned the area to escape the whine of the helicopters' engines.) The Argentine side offers the better close-up experience of the falls, with excellent hiking paths, catwalks that approach the falls, a sandy beach to relax on, and places to bathe in the froth of the Río Iguazú. Local travel agencies and tour operators offer trips that will take you to both sides. If you want to set your own pace, you can tour the Argentine side and then take a taxi or one of the regularly scheduled buses across the International Bridge, officially called the Ponte Presidente Tancredo Neves, to Brazil. Note that if you're a Canadian, British, or American citizen crossing into Brazil from Argentina or Paraguay, you don't need a visa for a short visit to the falls. You must, however, pay an entry fee and have your passport

Iguazú Falls

stamped. Always keep your passport handy, as immigration authorities keep the region under close watch.

The best way to immerse yourself in the falls is to wander the many access paths, which are a combination of bridges, ramps, stone staircases, and new metal catwalks set in a forest of ferns, begonias, orchids, and tropical trees. The catwalks over the water put you right in the middle of the action, so be ready to get doused by the rising spray. (Be sure to bring rain gear—or buy it from vendors along the trails on the Brazilian side.) If tropical heat and humidity hamper your style, plan to visit between April and October, though the falls are thrilling year-round. Five upstream Brazilian barrages (mini-dams) on the river Iguazú cast a man-made unreliability on the natural wonder: depending on the river flow and seasonal rains, barrages may affect the water volume in the falls anywhere from 1,500 cubic meters per second up to 8,000 or more (usually dam operators are careful not to shut down the falls on weekends or holidays).

The falls on the Argentine side are in the **Parque Nacional Iguazú** (Iguazú National Park), which was founded in 1934, declared a World Heritage Site in 1984, and refurbished by a private concession in 2001. There's a new **Visitor Center,** called Yvyra Reta ("country of the trees" in Guaraní tongue) with excellent facilities, including a good explanation of the region's ecology and human history. From here you can catch the gas-propelled **Tren de la Selva** (Jungle Train), which departs every 20 minutes. It makes a stop at **Estación Cataratas** and then proceeds to **Estación Garganta del Diablo** (Devil's Throat Station), where a new wheelchair-accessible, metal catwalk leads to a platform right beside one of the most dizzying spots in the world. Here the Iguazú river plummets, with an awesome roar, more than 230 feet into a horseshoe-shape gorge, amid a perennial cloud of mist.

If a more relaxed stroll is preferred, take the well-marked, ½ km (.3 mi) **Sendero Verde** (Green Path) past Estación Cataratas and connect with **Circuito Superior** (Upper Circuit), which stretches along the top of the falls for 1 km (½ mi). With six sightseeing balconies, this easy walk of about an hour and a half provides great upper views of the falls **Dos Hermanas, Ramírez, Bossetti, Méndez,** and the most impressive, named after the *Libertador* (Liberator) **San Martín.** Near the falls look for *vencejos,* swallows that nest behind the curtains of water. Note that the paths beyond the San Martín have more than a few stairways and, therefore, are not wheelchair-accessible.

The **Circuito Inferior** (Lower Circuit) starts by a water-and-watch tower and is a 1.7-km-long (1.1-mi-long) loop that consists of a metal catwalk, lots of stairways, and protected promontories at the best spots. At the beginning of this walk, you'll pass the small **Salto Alvar Núñez Cabeza de Vaca** falls, named after the Spanish conquistador who stumbled onto the spectacle in the 16th century; the **Peñón de Bella Vista** (Rock of the Beautiful View); and the **Salto Lanusse** (Lanusse Falls). These are just preliminaries to get you warmed up for the main event. Halfway along this circuit you get a panoramic peek at what's to come—through the foliage you can see the gigantic curtain of water in the distance. The trail leads along the lower side of **Brazo San Martín,** a branch of the Iguazú river that makes a wide loop to the south before following the same vertical fate as the main branch, along a mile-long series of falls. The last part of the trail offers the most exciting views of the main falls, including Garganta del Diablo in the background. Allow about an hour and a half to walk this circuit. There's no way to get lost on the catwalk, but English-speaking guides, found at the visitor center, can be hired to provide detailed explanations of the falls.

From Circuito Inferior you can reach the pier where a free boat service crosses the river to **Isla San Martín** (San Martín Island). This free boat service operates all day, except when the river is too high. On the island, after a steep climb up a rustic stairway, a circular trail opening presents three spectacular panoramas of Salto San Martín, Garganta del Diablo, and Salto Ventana (Window Falls). Few people make the effort to cross the river to Isla San Martín and do this climb, so you can often enjoy the show in solitary splendor.

The **Sendero Macuco** (Macuco Trail) extends 4 km (2½ mi) into the jungle, ending at the **Salto Arrechea** (Arrechea Falls) farther downriver from the main falls. The trail is very carefully marked, and descriptive signs in Spanish explain the jungle's flora and fauna. The closest you'll get to a wild animal is likely to be a paw print in the dirt, though you may be lucky enough to glimpse a monkey. The foliage is dense, so the most common surprises are the jungle sounds that seem to emerge out of nowhere. You can turn back at any point, or continue on to the refreshing view of the river and Salto Arrechea. The best time to hear animal calls and to avoid the heat is either early in the morning or just before sunset. The battalions of butterflies, also best seen in the early morning or late afternoon, can be marvelous, and the intricate glistening cobwebs crisscrossing the trail are a treat in the dawn light. Plan on spending about three hours for the whole trip. The **Centro de Investigaciones Ecológicas Subtropicales** (Center for Subtropical Ecological Investigation; ☏ 3757/421222) maintains the trail.

On the Brazilian side, the falls, known in Portuguese as the Foz do Iguaçu, can be seen from the **Parque Nacional Foz do Iguaçu,** Brazil's national park. The park runs for 25 km (16 mi) along a paved highway southwest of downtown Foz do Iguaçu, the nearest town. The **park entrance** (✉ Km 17, Rodovia das Cataratas ☎ 005545/529–8383) is the best place to get information; it's open daily 8–5, and the entrance fee is roughly 3 pesos. Much of the park's 457,000 acres is protected rain forest—offlimits to visitors and home to the last viable populations of panthers as well as rare flora such as bromeliads and orchids. The falls are 11 km (7 mi) from the park entrance. The luxurious, historic Hotel das Cataratas sits near the trailhead. Public parking is allowed on the highway shoulder and in a small lot near the hotel. The path to the falls is 2 km (1 mi) long, and its walkways, bridges, and stone staircases lead through the rain forest to concrete and wooden catwalks that take you to the falls. Highlights of the Brazilian side of the falls include first the **Salto Santa Maria,** from which catwalks branch off to the **Salto Deodoro** and **Salto Floriano,** where you'll be doused by the spray. The end of the catwalk puts you right in the heart of the spectacle at **Garganta do Diablo** ("Devil's Throat" in Portuguese), for a different perspective from the Argentine side. Back on the last section of the main trail is a building with facilities, including a panoramic elevator; it's open daily 8:30–6, and there's a small fee. A balcony brings you close to the far left of **Salto Deodoro.** The trail ends at the road some 35 feet above.

Where to Stay & Eat

$$ ✕ **Garganta del Diablo.** As the harpist plucks away, you can savor the expertly prepared dishes from the international menu at one of the area's finest restaurants. The trout in pastry and the surubí in banana leaves are exquisite. The restaurant, which is in the Sheraton Internacional Iguazú, only serves dinner (which starts after the last bus has left for Puerto Iguazú, which means an expensive taxi ride if you're not a guest at the hotel). ✉ *Sheraton Internacional Iguazú, Parque Nacional Iguazú* ☎ *3757/491800* 🖃 *AE, DC, MC, V* ☺ *No lunch.*

$$ ✕ **Zaragoza.** In a quiet neighborhood on a tree-lined street in Brazil's Foz do Iguaçu, this cozy restaurant is owned by Paquito, a Spanish immigrant. The Spanish fare includes a great paella, the house specialty, as well as several delicious fish options. The surubí definitely merits a try. ✉ *Rua Quintino Bocaiúva 882, Foz do Iguaçu, Paraná, Brazil* ☎ *045/574–3084* 🖃 *AE, V.*

★ $$$$ ✕🖻 **Tropical das Cataratas.** Not only is this stately hotel in the national park on the Brazilian side, but it also provides the more traditional comforts—large rooms, terraces, hammocks—of a colonial-style establishment. Galleries and gardens surround this pink building, and its main section has been declared a Brazilian national heritage sight. The restaurant serves traditional Brazilian food. ✉ *Km 25, Rodovia das Cataratas, 85850–970, Brazil* ☎ *005545/521–7000* ⊕ *www.tropicalhotel.com. br* ➳ *200 rooms* ♤ *2 restaurants, coffee shop, 2 tennis courts, pool, bar, shops, meeting room, business services* 🖃 *AE, DC, MC, V.*

$$$$
Fodor'sChoice
★

🖻 **Sheraton Internacional Iguazú.** Half of the rooms in this luxury hotel have direct views of the falls, so be sure to reserve one well in advance (they are about 30% more expensive). Floor-to-ceiling windows reveal the inspiring scene to the lobby, restaurants, bars, and even the pool. The spacious balconies are ideal for breakfast or a drink. Rooms are large and comfortable and have been refurnished recently under Sheraton management. ✉ *Parque Nacional Iguazú, 3372* ☎ *3757/491800* 🖷*3757/491810* ⊕*www.sheraton.com* ➳*180 rooms, 4 suites* ♤*2 restaurants, room service, minibars, 3 tennis courts, pool, sauna, bicycle, 2 bars, laundry service, meeting room, business services, Internet* 🖃 *AE, DC, MC, V.*

Minas de Wanda

② *43 km (27 mi) south of Puerto Iguazú.*

The Minas de Wanda (Mines of Wanda) are two of the largest sites for semiprecious stone in Argentina. Volcanic activity 120 million years ago created the deposits of amethyst, crystal, quartz, topaz, and agate. The two adjacent and nearly identical mines, the **Compañía Minera Wanda** (☎ 3752/437879 in Posadas) and the **Tierra Colorada** (☎ 3757/ 1554–5878) are both about 2 km (1 mi) off R12, where the bus from Puerto Iguazú lets you off and where you'll be greeted by representatives from both mines trying to steer you to their establishments. From the bus stop you can walk or take one of the taxis normally waiting there to the mines. On the tours (free) of the mines and workshops, guides (some speak English) explain how the stones are extracted, cut, and treated. The tours end in the gift shop, of course, where semiprecious stone clocks, paperweights, jewelry, mobiles, ashtrays, and other items are sold; don't count on any great bargains.

CHACO

The province of Chaco is so dry that it can hardly support human life. There's a large indigenous community, consisting mainly of the Wichi, and most of the province's inhabitants are of mixed European and indigenous heritage. As in most of the region, the major towns are not very interesting on their own; they're only places you'll need to pass through on your way elsewhere. The true gems are the utterly remote areas that serve as sanctuaries for an abundance of plants and wildlife.

Resistencia

㉓ *290 km (180 mi) west of Posadas, 1,019 km (632 mi) north of Buenos Aires.*

The capital of Chaco Province, with 300,000 inhabitants, is deservedly nicknamed *"la ciudad de las esculturas"* (the city of sculptures). Throughout the city—on street corners, in parks, on medians, and on lawns—are sculptures ranging from neoclassic busts to postmodern abstract figures. Every year for two weeks in late July and early August, the city hosts an international sculpting competition. It's fascinating to watch as the internationally renowned artists transform raw material (the medium changes every year) into fine sculptures. All work is performed in the enormous Plaza 25 de Mayo, which contains a beautiful fountain, towering palm trees, and, of course, many statues. If you're passing through Resistencia on your way to Presidencia Roque Sáenz Peña during this period, it may be worth spending a day and watching the artists at work. If not, there's little in this town to warrant an overnight stay.

Presidencia Roque Sáenz Peña

㉔ *168 km (104 mi) west of Resistencia.*

This small but sprawling town was originally called "Km 173" after the railway stop that created it. It was officially founded in 1912 and given the name of then Argentine president, a proponent of the region. Cotton used to be the town's chief industry, but now its 70,000 habitants make their living mostly through commerce, since the hinterland relies on its shops to provide everything from machinery to clothing. (Note that shops close from noon 'til 4 or 5 PM for *siesta*.) Efforts to draw in visitors appear to have been ineffective: neither the thermal baths at the main hotel nor the airstrip built in 1998 (still with no commercial flights) have attracted any significant tourism to Presidencia Roque Sáenz Peña.

The town's top attraction (6 km [4 mi] southeast of town) is the 370-acre **Complejo Ecológico Municipal** (Municipal Ecological Complex), one of Argentina's primary centers for the recuperation and reproduction of endangered animals. The enormous on-site zoo contains more than 2,000 animals and more than 208 species. The majority of these animals—including jaguars, monkeys, alligators, pumas, flamingos, and condors—come from the Parque Nacional Chaco (Chaco National Park), 150 km (93 mi) northeast (the park itself isn't that interesting). Animals, such as tigers, lions, a hippopotamus, and baboons, have also been brought here through an exchange program with many of the world's best zoos. The complex is very popular on weekends because it also has soccer fields, playgrounds, and cookout facilities by the lake. To get to the zoo, either take a taxi (about 5 pesos) or catch Linea 1, which passes through the central plaza on Calle 10. ⊠ *R95, Km 1,111 (1,000 feet from R16)* ☎ *3732/424284* ☜ *1 peso* ☉ *Daily 7 AM–8 PM.*

The **Complejo Termal** (Thermal Bath Complex) by the centric Gualok Hotel may be rather disappointing: it lacks maintenance and seems to attract very few customers. Thermal waters at a depth of 2,700 feet were discovered in the '30s during a severe drought, while drilling for drinkable water. The 105°F water contains chlorine, sulphur, calcium, magnesium, and iron, and is effective in relieving stress and symptoms of arthritis. There are private baths, saunas, and Turkish baths. Prices are very reasonable, starting at 5 pesos. ⊠ *Calle 23, No. 554* ☉ *Daily 6–12:30 and 2:30–9.*

The **Museo Histórico de la Ciudad** (City History Museum) has a variety of displays, including two extraordinary fossils. The first is a 200,000-year-old, 4-foot fossil of a glyptodon, which was a predecessor of the armadillo and became extinct 10,000 years ago; the second is a 10,000-year-old fossil of a 5-foot tortoise shell. Another noteworthy item is a small meteorite from Campos Cielo, a sight in southwest Chaco where an enormous meteorite shower fell 6,000 years ago. ⊠ *Calles 12 and 1* ☎ *3732/420654* ☜ *Free* ☉ *Weekdays 7–12:30 and 1:30–8, Sat. 6–9, Sun. 2:30–10.*

Where to Stay & Eat

$ ✕ **Café Bar El Patio.** This friendly café is in a small English-style colonial house. Dine outside on pizza, *minutas* (fast meals), and desserts. ⊠ *Calle 19 y Calle 10* ☎ *No phone* ▤ *MC.*

$ ✕▥ **Hotel Gualok.** This hotel isn't big on comfort—the pool might be dry or the air-conditioning not working—but it's cheap and clean, and one of only two options in town. The Hotel Gualok Restaurant ($) is somewhat somber and offers the usual fare of meat, poultry, and pasta dishes, along with *galeto* (chicken roasted Brazilian-style) on Wednesday. ⊠ *Calle 12, 1198, 3700* ☎ *3732/420521* ☜ *106 rooms, 2 suites.* ⌂ *Restaurant, minibars, pool, bar, laundry service, meeting room* ▤ *AE, DC, MC, V.*

★ $ ▥ **Hotel Presidente.** The cozy and clean rooms are a bargain at this hotel next to the tourism office. Included in the rate is an impressive breakfast and free laundry. This small hotel is very popular, especially with business travelers, so make reservations in advance. ⊠ *San Martín 12, 3700* ☎ *3732/424498* ☜ *16 rooms* ⌂ *Minibars, laundry service* ▤ *No credit cards.*

Nightlife & the Arts

A young crowd fills the dance club **Password** (✉ Calle 9 between Calles 12 and 14 ☎ 3732/425229), open weekends only. **Saravá** (✉ Calles 12 and 11 ☎ 3732/424266) is a dimly lighted bar near the main square. **Timotea y Divino** (✉ Calle 13 between Calles 12 and 14) is a noisy spot popular with a young crowd. **Vitamina** (✉ Calle 17 between Calles 12 and 10) is a dark, loud place with more provincial touches than your average club. **Teatro Septiembre** (✉ Calle 1 between Calles 8 and 10 ☎ 3732/421587) occasionally holds cultural events.

Shopping

At this writing, the **Mercado Artesanal** (✉ Calles 12 and 1), next to the history museum, appeared to be closed for good. But you can find stands selling handicrafts (mostly brightly colored pottery animals at bargain prices) around the gas station at the junction of R95 and R16.

El Impenetrable

25 *180 km (112 mi) northwest of Presidencia Roque Sáenz Peña.*

A desolate wilderness, El Impenetrable (The Impenetrable), in the northwest part of Chaco Province, covers nearly a third of the province, as well as much of the province of Formosa and part of Paraguay. It was named by Spanish explorers who couldn't traverse the area because of the scarcity of water. Indeed, the extremely arid climate and temperatures that commonly exceed 110°F make this a very unforgiving land. Even today it's sparsely populated, with just a few scattered villages, mostly inhabited by members of the indigenous Wichi. In fact, it's possible to drive for hours through the eerie-looking landscape without seeing any signs of other people: no telephone or electrical wires, no signs, no cars, and no houses. Then, out of nowhere a boy will appear on a bicycle, trudging through the red sandlike soil to an unimaginable destination.

Although life is barely sustainable for humans, many forms of flora and fauna thrive here. The landscape is marked by several types of cacti, specially adapted palm trees, thorny shrubs, and the famous *quebracho,* a strange, often gigantic tree that has an enormously convex trunk and is hollow inside. Its name, which means "axe breaker," is attributed to the toughness of its wood, once used as railroad ties. This is also the last frontier for some nearly extinct species, including wolves, anteaters, armadillos, jaguars, pumas, eagles, and many other birds. An especially impressive sight is the thousands of small blue, bright-yellow, and mint-green butterflies fluttering about.

Getting to the area is difficult. With even the slightest bit of rain, the dirt roads become impassible to all but specially equipped Jeeps and trucks. Presently, only one company, **Quiyoc** (☎ 3732/420721), organizes Jeep trips. Depending on the length of the trip, a tour may also include stops at Nueva Pompeya, an old Jesuit mission, and Villa Río Bermejito, a small village with a white-sand riverside beach; canoe rides on the river and hikes are also possible. With a group of at least three, the trip costs about 100 pesos per person per day. Because of the current lack of accommodations, tents are the only option. You probably won't feel a need to spend more than two or three days in the region. You could even take a day trip from Presidencia Roque Sáenz Peña (for 65 pesos per person), but you'll miss a lot if you're only here for such a short time.

THE NORTHEAST A TO Z

To research prices, get advice from other travelers, and book travel arrangements, visit www.fodors.com.

AIR TRAVEL

Aerolíneas Argentinas/Austral and LAPA each have two daily flights between Buenos Aires and Posadas; the trip takes about an hour and a half.

Daily flights depart from Aeropuerto Internacional de Rosario going to Buenos Aires and to Río on Aerolíneas Argentinas and Varig.

Aerolíneas Argentinas/Austral flies three times daily between Buenos Aires and the Argentine airport near Iguazú; the trip takes an hour and a half. LAPA also flies to and from Buenos Aires and is usually cheaper. Normal rates are about 200 pesos each way, but promotional rates, called *bandas negativas,* are sometimes available if you reserve ahead. The Brazilian airlines—Transbrasil, Varig, and Vasp—have offices in Foz do Iguaçu and offer connecting flights all over Brazil.

🛪 **Aerolíneas Argentinas/Austral** ⊠ Av. Victoria Aguirre 295, Puerto Iguazú ☎ 3757/420849 or 3757/420168. **LAPA** ☎ 3757/420390. **Varig** ☎ 5545/523-2111 in Foz do Iguaçu, 11/4329-9211 in Buenos Aires. **Vasp** ☎ 5545/529-6216.

AIRPORTS

Gualeguaychú's tiny airport, the Aerodromo, is 12 km (7 mi) west of town; the 15-minute taxi ride to town costs around 5 pesos.

Posadas's airport, the Aeropuerto Libertador General San Martín, is 10 km (6 mi) southwest of the town center; flights only go to and from Buenos Aires. A taxi from the airport into Posadas costs 10–15 pesos and takes a half hour. You could also take the Becivega Bus 28 from the airport to Calle Junín in front of Plaza San Martín.

Argentina and Brazil each have an airport at Iguazú. The Argentine airport is 20 km (12 mi) southeast of Puerto Iguazú, Argentina; the Brazilian airport is 11 km (7 mi) from Foz do Iguaçu and 17 km (11 mi) from the national park. The Colectivo Aeropuerto shuttle has service to hotels in Puerto Iguazú for 3 pesos. To get from the hotel to the airport, call two hours before your departure, and the shuttle will pick you up. Taxis to Puerto Iguazú cost 18 pesos.

🛪 **Aeropuerto Internacional de Rosario** ⊠ R9 ☎ 0341/451-2997. **Aeropuerto Libertador General San Martín** ⊠ Off R12 ☎ 3752/451903.

BUS TRAVEL

Traveling to the Northeast from Buenos Aires is relatively easy, and buses are one of the best ways to travel from town to town within the Northeast.

COLÓN Buses leave regularly from Buenos Aires to Colón, passing through Gualeguaychú and other towns on the Corredor del Uruguay. These include Jovibus and Nuevo Expreso–Flechabus. The trip from Buenos Aires takes close to five hours. Tata is the only company with a direct route between Colón and Presidencia Roque Sáenz Peña. The Colón Terminal de Omnibus is about 10 blocks northwest of the town center.

🚌 **Colón Terminal de Omnibus** ⊠ Paysandú and Sourigues ☎ 3447/421716.

GUALEGUAYCHÚ Buses between Buenos Aires and Gualeguaychú take about three hours, cost about 20 pesos, and run regularly. The two bus companies that travel this route most frequently are Nuevo Expreso–Flechabus and Tata. Nuevo Expreso and Jovibus have regular service between Gualeguaychú and Colón; the trip takes two hours. The Gualeguaychú Terminal de Omnibus is in the city center.

🚌 **Gualeguaychú Terminal de Omnibus** ⊠ Bv. Jurado and Av. Artigas ☎ 3446/440688. **Jovibus** ☎ 3446/440779. **Nuevo Expreso–Flechabus** ☎ 3446/440230.

MERCEDES From Mercedes to Presidencia Roque Sáenz Peña, there's only one direct bus—it's generally easier to go through Resistencia. The trip takes four hours to Resistencia from Mercedes and three more to Presidencia Roque Sáenz Peña. Nuevo Expreso–Flechabus goes once daily from Mercedes to Presidencia Roque Sáenz Peña and Resistencia. Flechabus goes from Mercedes to Resistencia three times a day, La Nueva Estrella only once. The Mercedes Terminal de Omnibus is in the town center.

🚌 **La Nueva Estrella** ☎ 03773/420531. **Mercedes Terminal de Omnibus** ⊠ San Martín and J. Alfredo Ferreyre ☎ 3773/420165. **Nuevo Expreso/Flechabus** ☎ 3773/422209.

POSADAS La Estrella and Crucero del Norte have several daily buses to Buenos Aires. Buses to Puerto Iguazú leave five times a day, and the trip takes five hours: Aguila Dorada runs the leading service. All of these buses pass by the three Jesuit ruins on R12, and some actually enter the town of San Ignacio, making an even more convenient trip. To get to Yacyretá Dam, you must take the bus to Ituzaingo; the trip is made nearly every hour, most frequently by Ciudad de Posadas. To Soberbio, take Aguila Dorada or Capital del Monte, each of which goes twice daily. The Posadas Terminal de Omnibus is 6 km (4 mi) southwest of the town center (a 4 peso taxi ride).

🚌 **Aguila Dorada** ☎ 3752/458888. **Crucero del Norte** ☎ 3752/455515. **La Estrella** ☎ 3752/453120. **Posadas Terminal de Omnibus** ⊠ R12 and Av. Santa Catalina, ☎ 3752/456106.

PRESIDENCIA
ROQUE SÁENZ
PEÑA
Four companies each have one daily bus to Posadas, which takes about eight hours: La Estrella, La Nueva Estrella, Ta-La Estrella, and Vosa. If no times are convenient, you can go through Resistencia, where buses regularly leave for Posadas. The Presidencia Roque Sáenz Peña Terminal de Omnibus is a few blocks and a 2 peso taxi ride from the center of town.

🚌 **La Estrella** ☎ 3732/425414. **La Nueva Estrella** ☎ 3732/429881. **Presidencia Roque Sáenz Peña Terminal de Omnibus** ⊠ Calles 19 and 21 ☎ 3732/420280. **Vosa** ☎ 3732/427676.

PUERTO IGUAZÚ Organized tours to Puerto Iguazú and the Cataratas del Iguazú by bus can be arranged through most Buenos Aires travel agencies. Via Bariloche has the quickest and most comfortable service between Puerto Iguazú and Buenos Aires; the trip takes 16 hours, costs about 75 pesos, and includes meals. Expreso Singer takes 18 hours and costs 82 pesos. The Puerto Iguazú Terminal de Omnibus is in the center of town.

From Puerto Iguazú to the falls, take El Práctico from the terminal; buses leave every 45 minutes 7–7 and cost 5.60 pesos round-trip. To get to the Minas de Wanda from Puerto Iguazú, you can take any bus going to Posadas. These buses leave nearly every hour and take about 45 minutes. For information call Agencia de Pasajes Noelia at the bus terminal.

🚌 **Agencia de Pasajes Noelia** ☎ 3757/422722. **Expreso Singer** ☎ 3757/422891. **El Práctico** ☎ 3757/422722. **Puerto Iguazú Terminal de Omnibus** ⊠ Avs. Córdoba and Misiones ☎ 3757/423006. **Via Bariloche** ☎ 3757/420854.

RESISTENCIA Between Resistencia and Buenos Aires, there are several buses daily on Flechabus and La Internacional. La Termal travels from Resistencia to Presidencia Roque Sáenz Peña five times a day, Estrella once a day. The Resistencia Terminal de Omnibus is 4 km (2 mi) west of the town center.

🚌 **Estrella** ☎ 3722/460905. **Resistencia Terminal de Omnibus** ⊠ Malvinas and Av. MacLean ☎ 3722/461098. **La Termal** ☎ 3722/460907.

ROSARIO Urquiza–Sierras de Córdoba links Rosario to Buenos Aires and other towns in the Pampas.

🚌 **Estación de Omnibus Mariano Moreno** ✉ Santa Fe between Caferata and Córdoba ☎ 0341/437-2384 ⊕ www.terminalrosario.com.ar. **Urquiza–Sierras de Córdoba** ✉ Estación de Omnibus Mariano Moreno, Window 11 ☎ 0341/439-8765.

CAR RENTAL

There aren't many places to rent cars in the region; you're better off renting a car in Buenos Aires and driving from there. Daniel Marrochi SRL has offices in Paraná, Posadas, and Puerto Iguazú.

🚗 **Daniel Marrochi SRL** ✉ Almafuerte 1300, Paraná ☎ 343/423-3885.

CAR TRAVEL

To get from Buenos Aires to Gualeguaychú by car, take R9 north to R14 north; the trip usually takes 2–3½ hours. R14 continues along the entire Corredor del Uruguay. The trip from Gualeguaychú to Colón along R14 takes about two hours. To get to Mercedes from Colón, take R14 north to R119 north; the trip takes about four hours. To get from Mercedes to Colonia Carlos Pellegrini, take R40 northeast; the trip is about 3½ hours. From Colonia Carlos Pellegrini you can take the R41, a dirt road, northeast until you hit paved R12, which leads east to Posadas. To reach San Ignacio Miní, Santa Ana, and Nuestra Señora de Loreto (3 km [2 mi] off R12) from Posadas, take R12 northeast. Continue on R12 to reach Puerto Iguazú. To get to Santa María la Mayor from Posadas, take R12 northeast to R4 and then southeast to R2 west. From Posadas to Soberbio, take R12 northeast to R7 and then east to R14 east to R212 southeast. Puerto Iguazú is a two-day, 1,363-km (848-mi) drive from Buenos Aires on R12 and R14 (it's quickest to take R14 to Posadas, then R12 to the falls). From Posadas, the R12 leads west toward Resistencia and the towns of Chaco Province. For the most part the roads are paved and rarely crowded.

CONSULATE

In Puerto Iguazú, the Brazilian consulate is open weekdays 8–12:30. If you're not an American, British, or Canadian citizen, a tourist visa is necessary to enter Brazil from Argentina, and it may take a couple of days, so do it ahead of time.

🏛 **Brazilian consulate** ✉ Av. Córdoba 264 ☎ 3757/421348.

EMERGENCIES

For ambulances call the hospitals directly. Several of the pharmacies listed are open 24 hours or share rotating 24-hour shifts with other pharmacies.

🚒 **Fire Colón** ☎ 3447/421112. **Gualeguaychú** ☎ 3446/423333. **Posadas** ☎ 100. **Presidencia Roque Sáenz Peña** ☎ 3732/421661.

🏥 **Hospitals Colón** ✉ Sanatorio Médico Quirúrgico, Artigas 211 ☎ 3447/421212. **Posadas** ✉ Hospital Dr. Ramón Madariaga, Av. Lopez Tones and Cabral ☎ 3752/447000, 107 emergencies. **Presidencia Roque Sáenz Peña** ✉ Hospital 4 de Junio, Malvinas Argentinas 1350 ☎ 3732/420667. **Puerto Iguazú** ✉ Hospital Samic, Av. Victoria Aguirre 131 ☎ 3757/420288.

💊 **Late-Night Pharmacies Colón** ✉ Farmacia Francia, San Martín 1050 ☎ 3447/422008. **Gualeguaychú** ✉ Farmacia Modelo, Urquiza 1788 ☎ 3446/423219. **Puerto Iguazú** ✉ Farmacia Bravo, Av. Victoria Aguirre 423 ☎ 3757/420479.

🚔 **Police Colón** ☎ 3447/421439. **Gualeguaychú** ☎ 3446/422222. **Posadas** ☎ 101. **Presidencia Roque Sáenz Peña** ☎ 3732/420710. **Puerto Iguazú** ☎ 3757/421224.

MAIL & SHIPPING

To send mail, look for the *correo* (post office). Most post offices are open weekdays until 8, with a siesta closing in mid-afternoon, and Saturday morning.

▪ Post Offices **Colón** ✉ 12 de Abril 431 ☎ 3447/421631. **Gualeguaychú** ✉ Urquiza and Angel Elias ☎ 3446/426387. **Posadas** ✉ Bolívar 193 ☎ 3752/424411. **Presidencia Roque Sáenz Peña** ✉ Calle 10, No. 602 ☎ 3732/420501. **Puerto Iguazú** ✉ Av. Victoria Aguirre 294 ☎ 3757/422454.

MONEY MATTERS

ATMs linked to the Cirrus system are found throughout the region.

In Colón there's nowhere to exchange money, but there are ATMs. In Gualeguaychú you can exchange money at COFIBAL, open weekdays 8–noon. A reliable bank in Gualeguaychú is Bank Boston, open weekdays 8–1. In Posadas, Cambio Mazza is open weekdays 8–noon and 3:30–6:30. For other banking needs in Posadas, go to Bank Boston; it has ATMs and is open weekdays 8–1. Dollars and pesos are used interchangeably in Puerto Iguazú; to exchange other currencies, but not traveler's checks, go to Argecam, open weekdays 8–7. For other banking needs in Puerto Iguazú, try Banco Macro, open weekdays 8–1; it has ATMs. There's nowhere to exchange foreign currency in Presidencia Roque Sáenz Peña, but for other banking needs, including ATM transactions, go to Banco Nación, open weekdays 7:30–11:30.

▪ Bank Information **Argecam** ✉ Av. Victoria Aguirre 562, Puerto Iguazú ☎ 3757/420273. **Banco Macro** ✉ Av. Victoria Aguirre 330, Puerto Iguazú ☎ 3757/420212. **Banco Nación** ✉ Calles 12 and 7, Presidencia Roque Sáenz Peña ☎ 3732/420300. **Bank Boston** ✉ Colón 1630, Posadas ☎ 3752/420113. **Cambio Mazza** ✉ Bolívar 1932, Posadas ☎ 3752/440505. **COFIBAL** ✉ Urquiza 834, Gualeguaychú ☎ 3446/426106.

SIGHTSEEING TOURS

From Colón, LHL organizes half-day trips to Parque Nacional El Palmar and Palacio San José.

A reliable travel agency for booking flights and tours in Gualeguaychú is Gualeguaychú Turismo. Lancha Ciudad de Gualeguaychú has a 40-person boat that goes for short trips along the Río Gualeguaychú four times per day for about 7 pesos per person. Siroco's 20-person sailboat travels along the Río Gualeguaychú for an hour-long trip several times a day for 5 pesos per person. Special trips to Río Uruguay can be arranged.

The only tour operator in Posadas is the reliable Abra, which arranges trips of varying length and price (they tend to be on the expensive side); the most popular are to the Jesuit mission ruins, Yacyretá Dam, Saltos de Moconá, and the Cataratas del Iguazú. English-speaking guides are available.

Tobas, in Presidencia Roque Sáenz Peña, is a reliable travel agency. At Quiyoc, owner Nestor Medina arranges personalized trips to El Impenetrable, Esteros del Iberá, and Campos de Cielo (a field where a meteorite shower fell 6,000 years ago), as well as fishing trips to several spots in Chaco and Corrientes.

All tour operators in Puerto Iguazú arrange basically the same trips: to Itaipú Dam, the San Ignacio ruins, a helicopter ride on the Brazilian side, and a circuit of falls on both sides. Two of the most reliable agencies are Aguas Grandes and IGR. Iguazú Explorer has four trips to the jungle and falls. The best is the Gran Aventura, which includes a truck ride through the forest and a boat ride to San Martín, Bossetti, and the Salto

Tres Mosqueteros (be ready to get soaked). Another tour takes you to Garganta del Diablo. Park ranger Daniel Somay organizes personalized Jeep tours through his Explorador Expediciones in Puerto Iguazú. Bring binoculars to see the birds.

🚩 Tour Companies **Aguas Grandes** ✉ Mariano Moreno 58, Puerto Iguazú ☎ 3757/421240. **Explorador Expediciones** ✉ Perito Moreno 217, Puerto Iguazú ☎ 3757/421632. **Gualeguaychú Turismo** ✉ Urquiza 786, Gualeguaychú ☎ 3446/424334. **Iguazú Explorer** ✉ Sheraton Internacional Iguazú Hotel, Puerto Iguazú ☎ 3757/421600. **Lancha Ciudad de Gualeguaychú** ✉ Plaza Colón, Gualeguaychú ☎ 3446/423248. **LHL** ✉ 12 de Abril 119, Colón ☎ 3447/422222. **Quiyoc** ✉ Las Heras 464, Sáenz Peña ☎ 3732/420721. **Tobas** ✉ Calle 17 (Superiora Palmira) 480, Presidencia Roque Sáenz Peña ☎ 3732/423105.

TAXIS

Taxis (*remises*) are generally inexpensive; the fare is based on the number of blocks traveled. Taxis can be hailed, but it's generally easier to call one. In Colón, try Remis-Palmar. A trip to and from Parque Nacional El Palmar, with a wait, should cost around 45 pesos; to the Palacio San José 40 pesos. In Gualeguaychú there's Remís Gualeguaychú, and in Posadas, Remises Nivel. In San Ignacio, independently owned taxis can often be found on Avenida San Martín near the ruins. A good way to explore the other ruins is to have a taxi take you from San Ignacio to Nuestra Señora de Loreto, wait, and then drop you off at Santa Ana. From there you can return to Posadas by catching a bus on the highway, a short walk from the ruins. It should cost about 15 pesos and take about two hours. If you want the taxi driver to wait at Santa Ana with you and then drop you off on the highway, it will probably cost an additional 10 pesos. In Presidencia Roque Sáenz Peña, try Remis Sáenz Peña. In Puerto Iguazú, one of the biggest taxi companies is Remis Unión; taxis are available for short rides and longer day trips. With a group of three or four, you may find this a more economical and certainly more convenient way to get around.

🚩 **Remís Gualeguaychú** ☎ 3446/422612. **Remises Nivel** ☎ 3752/428500. **Remis-Palmar** ☎ 3447/421278. **Remis Sáenz Peña** ☎ 3732/425041.

TELEPHONES & INTERNET ACCESS

Card-operated public phones are easy to find. Telephone cards can be purchased in many shops and kiosks. For long-distance calls and to send faxes, find the nearest *telecentro* (telephone center).

Colón's telecentro is open daily 8 AM–1 AM. Gualeguaychú's Visionet has Internet connections; it's open weekdays 7–noon and 4–7. In Posadas, Telecentro Plaza San Martín has long-distance calling, fax, and Internet access; it's open daily 6 AM–midnight. In Presidencia Roque Sáenz Peña, Telecentro Chaco has fax and Internet access; it's open Monday–Saturday 7 AM–midnight and Sunday 8:30 AM–midnight. Puerto Iguazú's telecentro is open daily 7 AM–midnight.

🚩 **Colón Telecentro** ✉ 12 de Abril 338 ☎ 3447/421479. **Puerto Iguazú Telecentro** ✉ Av. Victoria Aguirre 254 ☎ 3757/422454. **Telecentro Chaco** ✉ Calle 12, No. 1020, Presidencia Roque Sáenz Peña ☎ 3732/426630. **Telecentro Plaza San Martín** ✉ Ayacucho 2025, Posadas ☎ 3752/449719.

TRANSPORTATION AROUND THE NORTHEAST

Traveling by bus is the principal means of transportation in the region. If there's no public transportation to an out-of-town sight, you need to make other arrangements, such as a taxi or a tour.

VISITOR INFORMATION

The Cataratas del Iguazú visitor center, at the park entrance, is open daily 7 AM–8 PM. Colón's visitor center is open daily 6 AM–8 PM in winter, 6 AM–11 PM in summer. The visitor center in Gualeguaychú stays open 8–8 in winter and 8 AM–10 PM in summer. Presidencia Roque Sáenz Peña's visitor center is open weekdays and Saturday 7:30 AM–1 AM. Puerto Iguazú's visitor center is open daily 7–1 and 2–8. Secretaría de Turismo de la Provincia de Misiones in Posadas is the tourism authority for the province; it's open weekdays 7 AM–8 PM and weekends 8–noon and 4:30–8.

🚩**Cataratas del Iguazú** ✉ Visitor center at park entrance ☎ 3757/420180. **Colón** ✉ Av. Costanera and E. Gouchón ☎ 3447/421233. **Gualeguaychú** ✉ Plazoleta de los Artesanos, Paseo del Puerto ☎ 3446/423668. **Presidencia Roque Sáenz Peña** ✉ Calle 17, between Calles 10 and 12. **Puerto Iguazú** ✉ Av. Victoria Aguirre 311 ☎ 3757/420800. **Secretaría de Turismo de la Provincia de Misiones** ✉ Colón 1985, Posadas ☎ 3752/447540, 0800/555–0297 toll-free for local calls.

THE NORTHWEST

FODOR'S CHOICE

El Manantial del Silencio, *Purmamarca*

Hotel El Lagar, *Salta*

Iglesia San Francisco, *Salta*

Manos Jujeñas, *San Salvador de Jujuy*

Quebrada de Humahuaca

Tren a las Nubes, *Salta*

HIGHLY RECOMMENDED

El Solar del Convento, *restaurant in Salta*

Hotel Carlos V, *San Miguel de Tucumán*

Hotel Solar de la Plaza, *Salta*

Hotel Salta, *Salta*

La Leñita, *San Miguel de Tucumán*

Paseo de Siete Colores, *Purmamarca*

Updated by
Robin S.
Goldstein

THE HISTORY OF ARGENTINA BEGAN in the Northwest, in the provinces of Jujuy, Salta, and Tucumán, along the ancient road of the Incas. In the late 1400s, the Incan people traveled southward from Peru along this route to conquer the tribes of northern Argentina and Chile. Half a century later the Spaniards traveled the same route in search of gold and silver. By 1535 the Royal Road of the Inca had become a well-established trade route between the mines in the north and the agricultural riches of Argentina to the south. Examples of the pre-Hispanic and colonial cultures remain in the architecture, music, language, dress, and craftsmanship found in small villages throughout the region. Churches built by the Jesuits in the 17th century dot the landscape; Incan ruins lie half-buried in remote valleys and high plateaus; and pre-Inca mummies continue to be discovered in the highest peaks of the Andes near Salta.

The landscape, too, is incredibly varied—from 22,000-foot-high Andean peaks to the high, barren plateau known as the Puna, subtropical jungles, deserts with multicolor mountains, and narrow sandstone gorges cut by raging brown rivers. Much of the area is desert, cut and eroded by rivers that wash away everything in sight during summer rains, leaving deep red-rock canyons (*quebradas*) with strange rock formations and polychromatic mountainsides, resembling parts of the American Southwest. Snowcapped peaks, some more than 18,000 feet, in the Aconquija range in Tucumán, form a startling backdrop to the lush green subtropical jungle that climbs the slopes of the pre-cordilleras (foothills).

Exploring the Northwest

To fully appreciate the historical significance and the scenic and cultural diversity of the Andean Northwest, you must visit not only the major cities of Salta and San Miguel de Tucumán but also the high plateaus, deep canyons, and colonial villages wherein lie the stories of pre-Hispanic civilizations, conquering Spaniards, and the determining forces of nature.

Neighboring Bolivia calls the high-altitude Andean desert of this region by its Spanish name, the *altiplano,* but Argentina prefers the ancient Quechua term for the region, the Puna. The desert covers an area of 90,000 square km (34,750 square mi) from Catamarca north, across the Andes into Bolivia, Peru, and Chile. Alpaca, guanaco, llama, and vicuña are the only animals you'll see; dry grasses and thorny shrubs with deep roots searching for moisture the only plants. The wind is relentless. Who could live here? Just as you've asked yourself this question, the colorful red poncho of a *coya* (native woman of this region) momentarily brightens the barren landscape as she appears out of nowhere, herding llamas into an unseen ravine. Many people can't breathe at this altitude, let alone walk or sleep: luckily, ordinary mortals can experience a taste of the Puna from El Tren a las Nubes (The Train to the Clouds) in Salta, or by car driving north from Humahuaca to La Quiaca on the Bolivian border.

Down in the valleys, the colonial villages of Cafayate and Cachi bask in the warm, sunny Calchaquíes Valley on the border of Tucumán and Salta provinces. The soaring cliffs of the Talampaya Canyon in La Rioja, the Quebrada de Las Conchas between Salta and Cafayate, and the Quebrada de Humahuaca in Jujuy Province all impress with their peculiar rock formations.

About the Restaurants

The Northwest's indigenous heritage has influenced the unique cuisine: corn and potatoes are common ingredients in many of the region's dishes. Some dishes worth trying include *locro,* a soup of corn, beans, and red peppers, which becomes a stew when meat is added; *tamales,* ground corn baked with potatoes and meat and tied up in a corn husk; and *humitas,* grated corn with melted cheese cooked in a corn husk. Grilled *cabrito* (goat) is a specialty of the region. For dessert, you may come across *cayote,* an interesting concoction of green-squash marmalade served with nuts and local cheese.

About the Hotels

Hotels in the Northwest's major cities tend to be modern and comfortable. Most accept credit cards, though several offer discounts if you pay in cash. Many *estancias* (ranches) in the foothills accept guests and are listed with local tourist offices. ACA (Automóvil Club Argentino) maintains good campgrounds with numerous amenities. Note that as you travel farther north into smaller towns, English is rarely spoken at hotels.

WHAT IT COSTS In Argentina Pesos					
	$$$$	**$$$**	**$$**	**$**	**¢**
RESTAURANTS	over 3	25–35	15–25	8–15	under 8
HOTELS	over 300	220–300	140–220	80–140	under 80

Restaurant prices are for one main course at dinner. Hotel prices are for two people in a standard double room in high season.

Timing

The most agreeable times to visit are spring (October–December) and early autumn (April and May), when the weather is most pleasant. Winter (June–September) is brisk and downright cold on the Andean Puna but is actually the Northwest's peak tourist season. Rooms in better hotels may fill up at this time as well as during Semana Santa (Holy Week) and fiestas, so reserve ahead. Summer (January–March) is hot and rainy, and those rains frequently cause landslides that block mountain roads. (The Tucumán–Tafí del Valle route is notorious in that regard.) Most facilities do remain open year-round, but the region's famed Tren a las Nubes rail excursion from Salta does not operate at all in summer.

SALTA & JUJUY

The provinces of Salta and Jujuy make up the northern frontier of the vast Argentine territory. The farther north you progress, the more things start to feel Northern Andean, more evocative of Bolivia and Peru than of the modern industrialized capitals of the Argentine south. Indeed, many travelers wind up in these provinces by way of the Chilean Andes and the Puna, or one of the notorious border crossings from Bolivia and Paraguay. In this misty corner of Argentina, you'll come across Spanish-colonial plazas with hand-painted signs, cloud-shrouded river valleys, arid salt flats with craggy red rocks, train tracks into the clouds, Andean pan flute music, and locals munching on coca leaves—available at any corner store in the region, they're the ultimate antidote for altitude sickness.

Salta—the unofficial capital of the Argentine North and a growing hotspot for international tourism—is known throughout the country for its colonial architecture and its unassuming provincial appeal. The circuit south of Salta, including the smaller towns of San Lorenzo, Cachi, Cafayate, and Quilmes, has even more rural charm, although the roads connecting these villages are often unpaved. Progressing north from Salta, though, roads become yet narrower, prices get lower, and faces turn more indigenous as backpacker havens give way to rural villages so off-the-beaten-path, even the backpackers haven't discovered them yet. After the big provincial capital of Jujuy, towns get progressively smaller and wilder as you follow the R9 road, which snakes along the valley of the spectacular gorge, La Quebrada de Humahuaca. After passing the adobe villages of Purmamarca and Tilcara, Humahuaca is the most northerly destination featuring much in the way of modern amenities; north or west of that, you'll want a four-wheel-drive vehicle and an enterprising spirit. The intrepid will eventually arrive at the frontier outposts of Yavi and La Quiaca on the Bolivian border.

Salta

2 hrs from Buenos Aires by plane; 311 km (193 mi) north of Tucumán on R9 or 420 km (260 mi) north of Tucumán on R68 via Tafí del Valle, 92 km (57 mi) south of San Salvador de Jujuy on R9 or 311 km (193 mi) south of San Salvador de Jujuy on R34 (La Cornisa Rd.).

It's not just "Salta" to most Argentines, but "Salta la Linda" (Salta the Beautiful). That nickname is actually redundant—"Salta" already comes from an indigenous Aymara word meaning "beautiful"—but for the country's finest colonial city, it's worth stating twice. Walking among its well-preserved 18th- and 19th-century buildings, single-story houses, wooden balconies, and narrow streets, you could easily forget that this is a city of 500,000 people. But the ever-increasing traffic, the youthful population, and the growing contingent of international itinerants also give the city an irresistible cosmopolitan edge. All in all, it's a hard place to leave. Salta is also the best base for a thorough exploration of the Northwest.

a good walk

Plaza 9 de Julio ❶ ▶, the central park, is the logical starting point for any Salta tour. The magnificent **Catedral de Salta ❷** fronts the north side of the plaza on Avenida España. Head to the west side of the plaza to the **Museo de Arqueología de Alta Montaña ❸**, on Mitre. Walk west from the plaza on Caseros for one block, then south on La Florida. The **Museo de Bellas Artes ❹**, a fine arts museum, and **Casa de Hernández ❺**, showcasing city history, sit across from each other on La Florida. Backtrack to the plaza to see the **Cabildo ❻**, the seat of the city government, on the south side on Caseros. Walk one block farther east on Caseros to see the **Museo Presidente José Evaristo Uriburu ❼**, a fine example of a colonial-era dwelling; across the street is the **Iglesia San Francisco ❽**, the city's most recognizable church. Three blocks farther east on Caseros you'll come across the **Convento de San Bernardo ❾**. To finish off your tour, walk to the east end of Caseros, turn right onto Avenida H. Yrigoyen, and make a right onto Avenida San Martín, which leads to the **Teleférico a Cerro San Bernardo ❿**. Here, cable cars take you to the top of Cerro San Bernardo, from which you can look down over the entire valley.

TIMING   If you don't linger at the sights, you can do this walk in less than two hours, but spending more time inside the buildings adds perspective. Note that many places close for three or four hours in the afternoon. So either resign yourself to getting a very early start or split the walk in two. Weekdays are best; most places don't reopen on weekend afternoons.

What to See

❻ **Cabildo** (Town Hall). This whitewashed building, first constructed in 1582 and rebuilt many times since, houses Salta's municipal government. The **Museo Histórico del Norte** (History Museum of the North) occupies two floors of the Cabildo with an eclectic mix of exhibits about the pre-Hispanic, colonial, and religious history of city of Salta and the sur-

Numbers in the text correspond to numbers in the margin and on the North-west, Salta, and San Salvador de Jujuy maps.

4

If you have 5 days

If you have less than a week, begin your stay in 🖼 **Salta** ❶– ❿ with a city tour, spending your first night here. From Salta take a day trip or overnight excursion southwest to 🖼 **Cafayate** ⑫, in the Calchaquíes Valley. On Day 3, drive north on La Cornisa Road (R9) to the provincial capital of 🖼 **San Salvador de Jujuy** ⑭– ㉒. After a tour of the city and its historic landmarks, spend the night in town. Early the next morning head for the village of **Purmamarca** ㉓, behind which the Cerro de Siete Colores (Hill of the Seven Colors) rises in a polychromatic wall. Stay in Purmamarca for your fourth night. On the fifth day, follow the Río Grande up the colorful Quebrada to **Tilcara** ㉔ and then **Humahuaca** ㉕, a typical Quechua village at 9,000 feet. Both Tilcara and Humahuaca can be done as a day trip from Purmamarca, so if you have a fifth night, staying in Purmamarca again before returning to Salta is a possibility.

If you have 7 days

Begin your trip by exploring the lively university city of 🖼 **San Miguel de Tucumán** ㉘, your base for the first night. On the second day head to 🖼 **Tafí del Valle** ㉙ and spend the night there. The next day, travel over the mountains into the Calchaquíes Valley and on to 🖼 **Cafayate** ⑫, stopping for the night. On the fourth day continue north to 🖼 **Salta** ❶– ❿; spend two days here, ideally including a Saturday so that you can take El Tren a las Nubes. From Salta, follow the two-day excursion to 🖼 **San Salvador de Jujuy** ⑭– ㉒ and **Purmamarca** ㉓, with a day trip to **Tilcara** ㉔ and **Humahuaca** ㉕, as detailed in the five-day itinerary above.

If you have 10 days

Follow the seven-day itinerary above, but tack on an extra night in 🖼 **San Miguel de Tucumán** ㉘. Between Cafayate and Salta, follow the R40 and add a night in **Cachi** ⑪, using the day to visit the bodegas Etchart and Michel Torino. And if you're adventurous, at the end of the itinerary, tack on a day to add a trip farther north to **La Quiaca** ㉖ on the Bolivian border.

---

rounding province. The museum also highlights the works of regional artists in temporary exhibits. ✉ *Caseros 549* ☎ *387/421–5340* 🎫 *2 pesos* ⏱ *Tues.–Fri. 9:30–1:30 and 3:30–8:30, Sat. 9:30–1:30 and 5–8, Sun. 10–1.*

❺ **Casa de Hernández** (Hernández House). Inside an 1870 neocolonial house is the **Museo de la Ciudad.** The first floor displays an exceptional collection of musical instruments. Rooms upstairs document the history of Salta through paintings and photographs. ✉ *La Florida 97* ☎ *387/437–3352* 🎫 *1 peso* ⏱ *Weekdays 9–1:30 and 3–8, Sat. 9–1:30.*

❷ **Catedral de Salta** (Salta Cathedral). The city's 1882 neoclassical cathedral fronts the central plaza and is notable for the enormous frescoes on the portico around the altar, which portray the four gospel writers. On either side of the altar, small chapels hold the icons of the Señor y Virgen del Milagro, the patrons of Salta. Tradition credits these statues of Christ and the Virgin Mary with minimizing the damage of nine days of earth tremors in 1692. Inside the entrance is the Panteón de las Glorias del Norte, enclosing the tombs of General Martín Miguel de Güemes and other heroes from the War of Independence. ⊠ *España 537* ☎ *Free* ⊙ *Mon.–Sat. 6:30–12:30 and 4:30–8:15, Sun. 6:30–12:30 and 5:30–8:15.*

⑨ Convento de San Bernardo (Convent of St. Bernard). The oldest religious building in Salta served as a chapel first, then a hospital. Today a cloistered order of Carmelite nuns lives here, so the convent is closed to the public. The wooden rococo-style door, hand-carved by indigenous craftsmen in 1762, contrasts markedly with the otherwise stark exterior of the 1625 structure. ⊠ *Caseros 73.*

⑧ Iglesia San Francisco (St. Francis Church). Every Salteño's heart and soul belong to the town's landmark church, with its white pillars and bright terra-cotta–and-gold facade. The first temple and convent were built in 1625; the second, erected in 1674, was destroyed by fire; the present church was completed in 1882. The 173-foot-high belfry, with five independent sections piled on top of each other, houses the Campana de la Patria, a bell made from the bronze cannons used in the War of Independence, which rings with an atonal, strangely hypnotic rhythm, for more than 20 minutes, each afternoon at 5:30. In the sacristy, the **Museo Convento San Francisco** displays religious art and furniture from the colonial period. ⊠ *Córdoba 33* ☎ *387/432–1445* ☎ *Church free, museum 1 peso* ⊙ *Church daily 7–noon and 5–9; museum daily 9–noon and 5–8.*

FodorśChoice ★

③ Museo de Arqueología de Alta Montaña (Museum of High Mountain Archaeology). This museum exhibits the mummified remains of six children from a pre-Inca civilization and assorted funerary objects discovered at the summit of the 22,058-foot Volcán Llullaillaco, on the Argentine-Chilean border. The children are presumed to have been part of a ritual sacrifice; the burial site is thought to be the world's highest tomb. Museum hours, admission price, and phone number had not been determined at this writing. Contact the **tourist office** (☎ 387/431–0950) for details. ⊠ *Mitre 71.*

④ Museo de Bellas Artes (Fine Arts Museum). The 18th-century home of General Félix Árias Rengel now holds Salta's principal art museum. Its collection of colonial-era religious art includes figures from Argentina's Jesuit missions as well as Cuzco-style paintings from Peru and Bolivia. Another hall of the museum highlights 20th-century works by Salteño artists. ⊠ *La Florida 20* ☎ *387/421–4714* ☎ *1 peso* ⊙ *Weekdays 9–1 and 4–8:30, Sat. 10–1.*

⑦ Museo Presidente José Evaristo Uriburu (President José Evaristo Uriburu Museum). Fine examples of late-colonial architecture—an interior courtyard, thick adobe walls, a reed-and-tile roof—abound in this simple building, the 19th- and 20th-century home of the Uriburu family, which gave Argentina two presidents. Furniture, costumes, paintings, and family documents are on display in six rooms. ⊠ *Caseros 417* ☎ *387/421–8174* ☎ *1 peso* ⊙ *Tues.–Sun. 9:30–1:30 and 3:30–8:30.*

① Plaza 9 de Julio (July 9 Square). The heart of Salta is quintessential Latin America: a leafy, bustling central plaza named for the date of Argentina's independence. Arcaded buildings, many housing sidewalk cafés, line the streets surrounding the square, providing perfect spots to while away a warm afternoon.

need a break?

Van Gogh. This Parisian-style café, with reproductions of works of its namesake master, is one of the best coffee shops lining Plaza 9 de Julio. Come here to enjoy great coffee and cakes while writing

4

Folklore & Festivals

Several local festivals in the Northwest's high mountain villages and colonial cities celebrate Argentina's rich history. The parades, performances, costumes, music, and dancing of these festivals draw on 2,000-year-old Inca rituals, Catholic beliefs, political history, gaucho tradition, agricultural practices, local handicrafts, and regional food. **Inti Raymi** (Festival of the Sun), celebrated since Inca times on June 21 (winter solstice), marks the end of one year's planting and the beginning of the next. The indigenous residents, many of them dressed in traditional costumes handed down through generations, come from nearby villages to sing, dance, play music, and pay tribute to Pachamama (Mother Earth), and to pray to Inti, the Sun, for a good harvest. Festivities begin the night before in Huacalera on the tropic of Capricorn (105 km [65 mi] north of San Salvador de Jujuy in the Humahuaca Valley). The **Virgen de la Candelaria** (the patron saint of Humahuaca) is honored on February 2 in Humahuaca. During the event, *sikuris* (bands of young men playing Andean flutes) parade through the cobblestone streets accompanied by dancers and musicians. The **Fiesta del Poncho** (Gaucho Festival), a parade held on June 17 in Salta, is an impressive display of the power of the legendary gauchos and their fine horses. Pre-Lenten **Carnaval** is celebrated in towns and villages throughout the Northwest. In Salta, a parade of floats depicting historic events accompanies dancing characters wearing feathered and mirrored masks—some of them caricaturing local dignitaries. Beware of *bombas de agua* (water balloons) dropping from balconies. **El Éxodo Jujueño** (Jujuy Exodus), also known as the **Semana de Jujuy** (Week of Jujuy), is a historic festival held August 23–24 to commemorate General Belgrano's successful evacuation of the city in August 1812, before Spanish troops arrived. Salta celebrates the **Fiesta del Milagro** (Festival of the Miracle) September 6–15 in thanks for being spared damage from nine days of earth tremors in 1692. Figures of Christ and the Virgin Mary, credited with protecting the city, are paraded through the streets. In Tucumán, the cradle of Argentina's freedom, **Independence Day** is celebrated with special fervor on July 9 and the battle of Tucumán on September 24.

---

postcards to folks back home. ⊠ *España 502* ☎ *387/431–4659* ⊟ *AE, MC, V.*

❿ Teleférico a Cerro San Bernardo (Cable Car to San Bernardo Hill). The Cerro San Bernardo looms east of downtown Salta, a cool 880 feet higher than the city center. A cable car takes you from a station across from Parque San Martín to the top of San Bernardo in less than 10 minutes. Views of the entire Lerma Valley reward you at the top. ⊠ *San Martín and H. Yrigoyen* ☎ *387/431–0641* ⊠ *3 pesos one-way* ☉ *Daily 9–6:45.*

Fodor's Choice **Tren a las Nubes** (Train to the Clouds). A 14-hour round-trip train ex-★ cursion takes you to the high, desolate Puna and back. The trip begins at 4,336 feet as the train climbs out of the Lerma Valley into the mountains. As the train rattles over steel bridges that span wild rivers, it winds ever upward through many turns and tunnels and passes over the 210-foot-high **Viaducto La Polvorilla**, until it reaches the top at 13,770 feet,

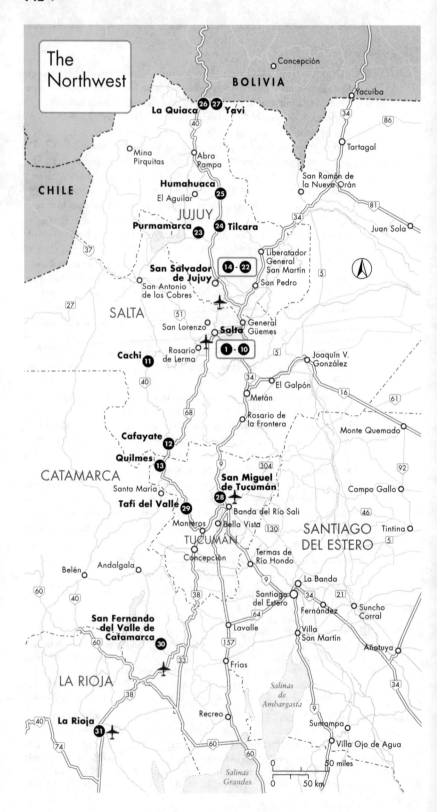

just beyond **San Antonio de los Cobres.** At this point you can disembark to test the thin air and visit a train-side market set up by locals. When the train returns the short distance to San Antonio de Los Cobres, it makes a second stop, and the market reappears. The only town of its size in the Puna, San Antonio de Los Cobres is an important customs and trucking stop on the road (R40) to Chile. For 160 pesos you get a guide, lunch in the dining car, a first-aid car equipped with oxygen for altitude sickness, and the experience of a lifetime. Reservations are essential; they can be made at most local tourism agencies, which are ubiquitous downtown. *In Salta ⊠ Caseros 431 ☎ 387/431–4984 🖷 387/431–6174 ⊠ In Buenos Aires ⊠ Esmeralda 1008 ☎🖷 11/ 4311–4282 ⊕ www.trenubes.com.ar ☉ Apr.–June and Aug.–Nov., most Sat. at 7 AM; July, Tues. and weekends at 7 AM; occasionally runs Sun. in June, Aug., and Sept.*

Nightlife & the Arts

El Rastro Peña (⊠ Av. San Martín 2555 ☎ 387/434–2987) is a big auditoriumlike dining hall—that is, until the lights dim and the beat of a drum, the whine of *quenas* (bamboo pipes), and the strumming of a guitar begin. National folk groups appear regularly. Shows begin at 10:30 PM, and reservations are advised.

Sports & the Outdoors

Turismo de Estancia provides the opportunity to stay on a working farm or ranch where you can you ride horses, hike, and get to know the countryside. At some estancias in the Calchaquíes and Lerma valleys, you can also participate in wine- and cheese making. The **tourist office** (⊠ Buenos Aires 93 ☎ 387/431–0950) in Salta has a list of farms and ranches.

Shopping

You could spend hours inside the 1882 Jesuit monastery that holds the **Mercado Artesanal** (✉ Av. San Martín 2555 ☎ 387/434–2808) and at the open stalls across the street. Goods range from red-and-black Salteño ponchos, alpaca knitwear and weavings, and leather goods to wood masks of animals and fine silver. It's open daily 9–9.

en route | If you're in the mood for a scenic drive north of Salta, you can even take the more rural **Route 9** between Salta and Jujuy, which is actually more direct than the highway, but will take a bit longer. Unless you're squeamish about narrow, winding roads, the extra time and wear and tear on your tires is worth it. Be sure to leave with a full tank of gas before embarking on this isolated, one-lane road, which winds through pine forests and hills. Keep your headlights on and honk before each of the many hairpin turns. Be sure to stop along the way at one or two sleepy little towns, such as **El Carmen**, about 27 km south of Jujuy; it has a shady little colonial plaza that time has left behind. Depending on your get-up, you may get some curious stares. There's a police checkpoint right along Route 9 about 5 km before El Carmen, where approximately one in three cars is stopped. If you look like a tourist, chances are you'll be the one in three. If you're given the fifth degree, however, a small bribe ("una colaboración") will help smooth things over—you might be asked outright for a small fee of 5 pesos or so; if not you may want to tactfully take the initiative by saying something along the lines of "Will it help to pay a fee?" Be polite and *don't* refer to the "fee" as a "colaboración," which might offend and get you into hotter water.

San Lorenzo

10 km (6 mi) northwest of Salta.

Salta is hardly an urban jungle, but some visitors opt to stay in the quieter hillside suburb of San Lorenzo a few miles away and a cooler 980 feet higher. It's a great place to stay if you have a car or can adhere to the every-30-minute bus service to and from Salta.

Where to Stay & Eat

¢–$ ✕ **Lo de Andrés.** Folks from Salta favor this bright, airy semi-enclosed brick-and-glass building with a vaulted ceiling for weekend dining. Andrés grills a lightly spiced Argentine-style parrillada, but if you're not up for such a feast, there are empanadas and *milanesas* (breaded steak) as well. ✉ *Juan Carlos Dávalos and Gorriti* ☎ *387/492–1600* ▣ *AE, DC, MC, V* ☉ *No lunch Mon.*

$–$$ ▥ **Eaton Place.** Despite appearances, this elegant Georgian-style mansion and its beautiful gardens are only a dozen years old. The bright and airy rooms in the main house and guest house have huge windows, hardwood floors, and period furniture. And you've likely never seen accommodations as huge as the dark-wood-paneled penthouse suite, complete with a vaulted ceiling. Rooms in the back guest house are smaller but still regal, in a more subdued way. Two of the guest-house double rooms share a sitting room, making them ideal for a family or group. Rates include a huge breakfast. ✉ *San Martín, 4401* ☎☎ *387/492–1347* ⊕ *www.redsalta.com/eatonplace* ☛ *8 rooms, 1 suite* ♨ *Pool* ▣ *No credit cards.*

¢–$ ▥ **Hostal Selva Montana.** A friendly German couple has created a quiet oasis in their hillside stucco house near the center of town. The white rooms, some with balcony, all have light-wood trim, pleasant pastel bedspreads and drapes, and stupendous views. The grounds extend down to a pool and tennis court, and even farther down into the Quebrada

San Lorenzo. Rates include a huge breakfast, and there's a 10% discount if you pay with cash. ✉ *Alfonsina Storni 2315, 4401* ☎ *387/492–1184* 🖷 *387/492–1433* ⊕ *www.iruya.com/ent/selvamontana* ↩ *28 rooms* ⚘ *Tennis court, pool, horseback riding, meeting room* ➟ *AE, DC, MC, V.*

> **en route**   Driving south toward Cafayate on R68 through the **Quebrada de Las Conchas** (Canyon of the Shells), notice the red-sandstone cliffs, sculpted by eons of wind and water into strange yet recognizable rock formations with imaginative names such as Los Castillos (The Castles), El Anfiteatro (The Amphitheater), and La Garganta del Diablo (The Devil's Throat).

Cachi

⑪ *157 km (97 mi) southwest of Salta.*

The long route to Cayafate on a narrow gravel road follows the Calchaquíes Valley along its river through colonial hamlets, untouched and little changed over the years. Cachi, on the site of a pre-Hispanic settlement of the indigenous Chicoana community, is the most interesting of these. Its charming **Iglesia San José**, with a cactus-wood altar, sits on the palm-and-orange–tree-lined central plaza. Watching over it all is the 20,800-foot Nevado del Cachi, a few miles away.

Cafayate

⑫ *185 km (115 mi) southwest of Salta via R68, 340 km (211 mi) southwest of Salta via R40, 230 km (143 mi) northwest of San Miguel de Tucumán.*

Basking in the sunny Calchaquíes Valley, Cafayate deserves much more than a day to absorb its colonial charm, see its fine museums, shop for authentic handicrafts, and visit some of the surrounding vineyards for which it's known. Street-side cafés, shaded by flowering quebracho trees, face the plaza, where a burro is likely to be tied up next to a car. Look for the five naves of the yellow-painted cathedral on the plaza.

For 66 years, Rodolfo Bravo collected and catalogued funerary and religious objects from local excavations. These objects, made out of clay, ceramic, metal, and textiles, are on display at the **Museo Regional y Arqueológico Rodolfo Bravo** (Rudolfo Bravo Regional and Archaeological Museum). Artifacts from the Incas (15th century) and Diaguitas of the Calchaquíes Valley are also part of the collection. ✉ *Colón 191* ☎ *3868/421054* 🎟 *1 peso* ☻ *By appointment only.*

Learn about wine making at the **Museo de la Vid y del Vino** (Museum of Grapevines and Wine), which was created in 1981 in a building dating back to 1881. Machinery, agricultural implements, and old photographs tell the history of wine making in this area. ✉ *R40, Av. General Güemes* ☎ *3868/421125* 🎟 *1 peso* ☻ *Daily 8–8.*

For a sample of Cafayate's Torrontés white wine, head to **Etchart Bodega** (✉ Finca La Florida), south of town on R40 and within walking distance. **Michel Torino Bodega** (✉ Finca La Rosa), on R68 northeast of town, offers tours and wine samples to familiarize you with Cafayate's most celebrated product.

Where to Stay & Eat

¢–$ ✕ **Juanita.** Everything is freshly made, on the spot, and served in the front room of this family house—it's the closest thing to home cooking among local restaurants. ⊠ *Camino Quintana de Niño 60* ☎ *No phone* ▤ *No credit cards.*

¢–$ ✕ **La Casona de Don Luis.** Come here to feast on humitas and locro and drink local Torrontés wine while listening to a guitarist playing gaucho laments. This restaurant with an interior, vine-covered patio is especially pleasant on a sunny afternoon. ⊠ *Salta and Almagro* ☎ *3868/421249* ▤ *No credit cards.*

¢ ▦ **Hotel Gran Real.** The swimming pool, patio, barbecue area, and quiet rooms with basic furnishings more than make up for the torn plastic furniture in the lobby. Rates include an ample breakfast. ⊠ *Av. General Güemes 128, 4427* ☎ *3868/421231* 🖷 *3868/421016* ⇗ *34 rooms* ♨ *Café, pool, bar* ▤ *MC, V.*

¢ ▦ **Hotel Tikunaku.** This small *residencial* (pension) with carpeted rooms is clean and comfortable and has an attentive staff. Note that there's a 10% discount if you pay with cash. ⊠ *Diego de Almagro 12, 4427* ☎🖷 *3868/421148* ⇗ *7 rooms* ♨ *Café* ▤ *V.*

Sports & the Outdoors

The town is flat, so bicycles are a common means of transportation. The tourist office on the plaza can suggest nearby destinations for hiking or biking. If you're ambitious, take a long ride along the Río Calchaquí on R40 (Argentina's longest highway and one of its longest rivers); along the way you'll pass through quiet colonial hamlets and ever-changing scenery. Bicycles and camping and fishing equipment can be rented at **Rudy** (⊠ Av. General Güemes 175). Horses are available from **La Florida** (⊠ at the Etchart Bodega), 2 km (1 mi) south of town on R40.

Quilmes

⑬ *50 km (31 mi) south of Cafayate.*

South of Cafayate, just over the border into Tucumán Province, lie Argentina's most well preserved ruins, home to a community of indigenous Quilmes between the 11th and 17th centuries. Some 5,000 people lived within this walled city at its peak (late 1600s). The Quilmes valiantly resisted the arrival of the Spaniards but were eventually subjugated and deported from the region. A small **museum** documents the history of the 75-acre site. ⊠ *Off R40* ☎ *3892/421075* 💲 *2 pesos* ☉ *Daily 9–dusk.*

San Salvador de Jujuy

1,643 km (1,020 mi) northwest of Buenos Aires, 97 km (60 mi) north of Salta, 459 km (285 mi) north of Tucumán.

San Salvador de Jujuy (simply Jujuy to most Argentines, and s. s. DE JUJUY on signs) is the capital of the province of Jujuy (pronounced "hoo-*hoo*-wee"). Founded by Spaniards in 1593, it was the northernmost town on the military and trade route between the Spanish garrisons in Peru and the northern cities of Argentina.

History has not been kind to the city: war and earthquakes over the centuries have taken their toll. San Salvador de Jujuy today is modern, with a large indigenous population and a few monuments to its proud past. The city lacks nearby Salta's colonial dreaminess, as well as its southern neighbor's wide selection of accommodations. That said, it has a pleasant downtown and unadulterated local culture with a bit of frontier-town charm; there's less tourist-oriented development here than in Salta, and it's a great base from which to explore the Puna region.

San Salvador de Jujuy

⑮ The whitewashed 1867 **Cabildo** (City Hall) houses the **Museo Histórico Policial** (Police-History Museum), a small collection of historical police uniforms and weapons. You may want to skip the gruesome second-floor exhibit of preserved body parts and fetuses. ⊠ *North side of Plaza General Belgrano* ☎ *388/423–7715* 💲 *Free* ⊙ *Mon.–Sat. 8–1 and 4–9.*

㉒ The austere 1777 **Capilla de Santa Bárbara** (Chapel of St. Barbara) houses a collection of paintings brought from Cuzco, one of which depicts the church's patron, St. Barbara. You can see the inside during Sunday mass at 8 and 10 AM; the building is locked the rest of the week (thefts have been a problem), but if you call ahead you can probably convince the key-bearers to let you in for a look around—a few pesos tip is appropriate. ⊠ *San Martín and La Madrid* ☎ *388/422–3009* 💲 *Free* ⊙ *Weekdays 10–noon and 5–10, weekends 7–noon and 5–10.*

⑰ The 1907 **Casa de Gobierno** (Government House) fronts the Plaza General Belgrano on San Martín and contains the offices of Jujuy's provincial government. A second-floor hall, the **Salón de la Bandera,** displays the original Argentine flag donated by General Belgrano in 1813, a gift to the city after its famed exodus during the War of Independence. You'll have to ask a guard to let you into the hall, which is always locked. ⊠ *San Martín 450* ☎ *388/423–9400* 💲 *Free* ⊙ *Weekdays 9–1 and 3–8.*

⑱ **Catedral de Jujuy** dates to 1763 but has been augmented and remodeled so many times that it's now a hodgepodge of architectural styles. The impressive interior contains the city's most stunning work of art, an ornately carved, gold-plated pulpit, said to be the finest in South America. A close look at the pulpit reveals an intricate population of carved figures, biblical and otherwise. It was inspired by the Cusqueña school of art from Cuzco, Peru, as were the building's ornate doors and confessionals. ⊠ *West side of Plaza General Belgrano* ☎ *388/423–5333* ☎ *Free* ⊙ *Weekdays 10–noon and 5–10, weekends 7–noon and 5–10.*

Harking back to the Northwest's rail heyday is the pink art-nouveau **⑭ Estación de Ferrocarril,** a former train station built in 1901. The building now houses Jujuy's friendly tourist office, the **Dirección Provincial de Turismo.** ⊠ *Urquiza 354* ☎ *388/422–1326* ⊙ *Daily 8–2 and 3–9.*

⑲ The centerpiece of the **Iglesia de San Francisco** (Church of St. Francis), two blocks west of Plaza General Belgrano, is an ornate 18th-century wooden pulpit with dozens of figures of monks. There's some debate about who carved the pulpit: it may have been local artisans, or the pulpit may have been transported from Bolivia. Despite the colonial appearance of the church and bell tower, the present structure dates only to 1930. ⊠ *Belgrano and Lavalle* ☎ *Free* ⊙ *Weekdays 10–noon and 5–10, weekends 7–noon and 5–10.*

⑳ The **Museo Arqueológico Provincial** (Provincial Archaeological Museum) contains archaeological treasures such as a 2,600-year-old ceramic goddess and a mummy of a two-year-old child dating back 1,000 years. Ceramic pots painted with geometric designs from Yavi and Humahuaca are constantly being added to the collection, and a diorama shows what life was like here 9,000 years ago. ⊠ *Lavalle 434* ☎ *388/422–1315* ☎ *1 peso* ⊙ *Weekends 8–1 and 3–8.*

㉑ Arms, trophies, and memorabilia from military campaigns collected from the 25 years of fighting for independence are on display at the **Museo Histórico Provincial Juan Lavalle** (Juan Lavalle Provincial History Museum). In this adobe building, General Juan Lavalle, a hero of the wars of independence and an enemy of the dictator Juan Manuel de Rosas, was assassinated. A replica of the door through which Lavalle was shot in 1746 is part of the exhibit. ⊠ *Lavalle 256* ☎ *388/422–1355* ☎ *1 peso* ⊙ *Weekdays 8 AM–9 PM, Sat. 9–1 and 3–9.*

off the beaten path

PARQUE SAN MARTÍN – An oasis of fountains and tree-shaded relaxation, this park will delight young children with horse rides, a miniature train, and a little amusement park. Young families flood the park on Sundays. It's within easy walking distance of downtown—just head west on Alvear or Güemes. ⊠ *Bounded by General Paz, Avenida España, and Avenida Córdoba.*

⑯ Orange trees and various vendors populate the city's central square, **Plaza General Belgrano,** which is lined with beautiful colonial buildings—including the imposing government palace—but strangely empty most of the time. ⊠ *Bounded by Belgrano, San Martin, Sarmiento, and Gorriti.*

Where to Stay & Eat

$ ✕ **Carena Resto Bar.** Probably the hippest spot in the entire Jujuy province, this restaurant-bar goes straight for New York chic, and in the process creates an exciting brand of Jujeña cuisine that's utterly unique in the region. Try the liver pâté with brioche and mango chutney or pork tenderloin with carmelized onions and brown sugar. Even the basics, like a dressed *lomito* sandwich, are well executed and even inexpensive. The lighting is appropriately muted and hip, and the big plate-glass windows and slick furniture only add to the 1980s-bond-trader effect; the clientele here is clearly the local bourgeoisie. ⊠ *Belgrano and Balcarce* ☎ *388/422–2529* ☐ *DC, MC, V.*

$ ✕ **Madre Tierra.** A vegetarian island in Argentina's sea of steak and empanadas, "Mother Earth" serves a meat-free fixed-price menu that rotates daily. A fairly bland salad, soup, juice, dessert, and whole-grain breads from the popular bakery accompany the main course, which could be spinach lasagna or stuffed eggplant. Don't expect culinary fireworks, but at least it's something different. Try to be seated in back, where you'll be lulled into the proper nature-loving mood by the view of a backyard garden. ⊠ *Otero and Belgrano* ☎ *388/422–9578* ⊟ *No credit cards* ⊘ *Closed Sun. No dinner.*

¢–$
Fodor'sChoice
★

✕ Manos Jujeñas. This is one of the best places in the entire region to try authentic Northwestern cooking. Ponchos on the walls, old paintings, native artifacts, stucco archways, and muted lighting are complemented by the piped-in Andean music. This is *the* place to try *locro*: maize, white beans, pork, chorizo, pancetta, and a wonderful red pepper oil glaze come together in a menage of savory, flowery, and starchy flavors that take this dish—which costs only 4.50 pesos—to another level. ⊠ *Senador Pérez 222* ☎ *388/422–2366* ⊟ *DC, MC, V* ⊘ *No lunch Sun. No dinner Mon.*

¢
✕ Royal Restaurant/Pub. With bustling tables both inside and out on the sidewalk, this is a deservedly popular local *confiteria* right in the thick of things downtown. It's a pleasant choice any time of day, whether just for a *cortado* (coffee with milk; here it's served in a tall glass), *medialuna* (croissant), and a morning newspaper or a quick lunch of a *lomito completo* (meat sandwich with ham, cheese, egg, lettuce, tomato, and mayonnaise). ⊠ *Av. Bolivia 1501* ☎ *388/423–5121* ⊟ *MC, V.*

$$
▣ Termas de Reyes. This countryside complex is improbably perched on the edge of a spectacular river valley. Life here focuses on the virtues of relaxation and panoramic views. The centerpiece is the natural thermal baths, indoor and out, bubbling up from underground hot springs. Rooms are clean and comfortable. It's located 19 km (12 mi) outside Jujuy on a road that's paved for all but 5 km (3 mi). ⊠ *Ruta 4, Km 19* ☎☎ *388/492–2522* ⊕ *www.termasdereyes.com* ⇱ *60 rooms* ⚐ *Restaurant, pool, spa, bar* ⊟ *AE, DC, MC, V.*

¢–$
▣ Jujuy Palace Hotel. Large rooms with impeccable facilities and balconies overlooking the street, a rooftop gym, a gated parking lot, and a formal second-floor dining room with first-class service add to the comforts of this exceptional hotel. Views from the top floors are outstanding, spanning the cloud-covered hills and Spanish colonial domes of the city center. You receive a 20% discount if you pay with cash. ⊠ *Belgrano 1060, 4600* ☎☎ *388/423–0433* ⊕ *www.imagine.com.ar/jujuy. palace/* ⇱ *54 rooms, 5 suites* ⚐ *Restaurant, gym, sauna, bar, meeting room, parking* ⊟ *AE, DC, MC, V.*

¢
▣ Gran Hotel Panorama. The modern Panorama, one of the nicer hotels in town, sits on a quiet corner a couple of blocks removed from the hubbub of Avenida Belgrano. It serves mostly businesspeople. Soft earth tones decorate the dark-wood-paneled rooms, which are a bit on the plain side. You get a 20% discount if you pay with cash. ⊠ *Belgrano 1295, 4600* ☎☎ *388/423–2533* ✑ *hotelpanorama@mail.com.ar* ⇱ *64 rooms, 3 suites* ⚐ *Café, pool, bar, laundry service, meeting room* ⊟ *AE, DC, MC, V.*

Nightlife & the Arts

The hip, modern hot spot **Carena Resto Bar** (⊠ Belgrano and Balcarce ☎ 388/422–2529) is the place, pre- and post-dinner, to sip imported scotch and discuss politics. If it's a musical evening you're after, though, you can hear local bands on Friday and Saturday at **Royal Restaurant–Pub** (⊠ Av. Bolivia 1501 ☎ 388/423–5121).

For something more elaborate and traditional, head for the amusingly named **Chung King** (⊠ Alvear 627 ☎ 388/422–8142), a restaurant that turns into an upscale dinner-entertainment venue with a good *peña* (folkloric music performance) on weekends.

Sports & the Outdoors
With its incredible canyons, painted mountains, wild rivers, and high Puna, the area around Jujuy is great for hiking and horseback riding. Miles of wild, open terrain separate the most interesting places, making driving a necessity. The tourist office in Estación de Ferrocarril can help you organize trips. Another solution is to stay at **Alojamiento El Refugio** (⊠ R9, Km 14, Yala 🕾🕾 388/490–9344), 15 km (9 mi) from town on the Río Yala; it has cabins and campsites, along with a pool and children's playground, and organizes hikes and horseback rides.

QUEBRADA DE HUMAHUACA

Fodor'sChoice ★ North of Jujuy, the inimitable Route 9 continues into the **Quebrada de Humahuaca** (Humahuaca Gorge), an explosion of improbable color stretched across over long stretches of craggy, bare rock, and one of Argentina's most distinctive landscapes. Variegated tones of pink, red, and gray color the canyon walls like giant swaths of paint. As the gorge deepens and narrows as it approaches Humahuaca on its northern tip, the colors become more vibrant, and mustard and green are added to the hues. Bright-green alamo and willow trees surround villages, contrasting with the deep red tones in the background. In summer and fall, torrential rains mixed with mud and melting snow from the high mountains rush down the mountainsides, carving deep ravines before pouring into the chalky gray Río Grande. Often this flow of water washes out the road, leaving it in constant need of repair.

Along the way, the R9 winds past the dusty villages of Purmamarca, Tilcara, Humahuaca, Tres Cruces, and ultimately La Quiaca and Yavi on the Bolivian border. The 65 km (40 mi) stretch between Jujuy and Purmamarca is half gravel, half pavement, and laden with detours for the ongoing construction of a fully paved thoroughfare. When workers hold a flag up above their heads, it means to stop your car; a waving flag means to go on. Another option is to take Route 9 as far as Purmamarca, and then turn off onto Route 52 and continue on to Route 16 to undertake a harrowing drive that will take away your breath—literally: across the Andes and the Jama Pass to Chile's San Pedro de Atacama, an adobe oasis town and backpackers' haven on the eastern edge of the driest desert on Earth. The R9, meanwhile, is fully paved between Purmamarca and Humahuaca, an easy 1½-hour drive through spectacular scenery.

Purmamarca

㉓ *65 km (40 mi) north of San Salvador de Jujuy.*

Nestled spectacularly in the shadow of craggy rocks and multicolored, cactus-studded hills with the occasional low-flying cloud happening by, the colonial village of Purmamarca (altitude 7,200 feet) is a great stopover along the Quebrada with a great hotel to boot. Here, blazing red adobe replaces the white stucco architecture you may be used to, and the simple, square buildings play off the matching red rock to create a memorable effect. The village is reached by a clearly marked 3-km (2-mi) detour off R9 onto R52. It's nothing more than a one-horse town with a few basic stores, places to eat, and artisans selling their wares in the pleasant, tree-shaded plaza. But Purmamarca's beauty is striking, and its few lights and dry air make it one of the best places in the region for star gazing.

The most notable item downtown on the central plaza is the landmark 1648 **Iglesia de Santa Rosa de Lima,** which was constructed from adobe and thistlewood. Looming above Purmamarca is the **Cerro de Siete Colores** (Hill of Seven Colors), with its lavenders, oranges, and yellows. Most people can pick out four of the seven colors. Look closely and see if you can find all seven—most people can only pick out four. The best way to see the hill is by driving a 3-km (2-mi) loop called the **Paseo de Siete Colores;** there's a turn-off just before the entrance to Purmamarca off R52. This spectacular gravel road winds precariously through bizarre, humanlike formations of bright, craggy, red rock, then opens up onto a series of stark, sweeping, Mars-like vistas with patches of verdant trees along the river valley. The road then passes a few family farms and ends with a striking view of the Cerro itself. The one-lane road can be traversed with most any car, though the ride is a bit bumpy. Better yet is to walk the Paseo; you'll see more, and it's an easy one-hour hike, start to finish. The loop ends up right back in the center of Purmamarca.

Where to Stay & Eat

$$ **✗⛐ El Manantial del Silencio.** It's like a song, the blend of verdant weeping willows, cornfields, red rocks, and chirping birds in the gardens of this spectacular stucco mansion, a tranquil retreat that's hemmed in on every side by the craggy Quebrada in utter calmness. The colonial-style splendor is balanced harmoniously with local artifacts and character; warm and spacious common areas are decked out in adobe colors. Service is first-rate, and there's a restaurant with fascinating local cooking—haute Andean, if you will—including a great llama steak. ⊠ *RN52, 3 km (2 mi) from RN9* ☎ *388/490–8080* ⊕ *www.newage-hotels. com* ➭ *12 rooms* ♻ *Restaurant, pool, bar* ⊟ *AE, DC, MC, V.*

FodorśChoice ★

Tilcara

㉔ *18 km (11 mi) north of Purmamarca, 83 km (51 mi) north of San Salvador de Jujuy via R9.*

The town of Tilcara (altitude 8,100 feet), founded in 1600, is on the eastern side of the Río Grande at its confluence with the Río Huasamayo. Many battles during the War of Independence were fought in and around Tilcara, as indicated on a monolith by the gas station. Purveyors of local artisanry crowd around the main plaza, and two museums on the town's main Plaza Alvarez Prado are worth visiting.

At the **Museo Arqueológico,** an archaeology museum run by the University of Buenos Aires, you can see pre-Hispanic tools and artifacts found in the nearby *pucará* (an indigenous fort). ⊠ *Belgrano 445* 🖾 *2 pesos* ⊙ *Daily 9–6.*

The **Museo Regional de Pintura José Antonio Terry** (José Antonio Terry Regional Museum of Painting), in an 1880 house, displays works by painter José Antonio Terry, who primarily focused on the scenery, people, and events in Tilcara. ⊠ *Rivadavía 459 at the Plaza de Tilcara* 🖾 *2 pesos* ⊙ *Daily 10–6.*

On a hill above the left bank of the Río Grande, about a mile from town, sit the remains of the **Pucará de Tilcara** (Tilcara Fort). This fortified, pre-Inca settlement was part of a chain throughout the Quebrada de Humahuaca.

Seven kilometers (4 mi) west of town is **La Garganta del Diablo** (The Devil's Throat), a narrow red-rock gorge where you can walk to many waterfalls. The tourist office in San Salvador de Jujuy can recommend guides and excursions to this area.

The cemetery of **Maimará** is a striking apparition in the middle of the Quebrada, right aside the R9 road. Crosses, shrines, and tombs are scattered haphazardly all across a barren hillside, making for a spooky, jarring sight in the shadow of a bigger, more colorful hill called La Paleta del Pintor (the Painter's Palette). ⊠ *R9, south of Tilcara, toward Purmamarca.*

Humahuaca

⑳ *126 km (78 mi) north of San Salvador de Jujuy.*

The narrow stone streets of the village of Humahuaca, enclosed by solid whitewashed walls, hark back to pre-Hispanic civilizations, when the first aboriginal tribes fought the Incas who came marauding from the north. Their struggle for survival continued into the 16th century, when the Spanish arrived and Jesuit missionaries built unpretentious little churches in villages throughout the valley. At 9,700 feet, Humahuaca is at the threshold of the Puna. Because of its choice location, Humahuaca has recently become a bit touristy, flooded with vendors hawking artisan wares and some jarring yuppie-style coffee joints. But it's also a fantastic place to buy handicrafts such as Andean weavings at low prices.

You can easily visit the town and nearby gorge as a day trip from San Salvador de Jujuy or Salta, either with a car or with a tour group. The town has a few extremely basic lodging options and one self-proclaimed luxury hotel (which really isn't, despite its high prices).

Humahuaca's picturesque **Cabildo** (town hall), on the main square, is the most striking building in the village, with a beautifully colored and detailed clock tower. Each day at about noon, everyone crowds into the plaza to watch as a life-size statue of San Francisco Solano pops out of the tower—it's kitschy fun. The interior can't be visited, but you can peer into the courtyard. ⊠ *Central plaza.*

The 1641 **Iglesia de la Candelaria** contains fine examples of Cusqueño art, most notably paintings depicting elongated figures of Old Testament prophets by 18th-century artist Marcos Sapaca. ⊠ *Calle Buenos Aires, west side of central plaza.*

off the beaten path

IRUYA – Those brave enough to endure the harrowing five-hour, 50-km (31-mi) drive east from Humahuaca on an unpaved cliffside road are rewarded with one of Argentina's most stunning settings. This cobblestoned town precariously clings to the edge of a valley on a rainbow of sheer rock and the community's remoteness has truly frozen it in time. Take the bus from Humahuaca rather than attempting to drive your own rental car to Iruya; one must know the road, as the bus drivers do, to negotiate it safely. There are some good hikes from Iruya, and a few basic places to stay and eat.

Where to Eat

¢ ✕ **Hostel El Portillo.** This restaurant-café-inn, which also rents out some nice little rooms, is representative of the tourist culture that has sprung up in Humahuaca, catering to the Quebrada- or Puna-bound travelers passing through town. However, this place retains a rustic, local feel despite its tourist clientele. Friendly service puts customers at ease, and a cute little adobe courtyard allows for a lazy lunch in the midday sun. The food is very local; you can get a llama steak or a hearty version of the classic regional dish, *locro* (here it's made with yellow squash, pureed beans and corn, and various types of pork). There's even a short wine list. ⊠ *Tucumán 69* ☎ *388/742–1299* ▭ *No credit cards.*

La Quiaca

26 *163 km (101 mi) north of Humahuaca, 289 km (179 mi) north of San Salvador de Jujuy on R9.*

On the Bolivian border, the frontier and former railroad town of La Quiaca, at 11,400 feet, is cold, windy, and not on most people's itinerary. The town, however, is the base for exploring the **Laguna de los Pozuelos,** the largest body of water in the Puna and home to more than 50,000 birds, mostly Andean flamingos.

Yavi

27 *15 km (9 mi) east of La Quiaca.*

Beginning in 1667, Yavi (altitude 11,600 feet) was occupied by noble Spanish families and was the seat of the marquis de Campero, a feudal lord with considerable property. The train tracks running along the side of the river once connected Argentina with Bolivia and Peru: those who remember this route (including Paul Theroux in his travel book *The Old Patagonian Express*) would like to see it rebuilt. In the town chapel, slabs of alabaster used in the windows cast a golden light on the gilded carvings of the altar and pulpit.

TUCUMÁN, CATAMARCA & LA RIOJA

Although Tucumán Province is the smallest in Argentina, it's one of the richest in industry, commerce, culture, and history. Sugar cane, tobacco, livestock, and citrus fruits all come from the region—in fact, Tucumán is the largest producer of lemons in the world. The high and dry plains in the eastern portion of the province contrast with green forests in the pre-cordillera, which rises to the snow-packed 8,000-foot Aconquija mountain range. Copious amounts of rainfall and the variety of climates have earned Tucumán the title "Garden of the Nation."

Catamarca Province has the most dramatic changes of altitude of any region in the country. The barren north has miles of *salinas grandes* (salt flats) at 1,300 feet. In the west, the Aconquija range has some of the highest mountains in the Andes, including the world's highest volcano, Ojos del Salado, at 22,869 feet. Fortified towns occupied first by the Diaguitas and later by the Incas are visible in the foothills.

San Miguel de Tucumán

28 *1,310 km (812 mi) northwest of Buenos Aires, 597 km (370 mi) north of Córdoba, 243 km (151 mi) north of Catamarca via R38, 311 km (193 mi) south of Salta via R9.*

In the center of Tucumán Province sits the bustling provincial capital and Argentina's fourth-largest city, San Miguel de Tucumán, or just Tucumán in local parlance. Local university students, combined with the constant flow of commercial activity, make the streets of this town crowded and traffic intense. The city is full of grand colonial architecture, broad avenues, and enormous, leafy plazas, all of which are overwhelmed with schoolchildren in uniform mid-day and early evening. Although the center of Tucumán is not quite beautiful by conventional standards, its youthful joie de vivre is infectious: it bursts with good restaurants, bars, outdoor cafés, and nightlife.

Tucumán is beloved by Argentines as the cradle of their independence. On July 9, 1816, congressmen from all over the country gathered in what is now called the **Casa Histórica de la Independencia** (Historical House of Independence) to draft Argentina's Declaration of Independence from Spain. Most of what you see here is a faithful reconstruction, not the original house, but the exterior is authentic, built from 1761 to 1780. A nightly sound-and-light show at 8:30 reenacts the arrival of these representatives and the historic signing; it's quite moving if you understand Spanish. ⊠ *Congreso 151* ☎ *381/431–0826* 🎫 *2 pesos* ⊙ *Wed.–Mon. 9–1 and 3:30–7.*

The monumental 1912 art-nouveau **Casa de Gobierno,** with fantastical onion-bulb cupolas almost evocative of Eastern Europe, housing Tucumán's provincial government, sits on one side of the central **Plaza Independencia.** Across the street are the cheery, bright-yellow **Iglesia de San Francisco** (St. Francis Church) and the more somber cathedral. Behind the government house and the church are two pedestrian-only shopping streets.

An escape to the **Parque 9 de Julio**—with its artificial lake for boating, tennis courts, and lovely gardens—provides a peaceful interlude, much in the spirit of New York's Central Park (without actually being centrally located). ⊠ *6 blocks east of the plaza, past Av. Soldati.*

Where to Stay & Eat

$ ✕ **El Fondo.** Generally acknowledged as the most distinguished place in town for grilled meat, El Fondo lives up to its billing with an impressive *parrilla* spread. A self-service salad bar and good wine list are among the accoutrements. The room and service are rather formal, but in an enjoyable way—you'll feel like you're in a huge, old Spanish colonial dining hall, and that's part of the experience here. Meat is cooked on the well-done side, so adjust your order accordingly. For a wine to accompany the meat, try the soft, round Montchenot, a Cabernet-Malbec-Merlot blend that's aged at least 12 years before its release. It's a unique Argentine red. ⊠ *Av. San Martín 848* ☎ *381/422–2161* 🍴 *AE, DC, MC, V.*

$ ✕ **La Corzuela.** Prices are a tiny bit higher here than elsewhere and the restaurant is a bit off the beaten path, but both things are justified by the fine fare on offer at this eclectic Argentine restaurant. Perhaps it's because Tucumán attracts so few tourists that this place is able to tack up all manner of regional artifacts, from weavings to horse paraphernalia, and pipe in regional music, and yet still not feel touristy, with a devoted crowd of older locals. You can't go wrong with anything on the menu, which features, in equal measures, regional specialties, grilled meats (the parrilla is king here, as elsewhere), seafood dishes (including trout and paella), and pasta. Even simple dishes such as *milanesa alla napoletana* (breaded, fried veal with mozzarella, ham, and tomato sauce) are satisfying. ⊠ *L'Aprida 866* ☎ *381/421–6402* 🍴 *AE, DC, MC, V.*

★ **$** ✕ **La Leñita.** This wonderful, lively parrillada also happens to be a great spot for some Argentine folk music, as each night around 11 PM, the waiters drop everything and break into song. The restaurant is rustic but welcoming, with red bricks, high ceilings, a country-lodge feel, and friendly service to boot. The *bife de chorizo* (sirloin steak) is juicy and tender, but the sublimely creamy grilled *mollejas* (sweetbreads), a parrilla appetizer, steal the show. There's also pasta and fish, and a salad bar. For dessert, the sweet, rich *panqueque* (crepe) with *dulce de leche* is glazed with burnt sugar for an unusual taste combination. ⊠ *Av. 25 de Mayo 377* ☎ *381/422–9241* 🍴 *AE, DC, MC, V.*

¢–$ ✕ **Restaurant Paquito.** If you're longing for good grilled beef, chicken, french fries, and fresh salad, this is the place for you. Pastas, pizzas, and regional specialties round out the menu. ⊠ *Av. San Martín 1165* ☎ *381/ 422–2898* 🍴 *AE, DC, MC, V.*

★ $ ✕🏠 **Hotel Carlos V.** Just steps off Tucumán's busiest street, this supremely central place is infinitely popular with Argentines, due in no small part to the fact that it's a spectacularly good value—book well in advance. The Carlos V has a bustling lobby and street-side café under an arched brick facade, along with a full-service restaurant that's good in its own right. Cream-color walls, dark wood, and well-appointed bathrooms make rooms feel more like an escape than just a place to drop your bags. Pay in cash for a 10% discount. ✉ *25 de Mayo 330, 4000* 🖨 *381/431–1566 or 381/431–1666* ⊕ *www.redcarlosv.com.ar* ↝ *70 rooms* ⚘ *Restaurant, café, minibars, bar, Internet, meeting room* ▭ *AE, DC, MC, V.*

$ 🏠 **Hotel del Sol.** Most of the rooms and the spacious, second-floor bar and buffet restaurant of this modern hotel look out over a leafy canopy of trees covering the main plaza. Polished granite floors, little nooks, and wood-paneled walls lend a distinctive air. A gallery lines the first-floor corridors, with displays by local artists. ✉ *Laprida 35, 4000* 🖨 *381/431–1755* 🖨 *381/431–2010* ✉ *hotel_delsol@arnet.com.ar* ↝ *88 rooms, 12 suites* ⚘ *Restaurant, pool, bar, meeting room* ▭ *AE, MC, V.*

$ 🏠 **Swiss Hotel Metropol.** The comfort-conscious Swiss owners have decreased the quantity of rooms and increased the quality by making them bigger. Modernity and taste pervades, and pastel colors decorate the bright and airy rooms. The friendly, English-speaking personnel and the hearty breakfasts add to the appeal of this hotel, only one block from the plaza. ✉ *24 de Septiembre 524, 4000* 🖨 *381/431–1180* 🖨 *381/431–0379* ✉ *metropol@arnet.com.ar* ↝ *75 rooms, 10 suites* ⚘ *Snack bar, room service, pool, piano bar, meeting room, car rental, travel services* ▭ *AE, DC, MC, V.*

Nightlife & the Arts

With so many students and businesspeople in town, there's plenty of nightlife—mostly in the form of late-night cafés, bars, and dance clubs. One of the most interesting bars in town is the **Plaza de Almas** (✉ Maipú 791, at Santa Fe), a remarkable art-nouveau bar (that also serves food) with warm lighting and multiple levels, nooks, crannies, and romantic courtyards that will keep you guessing—happily. Several other bars cluster around Plaza de Almas and even more are crammed into a four-block stretch of Avenida 25 de Mayo between Santiago del Estero and San Martín. Notable among those is **Club 25** (✉ 25 de Mayo 464 🖨 381/422–9785), a postmodern Internet café–bar–restaurant with crazy lighting, a hyper-cool vibe, and a raging scene on weekends. It's open just about all night, even weekdays, when it's much more relaxed; don't miss the romantic garden out back.

For the university crowd, though, weekends really get going in another area of town. Head out of the center on Avenida Mate de Luna, a continuation of 24 de Septiembre, and you'll eventually find yourself on Aconquija, which will lead you, after about a 15-minute drive, to a neighborhood called Yerba Buena. There, along Aconquija, you'll find an unparalleled proliferation of modern restaurants, musical peñas, bars, and nightclubs filled with young locals.

Shopping

Mendoza and **Muñecas** (which turns into Buenos Aires), two *peatonales* (pedestrians-only streets) that intersect one block west and one block north of the plaza, are good for shopping. The **Gran Vía** (✉ Entrance on Av. San Martín at Muñeca) shopping center is an immense, air-conditioned labyrinth of shops and restaurants. The clothing shops resemble those in Buenos Aires—stylish menswear, sportswear, and women's clothing oriented mainly toward teenagers.

Tafí del Valle

㉙ *143 km (89 mi) southwest of Tucumán via R38 and R307.*

This ancient valley was inhabited by the Diaguita people around 400 BC, later visited by the Incas, and settled by Jesuits in 1700 (until they were expelled in 1767). It remained isolated from the rest of the country until 1943, when a road was built from the town of Tucumán. The Sierra de Aconquija to the west and the Cumbres de Calchaquíes to the north enclose the high (6,600-foot) oval-shape valley and its artificial lake, Lago Angostura. You can best appreciate the size of this often fog-shrouded valley from El Pinar de los Ciervos (The Pinegrove of the Deer), just above the actual town of Tafí del Valle. Cerro Pelado (Bald Mountain) rises from the side of the lake to 8,844 feet.

Scattered about the landscape of the **Parque de los Menhires** (Menhirs Park) are stone monoliths said to be more than 2,000 years old. It's a good walk to the top of the hill, where you can see the reservoir from whose depths many menhirs were rescued and relocated when the dam was built. These ancient dolmens can still be found in the surrounding country, although many have been brought to the park in recent years. Some are 6 feet tall and carved with primitive cat or human motifs. The drive out of the valley on R307 toward the Calchaquíes Valley over a 10,000-foot pass gives you a glimpse of stone ruins, isolated menhirs, and then nothing but cactus as you leave the huge sweep of green valley and enter the desert landscape of the Puna. ⊠ *Park entrance 5 km (3 mi) from R307 into village of El Mollar.*

Where to Stay & Eat

The main street, **Calle Golero,** has several simple restaurants.

¢–$ ✕ **El Portal del Tafí.** Come to this café-restaurant for sandwiches and local specialties such as locro, humitas, and tamales, as well as fish from the region. ⊠ *Av. Diego de Rojas* ☎ *No phone* ▭ *No credit cards.*

$ ▦ **Hotel Mirador del Tafí.** Large urns filled with native plants, stone, and wood adorn this hotel overlooking the lake and valley. Rooms, done in soft desert pastels, with tile floors and wrought-iron lamps, open out onto a garden and a view of the valley. In winter, fireplaces in the lobby and the open-beam dining room keep out the cold. A string of horses for rent are tied to a hitching post at the entrance. ⊠ *Off R307, Km 61.2, 4137* ☎ *3867/421219* ⊕ *www.miradordeltafi.com.ar* ⌕ *32 rooms* ♤ *Restaurant, café, horseback riding* ▭ *AE, MC, V.*

Sports & the Outdoors

You can fish for trout or *pejerrey* (a narrow, silver fish, similar to a trout), sail, windsurf, water-ski, or row on **Lago Angostura.** Rentals, guided tours, and campground information are available in the nearby village of El Mollar, off R307. Horses can be rented December–March from **Otto Paz** (☎ 3867/421272); the tourist office or your hotel can also provide information.

Shopping

This region is famous for its cheeses, hand-loomed ponchos, blankets, and leather, all sold in the shops around the plaza.

San Fernando del Valle de Catamarca

㉚ *1,150 km (713 mi) northwest of Buenos Aires, 440 km (273 mi) northwest of Córdoba, 243 km (151 mi) south of Tucumán via R38.*

San Fernando del Valle de Catamarca is the capital of the Catamarca Province. Known by locals as Catamarca, the town was founded by the governor of Tucumán in 1683 (the fertile valley in which it sits used to be part of Tucumán Province). The valley has a mild climate year-round, and the agreeable colonial city has a nice unhurried feel. The pride of the town is the central **Plaza 25 de Mayo,** on which sits the bright, terra-cotta-color cathedral.

The **Museo Arqueológico Adán Quiroga** (Adán Quiroga Archaeological Museum), three blocks north of the plaza, has exhibits ranging from 10,000-year-old stone objects found in the nearby mountains to items from the Spanish conquest. You can also see stone and ceramic ceremonial pipes and offerings from the tombs of ancient cultures dating to the 3rd century. ⊠ *Sarmiento 450* ☎ *3833/437413* ⊒ *1 peso* ⊙ *Weekdays 8–12:30 and 2:30–8:30, weekends 8:30–12:30 and 3:30–5:30.*

Where to Stay & Eat

$ ✕ **Valmont.** Conservative pinks and grays lend this restaurant, in an old building on the plaza, a genteel, old-club feel. The food is truly international: French, Russian, Swiss, and Italian. At lunch time, you may only have room for the appetizer buffet. ⊠ *Sarmiento 683* ☎ *3833/450494* ⊟ *DC, MC, V.*

¢–$ ✕ **Viejo Bueno.** Good food and soccer on TV make this a local favorite. The grilled meats and chicken come in half and quarter portions. ⊠ *Esquiú 480* ☎ *3833/424224* ⊟ *DC, MC, V.*

$ ⊞ **Hotel Ancasti.** Good taste and attention to detail prevail throughout this ultramodern hotel, designed by the owner's architect son—from the sandstone walls covered with fine art (for sale) to the carpeted lobby to the custom-designed furniture. Rooms are sleek and spacious, with mostly built-in furniture. ⊠ *Sarmiento 520, 4700* ☎ *3833/435951* ⌨ *3833/430617* ⊕ *www.ancastihotel.com.ar* ⌁ *85 rooms, 5 suites* ⟂ *Restaurant, room service, gym, sauna, bar, meeting room* ⊟ *AE, DC, MC, V.*

¢ ⊞ **Hotel Leo III.** The regal crest of Leo III at the top of the brick-color tower of this modern hotel can be seen from almost every corner in Catamarca. The entrance is in a shopping arcade, which has a communications office with telephone, fax, and Internet service. From each of the nine floors, and the roof garden, you can see the Aconquija mountains. ⊠ *Sarmiento 727, 4700* ☎ *3833/432080* ⌁ *37 rooms* ⟂ *Restaurant, café, pool, bar, meeting room* ⊟ *AE, DC, MC, V.*

Sports & the Outdoors

Catamarca has just recently awakened to its potential for recreational tourism. The sparsely populated foothills and mountains west of town are ideal for mountain climbing, hiking, and horseback riding, and decent fishing can be found in the Calacaste and Punilla rivers to the northwest. For information, maps, and guides, contact the **tourism office** (⊠ General Roca and Mota Botello ☎ 3833/432647).

Shopping

Shops in town sell jewelry and other items made from local, semi-precious rose quartz as well as carvings out of teasel wood, ponchos, carpets, textiles, and blankets woven from alpaca, wool, and vicuña.

La Rioja

❸❷ *1,167 km (724 mi) northwest of Buenos Aires, 460 km (285 mi) northwest of Córdoba, 388 km (241 mi) southwest of Tucumán via R38, 155 km (96 mi) southwest of Catamarca via R38.*

In this province of red earth, deep canyons, and Argentina's former president Carlos Menem is the eponymous provincial capital of La Rioja. The town was founded in 1591 by Juan Ramírez de Velasco, a Spanish conqueror of noble lineage who named the city after his birthplace in Spain. Surrounding the town are high red mountains with many interesting shapes eroded into form by wind and water, and green valleys of vineyards and olive trees.

The central **Plaza 25 de Mayo** is named for the date the town was established. An earthquake in 1894 destroyed most of the town's colonial buildings, save the 1623 **Convento de Santo Domingo** church, which is the oldest building in Argentina (it's one block from the plaza).

The main attraction in the region is the **Parque Nacional Talampaya** (Talampaya National Park), which is 230 km (143 mi) from La Rioja (take R38 south to Patquía, head west on R150, and then northwest on R26). The 220-million-year-old gorge here is one of Argentina's most spectacular natural wonders; in one place it narrows to 262 feet between walls of solid rock 480 feet high. Pictographs and petroglyphs by pre-Hispanic cultures are preserved on canyon walls. Wind and erosion have produced strange columns and formations, providing nesting spots for condors. Tours by four-wheel-drive vehicles to the park can be arranged in La Rioja at the **Dirección General de Turismo** (⊠ Av. Perón y Urquiza ☎ 3822/428839). The nearest town with accommodations is Villa Unión, 55 km (34 mi) away from the park.

Where to Stay & Eat

¢–$ ✕ **Il Gatto.** Part of a chain based in Córdoba, this trattoria-style restaurant across the street from the plaza makes good pastas and fancy salads. ⊠ Pelagio B. Luna ☎ 3822/421899 ⊟ MC, V.

¢–$ ✕ **La Vieja Casona.** This big old house with wooden floors and a frontier character is a good place to try regional specialties, grilled meats, and pasta. ⊠ Rivadavía 427 ☎ 3822/425996 ⊟ DC, MC, V.

$ ⌂ **Hotel Plaza.** On Saturday nights, the whole town seems to circle the plaza—by foot, motorcycle, bicycle, or car. The hotel's café, which faces the square, is the perfect spot to watch this Riojano ritual. Although the exterior is a bland, whitewashed structure, inside, everything looks new and polished, and rooms are carpeted, quiet, and simply furnished. Drinks and snacks (excellent olives!) are served in the reception area, the small bar, and the restaurant-café. ⊠ San Nicolás de Bari and 9 de Julio, 5300 ☎ 3822/425215 ☎ 3822/422127 ➳ 60 rooms, 3 suites ⌂ Restaurant, café, pool, bar ⊟ AE, DC, MC, V.

Sports & the Outdoors

Hiking (guided or unguided) and camping in the Talampaya National Park can be arranged through the tourist office.

Shopping

The locally produced olives (*aceitunas aimugasta*) are outstanding, as are the dates and the date liqueur; these can be purchased in shops around the main plaza. A **crafts market** (⊠ Pelagio B. Luna 790) takes place Tuesday–Friday 9–noon and 3–8, weekends 9–noon. **Regionales El Changuito** (⊠ B. Mitre 315), on the plaza, sells antique spurs, knives, leather belts, old coins, *mate* (green tea–like beverage) gourds, and *bombillas* (the straw you drink mate through).

THE NORTHWEST A TO Z

To research prices, get advice from other travelers, and book travel arrangements, visit www.fodors.com.

AIR TRAVEL

Aerolíneas Argentinas has flights from Buenos Aires to Catamarca, La Rioja, Salta, San Salvador de Jujuy, and Tucumán. The only connecting flight is between La Rioja and Catamarca. Dinar flies from Buenos Aires to Salta, San Salvador de Jujuy, and San Miguel de Tucumán, with connecting flights among the three Northwest cities. LAPA flies from Buenos Aires to Catamarca, San Salvador de Jujuy, La Rioja, Salta, and Tucumán, with connecting flights between Catamarca and La Rioja, and between Salta and San Salvador de Jujuy. Southern Winds, based in Córdoba, flies to Salta and Tucumán.

All flights between Buenos Aires and the Northwest use the capital's Aeroparque Jorge Newbury domestic airport.

Airlines & Contacts **Aerolíneas Argentinas** ☎ 3833/424450 to Catamarca, 3822/426307 to La Rioja, 387/431-1331 to Salta, 3833/422-5414 to San Salvador de Jujuy, 381/431-1030 to Tucumán ⊕ www.aerolineas.com.ar. **Dinar** ☎ 387/431-0606 to Salta, 3833/423-7100 to San Salvador de Jujuy, 381/452-2300 to Tucumán ⊕ www.dinar.com.ar. **Lapa** ☎ 11/4819-6200 general line, 3833/434772 to Catamarca, 3822/435281 to La Rioja, 387/431-0780 to Salta, 388/423-8444 to San Salvador de Jujuy, 381/430-2630 to Tucumán ⊕ www.lapa.com.ar. **Southern Winds** ☎ 351/4775-0808 to Córdoba, 387/4210-8081 to Salta, 381/422-5554 to Tucumán ⊕ www.sw.com.ar.

Airports **Aeropuerto Benjamín Matienzo** ✉ 9 km (6 mi) east of Tucumán ☎ 381/426-4906. **Aeropuerto Dr. Horacio Guzmán** ✉ 30 km (19 mi) southeast of San Salvador de Jujuy ☎ 388/491-1101. **Aeropuerto El Aybal** ✉ 10 km (6 mi) southwest of Salta ☎ 387/437-5113. **Aeropuerto Felipe Varela** ✉ 22 km (14 mi) south of Catamarca ☎ 3833/437582. **Aeropuerto Vicente Almandos Almonacid** ✉ 7 km (4 mi) east of La Rioja ☎ 3822/427239.

BUS TRAVEL

Buses from all the major cities in Argentina have service to cities in the Northwest. Buses will even pick you up along the road when prearranged. All terminals are no more than a short taxi ride from downtown.

Buses in the Northwest are frequent, dependable, and convenient. Local tourist offices can advise which companies go where, or you can look up "Transportes" in the yellow pages. It's a good idea to buy tickets a day or two in advance; all bus companies have offices at town bus terminals.

Aconquija bus service links Tucumán to Tafí del Valle and Cafayate; to continue on to Salta you must change to El Indio.

Andesmar and La Estrella run from Catamarca to Tucumán and San Salvador de Jujuy and from La Rioja to Catamarca, San Salvador de Jujuy, and Tucumán. Andesmar also runs from San Salvador de Jujuy to Salta, Tucumán, Catamarca, La Rioja, and Mendoza (20 hours).

Atahualpa buses travel from Salta to San Salvador de Jujuy and La Quiaca.

Balut wins accolades from most locals for its efficient, punctual service. Buses connect Salta to San Salvador de Jujuy, Humahuaca, and Tucumán.

El Tucumano has bus service between Tucumán and Salta and San Salvador de Jujuy.

Mercobus has luxury double-decker buses for the overnight trip between Tucumán and Córdoba.

Panamericano links San Salvador de Jujuy to Salta, Humahuaca, and La Quiaca.

Catamarca Bus Information **Andesmar** ☎ 3833/423777. **La Estrella** ☎ 3833/423455. **Terminal de Omnibus** ✉ Güemes 850 ☎ 3883/423415.

La Rioja Bus Information **Andesmar** ☎ 3822/422430. **La Estrella** ☎ 3822/426306. **Terminal de Omnibus** ✉ Artigas and España ☎ 3822/425453.

Salta Bus Information **Atahualpa** ☎ 387/426-1926. **Balut** ☎ 387/432-0608. **El Indio** ☎ 387/421-9519. **Terminal de Omnibus** ✉ Av. Hipólito ☎ 387/401-1143.

🚌 San Salvador de Jujuy Bus Information **Andesmar** ☎ 388/423-3293. **Balut** ☎ 388/422-2134. **Panamericano** ☎ 388/427281. **Terminal de Omnibus** ✉ Dorrego and Iguazú ☎ 388/426229.

🚌 Tucumán Bus Information **Aconquija** ✉ Lavalle 395 ☎ 381/433-0205 in town, 381/422-7620 at terminal. **Balut** ☎ 381/430-7153. **Mercobus** ☎ 351/424-5717. **Terminal de Omnibus** ✉ Brígido Terán 350. **El Tucumano** ☎ 381/422-6442.

CAR RENTAL

Renting a car can be expensive, especially because agencies generally charge extra for miles, drop-off fees, and tax. But when you've come so far, the investment is probably worthwhile. You'll want a car with at least a 1.6 liter engine, such as a Volkswagen Gol (about 100 pesos per day), as the mountain roads can be demanding. Better yet is a 4x4, if you don't mind spending about 230 pesos per day. Salta Rent a Truck, which will allow dropoffs in Tucumán for an extra fee, is a good option for either the Gol or a 4x4, and offers good travel tips and advice. Stay away from the flimsy Ford Ka around here. Smaller local outfits can sometimes offer better deals and better cars than the big chains, but check the paperwork in the glove compartment (expiration dates of insurance and so on) before leaving.

🚗 **Ansa International** ✉ Caseros 374, Salta ☎ 387/421-7533. **Avis** ✉ Belgrano 715, San Salvador de Jujuy ☎ 388/422-5880. **Localiza** ☎ 0800/999-2999 central reservations ✉ Esquiú 789 and at the airport, Catamarca ☎ 3833/435838 ✉ Salta ☎ 387/431-4045 ✉ San Juan 935, Tucumán ☎ 381/421-5334. **Salta Rent a Truck** ✉ Buenos Aires 1, Salta ☎ 387/431-2097.

CAR TRAVEL

A long, monotonous drive across central Argentina to Córdoba or Santiago del Estero brings you within striking range of the Northwest. You then have to decide what route you want to go from here. North on R9, the ancient road of the Incas, takes you to Tucumán, Salta, San Salvador de Jujuy, and on to Bolivia. Southwest on R64 lie Catamarca and La Rioja. Another option is to fly to a major city in the Northwest (for instance, Salta) and then rent a car. The roads in the region are good and not very crowded. Before you set out, it's a good idea to visit an Automóvil Club Argentino office for maps and road information, especially during the January–March summer season when heavy rains can cause landslides on mountain roads.

Traveling outside of the Northwest's cities is easiest by car, as some villages, canyons, parks, and archaeological sites are neither on a bus route nor included in tours. For some short trips, like going from Tucumán to Tafí del Valle or Salta to Cafayate, it might be worth it to split the *remis* (taxi) fare with a companion. Most downtown hotels have enclosed garages, which is where you should leave your car.

🚗 **Automóvil Club Argentino (ACA)** ✉ Av. del Libertador 1850, Buenos Aires ☎ 11/4802-6061 ⊕ www.aca.org.ar.

EMERGENCIES

🚑 Emergency Services **Ambulance/Medical Assistance** ☎ 107. **Fire** ☎ 100. **Police** ☎ 101.

🏥 Hospitals **Hospital Angel C. Padilla** ✉ Alberdi 550, Tucumán ☎ 381/424-0848. **Hospital Pablo Soria** ✉ Av. General Güemes 1345, San Salvador de Jujuy ☎ 388/422-1228 or 388/422-1256. **Hospital Presidente Plaza** ✉ Av. San Nicolás de Bari Este 97, La Rioja ☎ 3822/427814. **Hospital San Juan Bautista** ✉ Av. Illia and Mariano Moreno, Catamarca ☎ 3833/423964. **Hospital San Bernardo** ✉ Tobís 69, Salta ☎ 387/431-0241.

💊 Pharmacies **Farmacia Centro** ✉ San Martín 1051, Tucumán ☎ 381/421-5494. **Farmacia Minerva** ✉ Sarmiento 599, Catamarca ☎ 3833/422415. **Farmacia Rivadavía** ✉ Rivadavía 740, Catamarca ☎ 3833/423126.

HEALTH

Soroche, or altitude sickness, which results in shortness of breath and headaches, can be a problem when you visit the Puna. To remedy any discomfort, walk slowly, eat carbohydrates, take aspirin beforehand, and drink plenty of fluids (but avoid alcohol). Locals have another solution that they swear by: *coqueando,* which means sucking on coca leaves (available in plastic bags at most little corner groceries in the region, and from street vendors in the smaller towns). Tear off the end of the stems, and then stuff a wad full of leaves into one side of your mouth, in the space between your teeth and cheek; leave them in for an hour or more, neither chewing nor spitting, but swallowing when you salivate. If symptoms don't subside, descend to a lower elevation immediately. If you have high blood pressure or a history of heart trouble, check with your doctor before traveling to high Andes elevations.

MAIL & SHIPPING

Correo Argentino provides reasonably efficient mail service. Letters sent from Salta or Tucumán take about a week to reach North America and two weeks to reach Europe. Add several days if you post from a smaller city in the Northwest.

FedEx and Western Union services are available in San Salvador de Jujuy at J. Storni & Associates.

🏠 Post Offices **Catamarca** ✉ San Martín 753. **La Rioja** ✉ Av. Perón 764. **Salta** ✉ Dean Funes 160. **San Salvador de Jujuy** ✉ La Madrid and Independencia. **Tucumán** ✉ 25 de Mayo and Córdoba.

🏠 Overnight Services **J. Storni & Associates** ✉ Av. Senador Pérez 197 P.A., San Salvador de Jujuy 📠 388/423-0103.

MONEY MATTERS

Dollars are not as changeable in this region as in Buenos Aires. For ATMs, look for the maroon BANELCO sign of Argentina's largest ATM network. You can use your Plus or Cirrus card to withdraw pesos. Banks are generally open weekdays 7–1 and 4–8.

Banco de Galicia and Banco de la Nación in Catamarca, Banco de Galicia in La Rioja, and Banco de la Nación in Salta all have ATMs. Banco de la Provincia in San Salvador de Jujuy changes dollars and will give you cash on your MasterCard only. Cambio Dinar and Horus in San Salvador de Jujuy change cash. Maguitur in Tucumán charges 2% to change money.

Tucumán and Catamarca provinces issue their own 2-, 5-, 10-, and 20-peso *bonos* (bonds), which circulate as currency within their respective jurisdictions along with pesos. They are worthless once you leave each province. Check your change carefully and spend the bonos quickly if you are about to leave. Luckily, they are easy to identify—there's mostly text on the back.

Traveler's checks are not recommended in the Northwest. Few places accept them, and with ATMs so easy to find, there's little need for them.

🏠 In **Catamarca Banco de Galicia** ✉ Rivadavia 554. **Banco de la Nación** ✉ San Martín 626.

🏠 In **La Rioja Banco de Galicia** ✉ S. Nicolás de Bari and Buenos Aires.

🏠 In **Salta Banco de la Nación** ✉ Mitre 151 at Belgrano. **Cambio Dinar** ✉ Mitre 101 on Plaza 9 de Julio.

🏠 In **San Salvador de Jujuy Banco de la Provincia** ✉ Lamadrid. **Cambio Dinar** ✉ Belgrano 731. **Horus** ✉ Belgrano 722. **Scotiabank Quilmes** ✉ Belgrano 904.

🏠 In **Tucumán Maguitur** ✉ San Martín 765.

SIGHTSEEING TOURS
Tours of Catamarca can be arranged through the Yocavil company.

In La Rioja, Velasco Tur arranges tours to the Parque Provincial Talampaya.

In Salta, La Veloz runs city tours on its own fleet of buses. It also organizes trips to San Antonio de Los Cobres (by car or by the Tren a las Nubes), to Cafayate and the Calchaquíes Valley, and to San Salvador de Jujuy and the Quebrada de Humahuaca.

San Salvador de Jujuy has NASA, a family-owned and -operated travel office with two generations of experience. The company arranges airport pickups, city guides, and excursions for individuals or groups in and around San Salvador de Jujuy; English is spoken.

In Tucumán, Duport Turismo runs four-hour city tours and three- to four-day excursions to Tafí del Valle and other nearby areas of interest and makes local, national, and international reservations.
🏢 **Duport Turismo** ✉ Mendoza 720, Galerí Rosario, Loc. 3, Tucumán ☏ 381/422-0000. **NASA** ✉ Av. Senador Pérez 154, San Salvador de Jujuy ☏🖨 388/223838. **Velasco Tur** ✉ Buenos Aires 253, La Rioja ☏ 3822/426052. **La Veloz** ✉ Caseros 402, Salta ☏ 387/431-1010 🖨 387/431-1114 ✉ Esmeralda 320, fl. 4, Buenos Aires ☏ 11/4326-0126 🖨 11/4326-0852. **Yocavil** ✉ Rivadavía 922, Loc. 14-15, Catamarca ☏ 833/430066.

TAXIS
Remises (taxis) can be found at airports, bus stations, and usually on the corner of the main plaza—or your hotel can call one for you.

TELEPHONES
Making calls from your hotel room is very expensive all over Argentina. Telecom's *telecentros* are plentiful in the provincial capitals and even small towns; Telfónica's *locutorios* are in the provincial capitals. Both have national and international phone service, fax service, and, in some instances, Internet access as well. If you're calling from outside the area code, add a 0 (0387 for Salta, for instance).

VISITOR INFORMATION
The Northwest's five provincial tourist offices are helpful, friendly sources of solid information. You'll see a lot of INFORMACIÓN TURÍSTICA signs around, but these are often storefront travel agencies interested in selling their own tours rather than providing general information.

The Catamarca tourism office is open weekdays 7–1 and 4–9 and weekends 9–1 and 5–9. It's difficult to find, so taking a taxi is recommended. La Rioja's tourism office is open weekdays 8–1 and 4–9 and on Saturday 8–noon. English is spoken at the tourism office in Salta, which is open weekdays 8:30 AM–9 PM and weekends 9–8. English is also spoken at San Salvador de Jujuy's tourism office, which stays open daily 8 AM–9 PM. The Tucumán tourism office is open weekdays 8–8 and weekends 9–9.
🏢 **Catamarca** ✉ General Roca and Mota Botello ☏ 3833/432647. **La Rioja** ✉ Av. Perón 715 ☏ 3822/428839. **Salta** ✉ Buenos Aires 93 ☏ 387/431-0950 🌐 www.turismosalta.gov.ar. **San Salvador de Jujuy** ✉ Urquiza 354 ☏ 388/422-1316. **Tucumán** ✉ 24 de Septiembre 484 ☏ 381/422-2199.

THE CUYO

5

FODOR'S CHOICE

1884 Restaurante, *Mendoza*

Parque Provincial Aconcagua

Posada San Eduardo, *Barreal*

HIGHLY RECOMMENDED

Azafrán, *Mendoza*

Bodega Escorihuela, *Mendoza*

Parque Provincial Ischigualasto

Updated by
Eddy Ancinas

IN THE CENTER OF ARGENTINA, on the dry side of the Andes, this semi-arid region is blessed with water from mountain glaciers that flows via rivers and canals into the fields and vineyards that surround the parks, plazas, and tree-lined streets of Mendoza, San Juan, and San Rafael.

Olive oil, garlic, melons, and a cornucopia of other fruits and vegetables are shipped from Mendoza all over the country and abroad. Argentina is the fifth-largest wine producer in the world (grapevines were first planted by Jesuit missionaries in 1556), and 80% of the country's vineyards thrive in the hot sun and sandy soil of Mendoza and San Juan provinces.

The Incas, who came south from Peru, had great difficulty subduing the Cuyo's first inhabitants, the Huarpes, Araucanos, and Pehuenches. But by the late 1400s, the Incas prevailed, extending their empire (Tahuantinsuyo) to its southernmost point (Collasuyo) in Argentina and Chile. The Huarpes lost much of their distinctive culture under the Incas, who imposed their language (Quechua) and their religion on the conquered tribes. Along the Inca roads across the Andes and north to Peru, forts and *tambos* (resting places), the remains of which can be seen throughout the region, gave shelter to travelers.

Spanish settlers from Chile founded the city of Mendoza in 1561, San Juan a year later, and San Luís in 1598. At that time, the Cuyo was part of the Spanish Viceroyalty of Peru. Most of the area was cattle country, and ranchers drove their herds over the Andes to markets in Santiago. Although the Cuyo became part of the eastern Viceroyalty of the Río de La Plata in 1776, the long, hard journey across the country by horse cart to Buenos Aires kept the region economically and culturally tied to Chile until 1884, when the railroad from Buenos Aires reached Mendoza.

Today the area is known not only for its wine but also for its outdoor activities. River-rafting, horseback riding, soaking in thermal baths, skiing at Las Leñas and Penitentes in Mendoza Province, and hiking on Aconcagua, the highest mountain in the Americas, attract outdoor enthusiasts year-round. Parque Provincial Ischigualasto, a World Heritage site in San Juan Province, is one of the richest paleontological areas in the world. San Luís Province has lakes and historic mountain villages as well as the immense Parque Nacional las Quijadas, with its great red-rock amphitheater—all relatively undiscovered.

Exploring the Cuyo

Mendoza, one of Argentina's prettiest cities, is a good base for exploring the Cuyo's lush vineyards and orchards, deep river gorges, and high mountain passes. Tours to vineyards, mountain spas, or the top of Uspallata Pass can be arranged through local tour companies. You can drive from Mendoza to Tupungato, San Juan, San Luís, and San Rafael and discover the region on your own, or you can take a bus between these cities, then take a guided tour or rent a car to explore.

About the Restaurants

Most of the Cuyo follows national culinary trends—beef, lamb, and pork—*a la parrilla* (grilled). Second- and third-generation Italian restaurants serve family recipes enhanced with fresh ingredients like wild asparagus and mushrooms. In fact, all ingredients in this region, including fine olive oil (look for Copisi), are produced locally. Juicy melons are ripe February–March. Spanish cuisine—hearty soups, stews, and casseroles—is a connection to the region's past, as is *clérico*, a white-wine version of sangria.

About the Hotels

The city of Mendoza has many good, small to medium-size hotels. The smaller cities of San Luís, San Juan, and San Rafael have at least one nice, modern hotel, and the rest are rather run of the mill. Tourist offices can recommend all kinds of *hospedajes* (lodgings), apart-hotels, *cabañas* (cabins), hostals, and *residenciales* (bed-and-breakfasts), all of which are generally well maintained and a good bargain. In the countryside is everything from campgrounds to small *hosterías* (inns) to large resorts and spa hotels. Owner-operated *posadas* (country inns) in villages and vineyards offer rural recreational activities in a natural setting.

WHAT IT COSTS In Argentina Pesos				
	$$$$	$$$	$$	$	¢
RESTAURANTS	over 35	25–35	15–25	8–15	under 8
HOTELS	over 300	220–300	140–220	80–140	under 80

Restaurant prices are for one main course at dinner. Hotel prices are for two people in a standard double room in high season.

Timing

Ski season is June through September: July is crowded with vacationing Argentines and Brazilians, August usually has plenty of snow, and September offers spring conditions and warmer weather. Weather in the Andes is unpredictable, so it's a good idea to contact the ski area for current conditions. Since the Cuyo is a desert region, summer (December–March) is hot. Wine is harvested March through April and celebrated with grand festivities, culminating in the annual *Vendinia* (wine festival), the last week of February or first week of March. If you're driving during summer months, be aware of flash floods and washed-out roads.

San Juan

❶ *1,140 km (708 mi) northwest of Buenos Aires, 167 km (104 mi) northeast of Mendoza via R40, 320 km (200 mi) northeast of San Luís via R20.*

In the Tulum Valley in the foothills of the Andes, San Juan Province's capital is set in an oasis of orchards and vineyards, surrounded by monotonous desert from which the shady streets and plazas of this easygoing town are a welcome reprieve. San Juan was founded in 1562 as part of the Chilean viceroyalty. Under Spanish rule, the Río San Juan was directed into canals that still run beneath the streets, cooling the city on hot summer days.

On January 18, 1817, General José de San Martín gathered his army of 16,000 men in the town's plaza and set out on his historic 21-day march over the Andes to Chile, where he defeated the royalist army at the battles of Chacabuco and Maipú. In Chile, San Martín commandeered ships from the British and North Americans and sailed north to Lima, Peru, liberating Peru and the rest of South America from the Spanish. A master of strategy, audacity, and sheer determination, San Martín proclaimed himself a liberator—not a conqueror. On returning to Buenos Aires in 1823, he received little acknowledgment for his feats, and he died in France, never having received the honors due him. Today, however, every town in Argentina has a street, school, or plaza named for San Martín, and paintings of the general crossing the Andes on a white mule hang in public buildings all over the country.

In January 1944 an earthquake destroyed San Juan (but helped to establish Juan Perón as a national figure through his relief efforts, which won him much popularity). The city was rebuilt with the low-rise buildings, tree-lined plazas, and pedestrian walkways you see today.

The **Casa Natal de Sarmiento** (Sarmiento Birthplace) was home to Domingo Faustino Sarmiento (1811–88), known in Argentina as the Father of Education for his fervent belief that public education was the right of every citizen. After teaching in local schools as a teenager, Sarmiento was forced to flee to Chile, having fought against the Federalists. On returning in 1836, he founded a girls' school and a newspaper, where he could voice his opinions on education, agriculture, and government. In 1840 Sarmiento returned to Chile, once again a political exile who opposed Rosas and his nationalist Caudillo government. Threatened with extradition back to Argentina, Sarmiento was sent by the Chilean government to the United States and Europe to observe their education systems. A prolific writer, Sarmiento was also a skilled diplomat and became senator of San Juan province in 1857, governor in 1862, and eventually president of the nation from 1869 to 1874. During this time, he passed laws establishing public education in Argentina. ⊠ *Sarmiento 21 Sur* ☎ *264/421–0004* 🖷 *264/422–5778* 💷 *$1, Sun. free* ☉ *Dec.–June, Tues.–Thurs. and Sun. 8–1 and 3–8, Mon. and Sat. 8–1; July–Nov., Tues.–Fri. and Sun. 9–7, Mon. and Sat. 9–2.*

Puerto del Sol (⊠ Entre Ríos 203 Sur ☎ 264/422–8264) conducts city tours and has information on other travel options. **Dirección Provincial de Turismo** (⊠ Sarmiento 24 Sur ☎ 264/422–7219 ⊕ www.ischigualasto. com) provides information on lodging, restaurants, places of interest, and recreational activities.

Where to Stay & Eat
Many of the town's best restaurants are on Avenida San Martín, about 15 blocks from downtown. A good local wine is Traviño, especially the Cabernet-Sirah.

$$ ✕ **Club Sirio Libanés.** Don't be dismayed by the bright lights and TV showing soccer games; just order a bottle of Malbec, head for the table of appetizers, and fill your plate with crab brochettes, pickled eggplant, fresh tomatoes and sliced tongue. Entrées include pastas, chicken, and beef prepared with a Mediterranean touch. ⊠ *Entre Ríos 33* ☎ *264/ 422–9884* ⊜ *AE, V* ☉ *No dinner Sun.*

$–$$ ✕ **Las Leñas.** This large, lively grill can serve up to 200 people under its high thatched roof and spinning fans. *Civita* (goat cooked asado style) is the specialty (it's available March and April). Otherwise, enjoy the grilled meats, sausages, and chicken, which arrive sizzling at your table, accompanied by salad, pasta, pizza, and tasty appetizers. On Sunday afternoon, families fill the long tables. ⊠ *Av. San Martín 1670 Oeste* ☎ *264/423–2100* ⊜ *AE, DC, MC, V.*

$ ✕ **Castillo de Oro.** The aroma of beef, lamb, chicken, and sausages grilling on the backyard patio wafts down the street. Meals here are served outdoors or inside under glaring fluorescent lights. *Tenedor libre* (free fork) means "all you can eat" for about 20 pesos, including meat, chicken or fish, pasta, potatoes, salad, and dessert. ⊠ *Av. J. I. de la Roza 199 Oeste* ☎ *264/427–3615* ⊜ *AE, DC, MC, V.*

$ 🏨 **Alkazar.** Chrome and glass shine in the lobby of this hotel on a quiet street two blocks from the main square. There are plenty of gathering places inside, including a small bar, streetside café, and restaurant. The modern rooms have views across the city to the mountains. ⊠ *Laprida 82 Este, 5400* ☎ *264/421–4965* 🖷 *264/421–4977* ⊕ *www.alkazarhotel. com.ar* ➭ *104 rooms, 8 suites* ♢ *Restaurant, café, in-room safes, mini-*

Numbers in the text correspond to numbers in the margin and on the Cuyo and Mendoza maps.

5

If you have
5 days

The ultimate ski holiday might be to ski in Chile, fly (or if possible, drive) from Portillo over the Andes to Mendoza, then fly south to Las Leñas (or the reverse). If you're not skiing, spend the first two days in 🖼 **Mendoza** ⑤–⑬ enjoying the city and visiting wineries. On Day 3, rise early (around 6 AM) and drive up the Panamerican Highway through Uspallata, stopping for lunch at the hostería in Puente del Inca, continuing on to Las Cuevas on the Chilean border, then returning to 🖼 **Uspallata** ⑭ for the night. On Day 4 go south through Potrerillos to 🖼 **Tupungato** ⑯, where you can visit some vineyards and spend the night before returning on the main highway to Mendoza for Day 5. You could also return from Uspallata to Mendoza via the northern route around Villavicencio—or spend a day relaxing in the hot springs at Termas de Cacheuta Spa.

If you have
7 days

Follow the five-day itinerary above, spending the night of Day 4 in **Tupungato** in the **Valle de Uco** ⑯, with its vineyards and orchards. On Day 5, continue south to R40, which follows the Andes to 🖼 **Malargüe** ⑱ and Las Leñas ski resort, or to R143, which goes directly to 🖼 **San Rafael** ⑰: choose the route to Malargüe for the drive and the sights along the way; pick the route to San Rafael for more vineyards and an excursion to the Cañón del Río Atuel. Another option is to spend the first two days in Mendoza, then drive to 🖼 **Uspallata** ⑭ on Day 3 by either route described above and spend the night. On Day 4, take R30 across a plateau bordered by some of the highest Andean peaks to 🖼 **Barreal** ④ in the Calingasta Valley. On Day 5, go to 🖼 **San Juan** ①. On Day 6, get up early (5 AM) for a day trip to the **Parque Provincial Ischigualasto** ③. Spend your last day relaxing in San Juan.

If you have
10
days

Fly to 🖼 **Mendoza** ⑤–⑬ and spend four days exploring the city and surrounding vineyards. If wine is your passion, go south to 🖼 **Tupungato** ⑯ on Day 5 and continue on to 🖼 **San Rafael** ⑰ the next day. On Day 8, visit more vineyards or go to 🖼 **Malargüe** ⑱ or the Cañón del Río Atuel, returning to Mendoza the next morning for a relaxing day at the hot springs at Cacheuta.

Alternatively, you can leave Mendoza on Day 3 and drive the extraordinary route to Aconcagua, returning to 🖼 **Uspallata** ⑭ for the night. On Day 4, visit the Bovedas in Uspallata, and then drive to 🖼 **Barreal** ④. Spend the next day exploring the Calingasta Valley, and on the afternoon of Day 6, continue on to 🖼 **San Juan** ①. On Day 7, drive to 🖼 **San Agustín del Valle Fértil**, visiting **Parque Provincial Ischigualasto** ③ and Parque Nacional Talampaya on Day 8 and returning to San Juan on Day 9. Spend your last day enjoying the town or a nearby lake.

---

bars, pool, health club, sauna, bar, airport shuttle, free parking 🛏 *AE, DC, MC, V* ❍ *CP.*

$ 🖼 **Hotel Nogaro.** This old hotel just off the main plaza has small and adequate if somewhat dreary rooms, but it's a good bargain. The pool on the second floor is surrounded by rather uninviting Astroturf. ✉ *Av.*

J. I. de la Roza, 5400 ☎ *264/422–7501* ⇨ *100 rooms, 3 suites, 9 apartments* ⚭ *Restaurant, indoor pool, bar* ▤ *AE, DC, MC, V* ⦿ *CP.*

Sports & the Outdoors

The **Presa de Embalse Quebrada de Ullum** (Ullum Valley Dam Reservoir), 15 km (9 mi) from town, is a huge hydroelectric complex with grand views of the Río San Juan. Windsurfing, sailing, swimming, rowing, fishing, and diving keep San Juaninos cool and active on hot summer days. You can rent boating equipment at the **Bahía Las Tablas** sports complex, just beyond the dam, where there's a café and change cabins. There's a **public beach** at the Embarcadero turnoff. You can white-water raft and kayak in the San Juan, Los Patos, and Jachal rivers. Fishing in Las Hornillas River can be arranged through local tour companies.

Ducher Viajes (✉ Mendoza 322 ☎ 264/420–0101 ⊕ www.ducherviajes. com) offers airport pickup, city and local tours, and tours to Parque Nacional Ischigualasto and Talampaya. **Dante Montes** (✉ Santa Fe 58 Galeria Estonell-Loc 32 ☎ 264/422–9019 🖷 264/421–5198) is a full service travel agency with local and regional tours, wine tours, and overnight excursions to Barreal and the mountains. **Fortuna EVyT** (✉ Mariano Moreno s/n, Barreal ☎ 264/844–1004), formerly Ossa Expeditions, has 20 years experience in educational outdoor adventures. Horseback trips to Aconcagua or over the Andes to Chile, mountaineering, rafting, fishing, sand-surfing, and photo safaris are a few of the activities offered.

San Agustín del Valle Fértil

❷ *247 km (153 mi) northeast of San Juan, 414 km (257 mi) northeast of Mendoza, 476 km (296 mi) south of La Rioja (via Villa Unión).*

In a valley formed by the Río San Juan and bordered on the west by the Sierra del Valle Fértil, the small town of San Agustín is a green and leafy surprise after miles of arid landscape, and an ideal base for exploring the Ischigualasto and Talampaya (⇨ Chapter 4) parks.

Where to Stay & Eat

There are inexpensive cafés on the main plaza, and the tourist office can suggest cabins, campgrounds, and small hotels.

$$ ▤ **Hostería Valle Fértil.** This low-rise, basic inn on a hill overlooking a lake is 80 km (50 mi) from the Parque Provincial Ischigualasto and a convenient stopover on the way to both Ischigualasto and Parque Nacional Talampaya. If you are not on a tour previously arranged in San Juan, you can hire a local Spanish-speaking guide and driver through the hotel or tourist office for about US$50 for one park or US$120 for both parks (not a bad price for two or more people). The hotel has a campground and playground; nearby are a pool and outdoor grills. There are also four cabins for rent; each sleeps eight people. ✉ *Rivadavia, 5400* ☎🖷 *2646/420015* ⊕ *www.alkazarhotel.com.ar* ⇨ *40 rooms, 4 cabins* ⚭ *Restaurant, mountain bikes, hiking, horseback riding, playground* ▤ *AE, DC, MC, V* ⦿ *CP.*

Parque Provincial Ischigualasto

★ ❸ *80 km (50 mi) north of San Agustín via R510, 315 km (196 mi) from San Juan.*

Popularly known as *Valle de la Luna* ("valley of the moon"), this 15,134-acre park is a World Heritage site. Two hundred twenty-five million years of wind and erosion have sculpted strange rock formations in the red sandstone and pale gray volcanic ash cliffs, laying bare a grave-

Wine Tasting *Los Caminos del Vino* (The Wine Roads) is a collection of 20 wineries in the major wine-producing areas of Mendoza Province: Maipú, Luján de Cuyo, Godoy Cruz, and Guaymallén, with extended tours south to Tupungato and the Valle de Uco, where old family vintners and state-of-the-art bodegas are planting grapes in wide swaths across this enormous open valley. Half- and whole-day tours usually include three or four bodegas and other cultural and historical sites. Hotels and local tour agencies can arrange tours, or you can hire a *remis* (taxi) and go on your own. Although unexpected visitors are greeted cordially, it's a good idea to call first if you're not on a tour. San Rafael's two major wineries, Suter and Valentín Bianchi, are just minutes by car or taxi from downtown San Rafael.

yard of extinct dinosaurs from the Triassic period of the Mesozoic era. When the 6-foot-long Dicinodonte roamed the valley, a large lake surrounded by trees and shrubs was the habitat for a variety of reptiles. Some of these fossils can be seen in the visitor center at the park entrance, where a diorama explains the paleontologic history of the area. You can take three routes through the park, one of which will lead you to a petrified forest. Early morning fog usually dissipates by mid-morning, and the varied colors of the rocks become more vivid in late afternoon. Roads inside the park are unpaved, unpatrolled, and difficult to follow, especially after rainstorms. A ranger must accompany all private cars. Tours can be arranged in San Agustín, San Juan, or Mendoza.

Barreal

4 *136 km (84½ mi) west of San Juan on R12, 133 km (82½ mi) north of Uspallata on R39.*

Whether you drive up from San Juan along the meandering San Juan River to Calingasta or choose the high route from Uspallata, you'll encounter a landscape of high mountain ranges, wild rivers, and deep gorges. The narrow road from San Juan climbs up and around 1,800 hairpin turns to dizzying precipices above the San Juan River gorge. Violent floods roaring down the barren mountainsides do major damage to this road (and probably to anyone on it at the time). The road is open westbound to Calingasta Sunday–Friday 4 AM–1 PM and Saturday until 2:30 PM; eastbound to San Juan Sunday–Friday 4 PM–8 PM and Saturday 4:30–8 PM. Check with police at either end for changes, fill your tank, and bring a picnic lunch. Beyond the tunnel of trees that cover the streets of Barreal lie orchards, vineyards, and fields of mint, lavender, and anise. Using Barreal as your headquarters, you can mountain bike, horseback ride, hike, climb, or drive a 4x4 east into the **Sierra Tontal,** where at 13,120 feet you can see the highest range of the Andes, including Aconcagua (22,825 feet) and Mercedario (22,205 feet) on the Chilean border.

Twenty-two kilometers (13½ mi) south on R412 toward Uspallata, a dirt road turns off into the **Reserva Natural El Leoncito** (Little Lion Natural Reserve), a vast, rocky area with little vegetation. Follow this road for 17 km (10½ mi) to the **observatory,** known for its exceptional stargazing on dark and cloudless nights. Near the turnoff, on the western side of R412 at **Pampa Leoncito,** the sport of *carrovelismo* (sand-surf-

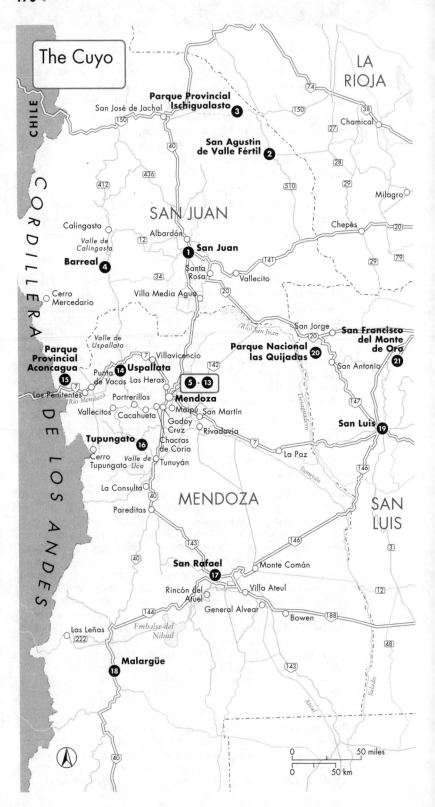

ing) is practiced in wheeled sand cars called wind yachts that sail at 150 kph (93 mph) across a windy expanse of white sand.

Where to Stay

$$$-$$$$
Fodor'sChoice
★
🏠 **Posada San Eduardo.** On a quiet corner under a canopy of trees sits a yellow adobe house with closed green shutters. Inside, a classic colonial patio is surrounded by spacious rooms decorated with local weavings and rustic pine furniture. Lunch is served anytime on the lawn by the pool. Ricardo Zunino, owner and former Formula One racer, inherited this 150-year-old estate from his family. ⊠ *Av. San Martín and Los Enamorados, 5500* ☎ *2648/441046 in Barreal, 264/423–0192 in San Juan* 🛏 *14 rooms* ⚐ *Restaurant, pool, horseback riding, paddle tennis, bar* ⊟ *V* ⏹ *CP.*

Mendoza

5–**13** *1,040 km (250 mi) west of Buenos Aires, 166 km (103 mi) south of San Juan.*

Mendoza, the capital of the province of the same name and the main city in the Cuyo, prides itself on having more trees than people. The result is a town with cool canopies of poplars, elms, and sycamores over its streets, sidewalks, plazas, and low buildings. Water runs in canals along the streets, disappears at intersections, and then reappears in bursts of spray from the fountains in the city's 74 parks and plazas. Many of these canals were built by the Huarpes and improved upon by the Incas long before 1561, when García Hurtado de Mendoza, governor of Chile, commissioned Pedro del Castillo to lead an expedition over the Andes with the purpose of founding a city and opening the way so that "knowledge could be brought back of what lay beyond."

Argentina's beloved hero, José de San Martín, resided here while preparing his army of 40,000 soldiers to cross the Andes in 1817 on the campaign to liberate Argentina from Spain. In 1861 an earthquake destroyed the city, killing 11,000 people. The city of Mendoza and the Cuyo remained isolated from eastern Argentina until 1884, when the railroad to Buenos Aires was completed and the city was rebuilt. Immigrants from Italy, Spain, and France then moved here in search of good land to farm and grow grapes, introducing their skills and crafts to the region.

Avenida San Martín is the town's major thoroughfare. Between it and the Plaza Independencia, Mendoza's central square, are many shops and restaurants. Maipú, Luján de Cuyo, and Godoy Cruz, notable for their wineries, and Las Heras and Guaymallén are all suburbs of Mendoza with shopping centers, restaurants, and hotels. Take a taxi: they're cheap and more direct than local bus service.

★ **7** Five minutes by car from the center of Mendoza, **Bodega Escorihuela** occupies several blocks of an urban area once covered with vineyards. This huge winery was founded in 1884 by Spaniard Miguel Escorihuela Gascón. Its 63,000-liter barrel, made in France, is the largest in the province. In the old house are art exhibits and a restaurant, 1884. ⊠ *Belgrano 1188, Godoy Cruz* ☎ *261/424–2282* ⊕ *www.escorihuela. com.ar* ⊗ *Weekdays 9:30–12:30 and 2:30–3:30; tours on the hr.*

12 The **Bodega la Rural,** founded in 1883 by Felipe Rutini, is still family-owned and -operated. It produces San Felipe, Rutini, and Trumpeter wines. Not to be missed is the outstanding **Museo del Vino** (Wine Museum), where everything from 100-year-old leather, wood, and copper tools to an ingenious mousetrap is displayed in the original adobe barns. ⊠ *Montecaseros 2625, Maipú* ☎ *261/497–2013* ⊕ *www.bodegalarural.com. ar* ⊗ *Mon.–Sat. and holidays 9:30–5, Sun. 10–1.*

CloseUp

ARGENTINE WINE

N THE DRY, SEMIDESERT VALLEYS *and foothills of Mendoza, San Juan, and San Rafael, the sun shines 300 days a year and pure mountain water from* melting snow rushes down from the Andes, irrigating miles of land. The province of Mendoza, by far the most important wine-producing region, lies at the foot of the Andes at southern latitudes similar to the northern latitudes of the best vineyards of France, Italy, and California. With 300,000 acres of vineyards, Mendoza alone produces 70% of the nation's wine—almost all of it grown at 2,000 to 5,000 feet, where the sun's rays ripen the grapes slowly, and cool nights maintain acidity for long lasting taste. Since this desert climate receives little rain, pests are minimal, and most vineyards could be classified organic, as chemicals are seldom used or needed.

Although chardonnays and sauvignon blancs are being improved and adjusted for export, and Torrontés (a dry fruity muscat grape from Spain) has its devotees, Argentina is best known for its red wines, and Malbec is the star of the show. This bold, dark, berry-flavor grape came to Argentina from Bordeaux as a blending grape and thrived in Mendoza's soil and climate. It has become the country's signature wine—some call it "Argentina's zinfandel." Fine cabernets, merlots, syrahs, and bonardas (similar to Italy's barbera) are remarkable on their own or blended with Malbec, and pair perfectly with Argentina's legendary beef.

With its 1,500 wineries (including those in the northern provinces of Jujuy, Salta, Catamarca, and La Rioja, and the southern province of Río Negro), Argentina is the fifth-largest wine producer in the world, yet its labels are just beginning to appear on the shelves and wine lists of stores and restaurants outside of the country. One reason is that Argentines have been the primary consumers of all they produced—only the French and the Italians drink more wine per capita—so there hasn't been much of an incentive to export. In addition, collective marketing of Argentine wine (or collective anything) goes against the grain in this land of stubborn individualists. While Chile formed cooperative marketing groups and aggressively sold their excellent wines in the United States and elsewhere, Argentines continued their individualistic approach to marketing. In 1989 the Argentine economy began to stabilize, and foreign investors such as Kendall Jackson and Domaine Chandon of California, Salentein (Holland), and many others took a new look at Argentina's potential wine industry. Then, in 2001, the economy went into a steep decline, resulting in the conversion from U.S. dollars back to a severely devalued peso. The good news is that with growing recognition and lower export prices, Argentine wines will soon be on the tables around the world.

Los Caminos del Vino (The Wine Roads) is a collection of 20 wineries in the major wine-producing areas of Mendoza Province. Bodegas Escorihuela, Trapiche, Chandon, Finca Flichman, Bodega Norton, and La Rural are some of the better-known ones. Kendall Jackson, Salentein, and Catena are vineyards in the scenic Valle de Uco, south of Mendoza, and Suter and Valentín Bianchi (champagne) are the major wineries in San Rafael. San Juan, whose largest bodega is Graffigna, has its own Camino del Vino and its own Vendimia (wine festival) held in early March.

Mendoza

Dolium is the Latin word for the amphoras used by the Romans to store wine underground. Hand-picked grapes are delivered to this underground winery, where processing, fermenting, storing, bottling, and packaging all take place underground. You can sample wine in a glass-and-steel reception area while looking down into the wine works. ✉ *R15, Km 30, Agrelo* ☎ *261/490–0200* ⊕ *www.dolium.com* ☉ *Weekdays 9–5, weekends by appointment.*

The first vines were planted at **Finca Flichman** in 1873, in the stony soil near the Mendoza River. Caballero de la Cepa wines are exported to the United States, Japan, and Europe. Stainless-steel tanks and computerized temperature controls make this one of Argentina's most modern wineries. ✉ *Munives 800, Barrancas/Maipú* ☎ *261/497–2039* ☉ *Wed.–Sun. 10–1 and 2–5.*

need a break?

Day or night (the later the better) is a good time for ice cream at **Soppelsa** (✉ Emilio Civit and Belgrano). Anything with *dulce de leche* (sweet caramelized milk) and *granizado* (chocolate chips) may make you want to visit every day.

On the site of the original civic center of Mendoza, the **Museo del Area Fundacional** (Foundation Museum) explains the social and historical development of the region, from the time of indigenous people through Spanish colonization to the present. Of special note is the display of a mummified child found on Aconcagua, with photos of his burial treasures—presumably an Inca or pre-Inca sacrifice. After the 1861 earthquake, the city center was moved from this location. Underground excavations, made visible by a glass-covered viewing area, reveal layers of pre-Hispanic and Spanish remains. ⊠ *Beltrán and Videla Castillo* ☎ *261/425–6927* ☜ *$1.50* ☉ *Tues.–Sat. 8 AM–10 PM, Sun. 3 PM–8 PM.*

❻ Twice governor and later senator Emilio Civit's 1873 mansion had 26 bedrooms and 4 courtyards and was the gathering place of the elite in the belle epoque. It's now the **Museo del Pasado Cuyano** (Museum of Cuyo's Past), a gallery and archive with paintings, antiques, manuscripts, and a library on Argentine and Chilean history. ⊠ *Montevideo 544* ☎ *261/ 423–6031* ☜ *Donation* ☉ *Weekdays 9–12:30.*

⓫ The **Museo Histórico de San Martín** (San Martín Historical Museum) has a token collection of artifacts from campaigns of the Great Liberator, as San Martín is known. ⊠ *Av. San Martín 1843* ☎ *261/425–7947* ☜ *$1* ☉ *Weekdays 8:30–1:30.*

❺ The **Parque General San Martín,** about 10 blocks from the city center, is a grand public space with thousands of species of plants and trees, tropical flowers, and a rose garden. A racecourse, golf club, tennis courts, observatory, rowing club, and museums are some of the attractions in the park. Atop **Cerro de la Gloria** (Glory Hill), in the center of the park, a monument depicts scenes of San Martín's historic Andes passage.

❽ **Plaza Independencia** is Mendoza's main square, filled daily with both visitors and Mendocinos alike. You may just sit on a bench in the shade of a sycamore tree and watch children playing in the fountains, browse the stands at a weekend fair, visit the **Museo de Arte Moderno** or perhaps cross the square after lunch at the historic **Plaza Hotel** (now a Hyatt) on your way to the shops and outdoor cafés on the pedestrian-only **Calle Sarmiento,** which bisects the square.

Where to Stay & Eat

$$–$$$ ✕ **1884 Restaurante Francis Mallman.** The soft glow of candles on the
Fodor'sChoice patio under the prune trees at the Godoy Cruz Winery's 100-year-old
★ Bodega Escorihuela sets the tone for one of Argentina's premier chefs to show what Patagonian cuisine can be. Born in Bariloche and trained in France and Italy, Francis Mallman put Argentina on the map of international *alta cocina* (haute cuisine). Students from his culinary school keep wineglasses full and forks flying as they attend to guests with discreet enthusiasm. The 36-page wine list has detailed information on grapes and bodegas. ⊠ *Belgrano 1188* ☎ *261/424–2698* ▤ *AE, DC, MC, V.*

$ ✕ **El Meson Español.** Stained-glass windows, bullfighting posters, reproductions of works by famous Spanish artists, and a well-trodden tile floor take you right back to Spain when you enter this old colonial house. Start with a cup of garlic soup, followed by paella or tapas, as Lucho, the blind piano player, plays blues, tango, swing, and Sinatra. ⊠ *Montevideo 244* ☎ *261/429–6175* ▤ *AE, DC, MC, V* ☉ *No lunch.*

$ ✕ **La Florencia.** Sidewalk tables invite strollers to stop and peruse the menu: grilled, baked, and broiled meats and fish; pastas; pizzas; game; and a variety of salads, along with a lengthy wine list. Step inside and admire the eclectic displays of antique weapons, telephones, and gaucho artifacts. Fine silver and crystal is stored in antique chests. An upstairs dining room has a breezy street view. ⊠ *Sarmiento and Perú* ☎ *261/429– 1564* ▤ *AE, DC, MC, V.*

$ ✕ **La Marchigiana.** Homemade pasta has been served since 1950 under the thatched roof and whirring fans of this cheerful Italo-Argentine eatery. Concoct your own salad and try a pitcher of sangria or clérico on hot summer afternoons. ⊠ *Patricias Mendocinas 1550* ☎ *261/423071* ⊠ *Palmares Shopping Mall, Godoy Cruz* ☎ *261/439–1961* ▤ *AE, DC, MC, V.*

★ ¢–$ ✕ **Azafrán.** In this wine bar (whose name means saffron), wooden stools surround an old wine press, which has been converted into a tasting table. Wines are displayed from floor to ceiling. Farther inside this 19th-century brick building, diners seated at small café tables enjoy cheeses, pâtés, and hot and cold tapas served on wooden platters. Shelves are stocked with Mendoza's finest: olive oils, smoked meats, dried herbs, mushrooms, olives, jams, and breads. Whether you view it as a gourmet grocery, wine shop, or restaurant, Azafrán is a pleasant diversion. ⊠ *Sarmiento 765* ☎ *261/429–4200* ⊠ *Park Hyatt Mendoza, Calle Chile 1124* ⊟ *MC, V* ⊗ *Closed Sun.*

⊛ **$$** ⊡ **Hotel Aconcagua.** Business travelers, tourists, and people in the wine trade appreciate the efficient service at this modern hotel on a quiet street near shops and restaurants. Serene tones of mauve and blue create a soothing atmosphere throughout the lobby and meeting and guest rooms. Although it doesn't have a bar for pre- or post-dinner schmoozing, friends and associates seem perfectly happy to gather in the lobby or in the restaurant, where a copious buffet is served, as well as regular entrées. ⊠ *San Lorenzo 545, 5500* ☎ *261/420–4499* ⊟ *261/420–2083* ⊕ *www. hotelaconcagua.com.ar* ⇆ *159 rooms, 9 suites* ⚬ *Restaurant, pool, massage, sauna, business services, meeting rooms, travel services, parking* ⊟ *AE, DC, MC, V* ⊦◯⊧ *CP.*

$$ ⊡ **Park Hyatt Mendoza.** Hyatt has preserved the 19th-century Spanish colonial facade of the landmark Plaza Hotel's grand pillared entrance and wide veranda, which extends to either side of the street. Lunch, afternoon tea, and dinner are served on this gracious terrace overlooking Mendoza's main square. A two-story wine wall separates the restaurant from the lobby. Minimalist bedrooms are softened by plump white pillows and duvets covering the simple ebony beds. Bathrooms have plenty of mirrors to compliment chrome and marble accents. ⊠ *Calle Chile 1124, 5500* ☎ *261/441–1234* ⊟ *261/441–1235* ⊕ *mendoza.park. hyatt.com* ⇆ *170 rooms, 15 suites* ⚬ *Restaurant, café, dining room, pool, health club, spa, bar, casino, meeting rooms, business services, parking* ⊟ *AE, DC, MC, V* ⊦◯⊧ *CP.*

$ ⊡ **Hotel Cervantes.** The simple rooms in this small downtown hotel are cheerfully decorated in floral prints. The hotel is owner-operated, and the front desk is helpful and knowledgeable. A big-screen TV in the living room makes you feel at home. Sancho, the hotel's excellent restaurant and bar is a popular lunch spot for the local wine trade. ⊠ *Amigorena 65, 5500* ☎ *261/520–0400* ⊟ *261/520–0458* ⊕ *www.hotelcervantesmza. com.ar* ⚱ *261/520–0446* ⇆ *60 rooms, 5 suites* ⚬ *Restaurant, bar, business services, meeting rooms, travel services, free parking* ⊟ *AE, DC, MC, V* ⊦◯⊧ *CP.*

⊛ **$** ⊡ **Hotel Crillón.** The loyal clientele of this small hotel returns for the tranquil neighborhood—within walking distance of plazas, restaurants, museums, and shops. Small suites with a separate work station are good for business travelers. The staff can help you plan excursions. ⊠ *Perú 1065, 5500* ☎ *261/429–8494* ⊟ *261/423–9658* ⊕ *www.hcrillon.com. ar* ⇆ *70 rooms, 6 suites* ⚬ *Café, pool, bar, meeting room* ⊟ *AE, DC, MC, V* ⊦◯⊧ *CP.*

¢ ⊡ **Damajuana.** The only property in Mendoza resembling a hostel has rooms for two, four, or six people, with lockers and shared bath. Guests feel at home inside or out: a bar, restaurant, and a fireplace and TV are in the living room, and the spacious backyard has a grill and hammocks. The neighborhood is the most popular among young Mendocinos, with bars, boutiques, and cafés just steps away. ⊠ *Aristedes Villanueva 282, 5500* ☎ *261/425–5858* ⊟ *261/425–5858* ⊕ *www. damajuanahostel.com.ar* ⇆ *8 rooms* ⚬ *Restaurant, pool, tennis court, bar, Internet; no a/c.*

Nightlife

The formerly sleepy **Avenida Arístedes Villanueva** is now a hot spot of inexpensive bars and cafés. The area wakes up around 6 PM, when the bars, boutiques, wine shops, and sidewalk cafés open their doors, and young Mendocinos, foreign tourists, and strolling couples converge on the area. As the evening progresses, crowds get bigger, and music—rock, tango, salsa—louder. The action peaks between 10 and midnight. Inexpensive, casual **El Bar del José** (⊠ Arístedes Villanueva 740 ☎ no phone) was the first gathering place in the trendy Villanueva neighborhood. **Por Acá** (⊠ Arístedes Villanueva 557 ☎ no phone) attracts a cosmopolitan crowd of locals and European travelers—many en route to hike or climb in the nearby Andes. Live rock music begins after 10 PM.

The **Regency Casino** at the **Park Hyatt Mendoza** has black jack, stud poker, roulette tables, slot machines, and an exclusive bar. (⊠ 25 de Mayo and Sarmiento ☎ 261/441–2844).

Cinemark (⊠ At the Palmeares shopping mall, Godoy Cruz ☎ 261/439–5555) has 10 screens. **Microcine Municipal "David Eisenchlass"** (⊠ 9 de Julio ☎ 261/449–5100) shows foreign films Thursday through Sunday. **Village** (⊠ Mendoza Plaza Shopping Center, Guaymallén ☎ 261/421–0700) has 10 movie screens.

Sports & the Outdoors

Along with local guides offering specific services, Mendoza also has several outfitters that seem to do it all. **Aymara Turismo** (⊠ 9 de Julio 1023 ☎☎ 261/420–5304 or 261/420–2064 ⊕ www.aymara.com.ar) organizes hikes, horseback riding trips, mountain climbing, white-water rafting, and mountain bike tours. They offer everything from day hikes to full mountaineering excursions to all the highest mountain peaks, including Mercederio and Aconcagua, plus volcano treks in Chile and Argentina. **Inka** (⊠ Av. Juan B. Busto 343 ☎ 261/425–0871) is an owner-operated company with ten years experience guiding hikers and mountaineers to the base camp at the foot of Aconcagua; an optional six-hour climb on Mt. Bonete, for an exceptional view of climbers making their way up Aconcagua, is also available. They also offer horseback riding trips.

HIKING Day-hikes or weeklong treks along rivers, canyons, on an Inca trail, through indigenous forests, or to the highest mountain peaks in the Andes can be arranged with local travel and tour offices. November through March is the best time to do these journeys. **Huentata** (⊠ Las Heras 680 ☎ 261/425–3108 ⊕ www.huentata.com.ar) offers day hikes out of Potrerillos in the pre-Cordillera.

HORSEBACK RIDING The beauty of the surrounding foothills, valleys, and mountains, combined with Mendoza's tradition of fine horsemanship, makes *cabalgatas* (horseback riding) an enjoyable and natural way to explore the area. You can ride to the foot of Aconcagua, Tupungato, or experience the grand adventure of a nine-day trip over the Andes following the hoof prints of San Martín. **Juan Jardel** (☎ 264/48303) takes riders from his ranch at Las Carditas in Potrerillos high into the mountains, where guanacos roam and condors soar. **Raúl Labat** (☎☎ 261/429–7257) takes groups from his ranch, El Puesto, near Tupungato, into the high rugged country where San Martín returned from Chile with his army.

MOUNTAIN BIKING Many of Mendoza's back roads lead through the suburbs and vineyards into the Andean foothills and upward to mountain villages—or all the way to Chile. The Valle de Uco slopes gently from the foothills down. **Betancourt Rafting** (⊠ Lavalle 36, Loc. No. 8 ☎☎ 261/429–9665 ⊕ www.betancourt.com.ar), has short trips into the mountains and valleys around Potrerillos, as well as an all-day trip to Vallecitos. **Huentata**

(⊠ Las Heras 680 ☎ 261/425–3108 ⊕ www.huentata.com.ar) also offers day excursions from Potrerillos into the surrounding mountains. **Travesía** (⊠ Montecaseros 699, Godoy Cruz ☎ 261/448–0289) conducts tours and provides maps for the suburbs and foothills outside of Mendoza.

Every February, **La Vuelta Ciclista de Mendoza,** a bicycle race around Mendoza Province, attracts cycling enthusiasts.

MOUNTAINEERING Mendoza offers challenging mountaineering adventures. Climbing in the Cordón de Plata or on Tupungato as well as Aconcagua can be arranged. Permits for climbing Aconcagua can be obtained personally in Mendoza at **Centro de Visitantes** (⊠ Av. de Los Robles and Rotondo de Rosedal), in Parque San Martín near the entrance. The center is open weekdays 8–6 and weekends 9–1.

Aymara Turísmo (⊠ 9 de Julio 1023 ☎ 261/420–5304 or 261/420–2064 ⊕ www.aymara.com.ar) offers a 19-day guided ascent of Aconcagua, which includes airport pickup, hotels, pack mules, and assistance in securing permits. They also offer shorter climbs for acclimatization. **Fernando Grajales** (⊠ 25 de Mayo 2985, Guaymallén ☎☎ 261/429–3830) is an experienced guide and veteran of many Aconcagua summits.

SKIING Skiers, bound for **Las Leñas,** in Malargüe near San Rafael arrive from July through September and use Mendoza as their base. Two resorts closer to Mendoza attract local clientele.

Los Penitentes is 153 km (95 mi) northwest of Mendoza on the Panamerican Highway. Day-trippers and weekenders from Mendoza and the surrounding provinces come for the 20 runs for all abilities and the cross-country skiing. Note that in spite of the elevation (10,479 feet), the snow is often thin and when it does snow a lot, the danger of avalanches is severe. At the base of the ski area are hotels, restaurants, ski rentals, day care, a first-aid clinic, and a disco. Between the Andes and the Cordon de Plata, a range that reaches 20,000 feet, **Vallecitos,** 80 km (49 mi) from Mendoza, attracts mostly families with nearby vacation homes, as well as summer hikers and mountaineers who come to train for an assault on Aconcagua.

WHITE-WATER RAFTING Many adventure tour companies organize rafting or kayaking trips on the Río Mendoza. They can be combined with horseback treks and often include an asado.

Argentina Rafting (⊠ Ruta Nacional 7, Luján de Cuyo ☎ 2624/482037 ⊕ www.argentinarafting.com.ar), located in Potrerillos, offers rafting and kayack classes and day trips. **Betancourt Rafting** (⊠ Lavalle 36, Loc. No. 8, Galería Independencia ☎☎ 261/429–9665 ⊕ www.betancourt. com.ar) has three small cabins and a lodge 25 km (15 mi) from Mendoza at the Cacheuta Hot Springs, which they use as a base for rafting trips on the Mendoza River. Their standard two-day trip, with medium to difficult rapids, includes an asado and accommodations in the cabins. Day trips vary from one to six hours. Transportation to and from Mendoza is included for all trips.

Shopping

Leather goods, shoes, and clothing can be found along the pedestrian part of Sarmiento, on Avenida Heras, and on side streets between. *Talabarterías* sell fine leather goods and everything equestrian, from saddles and hand-made tack to gaucho apparel—hats, vests, and many gaucho-inspired gift items.

Even Mendocinos shop at **La Matera** (⊠ Villanueva 314 ☎ 261/425–3332) for boots, vests, belts, scarves, and riding equipment. The **Mer-**

cado Central (⊠ Av. Heras and Patricias Mendocinas) has more of the same, plus ponchos and Indian weavings; it's open daily from 9 AM in the morning to 1:30 and again from 4:30 to 9. For all the things you forgot to pack, the indoor air-conditioned **Mendoza Plaza Shopping Center** (⊠ Lateral Accesso Este 3280, Guaymallén) has an American-style department store (actually Chilean owned), Falbella, plus shoe stores, cafés, and a bookstore (Yenny) with books in English. The children's indoor amusement park has a roller coaster, carousel, rides and games. South of Mendoza, **Palmares Shopping Mall** (⊠ Panamericano 2650) has 10 movie theaters and many good shops and restaurants.

en route

Forty-seven kilometers (29 mi) from Mendoza on R52, the springs at **Termas de Villavicencio** provide the mineral water that's sold all over northern Argentina. The **Hostería Villavicencio** (☎ 261/439–6487), a roadside inn just before the Gran Hotel de Villavicencio (closed), has a campground and serves lunch and dinner. This is a good place to stop before continuing up the narrow dirt road known as La Ruta de Año (Route of the Year), which winds around 365 sharp bends to the **Cruz de Paramillo pass** at 9,840 feet. From here, you can see three 20,000-foot giants of the Andes: Aconcagua, Tupungato, and Mercedario. At 67 km (41 mi), the road straightens out and descends into the Uspallata Valley and on into the town of Uspallata. You can return to Mendoza on R7 (95 km [59 mi]), continue west on R7 to Chile, or go north on R39 to Barreal in San Juan Province. **Mendoza Viajes** (⊠ Paseo Sarmiento 129, Mendoza ☎ 261/461–0210 ⊕ www. mdzviajes.com.ar) arranges tours of this route.

Uspallata

⓮ *125 km (77 mi) west of Mendoza on R7, 133 km (82 ½ mi) south of Barreal on R39.*

This small town in the Uspallata River valley between the foothills and the front range of the Andes is the last town before the Chilean border and ideally located at the crossroads of three important routes: R7 from Mendoza across the Andes to Chile, R57 from Mendoza via Villavicencio, and R39 from San Juan via Barreal in the Calingasta Valley. More than an overnight stopover, however, Uspallata is a good base for excursions into the mountains by 4x4 or on horseback to abandoned mines, a desert ghost town, and spectacular mountain scenery where the 1997 movie *Seven Years in Tibet* was filmed.

Las Bóvedas, a few miles north of town, are pointed adobe cupolas where metals have been forged since pre-Columbian time. Arms and canons for San Martín's army were made there. In the surrounding valley and the Aconcagua area, guided horseback riding, trekking, mountain climbing, and ice climbing are expertly handled by **Límite Zero** (☎ 261/429–9165 in Mendoza, 261/1566–21516 cell).

Driving north on RN 39 from Uspallata to Barreal in San Juan Province (108 km/67 mi), you cross a high desert valley, where the only sign of life is an occasional estancia partially hidden in a grove of alamos. The first 63 km (39 mi) are on a dirt road (R39). At **Los Tambillos,** about 40 km (25 mi) from Uspallata, the Inca road that ran from Cusco, Peru, through Bolivia and into northern Argentina crosses the road. The site is surrounded by a fence that protects traces of the original road and remains of an Inca *tambo* (resting place). A map shows the route of the Incas. The mountains to the west, including Mercedario (22,205 feet), get higher and more spectacular as you approach Barreal. At the San

Juan Province border, the road becomes R412 and is paved the remaining 50 km (31 mi) to Barreal.

Where to Stay & Eat

¢–$ ✕ **Lo de Pato.** This casual roadside grill and café serves cafeteria-style lunches and grilled meat and pasta dinners to bus drivers, tourists, and locals; get yourself a cold drink from the refrigerator. The souvenir shop sells candy bars, postcards, T-shirts, and other mementos. There's even an in-house telefónica. ⊠ *R7* ☎ *264/420249* 🖃 *AE, MC, V.*

$$ 🏨 **Hotel Uspallata.** Cavernous hallways, minimal decor, barren walls, and dim lighting are the legacies of the Perón era, when the government built grand hotels for its employees and cronies; the hotel is still visited by *sindicalístas* (union members). The grounds and gardens remain impressive, the dining room is grand, and the large rooms with closets for a month's stay are pleasant—in a nostalgic kind of way. ⊠ *R7, Km 1149, 5500* 🖃🖴 *264/420003* ⊕ *www.hotelescadenadelsol.com.ar* ↝ *73 rooms* ⚪ *Restaurant, café, pool, bar, recreation room, travel services* 🖃 *No credit cards* ◉ *CP.*

$ 🏨 **Hotel Valle Andino.** A brick building with a pitched tile roof and wood trim looks inviting by the side of R7. Inside you'll find an open, airy living room with places to sit around a woodstove. Outside, a large glass-enclosed swimming pool is surrounded by a lawn big enough for a soccer game. Rooms are modern, some with bunk beds, all with brick walls and minimalist furniture. ⊠ *R7, 5500* ☎ *2624/420033* ⊕ *www.hotelguia.com/hoteles/valleandino* ↝ *26 rooms* ⚪ *Restaurant, pool, bar, recreation room* 🖃 *AE, MC, V* ◉ *CP.*

Parque Provincial Aconcagua

⑮ *195 km (121 mi) northwest of Mendoza via R7, 86 km (54 mi) west of*
Fodor'sChoice *Uspallata on R7.*
★

The Parque Provincial Aconcagua extends for 165,000 acres over wild, high country with few trails other than those used by climbing expeditions up the impressive Cerro Aconcagua (Aconcagua Mountain). Organized tours on horse or foot can be arranged in Mendoza or at the Hostería Puente del Inca.

The drive up the Uspallata Pass to the Parque Provincial Aconcagua is as spectacular as the mountain itself. Tours can be arranged, but renting a car is well worth it, as there are many sights to stop and photograph along the way. You can make the trip from Mendoza in one long, all-day drive or stay a night en route. Note that driving in winter on the icy roads can be treacherous and that you should be aware of the change in altitude from 2,500 feet in Mendoza to 10,446 feet at the top.

Leaving Mendoza early in the morning, head south on Avenida San Martín to the Panamerican Highway (R7) and turn right. Green vineyards soon give way to barren hills and scrub brush as you follow the river for 30 km (19 mi) to the **Termas Cacheuta.** If you're still engulfed in fog and drizzle, don't despair: it's likely that you'll break through into brilliant sunshine when you reach the **Potrerillos Valley** at 39 km (24 mi). The road follows the Río Mendoza and an abandoned railroad track that once crossed the Andes to Chile. In 1934 an ice dam broke and sent a flood of mud, rocks, and debris down the canyon, carrying off everything in its path. Evidence of this natural disaster is still visible all along the river.

After passing Uspallata, the last town before the Chilean frontier, the road goes through rolling hills and brooding black mountains. The Ríos Blanco and Tambillos rush down from the mountains into the Río

Mendoza, and remnants of Inca tambos remind you that this was once an Inca route. At **Punta de Vacas,** the corrals that once held herds of cattle on their way to Chile lie abandoned alongside now defunct railway tracks. Two kilometers (1 mi) beyond the army barracks and customs office, three wide valleys converge. Looking south, you can see the second-highest mountain in the region, **Cerro Tupungato** (22,304 feet). The mountain is accessible from the town of the same name, 73 km (45 mi) southwest of Mendoza.

After passing the ski area at Los Penitentes (named for the rock formations on the southern horizon that resemble penitent monks), you arrive at **Puente del Inca** (9,000 feet), a natural bridge of red rocks encrusted with yellow sulphur that spans the river. The hot springs below are slippery to walk on but fine for soaking tired feet. A splendid hotel was once here, but it, too, was a victim of the 1934 flood. A few miles farther west, after you pass the customs check (for Chile), is the entrance to the park and a cabin where the park ranger lives. About 15 km (9 mi) beyond the park entrance, the highway passes Las Cuevas, a settlement where the road forks right, to a tunnel and the road to Chile, or left, to the statue of **Cristo Redentor** (Christ the Redeemer) on the Chilean border (13,800 feet), commemorating the 1902 peace pact between the two countries.

The main attraction of the Parque Provincial Aconcagua is **Cerro Aconcagua** itself. At 22,825 feet, it's the highest mountain in the Americas and it towers over the Andes, its five gigantic glaciers gleaming in the sun. Although it seems amazingly accessible from the roadside, Aconcagua has claimed 37 climbers from the more than 400 expeditions that have attempted the summit. Nevertheless, every year hundreds of mountaineers arrive, ready to conquer the "giant of America." A trail into the park begins at the ranger's cabin and follows the **Río Horcones** past a lagoon and continues upward to the **Plaza de Mulas** base camp at 14,190 feet, where there's a **hotel** (☎ 261/423–1571 in Mendoza for reservations).

Where to Stay & Eat

$$$ ✕🏨 **Hotel Termas Cacheuta.** Stop at this mountain spa for a sauna in a natural grotto, a volcanic mud bath, a hydromassage, and a soak in the large swimming pool filled with water from the hot springs that have been curing devotees since 1902. Rooms overlook the lawn and swimming pool. The restaurant serves healthful, natural cuisine using vegetables from its own garden. Rates include three meals, two thermal baths, and one massage per day; hiking, river rafting, and mountain biking can be arranged. ⌧ *R7, Km 38, Cacheuta, 5500* ☎ *2624/482082* ⌧ *Reservations: Rodríguez Peña 1412, Godoy Cruz, 5501* ☎ *261/431–6085* 🖷 *261/431–6089* ⤳ *16 rooms* ᠔ *Restaurant, massage, sauna* ▭ *No credit cards* �‖ *FAP.*

¢ 🏨 **Hostería Puente del Inca.** Mountaineers gather here to assemble equipment before climbing Aconcagua and return here afterward to relate their adventures. The hostel's history as a mountaineering outpost is told in vintage photos on the dining room walls. Guides and mules can be arranged. ⌧ *R7, Puente del Inca* ⌧ *Turismo Aymara SRL, 9 de Julio 1023, Mendoza, 5500* ☎ *261/420–2064* ✉ *info@aymara.com.ar* ⤳ *82 beds in doubles, 4- to 6-person dorms* ᠔ *Dining room* ▭ *MC.*

Outdoor Activities

To climb Aconcagua, you must first get a permit in Mendoza. Horseback rides and hikes can be arranged with a guide or on your own. *See* Mountaineering *in* Mendoza. The best time to climb is in mid-January to mid-February.

Tupungato & the Valle de Uco

⑯ *78 km (48 mi) south of Mendoza on R40, turning west at Ugarteche onto R86.*

From Mendoza, you can drive south on R40, then go west on R86. You can also drive first to the small town of Potrerillos and turn south on R89 to Tupungato; the road passes clusters of vacation cottages, brimming with flowers in summer and covered with snow in winter. The nearby ski area at **Vallecitos** is popular with local families and ski clubs. As the road climbs out of the canyon, the Valle de Uco unfolds before you: estancias extending to the Chilean border, miles of potato fields, and acres upon acres of vineyards cover the gently sloping terrain from the desert to the Andes. The major wineries of Catena, Chandon, La Rural, and Salentein grow different varieties of grapes in this high-altitude region, where grapes spend more time on the vine, ripening slowly and deepening the flavor of the wines produced. The snow-covered cone of **Tupungato volcano** (22,304 feet) watches over the valley on the western horizon.

Where to Stay & Eat

¢ ✕🏠 **Don Romulo.** Don Romulo is the president of the local Gaucho Association, which works to preserve the traditions and activities of his ancestors. His sons run the hotel and restaurant with warmth and enthusiasm and organize horseback rides at a nearby ranch, hikes, 4x4 excursions, and visits to wineries. Rooms are clean and basic, and the food is pure *criollo* (country cooking): empanadas, grilled meat, sausages, and salads. On weekends, lamb, goat, and beef are cooked out back on the *asador*. ✉ *Almirante Brown 1200* 📠 *2622/489020* ⊕ *www. donromulo.com.ar* 🛏 *6 rooms* ⌂ *Restaurant, no a/c, no room phones, travel services* ⊟ *No credit cards.*

$$$$ 🏠 **Chateau d'Ancon.** Curved oak doors open onto marble halls filled with antiques, statues, paintings, tapestries, and family photographs. You can taste the estate bottled wine in the English pub and dine in an exquisite room furnished with some of the contents of the 200 containers the Bombal family shipped home from Europe in 1933 when they returned from England. Lucy Bombal, the granddaughter of the original owners, entertains guests with stories of her family's history. The place isn't cheap, but the price includes all meals, tea, cocktails, a wine-tasting, a vineyard tour in a 4x4, and a horseback ride. Children under 10 are not permitted. ✉ *R89, 2 km (1 mi) west of the village of San José and R86* 📞 *261/429–5035 in Mendoza, 2622/488245 in Tupungato* ⊕ *www. estanciancon.com* 🛏 *6 rooms* ⌂ *Pool, horseback riding* ⊟ *No credit cards* ⊙ *Closed mid-May–mid-Oct.* ❘⊙❘ *FAP.*

¢ 🏠 **Posada Salentein.** Fifteen kilometers (9 mi) south of Tupungato on RN 94, this posada is close to the ultra-modern Bodega Salentein. An old adobe farm house, shaded by ancient chestnut trees, has been converted into an inn with pleasant pastel rooms that open onto a veranda with cool terra-cotta tile floors and a view of the vineyards. ✉ *Reservations: Emilio Civit 778, Mendoza* 📞 *261/423–8514* ⊕ *www. salenteintourism.com* 🛏 *4 rooms, 1 cottage* ⌂ *Dining room, bicycles, horseback riding* ⊟ *AE, V* ❘⊙❘ *FAP.*

San Rafael

⑰ *240 km (150 mi) south of Mendoza, 1,000 km (620 mi) northwest of Buenos Aires.*

A series of dams along the Ríos Atuel and Diamante has created an agricultural oasis surrounding the second-largest city in Mendoza Province.

Cold winters, warm summers, and late frosts guarantee high-quality grapes for the area's major vineyards, such as Suter and Valentín Bianchi, not to mention the many smaller, family-owned operations.

Two avenues, Hipólito Yrigoyen and Bartolomé Mitre, meet head-on in the center of town at the intersection with Avenida San Martín, where shops and restaurants are found. Note that siesta time lasts from lunch until 4:30, after which shops reopen and people go back to work.

Bodega Valentín Bianchi, on R143 near the airport, is a high-tech *champañera* (champagnery) sparkling with stainless-steel vats, pipes, and walkways. The bodega has extensive underground tunnels and a vaulted tasting room. ⊠ *Ortiz de Rosas and Comandante Torres* ☎ 2627/ 422046 ⊕ *www.vbianchi.com* ⊙ *Tours weekdays on the hr 9–1 and 3–5.*

Suter, which produces fine wine and champagne, is owned by the fourth generation of its Swiss founders. A tour through this spotless showcase winery leads you through a labyrinth of underground caves where wines mature at a constant temperature. ⊠ *H. Yrigoyen 2900, near the airport* ☎ 2627/424008 ⊙ *Weekdays 8–3:30, Sat. 9–5.*

A nice excursion out of town is a drive through the **Cañón del Atuel** (Atuel Canyon), a 160-km (102-mi) round-trip on R173. Sandstone cliffs enclose the canyon as you follow the Río Atuel past swimming holes, shady picnic spots, and campsites. Shops along the way rent rafting and kayaking equipment, and some organize rafting trips. About halfway up the canyon is the Hotel Valle Grande. The road continues up to **Lago Valle Grande** (Valle Grande Lake) and passes a series of dams before descending into a labyrinth of red, brown, and gray sandstone rock formations. Unfortunately, the river then disappears underground—sacrificed to the demand for hydroelectric power.

Where to Stay & Eat

$–$$ ✕ **Cabaña Dos Amigos.** At this restaurant 6 km (4 mi) from town, the owner-chef greets you at the door and starts you off with bowls of appetizers, followed by salad, homemade prosciutto with melon, empanadas, chorizos fresh off the grill, and, finally, your choice of meat. ⊠ *Off R143* ☎ 2627/441017 ▤ *No credit cards* ⊙ *Closed Mon. No dinner Sun.*

$ ✕ **A Mi Manera.** Two tall doors open into this colonial-era building where the Spanish Club, a holdover from colonial days, has met since 1910. With its 18-foot ceilings, soft gold tones, wood trim, and Spanish *escudos* (emblems of Spanish and Argentine provinces) on the walls, the restaurant is very traditional. So is the food: roasted and grilled meats, marinated vegetables, pasta, and paella. ⊠ *Comandante Salas 199 and Colonel Day* ☎ 2627/423597 ▤ *AE, DC, MC, V.*

¢–$ ✕ **Friends.** This popular local café is good for a coffee or a light lunch. Try the *barroluco* sandwich: steak, ham, cheese, and tomato compressed between thin slices of white bread. ⊠ *H. Yrigoyen and San Martín* ☎ *No phone* ▤ *No credit cards.*

$$$$ ▦ **Finca los Alamos.** When this 150-year-old estancia was established by the great-grandparents of César and Camilo Aldao Bombal in 1820, San Rafael was still a fort. The Bombal brothers inherited the vineyards and ranch from their mother, who grew up here. The ranch house is filled with an eclectic collection of art and artifacts from around the world. Prices include all meals plus tea on the veranda, open bar, wine, and conversations (in English) with the owners. Horses are available for an extra charge. ⊠ *Bombal (R165), 10 km (6 mi) from town,* ✉ *Box 125, 5600* ☎☎ 2627/442350 ⇴ *6 rooms* ⌂ *Dining room, pool, horseback riding, bar* ▤ *No credit cards* ¶ *FAP.*

$$$ ⊞ **Hotel Kalton.** Polished floors and a hall lined with local photographs lead you to the quiet, leafy lobby. Rooms are plainly furnished in somber colors and have large windows. Lunch and dinner can be arranged for groups along with wine tours. ✉ *H. Irigoyen 120, 5600* ☎ *2627/430047* ✏ *20 rooms* ⚐ *Minibars, laundry service* ☰ *AE, DC, MC, V.*

$$$ ⊞ **Hotel San Rafael.** Just off busy Avenida San Martín, this half-old and half-new hotel has views of the Andes and vineyards from the top floor, where it's quietest. The reception area has plants, native stone floors, and wood trim. The newer half of the hotel has carpeted rooms with sparse but adequate furnishings in soft pastels. ✉ *Colonel Day 30, 5600* ☎ *2627/430127* ✏ *60 rooms* ⚐ *Café, minibars, free parking* ☰ *AE, DC, MC, V* ⦿ *CP.*

Sports & the Outdoors
Atuel Travel (✉ Av. Mitre 439 ☎ 2627/429282) arranges horseback riding, biking, and bus expeditions as well as rafting trips on the Río Atuel and windsurfing and kayaking on Lago Valle Grande. **Bessone Viajes** (✉H. Yrigoyen 423 ☎ 2627/436439) organizes local hiking, rafting, mountain biking, and ski trips.

Malargüe & Las Leñas

⑱ *193 km (120 mi) south of San Rafael via R40.*

In the southwestern part of Mendoza Province, the small town of Malargüe was populated by the Pehuenche until the Spanish arrived in 1551, followed by ranchers, miners, and petroleum companies. In 1981 an airport was built to accommodate skiers headed for nearby Las Leñas ski area, and since then Malargüe has made strides toward becoming a year-round adventure-tourism center.

The **Las Leñas** ski area—an hour-and-a-half flight from Buenos Aires, 70 km (43 mi) from Malargüe, 445 km (276 mi) south of Mendoza (7 hours by car or less by charter plane), and 200 km (124 mi) south of San Rafael—is the biggest and the highest ski area in Argentina. In fact, with a lift capacity of 9,200 skiers per hour, Las Leñas is the largest ski area served by lifts in the western hemisphere—bigger than Whistler–Blacomb in British Columbia, and Vail and Snowbird combined. From the top, at 11,250 feet, a treeless lunar landscape of lonely white peaks extends in every direction. Numerous long runs (the longest is an 8-km [5-mi] drop, 4,000 feet) extend over the 10,000 acres of skiable terrain. There are steep, scary, 2,000-foot vertical chutes for experts; machine-packed routes for beginners; and plenty of intermediate terrain in between.

Where to Stay & Eat
Las Leñas is a ski village with five full-service hotels, two apart-hotels, four condominium complexes, and four *dormy* (dorm) buildings. Shuttle buses run between lifts, hotels, restaurants, and shops. Less expensive lodging is in the nearby hot-springs resort town of Los Molles, 19 km (12 mi) away; there's bus service from there to the ski area. **Lodging information:** (☎ 11/4816–6999 in Buenos Aires, 2627/471100 in Mendoza).

Day-trippers most likely will dine slopeside during the day, at the central **El Brasero** (cafeteria by day, grill at night) or at restaurants in hotels or in the **Pirámide** shopping center.

$$$$ ⊞ **Aries.** Even if you don't ski, you'll find plenty of diversions in this slopeside hotel. There is a separate space for children's games and activities; a piano bar in the lobby and a wine bar serving cheese and re-

gional smoked meats for adults; and a movie theater for the whole family. Rooms are spacious with large windows overlooking the slopes. For the adventurous, heli-skiing can be arranged here. ⊠ *Las Leñas Ski Area* ☎ *11/4816–6999 in Buenos Aires* ⊕ *www.laslenas.com/hoteles* ⤵ *72 rooms, 5 suites* ♦ *Restaurant, indoor pool, hot tub, massage, sauna, spa, downhill skiing, ski shop, 2 bars, pub, cinema, recreation room, shop, children's program (ages 1–12), travel services* ⊟ *AE, DC, MC, V* ⊙ *Closed Oct.–June* ⦿ *MAP.*

$$$$ ⊞ **Escorpio.** Smaller and intimate, this ski lodge is right on the slopes. Its terrace is a great spot to watch the action while lunching or taking a break. Many rooms have balconies and views of the mountains. ⊠ *Las Leñas ski area* ☎☎ *2627/471100* ⤵ *47 rooms, 1 suite, 2 apartments* ♦ *Restaurant, bar, shop* ⊟ *AE, DC, MC, V* ⦿ *MAP.*

$$$$ ⊞ **Piscis.** The most deluxe hotel at Las Leñas pampers its guests with spa services, ski equipment delivered to the slopes, and a large indoor-outdoor pool. The hotel has supervised indoor play activities for kids as well as all levels of ski instruction. Complimentary hot wine and hot chocolate are served in the afternoon. ⊠ *At Las Leñas ski resort* ☎☎ *2627/471100* ⤵ *90 rooms* ♦ *2 restaurants, indoor-outdoor pool, gym, hair salon, hot tub, sauna, 3 bars, casino, recreation room, shop, baby-sitting, Internet, airport shuttle* ⊟ *AE, DC, MC, V* ⦿ *MAP.*

Sports & the Outdoors

The ski season usually runs from June to October. Most South Americans take their vacation in July, the month to avoid if you don't like crowds and higher prices. August has the most reliable snow conditions, September the most varied—a blizzard one day, sunshine the next. Seven-night ski packages are sold through travel offices in the United States, Buenos Aires, Mendoza, and San Rafael. Lift-ticket prices are lowest mid-June–early July and mid-September–early October, and highest mid- to late July. For information, contact **Las Leñas Central de Reservas** (⊠ Reconquista 616, fl. 5, Buenos Aires ☎ 11/4313–1300 ⊟ 11/4315–2070). The **information office** (☎☎ 2627/47100) at Las Leñas can also provide you with information on lift tickets and snow conditions.

Badino (⊠ Paraguay 930, Buenos Aires ☎ 11/4326–1351 ⊟ 11/4393–2568 ⊕ www.badino.com.ar) offers package tours to ski areas in Argentina and Chile.

San Luís

⑲ *820 km (509 mi) northwest of Buenos Aires, 258 km (160 mi) east of Mendoza via R7, 212 km (131 mi) northwest of San Rafael via R146.*

In the northeast corner of the Pampas, the busy capital of the San Luís Province (founded in 1594) has been the crossroads between the Northwest, Mendoza, and Buenos Aires for centuries. A growing petroleum industry, national investment in manufacturing, government tax incentives, and a university attract a lively mix of businesspeople, students, and tourists.

In the center of town, surrounded by shady sidewalks, is the **Plaza Pringles,** a good place to start a half-day walk. The square is named for Colonel Juan Pascual Pringles, a soldier in the battle for independence, whose statue is in the center of the plaza and whose tomb is in the cathedral across the street. Begun in 1883 and finished in 1944, the monumental **Iglesia Catedral** has a lovely interior, decorated with green onyx, marble, and dark *algarrobo* (carob) wood from the region.

The **Colegio Nacional Juan Crisóstomo Lafinur** (Juan Crisóstomo National High School), across from the plaza at Junín and San Martín, was built in 1869. Surrounded by halls and galleries, it's the finest example of colonial architecture in the city and reflects the educational ideals of Domingo Sarmiento, Argentina's Father of Education. It also has a splendid vestibule and theater. Ask permission within to enter.

Where to Stay & Eat

$–$$ ✕ **Sofia.** By 10:30 on Saturday night, the tables are filled with families in their Sunday best. They come for the supreme steaks, baby goat, lamb, fresh trout, and chicken cooked in a variety of sauces. A roast pig on a platter—stuffed and coiffed with fruits and vegetables—is paraded around the room on a cart accompanied by tempting appetizers. ⊠ *Colón and Bolívar* ☎ *2652/427960* ▭ *AE, DC, MC, V.*

¢–$ ✕ **La Ragazza.** At this small, street-side café close to most hotels, you can enjoy Argentine home cooking made with loving care by the owner-chef. Outstanding empanadas, pizzas, and pastas are served with fresh vegetables. ⊠ *Av. Pte. Arturo Illia 210* ☎ *2652/433732* ▭ *No credit cards.*

▥ **Gran Hotel San Luís.** Rooms are adequate if small, dark, and drab at this business traveler's hotel. But the business center with a fax machine and Internet access is a significant asset in this part of the country. ⊠ *Av. Pte. Arturo Illia 470, 5700* ☎ *2652/425049* ▤ *2652/430148* ⇌ *63 rooms, 2 suites* ⚒ *Laundry service, business services, free parking* ▭ *AE, DC, MC, V* ¶⊙¶ *CP.*

$$ ▥ **Hotel Potrero de los Funes.** Only 15 km (9 mi) from San Luís on R18, this large (bordering on grandiose) resort complex built by the government during Perón's time caters to company meetings and groups. Some rooms have antiques and others are slightly antiseptic, though all are comfortable. ⊠ *R18, Km 16, Potrero de los Funes, 5700, 15 km (9 mi) north of San Luís* ☎☎ *2652/495001* ⇌ *94 rooms, 7 suites* ⚒ *Restaurant, café, 5 tennis courts, gym, sauna, windsurfing, boating, horseback riding, soccer, bar, casino, business services, meeting rooms* ▭ *AE, D, MC, V* ¶⊙¶ *CP.*

$$ ▥ **Quintana Hotel.** This modern hotel is on a wide, quiet boulevard within walking distance of downtown. The staff is attentive and well informed. Sunlight shines through tall windows into the interior garden where breakfast, drinks, and snacks are served. The spacious rooms are done in desert colors with light wood. ⊠ *Av. Pte. Arturo Illia 546, 5700* ☎☎ *2652/438400* ⇌ *84 rooms, 12 suites* ⚒ *Restaurant, café, room service, pool, massage, sauna, bar, laundry service, business services, car rental, travel services* ▭ *AE, DC, MC, V* ¶⊙¶ *CP.*

Sports & the Outdoors

Nine kilometers (5 mi) northeast of San Luís on R20 is a sports complex called **Avenida Fénix en Koslay** (also the address), with a swimming pool, tennis courts, five soccer fields, Ping-Pong tables, and a picnic area with grills. Farther northeast, in the Sierra de San Luís, are dams that have been built to store precious water. Two of these dams, the **Embalse de Cruz de Piedra** (16 km [21 mi] northeast of San Luís on R20) and the **Embalse Potrero de los Funes** (18 km [11 mi] northeast of San Luís on R20 and R18), are good for fishing, sailing, swimming, and canoeing. Canoes can be rented at the hotel **Potrero de los Funes** (⊠ R18, Km 16, Potrero de los Funes ☎☎ 2652/495001). For fishing licenses and information, contact the **Club Nautico La Florida** (☎ 2652/483042).

Shopping

Local artisans sell handwoven rugs at the **Mercado Artesanal** (⊠ 25 de Mayo), facing the Plaza Independencia. Next to the tourist office, a shop also called the **Mercado Artesanal** (⊠ Av. San Martín and Av. Pte. Arturo Illia) sells regional handcrafts.

Parque Nacional las Quijadas

⑳ *127 km (76 mi) northwest of San Luís via R154.*

You might find yourself all alone—but for a few gray foxes, snakes, and passing condors—staring into the colossal red-rock amphitheater called the Potrero de la Aguada, (named for a corral with a watering hole), which is surrounded by wind-and-rain–eroded red and gray cliffs. You can follow the semi-marked trail (it has no guardrails or constructed steps) through the canyon on your own or go with a guide. Spring and summer bring torrential rains and intense thunderstorms. In summer, the couple that lives at the end of the road into the park manages the campground and a small kiosk where soft drinks, beer, and snacks are sold. The couple's son is a guide with **Daniel Rodriguez Guía Turístico** (☎ 2652/1554–7328). You can get information in San Luís about the Parque Nacional las Quijadas at **Las Quijadas** (✉ San Martín 974 ☎ 2652/461683).

San Francisco del Monte de Oro

㉑ *112 km (69½ mi) northeast of San Luís via R146.*

At the foot of the Sierra de Michilingue, San Francisco del Monte de Oro is split in two by the Río San Francisco. Colonial buildings line the narrow streets of the southern portion of town. **El Ranchito de Sarmiento** is an adobe house where in 1826, at age 15, Domingo Sarmiento taught adults to read and write in a school founded by his uncle.

About 14 km (8 mi) from town, deep gorges cut through by crystal streams entice both trout anglers and rock climbers. Look for the **Salto Escondido** ("hidden falls"), a waterfall that drops 243 feet into a pool where you can bathe or fish.

Where to Stay

$ 🏠 **Hostería del Valle de San Francisco.** This family-run inn in a remodeled country home has flowery guest rooms and a blue-and-yellow-tiled restaurant–bar. Vacationing Argentine families come here to horseback ride, bird-watch, stargaze, mountain bike, and fish. You can arrange tours of the area at the inn. ✉ *San Francisco del Monte de Oro 5705* ☎ *2652/ 426137* ➷ *24 rooms* ☖ *Restaurant, pool, travel services* ▭ *No credit cards* ¶◎¶ *CP.*

THE CUYO A TO Z

To research prices, get advice from other travelers, and book travel arrangements, visit www.fodors.com.

AIR TRAVEL

Mendoza's Aeropuerto Internacional Francisco Gabrielli is 6 km (4 mi) from town on R40. Aerolíneas Argentinas has flights to Mendoza from Buenos Aires and connects to San Juan and San Luís. AIRG (formerly LAPA) and Southern Winds fly from Buenos Aires and Santiago, Chile to Mendoza.

🛫 Airlines & Contacts **Aerolíneas Argentinas** ✉ Sarmiento 82, Mendoza ☎ 261/420–4100 ✉ Av. San Martín 215 Oeste, San Juan ☎ 264/427–4444, 2627/430036 in San Rafael. **Aeropuerto Internacional Francsico Gabarielli** ☎ 261/448–2603 in Mendoza. **AIRG** ✉ España 1002, Mendoza ☎ 261/423–1000 ✉ Av. J. I. de la Roza, San Juan ☎ 264/ 421–6039 ✉ Pedernera 863, San Luís ☎ 2652/431753. **Southern Winds** ✉ España 943, Mendoza ☎ 261/429–3200.

BUS TRAVEL

Mendoza's big and busy Terminal del Sol is in Guaymallén, a suburb east of downtown. Buses go from Mendoza to every major city in Argentina. Some transport companies are as follows: Andesmar, with service to Bariloche, Salta–Jujuy, and San Juan; Chevallier, with daily service to Buenos Aires; La Cumbre, with daily service to San Juan and Córdoba along a scenic route; La Estrella, with buses via San Juan to La Rioja, Tucumán, and Jujuy, and to Buenos Aires via San Luís; Jocoli, which has a sleeper via San Luís to Buenos Aires; El Rápido, with daily buses to Buenos Aires and Santiago, Chile, and three trips weekly to Lima, Peru; and T.A.C., with service to Bariloche, Buenos Aires, and Córdoba.

Every town has local buses, and if you can express where you want to go and understand the reply, you can travel cheaply (but slowly). A number in brackets on the bus indicates the route. Almost every tour agency runs minivans to local sights.

Andesmar ☎ 261/438-0654. **Chevallier** ☎ 261/431-0235. **El Rápido** ☎ 261/431-4094. **La Cumbre** ☎ 261/431-9252. **La Estrella** ☎ 261/431-1324. **Jocoli** ☎ 261/431-4409. **Mendoza Viajes** ☎ 261/438-0480. **T.A.C.** ☎ 261/431-1039. **Terminal del Sol** ✉ Av. Gobernador Videla and Av. Acceso Oeste ☎ 261/448-0057.

CAR RENTAL

Cars and 4x4s can be rented in all major cities. It's a good idea to make reservations in advance during peak season. Avis has a large fleet at the Mendoza airport.

Rental Agencies A. Sanchez ✉ Rodoviária, Loc. No. 4, San Rafael ☎ 2627/428310. **Andina Rent A Car** ✉ Sarmiento 129, Mendoza ☎ 261/461-0210 ⊕ www.andinarentacar. com.ar. **Avis** ✉ Primitivo de la Reta 914, Mendoza ☎ 261/420-3178, 261/447-0150 airport ⊕ www.avis.com. **Dollar Rent A Car** ✉ Primitivo de la Reta 936, Loc. No. 6, Mendoza ☎ 261/429-9939 ⊕ www.dollar.com. **Localiza** ✉ San Juan 931, Mendoza ☎ 261-429-0876 ⊕ www.localiza.com.ar.

CAR TRAVEL

The trip from Buenos Aires to Mendoza is 1,060 km (664 mi) along lonely, paved R7. From Santiago, Chile, it's 250 km (155 mi) east (the road is sometimes closed in winter) on R7. Mendoza locals are known for their cavalier attitude toward traffic rules. Outside the major cities, however, there's very little traffic.

You can drive to most sights and wineries in the Cuyo, although finding wineries on your own requires a good map and some knowledge of Spanish. Driving to the high Andean villages and the border with Chile is a remarkable experience and worth the expense of a rental car. If you fear getting lost or breaking down in remote areas, hire a remis—a car with a driver.

Pay attention to weather and road information. In winter, snow and avalanches close some roads. Torrential rainstorms cause flash floods and can obliterate seldom-used dirt roads. Good maps can be found in bookstores and at Automóvil Club Argentino.

Auto Club Automóvil Club Argentino (ACA) ✉ Av. del Libertador 1850, Buenos Aires ☎ 11/4808-4460 🖶 11/4808-4601 ✉ Gdor. Videla and Reconquista, Mendoza ☎ 261/431-4100 ⊕ www.aca.org.ar. **Roadside Assistance** ☎ 0800/888-9888.

EMERGENCIES

Ambulance-Medical Emergencies ☎ 107. **Fire** ☎ 100. **Police** ☎ 101.

HOSPITALS & PHARMACIES **In Mendoza Hospital Central** ✉ José F. Moreno and Alem, near the bus station ☎ 261/420-0600. **Farmacia del Puente (open 24 hrs)** ✉ Av. Las Heras 201 ☎ 261/425-9209.

In San Juan Hospital Dr. G. Rawson ✉ General Paz and E.E.U.U. ☎ 264/422-2272.

🔳 In San Luís **Clínica Privada Italia** ✉ Italia Esq. Martín de Loyola ☎ 2652/421241 or 2652/425825. **Hospital Materno Infantil** ✉ Av. Republica Oriental del Uruguay 150 ☎ 2652/425045. **Sanatorio y Clínica Rivadavía** ✉ Rivadavía 1059 ☎ 2652/436624 or 2652/436631.

🔳 In San Rafael **Hospital Schestakow** ✉ Emilio Civit 151 and Corrientes ☎ 2627/424290 or 2627/424291.

ENGLISH-LANGUAGE BOOKSTORES

🔳 **Librerías Y** ✉ Upstairs in the Mendoza Plaza Shopping Center, Av. Acceso Este 3280, Guaymallén. **Y Libros** ✉ Av. San Martín 1252, Mendoza ☎ 261/425-2822.

HEALTH

Good water and fresh fruits and vegetables are part of Cuyano life. Bottled water is available in bars, stores, restaurants, and kiosks. If you're heading into high altitude, carry aspirin for headaches and drink plenty of water. Herbal teas such as té de boldo, té de coca, and cachimay soothe upset stomachs. Sunscreen is a must wherever you go in this hot, dry, sunny climate.

MAIL & SHIPPING

Post offices are generally open 8 AM to 8 PM, but it's best to ask at your hotel. UPS, DHL, and Federal Express have offices in Mendoza. American Service Pack is a private postal service in Guaymallén (in Mendoza).

🔳 **American Service Pack** ✉ Casa Central, O'Brien 508 and San José ☎ 261/445-3178. **Mendoza Post Office** ✉ Av. San Martín and Colón ☎ 261/449-9500. **San Juan Post Office** ✉ Av. J. I. de la Roza 259 Este ☎ 264/422-4430. **San Rafael Post Office** ✉ San Lorenzo and Barcala ☎ 2627/421119.

MONEY MATTERS

Banks in the region are generally open weekdays 10–4. ATMs are available everywhere (Banelco and LINK have ATMs in most cities). Hotels and sometimes travel agencies will change dollars to pesos. Traveler's checks are inconvenient; you have to go to the bank to change them and pay a fee.

🔳 Mendoza Bank Information **Banelco** ✉ Av. San Martín 831 ✉ Sarmiento 29. **Banco de la Nación** ✉ Av. San Martín and Gutiérrez ☎ 261/423-4500 ✉ At bus terminal. **Citibank** ✉ Av. San Martín 1098 ☎ 261/420-4113. **Exprinter** ✉ Espejo 74 ☎ 261/429-1200.

🔳 San Juan Bank Information **Banco de Boston** ✉ Laprida and Mendoza ☎ 264/421-0708. **Banco de Galícia** ✉ General Acha and Rivadavía ☎ 264/421-2490. **Citibank** ✉ Av. J. I. de la Roza 211 Oeste ☎ 264/427-6999. **Lloyd's Bank** ✉ General Acha 127 Sur ☎ 264/420-6480.

🔳 San Luís Bank Information **Banco de Galícia** ✉ Rivadavía and Belgrano ☎ 2652/423479.

🔳 San Rafael Bank Information **Banco de la Nación** ✉ El Libertador and Mitre ☎ 2627/422265 ✉ H. Yrigoyen 113 ☎ 2627/43009.

TAXIS

Taxis in the region are inexpensive, metered, and plentiful. There's usually a taxi stand near the central plaza, and you can always have one called at hotels and restaurants. For tips—give the fare rounded up. Although drivers are generally honest, it's a good idea for long trips to agree upon the fare before you go. Remises cost a little more than a taxi, but they are reliable, and a good value for groups sharing expenses. Arrangements can be made through your hotel or at the airport or bus station.

🔳 Remises **Class Remise** ☎ 261/431-8238 local guided tours, 261/431-8244 airport transfers, 261/431-5810 business trips 🖨 261/431-9264. **Imperio Remises** ✉ At the bus station, Loc. D23 ☎ 261/432-2222 or 0800/433368. **La Veloz del Este** ✉ Alem 439 ☎ 261/423-9090.

TELEPHONE & INTERNET

Most *locutorios* (long-distance telephone centers) are large, modern, and user-friendly, with Internet access and fax machines. Local calls can be made on public phones with tokens or phone cards available at kiosks. The cybercafé in San Rafael has few machines, but it does have good coffee and helpful, English-speaking attendants.

🚺 In Mendoza **Cyber Café** ⊠ Av. San Martín and Garibaldi 7 ☎ 261/425-4020. **Internet Mendoza** ⊠ Sarmiento 25 ☎ 261/429-0143. **Telefónica** ⊠ Av. San Martín 650. 🚺 In San Juan **Casino Cyber Café** ⊠ Rivadavía 12 Este ☎ 264/420-1397. **Interredes** ⊠ Laprida 362 Este ☎ 264/427-5790. **Telefónica** ⊠ Laprida 180 Oeste. 🚺 In San Rafael **Cybercafé** ⊠ In gallería on Av. San Martín 120. **Locutorio I** ⊠ Avellaneda 76 ☎☎ 2627/43016. **Locutorio III** ⊠ Terminal de Omnibus, Loc. No. 35 ☎☎ 2627/435809. **Telefónica Argentina** ⊠ San Lorenzo 131.

TOURS

For ski tours in Mendoza, contact Mendoza Viajes, Badino, or Feeling Turísmo.

Aymará Turismo and Mendoza Viajes organize wine tours, excursions to mountains and villages and outdoor adventures. Huentata and Inka offer local excursions and outdoor adventures. Argentine Rafting and Betancourt Rafting specialize in rafting, kayaking, and trekking.

Puerto del Sol in San Juan, a full-service travel agency, organizes many local tours. Dasso Viajes rents cars and makes foreign, domestic, and local travel arrangements in and around San Luís. For tours of San Rafael, contact Atuel Travel or Bessone Viajes y Turismo.

🚺 **Argentina Rafting Expeditions** ⊠ Ruta Nacionál 7, Km 53, Potrerillios-Luján de Cuyo ☎ 262/448-2037 ⊕ www.argentinarafting.com. **Atuel Travel** ⊠ Av. Mitre 439, San Rafael ☎☎ 2627/429282 ⊕ www.atueltravel.com.ar. **Aymará Turismo** ⊠ 9 de Julio 1023, Mendoza ☎☎ 261/420-2064 ⊕ www.aymara.com.ar. **Badino** ⊠ Paraguay 930, Buenos Aires ☎ 11/4326-1351 ⊕ www.badino.com.ar/patagonia/. **Bessone Viajes y Turismo** ⊠ H. Yrigoyen 423, San Rafael ☎☎ 2627/436439. **Betancourt Rafting** ⊠ Lavalle 36, Galería Independencia Loc. No. 8, Mendoza ☎☎ 261/429-9665 ⊕ www.betancourt. com.ar. **Dasso Viajes** ⊠ Rivadavía 615, San Luís ☎ 2652/421017. **Huentata** ⊠ Av. Las Heras 680, Mendoza ☎☎ 261/425-3108 ⊕ www.huentata.com.ar. **Inka** ⊠ Av. Juan B. Busto, Mendoza ☎ 261/425-0871 ⊕ www.inka.com.ar. **Mendoza Viajes** ⊠ Paseo Sarmiento 129, Mendoza ☎☎ 261/461-0210 ⊕ www.mdzviajes.com.ar. **Puerto del Sol** ⊠ Entre Ríos 203 Sur, San Juan ☎☎ 264/427-5060.

VISITOR INFORMATION

🚺 **Mendoza** ⊠ Av. San Martín 1143 at Garibaldi ☎ 261/420-2800 🖶 261/420-2243 ⊕ www.turismo.mendoza.gov.ar. **San Juan** ⊠ Sarmiento 24 Sur ☎ 264/421-0004 ⊕ www.ischigualasto.com. **San Luís** ⊠ Av. Presidente Illía and Av. Junín ☎ 2652/423957 or 800/666-6176 ⊕ www.turismoensanluis.com. **San Rafael** ⊠ Av. H. Yrigoyen 745 ☎☎ 2627/424217.

PATAGONIA

6

FODOR'S CHOICE

Bosque Petrificado, *Atlantic Patagonia*

Cruce a Chile por Los Lagos, *Atlantic Patagonia*

El Viejo Molino, *Trelew*

Glaciar Moreno, *Atlantic Patagonia*

Hostería Los Notros, *El Calafate*

Hotel Correntoso, *Villa La Angostura*

Hotel y Resort Las Hayas, *Ushuaia*

Llao Llao Hotel & Resort, *near Bariloche*

Museo Marítimo, *Ushuaia*

Museo Paleontológico, *Trelew*

Península Valdés, *Atlantic Patagonia*

Reserva Faunistica Punta Tombo

HIGHLY RECOMMENDED

Bahía Nueva Hotel, *Puerto Madryn*

El Patacón, *restaurant in Bariloche*

Hostería Paimún, *San Martín de los Andes*

Hostería Patagonia Jarké, *Tierra del Fuego*

Hotel Edelweiss, *Bariloche*

La Marmite, *restaurant in Bariloche*

La Vieja Cuadra, *restaurant in Gaiman*

Parque Nacional Tierra del Fuego

Reserva Faunistica de Punta Bermeja, *Viedma*

Ty Te Caerdydd, *restaurant in Gaiman*

Ty Gwyn, *restaurant in Gaiman*

Volver, *restaurant in Ushuaia*

Updated by
Eddy Ancinas
and Michael
de Zayas

PATAGONIA, THAT FABLED LAND of endless, empty, open space at the end of the world, has humbled the most fearless explorers. Many have described it as a cruel and lonely windswept place unfit for humans. Darwin called Patagonia "wretched and useless," yet he was deeply moved by its desolation and forever attracted to it. Today, the 800,000 square km (309,000 square mi) that make up Argentine Patagonia continue to challenge and fascinate explorers, mountaineers, nature lovers, sports enthusiasts, and curious visitors from around the world.

From the Río Colorado (Colorado River) in the north to Cape Horn, 2,000 km (1,200 mi) south, this vast territory may seem monotonously devoid of life—uninhabited and inhospitable—but these very characteristics make it one of the most amazing natural preserves on earth. Because the population in Patagonia is small relative to its land mass, a staggering variety of plants and wildlife exists in pristine habitats.

The Andes mountains on the western border with Chile form a natural barrier to Pacific storms, and runoff from their eternal snows pours into lakes and streams, eventually spilling into major rivers that wind their way for hundreds of miles across the great arid plateau, until finally flowing into the Atlantic. Farther south, the continental ice cap spreads over 13,500 square km (8,400 square mi), forming the only glacier (Perito Moreno) in the world that is still growing after 30,000 years.

Ushuaia, on the Canal Beagle (Beagle Channel) in Tierra del Fuego, prides itself on being the southernmost city in the world. Puerto Madryn, on the Atlantic coast in the province of Chubut, is the gateway to the Península Valdés and its unending show of marine life. San Carlos de Bariloche, at the foot of the Andes in the northern lake district, is by far the largest and most frequently visited city in Patagonia and is undeniably picturesque. Yet its beauty lies outside the city limits—on a mountain road, by a lake or stream, in the forest, or in the surrounding mountains.

Exploring Patagonia

A new airport in Calafate, with direct flights from Buenos Aires and Bariloche has made the far reaches of Patagonia much more accessible to tourists. Covering the great distances between Bariloche, in the north; Ushuaia, in the south; and El Calafate, Río Gallegos, and Trelew–Puerto Madryn, in the middle, requires careful planning—air travel is essential. Tours to popular sights along the Atlantic coast, to the glaciers, or in and around Bariloche, can be arranged in Buenos Aires or in each destination. If you want to see it all, packaged tours can make the whole trip easier.

About the Restaurants

Since sheep and cattle far outnumber humans in Patagonia, expect lamb and beef to appear on almost every menu. Often cooked on a *parrilla* (grill) before your eyes, beef, lamb, and *chorizos* (homemade sausages) are enhanced by a spoonful of *chimichurri* sauce (made from olive oil, garlic, oregano, and sometimes chopped tomatoes and onions). On ranches and in some restaurants, you may have the opportunity to try gaucho-style *carne al asador,* where the meat is attached to a metal cross placed in the ground over hot coals. The heat is adjusted by raking the coals as the meat cooks, and the fat runs down to create a natural marinade. Lamb and goat cooked in this manner are delicious, and the camaraderie of standing around the fire sipping *mate* (a traditional Argentine drink) or wine while the meat cooks is part of the gaucho tradition.

Throughout the northern Andean lake district, local trout, salmon, and hake are grilled, fried, baked, smoked, and dried. Wild game such as hare, venison, and boar is prepared in a variety of marinades and sauces. Smoked fish and game from the region are popular appetizers throughout Argentina. Pasta also appears on every menu, often with homemade (*casera*) sauces, which are listed separately.

If the 10 PM dinner hour seems too great a gap, tea is a welcome break around 4 PM. Patagonia's Welsh teahouses, a product of Welsh immigration in the 19th century, serve delicious cakes, tarts, and cookies from recipes that have been handed down for generations. Jams made from local berries spread on homemade bread and scones are a welcome treat on a blustery day.

Reservations are seldom needed except during school, Easter, and summer holidays (July, January, and February). Attire is informal, and tipping is the same as in the rest of the country (about 10%).

About the Hotels
Idyllic lake-view lodges, cozy *cabañas* (cabins), vast *estancias* (ranches), and inexpensive *hospedajes* or *residenciales* (bed-and-breakfasts) are found in towns and in the countryside throughout Patagonia. Luxurious hotels in the northern lake district and near the glaciers attract outdoor enthusiasts from all over the world, as do small family-run hostals, where backpackers squeeze five to a room. Fishing lodges on the lakes near Bariloche, San Martín de los Andes, and Junín de los Andes are not only for anglers; they make great headquarters for hiking, boating, or just getting away. In cities, avoid hotel rooms on lower floors that face the street. *Apart-hotels* have small, furnished apartments with kitchenettes. Local tourist offices are most helpful in finding anything from a room in a residence to a country inn or a downtown hotel. Patagonia has become such a popular tourist destination that advance reservations are highly recommended if you're traveling during peak times (December–March; July–August for the ski resorts). Note: lodging prices include tax; most include Continental breakfast as well, unless otherwise noted.

Staying at an estancia is a unique way to experience Patagonian life on the range. Sheep shearing, cattle round-ups, horseback riding, and sharing ranch chores are typical activities; a lamb asado is often an added attraction. Estancias are in remote areas, and accommodations are limited, so reservations are essential. For information on estancias in Santa Cruz province, contact the **Centro de Información de la Provincia de Santa Cruz** (✉ Suipacha 1120, Buenos Aires ☏ 11/4325–3098 ⊕ www.estanciasdesantacruz.com). The regional tourist office, **Subsecretaría de Turismo de Santa Cruz** (✉ Av. Roca 1551, Río Gallegos ☎ 2966/422702) also has information on estancias.

For information on estancias or lodging in Santa Cruz province, contact the **Centro de Información de la Provincia de Santa Cruz** (✉ Suipacha 1120, Buenos Aires ☏ 11/4325–3098). The **Subsecretaría de Turismo de Santa Cruz** (✉ Av. Roca 1551, Río Gallegos ☏ 2966/422702 ⊕ www.sectur.gov.ar) has accommodations information for Santa Cruz province. For information on estancias in all of Patagonia, try their web site and click on patagonia/active tourism/rural tourism.

For more general information, (⊕ www.interpatagonia.com) has everything from ski resorts, to fishing lodges, restaurants to tourist attractions.

Numbers in the text correspond to numbers in the margin and on the Patagonia and Bariloche and the Parque Nacional Nahuel Huapi maps.

If you have 5 days

Fly to ▦ **Bariloche** ❶ and make it your base. In the afternoon of the day you arrive, take in the view of the lake in front of the Civic Center, where you can find the tourist office and the fine **Museo de la Patagonia**; then stroll past the shops on Calle Mitre. You can set up excursions for the following days either through the tourist office or your hotel. On Day 2, follow the Circuito Chico along the shore of the lake, with a side trip to **Cerro Otto** ❹ or the ski area at **Cerro Catedral** ❸. Take a boat trip on the third day to **Isla Victoria** ❷ and the Península Quetrihué to see the Arrayanes forest. On Day 4, consider going hiking, fishing, horseback riding, river rafting, or mountain biking in the surrounding area; or you might just want to stay and shop in Bariloche. The Circuito Grande combined with the Circuito de los Siete Lagos can be done in a long day or with an overnight in ▦ **San Martín de los Andes** ⓫ or **Villa La Angostura** ❽. Yet another option is to take an overnight trip to ▦ **Esquel** ⓭, stopping in **El Bolsón** ⓬ and the Parque Nacional los Alerces along the way. If you have a day left, take a lake cruise to **Puerto Blest** ❼ and Laguna Frías at the foot of **Monte Tronadór** ❺. (Note: If you're arriving or leaving Bariloche via the Chilean lake crossing, you'll have traveled this route.)

If you visit Bariloche in winter (June–September) for a ski vacation, arrange on arrival at your hotel to take the bus the next morning to the ski area at Cerro Catedral. To add some variety to your ski week, you can do the Circuito Chico on your return trip from the ski area, stopping at a teahouse en route. Or take a day off for the lake excursion mentioned above. Across the lake, **Villa La Angostura** ❽ has a smaller ski area, Cerro Bayo.

If you'd prefer to spend five days in the Tierra del Fuego, fly to ▦ **Ushuaia** ⓲ and spend three days exploring the national park, taking a boat to the wildlife preserve on Isla Redonda, and visiting the Maritime Museum at the Almirante Berisso Naval Base. Fly on the fourth day to ▦ **El Calafate** ⓰ and take two days to see the impressive glaciers in the Parque Nacional los Glaciares.

If you have 7 days

Spend the first four days in and around ▦ **Bariloche** ❶–❼, as described in the five-day itinerary. On Day 5, fly to ▦ **El Calafate** ⓰. Allow one day each for excursions to the Glaciar Upsala and the Glaciar Moreno. Check flight schedules from Bariloche well ahead of time.

Another seven-day option, depending on the season and your preference for wildlife versus glaciers, would be to spend four days in Bariloche as described above, then fly to **Trelew** ㉕ and transfer to ▦ **Puerto Madryn** ㉖, leaving two days to view wildlife along the coast.

A third possibility is to spend your first three days in ▦ **Ushuaia** ⓲ exploring the Tierra del Fuego and then two days in ▦ **El Calafate** ⓰ seeing the glaciers in the Parque Nacional los Glaciares. Fly to ▦ **Bariloche** ❶ on the sixth day and spend your last two days in this area.

6

Fly from Buenos Aires to 🚇 **Bariloche** ❶ for four days and do the Circuito Chico or Circuito Grande as described in the five-day itinerary, or consider a two-day (one-night) excursion by lakes and land from Bariloche to Puerto Montt, Chile, returning by bus. On Day 5, fly from Bariloche to **El Calafate** ⓰ and spend two days exploring the glaciers. From there fly on to **Trelew** ㉕ or 🚇**Gaiman** ㉓ your base for the next three days, taking time to visit **Península Valdés** ㉗ or 🚇 **Punta Tombo** ㉒. On Day 8, continue on to and visit the Glaciars Moreno and Upsala, returning to Buenos Aires on the evening of Day 10.

If you enjoy hiking, you could extend your time in El Calafate for an overnight in **El Chaltén** ⓱ at the base of Cerro Fitzroy. If you're an avid angler, use Bariloche as your headquarters and hire a guide to take you to nearby lakes and streams—or go on a real fishing odyssey to Lago Traful; then spend three days in 🚇 **San Martín de los Andes** ⓫ and three days at the Paimún Lodge north of 🚇 **Junín de los Andes** ⓾. If that's not enough fishing, drive south to the Parque Nacional los Alerces for a week of fishing in the streams and lakes around Lago Futalaufquen.

WHAT IT COSTS In Argentina Pesos				
$$$$	**$$$**	**$$**	**$**	**¢**
RESTAURANTS over 35	25–35	15–25	8–15	under 8
HOTELS over 300	220–300	140–220	80–140	under 80

Restaurant prices are for one main course at dinner. Hotel prices are for two people in a standard double room in high season.

Timing

January and February are the peak summer months in Patagonia, and for good reason: the wind dies down and long, warm days (the sun sets at 10 PM) ensure plenty of time to enjoy a multitude of activities. Hotel and restaurant reservations are necessary in popular destinations, and campgrounds get crowded. March and April are still good months to visit, although rainy, cloudy days and cold nights might curtail some activities. The rewards, however, are fewer crowds and the great colors of fall. Some hotels in remote areas close from May through September, as few want to brave the knock-down winds, rain, sleet, and snow of Patagonian winters.

In Bariloche and the northern lake district, ski season begins in June. The snow-covered mountains reflected in the blue lakes are spectacular, and the weather is typical of any alpine region—tremendous snowstorms, rain, and fog punctuated by days of brilliant sunshine. August and September are the best months for skiing. In July, the slopes are crowded with vacationing schoolkids and their families.

December is spring in Patagonia. The weather might be cool, breezy, overcast, or rainy, but the rewards for bringing an extra sweater and rain gear are great: an abundance of wildflowers and very few tourists. The December–June period is the best time to visit Península Valdés—this is when you can see the whales. Tierra del Fuego has different charms year-round: in summer it's warm during the day and cool at night, which is ideal for outdoor activities but also means big crowds; in winter it's great for skiing, sledding, visiting dog-sledding camps, and hiking through beautifully desolate woods. If you want to whale-watch and do winter sports, consider combining a trip to Tierra del Fuego and Puerto

Madryn sometime between June and September. Tierra del Fuego winters are not as harsh as you might think: the average temperature in August, the dead of winter, is about 36°F.

ANDEAN PATAGONIA

Updated by
Eddy Ancinas

Snow-packed peaks, a white volcano mirrored in a still lake, chalk-white glacial streams cascading over polished granite, meadows filled with chin-high pink and purple lupine, fast-flowing rivers, and thousands of lakes, with no houses, no piers, no boats: this could be paradise on Earth.

Andean Patagonia's northern lake district seems like one big national park: the Parque Nacional Lanín, just north of San Martín de los Andes in Neuquén Province, combined with the neighboring Parque Nacional Nahuel Huapi, in Río Negro Province, with Bariloche as its headquarters, adds up to 2.5 million acres of natural preserve—about the size of New England. South of the Cholila Valley and northwest of Esquel is the Parque Nacional los Alerces, named for its 2,000-year-old *alerces* (*Fitzroya cupressoides*), which are similar to California redwoods. The park covers 1,610 square km (1,000 square mi) of true wilderness, with only one dirt road leading into it.

Along the eastern edge of the northern lake district, mountain streams flow into rivers that have carved fertile valleys into deep canyons. Welsh farmers have been growing wheat and raising sheep in the Chubut Valley since 1865. Rain diminishes as you move eastward, and the land flattens into a great plateau, running eastward into dry, desolate Patagonia. This is sheep-breeding country, and Benetton owns a large portion of it. In summer (December–March), the towns of El Calafate and El Chaltén, in the southern lake district, come alive with the influx of visitors to the Parque Nacional los Glaciares and climbers headed for Cerro Torre and Cerro Fitzroy.

Bariloche & the Parque Nacional Nahuel Huapi

1,615 km (1,001 mi) southwest of Buenos Aires (2 hrs by plane), 432 km (268 mi) south of Neuquén on R237, 1,639 km (1,016 mi) north of Río Gallegos, 876 km (543 mi) northwest of Trelew, 357 km (221 mi) east of Puerto Montt, Chile, via lake crossing.

In 1620, the governor of Chile sent Captain Juan Fernández and his troops across the Andes in search of the "Enchanted City of the Caesars," a mythological city alleged to be somewhere in Patagonia. By 1670, the Jesuits had established a mission on the shores of the lake, near what is now Isla Huemúl. They attempted to convert the Tehuelches, who ultimately massacred the missionaries in 1717, including the missions' founder, Father Mascardi. No Europeans returned to the area until the next century, when Captain Cox arrived by boat from Chile in 1870. Later, in 1876, *perito* (expert) Francisco Moreno led an expedition from the Atlantic, becoming the first explorer to arrive from the East.

Most of the indigenous people of the area were massacred during the infamous Campaña del Desierto (Desert Campaign, 1879–83). Settlers then felt safe to colonize, and a fort (called Chacabuco) was built at the mouth of the Río Limay in 1883. Many settlers were German farmers immigrating from Chile, followed by Swiss, Scandinavian, and northern Italian immigrants. They found a rugged and relatively unexplored land similar to their mountainous homelands and built chalets ❶ in the town that would become **Bariloche** and along the shore of Lago Nahuel Huapi.

Bariloche's first house, built by a German immigrant named Karl Wiederhold (1867–1935), also became the town's first hotel, called La Cuchara Sucia ("the dirty spoon"). By 1924 tourists could travel two days from Buenos Aires by train, then drive 560 km (350 mi) on dirt roads. The railway finally reached Bariloche in 1934, and by 1938 people from all over the world were coming to ski on the slopes at nearby Cerro Catedral.

These days, Bariloche is the gateway to all the recreational and scenic splendors of the northern lake district. Although planes, buses, trains, boats, and tour groups arrive daily, you can escape into the stunning wilderness of clear blue lakes, misty lagoons, rivers, waterfalls, mountain glaciers, forests, and flower-filled meadows on foot, mountain bike, or horseback or by boat. You can also fish peacefully in one of the 40 nearby lakes and countless streams. It's also possible to get around on your own with a rented car or go on a planned excursion with a local tour company.

The rustic gray-green stone-and-log buildings of the Centro Cívico (Civic Center) were designed by Alejandro Bustillo, the architect who also designed the Llao Llao Hotel and the National Park office in San Martín de los Andes. His Andean-Swiss style is recognizable in lodges and buildings throughout the lake district. The spacious square in front of the Civic Center, with an equestrian statue of General Roca (1843–1914) and a wide-angle view of the lake, is a good place to begin exploring Bariloche. Note that the Civic Center is Km 0 for measuring points from Bariloche.

For information on mountain climbing, trails, *refugios* (mountain cabins), and campgrounds, visit the **Intendencia de Parques Nacional Nahuel Huapi** (✉ Av. San Martín 24 ☎ 2944/423111 ⊕ www.parquesnacionales. gov.ar) at the Civic Center. Another source of information on local activities, excursions, lodging, and private and public campgrounds is the **Oficina Municipal de Turismo** (✉ Centro Cívico, across from clock tower ☎ 2944/429850), open daily 8:30 AM–9 PM.

The **Museo de la Patagonia** (Patagonia Museum) tells the social and geological history of northern Patagonia through displays of Indian and gaucho artifacts and exhibits on regional flora and fauna. The history of the Mapuche and the Conquista del Desierto (Conquest of the Desert) is also explained in detail. ✉ *Centro Cívico, next to arch over Bartolomé Mitre* ☎ 2944/422309 ⊴ *10 pesos* ⊙ *Mon. and Sat. 10–1, Tues.–Fri. 10–12:30 and 2–7.*

The **Parque Nacional Nahuel Huapi,** created in 1943, is Argentina's oldest national park, and **Lago Nahuel Huapi** is the sapphire in its crown. The park extends over 2 million acres along the eastern side of the Andes in the provinces of Neuquén and Río Negro, on the frontier with Chile. It contains the highest concentration of lakes in Argentina. The biggest is Lago Nahuel Huapi, a 897-square-km (557-square-mi) body of water, whose seven long arms (the longest is 96 km [60 mi] long, 12 km [7 mi] wide) reach deep into forests of *coihué* (a native beech tree), *cyprés* (cypress), and *lenga* (deciduous beech) trees. Intensely blue across its vast expanse and aqua green in its shallow bays, the lake meanders into distant lagoons and misty inlets where the mountains, covered with vegetation at their base, rise straight up out of the water. Every water sport invented and tours to islands and other extraordinarily beautiful spots can be arranged through local travel agencies, tour offices, and through hotels. Information offices throughout the park offer help in exploring the miles of mountain and woodland trails, lakes, rivers, and streams.

Outdoor Activities

With some of the most wild and remote places left on earth, Patagonia has plenty of opportunities to experience the great outdoors. Many ranches near Bariloche, El Calafate, and Chaltén have horseback riding (*cabalgatas*) as well as organized excursions. Horses are available to rent for a day or a week through tour operators in Bariloche, Esquel, San Martín de los Andes, and El Calafate. The animals are well trained and so much a part of Argentine culture that horseback-riding trips are a natural way to explore the mountains, forests, and lakes of Nahuel Huapi, Lanín, Los Alerces, and the Parque Nacional los Glaciares.

6

Hiking trails are well marked in all the national parks of the lake district as well as in the area around Ushuaia and Chaltén in southern Patagonia, where Cerro Fitzroy and Cerro Torre attract serious mountain climbers from the world over. Trail maps are available at park offices. Fishing in the lakes and streams of the Andes, from Bariloche all the way south to Tierra del Fuego, is legendary; lodges devoted to fishing enthusiasts are booked well in advance. River rafting on the Río Limay (Limay River) or on the more rapid Manso, which runs west into Chile, can be arranged with outfitters in Bariloche. The Hua-Hum also flows into Chile from San Martín de los Andes, as does the exciting Futaleufú, south of Esquel. Mountain biking, whether on the slopes of the ski runs at Cerro Bayo in Villa La Angostura, Catedral in Bariloche, or Chapelco in San Martín, or over mountain passes, through forests, and along rocky streams, can be enjoyed for a day or a week anywhere in the Andes. Rentals and excursions can be arranged in Bariloche, San Martín, Esquel, Villa La Angostura, El Bolsón, and El Calafate.

Wildlife

From the mountain aeries of the Andean east to the desolate Atlantic shoreline to the west, Patagonia provides a great chance to see animals in their natural habitats. The greatest concentration of easily viewed wildlife is along the Atlantic shoreline. At Península Valdés, countless species of marine life cavort in the sea and on land. In January, sea lions breed in rookeries, followed by killer whales, which come to feed on elephant seals on the coast. The spectacle of this feeding is matched in later months by close-up viewing of thousands of right whales that come here to mate and give birth. To the south, at the world's largest penguin rookery, in Punta Tombo, over 300,000 little Magellanic penguins waddle back and forth on "penguin highways."

On land you'll see foxes, opossum, hares, lizards, armadillos, and guanacos (relatives of the camel). The hunting of guanacos for their fur and meat has gone on for centuries, and continues legally to the present day, even in such reserves as Península Valdés. Despite a drastic depletion in their numbers, there are still hundreds of thousands of these animals left in Patagonia. The guanaco's main non-human predator, the puma, travels the length of Patagonia as far south as Tierra del Fuego. Don't expect to spot one along the road, though—this solitary and secretive cat is rarely seen by humans.

All kinds of birds can be spotted, especially at high altitudes. Condors spread their massive wings and coast along the Andes at altitudes of 10,000 to 16,000 feet. Other common Patagonians include hawks, black eagles, peregrine falcons, snowy sheathbills, cormorants, and upland geese.

Patagonia

The most popular excursion on Lago Nahuel Huapi is the 30-minute ❷ boat ride to **Isla Victoria** (Victoria Island), the largest island in the lake. A grove of redwoods transplanted from California thrives in the middle of the island. After a walk on trails that lead to enchanting views of emerald bays and still lagoons, the boat crosses to the tip of the **Península Quetrihué** for a visit to the **Parque Nacional los Arrayanes**, a unique forest of cinnamon-color myrtle trees.

❸ The renowned ski area at **Cerro Catedral** (Mt. Cathedral) is 46 km (28½ mi) west of town on Avenida Ezequiel Bustillo (R237); turn left at Km 8½ just past Playa Bonita. The mountain was named for the Gothic-looking spires that crown its peaks. Though skiing is the main activity here, the view from the top of the chairlift at 6,600 feet is spectacular any time of year. To the southwest, Monte Tronadór, a 12,000-foot extinct volcano, straddles the border with Chile, towering above lesser peaks that surround Lago Nahuel Huapi as it meanders around islands and disappears into invisible bays beneath mountains and volcanoes miles away. Lanín Volcano is visible on the horizon.

❹ You can reach the summit of **Cerro Otto** (Mt. Otto; 4,608 feet), a small ski area, by hiking, mountain biking, or driving 8 km (5 mi) up a gravel road from Bariloche. Hiking to the top of the mountain takes you through a forest of lenga trees to Argentina's first ski area, at Piedras Blancas. Here Herbert Tutzauer, Bariloche's first ski instructor, won the first ski race by climbing the mountain, then skiing down it through the forest in 1½ hours. You can also take the **Teleférico Cerro Otto** (⌂ Av. de Los Pioneros), 5 km (3 mi) west of town; a free shuttle bus leaves from the corner of Mitre and Villegas, and Perito Moreno and Independencia. The ride to the top takes about 12 minutes. All proceeds go to local hospitals. At the top, a revolving cafeteria with a 360-degree panorama takes in Monte Tronadór, lakes in every direction, and Bariloche. In winter, skis and sleds are available for rent at the cafeteria. In summer, hiking and mountain biking are the main activities. For a real thrill, try soaring in a paraplane out over the lake with the condors. Call for **information** (☎ 2944/41031) on schedules and sled or ski rentals.

⑤ A visit to **Monte Tronadór** (Thunder Mountain) requires an all-day outing of 170 km (105 mi) round-trip from Bariloche. The 12,000-foot extinct volcano, the highest mountain in the northern lake district, sits astride the frontier with Chile, with one peak on either side. Take R258 south along the shore of **Lago Gutiérrez** and **Lago Mascardi**. Between the two lakes the road crosses from the Atlantic to the Pacific watershed. At Km 35, turn off onto a road marked TRONADÓR and PAMPA LINDA and continue along the shore of Lago Mascardi, passing a village of the same name. Just beyond the village, the road forks and you continue on a gravel road, R254. Near the bridge the road branches left to **Lago Hess** and **Cascada Los Alerces**—a detour you might want to take on your way out. As you bear right after crossing Los Rápidos Bridge, the road narrows to one direction only: it's important to remember this when you set out in the morning, as you can only go up the road before 2 PM and down it after 4 PM. The lake ends in a narrow arm (Brazo Tronadór) at the Hotel Tronadór, which has a dock for tours arriving by boat. The road then follows the **Río Manso** (Manso River) to **Pampa Linda,** which has a lodge, restaurant, park ranger's office, campsites, and the trailhead for the climb up to the **Refugio Otto Meiling** at the snow line. Guided horseback rides are organized at the lodge. The road ends 7 km (4 mi) beyond Pampa Linda in a parking lot that was once at the tip of the now receding **Glaciar Negro** (Black Glacier). As the glacier flows down from the mountain, the dirt and black sediment of its lateral moraines are ground up and cover the ice. At first glance, it's hard to imagine the tons of ice that lie beneath its black cap.

⑥ The detour to **Cascada Los Alerces** (Los Alerces Falls), 17 km (10 mi) from the turnoff at the bridge near Mascardi, follows the wild Río Manso, where it branches off to yet another lake, **Lago Hess.** At this junction are a campground, refugio, restaurant, and trailhead for the 1,000-foot climb to the falls. The path through dense vegetation over wooden bridges crosses a rushing river as it spills over steep, rocky cliffs in a grand finale to a day of viewing nature at its most powerful and beautiful.

A possible excursion from Bariloche is the **Circuito Chico** (Small Circuit), a half-day, 70-km (43½-mi) scenic trip along the west shore of Lago Nahuel Huapi. You can do it by car, tour bus, or mountain bike. First, head west on Avenida Bustillo (R237) toward Península Llao Llao. At Km 20, you can take a brief side trip on an 11-km-long (7-mi-long) dirt road to the **Península San Pedro,,** then follow the coast road that passes some fine homes set back in the woods. At the **Ahumadero Familia Weiss** (Weiss Family Smokehouse), along the way, you can buy smoked fish and game. Back on R237, continue west to **Puerto Pañuelo** (Km 25½) in a little bay on the right; it's the embarkation point for lake excursions and for the boat crossing to Chile. Across from the port, a long driveway leads up a knoll to the Hotel Llao Llao, which is worth a visit even if you're not staying here. The Circuito Chico then follows R77 to Bahía Lopez, winding along the lake's edge through a forest of ghostly, leafless lenga trees. After crossing the bridge that links **Lago Moreno** (Lake Moreno) and Lago Nahuel Huapi at Bahía Lopez, the road crosses the Arroyo Lopez (Lopez Creek). Here you can stop for a hike up to a waterfall and then climb above Lago Moreno to **Punto Panoramico,** a scenic overlook well worth a photo stop. Just before you cross Lago Moreno, an unmarked dirt road off to the right leads to the rustic village of **Colonia Suiza,** a good spot to stop for tea or lunch. After passing **Laguna El Trebol** (a small lake on your left), R77 joins R237 from Bariloche.

need a break? The window of the **Bellevue Casa de Te** holds the mirrored image of Monte Tronadór, framed by a forest of cypress and lenga trees. It's hard to say which is better—the view, the rich chocolate cake, the fruit tarts, or the garden. The bus stops across from Hotel Tunquelen; a sign here will direct you down a dirt road to the house. ⊠ *Av. Bustillo (R237), Km 25* ☎ *2944/448389* ⊗ *Closed Mon. and Tues. No lunch* ⊟ *No credit cards.*

The **Circuito Grande** (Large Circuit), a more ambitious excursion than the Circuito Chico that's particularly lovely in spring or fall, covers 250 km (155 mi). Along the way there are plenty of spots to stop and enjoy the view, have a picnic lunch, or even stay overnight. Leaving Bariloche on R237, follow the **Río Limay** into the **Valle Encantado** (Enchanted Valley), with its magical red-rock formations. Before crossing the bridge at **Confluéncia** (where the Río Traful joins the Limay), turn left onto R65 to Lago Traful. Five kilometers (3 mi) beyond the turnoff, on a dirt road heading toward Cuyín Manzano, are some astounding sandstone rock formations. As you follow the shore of Lago Traful, a sign indicates a *mirador* (lookout) on a high rock promontory, which you can climb up to on wooden stairs. The road from Villa Traful dives into a dense forest until it comes to the intersection with the Seven Lakes Circuit (R237). Turn right if you want to add the Seven Lakes Circuit. Otherwise, turn left and follow the shore of **Lago Correntoso** to the paved road down to the bay at **Villa La Angostura.**

The **Circuito de los Siete Lagos** (Seven Lakes Circuit) is an all-day trip of 360 km (223½ mi) round-trip, which could be extended to include an overnight in San Martín de los Andes or Villa La Angostura). Drive north on R237 for 21 km (13 mi), and turn left on R231 to **Villa La Angostura,** 65 km (40 mi) from Bariloche. About 11 km (7 mi) farther along the same road is the Seven Lakes Road (R234), which branches right and along the way passes **Lago Correntoso, Lago Espejo, Lago Villarino, Lago Falkner,** and **Lago Hermoso.** After lunch or tea or an overnight in San Martín de los Andes, head south to Bariloche on the dirt road over Paso Córdoba, passing **Lago Meliquina** on the way. At Confluéncia, the road joins R237, following the Río Limay through Valle Encantado to Bariloche.

❼ A longer, less traveled, all-day boat excursion to **Puerto Blest** leaves from Puerto Pañuelo on the Península Llao Llao (accessible by bus, car, or tour). The boat heads west along the shore of Lago Nahuel Huapi to Brazo Blest, a 1-km-long (½-mi-long) fjordlike arm of the lake. Along the way, waterfalls plunge down the face of high rock walls. A Valdivian rain forest of coihués, cypress, lengas, and *arrayanes* (myrtle) covers the canyon walls. After the boat docks at Puerto Blest, a bus transports you over a short pass to Puerto Alegre on **Laguna Frías** (Cold Lagoon), where a launch waits to ferry you across the frosty green water to **Puerto Fríos** on the other side. Monte Tronadór towers like a great white sentinel. The launch returns to the dock at Puerto Alegre, where you can return by foot or by bus to Puerto Blest. From there, the trail to **Cascada Los Cántaros** (Singing Waterfalls) climbs 600 steps to a series of waterfalls cascading from rock to pool to rock. After lunch in **Puerto Blest** at its venerable old hotel, the boat returns to Bariloche. Note: this is the first leg of the Cruce a Chile por Los Lagos.

The **Cruce a Chile por Los Lagos** (Chile Lake Crossing) is a unique excursion by land and lakes that began in the 1930s when oxcarts used to haul people. These days you can do the tour in one or two days. Follow the itinerary above, stopping for lunch in **Puerto Blest** and then continuing on to **Puerto Fríos** on **Laguna Frías**. After docking at Puerto Fríos and clearing Argentine customs, get on another bus that climbs through lush rain forest over a pass, then descends to **Peulla**, where Chilean customs is cleared (bring your passport). A little farther on is a comfortable lodge by **Lago Todos los Santos**. Early the next morning a catamaran sets out across the lake, providing views of the volcanoes **Putiagudo** (which lost its *punto* [peak] in an earthquake) and **Osorno**. The boat trip ends at the port of **Petrohué**. Another (and final) bus skirts **Lago Llanquihue**, stopping for a visit at the rockbound Petrohué waterfalls, passing through the town of **Puerto Varas** (famous for its roses) and arriving, at last, at the Chilean port town of Puerto Montt. Catedral Turismo specializes in this trip and can arrange a one-day return by bus to Bariloche.

Where to Stay & Eat

Accommodations range from family-run *residenciales* (bed-and-breakfasts) to resort hotels. If you don't have a car, it's better to stay in town. If you're looking for serenity, consider a lake-view hotel, inn, or cabins along the route to the Llao Llao Peninsula. Addresses for out-of-town dining and lodging properties are measured in kilometers from the Bariloche Civic Center. The most crowded time of the year is during school vacations (July and January). Of the many fine restaurants, most are casual and open noon–3 for lunch and 8–midnight for dinner.

$$$$ ✕ **Kandahar.** A rustic wood building with a woodstove and cozy window seats in alcoves around the bar is the perfect setting for a pisco sour, smoked meats, and guacamole. Former ski champion, Marta Peirano, prepares and presents her tasty creations while greeting friends and guests. Start with unusual appetizers such as *tarteleta de hongos* (mushroom tart), followed by wild game and profiteroles with hot chocolate sauce. ⊠ *20 de Febrero 698* ☎ *2944/424702* ▭ *AE, MC, V.*

★ **$$–$$$** ✕ **El Patacón.** Constructed of local stone and wood, with large picture windows looking out over the lake, this ranch-style restaurant displays gaucho tools, local art, and weavings on its wood and stucco walls. Leather and sheepskin furniture add to the country atmosphere. An organic garden with fresh herbs, berries, and vegetables enhances the menu of meats, game, and fish. ⊠ *Av. Bustillo, Km 7* ☎ *2944/442800* ▭ *AE, DC, MC, V.*

$$–$$$ ✕ **Jauja.** Big, friendly, and casual, this spot is a favorite with locals and families for its great variety of entrées: meats from the Pampas, fish from both oceans, local game, and pasta dishes are enhanced by fresh vegetables and salads. Take-out food is available around the corner at the Quaglia address. ⊠ *Elflein 128* ☎ *2944/429986* ⊠ *Quaglia 366* ☎ *2944/422952* ▭ *AE, DC, MC, V.*

★ **$$–$$$** ✕ **La Marmite.** If there's a Euro-Argentine cuisine, this is it: wild boar in wine with local mushrooms served with cabbage and elderberry jam, and venison, trout, and lamb prepared equally imaginatively. Argentina's famous malbecs and cabernets are the perfect companion for this international fare. ⊠ *Mitre 329* ☎ *2944/441008* ▭ *AE, DC, MC, V* ☾ *No lunch Sun.*

$ ✕ **El Boliche de Alberto.** Just point at a slab of beef, chicken, lamb or sausages, and have it grilled to your liking. It'll arrive sizzling on a wooden platter, accompanied by empanadas, salad, fried potatoes, and chimichurri sauce (slather it on the bread). ⊠ *Villegas 347* ☎ *2944/431433* ▭ *AE, DC, MC, V.*

★ $$$ ✕🏨 **Hotel Edelweiss.** Fresh flowers from the owner's nursery are arranged throughout this excellent medium-size hotel, which is three blocks from the Civic Center and within walking distance of tour offices, restaurants, and shops. The modern, spacious rooms and suites have lake views from their bay windows. Breakfast includes eggs, bacon, sausages, fresh fruits, and juices—unusual in this country of *medias lunas* (croissants) and coffee. Both lunch and dinner consist of good salads, grilled fish, fowl, game, and beef prepared with fresh vegetables and tasty sauces. Most ski and tour buses, whether arranged through the hotel or other travel agencies, pick up passengers at this hotel. ⊠ *Av. San Martín 202, 8400* 🕿 *2944/426165* 🖷 *2944/425655* ⊕ *www.edelweiss.com.ar* ⇘ *94 rooms, 6 suites* ⚫ *Restaurant, in-room safes, indoor pool, gym, hair salon, massage, sauna, bar, meeting room, travel services, free parking* ⊟ *AE, DC, MC, V* ⦿ *CP.*

$$$$ 🏨 **Hotel Catedral.** Popular with Argentine and Brazilian skiers (so book well in advance), this venerable stone-and-wood apart-hotel sits on a hill just beyond the tram building across the road from the Cerro Catedral ski area. The gracious former dining room, with its large windows framing a perfect postcard view of the lake and surrounding mountains, has been reinvented as a living room. Apartments sleep up to four people. ⊠ *Base Cerro Catedral, 8400* 🕿 *2944/460006* 🖷 *2944/460137* ✎ *hcatedral@bariloche.com.ar* ⊠ *Av. Córdoba 1345, fl. 7, Buenos Aires, 1055* 🕿 *11/4816–4811* ⇘ *60 apartments* ⚫ *2 restaurants, kitchenettes, 2 tennis courts, pool, sauna, bar, travel services* ⊟ *AE, DC, MC, V* ⊘ *Closed Apr.–May and Oct.–Nov.*

$$$$
Fodor'sChoice
★
🏨 **Llao Llao Hotel & Resort.** This masterpiece by architect Alejandro Bustillo sits on a grassy knoll surrounded by three lakes with a backdrop of rock cliffs and snow-covered mountains. Local wood—alerce, cypress, and hemlock—has been used for the walls along the 100-yard hallway, where paintings by local artists are displayed between fine boutiques. Every room has a view worth keeping the curtains open. A hospitality suite at Cerro Catedral allows hotel guests to buy tickets and store equipment while skiing. ⊠ *Av. Ezequiel Bustillo, Km 25, 25 km (15½ mi) west of Bariloche, 8400* 🕿 *2944/448530* 🖷 *2944/445781* ⊕ *www.llaollao.com* ⇘ *162 rooms, 12 suites, 1 cabin* ⚫ *Restaurant, café, in-room safes, minibars, cable TV, 18-hole golf course, tennis court, pool, fitness classes, gym, hair salon, hot tub, massage, sauna, spa, dock, windsurfing, boating, mountain bikes, archery, paddle tennis, bar, piano bar, recreation room, baby sitting, children's programs (ages 2–12), business services, convention center, meeting rooms, travel services, no-smoking rooms* ⊟ *AE, DC, MC, V* ⦿ *CP.*

$$$–$$$$ 🏨 **Hotel Nevada.** Right in the middle of town, this traditional hotel is a favorite of both business travelers and tourists alike. Rooms are high enough up to avoid street noise, and, although the hotel is old, have modern furniture and cheerful floral prints. Breakfast, snacks, tea, and drinks are served in the café and bar. ⊠ *Rolando 250, 8400* 🕿 *2944/ 522778 or 2944/527914* 🖷 *2944/427914* ⊕ *www.nevada.com.ar* ⇘ *81 rooms, 14 suites* ⚫ *Restaurant, gym, sauna, lobby lounge, recreation room, theater, business services, meeting room, free parking* ⊟ *AE, DC, MC, V* ⦿ *CP.*

$$$–$$$$ 🏨 **La Cascada.** Named for its lovely waterfall plunging into an idyllic pool a few steps from the entrance, this lake-view hotel 6 km (4 mi) from Bariloche on the road to Llao Llao brings the outdoors inside through its floor-to-ceiling windows in the living room, dining room, and bar. Views through the trees of blue Nahuel Huapi Lake and distant peaks are enhanced by bay windows in most of the bedrooms. ⊠ *Av. E. Bustillo, Km 6, CC 279, 8400* 🕿 *2944/441088* 🖷 *2944/441076* ⊕ *www.*

lacascada.com 22 rooms ⚬ *Restaurant, indoor pool, gym, sauna, bar* ▭ *DC, MC, V* ⦿ *CP.*

$$$–$$$$ 🏨 **Villa Huinid.** The two-story log and stucco cabins (one, two, or three bedrooms), with their stone chimneys and wooden decks, look like private homes surrounded by lawns and well-tended gardens. Well-equipped kitchens with large family dining tables invite week-long stays with family and friends. Cypress plank floors with radiant heat, carved wooden counters, slate floors in the bathroom, and cozy plaids and prints in the bedrooms add to the total comfort—all this and a view of Nahuel Huapi Lake. ⊠ *Av. Bustillo, Km 2.5, R8402* 📠 *2944/523523* ⊕ *www.villahuinid.com.ar* 11 cabins ⚬ *IDD phones, kitchens, cable TV, library, playground* ▭ *AE, MC, V.*

$ 🏨 **Hotel Tunquelen.** Surrounded by 20 acres of woods and gardens, this châteaulike hotel outside Bariloche is visible from the lake but not from the busy road to Llao Llao. An uninterrupted view across the water to distant peaks—even from the indoor pool—has a calming effect. Rooms are small, but adequate, with whitewashed stucco and native wood, and open onto the garden or overlook the lake. A downstairs dining room serves breakfast and dinner, and cocktails are served in the garden, weather permitting. ⊠ *Av. Bustillo, Km 24½, 24½ km (13 mi) west of Bariloche on the road to Llao Llao, 8400* 📠 *2944/448400* ⊕ *www.maresur.com* 31 rooms, 1 suite, 8 apartments ⚬ *Restaurant, cable TV, indoor pool, dock, bicycles, piano bar, meeting rooms, travel services, free parking* ▭ *AE, DC, MC, V* ⦿ *CP.*

¢–$ 🏨 **Casita Suiza.** Swiss-owned and -operated since 1961, this charming downtown chalet exudes old-world hospitality. The owners have lovingly painted flowers on the walls. Rooms are well maintained, and rates include a hearty breakfast with homemade wheat bread, jams, and juices. In summer and spring the street-side terrace explodes with blossoming pansies and violets. ⊠ *Quaglia 342, 8400* 📠 *2944/23775 or 2944/426111* ✉ *cassuiza@bariloche.com.ar* 13 rooms ⚬ *Restaurant, cable TV, bar, laundry service* ▭ *AE, DC, MC, V* ⦿ *CP.*

¢–$ 🏨 **Patagonia Sur.** This tall, slender seven-story structure sits high on a hill overlooking the town and the lake. The view of the church spire, rooftops, and blue lake make the five-block walk from town worth the effort. Inside and out it's clean and modern, from the softly upholstered benches in the lobby to the sparsely furnished rooms. The fifth floor is accessible by elevator from Aguas del Sur Hotel on the street below (Moreno). ⊠ *Elfleín 340, 8400* 📞 *2944/422995* 📠 *2944/424329* 55 rooms ⚬ *Café, cable TV, business services, meeting room, free parking* ▭ *DC, MC, V* ⦿ *CP.*

¢ 🏨 **Aconcagua Hotel.** A tidy wood-and-stucco building close to the Civic Center, this four-story hotel has weekly rates for its simple basic rooms, some with lake views. ⊠ *Av. San Martín 289, 8400* 📞 *2944/424718* 📠 *2944/424719* ✉ *aconcagua@infovia.com.ar* 32 rooms ⚬ *Snack bar, free parking* ▭ *AE, MC, V* ⦿ *CP.*

¢ 🏨 **Albergue La Bolsa.** Cyclists, mountaineers, skiers, and friends from around the world have been staying at this popular family home for years. This lively hostal provides beds and lockers in rooms for two, four, or five—each room has its own bathroom. Walls are decorated with photos of guests and friends enjoying every sport invented, and information on outings and excursions with sign-up sheets invite an active clientele to participate. Meals are prepared by guests in a large kitchen and eaten on bicycle seats at the counter, outdoors in the enclosed front yard or around the living room. ⊠ *Palacios 405, 8400* 📞 *2944/423520* ⊕ *www.labolsadeldeporte.com* 4 rooms ⚬ *Kitchen, Internet* ▭ *No credit cards.*

CROSSING INTO CHILE

WHETHER YOU want to experience another culture, make a loop through the lakes, or hook up with a tour, you'll find crossing into Chile simple and efficient—provided you have your passport and are not carrying any fresh food (meat, cheese, fruits, or vegetables). Rental car companies should give you the proper documents for your car, but it's a good idea to double-check that you have all the necessary paperwork. It's also a good idea to have some Chilean pesos with you, as it is can be expensive to change them at the border. Be aware of the weather, as lake crossings are not fun when you have to deal with driving rain and high waves. Snow may close some passes in winter.

In the northern lake district, there are seven border crossings. Paso Pérez Rosales is part of the popular 12-hour bus and boat tour from Bariloche to Puerto Montt, Chile. The quickest way to return by paved road to Bariloche is via Osorno, crossing at Cardenal Samoré (a.k.a. Paso Puyehue) to Villa Angostura (125 km [78 mi] from the border to Bariloche on RN231).

Paso Hua Hum is the only crossing open year-round. It may be the shortest route—only 47 km (29 mi) from San Martín de Los Andes on RP48—as the condor flies, but it's the longest journey by road, after factoring in the 1½-hour-long ferry ride across Lake Pirehueico on the Chilean side. There are three ferries daily, and buses leave regularly from San Martín de Los Andes. You can also make this crossing by raft in the river Hua Hum.

Farther north, and accessible via Junín de los Andes, are two passes that require a longer excursion. Mamuil Malal (a.k.a. Paso Tromen) is 67 km (41.5 mi) northwest of Junín de los Andes on RP60. This dirt road crosses Lanín National Park and passes through a forest of ancient Arucaria trees as it heads for the foot of Lanín Volcano. Just before the park office, a road leads to good picnic and campsites on Lago Tromen. If you continue on to Chile, you'll see the Villarica and Quetupillán volcanoes to the south and Pucón to the north.

Paso Icalma is 132 km (20 mi) west of Zapala on RN13. Villa Pehuenia, (10 km [6 mi]) before the pass, is a small village on the shore of Lake Alluminé with modern accommodations and restaurants. Rafting or fishing the Alluminé River, a visit to a Arucaria nursery, plus horse, bike, and raft rentals might tempt you to stay awhile.

The combination of Argentina's glaciers and Chile's Torres del Paine National Park are on many travelers' itineraries. Crossing at Cancha Carrera is quick and simple. From Río Gallegos, it's 161 km (100 mi) northwest on RP5 to La Esperanza, then 129 km (80 mi) west on PR7 to Cancha Carrera. From Calafate, you can take a shortcut (closed in winter) on RN40 south to El Cerrito, which then runs 70 km (43 mi) southwest to RP7 at Estancia Tepi Aike, 78 km (48 mi) west of Esperanza. The longer but easier alternative is to drive 161 km (100 mi) to La Esperanza on the main road to Río Gallegos, then west on PR7. As you approach the border, the grey granite spires of Torres del Paine are visible for miles across the empty plain. You will pass (and can stop and visit) the 100-year-old Tapi Aike ranch. Puerto Natales, in a sound on the Chilean coast, is the access city for Torres del Paine and Chilean coastal cruises. Río Túrbio, a coal-mining town with huge fields and a miner's museum, is 257 km (159 mi) west of Río Gallegos, and from there 30 km (19 mi) north to Puerta Natales. At Monte Aymond, 68 km (42 mi) south of Río Gallegos on RP68, you can cross into Tierra del Fuego via Punta Delgada in Chile.

— Eddy Ancinas

Nightlife & the Arts

Three of the town's most popular *discotecas* (discos) are all on the same street, Avenida J. M. de Rosas. Whole families—from children to grand-parents—go to discos, though on Saturday night only people 25 years and older are admitted. The clubs are especially busy during school holidays and ski season. You can dance the night away at **Cerebro** (⊠ 405 Av. J. M. de Rosas ☎ 2944/424965). Bariloche's oldest disco is **El Grisu** (⊠ 574 Av. J. M. de Rosas ☎ 2944/422269). **Roket** (⊠ 424 Av. J. M. de Rosas ☎ 2944/420549 day; 2944/431940 night) has blue-and-purple lights and a cutting-edge sound system. Around the corner from the Avenida J. M. de Rosas strip of clubs is the **Casino Worest** (⊠ España 476 ☎ 2944/424421), which is open daily 10 PM–4 AM.

Sports & the Outdoors

FISHING Fishing season runs November 15–May 1. In some areas, catch-and-release is allowed year-around; in some places it's compulsory, and in some, catches may be kept. Guides are available by the day or the week. Nahuel Huapi, Gutiérrez, Mascardi, Correntoso, and Traful are just a few of the many lakes in the northern lake district that attract fishing fanatics from all over the world. If you're seeking the perfect pool or secret stream for fly-fishing, you may have to do some hiking, particularly along the banks of the Chimehuín, Limay, Traful, and Correntoso rivers. Near Junín de los Andes, the Río Malleo (Malleo River) and the Currihué, Huechulafquen, Paimún, and Lácar lakes are also good fishing grounds. Near El Bolsón and Esquel in the Parque Nacional los Alerces, many remote lakes and streams are accessible only by boat or seldom-traveled dirt roads. Fishing lodges offer rustic comfort in beautiful settings; boats, guides, and plenty of fishing tales are usually included. Make reservations early, as they're booked well in advance by an international clientele of repeat visitors.

Fishing licenses allowing you to catch brown, rainbow, and brook trout as well as perch and *salar sebago* (landlocked salmon) are available in Bariloche at the **Direcciones Provinciales de Pesca** (⊠ Elfleín 10 ☎ 2944/425160). You can also get licenses at the Nahuel Huapi National Park office and at most tackle shops. Boats can be rented at **Charlie Lake Rent-A-Boat** (⊠ Av. Ezequiel Bustillo, Km 16.6 ☎🖷 2944/448562).

Oscar Baruzzi at **Baruzzi Deportes** (⊠ Urquiza 250 ☎ 2944/424922 🖷 2944/428374) is a good local fishing guide. **Martín Pescador** (⊠ Rolando 257 ☎ 2944/422275 🖷 2944/421637) has a shop with fishing and hunting equipment. Ricardo Almeijeiras, also a guide, owns the **Patagonia Fly Shop** (⊠ Quinchahuala 200, Av. Bustillo, Km 6.7 ☎🖷 2944/441944).

Arturo Domínguez is a professional English-speaking guide (☎ 2944/15552237 cell 🖷🖷 2944/461937).

For trolling or spinning contact **Jorge Lazzarini** (☎ 2944/294411). **Luís Navarro** (☎ 2944/0668–55044) also knows good spots on Nahuel Huapi Lake for spinning and trolling.

HIKING Nahuel Huapi National Park has many forest trails that lead to hidden lakes, tumbling streams, waterfalls, glaciers, and mountaintop vistas. For maps and information in English on trails, distances, and degree of difficulty, visit the **Parques Nacionales** (⊠ Av. San Martín 24 ☎ 2944/423111) office at the Civic Center. For ambitious treks, mountaineering, or use of mountain huts and climbing permits, contact **Club Andino Bariloche** (⊠ 20 de Febrero 30 ☎ 2944/422266).

HORSEBACK RIDING	*Cabalgatas* (horseback outings) can be arranged by the day or the week. Argentine horses are sturdy and well trained, much like American Quarter Horses, and saddles are typically covered with a thick sheepskin. *Tábanas* (horseflies) attack humans and animals in summer months, so bring repellent. **El Manso** (☎ 2944/523641 or 2944/441378) combines riding and rafting over the border to Chile. Tom Wesley at the **Club Hípico Bariloche** (✉ Av. Bustillo, Km 15.5 ☎☎ 2944/448193 ⊕ www.bariloche.org/twesley.html) does rides lasting from one hour to a week. **Cumbres Patagonia** (✉ Villegas 222 ☎ 2944/423283 🖷 2944/431835) arranges day trips to Monte Tronadór and other sights.
MOUNTAIN BIKING	The entire Nahuel Huapi National Park is ripe for mountain biking. Whether you're a beginner or an expert, you can find a trail to suit your ability. Popular rides are from the parking lot at the Cerro Catedral ski area to Lago Gutiérrez and down from Cerro Otto. Local tour agencies can arrange guided tours by the hour or day and even international excursions to Chile. Rental agencies provide maps and suggestions and sometimes recommend guides.

Adventure World (✉ Base of Cerro Catedral ☎ 2944/460164 or 2944/422637) rents bikes at the ski area. From there you can ride off on your own or follow a guide down to Lago Guitérrez. **Alunco** (✉ Moreno 187 ☎ 2944/422283) is a full service travel agency that arranges bike tours with local companies. **Cumbres Patagonia** (✉ Villegas 222 ☎ 2944/423283) offers guided bike tours for a day or a week. **Dirty Bikes** (✉ Vice Almirante O'Conner 681 ☎ 2944/425616) rents, repairs, and sells bikes and arranges local tours. **La Bolsa del Deporte** (✉ Diagonal Capraro 1081 ☎ 944/433111) rents and sells new and used bikes.

PARAGLIDING	*Parapente* (paragliding) gives you the opportunity to soar with the condors through mountains and out over lakes, lagoons, and valleys. Cerro Otto and Cerro Catedral (both accessible by ski lifts) are popular launch sites. For equipment and guide information, contact **Parapente Bariloche** (☎ 2944/462234; 2944/15552403 cell).
SKIING	**Cerro Catedral** is the largest and oldest ski area in South America, with 29 lifts, mostly intermediate terrain, and a comfortable altitude of 6,725 feet. The runs are long, varied, and very scenic. Two ski areas share 4,500 acres of skiable terrain, making it necessary to purchase two separate tickets. **Lado Bueno** (The Good Side) has a vertical drop of 3,000 feet, mostly in the fall line. **Robles** goes about 300 feet higher, offering open bowls and better snow for beginners and intermediates at higher elevation. From the top of the second Robles chair, a Poma Lift transports skiers to a weather station at 7,385 feet, where a small restaurant, **Refugio Lynch,** is tucked into a wind-sculpted snow pocket on the edge of an abyss with a stupendous 360-degree view of Nahuel Huapi Lake, Monte Tronadór, and the Andes. **Villa Catedral,** at the base of the mountain, has ski retail and rental shops, information and ticket sales, ski school offices, restaurants, private ski clubs, an ice rink, and even a disco. Frequent buses transport skiers from Bariloche to the ski area. For information and trail maps, contact **La Secretaría de Turismo de Río Negro** (✉ 12 de Octubre 605 ☎ 2944/423188). **Club Andino Bariloche** (✉ 20 de Febrero 30 ☎ 2944/422266) also has information and trail maps.
WHITE-WATER RAFTING	With all the interconnected lakes and rivers in the national park, there's something for everyone—from your basic family float down the swift-flowing, scenic Río Limay to a wild and exciting ride down Río Manso (Class II), which takes you 16 km (10 mi) in three hours. If you're really adventurous, you can take the Manso all the way to Chile (Class IV)

through spectacular scenery. Some tour companies organize a trip down the Manso with return by horseback and a cookout at a ranch. **Adventure World** (⊠ At the Base of Cerro Catedral ☎ 2944/460164) does one-day and three-day raft trips on the Río Manso, with a combination horseback trip to the Chilean border available. **Alunco** (⊠ Moreno 187 ☎ 2944/422283 🖷 2944/422782) arranges rafting trips throughout the area. **Bariloche Rafting** (⊠ Mitre 86, Room 5 ☎ 2944/435708) offers trips along the Limay. **Cumbres Patagonia** (⊠ Villegas 222 ☎ 2944/423283 🖷 2944/431835) arranges trips on the Ríos Limay and Manso. **El Manso** (☎ 2944/523641 or 2944/1558–3114 cell) specializes in white-water rafting trips on the Manso River.

Shopping

Along Bariloche's main streets, Calle B. Mitre and Moreno, and its cross streets from Quaglia to Rolando, you can find shops selling sports equipment, leather goods, hand-knit sweaters, and gourmet food like homemade jams, dried meats, and chocolate. **Ahumadero Familia Weiss** (⊠ Palacios 401 ☎ 2944/435789) makes pâtés, cheeses, smoked fish, and wild game.

You can't avoid the chocolate supermarkets on both sides of Mitre. Grandmother Goye and her descendants have been creating chocolate delicacies at **Abuela Goye** (⊠ Mitre 258 ☎ 944/423311) since the 1960s. **Del Turista** (⊠ Mitre 239) is *the* supermarket chocolate store, with every chocolate concoction imaginable. **Fenoglio** (⊠ Mitre and Rolando ☎ 544/423119) has ice cream and a café to compliment the chocolate confections.

Talabarterís sell items for the discerning equestrian or modern gaucho. **Cardon** (⊠ Villegas 216) has leather bags, belts, boots, jackets, and coats, as well as silver buckles, jewelry, and tie rings. At **El Establo** (⊠ Mitre 22), look for shoes, hand bags, belts, wallets, and wall coverings featuring distinctive black-and-white Mapuche designs. These make nice mementos or gifts, as do hand woven rawhide scarf holders and key chains.

Cerámica Bariloche (⊠ Mitre 112) has been creating fine ceramics inspired by colorful local flora and fauna for 50 years. **Cultura Libros** (⊠ Elfleín 78 ☎ 944/420193) carries books in English and coffee table books with superb photos of the lake district and Patagonia, as well as local guidebooks. **Fitzroy** (⊠ Mitre 18), just past the Civic Center, has a good selection of ponchos, Mapuche blankets, and regional articles. **La Barca Libros** (⊠ Quaglia 247) has used books in English and photography and guide books.

Villa La Angostura

❽ *In Neuquén Province, 81 km (50 mi) northwest of Bariloche (a 5-hr drive on R237 around the east end of Lago Nahuel Huapi; also accessible by boat from Bariloche); 90 km (56 mi) southwest of San Martín de los Andes.*

Thoughtful planning and strict adherence to building codes have made this lakeside hamlet an attractive escape from the bustle of Bariloche. Log art abounds—over doorways, under window sills, on signposts, and on fences—there's even a large hand-carved wooden telephone on the street in front of the telephone office. The modern, medium-size convention center is constructed of native rock and stone. Most shops and restaurants are on Avenida Arrayanes (R231), in a commercial area called El Cruce (the Crossing)—the name refers to the crossing of R231, which goes from Bariloche to the Chilean border, with the road to the port, Nahuel Huapi, and the Seven Lakes Road, R234, to San Martín de los

Andes). The **Secretaría de Turismo y Cultura** (✉ Av. Siete Lagos 93 ☎ 2944/494124) is at the southern end of Avenida Arrayanes. At the intersection of Avenida Arrayanes and Avenida Siete Lagos, turn left onto Bulevar Nahuel Huapi to get to the original **Villa Angostura** (Narrow Village) on the lake—so named because it occupies a narrow isthmus connecting it to the Península Quetrihué.

The **Parque Nacional los Arrayanes** (12 km [7½ mi] along a trail from the Península Quetrihué) is the only forest of arrayanes in the world. These native trees absorb so much water through their thin skins that they force all other vegetation around them to die, leaving a barren forest of peeling cinnamon-color trunks. You can make this excursion by boat from Bariloche via Isal Victoria or from the pier at Bahía Brava in Villa La Angostura; or walk (three hours) or ride a bike or horse across the isthmus. A nice combination is to go by boat and return by bicycle (it's all downhill that way).

The ski area at **Cerro Bayo** (Bay-Color Mountain), named for its dirt-brown color, is 9 km (5½ mi) northeast of town and open year-round for skiers (it's open to snowboarders in winter only), and also for mountain biking in the summer. Two chairlifts take you to the top (5,000 feet), where a 5-km (3-mi) panoramic trail wends its way around the mountain, affording a wide-angle view of Nahuel Huapi Lake. Four surface lifts transport skiers and snowboarders to easy and intermediate runs. The El Tronadór café at the mid-station serves, among other fare, waffles with local jams. El Refugio Chaltén, at the base of the mountain, serves goulash, lamb stew, snacks, and beverages.

Where to Stay & Eat

$-$$ ✗ **El Esquiador.** A *tenedor libre* (salad and appetizer bar) makes for easy pickings at this simple family-run café and restaurant one block from Avenida Arrayanes. Photos of local skiers and fishing conquests add local color. ✉ *Las Retamas 142* ☎ 2944/49433 ☰ AE, DC, MC, V.

$-$$ ✗ **Waldhaus.** This Hansel and Gretel dark-timbered log house with a sod roof is open for lunch, tea, and dinner. It serves Argentine food with a Germanic flavor: goulash, spaetzle, fondue, and Patagonian lamb. The interior is a riot of hearts and flowers with Swiss canton shields on the walls and ceilings. ✉ *Av. Arrayanes 6431 (R231)* ☎ 2944/495123 ☰ AE, DC, MC, V ⊘ Closed Mar.–June.

¢-$ ✗ **La Casita de la Oma.** Between the bay and the main street, this tea-house serves homemade soups, sandwiches, salads, and a tempting array of cakes, pies, and scones. Jars of jams line the shelves. ✉ *Inacayal 303* ☎ 2544/494602 ☰ MC, V ⊘ Closed May.

$$$$ ✗▥ **Las Balsas.** A short drive down a secluded road brings you to this Relais & Châteaux hotel right at the edge of Lago Nahuel Huapi. Afternoon tea and evening cocktails are served in the living room, which is a homey blend of wicker, natural wood, kilim rugs, and old photographs. Every room has a different decor, but all have views of the woods or the lake. In the candlelit dining room, fresh trout and game are accompanied by vegetables and spices grown in the hotel's organic garden; dinner reservations are advised if you're not a guest. ✉ *Bahía las Balsas, 8407* ☎☎ 2944/494308 ⊕ www.lasbalsas.com ⤶ 13 rooms, 2 suites ⚘ Restaurant, pool, gym, hot tub, sauna, beach, dock, bicycles, bar, recreation room, baby-sitting, laundry service, Internet, meeting rooms ☰ AE, MC, V ⊘ Closed May–Aug. ⑩ CP.

$$$-$$$$
Fodor'sChoice
★ ▥ **Hotel Correntoso.** You can see the fish jump from your bedroom window, your dining table, through the glass panels of the encircling deck, or from the refurbished 100-year-old fishing bar down by the lake. Perched on a hill where the Correntoso River runs into Nahuel Huapi Lake, this landmark hotel celebrates its place in history with old pho-

tos, light fixtures made from coihue branches, hand-woven Mapuche fabrics, and custom-made furniture covered in leather and linen. The restaurant overlooking the lake serves Patagonian specialties such as hare, wild boar, lamb, beef, and, of course, fish from local lakes and streams. ⊠ *RN 231 (Km 86), Puente Correntoso, 8407* ☎ *2944/156–19727; 11/4803–0030 in Buenos Aires* 🖷 *11/4803–0030* ⊕ *www.correntoso.com* ⤴ *16 rooms, 16 suites* ⚴ *Restaurant, dining room, cable TV, marina, fishing, bar, pub, library, Internet* ⊟ *AE, MC, V.*

$$ ▢ **Hostería la Posada.** Wrapped around a steep slope, this delightful inn overlooks terraced lawns and gardens, a pool, a beach, and across an emerald-color bay to distant mountains. There's no reason to close the flowery curtains in your room's bay windows—there's nothing out there but forest, lake, and stars. ⟐ *Box 12, 8407* ☎☎ *2944/494450 or 2944/494368* ⊕ *www.hostarialaposada.com* ⤴ *18 rooms, 2 suites* ⚴ *Restaurant, pool, beach, dock, boating, bicycles, bar* ⊟ *AE, DC, MC, V* ⊘ *Closed June* ⦿ *CP.*

$$ ▢ **Naranjo en Flor.** This tranquil mountainside retreat in a forest above Lago Nahuel Huapi is close to the ski area at Cerro Bayo. It looks like a Norman hunting lodge and feels like home, with a fireplace in the living room and a piano bar and playroom for bad-weather days. The modern carpeted bedrooms have big windows and tasteful antiques. ⊠ *Chucao 62, Puerto Manzano, 8407* ☎☎ *2955/494863* ⟐ *naranjoenflor@infovia.com.ar* ⤴ *8 rooms* ⚴ *Restaurant, pool, bar, travel services* ⊟ *AE, V* ⦿ *CP.*

¢ ▢ **Hostel La Angostura.** This friendly hostel near the bus station and tourist office is configured like a motel, with rooms opening onto a radiant heated tile hall way. Guests can gather in the living room for a game of pool, to watch a video or plan the day's activities. Family-style dinners are served in the cafeteria. ⊠ *Barbagelata 157, 8407* ☎☎ *2944/494834* ⊕ *www.hostellaangostura.com.ar* ⤴ *9 rooms for up to 6 people, 1 double with private bath* ⚴ *Cafeteria, bicycles, bar, library, recreation room* ⊟ *AE, MC, V* ⦿ *CP.*

¢ ▢ **Pichi Rincón.** Meaning "Little Corner" and in a grove of trees just beyond the village, this simple two-story inn looks across a spacious lawn through the forest and to the lake. Two columns of gray river rock guard the comfortable sitting area, which has a fireplace. Hefty pine furniture decorates the rooms. ⊠ *Off Av. Quetrihué, 3 km (2 mi) south of town on R231; just before Correntoso, turn left on Av. Quetrihué, 8407* ☎☎ *2944/494186* ⊕ *www.pichirincon.com* ⤴ *12 rooms, 3 cabins* ⚴ *Dining room* ⊟ *MC, V* ⦿ *CP.*

Sports & the Outdoors

FISHING The bays and inlets of Lago Nahuel Huapi are ideal for trolling and spinning, and the mouth of the Río Correntoso (Correntoso River) is famous for its trout. For trolling, spinning, or fly-fishing equipment rental or purchase, or for guides, contact the **Banana Fly Shop** (⊠ Av. Arrayanes 282 ☎ 2944/94634). **Jorge Lazzarini** (☎ 2944/294411) in Bariloche is a professional guide.

HORSEBACK Most trails used for hiking and mountain biking are also used for horse-
RIDING back riding. Picnic stops with a swim in a river, and an asado at the end of the ride are added attractions. Horses are available from **Los Saucos** (⊠ R231, Km 61.8 (Av. Arrayanes 1810) ☎ 2944/494853).

MOUNTAIN In and around the village are more bike rental shops than gas stations.
BIKING You can easily ride from the village to such places as Laguna Verde, near the port, or off the Seven Lakes Road to Mirador Belvedere and on to the waterfalls at Inacayal. The tourist office has a brochure, *Paseos y Excursiones*, with maps, distances, and descriptions (in Spanish) of mountain biking, hiking, and horseback-riding trails throughout the area.

Maps, information, and rentals are available in Las Cruces at **Free Bikes** (✉ Las Retamas 121 ☎ 2944/495047) and **IAN Bikes** (✉ Topa Topa 102 and Las Fucsias ☎ 2944/495005). Bikes are also available at the base of Cerro Bayo, at **Mountain Bike Cerro Bayo** (☎ 2944/495047).

SKIING **Cerro Bayo** (☎☎ 2944/494189), 9 km (5½ mi) from El Cruce via R66, has good skiing from July through September. Day rates are less than at most other ski areas. Rental equipment and lessons are available at the base facility. You can cruise on skis in winter or mountain bike in summer down a long road with spectacular views of the lake and surrounding mountains.

Shopping

Shops along Avenida Arrayanes carry products that are typical of the area—chocolate, smoked meats, dried mushrooms, handicrafts, sporting goods, and knitwear. Delicious homemade jams (*dulces caseros*) are found in nearly every shop, at roadside stands, and at teahouses.

en route Just beyond El Cruce, **R231** crosses the world's shortest river between Lakes Nahuel Huapi and Correntoso. Eleven kilometers (7 mi) from El Cruce, **R65** goes north past Lago Espejo, then turns east for 22 km (14 mi), when it meets R234 to San Martín de los Andes. Continuing on R65, the road (sometimes closed in winter) goes over a pass and descends through a forest of coihués to Lago Traful.

Villa Traful

❾ *60 km (37 mi) north of Villa La Angostura on R231 and R65, 100 km (60 mi) northwest of Bariloche on R234 and R65.*

Small log houses built by early settlers peek through the cypress forest along the way to Villa Traful, a village on Lago Traful. The town consists of about 50 log cabins, horse corrals, two fishing lodges, shops for picnic and fishing supplies, and a park ranger's office. Less visited than those in neighboring villages, the fine ranches and private fishing lodges here are tucked back in the surrounding mountains. By day swimmers play on sandy beaches on the lake, a lone water skier cuts the still blue water, and divers go under to explore the mysteries of a submerged forest. Night brings silence, thousands of stars, and the glow of a lakeside campfire. The **Oficina Municipal de Turismo** (✉ Across from municipal pier ☎ 2944/479020) can assist you with planning excursions.

Only 3 km (2 mi) from the village is **Arroyo Blanco**, a waterfall that cascades 66 feet over the rocks into a natural pool. You can walk or ride (a bike or a horse) through 1,000-year-old forests above and beyond the village to this waterfall as well as to nearby caves and mountain lookouts.

Where to Stay & Eat

Besides staying in the resorts outside town, you can also pitch a tent and throw your sleeping bag down just about anywhere along the lake. Good campsites, however, with rest rooms, benches, tables, and fire pits are plentiful along the southern shore of the lake. For exquisite beauty, look for Puerto Arrayanes at the western end of the lake. A large campground near the village is **Camping Vulcanche** (☎ 2944/479061).

¢–$$ ✕ **Ñancu-Lahuen.** The carved-wood sign says TEAHOUSE, but it's much more. Sandwiches, omelets, homemade ice cream, tarts, pies, and anything chocolate are served from noon until sundown, when salmon, trout, and steak dinners are served in an adjacent log house with a hand-hewn thatched roof and a floor of trunk rounds. ✉ *R65* ☎☎ *2944/49017* ▭ *AE, DC, MC, V.*

¢ ✕🏠 **Hostería Rincón del Pescador.** This long, low, white lodge in the middle of an ample lawn attracts fishing and outdoor enthusiasts. Enjoy afternoon tea and dinners of fresh-caught fish. Fishing guides are also available. ✉ On R65, 9006 🏠🏠 2944/479020 ➘ 12 rooms ⌂ Restaurant, fishing, mountain bikes, horseback riding ▭ No credit cards ⊙ Closed May–Oct.

¢ ✕🏠 **Hostería Villa Traful.** Across the road from the lake is a large log house, constructed in the 1940s as a fisherman's inn. Cabins that sleep two to six people are also available for rent. Afternoon tea is served, as are dinners of trout and salmon. The hotel can arrange fishing guides and lake tours. ✉ R65, 9006 🏠 2944/479006 🏠🏠 2944/479005 ⌨ turismo@neuquen.gov.ar ➘ 5 cabins ⌂ Fishing, mountain bikes ▭ No credit cards ⊙ May–Oct.

Sports & the Outdoors

Trails through forests to lakes, lagoons, streams, and waterfalls are accessible on foot, horseback, or mountain bike.

You can dive to 30 meters (98 feet) in crystalline water and explore a submerged cypress forest. For information, contact **Cabañas Aiken** (🏠 2944/479048).

This area is famous for its land-locked salmon and record-breaking-size trout in Lago Traful and the Laguna Las Mellizas (Twins Lagoon), 5 km (3 mi) north of town. Fishing season runs from November 15 to April 15. **Osvaldo Brandeman** (✉ Villa Trafúl 🏠 2944/442864 or 2944/479048) is a local fishing guide.

Junín de los Andes

❿ 41 km (25 mi) northeast of San Martín on paved R234, 219 km (136 mi) north of Bariloche on paved R237 and R234.

The quickest route between Bariloche and San Martín de los Andes is the paved road that runs through this typical agricultural town, where gauchos ride along the road, their dogs trotting faithfully behind. Once a fort in a region inhabited by the Mapuche, Junín de los Andes became a town during the last phase (1882–83) of the Conquista del Desierto, making it the oldest town in Neuquén Province. For centuries the valley where the town lies was the trading route of the Mapuche between mountainous Chile and the fertile plains of Argentina. Today Mapuche descendants sell their handicrafts and weavings in local shops and fairs, and the town's main attraction is its proximity to the Río Chimehuín (Chimehuín River), lakes Huechulafquen and Paimún, the Parque Nacional Lanín, and Lanín Volcano.

Where to Stay & Eat

The **Dirección Municipal de Turismo** (✉ Coronel Suárez and Padre Milannensio 🏠🏠 2972/491160) has information on lodging, dining, campgrounds, and nearby fishing lodges, which are open November–April. The best restaurants are in hotels, except for **Ruca Hueney** (🏠 2972/49113) on Suárez and P. Milanesia.

San Martín de los Andes

⓫ 260 km (161 mi) northwest of Bariloche on R237 via Junín de los Andes, 160 km (99 mi) northwest of Bariloche on R237 over the Córdoba Pass (69 km [42 mi] is paved), 184 km (114 mi) northwest of Villa La Angostura on R234 (the Seven Lakes Rd., only 66 km [41 mi] is paved).

Surrounded by mountains, lakes, and dense forests, San Martín de los Andes lies in a natural basin at the foot of Lake Lácar. It's the major tourist center in Neuquén Province and the gateway for exploring the Parque Nacional Lanín. San Martín was founded in 1898 by General Rudecindo Roca, who moved the original fort, built in 1883, from Vega de Maipú, 3 km (2 mi) north, to the present city. With a population of 20,000, San Martín is much like Bariloche was 30 years ago. Wide, flat streets run from the town pier on the eastern shore of Lago Lácar, along sidewalks lined with rosebushes, to a four-block commercial area of shops and chalets. Private gardens, stores, and the town square all display a colorful profusion of native flowers from spring until the snow first falls in June. Early Patagonian houses built with local timber and covered with corrugated metal to keep the wind out are still visible around the Plaza San Martín. One house of note, the **Obeid family mansion** (⌧ Roca and Coronel Perez), was built in 1903 with materials brought from Valdivia (Chile). For information on tours, lodging, and other services, contact the **Dirección Municipal de Turismo** (⌧ Av. San Martín and J. M. Rosas 790 ☎ 2972/427347 ⊕ www.smandes.gov.ar); it's open daily 8 AM–9 PM.

The **Museo Pobladores** (Pioneer Museum), next to the tourist office, gives you an idea of what life was like for the early pioneers. ⌧ J. M. de Rosas 700 ☎ No phone ▨ Free ☉ Weekdays 10–3 and 6–9.

The **Parque Nacional Lanín** (Lanín National Park), north of Nahuel Huapi National Park, runs north–south for 150 km (93 mi) along the Chilean border and covers 3,920 square km (1,508 square mi) of mountain lakes, rivers, and ancient forests. Giant *Araucaria araucana* (monkey puzzle trees) grow in thick groves in the northern region of the park. These spiky conifers, also known as *pehuén* to the Mapuche and Pehuenche, were so named because the Pehuenche depended on the nutritious *piñon* nuts as a dietary staple during long winters. Towering over the entire park and visible from every direction, **Volcán Lanín** (Lanín Volcano) rises 12,378 feet in solitary snow-clad splendor—an imposing white cone on the western horizon.

The **Intendencia de Parques Nacionales** (National Park Office) building is a classic example of Andean-alpine architecture in the style of Bustillos, who did the Civic Center in Bariloche and the Llao Llao Hotel. Here you can get maps and information on all the parks and trails in the region, as well as fishing permits and information on big-game hunting. ⌧ E. Frey 749 ☎ 2972/427233 ☉ Weekdays 7–1.

From town you can walk, mountain bike, or drive to the **Mirador de las Bandurrias** (Bandurrias Overlook), 7 km (4 mi) away, where you get a magnificent view of the town and the lake. To walk there, take Avenida San Martín to the lake, turn right, cross the bridge over Puahullo Creek, and then head uphill on a path around the mountain.

The rather long (200 km [124 mi] round-trip) but infinitely rewarding excursion to **Lago Huechulafquen** and **Lago Paimún** (Paimún Lake) can be made via Junín de los Andes. An overnight stay is recommended. From San Martín, take R234 north to Junín, and then take the dirt road (R61) west. As you speed across the open range following the **Río Chimehuín** toward the lake, Lanín Volcano plays hide-and-seek on the horizon. This is serious fishing country. Numerous beaches and campsites along the lakeshore make good picnic stops.

Where to Stay & Eat

Restaurants in San Martín are mostly parrillas, pizzerias, and simple cafés. Lodging consists of well-equipped, medium-size hotels, inns, residenciales, and cabins. Rates are highest in July, when Argentine families take ski vacations, lower in August, and even lower December–March, which is summer and perhaps the best time to visit. There are two beach camp-grounds with electricity, hot water, showers, rest rooms, and a store at **Playa Catrite** (⊠ R234, Km 4 ☎ 2972/423091). **Quila Quina** (⊠ R108, Km 12 ☎ 2972/426919) also has a dining room and some water-sports equipment rental.

$$$$ ✕ **La Tasca.** With tables scattered about the black stone floor, and wine barrels, shelves, and every other imaginable surface stacked with pick-led vegetables, smoked meats, cheese rounds, dried mushrooms and herbs, olive oils in cans and bottles, and wine bottles displayed in 40 different ways, you might think you're in a Patagonian deli. The set-up encour-ages diners to be bold and try local wild game dishes; especially good is the appetizer platter of smoked salmon, deer, boar, and trout pâté. ⊠ *Mariana Moreno 866* ☎ *2972/428663* ▭ *AE, MC, V.*

$$–$$$ ✕ **Posta Criolla.** In the front window, an asador slanted over hot coals cooks lamb and beef gaucho-style; the grill is filled with sausages, meats, and fish. This is the best parrilla in town. Locally cured cold cuts, trout, and chicken are also available for lunch, dinner, and takeout. ⊠ *Av. San Martín 501* ☎ *272/429515* ▭ *AE, DC, MC, V* ☉ *Closed Wed.*

$–$$ ✕ **Mendieta.** This may be the friendliest parrilla in Patagonia: cooks, wait-ers, and even the owners scurry about with sizzling meats from the grill and fresh, steaming pasta with various sauces. By 2 PM the tables are filled with locals, who all seem to know each other. Pine racks around the dining room display a good selection of Argentina's fine wines. ⊠ *Av. San Martín 713* ☎ *2972/429301* ▭ *DC, MC, V.*

¢–$ ✕ **La Casa de Alicia.** This adorable little Victorian teahouse on a side street across from the Residencial Anay sells homemade cakes, tarts, salads, sandwiches, and frozen desserts. You can eat outside on the patio in sum-mer. ⊠ *M. Cap. Drury 814* ☎ *2972/1561–6215* ▭ *AE, DC, MC, V.*

★ **$$$$** ✕▣ **Hostería Paimún.** A field of lupine almost hides the low-lying build-ings of this remote fishing lodge on the shore of Lago Paimún. Lanín Volcano, mirrored in the lake, towers above giant arucaria trees. Rooms are cozy and lodgelike (everything is made of wood). You can explore the lake by boat, ride a horse, hike to a waterfall or up the volcano. Af-ternoon tea includes fresh-baked bread and homemade jams. Dinners feature home-cooked meats, vegetables from the garden, and fresh fish—perhaps your own! ⊠ *C/c 31, Camino al Lago Paimún (R61), 8371* ☎ *2972/491211* 🖷 *2972/491201* ⊕ *www.interpatagonia.com/hosteriapaimun* ⇌ *16 rooms* ⌂ *Dining room, fishing, horseback rid-ing* ▭ *No credit cards* ☉ *Closed May–Nov. 15* ▣ *FAP.*

$$$$ ▣ **Hotel la Cheminée.** Two blocks from the main street is this comfortable inn with pink-floral chintz and lace curtains. Plump pillows, fresh flow-ers, and fireplaces in some rooms add to the coziness. A sumptuous break-fast and an afternoon tea of homemade breads, scones, cakes, cookies, and jams are served. ⊠ *M. Moreno and Gral. Roca, 8370* ☎☎ *2972/427617* ✉ *lacheminee@smandes.com.ar* ⇌ *15 rooms, 3 suites, 1 cot-tage* ⌂ *Café, pool, sauna, bar, free parking* ▭ *AE, MC, V* ▣ *CP.*

$$ ▣ **Hosteria Anay.** *Anay* means "friendship" and that's what you feel when you step inside this small, white stucco–and–log house. Guests gather around the fireplace for tea, in the cozy sitting area or in the bright, cheer-ful breakfast room. Rooms have simple whitewashed walls, beamed ceil-ings, and carpeted floors. ⊠ *Capitán Drury 841, 8370* ☎☎ *2972/427514* ✉ *anay@smandes.com.ar* ⇌ *15 rooms* ⌂ *Baby-sitting, laun-dry service, free parking* ▭ *No credit cards* ▣ *CP.*

$$ ▣ **Terrazas del Pinar.** Renting a cabin here for two to six people can be economical and fun. Located on a quiet street, just steps from Lago Lácar, the stone-and-log cabins are available by the week or month. Each unit has a kitchen and an outdoor grill; neighbors often join each other for barbecues. Note that prices here are substantially lower in the off-season (March–April and October–November). ✉ *Juez del Valle 1174, 8370* ☎📠 *2972/429316* 🌐 *www.interpatagonia.com/terrazasdelpinar* *8 cabins* *Kitchens, boating, baby-sitting, playground* *No credit cards* *CP.*

$–$$ **Hotel Caupolican.** In season, flowers cascade from the wooden window boxes of this hotel on the main street. In the reception and sitting area, locally carved wooden chairs are covered with sheepskin. The simple, comfortable rooms, done in deep red and blue tones, are off the street and thus quiet. A game room with a fireplace, two meeting rooms, and the reception and bar area face the street. ✉ *Av. San Martín 969, 8370* ☎ *2972/427658* 📠 *2972/427090* *hotelcaulalican@smandes.com.ar* *42 rooms, 2 suites* *Café, sauna, bar, meeting room, free parking* *AE, DC, MC, V* *CP.*

Sports & the Outdoors

BEACHES **Playa Catrite,** 4 km (2½ mi) from San Martín on R234, on the south side of Lago Lácar, is a sandy beach with a campground, a store with picnic items, and a café. **Playa Quila Quina,** 18 km (11 mi) from San Martín, is reached by turning off R234 2 km (1 mi) before the road to Catrite and then getting on R108. On the 12-km (7-mi) drive to the lake you'll pass through Mapuche farm lands and forests. The soft, sandy beach and clear water attract both day-trippers and campers as well as residents with vacation homes. Both beaches can also be reached by boat.

BOATING You can rent small boats, canoes, and kayaks at the pier from **Lacar Nonthue** (✉ Av. Costanera ☎ 2972/427380). You can also rent a bicycle and take it with you on an all day excursion to the other side of Lake Lacar.

FISHING During the fishing season (November 15–April 15, and sometimes extended to the end of May in certain areas), local guides can take you to their favorite spots on Lácar, Lolog, Villarino, and Falkner lakes and on the Caleufu, Quiquihue, Malleo, and Hermoso rivers, or farther afield to the Chimehuín River and Lakes Huechulafquen and Paimún. Permits are available at the **Parque Nacional Intendencia** (✉ Emilio Frey 749 ☎ 2972/427233) or any licensed fishing stores along Avenida San Martín. Most stores can suggest guides. **Jorge Cardillo** (✉ Gral. Roca 626 ☎ 2972/428372) is a well-known local guide. **Augusto Matus** (☎ 2972/429143; 2944/1556–3429 cell 🌐 tiempodepesca.com) offers guidance on wading and trolling for all levels of experience as well as fly-fishing trips for experts.

HORSEBACK RIDING Horseback riding is a great way to see the areas you can't get to by car or boat. Hour-, day-, and week-long organized and guided rides, often with an *asado* (barbecue) included, can be arranged through local tour offices. **Abuelo Enrique** (✉ Callejón Ginsgins, ☎ 2972/426465) offers rides with a guide for two hours or all day, asado included. To get there, take Avenida Dr. Koessler (R234) toward Zapala, turn left at the polo field and head toward Lago Lolog, then take a right past the military barracks to Callejón Ginsgins.

Adventure tour agencies in town can arrange canoeing, rafting, mountain bike, horseback riding, and fishing tours. **El Refugio** (✉ Tte. Colonel Perez 1124 ☎📠 2972/425140) is recommended. **Las Taguas Turismo** (✉ Perito Moreno 1035 ☎ 2972/427423 🌐 www.lastaguas.com) operates in both Lanín and Nahuel Huapi national parks. **Tiempo Patagónico** (✉ Av. San Martín 950 ☎ 2972/427114 📠 2972/425125) offers excursions throughout the area.

MOUNTAIN BIKING San Martín is flat, but everything goes up from it. Dirt and paved roads and trails lead through forests to lakes, waterfalls, and higher mountain valleys. In town you can rent bikes at **HG Rodados** (✉ Av. San Martín 1061 ☎ 2972/427345). Bikes are also available at **Enduro Kawa & Bikes** (✉ Elordi and Perito Moreno ☎ 2972/427093). **Chapelco Ski Area** has good trails and mountain-biking lessons.

SKIING The ski station and summer resort of **Cerro Chapelco** (✉ Information office: San Martín 876 ☎☎ 2972/427845 ⊕ www.nievesdelchapelco. com.ar) is 15 km (9 mi) above town along a dirt road. Ideal for families and beginning and intermediate skiers, the resort has modern facilities and lifts. Almost all the runs are visible from the top (6,534 feet), and Lanín Volcano dominates the horizon. The summer Adventure Center has mountain biking for experts and classes for beginners, horseback rides, hiking, archery, a swimming pool, an alpine slide, and numerous other children's activities.

WHITE-WATER An all-day rafting trip that crosses into Chile on either Río Aluminé or
RAFTING Río Hua Hum can be arranged by **Tiempo Patagónico** (✉ Av. San Martín 950 ☎ 2972/427114 ☎ 2972/425125).

El Refugio (✉ Tte. Colonel Perez 1124 ☎ 2972/425140) leads rafting trips on nearby rivers. **Las Taguas Turismo** (✉ Perito Moreno 1035 ☎ 2972/427423 ⊕ www.lastaguas.com) does combination rafting and mountain biking trips.

Shopping
Along Avenida San Martín, numerous fishing and sporting goods stores are interspersed with authentic regional *artesanías* (handicrafts) of exceptional quality. Next to the tourist office, **Artesanías Neuquinas** (✉ Av. J. M. de Rosas 790 ☎ 2972/428396) carries Mapuche ceramics, weavings, and wood carvings; authenticity is guaranteed.

El Bolsón

⑫ *131 km (80 mi) south of Bariloche via R258.*

El Bolsón ("the purse"), in southwestern Río Negro Province, is so named because it's surrounded by high mountain ranges. This narrow mountain valley was first settled by Chilean farmers in the late 1800s and remained isolated until the 1930s, when a long, winding dirt road (often closed in winter) connected it to Bariloche. Basque, Spanish, Polish, Arab, English, Swiss, and American hippies, attracted by the bucolic setting, pleasing (for Patagonia) microclimate, and the productive land, have all contributed to the cultural identity of the community. The first in Argentina to declare their town a non-nuclear zone, the forward-thinking citizens have preserved the purity of its air, water, and land, creating an environment where the country's largest crops of hops thrive along with strawberries, raspberries, gooseberries, boysenberries, cherries, and plums. Canneries export large quantities of jams and syrups.

As you travel here from Bariloche, the road passes Lago Gutiérrez and enters the Pacific watershed. Lago Mascardi flows into Lago Guillelmo just before the road climbs gently to a pass. Sixty-six kilometers (41 mi) from Bariloche, the first glimpse of the valley opens below you. As you descend into the valley and look south and west, the frozen glaciers of Perito Moreno and Hielo Azul (both more than 6,500 feet) appear on the horizon.

The **Secretaría de Turismo** (✉ Plaza Pagano and Av. San Martín ☎ 2944/429850 ⊕ www.bolsonturistico.com.ar) has information about lodging, activities, and excursions in the area.

need a
break? Stop at **Tacuifi** in the town of El Foyel, 88 km (54½ mi) south of Bariloche and 43 km (27 mi) north of El Bolsón. Lunch, tea, and snacks are available all day in the little log house with a metal roof surrounded by a prodigious garden.

The **Cascada de la Virgen** (Waterfall of the Virgin), 18 km (11 mi) north of El Bolsón, is visible from the road. Nearby is a **campground** (☎ 2944/492610 information) with cabins, grills, and a restaurant.

The **Cascada Mallín Ahogado** (Drowned Meadow Waterfall), 10 km (6 mi) north of El Bolsón on R258, makes a great picnic spot. The ski area at **Cerro Perito Moreno** is farther up the gravel road from the Cascada Mallín Ahogado.

A 39-km (24-mi) round-trip (mostly on dirt roads) to the **Parque Nacional Lago Puelo** (Puelo Lake National Park) is a good all-day excursion from El Bolsón. Information is available at the **park ranger's office** (☎ 2944/499183), and picnic and fishing supplies can be purchased at the roadside store, 4 km (2½ mi) before you reach the sandy beach at **Lago Puelo** (Puelo Lake). Three launches, maintained by the Argentine navy, wait at the dock to take you on one- to three-hour excursions on the lake. The trip to **El Turbio,** an ancient settlement at the southern end of the lake on the Chilean border, is the longest. On the return trip, a branch to the right leads down a narrow arm to a river connecting Lago Puelo with **Lago Epuyén** (Epuyén Lake). A cruise along the shore of the Brazo Occidental (Western Arm) ends at the Chilean border, where the lake runs into a river bound for the Pacific Ocean. You can return by horse or on foot. One side of the lake is inaccessible, as the Valdivian rain forest grows on steep rocky slopes right down into the water. Campgrounds are at the park entrance by the ranger's station, in a bay on the Brazo Occidental, and at the Turbio and Epuyén river outlets.

Where to Stay & Eat
Many campgrounds line the banks of the Río Los Repollos (Los Repollos River), just before you enter town. More hotels and restaurants are being renovated or constructed along the rosebush-lined main street, and numerous small guest houses in and about the town take small groups. Lodges in the surrounding mountains open for fishing season in summer (November–April) and close in winter (May–October). Information about hotels, cabins, guest houses, and campgrounds is available at the **Secretaría de Turismo** (✉ Plaza Pagano and Av. San Martín ☎ 2944/492604).

$$–$$$ ✕ **Parilla Amancay.** You can get your beef, trout, and fresh vegetables cooked any way you like here. Fresh pasta, pizzas, and a good fixed-price menu are also available. ✉ *Av. San Martín, next to Hotel Amancay* ☎ *2944/492222* ▭ *AE, MC, V.*

¢–$$ ✕ **Jauja.** Homemade chocolates and jams are sold at the ice cream counter, where locals and tourists line up for dulce de leche or any of the other 40 flavors. If you're feeling guilty, you can start with a low-calorie entrée or vegetable platter inside the adjoining café. If guilt isn't your thing, try the trout mousse, patagonian lamb, and rose mosqueta soup. ✉ *Av. San Martín 2867* ☎ *2944/492448* ▭ *AE, MC, V.*

$ ✕ **Arcimboldo.** This basic family restaurant on the main street has good pastas and steak and fries. In summer you can dine on the front patio. ✉ *Av. San Martín 27* ☎ *2944/492137* ▭ *DC, MC, V.*

¢ ▦ **Hotel Amancay.** A rose garden and masses of flowers greet you at the door of this pretty white-stucco hotel with a tile roof, three blocks from the center of town. The warm, casual lobby, with its tile floors and dark-wood furniture with bright cushions, looks Spanish. The Parilla Amancay restaurant adjoins the hotel. ✉ *Av. San Martín 3217, 8430* ☎ *2944/492222* 🖷 *2944/492374* ⮐ *15 rooms* ⚲ *Restaurant, café, free parking* ▭ *AE, DC, MC, V* ⦿⦿ *CP.*

Sports & the Outdoors

Fishing in the lakes and streams that surround this area can be arranged with guides locally or in Bariloche. Hiking, rock climbing, mountain biking, and horseback riding (sometimes all combined in one trip) lead you to waterfalls, high mountain huts, deep canyons, and hidden lakes; trips can last a day or a week. Often you'll encounter a little teahouse or an asado at the end of your day. The tourist office can supply maps and directions or direct you to local outfitters. Both cross-country and downhill skiing are winter options at Cerro Perito Moreno, 22 km (13½ mi) north of town on R258. At the base is a refuge belonging to the Club Andino Piltriqitrón, as well as a restaurant and a rental shop. Three lifts service the trails for downhill skiing (3,000 feet–10,000 feet).

Shopping

At the local market on the main plaza, local artisans sell ceramics, leather goods, wood handicrafts, objects made from bone and clay, and agricultural products. El Bolsón is known for its delicious small strawberries. Music and folk dancing often enliven the scene.

---

en route | If you're heading south from El Bolsón to the Parque Nacional los Alerces on R71, just north of Cholila, take the turnoff for the Casa de Piedra teahouse. Turn right onto the road in front of the police station. A path through a gate leads to a group of small log houses where Butch Cassidy, Etta Place, and the Sundance Kid lived and ranched between 1901 and 1905. They kept a low profile here until they attended a Governor's Ball in Esquel. The governor so enjoyed their company, he asked to pose with them in a photograph that later appeared in a Buenos Aires newspaper, where Pinkerton detectives, after years of searching, saw the pictures. After robbing the bank in Río Gallegos, they fled to Bolivia, where they were finally shot.

Esquel

⓭ *180 km (112 mi) southeast of El Bolsón via R258 and R71, 285 km (177 mi) south of Bariloche via R259 and R40.*

In 1906 Esquel was a small village where sheep ranchers, many of them Welsh, came to buy supplies and visit with seldom-seen neighbors from the huge ranches, which still operate on the endless steppes east of the Andes. In 1910 the British owners of the approximately 2,538,202-square-km (980,000-square-mi) Leleque Ranch (now owned by Benetton) brought merino sheep from Australia to the region, establishing this breed in Patagonia. Although Esquel is now the most important town in northern Chubut Province and the gateway to unlimited recreational activities, it retains much of its frontier-town feeling. Along the roads outside town, for instance, you often see gauchos herding their sheep or "riding the fences" (checking to see that they aren't broken) of their vast ranches. Note that when you leave El Bolsón and enter the Province of Chubut, gas costs 40 percent less. For information about activities in the area, go to the **Secretaría de Turismo y Medio Ambiente** (✉ Alvear and Sarmiento ☎☎ 2945/451927 ⊕ www.esquel.gov.ar).

In 1905, when Patagonia was still a territory, a railway project was conceived to facilitate the transport of wool, cattle, and lumber from the far-flung villages of El Maitén, Trevelín, and Esquel to Ingeniero Jacobacci, where it would link up with the national railway and the rest of the country. German and American companies worked with the Argentine railroad from 1922 until 1945, when the last section was completed. Today, **El Trocha Angosta,** known as La Trochita or the Great Patagonia Express, puffs clouds of steam and toots its horn as its 1922 Belgian Baidwin and German Henschell engines pull the vintage wooden cars 402 km (249 mi) between Esquel and Ingeniero Jacobacci (194 km [120 mi] east of Bariloche). Inside the cars, passengers gather around the woodstoves to add wood, sip mate, and discuss the merits of this rolling relic. The trip from Esquel to **Nahuel Pan** (20 km [12 mi] round-trip) leaves Esquel in summer Monday–Wednesday and weekends at 9 AM and 2 PM, returning at 12:30 and 4:30. It includes a visit to Mapuche handcraft market. The schedule for the rest of the year varies, so check ahead of time. The train to **El Maitén** (165 km [102 mi] one-way) leaves Monday, Wednesday, and weekends at 3 (returning at 5:30), and includes a guided visit to the railroad museum and repair shop—a must for train buffs. For current schedules and reservations, contact the **Estación Esquel Train Station** (⊠Brown and Roggero ☎2945/451403 ⊕www.paginade/latrochita).

---

need a break?

Homemade ice cream and pastries, coffee and tea, and two computers with Internet access will keep you busy for an afternoon at **Mayor** (⊠ Rivadavía 1943, at the corner of Sarmiento).

The **Parque Nacional los Alerces** (Los Alerces National Park) is 50 km (30 mi) west of Esquel on R258 (and 151 km [94 mi] south of El Bolsón). The park is named for its 2,000- to 3,000-year-old *alerces* (*Fitzroya cupressoides*), which are similar to redwoods. Covering 2,630 square km (1,012 square mi) of lakes, rivers, and forests, most of the park is accessible only by boats and trails. Wild, rugged, and astoundingly beautiful, this park is mostly untouched. The dirt road (the only one) into the park takes you to **Villa Futalaufquen** (Futalaufquen Village), on the lake of the same name. The park has only four small hotels and a few cabins; most people camp or come from Esquel or El Bolsón for the day. For camping and fishing information, visit the **park information office** (☎ 2945/471020) in Villa Futalaufquen. Fishing in the 14 lakes and connecting rivers is legendary; licenses are available in the village at two small shops, Kiosco and Almacén, at the fishing lodges, and the campgrounds at Bahía Rosales.

A boat excursion from Puerto Limonao, the principal port on Lago Futalaufquen, takes you to **Lago Menendez** (Menendez Lake). Along the way you see the glaciers of the **Cerro Torrecillos** and stop at a grove of giant alerces. Tour operators in Esquel and lodges in the park can arrange lake excursions.

Where to Stay & Eat

Besides downtown hotels, there are hosterías, cabins, and campgrounds in the surrounding countryside. For information contact the tourist office.

$ ✕ **De Maria Parrilla.** Popular with local ranchers, fishermen, and town folk, this typical grill has a salad bar at dinner and Patagonian lamb is often cooked out back on an asador. The owner, also a ski instructor, studied cooking in Buenos Aires and returned home to open this restaurant. The local lamb, pork, and game dishes are all prepared with a personal touch. ⊠ *Rivadavía 1024* ☎ *2945/454247* ▤ *AE, DC, MC, V.*

$$$$ ✕▦ **Villa Futalaufquen.** From this stone-and-log lodge on top of a hill, you can look through tall alamo trees across miles of blue lake. Six-foot-tall lupines almost hide the little log cabins strewn across the lawn. In-

side, worn leather, wicker furnishings, and wooden beams evoke a rustic elegance, reminiscent of an English hunting lodge. The rooms are simple—white walls, wood trim, a chair, and a bed—all you need, really, because the place to be is outside. In addition to offering equipment rentals, the hotel can arrange hiking and lake excursions. ⊠ *Villa Futalaufquen, 4 km (2 mi) from the village, 9200* 🏠 *2945/471008* 🛏 *12 rooms, 3 cabins* ♿ *Restaurant, waterskiing, fishing, bicycles, mountain bikes, horseback riding, bar* 🚬 *AE, DC, MC, V* ⦿*I CP.*

$–$$ 🏨 **Hostería Cumbres Blancas.** After a day of skiing, hiking, or exploring the nearby parks, the big carpeted rooms here exude unexpected extravagance. Most have views beyond the ample lawn to windswept plains and lonely mountains. The top-floor suite has a mountain view, balcony, and fireplace. A good restaurant adjoins the hotel. ⊠ *Av. Ameghino 1683, 9200* 🏠 *2945/455100* 🖨 *2945/455400* 🌐 *www. cpatagonia.com/esq/cblancas* 🛏 *19 rooms, 1 suite* ♿ *Restaurant, room service, sauna, bar, recreation room, playground, free parking* 🚬 *AE, DC, MC, V* ⦿*I CP.*

$ ✕🏨 **Hostería Cume Hué.** Owner Camilo Braese was born in this stucco-and-wood inn overlooking the lake. Having hiked and fished the area since he was a boy, Braese is much sought after as a guide. Breakfast, lunch, and tea are served in the living room, and dinner is eaten in the *quincho* (a room with a fireplace for asados). Rooms are basic, with small beds and lots of blankets. Some rooms have lake views and most share a bath. There are no telephones and no electricity during the day (at night a generator provides electricity). Good campsites along the river behind the inn include use of the hotel's facilities (sign up at the inn for a site). ⊠ *Off R71 on Lago Futalaufquen's north shore, 70 km (43½ mi) southwest from Esquel, 9200* 🏠*2945/453639* 🛏 *13 rooms* 🚬 *No credit cards* ☾ *Closed May–Oct.* ⦿*I FAP.*

$ 🏨 **Hotel Sol del Sur.** This large brick building right in downtown Esquel was a casino until 1987, when the top floor was converted into a large dining area and a meeting room and guest rooms were added on the floors in between. The building is still old and austere, as are the rooms. The convenience of having an adjoining tour agency and ski retail and rental shop makes up for the plain furnishings. ⊠ *9 de Julio and Sarmiento, 9200* 🏠*2945/452189* 🖨*2945/452427* ✉ *soldelsur@ar.inter. net* 🛏 *50 rooms, 2 5-person apartments* ♿ *Restaurant, bar* 🚬 *AE, DC, MC, V* ⦿*I CP.*

¢ 🏨 **Hostería los Tulipanes.** On a quiet side street in Esquel but close enough to the center of town, the owners make you feel like a guest in their home at this family-run *residencial* (pension). There's a small sitting room with a fireplace and dining rooms. Rooms are very small and basic. ⊠ *Av. Fontana 365, 9200* 🏠 *2945/452748* 🛏 *7 rooms, 1 apartment* 🚬 *No credit cards* ⦿*I CP.*

Sports & the Outdoors

With all the remote lakes and rivers to explore, canoeing, kayaking, fishing, and rafting are limitless, as are hiking, horseback riding, and mountain biking opportunities. Skiing and snowboarding are popular winter sports.

FISHING   Fishing fanatics from the world over have come to battle with the stubborn trout or catch and release the wily rainbow in the remote lakes, tranquil lagoons, shallow rushing rivers or deep quiet ones of Los Alerces National Park. For fishing information on the Ríos Grande or Futaleufú (near Chile), and a list of licensed guides, contact the tourist office in Esquel. Permits are available at gas stations, fishing shops, and at the **Dirección de Pesca Continental** (⊠ Pasteur 538 🏠 2945/42468).

RAFTING, The white-water rafting season begins in November, when the rivers are
KAYAKING & full and fast, and lasts into March. **Frontera Sur** (✉ Avenida Alvear y
CANOEING Salmiento ☎ 2945/450505 ⊕ www.fronterasur.net) organizes rafting
trips for a day on the Corcovado or a week on the Futaleufú, ending in
Chile; sometimes kayak and canoe instruction is included. **Sol del Sur**
(✉ 9 de Julio 1086 ☎☎ 2945/42189 ⊕ www.hsoldelsur.com.ar) also
offers rafting trips on the Corcovado and Futaeufú rivers.

SKIING Only 13 km (8 mi) from Esquel and generally blessed with a long ski
season (July–mid-November), La Hoya is a popular ski resort for its reasonable prices and uncrowded slopes—2,200 acres of skiable terrain. Four
chairlifts and five surface lifts take you up 2,624 feet. Runs are long and
above the tree line, and off-piste skiing is often possible. For information about the ski area, contact the Esquel tourist office, or **La Hoya Esquel** (✉ Rivadavía 1003 ☎ 2945/453018 ⊕ www.camlahoya.com.ar).

Shopping

At **Casa los Vascos** (✉ 25 de Mayo and 9 de Julio) you can outfit yourself in gaucho attire: black hat, scarf pulled through leather knot, *bombachas* (baggy, pleated pants, gathered at the ankle), and boots. **Braese**
(✉ 9 de Julio 1540) has the best selection of jams, cakes, chocolates,
and smoked meats. Local dried flowers, hand-knit sweaters, and handicrafts are for sale at **Ramos Generales** (✉ 25 de Mayo 528).

Trevelín

⑭ *25 km (15½ mi) south of Esquel on R259.*

The Welsh came to Trevelín in 1888, when 30 men were sent out to explore the region. Their ancestors, beginning in 1865, had set sail across
the Atlantic to seek a better life and to escape the economic, religious,
and social oppression in their homeland. Expecting to find the Promised
Land, they instead found a windswept empty expanse with little or no
arable land—nothing like the fertile green valleys they had left behind.
Undaunted, these hardy pioneers settled in the Chubut Valley. As the
population grew, although land for farming grew scarce, they looked
westward toward the Andes. They found their *cwn hyfryd* ("beautiful
valley" in Welsh) between the present towns of Esquel and Corcovado.
Fifty families settled in the area, building their town around a flour mill—
Trevelín in Welsh means "mill town." Today the town is still a pleasant and quiet place.

The **Secretaría de Turismo** (✉ Plaza Coronel Fontana ☎ 2945/480120
⊕ www.trevelin.org) has information on the history of the region and
its Welsh settlers. Hardworking, honest, faithful, and as proud to be Argentine as they are to have their own traditions, many descendants of
those first families still live here, and the tourist office can arrange in-
terviews with some of them. Many family-run residenciales and small
hotels closed down during the economic crisis in 2000–2002. Check at
the tourist office for new ones opening up as the economy stabilizes.

Once a four-story brick mill and now a regional museum, **El Molino Viejo**
houses agricultural tools, photos, a Welsh bible, and artifacts from everyday life during the early settlement years. ✉ *25 de Mayo* ☎ *2945/
480145* 🏷 *Free* 🕐 *Dec.–Mar., daily 11–8:30; Apr.–Nov., Wed. 10–4,
Thurs.–Sun. 2–8.*

Where to Eat

$ ✕ **Pizzería Küsimey Ruca.** The name of this restaurant means "beauti-
ful house" in Mapuche. With 36 kinds of pizzas and nine kinds of empanadas created by owner-chef Hugo Molares, it's easy to eat well.

Molares's fine photographs decorate the walls under the imposing log ceiling. ⊠ *Av. Fortín Refugio, on the Plaza* ☎ *2945/480088* ▭ *DC, MC, V* ⊘ *Closed Mon.*

¢–$ ✕ **Casa de Te Nain Maggie.** *Nain* (grandma) Maggie (1878–1981) handed down the old family recipes to her granddaughter who, with her daughter, continues to make the same fruit tarts, cakes, breads, and scones with currant or gooseberry jam, which are just a few of the confections you'll find in this typical Welsh teahouse. ⊠ *Perito Moreno and Sarmiento 179* ☎ *2945/480232* ▭ *No credit cards* ⊘ *No lunch.*

Río Gallegos

⑮ *2,640 km (1,639 mi) south of Buenos Aires, 1,034 km (640 mi) south of Comodoro Rivadavia via R3, 319 km (197 mi) south of El Calafate, 596 km (370 mi) north of Ushuaia, and 251 km (157 mi) east of Puerto Natales, Chile, via R40.*

The administrative and commercial capital of Santa Cruz Province and perhaps the windiest town in the world (from September to November), Río Gallegos was founded in 1885 and served as a port for coal shipments from Río Túrbio (Túrbio River), on the Chilean border. Wool and sheepskins were its only other economic factors. As the gateway city to southern Patagonia, travelers en route south to Ushuaia, north to the Parque Nacional los Glaciares, or west to Chile, are often obliged to spend a night here. A desk at the airport has information on all the tourist attractions in the area, and helpful attendants will also make hotel reservations. More information is available at the **Subsecretaría de Turísmo** (⊠ Av. Roca 863 ☎ 2966/438725 🖷 2966/422702 ⊕ www.scruz. gov.ar) in town.

If you're into dinosaurs, visit the **Museo Regional Provincial Padre Manuel Jesus Molina** (Provincial Museum), which exhibits reconstructed skeletons excavated at sites in Patagonia. Exhibits on biology, geology, history, paleontology, and Tehuelche ethnology are displayed in different sections of the museum. ⊠ *Ramón y Cajal 51* ☎ *2966/423290* 🖅 *Free* ⊘ *Weekdays 10–5, weekends 11–7.*

| off the beaten path | **CABO VIRGENES** – From September through April, this provincial nature preserve plays host to 150,000 mating Magellanic penguins— the second largest penguin colony in Patagonia. A lighthouse guarding the entrance to the Strait of Magellan has a tea house inside. You can go on an organized tour or on your own by following the signed interpretive trail. ✛ *128 km (79 mi) south on RN3. At 17 km, branch left on to RP1, a dirt road, and continue past the ranches to the Reserva Faunística Provincial (Provincial Nature Preserve).* |

Where to Stay & Eat

$$–$$$ ✕ **El Horreo.** A well-heeled clientele begins to fill this rather classy Spanish-looking restaurant around 10:30 PM. Complimentary pisco sours begin your repast. It's hard to beat the local spring lamb, the steaks, or the mountain trout, crab, and seafood—grilled or in homemade sauces. ⊠ *Av. Roca 862* ☎ *2966/426462* ▭ *MC, V.*

$ ✕ **Trattoría Diaz.** This big, open family-style café in the center of town has been serving grilled lamb and beef, homemade pastas, seafood, and fish since 1932. ⊠ *Av. Roca 1157* ☎ *2966/420203* ▭ *DC, MC, V.*

$$$$ 🏨 **Costa Río.** Flags flutter above the entrance to this modern white-brick apart-hotel on a quiet side street. For business travelers and families in town for an extended stay, having a room with chairs, sofas, and tables makes the hotel worth the extra money. A kitchenette and eating area

provide an alternative to going out for every meal. All rooms are carpeted and have comfortable, contemporary furnishings. ⊠ *Av. San Martín 673, 9400* ☎ *2966/423412* ✉ *costario@infivia.com.ar* 🛏 *54 apartments* ⚥ *Café, kitchenettes, minibars, baby-sitting, dry cleaning, laundry service, free parking* ⊟ *AE, DC, MC, V.*

¢ 🏨 **Hotel Santa Cruz.** Although the hotel looks old, rooms are comfortable, if a little utilitarian. Intimate seating areas, plants, and a friendly staff make the lobby bar a pleasant retreat on a windy day. Avoid rooms on the Avenida Roca side, as they can be noisy. ⊠ *Av. Roca 701, 9400* ☎ *2966/420601* ᕸ *2966/420603* 🛏 *53 rooms, 1 suite* ⚥ *Restaurant, sauna, free parking* ⊟ *AE, DC, MC, V* ⦿ *CP.*

Shopping

Monte Aymond (⊠ Maipú 1320 ☎ 2966/438012) is a factory outlet for sheepskin and leather coats; the children's jackets, hats, and little sheepskin booties make great gifts. There's also a branch at the airport.

El Calafate & the Parque Nacional los Glaciares

⓰ *320 km (225 mi) north of Río Gallegos via R5, 253 km (157 mi) east of Río Turbio on Chilean border via R40, 213 km (123 mi) south of El Chaltén via R40.*

Founded in 1927 as a frontier town, El Calafate is the base for all excursions to the Parque Nacional los Glaciares (Glaciers National Park), which was created in 1937. Because of its location on the southern shore of Lago Argentino, the town enjoys a microclimate much milder than the rest of southern Patagonia. During the long summer days between December and February (when the sun sets around 10 PM), and during Easter vacation, thousands of visitors come to see the glaciers and fill the hotels and restaurants. This is the area's high season, so be sure to make reservations well in advance. October, November, March, and April are less crowded and less expensive periods to visit. March through May can be rainy and cool and sometimes quite pleasant. Winter lasts through September.

Daily flights from Buenos Aires, Ushuaia, and Río Gallegos, as well as direct flights from Bariloche, transport tourists in a few hours to Calafate's modern glass and steel airport—an island of modernity surrounded by the lonely expanse of Patagonia—with the promise of adventure and discovery in distant mountains and unseen glaciers.

Driving from Río Gallegos takes about four hours across desolate plains, enlivened occasionally by the sight of a gaucho, his dogs, and a herd of sheep, as well as *ñandú* (rheas), shy llamalike guanacos, silver-gray foxes, and fleet-footed hares the size of small deer. **Esperanza** (Hope) is the only gas, food, and bathroom stop halfway between the two towns.

Avenida del Libertador San Martín (known as Libertador or San Martín) is the main street, with tour offices, restaurants, and shops selling regional specialities, sportswear, camping and fishing equipment, souvenirs, and food. A staircase in the middle of San Martín ascends to Avenida Julio Roca, where you'll find the bus terminal and a very busy **Oficina de Turismo** (⊠ Av. Julio Roca 1004 ☎ 2902/491090 ⊕ www.elcalafate. gov.ar) with a board listing available accommodations and campgrounds; you can also get brochures and maps, and there's a multilingual staff to help plan excursions. It's open daily 7 AM–10 PM. The **Parques Nacionales** (⊠ Av. Libertador 1302 ☎ 2902/491545), open weekdays 7–2, has information on the entire park, the glaciers, area history, hiking trails, and flora and fauna.

The Hielo Continental (Continental ice cap) spreads its icy mantle from the Pacific Ocean across Chile and the Andes into Argentina, covering an area of 21,700 square km (8,400 square mi). Approximately 1.5 million acres of it are contained within the **Parque Nacional los Glaciares**, a UNESCO World Heritage site. Extending along the Chilean border for 350 km (217 mi), the park is 40% covered with ice fields that branch off into 47 major glaciers that feed two lakes—the 15,000-year-old **Lago Argentino** (Argentine Lake, the largest body of water in Argentina) in the southern end of the park and **Lago Viedma** (Lake Viedma) at the northern end near **Cerro Fitzroy**, which rises 11,138 feet. Visits to the park are usually by tour, though you could rent a car and go on your own. Travel agents in El Calafate, Río Gallegos, or Buenos Aires can book tours if you haven't made arrangements from home. Plan on a minimum of three days to see the glaciers and enjoy the town—more if you plan to visit El Chaltén or any of the other lakes.

FodorśChoice
★
One of the few glaciers in the world still growing after 3,000 years, the **Glaciar Moreno** lies 80 km (50 mi) away on R11, which is paved from El Calafate to the national park entrance. From there, a dirt road winds through hills and forests of lengas and ñires, until suddenly, the startling sight of the glacier comes into full view. Descending like a long white tongue through distant mountains, it ends abruptly in a translucent blue wall 3 km (2 mi) wide and 165 feet high at the edge of frosty green Lago Argentino. A viewing area, wrapped around the point of the **Península de Magallanes**, allows you to wander back and forth, looking across the **Canal de los Tempanos** (Iceberg Channel). Here you listen and wait for nature's number one ice show—first, a cracking sound, followed by tons of ice breaking away and falling with a thunderous crash into the lake. Sometimes the icy water splashes onlookers across the channel! As the glacier creeps across this narrow channel and meets the land on the other side, an ice dam builds up between the inlet of **Brazo Rico** on the left and the rest of the lake on the right. As the pressure on the dam increases, everyone waits for the day it will rupture again. The last time was in 1986, when the whole thing collapsed in a series of explosions that lasted hours and could be heard in El Calafate. Videos of this event are sold locally.

Glaciar Upsala (Upsala Glacier), the largest glacier in South America, is 60 km (37 mi) long and 10 km (6 mi) wide, and accessible only by boat. Daily cruises depart from **Puerto Banderas** (40 km [25 mi] west of El Calafate via R11) for the 2½-hour trip. While dodging floating icebergs (*tempanos*), some as large as a small island, the boats maneuver as close as they dare to the wall of ice rising from the aqua-green water of Lago Argentino. The seven glaciers that feed the lake deposit their debris into the runoff, causing the water to cloud with minerals ground to fine powder by the glacier's moraine (the accumulation of earth and stones left by the glacier). Condors and black-chested buzzard eagles build their nests in the rocky cliffs above the lake. When the boat stops for lunch at **Onelli Bay**, don't miss the walk behind the restaurant into a wild landscape of small glaciers and milky rivers carrying chunks of ice from four glaciers into Lago Onelli.

Where to Stay & Eat

$$ ✕ **Barricas de Enopio.** The emphasis in this restaurant-bar is on the extensive wine list and great cheeses to accompany each glass. A variety of brochettes and dinner entrées are big enough to split or share. The space is chic, casual, and cozy, with natural cotton curtains and table cloths, handmade lamps, and Tehuelche influences. ⊠ *Av. Libertador 1610* ☎ *2902/493414* ▱ *AE, MC, V.*

$$ ✕ **La Tablita.** This typical parrilla lets you watch your food as it's prepared: Patagonian lamb and beef ribs cook gaucho-style on an asador;

steaks, chorizos, and chicken sizzle on the grill. Grilled fish and home-made pastas are alternatives to the Patagonian fare. ⊠ *Coronel Rosales 28* ☎ *2902/491065* ▤ *AE, DC, MC, V.*

$ ✕ **La Cocina.** This casual café on the main shopping street serves home-made pasta, quiches, crepes, and hamburgers. Homemade ice cream and delicious cakes make good snacks any time of the day. "*Postre Chancho*" (Pig's Dessert) is ice cream with hot dulce de leche sauce. Note that there is a long siesta daily from 2 to 7:30. ⊠ *Av. Libertador 1245* ☎ *2902/491758* ▤ *MC, V.*

$$$$ ✕▦ **Hostería los Notros.** Weathered wood buildings cling to the moun-
Fodor'sChoice tainside that overlooks the Moreno Glaciar as it descends into Lago Ar-
★ gentino. This inn, seemingly at the end of the world, is 73 km (45 mi) west of El Calafate. With the glacier framed in the window of every room, and a fireplace in some, inside is as nice as out. A path, through the garden and over a bridge spanning a canyon with a waterfall, connects rooms to the main lodge. Appetizers and wine are served in full view of sunset (or moonrise) over the glacier, followed by innovative pastas, fish, and game dishes accompanied by local mushrooms, vegetables, and herbs from the garden. Note that a two-night minimum stay is required. This property is extremely expensive (up to US$674 per night); prices include all meals, cocktails, park entry, and a glaciar excursion. ⊠ *Reservations in Buenos Aires: Arenales 1457, fl. 7, 1961* ☎ *11/4814–3934 in Buenos Aires; 2902/499510 in El Calafate* 🖷 *11/4815–7645 in Buenos Aires; 2902/499511 in El Calafate* ⊕ *www.losnotros.com* 🛏 *32 rooms* ⌂ *Restaurant, fishing, hiking, horseback riding, bar, recreation room, playground, Internet, airport shuttle, travel services* ▤ *AE, DC, MC, V* ✺ *Closed mid-May–mid-Sept.* ⊺◎⊺ *FAP.*

$$$$ ✕▦ **Hotel Kau-Yatun.** Books, games, and magazines clutter the tables in the large living room of this former ranch house; guests congregate at the bar or in front of the fireplace. Rooms vary in size, shape, and decor, with all following a casual ranch theme. Country cuisine (meat, pasta, and vegetables) is served in the dining room, and wild game dishes are available at La Brida restaurant. On weekends, steaks and chorizos sizzle on a large open grill in the *quincho* (combination kitchen, grill, and dining room), while lamb or beef cooks gaucho style on an asador. ⊠ *Estancia 25 de Mayo, 9405* ☎ *2902/491059* 🖷 *2902/491260* ✉ *kauyatun@cotecal.com.ar* 🛏 *45 rooms* ⌂ *Restaurant, bar, Internet access, horseback riding, airport shuttle* ▤ *AE, MC, V* ⊺◎⊺ *CP.*

$$$$ ▦ **Kosten Aike.** The stone-and-brick accents and wood balconies outside, and the slate floors, wood-beamed ceilings, and unfailing attention to detail inside, will please aficionados of Andean Patagonian architecture. Tehuelche symbols and designs are used in everything from the curtains to the room plaques. A lobby bar and living room with fireplace, card tables, magazines, and a large TV is conducive to lounging about indoors anytime of day. ⊠ *G. Moyano y 25 de Mayo, 9405* ☎ *2902/492424; 11/4811–1314 in Buenos Aires* 🖷 *2902/491538* ⊕ *www.kostenaike.com.ar* 🛏 *58 rooms, 2 suites* ⌂ *Restaurant, gym, bar, shop, Internet, business services, meeting room, car rental* ▤ *AE, DC, MC, V.*

$$$$ ▦ **Posada los Alamos.** Surrounded by tall, leafy alamo trees and constructed of brick and dark *quebracho* (ironwood), this attractive country manor house uses rich woods, leather, and handwoven fabrics to produce conversation-friendly furniture groupings in the large lobby. Plush comforters and fresh flowers in the rooms, and a staff ready with helpful suggestions make this a top-notch hotel. Lovingly tended gardens surround the building and line a walkway through the woods to the restaurant and the shore of Lago Argentino. ⊠ *Moyano 1355, 9405* ☎ *2902/491144* 🖷 *2902/491186* ⊕ *www.posadalosalamos.com* 🛏 *140 rooms, 4 suites*

⚙ *Restaurant, 3-hole golf course, tennis court, 2 bars, travel services* ☰ *AE, MC, V* 🍽 *CP.*

$$$–$$$$ 🏨 **El Mirador del Lago.** The best thing about this hotel is not the zigzag brick facade offering all the front rooms a corner view of Lago Argentino, nor the cozy bar and sitting room, nor the collection of games, books, videos, and magazines to enjoy on stormy days. The best thing is the unfailingly friendly staff. They're all related and take great pride in helping their guests enjoy everything the region has to offer. They know the roads, the restaurants, and the best way to get to all the attractions. ✉ *Av. Libertador 2047, 9405* ☎ *2902/491045* 📠 *2902/493176* 🌐 *www. miradordellago.com.ar* ↪ *20 rooms* ⚙ *Dining room, sauna, bar, recreation room, travel services* ☰ *AE, DC, MC, V* 🍽 *CP.*

$$$ 🏨 **El Quijote.** Sun shining through picture windows onto polished slate floors and high beams gives this modern hotel, on a quiet side street in town, a light and airy feel. The carpeted rooms with plain white walls and wood furniture provide peaceful comfort. It's right next to Sancho restaurant and a few blocks from the main street. ✉ *Gregores 1155, 9405* ☎ *2902/491017* 📠 *2902/491103* 📧 *elquijote@cotecal.com.ar* ↪ *80 rooms* ⚙ *Café, bar, travel services* ☰ *AE, DC, MC, V* 🍽 *CP.*

$$ 🏨 **Michelangelo.** Bright red and yellow native flowers line the front of the low log-and-stucco building with its distinctive A-frames over rooms, restaurant, and lobby. A fine collection of local photographs is displayed on the walls next to a sunken lobby, where easy-chairs and a banquette surround the fireplace. Motel-style rooms have individual heaters, and there's an excellent restaurant next door. ✉ *Moyano 1020, 9405* ☎ *2902/491045* 📠 *2902/491058* 📧 *michelangelo@cotecal.com.ar* ↪ *20 rooms* ⚙ *Restaurant, café, cable TV* ☰ *AE, MC, V* 🕓 *Closed June* 🍽 *CP.*

$ 🏨 **Ariel.** This small hotel on a hill at the edge of town is surrounded by a carefully tended garden. The small, wall-papered bedrooms open onto a wide indoor passageway that is more like a solarium, protecting guests from Patagonian winds and chill. Breakfast and afternoon tea with homemade cakes are served in a homey dining room conducive to sharing conversation with other guests. ✉ *Casimiro Biguá 35, 9405* ☎ *2902/ 493131* 📠 *2902/493131* 📧 *hoyelariel@cotecal.com.ar* ↪ *5 rooms* ⚙ *Cable TV* ☰ *No credit cards.*

Sports & the Outdoors

HIKING You can hike anywhere in the Parque Nacional los Glaciares. Close to El Calafate are trails along the shore of Lago Argentino and in the hills south and west of town. El Chaltén is usually a better base than El Calafate for hikes up mountain peaks like Cerro Torre.

HORSEBACK RIDING Anything from a short day-ride along Lago Argentino to a weeklong camping excursion in and around the glaciers can be arranged in El Calafate by **Gustavo Holzmann** (✉ Av. Libertador 3600 ☎ 2902/493203; 2966/1562–0935 cell) or through the tourist office. *Estancias Turísticas* (tourist ranches) are ideal for a combination of horseback riding, ranch activities, and local excursions. Information on **Estancias de Santa Cruz** is available in Buenos Aires at the **Provincial tourist office** (✉ Suipacha 1120 ☎ 11/4325–3098 🌐 www.estanciasdesantacruz.com). **Estancia Alice** (✉ Ruta 11, Km 22 ☎ 2902/491793 Calafate; 11/4312–7206 Buenos Aires) welcomes guests overnight or for the day—for a horseback ride, bird-watching, or an afternoon program that includes a demonstration of sheep dogs working, a walk to the lake with a naturalist, sheep-shearing, and dinner in the former sheep-shearing barn, served right off the grill and the asador by knife-wielding gauchos. Other estancias close to Calafate are **Nibepo Aike** (⌖ 60 km/37 mi from Calafate

☎ 2966/422626), **Alta Vista**(⊹ 33 km/20 mi from Calafate ☎ 2966/ 491247), and **Huyliche** (⊹ 3 km/2 mi from Calafate ☎ 2902/491025).

ICE TREKKING A two-hour minitrek on the Moreno Glacier involves transfer from El Calafate to Brazo Rico by bus and a short lake crossing to a dock and refugio, where you set off into the woods, with a guide, through the treacherous terrain. Crampons (provided) are attached over hiking boots and the climb commences. The entire outing lasts about five hours, culminating with cocktails over 1,000-year-old ice cubes. Most hotels arrange minitreks, as does **Hielo y Aventura** (✉ Av. Libertador 935 ☎ 2902/492205 🖷 2902/491053), which also organizes much longer, more difficult trips of eight hours to a week to other glaciers.

MOUNTAIN BIKING Mountain biking is popular along the dirt roads and mountain paths that lead to the lakes, glaciers, and ranches. Rent bikes and get information at **Alquiler de Bicicletas** (✉ Av. Libertador 689 and Comandante Espora ☎ 2902/491398).

Shopping

Along Avenida Libertador shops sell sporting goods, Tehuelche handcrafted items, leather goods, and gaucho apparel. The **Mercado Artesanal** (✉ Av. Libertador 1208) has books about the area and Patagonia memorabilia. The **Patagonia Supermercado** (✉ Libertador and Perito Moreno) has all kinds of Patagonia-related items. On the same side of Libertador as the stair to the bus station, in the 1000 block, a minimall with boardwalk and waterfall has an excellent book store **Lechuza** (*owl*) and a super slipper shop—Patagonian sheepskin in all shapes and sizes.

El Chaltén & Cerro Fitzroy

🔞 *222 km (123 mi) north of El Calafate (35 km [22 mi] east on R11 to R40, then north on R40 on a dirt road to R23 north).*

The four-hour one-way bus or car trip to El Chaltén from El Calafate makes staying at least one night here a good idea. The only gas, food, and rest room facilities en route are at La Leona (110 km [68 mi] from El Calafate). As you follow the shore of Lago Viedma, look north for the glacier of the same name descending into the lake. Visible for hundreds of miles (weather permitting) on the northern horizon as you approach the frontier village of El Chaltén, the granite hulk of **Cerro Fitzroy** (11,286 feet and named after the captain of the *Beagle,* on which Charles Darwin served as a naturalist) rises like a giant arrowhead next to the slender spires of **Cerro Torre** (10,174 feet). The Tehuelche called Cerro Fitzroy Chaltén ("smoke") for the snow constantly blowing off its peak. The village was founded in 1985 as a hiking mecca at the base of the range. Before you cross the bridge to town over Río Gallegos, stop at the **Parque National office** (☎🖷 2962/493004) for information on excursions and accommodations. Information is also available at the Río Gallegos and El Calafate tourist offices. The **Laguna del Desierto** (Lake of the Desert), a lovely lake surrounded by forest, is 37 km (23 mi) north of El Chaltén on R23, a dirt road.

Where to Stay & Eat

$–$$ ✕ **Ahumados Patagonia.** This small restaurant, in a grassy field next to the Albergue Patagonia hostel, serves smoked meats, hearty soups, chicken, lamb, beef kabobs, and fresh trout. ✉ *Av. San Martín 493* ☎ *2962/493019* 🖃 *MC, V.*

¢ 🏠 **Albergue Patagonia.** Just steps from hiking and mountain-biking trails stands this simple wood-frame farm house, with rooms that sleep two to six people. You can cook your own meals here, prepare picnic lunches, peruse trail maps, and share information with fellow guests, all for under US$15. The hostel also arranges horseback riding, hiking, and biking excursions. ☒ *Av. San Martín 493, 9301* 🖾 *2962/493019* ✉ *alpatagonia@infovia.com.ar* 🛏 *7 rooms* ⚵ *Restaurant, bicycles, horseback riding, bar, library, laundry facilities* ▭ *No credit cards.*

Sports & the Outdoors

HIKING Both long and short hikes on well-trodden trails lead to lakes, glaciers, and stunning viewpoints. A three-hour hike that includes all of the above takes you to El Mirador ("the lookout"). The six-hour hike to the base camp for Cerro Torre at **Laguna Torre** has (weather seldom permitting) dramatic views of Torres Standhart, Adelas, Grande, and Solo. The eight-hour hike to the base camp for **Cerro Fitzroy** passes Laguna Capri, which mirrors the granite tower framed by ghostly lenga trees. Beyond El Chaltén (37 km [23 mi]), Lago del Desierto has an easy 5-km (3-mi) hike to **Chorillo del Salto** (Trickling Falls). Other hikes to and around Lago del Desierto are described in brochures and maps obtainable at the tourist office in El Chaltén) or at the tourist office or national park office in El Calafate.

HORSEBACK Most of the hiking trails up, to, and around Fitzroy are used to transport
RIDING mountaineering equipment by horse to base camps. Make arrangements for trail rides through local outfitters and guides, including **Rodolfo Guerra** (☒ Northwest of town at Fitzroy trailhead 🖾 2962/493020).

MOUNTAIN Lionel Terray and Guido Magnone were the first to climb **Cerro Fitzroy**,
CLIMBING in 1952. Terray remarked, "Of all the ascents in my life, Fitzroy was the one that took me closest to my limits of strength and endurance. Climbing it is mortally dangerous; its ascent more complex, risky, and difficult than anything in the Alps." **Cerro Torre** is also a difficult mountain, and expert mountaineers from every corner of the globe come to climb this illusive peak. They sometimes camp for weeks, even months, at Laguna Torre, waiting for the wind to die down, the rain to stop, or the clouds to disperse. The best time to climb is February through March. Climbing permits are available at the national **park office** (☒ Before bridge into town 🖾 2962/493004). **Fitzroy Expeditions** (☒ Lionel Terray 212, El Chaltén, 9301 🖾 2962/493017 🖾 2962/49136 ⊕ www.elchalten.comfitzroy) has English-speaking guides for glacier and mountain treks.

For maps, hiking, and lodging information, contact the **Comisión de Fomento** (☒ Av. Güemes 21 🖾 2962/493011 ⊕ www.elchalten.com).

ATLANTIC PATAGONIA

Updated by Michael de Zayas

From the immense whales at Península Valdés to the 325,000 penguins of Punta Tombo, traveling through Atlantic Patagonia is like being on an adventure aboard Jacques Cousteau's boat. The scattered giant dinosaur bones, fossils, and petrified forests witnessed an era extinct for millions of years but display a continuity with the current species on the beaches and in the waters. Experiencing Atlantic Patagonia means crossing vast, flat, windswept deserts to reach oases of isolated population centers. It means traveling to the end of the world—Tierra del Fuego (Land of Fire) and its dramatic Alps-like scenery of picturesque lakes, streams, mountains, and wildlife. It means being embraced by independent, pioneering souls just beginning to understand the importance of tourism as traditional industries—wool, livestock, fishing, and oil—are drying up.

The culture of Atlantic Patagonia, like that of other parts of the region, is a hybrid of the cultures of primarily European immigrants, who came here in the 19th century, and the cultures of the indigenous peoples, mainly the Mapuche. This area's history is in large part the fascinating story of the Welsh who left Great Britain in 1865 as a result of religious persecution and came to Patagonia to establish a colony of their own in Chubut Province. It's also a tale of rugged, pioneering Italians, Spanish, Croats, Germans, Lebanese, and Portuguese, among others, who staked a claim in inhospitable, uncharted territories upon invitation from the Argentine state beginning in the mid-19th century. Argentina, in an effort to thwart Chilean and European ambitions for the land and to quell the indigenous population, sought to settle the territory by actively courting European immigration, instituting customs and tax incentives, and even shipping over hundreds of prisoners as colonizers. The settlers who came built water channels, ports, and chapels while baking the breads and planting the crops of their homelands; these cultural traditions still remain. The indigenous populations are long gone; they were wiped out by the four-year military campaign (1879–83) led by General Roca and known as the Conquest of the Desert.

Ushuaia & the Tierra del Fuego

⑱ *230 km (143 mi) south of Río Grande, 596 km (370 mi) south of Río Gallegos, 914 km (567 mi) south of El Calafate, 3,580 km (2,212 mi) south of Buenos Aires.*

Ushuaia—which at 55 degrees latitude south is closer to the South Pole (2,480 mi) than to Argentina's northern border with Bolivia (2,540 mi)—is the capital and tourism base for Tierra del Fuego, an island at the southernmost tip of Argentina. Although its physical beauty is tough to match, Tierra del Fuego's historical allure is based more on its mythical past than on reality. The island was inhabited for 6,000 years by Yamana, Haush, Selk'nam, and Alakaluf Indians. But in the late 19th century, after vanquishing the Indians in northern Patagonia, the Argentine Republic was eager to populate Patagonia to bolster its territorial claims in the face of European and Chilean territorial ambitions. An Anglican mission had already been established in Ushuaia in 1871, and Argentina had seen Great Britain claim the Falklands, a natural Argentine territory. Thus, in 1902 Argentina moved to initiate an Ushuaian penal colony, establishing the permanent settlement of its most southern territories and, by implication, everything in between.

At first, only political prisoners were sent to Ushuaia. Later, however, fearful of losing Tierra del Fuego to its rivals, the Argentine state sent increased numbers of more dangerous criminals. When the prison closed in 1947, Ushuaia had a population of about 3,000, made up mainly of former inmates and prison staff. Another population boom occurred after Argentina's 1978 industrial incentives law, which attracted electronics manufacturers like Philco and Grundig to Ushuaia. Many of these television and home-appliance factories have shut down because they weren't able to compete in the global marketplace, but the children those boom times produced now populate Ushuaia's streets.

Today the Indians of Darwin's "missing link" theory are long gone—wiped out by disease and indifference brought by settlers—and the 50,000 residents of Ushuaia are hitching their star to tourism. The city rightly promotes itself as the southernmost city in the world (Puerto Williams, a few miles south on the Chilean side of the Beagle Channel, is but a tiny town). Ushuaia feels a bit like a frontier boomtown, with the heart of a rugged, weather-beaten fishing village and the frayed edges of a city that quadrupled in size in the '70s and '80s. In the late '90s the local government completed an airport that has the capacity to handle direct flights from abroad and finished a deep-water pier that welcomes cruise ships stopping for provisions in Ushuaia on their way to the Antarctic. Unpaved portions of R3, the last stretch of the Panamerican Highway, which connects Alaska to Tierra del Fuego, are finally, albeit slowly, being paved. The summer months—December to March—draw 120,000 visitors, and the city is trying to extend those visits with events like March's Marathon at the End of the World.

Tierra del Fuego could be called picturesque, at a stretch. A chaotic and contradictory urban landscape includes a handful of luxury hotels amid the concrete of public housing projects. Scores of "sled houses" (wooden shacks) sit precariously on upright piers, ready for speedy displacement to a different site. Many of the newer homes are built in a Swiss-chalet style, reinforcing the idea that this is a town that tourism has breathed new life into. At the same time, the weather-worn pastel colors that dominate the town's landscape remind you that Ushuaia was once just a tiny fishing village, populated by criminals, snuggled at the end of the Earth.

As you stand on the banks of the Canal Beagle (Beagle Channel) near Ushuaia, as Captain Robert Fitzroy—the captain who was sent by the English government in 1832 to survey Patagonia, including Tierra del Fuego—must have done, the spirit of the farthest corner of the world takes hold. What stands out is the light: at sundown the landscape is cast in a subdued, sensual tone; everything feels closer, softer, more human in dimension despite the vastness of the setting. The snowcapped mountains of Chile reflect the setting sun back onto a stream rolling into the channel, as nearby peaks echo their image—on a windless day—in the still waters.

Above the city, the last mountains of the Andean Cordillera rise, and just south and west of Ushuaia they finally vanish into the often stormy sea. Snow dots the peaks with white well into summer. Nature is the principal attraction here, with trekking, fishing, horseback riding, and sailing among the most rewarding activities, especially in the Parque Nacional Tierra del Fuego (Tierra del Fuego National Park).

As Ushuaia converts to a tourism-based economy, the city seeks ways to utilize its 3,000 hotel rooms in the lonely winter season. Though most international tourists stay home to enjoy their own summer, the adventurous have the place to themselves for snowmobiling, dogsledding, and cross-country and downhill skiing at new ski resorts just outside town.

The **tourist office** (✉ Av. San Martín 674 ☎ 2901/424550 ⊕ www.tierradelfuego.org.ar/ushuaia or www.e-ushuaia.com) is a great resource for information on the town's and Tierra del Fuego's attractions. It's open weekdays 8 AM–10 PM, weekends 9–8. Several people on the cheerful staff speak English. While the office also has a stand at the airport that greets all flights, it's worth a stop into the main office to plan a stay in the area.

The **Antigua Casa Beben** (Old Beben House) is one of Ushuaia's original houses, and long served as the city's social center. Built between 1911 and 1913, Fortunato Beben is said to have ordered the house through a Swiss catalog. In the 1980s the Beban family donated the house to the city to avoid demolition. It was moved to its current location along the coast and restored, and is now a cultural center with art exhibits.

✉ *Maipú and Pluschow* ☎ *No phone* 💲 *Free* ⊙ *Tues.–Fri. 10–8, weekends 4–8.*

Rainy days are a reality in Ushuaia, but two museums give you an avenue for urban exploration and a glimpse into Tierra del Fuego's fascinating past. Part of the original penal colony, the Presidio building was built to hold political prisoners, street orphans, and a variety of other social undesirables from the north. Today it holds the **Museo Marítimo** (Maritime Museum), within Ushuaia's naval base, which has exhibits on the town's extinct indigenous population, Tierra del Fuego's navigational past, Antarctic explorations, and life and times in an Argentine penitentiary. You can enter cell blocks and read the stories of the prisoners who lived in them while gazing upon their eerie effigies. Well-presented tours (in Spanish only) are conducted at 3:30 daily. ✉ *Gobernador Paz and Yaganes* ☎ *2901/437481* 💲 *13 pesos* ⊙ *Daily 9–8.*

FodorsChoice ★

At the **Museo del Fin del Mundo** (End of the World Museum), you can see a large stuffed condor, as well as other native birds, indigenous artifacts, maritime instruments, and such seafaring-related objects as an impressive mermaid figurehead taken from the bowsprit of a galleon. There are also photographs and histories of El Presidio's original inmates, such as Simon Radowitzky, a Russian immigrant anarchist who received a life sentence for killing an Argentine police colonel. The museum is in the 1905 residence of a Fuegonian governor. The home was later converted into a bank, and some of the exhibits are showcased in the former vault. ✉ *Maipú 173 and Rivadavía* ☎ *2901/421863* 💲 *5 pesos* ⊙ *Daily 10–1 and 3–7:30.*

Tierra del Fuego was the last land mass in the world to be inhabited—until 9,000 BC, when the ancestors of those native coastal inhabitants, the Yamana, arrived. The **Museo Yamana** chronicles their lifestyle and history. The group was decimated in the late 19th century, mostly by European disease. (There is said to be, at this writing, one remaining Yamana descendant, who lives a few miles away in Puerto Williams.) Photographs and good English placards depict the unusual, hunched posture of the Yamana; their unusual, wobbly walk; and their hunting of cormorants, which were killed with a bite through the neck. ✉ *Rivadavía 56* ☎ *2901/422874* ⊕ *www.tierradelfuego.org.ar/mundoyamana* 💲 *5 pesos* ⊙ *Daily 10–8.*

The **Tren del Fin del Mundo** (End of the World Train) takes you to the Parque Nacional Tierra del Fuego, 12 km (7½ mi) away. The two-hour train ride is a simulation of the trip on which El Presidio prisoners were taken into the forest to chop wood; but unlike them, you'll also get a good presentation of Ushuaia's history (in Spanish and English). The train departs daily at 10, noon, 3, and 7 in summer, and just once a day, at 10 AM, in winter, from a stop near the national park entrance. ✉ *Ruta 3, Km 3042* ☎ *2901/431600* 🖷 *2901/437696* ⊕ *www.trendelfindelmundo.com.ar* 💲 *72 pesos first class ticket, 58 pesos tourist-class ticket, 12 pesos national park entrance fee.*

Tour operators run trips along the **Canal Beagle,** on which you can get a startling close-up view of all kinds of sea mammals and birds on **Sea Lion's Island** and near **Les Eclaireurs Lighthouse.**

One good excursion in the area is to **Lago Escondido** (Hidden Lake) and **Lago Fagnano** (Fagnano Lake). The Panamerican Highway out of Ushuaia goes through deciduous beechwood forest and past beavers' dams, peat bogs, and glaciers. The lakes have campsites and fishing and are good spots for a picnic or a hike. A rougher, more unconventional tour of the lake area goes to **Monte Olivia** (Mt. Olivia), the tallest mountain along the Canal Beagle, rising 4,455 feet above sea level. You also pass the **Five Brothers Mountains** and go through the **Garibaldi Pass,** which begins at the Rancho Hambre, climbs into the mountain range, and ends with a spectacular view of Lago Escondido. From here you continue on to Lago Fagnano through the countryside past sawmills and lumberyards. To do this lake tour in a four-wheel-drive truck with an excellent bilingual guide, contact **Canal Fun** (⊠ Rivadavía 82 ☎ 2901/437395); you'll drive *through* Lago Fagnano (about 3 feet of water at this point) to a secluded cabin on the shore and have the best asado of your life, complete with wine and dessert. For a more conventional tour in a comfortable bus with a bilingual guide and lunch at Las Cotorras, try **All Patagonia** (⊠ Juana Fadul 26 ☎ 2901/433622 or 2901/430725 🖷 2901/430707).

Estancia Harberton (Harberton Ranch; ☎ 2901/422742) consists of 50,000 acres of coastal marshland and wooded hillsides. The property was a late-19th-century gift from the Argentine government to Reverend Thomas Bridges, officially considered the Father of Tierra del Fuego. Today the ranch is managed by Bridges's great-grandson, Thomas Goodall, and his American wife, Natalie, a scientist and author who has cooperated with the National Geographic Society on conservation projects. Most people visit as part of organized tours, but you'll be welcome if you arrive alone. They serve up a solid and tasty tea in their home, the oldest building on the island. For safety reasons, exploration of the ranch can only be done with a guide. Lodging is not available, but you can arrange to dine at the ranch by calling ahead for a reservation. Most tours reach the estancia by boat, offering a rare opportunity to explore the **Isla Martillo** penguin colony, in addition to a sea lion refuge on **Isla de los Lobos** (Island of the Wolves) along the way.

If you've never butted heads with a glacier, check out **Glaciar Martial,** in the mountain range just above Ushuaia. Named after Frenchman Luís F. Martial, a 19th-century scientist who wandered this way aboard the warship *Romanche* to observe the passing of planet Venus, the glacier is reached via a panoramic ski lift. Take the Camino al Glaciar (Glacier Road) 7 km (4 mi) out of town until it ends. Even if you don't plan to hike to see the glacier, it's a great pleasure to ride the 15-minute lift (locally called Aerosilla), which is open daily 10–6:30 and costs 7 pesos round-trip. If you're afraid of heights, you can instead enjoy a small nature trail here, and a teahouse. You can return on the lift, or continue on to the beginning of a 1-km (½-mi) trail that winds its way over lichen and shale straight up the mountain. After a strenuous 90-minute hike, you can cool your heels in one of the many gurgling, icy rivulets that cascade down water-worn shale shoots or enjoy a picnic while you wait for an early sunset. When the sun drops behind the glacier's jagged crown of peaks, brilliant rays beam over the mountain's crest, spilling a halo of gold-flecked light on the glacier, valley, and channel below. Moments like these are why this land is so magical. Note that temperatures drop dramatically after sunset, so come prepared with warm clothing.

★ The pristine **Parque Nacional Tierra del Fuego,** 21 km (33½ mi) west of Ushuaia, offers a chance to wander through peat bogs; stumble upon hidden lakes; trek through native *canelo,* lenga, and wild cherry forests; and experience the wonders of Tierra del Fuego's rich flora and fauna. Visits to the park, which is tucked up against the Chilean border, are commonly arranged through tour companies. Trips range from bus tours to horseback riding to more adventurous excursions, such as canoe trips across Lapataia Bay. Another way to get to the park is to take the Tren del Fin del Mundo. **Transporte Kaupen** (☎ 2901/434015), one of several private bus companies, has buses that travel through the park, making several stops within it; you can get off the bus, explore the park, and then wait for the next bus to come by or trek to the next stop. Yet one more option is to drive to the park on R3 (take it until it ends and you see the last sign on the Panamerican Highway, which starts at Alaska and ends here). Trail and camping information is available at the park-entrance ranger station or at the Ushuaia tourist office. A nice excursion in the park is by boat from lovely **Ensenada Bay** to **Isla Redonda,** a wildlife refuge where you can follow a footpath to the western side and see a wonderful view of the Canal Beagle. While on Isla Redonda you can send a postcard and get your passport stamped at the world's southernmost post office. Tours to the park are run by **All Patagonia** (✉ Juana Fadul 26 ☎ 2901/433622 or 2901/430725 🖶 2901/430707).

Where to Stay & Eat

Dotting the perimeter of the park are five free campgrounds, none of which has much more than a spot to pitch a tent and a fire pit. Call the **park office** (☎ 2901/421315) or consult the ranger station at the park entrance for more information. **Camping Lago Roca** (✉ South on R3 for 20 km [12 mi] ☎ No phone), also within the park, charges 8 pesos per person per day and has bathrooms, hot showers, and a small market. Of all the campgrounds, **La Pista del Andino** (✉ Av. Alem 2873 ☎ 2901/435890) is the only one within the city limits. Outside of town, **Camping Río Pipo** (☎ 2901/435796) is the closest to Ushuaia (it's 18 km [11 mi] away).

Choosing a place to stay depends in part on whether you want to spend the night in town or 3 mi uphill. Las Hayas Resort, Hotel Glaciar, and Cumbres de Martial have stunning views, but require a taxi ride to reach Ushuaia.

$$–$$$ ✕ **Chez Manu.** Provence herbs in the greeting room tip French owner chef Manu Herbin's hand: he uses local seafood with a French touch to create some of Ushuaia's most memorable meals. Perched a couple of miles above town, across the street from the Hotel Glaciar, the all-glass restaurant has grand views of the Beagle Canal. The rest of the restaurant is understated, with an aquarium in the center of the dining room, a kind of throne to the king crab. The menu's highlights include *centolla* (king crab) au gratin and a seafood and fish bouillabaisse. ✉ *Camino Luís Martial 2135* ☎ *2901/432253* ⊕ *www.chezmanu-ushuaia.ifrance.com* 🖃 *AE, MC, V* ☉ *Closed Mon. and May–Sept.*

$–$$$ ✕ **La Cabaña Casa de Té.** This cottage, in a verdant wood of lenga trees beside the surge of a powerful river, overlooks the Beagle Channel and provides a warm, cozy spot for tea or snacks before or after a hike to the Martial glacier—it's at the end of the Martial road that leads up from Ushuaia. Fondues are a specialty at lunch time; at 8 PM the menu shifts to pricier dinner fare with dishes like salmon in wine sauce. ✉ *Camino Luís Martial 3560* ☎ *2901/434699* 🖃 *AE, DC, MC, V* ☉ *Closed Mon.*

★ $–$$$ ✕ **Volver.** A giant plastic king crab sign beckons you into this red tin restaurant, which provides some major relief from Avenida San Martin's row of all-you-can-eat parrillas. The name means "return" and it's the kind of place that calls for repeat visits. Newspapers from the 1930s line the walls in this century-old home; informal table settings have placemats depicting old London landmarks; and fishing nets hang from the ceiling, along with hams, a disco ball, tricycles, and antique lamps. The culinary highlight is, of course, king crab (*centolla*), which comes served with a choice of five different sauces. ✉ *Maipú 37* ☎ *2901/423977* 🖃 *AE, DC, MC, V.*

$ ✕ **La Estancia.** This restaurant in the center of town has mouth-watering lamb and other typical Patagonian meats. Sit by the glass wall to see the chef artfully coordinate the flames, the cooking, and the cutting of tender pieces of lamb and parrilla-style meats. Don't be bashful about requesting more lamb if you're still hungry—all-you-can-eat is implied for all entrées. ⊠ *Av. San Martín 253* ☎ *2901/432700* ▤ *AE, DC, MC, V.*

$$$$ ▦ **Cumbres de Martial.** This charming wood complex, painted fire-engine red, is high above Ushuaia at the foot of the ski lift that leads to the Martial glacier. Depending on your take, the hotel can seem desolate and removed from town, or a peaceful sanctuary close to glacier hiking. Each spacious room has a small wooden deck with terrific views down to the Beagle Channel. There are also a teahouse and a small nature trail beside the Martial River. There is, however, no complimentary shuttle service to town, so you'll need to take a (cheap) taxi to access Ushuaia. ⊠ *Camino Luís Martial 3560, 9410* ☏ *2901/434699* ⊕ *www.tierradelfuego.org.ar/cumbresdemartial* ↻ *14 rooms* ⟳ *Restaurant, tea shop, in-room safes, bar, lounge, laundry service, airport shuttle* ▤ *AE, DC, MC, V* ⦿ *BP.*

$$$$ ▦ **Hotel del Glaciar.** Just above the Las Hayas hotel in the Martial Mountains, this hotel has the best views of Ushuaia and the Canal Beagle. The rooms are bright, clean, and very comfortable. After a long day in the woods, you can curl up on the large sofa next to the fire pit or make your way over to the cozy wood-paneled bar for a drink. Hourly shuttle buses take you to the town center. ⊠ *2355 Camino Glaciar Martial, Km 3.5, 9410* ☎ *2901/430640* ⊕ *www.tierradelfuego.org.ar/delglaciar* ☏ *2901/430636* ↻ *73 rooms, 4 suites* ⟳ *Restaurant, café, minibars, cable TV, bar, laundry service, Internet, convention center, airport shuttle, travel services* ▤ *AE, DC, MC, V* ⦿ *CP.*

$$$$ ▦ **Hotel y Resort Las Hayas.** Las Hayas is in the wooded foothills of the
Fodor'sChoice Andes, overlooking the town and channel below. Every single one of its
★ rooms is decorated differently; you're bound to run into such luxurious details as Portuguese linen, solid oak furnishings, and fabric-padded walls. A suspended glass bridge connects the hotel to a complete health spa. Frequent shuttle buses take you into town. ⊠ *1650 Camino Luís Martial, Km 3, 9410* ☎ *2901/430710; 11/4393–4750 in Buenos Aires* ☏ *2901/430710 or 2901/430719* ⊕ *www.lashayas.com* ↻ *102 rooms, 8 suites* ⟳ *Restaurant, coffee shop, in-room safes, golf privileges, indoor pool, health club, hot tub, massage, sauna, spa, squash, bar, laundry service, convention center, meeting rooms, airport shuttle, travel services* ▤ *AE, DC, MC, V* ⦿ *CP.*

$$$ ▦ **Hostería Petrel.** At this small, isolated lodge along the shores of Lago Escondido—in fact, it's the only lodging choice on the lake—fishing, hiking, and relaxing are the order of the day; the hotel can arrange for guides. Ten cozy cabins overlook the lake. The lodge's upstairs rooms have pleasant balconies over the lake; downstairs rooms have a large hot tub but no balcony. The restaurant and asador services tour buses stopping on their way to visit Escondido and Fagnano lakes. ⊠ *R3, Km 3, 086, 9410 (50 km [31 mi] from Ushuaia)* ☏ *2901/433569* ↻ *20 rooms* ⟳ *Restaurant, snack bar, laundry service* ▤ *AE, MC, V.*

★ **$$** ▦ **Hostería Patagonia Jarké.** Jarké means "spark" in a local native language, and indeed this B&B is a vibrant addition to Ushuaia proper. This two-story lodge, on a dead-end street in the heart of town, is an amalgam of alpine and Victorian styles on the outside; inside, a spacious contemporary design incorporates a glass-roofed lobby, lounge, and breakfast room. Rooms have polished wood floors, peaked-roof ceilings, artisanal soaps, woven floor mats, and lovely views. ⊠ *Sarmiento 310, 9410* ☏ *2901/437245* ✎ *hpatagoniaj@speedy.com.ar* ↻ *10 rooms* ⟳ *Café,* *in-room safes, cable TV, bar, laundry service, Internet* $\equiv$ *AE, DC, MC, V* |O| *BP.*

$$ ▦ **Hotel Albatros.** The best part about this hotel is the view from the restaurant and bar; otherwise, services are solid but unremarkable. Originally constructed of lenga, a local hardwood, the Albatros burned to the ground in 1982 and was rebuilt, but without the same charm. Rooms are clean and standard issue, with reasonably comfortable beds, plain wood furniture, and TVs. Some rooms have views of the dock and channel. ⊠ *Av. Maipú 505, 9410* 🕾 *2901/430003 or 2901/430637* 🖷 *2901/430666* 🖙 *73 rooms, 4 suites* ♧ *Restaurant, café, minibars, cable TV, bar, laundry service, travel services* $\equiv$ *No credit cards* |O| *CP.*

$$ ▦ **Hotel Cabo de Hornos.** Cabo de Hornos is a cut above other downtown hotels in the same price category. The rooms are clean and simple, and all have cable TV and telephones. The lobby-lounge is tacky and tasteful at the same time, decorated with currency and postcards from all over the world. Its old ski-lodge feel makes it a nice place to relax and watch *fútbol* with a cup of coffee or a beer. ⊠ *San Martín and Rosas, 9410* 🕾 *2901/422187* 🖷 *2901/422313* 🖙 *30 rooms* ♧ *Restaurant, bar* $\equiv$ *AE, MC, V* |O| *CP.*

$$ ▦ **La Posada.** This family-run hotel in the middle of town is a decent, lower-cost alternative to the bigger, more costly hotels, but don't expect much in the way of amenities. Rooms on one side face the mountains; on the other side they face the bay and more mountains. ⊠ *Av. San Martín 1299, 9410* 🕾🖷 *2901/433222 or 2901/433330* 🖙 *17 rooms* ♧ *Some room TVs, travel services* $\equiv$ *AE, MC, V* |O| *CP.*

Nightlife & the Arts

Ushuaia has a lively nightlife scene in summer, with its casino, discos, and cozy cafés all within close proximity of each other. The biggest and most popular disco is **El Nautico** (⊠ Maipú 1210 🕾 2901/430415), which plays all kinds of music, from Latin to techno. It's pumping Thursday through Saturday nights from midnight to 6 AM.

Another popular nightspot is **Lenon Pub** (⊠ Maipú 263 🕾 2901/435255), which serves drinks and food to those 21 and older. It's open 11 AM–6 AM. Try your luck at the only full-fledged casino, **Casino Club S.A.** (⊠ Av. San Martín 638 🕾 2901/430415), which features roulette and blackjack tables. There's a 5 peso entrance fee in the evening. The casino is open Sunday–Thursday 11 AM–4 AM and weekends 11 AM–5 AM. For more traditional Argentine entertainment, **Hotel del Glaciar** (⊠ 2355 Camino Glaciar Martial, Km 3½) has tango shows Saturday at 11 PM.

Sports & the Outdoors

FISHING The rivers of Tierra del Fuego are home to trophy-size freshwater trout—including browns, rainbows, and brooks. Both fly- and spin-casting are available. The fishing season runs November–March; fees range from 10 pesos a day to 40 pesos for a month. Fishing expeditions are organized by the following companies. Founded in 1959, the **Asociación de Caza y Pesca** (⊠ Av. Maipú 822 🕾 2901/423168) is the principal hunting and fishing organization in the city. **Rumbo Sur** (⊠ Av. San Martín 342 🕾 2901/422441 or 2901/421139) is the city's oldest travel agency and can assist in setting up fishing trips. **Wind Fly** (⊠ Av. San Martín 54 🕾 2901/431713 or 2901/1556–1573 ⊕ www.windflyushuaia.com.ar) is dedicated exclusively to fishing, and offers classes, arranges trips, and rents equipment.

FLIGHT-SEEING The gorgeous scenery and island topography is readily appreciated on a Cessna tour of the area. A half-hour flight (US$50 for two) with a local pilot takes you over Ushuaia and the Beagle Channel with views of area glaciers and snow-capped islands south to Cape Horn. A 60-

minute flight crosses the Andes to the Escondida and Fagnano lakes. **Aero Club Ushuaia** (✉ Antiguo Aerpuerto ☏ 2901/421717 ⊕ www. aeroclubushuaia.org.ar) offers half-hour and hour-long trips.

MOUNTAIN
BIKING
A mountain bike is an excellent mode of transport in Ushuaia, giving you the freedom to roam without the rental car price tag. Good mountain bikes normally cost about 5 pesos an hour or 15–20 pesos for a full day. They can be rented at **D. T. T. Ushuaia** (✉ Av. San Martín 1258 ☏ 2901/434939). Guided bicycle tours (including rides through the national park), for about 50 pesos a day, are organized by **All Patagonia** (✉ Fadul 26 ☏ 2901/430725 🖷 2901/430707). **Rumbo Sur** (✉ Av. San Martín 342 ☏ 2901/422441 or 2901/421139) is the city's biggest travel agency and can arrange trips. **Tolkeyén Patagonia** (✉ Av. Maipú 237 ☏ 2901/437073) rents bikes and arranges trips.

SKIING
Ushuaia is the cross-country skiing (*esqui de fondo* in Spanish) center of South America, thanks to enthusiastic **Club Andino** (☏ 2901/422335) members who took to the sport in the 1980s and made the forested hills of a high valley about 20 minutes from town a favorite destination for skiers. **Hostería Tierra Mayor** (☏ 2901/423240), **Hostería Los Cotorras** (☏ 2901/499300), and **Haruwen** (☏ 2901/424058) are three places where you can ride in dog-pulled sleds, rent skis, go cross-country skiing, get lessons, and eat; contact the Ushuaia tourist office for more information. **Glaciar Martial Ski Lodge** (☏ 2901/2433712), open year-round, Tuesday–Sunday 10–7, functions as a cross-country ski center from June to October. Skis can also be rented in town, as can snowmobiles.

For downhill (or *alpino*) skiers, Club Andino has bulldozed a couple of short, flat runs directly above Ushuaia. The area's newest downhill ski area, **Cerro Castor** (☏ 2901/422335 ⊕ www.cerrocastor.com), is 26 km (16 mi) northeast of Ushuaia on R3, and has 15 trails and four high-speed ski lifts. More than half the trails are at beginner level, three are for intermediate skiers, and the rest are for experts. You can rent skis and snowboards and take ski lessons here.

Shopping

For typical regional chocolates and other sugars and sweets, head for **Laguna Negra** (✉ Av. San Martín 513). **Mascaras Aborigenes Fueguinas** (✉ Piedrabuena 25) has masks made from local lenga—copies of aboriginal masks used for the *hain* ceremony, in which adolescents were initiated into sexual life. **Patacón** (✉ Av. San Martín 705 ☏ 2901/435588) carries an array of antique Patagonian furnishings and paintings, wood carvings, and picture frames. **Poncho** (✉ Maipú and Laserre ☏ 2901/ 424028) sells some interesting local artisan goods and other knick-knacks from the area. **Tierra de Humos** (✉ Av. San Martín 861 ☏ 2901/ 2433050) has a wide-variety of locally produced leather and ceramic handicrafts, wool sweaters and rugs, postcards, T-shirts, and Patagonian jams. **Ushuaia** (✉ Av. San Martín 785) sells chocolates and sweets.

Comodoro Rivadavía

⓭ *1,854 km (1,149 mi) south of Buenos Aires, 1,726 km (1,070 mi) north of Ushuaia, 945 km (586 mi) north of Río Gallegos, 397 km (246 mi) south of Rawson.*

Argentina's answer to Houston, Comodoro Rivadavía is the town that oil built. Argentina's first oil discovery was made here in 1907 during a desperate search for water because of a serious drought. It was an event that led to the formation of Yacimientos Petroliferos Fiscales (YPF), among the world's first vertically integrated oil companies. After YPF's privatization in 1995, however, thousands were laid off, and record-low oil prices prompted a halt in drilling, which has brought hard times to Comodoro's 130,000 residents. Even as authorities hope for a comeback in oil prices, they are counting on the city's proximity to natural wonders, including the Petrified Forest in Sarmiento, to attract tourists and help compensate for the lost petro-dollars. The city has published several slick-looking brochures detailing the area's sights. The **Tourist Office** (⊠ Moreno and Av. Yrigoyen ☎ 0297/446–2376 ⊕ www.comodoro. gov.ar) has a friendly staff that can help you plan day trips. The building also serves as a cultural center displaying some outstanding local and regional artwork. Across the street, overlooking the Golfo San Jorge, are several statues commemorating the Argentine soldiers who died during the Falkland Islands War in the 1980s.

Surrounded by dry hills and sheer cliffs off the Golfo San Jorge (San Jorge Gulf), Comodoro looks dramatic from a distance. Up close, it's a little frayed around the edges. The main commercial streets, where restaurants and bars can also be found, are San Martín and Comodoro Rivadavía. A relative urban newcomer, Comodoro has little of the old-world charm found in colonial Latin American cities, and it lacks a main central plaza with a traditional church. Residents congregate around the port, with its promenade, park, and basketball and volleyball courts.

You can learn more about petroleum than you probably ever wanted to know at the **Museo Nacional del Petroleo** (National Petroleum Museum). It's well worth a visit, though unfortunately English-language information is scarce. ⊠ *San Lorenzo 250* ☎ *0297/455–9558* ☜ *4.50 pesos* ☉ *June–Oct., Tues.–Fri. 8–6, weekends 2–6; Nov.–May, Tues.–Fri. 9–12 and 3–8, weekends 3–8.*

The windmills at **Parque Eolicó,** a 20-minute drive east of the city, are some of the world's most efficient and modern. Taking advantage of the windy conditions in this area, these windmills generate electricity for the rest of the country.

Where to Stay & Eat

$–$$ ✕ **Tunet.** Though this is Comodoro Rivadavía's best seafood restaurant, the fish, ironically, is mostly imported, owing to the lack of a consistent supply of good-quality local fish. Nonetheless, the food is very good, the service attentive, and the ambience elegant if not too formal. ⊠ *Austral Hotel, Moreno 725* ☎ *0297/447–2200* ▭ *AE, DC, MC, V.*

$ ✕ **La Estancia.** This restaurant—made to look like a typical Argentine ranch—has been serving finely prepared, traditionally cooked meats for 34 years and is the city's oldest. Try the *cordero* (lamb) with chimichurri sauce and mashed potatoes, the seafood, or the homemade pasta. Desserts are extravagant, especially the pancakes with *dulce de leche* (sweet milk). The owners, the friendly Dos Santos family, provide excellent service. Unlike other restaurants, it has a menu in English. ⊠ *Urquiza 863* ☎ *0297/447–4568* ▭ *AE, DC, MC, V.*

$ ✕ **Restaurant Patagonia.** This newcomer gives the well-established Tunet restaurant across the street a run for its money. Though the decor and dishes (fish, chicken, and meat) are outstanding, the service is slow, even by Argentine standards. Don't leave without trying the fabulous "Symphony of Chocolate Mousse." ⊠ *Lucania Palazzo Hotel, Moreno 676* ☎ *0297/449–9300* ▭ *AE, DC, MC, V.*

$$ 🏨 **Lucania Palazzo Hotel.** The newest and most luxurious hotel in town is also blessed with the best waterfront views. Large white pillars, marble floors, and cushy white-leather chairs in the lobby add elegance. The spacious suites, with corner views on both sides, are particularly attractive, and other rooms are a cut above those everywhere else, too. ⊠ *Moreno 676, 9000* ☎ *0297/449–9300* 🖷 *0297/449–9340* ⊕ *www.lucania-*

palazzo.com ↪ *79 rooms, 6 suites* ⌂ *Restaurant, in-room safes, mini-bars, cable TV, gym, sauna, bar, Internet, business services, meeting room, free parking* ⊟ *AE, DC, MC, V* ¶⊙¶ *CP.*

$–$$ ⌨ **Austral Hotel.** This is really two hotels in one: a 42-room luxury hotel with marble floors and plush towels in the rooms and a modest 108-room hotel adequate for its class. The older portion has the advantage of being cheaper while allowing access to some of the newer portion's amenities, such as fax and Internet services. The Austral also has perhaps the city's finest seafood restaurant, Tunet. ⊠ *Moreno 725, 9000* ☎ *0297/447–2200* ⎙ *0297/447–2444* ⊕ *www.australhotel.com.ar* ↪ *150 rooms* ⌂ *Restaurant, gym, sauna, business services, free parking* ⊟ *AE, DC, MC, V* ¶⊙¶ *CP.*

$ ⌨ **Comodoro Hotel.** Among the city's oldest lodgings, this hotel is also one of the most reliable. Rooms are clean and unremarkable, though those higher up have lovely views. If you have trouble finding it, just look for the huge Coke advertisement on one of its side walls. ⊠ *Av. 9 de Julio 770, 9000* ☎ *0297/447–2300* ⎙ *0297/447–3363* ↪ *104 rooms* ⌂ *Cafeteria, bar, cable TV, Internet, business services* ⊟ *AE, DC, MC, V* ¶⊙¶ *CP.*

Sports & the Outdoors

The **beach** at Rada Tilly is about 8 km (5 mi) south of Comodoro. You can get a bus there or drive (take Avenida Yrigoyen along the water).

Shopping

Many of Comodoro's shops sell baby clothes—a holdover from the population explosion during the oil boom days. Some sell regional artisan items. **Doris Hughes Decoraciones** (⊠ Av. San Martín 282) carries regional paintings and international artisan goods.

Tierra Viva (⊠ Moreno 912 ☎ 0297/1562–48211) looks like a natural foods store you might find in Vermont or Oregon—it's filled with grains, herbs, dried fruit, and local microbrews.

Sarmiento & the Bosque Petrificado José Ormaechea

⓴ *150 km (94 mi) west of Comodoro Rivadavía.*

Fodor'sChoice
★

Sarmiento is a one-horse town of dirt and paved roads, with small, low structures—primarily houses, a couple of churches, a gas station, a few small restaurants, and some no-frills hotels. It's also the jumping-off point for the Bosque Petrificado José Ormaechea (José Ormaechea Petrified Forest), about 30 km (19 mi) from Sarmiento on R26. There, you can see trunks of petrified wood 65 million years old, with their colorful stratifications, and feel the overpowering wind. Let the park's resident attendant and self-professed "Patagonia fanatic," Juan José Balera, give you a whirl through the eerily lonely landscape in his Mercedes-Benz bus (just show up; he's usually there). If you rent a car, make it a four-wheel-drive vehicle because you'll have to drive a half hour on a rough, unpaved road once you leave Sarmiento. For more information about the park, contact the **tourist office** (☎ 0297/489–8220) in Sarmiento. While you're in the area, stop at **Lago Musters** (Musters Lake), 7 km (4 mi) from Sarmiento, and **Lago Olhue Huapi** (Olhue Huapi Lake), a little farther on. At Lago Musters you can take an isolated swim or go fishing.

Where to Stay & Eat

¢ ✕ **Restaurant Heidy's.** About a mile off the main highway in Sarmiento is this restaurant owned by Luís Kraan, of Dutch heritage, and his German-descended wife, Kathy Mueller. Enjoy delicious vegetable broth, called *puchero*, homemade pasta, and steak. And don't skip their delicious chimichurri sauce. ⊠ *Perito Moreno and Patagonia* ☏ *2965/ 489–3308* ☱ *No credit cards.*

¢ ⊡ **Hotel Ismar.** This is the best lodging in Sarmiento. Rooms are clean and have simple wood furnishings and cable TV. ⊠ *Patagonia 248, 9020* ☏ *0297/489–3293* ♿ *Cable TV, free parking* ☱ *MC, V* ⦿ *CP.*

Camarones

㉑ *252 km (156 mi) south of Trelew, 105 km (65 mi) south of Punta Tombo, 258 km (160 mi) north of Comodoro Rivadavia.*

Camarones is a tiny and dilapidated but charming fishing town whose main attractions are the particular blueness of the sea and the nearby nature reserve. Every year, on the second weekend in February, the town celebrates the Fiesta Nacional de Salmon (National Salmon Festival) with all kinds of events and a fishing contest. Camarones is difficult to reach by public transportation, though at least one bus company, Don Otto, passes through here on its 3½-hour trip from Trelew. The **Cabo Dos Bahías Fauna Reserve,** 30 km (19 mi) southeast of town, has all kinds of wildlife, including penguins, sea lions, birds, seals, guanacos, rheas, and foxes.

Where to Stay

Camping is free in the municipal campgrounds that front the Bay of Camarones; call the **Chubut Province Tourism Agency** (☏ 11/4432–8815 in Buenos Aires; 2965/481113 in Rawson) for more information.

Punta Tombo

㉒ *120 km (74 mi) south of Trelew, 105 km (65 mi) north of Camarones.*

FodorśChoice The **Reserva Faunística Punta Tombo** (Punta Tombo Wildlife Reserve) has
★ the largest colony of Magellanic penguins in the world and one of the most varied seabird rookeries. Roughly 325,000 penguins live here from the middle of September to March. You can walk among them (along a designated path) as they come and go along well-defined "penguin highways" that link their nests with the sea, and you can see them fishing near the coast. Other wildlife found here in abundance includes cormorants, guanacos, seals, and Patagonian hares. Although December is the best month to come—that's when the adult penguins are actively going back and forth from the sea to feed their newborns—anytime is good, except from April through August when the penguins feed at sea. Other than driving, the easiest way to get to Punta Tombo is with a tour guide from Trelew, Rawson, Gaiman, or even Puerto Madryn, the stopover points for the reserve.

Gaiman

㉓ *17 km (10½ mi) west of Trelew.*

The most Welsh of the Atlantic Patagonian settlements, Gaiman (pronounced GUY-mon) is far more charming than nearby Trelew and Rawson. The Welsh colony's history is lovingly preserved in museums and private homes; Welsh can still be heard on the streets (though residents speak accentless Spanish); and there continues to be a connection to Wales, with teachers, preachers, and visitors going back and forth frequently. Even the younger generation maintains an interest in the culture and language.

Perhaps the town's greatest draw is its five Welsh teahouses (*casas de te*)—Ty Gwyn, Plas-y-Coed, Ty Nain, Ty Cymraeg, and Ty Te Caerdydd. Teahouses were established in Wales as an alternative to having a full-fledged family meal on Sunday. The ones in Gaiman all serve a similar menu for about the same price (around 15 pesos will buy a *completo* sampling, which should serve two), but have different atmospheres. Tea-houses are usually open daily 2–8; if you're anywhere nearby, they're worth a special trip.

Gaiman was founded in 1874, a few years after the Welsh arrived in Patagonia seeking escape from religious persecution in Britain. Since then, Welsh, German, and British immigrants, the indigenous population, and, more recently, Bolivians, who have renewed the agriculture industry, have made Gaiman home.

For a fee of 1 peso, a tour guide at the **tourist office** (⊠ Corner of Riva-davía and Belgrano Sts. ☎ 02965/491152 ⊙ Dec.–mid-Mar., Mon.–Sat. 9–9, Sun. 3–8; mid-Mar.–Nov., Mon.–Sat. 9–6, Sun. 3–6) will hop in the passenger seat of your car to lead you through a few sights in town, including the now-unused train tunnel (which you drive through) and the **Museo Antropológico de Gaiman,** a two-story brick house built in 1910 by the pioneering Nichols family. Inside are pre-Hispanic skulls, Patagonian stone tools, and displays of other artifacts from the region. Note that this museum can only be visited with a tour guide.

The **Museo Histórico Regional de Gaiman** (Gaiman Regional Historical Museum) has photographs of Gaiman's original 160 settlers; stock certificates from the Companía Unida de Irrigación del Chubut (United Company for Chubut Irrigation), which was nationalized by Perón in the '40s; and other interesting memorabilia. Tegai Roberts, the English-speaking octogenarian who gives tours here, is the great-granddaughter of Michael D. Jones, one of the original settlers of the Patagonian colony. If you strike up a conversation with her, you're likely to get a complete oral history of Gaiman and its inhabitants. ⊠ *Av. Sarmiento and Av. 28 de Julio* 🎫 *1 peso* ⊙ *Jan. and Feb., Tues.–Sun. 10–11:30 and 3–7; Mar.–Dec., Tues.–Sun. 3–7.*

Argentina's weirdest attraction is Gaiman's **Parque Desafío.** Colorful, kitschy, and entirely creative, the park is filled with recycled goods— 80,000 bottles, 15,000 tin cans, and the remains of several automobiles. Its mastermind is Joaquin R. Alonso, an eccentric octogenarian whose optimistic outlook on life is clearly conveyed in his artwork. The park has found international fame in the pages of the *Guinness Book of Records* for using tens of thousands of pieces of refuse in its creation. Alonso and his wife Maria del Carmen Caballero, who live here, welcome you to the park and invite you to stroll the paths lined with Alonso's alternately pensive and humorous musings. One reads, "Cows affirm that artificial insemination is boring." A visit here is anything but. ⊠ *Av. Brown at Calle Espora* 🎫 *5 pesos* ⊙ *Daily 8:30–8:30.*

Throughout the Chubut Valley are three dozen or so chapels where the Welsh went to school, held meetings, trials, and social events, sang religious hymns, and even had their tea—some of them are still functioning as teahouses. Two of these chapels are in Gaiman. The **Capilla Vieja** was built in 1880. Three times a year it's used in a traditional event called Eisteddfod, when townspeople gather to celebrate Welsh traditions with song, poetry, and dance below the chapel's wooden vaulted ceilings. Next to the Capilla Vieja is the **Capilla Bethel,** built in 1914 and used today by Protestants for Sunday service. To reach the chapels take the first right after the bridge heading out of town and follow the dirt road around several bends.

The **Parque Paleontológico Bryn Gwyn** (Bryn Gwyn Paleontology Park), outside town, is the companion to the Museo Paleontológico Egidio Feruglio in Trelew. Here you can see 40 million years of geological history in a natural setting. Call ahead to make arrangements for getting into the park and going on a tour. ⊠ *11 km (7 mi) south of town* ☎ *2965/ 435464* ⚌ *4 pesos.*

BOD IWAN FARM – Want to spend a day on the same farm where Bruce Chatwin stayed while researching his famed travelogue *In Patagonia*? Contact Waldo Williams at Bod Iwan Farm, a working Welsh farm 15 minutes east of Gaiman, where you can walk among cows, sheep, wagons, and tractors. Waldo will also host an asado or Welsh tea for you and give you a tour of his century-old home. Stick around until dusk; watching the sunset in the Chubut River valley is quite an experience and you'll understand why Patagonia has been a source of both desperation and inspiration for so many. ☎ *2965/ 491251 or 2965/1566–1816.*

Where to Stay & Eat

For a small town, Gaiman has a good choice of eateries, from parrillas to pizzerias. The town's true joy, however, is a visit to one—or all—of Gaiman's teahouses.

★ **$–$$** ✕ **La Vieja Cuadra.** Implements from Gaiman's old bakery—a 25-foot-long kneading trough, a butter churner, scales, the old brick oven—add warmth to the town's best restaurant. Though these implements were used at the *panadería* from the mid-1970s to as late as 1994, they seem more like relics from the 19th century. Four large wooden wheels that formed part of a bread-delivery carriage form modified chandeliers above the dining room. The house specialty is homemade pizzas and pastas, including ham and cheese stuffed *sorrentinos*. If you crave sirloin, try the *lomo a los tres pimientos* (pork loin with three types of peppers). ⊠ *M. D. Jones 418* ☎ *2965/1568–2352* ⊟ *AE, MC, V* ☺ *Closed Mon. No lunch Tues.–Sat.*

$ ✕ **Ty Cymraeg.** Photographs of the Thomas family's ancestors hang proudly on the walls of the wood-paneled rooms in this teahouse on the banks of the Chubut River. An enormous Bible written in Welsh is at your disposal, as is an outdoor patio with tree-shaded benches. ⊠ *Av. Matthews 74* ☎ *2965/491010* ⊟ *AE, DC, MC, V.*

★ **$** ✕ **Ty Te Caerdydd.** Cypress trees, fountains, and sculpted gardens mark the grounds of Gaiman's largest teahouse, which looks like a mini palatial estate on the south bank of the Chubut River. It succeeds in impressing, though the dining rooms here are larger and less homey than the town's other teahouses. A separate *casa de artesanias* is the best place to pick up jams, handicrafts, and souvenirs. ⊠ *Av. Fontana s/n, Zona de Chacras* ☎ *2965/491510* ⊟ *AE, DC, MC, V.*

¢–$ ✕ **Gustos Pizzeria y Confitería.** Surprisingly good pizza can be found at Gustos. Besides the usual, toppings include Roquefort cheese, ham, hard-boiled eggs, red pepper, onion, and tuna fish. An individual pizza is 5 pesos. ⊠ *Av. Eugenio Tello 156* ☎ *2965/491828* ⊟ *No credit cards.*

★ **$** ✕▥ **Ty Gwyn.** This wood-and-brick teahouse was opened in 1974 by Maria Elena Sanchez Jones, who still directs the kitchen. It serves delicious scones, breads, and jams lovingly made from local fruits, and other elaborate sweets, including the classic Argentine-Welsh tea accompaniment, *torta negra* (black cake), a kind of fruitcake. A sure bet is to order a *completo* and get a taste of each. An interior garden leads to a staircase above which Ms. Sanchez Jones maintains four bedrooms that form the town's best lodging. The quarters are spotless, affordable, and have wood floors, soothing mint-colored walls, and small private balconies with river views. Room 4 has antique furnishings. ⊠ *Av. 9 de Julio 111* ☎ *2965/491009* ⊕ *www.cpatagonia.com/cp/ty-gwyn* ⇲ *4 rooms*

⚐ *Restaurant, bar, laundry service; no room phones, no room TVs* ⊟ *AE, MC, V* ⦿ *BP.*

$ 🏨 **Posada Los Mimbres.** An alternative to staying in town—and a great choice if you're seeking a little space and solitude—is this ranch on the Chubut River. Guests can choose to stay in one of two three-bedroom homes, one of which is a century old. You reach the ranch by following signs from town to the "Zona de Chacras," or farmhouse zone. It's a 5-km (3-mi) ride down a dirt road. ⊠ *Chacra 211, 9105* 📠 *2965/ 491299* ⊕ *www.posadalosmimbres.com.ar* ⚐ *2 houses* ⊟ *No credit cards* ⦿ *BP.*

¢ 🏨 **Hostería Gwesty Tywi.** If the rooms at Ty Gwyn are full, the six rooms at this private home are the next-best bet for a pleasant, reliable stay within town. The innkeepers are friendly and will fill you in on local lore. Gaiman is small, and you can walk from the front door to any destination. ⊠ *M. D. Jones 342, 9105* 📠 *2965/491292* ⊕ *www.advance. com.ar/usuarios/gwestywi* ⚐ *6 rooms* ⊟ *No credit cards* ⦿ *CP.*

Sports & the Outdoors

If you'd like to go horseback riding in the outskirts of Gaiman, call Horacio Symonides at the **Escuela de Equitación** (☎ 2965/1576–2462). Two hours of riding will cost you around 10 pesos.

Trelew

㉔ *17 km (10½ mi) east of Gaiman, 250 km (155 mi) north of Camarones, 1,800 km (1,116 mi) north of Ushuaia, 67 km (41½ mi) south of Puerto Madryn.*

Trelew (pronounced Tre-LEH-ew) is a commercial, industrial, and service hub with hotels, restaurants, gas stations, mechanics, and anything else you might need as you travel from point to point. Its biggest attractions are its paleontology museum and its proximity to the Punta Tombo Reserve and Península Valdés. Like Gaiman, Trelew has a strong Welsh tradition. If you come in the second half of October, you can participate in the Eisteddfod, a Welsh literary and musical festival, first held in Patagonia in 1875. Trelew itself was founded in 1886 as a result of the construction of the Chubut railway line, which joined the Chubut River valley with the Atlantic coast. It's named after its Welsh founder, Lewis Jones (Tre means "town" in Welsh, and Lew stands for Lewis), who fought to establish the rail line. Trelew gained another kind of infamy in 1974 for the massacre of political prisoners who had escaped from the local jail. For more information about the town, contact the **tourist office** (⊠ Mitre 387 📠 2965/420139 ⊕ www. trelewpatagonia.gov.ar).

The tourist office is in front of the town's main square, **Plaza Independencia,** which features a central gazebo with intricate woodwork and a steeple. In 1910 the plaza and gazebo were inaugurated in a spot formerly used for grazing by horses of the train station's employees.

The **Teatro Español** (Spanish Theater), on the north side of Plaza Independencia, was constructed by the city's Spanish immigrants in 1918. Today it's a cultural center that hosts drama, dance, and musical events. ⊠ Av. 25 de Mayo 237 ☎ 2965/434336.

The **Museo de Arte Visuales de Trelew** (Museum of Visual Arts) is east of the plaza and hosts good monthly contemporary art exhibitions. It's in a Flemish- and German-influenced building designed by a French architect in 1900. From 1913 to 1932, this was city hall. ⊠ *Mitre 389* 📠 *No phone* ⊕ *http://ar.geocities.com/museotw* ⊙ *Daily 8–8.*

At Trelew's most prominent attraction, **Museo Paleontológico Egidio Fer-uglio (MEF)**, the most modern display is 2 million years old. This state-of-the-art educational extravaganza features exhibits on extinct dinosaurs from Patagonia. There's a fossil of a 290-million-year-old spider with a 3-foot leg span and the 70-million-year-old petrified dinosaur eggs of a carnotaurus. The museum's tour de force is the bones of a 100-ton, 120-foot-long dinosaur. You can also glimpse into a workshop where archaeologists study newly unearthed fossils. Tours in English are available. ⊠ *Av. Fontana 140* ☎ *2965/432100 or 2964/420012* ⊟ *8 pesos* ⊙ *Oct.–Feb. daily 10–8; Mar.–Sept. daily 10–6.*

Across the street from MEF is Trelew's old train station, which operated from 1889 to 1961, when the government shut down the country's rail service. The national historic landmark now holds a small museum of town history, the **Museo Regional Pueblo de Luís** (Lewistown Regional Museum). It has a mishmash of displays on the European influence in the region, the indigenous populations of the area, and wildlife. ⊠ *Avs. 9 de Julio and Fontana* ☎ *2965/424062* ⊟ *2 pesos* ⊙ *Weekdays 8–8, Sun. 5–8.*

Where to Stay & Eat

$ ✕ **El Viejo Molino.** It's fun to find a restaurant that outclasses its city. The thoughtful design and renovation of this 1886 mill have set a new benchmark for dining on the Patagonian coast. Beneath the Alexander Calder–inspired mobiles that hang from the two-story-high ceilings, elegant hostesses and courteous waiters deliver cosmopolitan service. The interior's coup de grace is a glassed-in parrilla, where you can watch an attendant pour wine over the roast and attend to it lovingly. Old black-and-white photos on the wall document this location's history from a brick cube into an ivy-hung gem of a steak house. ⊠ *Mitre and Av. Galés* ☎ *2965/428019* ⊟ *AE, MC, V.*

¢–$ ✕ **Touring Club.** This classic old *confitería* was founded in 1907 by the Chubut Railway Company as a restaurant and became Chubut's first hotel in 1926. In its heyday it was one of Patagonia's most luxurious options. It was the choice of Argentine presidents Juan Perón and Arturo Frondizi, both of whose photos grace the restaurant walls. Now, the hotel's rooms are too shabby to recommend. But the café staff is proud of its past; after a coffee, ask to see the old ballroom, which hasn't been used in 12 years: it's a spectacle of grace in ruins. ⊠ *Av. Fontana 240, 9100* ☎ *2965/433997 or 2965/433998* ⊟ *AE, DC, MC, V.*

$ ⊞ **Hotel Libertador.** This big hotel has seen better days, but because it caters to tour groups, the friendly, English-speaking staff is very reliable. Rooms are clean and light and reasonably modern. Fourteen "superior" rooms are more recently renovated and are worth the modest increase in price. ⊠ *Av. Rivadavia 31, 9100* ☎ *2965/420220 or 2965/426026* ⊕ *www.hotellibertadortw.com* ⊷ *90 rooms* ⊖ *Restaurant, snack bar, in-room data ports, cable TV, laundry service, business services, car rental, free parking* ⊟ *AE, DC, MC, V* ⊠ *CP.*

$ ⊞ **Rayentray.** The nicest, and most expensive, hotel in Trelew is this 22-year-old building, part of an Argentine chain. Rayentray, which means "stream of flowers" in Mapuche, has more amenities than any other local hotel. It's a block from Plaza Independencia. ⊠ *San Martín 101, 9100* ☎ *2965/434702* ⊕ *www.cadenarayentray.com.ar* ⊷ *110 rooms* ⊖ *Restaurant, minibars, cable TV, pool, massage, sauna, laundry service, business services* ⊟ *AE, DC, MC, V* ⊠ *CP.*

Nightlife & the Arts

Trelew's biggest discoteca is **La Recova** (⊠ Av. Yrigoyen and Av. Los Mártires). For people 25 years and older, the pub turns into a big dance floor after midnight. You can give gaming a try at **Casino Club Trelew** (✉ Belgrano 477 ☎ 2965/425236), which has eight roulette and two blackjack tables along with 100 slot machines.

Puerto Madryn

➎ *67 km (41½ mi) north of Trelew, 450 km (279 mi) north of Comodoro Rivadavia, 104 km (64 mi) west of Puerto Pirámides, 1,380 km (856 mi) south of Buenos Aires.*

The Welsh people, who came to Patagonia to seek refuge from religious persecution in Great Britain, landed first in Puerto Madryn in 1865 (and the anniversary of their arrival is celebrated every July 28 here and in other Chubut towns). You can still find many of their descendants today, but there isn't much evidence of the indigenous people who helped the Welsh survive and become the first foreigners to unveil the secrets of Patagonia's interior.

Puerto Madryn's first economic boom came in 1886, when the Patagonian railroad was introduced, spurring the town's port activities and the salt and fishing industries. Customs taxes were removed in the 1960s, attracting manufacturers (mainly of salt) to the town, but many folded within a decade or so because of inefficient operations and low international commodity pricing for salt. The construction of Argentina's largest aluminum plant, Aluminios Argentinos S.A., however, prompted a population explosion in the 1970s, and at this writing the plant was expanding its operations. The fishing and mining industries, too, continue to provide jobs. But most recently Puerto Madryn residents have been riding the tourism boom, a result of the town's proximity to the nature reserves at Península Valdés.

Puerto Madryn's main hotels and residences are on or near the 3½-km-long (2-mi-long) Rambla, the pedestrian stretch that hugs Golfo Nuevo; it's also a favorite place for joggers and strollers. In high whale-watching season—from September to December—the city's nearly 5,000 hotel rooms and its campgrounds usually fill up.

The **Museo Oceonográfico y Sciencias Naturales** (Oceanographic and Natural Science Museum) is worth a visit if you have the time. Housed in a lovely 1917 colonial building once owned by the Pujol family (original settlers), the museum focuses on marine life. You can see a giant squid preserved in formaldehyde and learn how fish breathe. ✉ *Domecq García and Menéndez* ☎ *2965/451139* 🎫 *Free* ☉ *Weekdays 9–noon and 2–7, Sat. 2:30–7.*

Furthering Puerto Madryn's reputation as the eco-conscious center of Patagonia is the spectacular **EcoCentro,** a modern hands-on museum and research center that strives to promote the protection of the sea and its inhabitants through education. Exhibits provide background on local marine life, and the invertebrates "touch pool" allows visitors to get a real feel for the fish. The center is on a cliff at the north end of the city's beach. ✉ *Julio Verne 3784* ☎☎ *2965/457470* 🌐 *www.ecocentro.org. ar* 🎫 *7 pesos* ☉ *Mid-Dec.–mid-Mar., Tues.–Sun. 6 PM–10 PM; mid-Mar.–Sept., Tues.–Sun. 3–8; Oct.–mid-Dec., daily 9–noon and 3–8.*

Where to Stay & Eat

$–$$ ✕ **Ambigú.** This stylish place to eat and drink is across the street from the beach. The menu has 60 pizzas to choose from, as well as entrées like sirloin medallion (medallón de lomo) with pumpkin puree. A clean, contemporary style complemented by well-mounted photographs documenting the history of the building (note the art deco detailing, including original iron cresting, on the exterior) lends the restaurant both authenticity and sophistication. ☒ *Av. Roca at Av. Saenz Peña* ☎ *2965/472541* ⊟ *AE, MC, V.*

$–$$ ✕ **Placido.** For an elegant dining experience and nouvelle cuisine, head to this glass-front restaurant overlooking the water and the bay's fishing ships. It specializes in seafood but also has pasta, chicken, and meat dishes. ☒ *Av. Roca 506* ☎ *2965/455991* ⊟ *AE, DC, MC, V.*

$ ✕ **El Restaurant Pequeño.** This restaurant does it all pretty well: pastas, beef, and fresh fish. Try the delicious salmon or perhaps the *lenga* (tongue) in a tasty sauce of onions, chives, peppers, and other herbs. ☒ *Av. Roca 820* ☎ *2965/454475* ⊟ *AE, MC, V.*

¢–$ ✕ **Cantina El Nautico.** Don't let the corny, yellow-neon sign outside dissuade you; this local favorite run by three generations of a French Basque family has hosted a variety of celebrities over the years, from Juan Manuel Fangio (a Formula One race car driver) to one of Hemingway's daughters. The homemade pasta and the fresh seafood are especially good, as is the "butter"—a mixture of mayonnaise with garlic, parsley, and pepper—that accompanies the bread. For dessert, try the outstanding *Macedonia* (fruit salad with ice cream). ☒ *Av. Roca 790* ☎ *2965/471404* ⊟ *AE, DC, MC, V.*

¢–$ ✕ **Restaurant Estela.** Run lovingly by Estela Guevara, who could easily pass for anybody's favorite aunt, this restaurant is a real pleasure. There are menus in English, German, French, and Italian; the postcards from all over the world sent by dinner guests and displayed on the walls attest to the owner's popularity. Ms. Guevara, who is of Ukrainian descent and speaks perfect English, tends to all her guests personally and will even offer travel advice. The restaurant serves hearty meals of beef, chicken, and fish at reasonable prices. ☒ *R. S. Peña 27* ☎ *2965/451573* ⊟ *AE, MC, V* ☉ *Closed Mon.*

$$$ ✕▦ **Estancia San Guillermo.** If you want to experience a Chubut farm filled with snorting pigs, overfriendly guanacos, and strutting roosters, head for Estancia San Guillermo. Just a few miles outside Puerto Madryn, owners Alfredo and Cristina Casado make you feel at home with their 1,200 sheep, which roam their 7,400-acre fossil-filled farm. Watch Alfredo shear a sheep (from September through December only) or his helpers prepare the parrilla. Stay in roomy, comfortable villas with kitchens and bathrooms; rates include all meals. The estancia has a dining room, too, if you're just coming for the day. ☒ *Contact info in Puerto Madryn: Av. 28 de Julio 90, 9120* ☎ *2965/452150* 🖷 *2965/473583* ⊕ *www.san-guillermo.com* ⚹ *Dining room, horseback riding* ⊟ *No credit cards* ⏀ *FAP.*

★ $ ▦ **Bahía Nueva Hotel.** Clean and spacious rooms, a great location, a pool table, and friendly service make this hotel on the bay front a good option. The English-speaking staff are eager to please, and the eco-conscious literature and decor make guests aware of their awesome natural surroundings. The warm brick lobby area features a library, comfortable armchairs, and a fireplace. ☒ *Av. Julio A. Roca 67, 9120* 🖷🖷 *2965/451677 or 2965/450145* ⊕ *www.bahianueva.com.ar* ⚹ *40 rooms* ⚹ *Cable TV, bar, library, Internet, laundry service, business services* ⊟ *AE, DC, MC, V* ⏀ *CP.*

$ ▦ **Hotel Aguas Mansas.** This hotel is one block from the beach in a pretty residential neighborhood and a few blocks from the center of town. It's nothing fancy—just clean, quiet rooms and good, personable service. It's one of the few lodgings with a pool, especially in this price range. ☒ *José Hernandez 51, 9120* ☎ *2965/473103* 🖷 *2965/473103* ⊕ *www.aguamansas.com* ⚹ *20 rooms* ⚹ *Cable TV, pool, bar, laundry service* ⊟ *MC, V* ⏀ *CP.*

Nightlife & the Arts
La Oveja Negra (✉ Irigoyen 144) is a small, cozy bar and literary café; Thursday through Sunday nights you can attend poetry readings or hear good local bands. At the **Margarita Bar** (✉ Av. Peña 15), you'll find a hip crowd, cheap beer, and a DJ spinning tunes by the likes of the Red Hot Chili Peppers and Beck. For a totally different experience, try your luck at the **Casino Puerto Madryn** (✉ Av. Roca 639).

Sports & the Outdoors
There are all sorts of sports in and around Puerto Madryn, ranging from bicycling and fishing to sand-boarding (basically, surfing on the sand). Puerto Madryn is also Argentina's scuba-diving capital. In an effort to further boost interest in scuba diving—by giving divers something else to explore—town officials sank the *Albatros,* a large fishing vessel, off the coast in Golfo Nuevo. Several scuba shops rent equipment and can arrange dives for you. Most of them are found on Boulevard Brown, which runs along the beach; almost all of them have small restaurants and bars complete with tiki huts, reclining chairs, and music. **Na Praia** (✉ Blvd. Brown 860 ☎ 2965/473715) rents scuba gear. **Ocean Divers** (✉ Blvd. Brown 700 ☎ 2965/472569 or 2965/1566–0865) is another reliable place to find scuba equipment. **Scuba Duba** (✉ Blvd. Brown 893 ☎ 2965/452699), as the name implies, is an established dive shop.

Several companies rent bicycles for about 20 pesos a day, including **XT Mountain Bike** (✉ Av. Roca 742 ☎ 2965/472232). **Na Praia** (✉ Blvd. Brown 860 ☎ 2965/473715) also rents mountain bikes.

Costas Patagonicas (☎ 2965/451131) organize fishing trips. **Jorge Schmid** (☎ 2965/451511), a respected guide in the area, offers fishing trips, as well as whale-watching and dolphin-viewing trips.

Shopping
Puerto Madryn is one of the better shopping cities on the eastern coast of Patagonia. The best shopping is found on the streets that intersect with the Rambla, like **Avenida 28 de Julio,** at the corner of which is a pleasant, three-story upscale mall, Portal de Madryn. **Artesanias Mag** (✉ Portal de Madryn, Av. Roca and Av. 28 de Julio), makes its own pots and craft items from a local white clay known as *arcilla.* It also sells leather goods, hand-drawn postcards, and unique knives. **Barrika** (✉ Av. Roca 109 ☎ 2965/450454) is a lovely boutique wine shop. Its helpful staff will guide you to the choicest Argentine bottles. On the second floor of Portal de Madryn is **Yenelen,** which sells regional culinary goodies, such as torta *galetas,* chocolates, jellies made from wild Patagonian fruits, and teas. Yenelen runs the city's only **chocolate factory** (✉ Av. Roca 672 ☎ 2965/457779), which is free and open to the public daily from 9:30 to 1 and 4:30 to 10. Yenelen also sells Welsh cakes and other local crafts.

Península Valdés

㉖ *Puerto Pirámides is 104 km (64 mi) northwest of Puerto Madryn.*

Fodor's Choice
★
The Península Valdés is one of Argentina's most important wildlife reserves. Its biggest attractions are the 1,200 southern right whales that feed, mate, give birth, and nurse their offspring here. One unique characteristic of these whales is that they have two external blowholes on top of their heads, and when they emerge from the water, they blow a V-shape water blast that can be seen for miles away. The protected mammals attract some 100,000 visitors every year from September through December, when people crowd into boats small and large to observe at close range the 30- to 35-ton whales leap out of the water and blow water from their spouts. Once 100,000-strong, the worldwide popula-

tion of these giant mammals has declined to only 4,000, a result of being hunted for their blubber.

Off-season the peninsula is still worth visiting: sea lions, elephant seals, Magellanic penguins, egrets, and cormorants as well as land mammals like guanacos, gray fox, and Patagonian *mara*, a harelike animal, all make their home here. Discovered by Spanish explorer Hernando de Magallanes in 1520 and named after Don Antonio Valdés, minister of the Spanish navy in the late 18th century, Península Valdés is a protected zone. So valued is the peninsula's animal population that UNESCO is considering declaring it a site of universal patrimony. It's also the lowest point on the South American continent, at 132 feet below sea level.

To get to the peninsula, you must drive along desolate, unpaved roads surrounded by vast estancias dotted with sheep and a handful of cows. The biggest landholder since the late 19th century, the Ferro family owns one-quarter of Península Valdés—3,625 square km (5,850 square mi), with five airstrips from which they can visit their property. You also pass abandoned salt mines, an important industry in the early 1900s. But the salt is a reminder of the at least 260,000 sea lions killed in the peninsula between 1917 and 1953, at which point hunting was prohibited: salt was used to preserve the sea lions' blubber. Today only about 20,000 sea lions remain.

Puerto Pirámides, the only village on Península Valdés, is a more tranquil, isolated base than Puerto Madryn from which to explore the area's natural attractions. For ecological reasons, only 200 people are allowed to live here, but there are a handful of campsites, hotels, and restaurants. Aside from lounging around with a beer in hand and looking out on the pyramid-shape cliffs of Valdés Bay, the only activities in town are scuba diving and surfing.

Where to Stay & Eat

$$ ✕⬚ **The Paradise.** This hotel and restaurant is overpriced, but lacks competition. If you're seeking reliability, look no further. Rooms are clean and spare; those on the second floor have cable TVs. The restaurant is the most fun in town, with postcards and photographs left behind by visitors, and a fireplace in the back. Two bars create atmosphere enough to cover for seafood dishes like squid or prawns in garlic sauce that lack flair. The hotel can organize scuba-diving tours and activities like sand surfing. ⊠ *Av. Julio A. Roca, 9121* 🕿 *2965/495030 or 2965/495003* ⊕ *www.puerto-piramides.com.ar* 🛏 *12 rooms* ⚭ *Restaurant, some room TVs, some in-room hot tubs, fishing, bar, laundry service* ▤ *AE, MC, V* ⅋⊙⅋ *CP.*

$ ⬚ **Cabañas en el Mar.** Families would do well to stay in one of these wooden cabañas that have small private balconies that look toward the sea. They come with small kitchens and can accommodate up to six people. Since the food options in town are limited, the cabañas are popular with biologists on extended stays. A recent group was a team from National Geographic working on a documentary about orcas. ⊠ *Av. de las Ballenas s/n, 9121* 🕿 *2965/495049* ⌁ *cabanas@piramides.net* 🛏 *6 cabañas* ⚭ *Cafeteria, laundry service; no room TVs* ▤ *No credit cards.*

$ ⬚ **Posada Aguamarina.** The three rooms at this friendly and accommodating inn are converted classrooms from Puerto Principe's first school, built in 1914. Instead of school desks, you'll find now the town's most comfortable beds. Owners and environmentalists Gabriela and Fabian couldn't be more hospitable or knowledgeable about the area; they speak English. ⊠ *Av. de las Ballenas s/n, 9121* 🕿 *02965/495008* ⌁ *fauna@wef.org.ar* 🛏 *3 rooms* ⚭ *Cafeteria, laundry service* ▤ *No credit cards.*

Sports & the Outdoors

Scuba-diving equipment is easy to find in Puerto Pirámides. **Jorge Schmid** (📞 2965/295012 or 2965/295112) rents scuba-diving equipment and organizes whale-watching tours. **Mar Patag** (📞 2965/1545–798963 🌐 www.crucerosmarpatag.com) offers multiday luxury boat tours of Valdés Bay and the Atlantic Ocean. Its brand-new ship has seven well-equipped rooms and can accommodate up to 50 people. The all-inclusive cruises run two to three days and cost about $150 per person per day.

en route

Heading north on R3 toward Viedma will take you through the small town of Sierra Grande and its vast supply of iron, said to be among the world's largest. You can tour a mine here for 15–20 pesos, hiking 300 feet beneath the Earth's crust, rappelling, and rafting in underground waters while learning about iron mining. Contact **Area Natural Recreativa Movil 5** (📞 2934/481–0212 or 2934/481333 📠 2934/481095) for information. Other hiking and camping options are nearby; the folks at Area Natural Recreative Movil 5 will give you more information.

Viedma

㉗ *528 km (327 mi) north of Puerto Madryn, 176 km (109 mi) south of Bahía Blanca, 662 km (410 mi) east of Neuquén, 960 km (595 mi) south of Buenos Aires.*

Landing amid the desert thistle that surround's Viedma's airport, you might think that you've made an unscheduled stopover. But within minutes of the airport, you get to the vibrant, albeit small, provincial city of Viedma whose 50,000 residents go about their daily routines unaware of the tourism boom that their Patagonian neighbors are undergoing. The ½-km-wide (¼-mi-wide) Río Negro (Black River), which separates Viedma from its sister city, Carmen de Patagones, is the heart of the town. By day people swim and boat in the river and picnic and play ball by it; by night people stroll along the river and fill the restaurants and bars lining it. Aside from La Costanera (roughly "Riverwalk"), as the area is known, the other center of activity in town is Avenida Buenos Aires, along which are hotels, restaurants, shops, and the Catedral Cardenal Cagliero.

In 1779 Francisco de Viedma y Narvaez, with his men dying of fever amid a critical water shortage in Península Valdés, decided to anchor along the shores of the Río Curru Leuvu, now the Río Negro. Viedma, who was aiming to claim Patagonia for Spain, was attracted by the lush conditions and abundance of fresh water. The date of which the town's residents are the most proud, however, is the victorious 1885 battle against Portuguese settlers from Brazil who were seeking to claim this strategic site along the river. In 1879 Viedma became the administrative and political capital of all of Patagonia. Five years later Patagonia was divided into five separate provinces, at which point Viedma became simply the capital of the Río Negro Province, which it still is today. In the mid-1980s, Viedma was slated by President Raúl Alfonsín to become the new capital of the Argentine Republic—the Argentine Brasília—but the plan was abandoned because of the cost. Legislation for such a move is still floating around Buenos Aires, but the new frontrunner for capital status is Córdoba.

At Viedma's unusual **Museo Tecnológico del Agua y del Suelo** (Museum of Water and Soil Technology), you can meet its founder and caretaker, Osvaldo Casamiquela, an engineer and retired bureaucrat with a passion for water. It's an important subject in a province that is 95% arid and where only 345,000 of 55 million acres are under agricultural production because of a lack of irrigation. ✉ *Av. Colón 498, fl. 1* ☎ *2920/ 431569* 🖃 *Donation* ⊙ *Weekdays 9* AM–11 AM.

The **Golfo San Matías,** 30 km (19 mi) south of Viedma, is a stretch of coast favored by Viedma and Carmen de Patagones residents for its beaches and wildlife. **Balneario El Cóndor,** a nice beach area, is bordered by sheer cliffs and has a number of small hotels, restaurants, campgrounds, and even a little casino. About 1 km (½ mi) from where the cliffs begin is a fishing pier that was constructed by blasting out a large area of sheer rock and stone. From high above the water, you can catch all kinds of fish, even sharks. A little restaurant nearby serves up the day's catches; the proprietor is an old Chilean man prone to relating his past triumphs at sea. If you walk the kilometer (½ mi) toward the pier on the beach at low tide, you'll be surrounded by the screeching sounds of the yellow parakeets called *loros* (Hitchcock's *The Birds* may come to mind). On your way back to town head toward the top of the cliffs and you'll see the first lighthouse in Patagonia, the **Faro Río Negro,** which was built in the 1880s to aid ships coming into Río Negro. If you catch the caretaker on a good day, you may be able to climb the 64 steps to the top for a good view of the coast.

★ Another 30 km (19 mi) south is the **Reserva Faunística de Punta Bermeja** (Point Bermeja Wildlife Reserve), more commonly known as La Lobería ("seal home") for the 3,500 sea lions that line its shores in high season. If you can, bring binoculars to better observe from the breezy bluffs the sea lions and the striking scenery (it's prohibited to go down to the beach). If you're here from May to November, you might even see a sea lion being pursued—or even eaten—by an orca whale, its only natural predator. Look out for the *loros barranqueros,* a type of parakeet that nests in the soft cliff rocks. You'll see the holes of the parakeets' nests and possibly the black eagles, peregrine falcons, and turkey vultures that prey on them. Other birds commonly seen in the reserve are snowy sheathbills, cormorants, gulls, sandpipers, and oystercatchers. Land-based wildlife includes guanacos, rheas, maras, wildcats, skunks, foxes, armadillos, and small reptiles. You can also bathe in the natural-stone tidal pools and walk on the black, iron-tinged sand at the beach at **La Lobería,** which is about a mile down the road. There are lifeguards in summer, as well as showers, rest rooms, and a restaurant. After La Lobería, the highway is no longer paved, and the farther you go, the more desolate it gets.

Where to Stay & Eat

For accommodation information, including campsites, contact the **tourist office** (✉ On the Costanera between 7 de Marzo and Urquiza ☎☎ 2920/ 427171).

$ ✕ **La Balsa Restaurant.** As at many other good restaurants, the bread and butter at this local favorite are exceptional—though it's not really butter but a delicious, artery-hardening mixture of Roquefort cheese, cream, olive oil, and a drop of whiskey. The food is fresh and good—steak, mashed potatoes, fish, and pasta. It's on the Río Negro in a breezy, pleasant spot. ✉ *Villarino 27, at Av. Costanera* ☎ *2920/431974* ▭ *AE, DC, MC, V.*

¢–$ ✕ **El Tío.** This is a real neighborhood joint, frequented by locals who eat the meat off the parrilla, drink beer, and watch soccer. Note the many stuffed animal heads that line the walls; the rest of the animals were no doubt grilled and served at the restaurant in years past. ✉ *Av. Colón and Zatti* ☎ *2920/420757* ▭ *V.*

$ ⌨ **Hotel Austral.** Though it's a tad shabby for the price, this hotel's the best in town (and rooms have cable TV and are bright). Its location is also excellent: across the street from the Río Negro, with great northward views of Carmen de Patagones and its cathedral (ask to be lodged on this side) and of Viedma to the south. The tiny boat that takes you to Carmen de Patagones for 1.50 pesos is just steps from the hotel, as are most of the town's other attractions. The large lobby is comfortable, and there's a full-service restaurant with Argentine basics: steak, chicken, and pasta. ☒ *Av. 25 de Mayo and Av. Villarino, 8500* ☎ *2920/ 422615, 2920/422616, 2920/422617, or 2920/422618* 🖷 *2920/422619* ⊕ *www.hoteles-austral.com* ➸ *100 rooms* ♿ *Restaurant, dry cleaning, laundry service, business services, meeting room* ▤ *MC, V* ❍❘ *CP.*

¢ ⌨ **Hotel Nijar.** Although a few blocks from the town center, this place is great for a great price. The rooms are clean and quiet; all have cable TV and telephones. There's a bakery next door to the lobby. ☒ *Mitre 490, 8500* ☎🖷 *2920/422–2833 or 2920/426864* ➸ *45 rooms* ♿ *Restaurant, bar, business services* ▤ *AE, DC, V* ❍❘ *CP.*

¢ ⌨ **Hotel Peumayén.** Though it's nothing out of the ordinary, this hotel is a good value for the money. Rooms are on the small side, with basic wood furniture; all have TVs. It's in front of a pleasant, tree-lined park on the main drag and just three blocks from the river. The staff is helpful. ☒ *Av. Buenos Aires 334, 8500* ☎ *2920/425222* 🖷 *2920/425243* ♿ *In-room safes, bar* ▤ *AE, DC, MC, V* ❍❘ *CP.*

Nightlife

Viedma can get lively on weekends: youngsters and families walk and play alongside the riverfront, while processions of cars blast music as they cruise down the main streets. One popular stop is **Fiore Helados,** an ice cream shop where throngs of people line up for Italian-style delights. The younger set (teens to mid-20s) heads to the **Maroco Tropical** (☒ Caseros 1689). Others go to **Zion** (☒ Caseros 1738) to drink, primp, and dance the night away. For a more laid-back bar with occasional live music and a big-screen TV showing sports, head to **Codigos Café Concert** (☒ E. Garrone 245).

Sports & the Outdoors

Kayaking, canoeing, fishing, and swimming in the Río Negro are the main outdoor activities in Viedma. You might even be able to join in a soccer game being played in the street alongside the Río Negro. The tree-lined promenade along the river is also a lovely place for a bike ride. Dario Santos at **Todobici** (☒ A. Barros 567 ☎ 2920/423158) will let you borrow (for free) one of his bikes for a few hours if you leave him a valid ID. You may be able to rent a bike (though they primarily sell them) at the **Bike Shop del Vecchio** (☒ Calle Saavedra and Calle Garrones ☎ 2920/424466). The one-stop shop for all kayaking, fishing, and camping needs is **Patagonia Outdoor Life** (☒ 25 de Mayo, 340 ☎ 2920/ 431442). Every year during the second week of January is the **Regatta Río Negro,** when dozens, if not hundreds, of boats strut their stuff down the river.

Carmen de Patagones

❷❽ *On the north bank of the Río Negro across from Viedma; it can be reached from Viedma by taking the 5-minute ferry ride across the river; service ends at about 10 PM. If you're going by car or taxi, there are two bridges on the town's outskirts.*

More picturesque, quieter, and smaller than its neighbor Viedma, Carmen de Patagones still conserves much of the early-19th-century colonial heritage that Viedma lost in an early-1900s flood. It was founded, with Viedma, in 1779 with the construction of a fort. For four decades the early settlers lived in caves, one of which is preserved in the Museo Histórico Regional Francisco de Viedma. Residents are sometimes called Maragatos, a reference to the many settlers who came from the Spanish area of Maragateria, in the León Province. The town is oriented around its cathedral, which is fronted by a park and a bench-lined waterfront, where kids can often be found jumping off an old pier into the water. For more information about activities in the area, contact the **tourist office** (✉ Bynon 186 ☎ 2920/461777).

At the **Museo Histórico Regional Francisco de Viedma** (Francisco de Viedma Historical Regional Museum) the biggest attraction is the *craneo fletchado,* the skull of an 18th-century Tehuelche Indian, with a Mapuche Indian arrow in place of its nose; it will give you more appreciation for the struggles of indigenous people even before the arrival of the colonizers. Also here is one of the actual caves in which the earliest settlers lived before moving into houses. ✉ *J. J. Biedma 64, in front of ferry landing* ☎ *2920/462729* 🎟 *Free, donations accepted* ⊙ *Weekdays 10–12 and 2:30–4:30.*

The early-19th-century adobe-walled **Casa Historica La Carlota** (La Carlota Historical Home) last belonged to Dona Carlota, a stern-looking Spanish immigrant seen in a hallway photo, who died in the early 1900s. The city's early immigrants built houses like this one with their earnings from working in the salt mines; this is one of the three earliest remaining houses. Still standing are the well, the wheat-grinding stones, the stone oven used for baking bread, and other rudimentary tools. In preparation for Indian attacks, which never happened, the house is ringed with thick cacti and outfitted with a secret compartment where the children were to hide. ✉ *Bynon 112* ☎ *2920/462729* ⊙ *Weekdays 9–noon and 7–9, by guided tour only* ☞ *Tours can be arranged by request at the Museo Regional Francisco de Viedma.*

In 1827 the locals fought off a Brazilian invasion headed by the Portuguese. To understand the importance of this battle to residents on both sides of the Río Negro, visit the **Iglesia Parroquial** (Parochial Church), built by Salesian priests and inaugurated in 1885. You can't miss the two immense Brazilian flags on either side of the main altar, which were captured in the battle. ✉ *Av. Comodoro Rivadavia and Av. 7 de Marzo.*

Where to Stay & Eat

¢–$ ✕ **Morena's Pizzeria.** Reminiscent of a New York pizzeria, Morena's is a good place to come in from the heat and cool off with a soda and a well-prepared salad or pizza. There's also a *heladeria* (ice cream shop) next door. ✉ *Olivera 11* ☎ *2920/461378* 🖃 *No credit cards.*

¢–$ ✕ **Novecento.** This charming but dark one-room restaurant sits across from the ferry launch. Eclectic artwork decorates the walls. The burly owner and chef proudly serves up homemade empanadas and pizza prepared in his wood-burning stove. ✉ *J. J. Biedma 34* ☎ *2920/462960* 🖃 *No credit cards.*

¢–$ ✕ **Rigolleto.** A favorite local spot, this bar feels like a Western saloon, with lots of dark wood. Come here for good oven-baked pizza, light snacks, and the location overlooking the water; on a hot day you can stroll with your cool Quilmes beer out to the waterfront. ✉ *J. J. Biedma 2* ☎ *No phone* 🖃 *No credit cards.*

¢ 🏨 **Hotel Percaz.** Like it or not, this hotel is the only game in town. Rooms are simple but clean and have cable TV, and breakfast is included in the price. The hotel is a few short blocks from the central square. ✉ *Comodoro Rivadavia and Irigoyen, 8504* ☎ *2920/254104* 🛏 *20 rooms* ♿ *Snack bar* 🖃 *AE, DC, MC, V* ⫟ *CP.*

Nightlife & the Arts

Every year during the week of March 7, the weeklong **Fiesta de Soberanía y la Tradición** (Sovereignty and Tradition Festival) celebrates the city's defense against the Brazilian incursion in 1827. People from all over the region come here for the food, crafts, and carnival rides. It's part statefair, part flea-market, and all fun. There's also live music every night, with some of the biggest names in Argentine music, like Soledad, making appearances.

PATAGONIA A TO Z

To research prices, get advice from other travelers, and book travel arrangements, visit www.fodors.com.

AIR TRAVEL

The best way to get to Patagonia is to fly from Buenos Aires. The country's major airline, Aerolíneas Argentinas (and Austral, its regional offshoot), flies from Buenos Aires to Ushuaia with stops in Trelew and El Calafate. It also flies to Bariloche, Comodoro Rivadavía, Puerto Madryn, Río Gallegos, San Martín's Chapelco airport, and Viedma. Aerolíneas Argentina's "Visit Argentina" pass allows you to fly to multiple destinations at a discount; it must be purchased outside of Argentina.

Aerolíneas Argentinas flies daily from Buenos Aires to Bariloche, with service from Bariloche to Calafate, Trelew, Río Gallegos and Ushuaia. LADE (Líneas Aéreas del Estado) flies from Bariloche to Chapelco (San Martín) and Esquel, and from Buenos Aires to Trelew, Puerto Madryn, El Calafate, Río Gallegos, Comodoro Rivadavía, Puerto Deseado, and Viedma. Airg (formerly LAPA) flies between Buenos Aires and Trelew, El Calafate, Comodoro Rivadavía, Río Gallegos, and Ushuaia. Southern Winds flies round-trip Buenos Aires and Neuquén.

🛫 **Aerolíneas Argentinas** ☎ 0810/2228-6527 24-hr reservations and sales in Argentina; 11/4317-3000 in Buenos Aires; 2944/423161 in Bariloche; 2966/422020 in Río Gallegos. **Airg (formerly LAPA)** ☎ 11/4114-5272 24-hr reservations and sales in Argentina; 11/4819-5272 in Buenos Aires; 2944/425032 in Bariloche; 2902/491171 in El Calafate; 2966/430446 in Río Gallegos. **LADE** ☎ 11/4361-7071 in Buenos Aires; 2944/423562 in Bariloche, 2966/422326 in Río Gallegos; 2902/491262 in Calafate; 2901/421123 in Ushuaia. **LanChile** ☎ 562/632-3211 in Santiago. **Southern Winds** ☎ 810/777-7979 in Buenos Aires; 2944/423704 in Bariloche; 2901/437073 in Ushuaia.

BOAT & FERRY TRAVEL

Traveling between Bariloche and Puerto Montt, Chile, by boat is one of the most popular excursions in Argentina. It requires three lake crossings and various buses and can be done in a day or overnight. Travel agents and tour operators in Bariloche and Buenos Aires can arrange this trip and many foreign tour companies include it in their itineraries. Cruises to Antarctica and the Malvinas (Falkland Islands) rarely stop at Ushuaia nowadays; they call instead at Punta Arenas, Chile.

BUS TRAVEL

Every Patagonian town, no matter how small or insignificant, has a bus station; and it's not uncommon for buses to stop and pick up a passenger standing by the road where there's nothing in sight for hundreds of miles. Andesmar Autotransportes and La Puntual are two of the main regional bus companies. They stop at almost every major and minor city along the coast and also cross Patagonia between Bahía Blanca and Neuquén. To the west, buses reach Chile's cities of Los Andes and Santiago, among others, and they go as far south as Río Gallegos. You can pick up schedules at bus stations.

Buses arrive in Bariloche from every corner of Argentina—from Jujuy in the north, Ushuaia in the south, and everywhere in between. Several companies have daily service to Buenos Aires. Bariloche's Terminal de Omnibus is in the Estación de Ferrocarril General Roca (Railroad Station) east of town, where all bus companies have offices. Most have downtown offices, too, but your best bet is to go directly to the terminal. The following bus companies run comfortable and reliable overnight buses between Buenos Aires and Bariloche (the trip takes 22 hours): Chevallier, El Valle, and Via Bariloche. Buses also run daily between Bariloche and Chile (Osorno, Puerto Montt, Valdivia, and Santiago) via the Puyehue Pass; contact Tas–Choapa.

To travel from Bariloche south to El Bolsón and Esquel, contact Don Otto, Andesmar at the bus terminal, and TAC. For travel north to Villa Angostura, Traful, and San Martín de los Andes, contact TAC. Algarrobal has daily trips to Villa Angostura.

The following bus companies connect Buenos Aires to Río Gallegos and El Calafate: Don Otto, Interlagos, El Pingüino, and TAC. In summer, Bus Sur and Turismo Zaahj make the five-hour run from Puerto Natales, Chile, to El Calafate. El Pingüino also has service to Trelew and Puerto Madryn and to Bariloche with a change in Comodoro Rivadavia.

You'll probably want to fly to Ushuaia to make the most of your time in the Tierra del Fuego (besides being much faster, it's also cheaper to fly), but direct bus service between Buenos Aires and Ushuaia exists. Trans los Carlos and Turismo Ghisoni make the 12-hour run between Punta Arenas, Chile, and Ushuaia.

🚌 Bus Companies **Algarrobal** ✉ Bus Terminal, Bariloche ☎ 2944/427698. **Andesmar** ✉ Mitre 385, Bariloche ☎ 2944/422140; 2944/430211 at bus terminal. **Bus Sur** ✉ At the bus station, Av. Julio A. Roca 1004, Río Gallegos ☎ 2966/442687; 2902/491631 in Calafate. **Chevallier** ✉ Moreno 105, Bariloche ☎ 2944/423090 or 11/4314-0111; 11/4314-5555 in Buenos Aires. **Don Otto** ✉ At the bus terminal in Bariloche, B. Mitre 321 ☎ 2944/437699. **El Pingüino** ✉ 11/4315-4438 in Buenos Aires; 2966/442169 in Río Gallegos. **Interlagos** at the bus terminals: ☎ 2902/491179 in El Calafate; 2966/442080 in Río Gallegos. **La Puntual** ☎ 11/4313-2441 in Buenos Aires; 297/429176 in Comodoro Rivadavía. **TAC** ✉ Moreno 138, Bariloche ☎ 2944/434727; 2972/428878 in San Martín de los Andes; 2966/29805 in Río Gallegos; 11/4313-3627 in Buenos Aires. **Tas–Choapa** ✉ Moreno 138, Bariloche ☎ 0944/26663; 562/697-0062 in Santiago. **Trans los Carlos** ✉ Av. San Martín 880, Ushuaia ☎ 0901/22337. **Turismo Ghisoni** ✉ Lautaro Navarro 975, Punta Arenas ☎ 5661/223205. **Turismo Zaahj** ☎ 5661/412260 in El Calafate. **El Valle** ✉ 12 de Octubre 1884, Bariloche ☎ 2944/431444; 11/4313-3749 in Buenos Aires. **Via Bariloche** ✉ Mitre 321, Bariloche ☎ 2944/432444; 2972/422800 in San Martín de Los Andes; 11/4663-8899 in Buenos Aires.

🚌 Bus Terminals **Bariloche Terminal de Omnibus** ✉ Av. 12 de Octubre ☎ 2944/432860. **San Martín de Los Andes** ✉ Villegas & Juez de Valle ☎ 427044. **Río Gallegos** ✉ Av. Eva Perón.

CAR RENTAL

For short excursions, renting a car gives you the freedom to stop when and where you want. Gas is 30% less south of El Bolsón. Almost all hotels have off-street parking, some in locked yards—a good idea at night.

A number of U.S. car rental agencies can be found in Patagonia's major cities and tourist centers, as well as locally owned agencies with knowledgable staff that can help you plan excursions, suggest hotels, and even make reservations. For winter travel, it's a good idea to rent a 4x4, especially if you're traveling on dirt roads.

Hiring a *remis* (car with driver) is another option; it costs a little more, but you get a bigger vehicle and the rate is set before you depart on your trip.

Major Agencies Avis 11/4326-5542 in Buenos Aires At the airport, Bariloche 2944/431648 Av. 9 de Julio 687, Comodoro Rivadavia 0297/447-6382 Paraguay 105, Trelew 2965/434634. **Budget** 11/4313-9870 in Buenos Aires Mitre 106, Bariloche 2944/422482; 2944/15551168 cell www.budgetbariloche.com.ar. **Dollar** 11/4315-8800 in Buenos Aires Villegas 282, Location 6, Bariloche 2944/430333 www.patagoniarentacar.com. **Hertz** 11/4312-1317 in Buenos Aires; 2944/434543 in Bariloche. **Localiza** 11/4327-5288 in Buenos Aires; 0800/999-2999 toll free Av. San Martín 531, Bariloche 2944/424767 Av. del Libertador 687, El Calafate 2902/491398 Av. 9 de Julio 770, Comodoro Rivadavia 0297/446-0334 Av. Rivadavia 1168, Esquel 2945/453276 Av. Roca 536, Puerto Madryn 2965/456300 Sarmiento 237, Río Gallegos 2966/424417 Urquiza 310, Trelew 2965/435344 Av. San Martín 1222, Ushuaia 2901/430739 or 2901/432136.

Local Agencies Ai Rent A Car International Av. San Martín 235, across from Edelweiss Hotel, Bariloche 2944/427494 www.rentacarbariloche.com. **Aonik'Enk de Patagonia** Av. Rawson 1190, Comodoro Rivadavia 0297/446-6768. **Bariloche Rent a Car** Moreno 115, fl. 1, No. 15, Bariloche 2944/427638 2944/427638. **Cristina** Av. del Libertador 695, El Calafate 2902/491674 Libertad 123, Río Gallegos 2960/425709. **Freelander** Av. del Libertador 1329, El Calafate 2902/491437. **Rastro** Maipú 13, Ushuaia 2901/422021. **Rent-A-Car** Av. Roca 277, Puerto Madryn 2965/450295 Av. San Martín 125, Trelew 2965/420898. **Visita Rent-a-Car** Maipú, Ushuaia 2901/235181.

Remis Calafate Av. Julio A. Roca 2902/492005. **Centenario** Maipú 285, Río Gallegos 2966/422320. **De La Ciudad** Quaglia 268 Bariloche 2944/428000. **Del Oscar** Av. San Martín 1254, San Martín 2972/428774. **Patagonia Remises** Av. Pioneros 4400, Bariloche 2944/443700.

CAR TRAVEL

Driving to any of the towns in Patagonia from Buenos Aires is a long haul (1,593 km [990 mi]; two–three days) of interminable stretches without motels, gas stations, or restaurants. Fuel in Argentina is expensive and if you break down in the hinterlands, it's unlikely that you'll find anyone who speaks much English. Note, too, that what seem like towns marked on the map may just be private estancias not open to the public. On the other hand, driving exposes you to the heart of the country (and roads are paved all the way to Bariloche). Planning is essential, and Automóvil Club Argentino can provide maps and advice. To get to Bariloche from Buenos Aires: take R5 to Santa Rosa (615 km [382 mi]), then R35 to General Acha (107 km [66 mi]), then R20 to Colonia 25 de Mayo, then R151 to Neuquén (438 km [272 mi]), and then R237 to Bariloche (449 km [279 mi]).

Driving to Río Gallegos (2,504 km [1,555 mi] from Buenos Aires) is even more daunting, more isolated, and more monotonous. The most sensible solution is to fly and rent a car at your destination. Roads between towns and sights in both the northern and southern lake districts are mostly paved, and if not, generally kept in good condition, except in rainy seasons, when it's a good idea to seek local advice about road conditions.

Auto Club Automóvil Club Argentino (ACA) Av. del Libertador 1850, Buenos Aires 11/4802-6061 www.aca.org.ar.

EMERGENCIES

Coast Guard 106. **Fire** 100. **Forest Fire** 103. **Hospital** 107. **Police** 101.

HOSPITALS & PHARMACIES **In Bariloche Farmacia Suizo Andino** Rolando 699, Bariloche 2944/524040. **Farmacia Zona Vital** Moreno 301 and Rolando, Bariloche 2944/420752. **Hospi-**

tal Ramón Carillo ⊠ Moreno 601 ☎ 2944/426117 or 2944/426119. **Hospital Sanatorio del Sol** ⊠ 20 de Febrero 640 ☎ 2944/525000 or 2944/524800.

🚩 In El Calafate **Farmacia El Calafate** ⊠ Av. Libertador 1190 ☎ 9405/491407. **Hospital Municipal** ⊠ Av. Roca 1487 ☎ 2902/492101 or 2902/491173.

🚩In Esquel **Farmacia Atenas** ⊠Av. Fontana 779 ☎2945/451004. **Farmacia Dra. Bonetto** ⊠ 25 de Mayo 150, Esquel ☎ 2945/450662. **Hospital Zona Esquel** ⊠ 25 de Mayo 150 ☎ 2945/450222 or 2945/451224.

🚩 In Río Gallegos **Hospital Regional** ⊠José Ingeniero 98 ☎2966/420025 ☎☎2966/420641.

🚩 In San Martín **Farmacia del Centro** ⊠San Martín 896 and Belgrano ☎2972/428999. **Hospital Ramón Carillo** ⊠ San Martín and Rodhe ☎ 2972/427211.

HEALTH

The water in Bariloche and throughout Patagonia is generally safe. But if you're susceptible to intestinal disturbances, it's best to stick to bottled water, which is available in stores, restaurants, and at some kiosks. *Tabanas* (horseflies) are pests around horses and in the woods in summer. Horsefly repellent is more effective than general bug spray; bring enough for yourself and the horse.

MAIL & SHIPPING

Post offices in bigger towns are usually open 10 AM to 6 PM; smaller towns generally make their own rules. Stamps can also be purchased at kiosks.

🚩 Post Office (Correo) Information **Bariloche** ⊠ Moreno 175. **El Calafate** ⊠ Av. Libertador 1133. **Carmen de Patagones** ⊠ Paraguay 38. **Esquel** ⊠ Alvear 1192, across from the bus station. **Gaiman** ⊠ Juan C. Evans 110. **Puerto Madryn** ⊠ Belgrano and Maíz ⊠ Av. Julio A. Roca 223. **Río Gallegos** ⊠ Av. Julio Roca and Av. San Martín. **San Martín** ⊠ At the Civic Center, General Roca and Pérez. **Trelew** ⊠ 25 de Mayo and Mitre. **Ushuaia** ⊠ Belgrano 96. **Viedma** ⊠ Moreno and 25 de Mayo ⊠ Av. Rivadavía 151 ⊠ Oca and Zatti 545.

MONEY MATTERS

Banks are open weekdays 10–4 in most towns and most have ATMs.

BANKS 🚩 In Bariloche **Citibank** ⊠ Mitre 694 ☎ 2944/436301. **Frances BBV** ⊠ Av. San Martín 336 ☎ 2944/430325. **Scottiabank Quilmes** ⊠ Mitre 433 ☎ 2944/422792.

🚩 In Comodoro Rivadavía **Banco Nación** ⊠ Av. San Martín 102 ☎ 0297/444–2310. **Banco Patagonia** ⊠ Av. Rivadavía 202 ☎ 0297/446–5883. **Lloyds Bank** ⊠ Av. Rivadavía 266 ☎ 0297/447–2061.

🚩 In El Calafate **Provincia de Santa Cruz** ⊠ Av. Libertador 1285 ☎ 2902/491168.

🚩 In Esquel **Banco Nación** ⊠ Alvear and Roca ☎ 2945/452105.

🚩 In Puerto Madryn **Banco Nación** ⊠ 9 de Julio 117 ☎ 2965/450465. **Credicoop** ⊠ Roque Sanez Peña and 25 de Mayo ☎ 2965/452194.

🚩 In Río Gallegos **Bancos de Galicia** ⊠ Av. Roca 802. **Banco de Santa Cruz** ⊠ Roca 802. **Hipotecario Nacional** ⊠Zapiola 49. **Nazionale de Lavoro** ⊠Fagnano off Av. Roca.

🚩In San Martín **Banco de la Nación Argentina** ⊠Av. San Martín 687 ☎2972/427292. **Banelco** ⊠ Av. San Martín 780 ☎ 2972/427292.

🚩 In Trelew **Banco Nación** ⊠ Fontana and 25 de Mayo ☎ 2965/449114 or 2965/449101. **Lloyds Bank** ⊠ 9 de Julio 102 ☎ 2965/434264 or 2965/434058.

CURRENCY *Banelco* and *Link* are ATMs throughout Patagonia. Dollars can be changed to pesos in *Casas de Cambio* (Change Houses), banks and small amounts in hotels. Torn or marked dollars may not be accepted.

SAFETY

Argentina is safer than almost any country in South America, and Patagonia even more so. Reasonable precautions, such as locking your car and leaving nothing inside, leaving large amounts of cash and travel documents in hotel safes, and carrying money in a money belt are advised.

In bus stations and airports, keep an eye on your luggage and wear back-packs in front. To avoid car break-ins, park in hotel garages off the street.

TAXIS

Since taking a taxi doesn't cost much and drivers know their way around, arranging tours or quick trips by taxi to sights near Bariloche, San Martín de Los Andes, El Calafate, Esquel, or other locales makes sense. If you're in El Calafate and have a sudden urge to see the Moreno Glacier, for example, or if you missed the bus to a boat departure on Lago Nahuel Huapi, taking a taxi is a good solution. In Bariloche, there are taxi stands at the Civic Center and at Calles Mitre and Ville-gas. In other towns, taxis line up at the airport, the bus terminal, and at main intersections. Your hotel can also call a taxi for you.

TELEPHONES & INTERNET ACCESS

When you call from outside a particular area code within Argentina, a 0 precedes the area code. Local calls can be made from *telecabinas* (phone booths) with a phone card purchased at kiosks. There are numerous *locutorios* (telephone offices) in all towns. They're easy to use: an attendant sends you to a booth where you can call all over the country or the world, and then pay one bill when you leave. Since hotels charge exorbitant rates for long-distance calls, it's best to go to one of the closest locutorios, which are centrally located and open late into the night. Most locutorios now have fax machines and Internet access. The lowest price for Internet use is 1 peso an hour; you're liable to find the best rates at small, privately run Internet cafés. Of those listed below, only Mas in Bariloche doesn't have Internet access (it has photocopy and fax services). Locutorio Quaglia, also in Bariloche, has Western Union services as well and is open daily from 7 AM to 1 AM. It's possible to rent a cellular phone in Buenos Aires that you can use for both local and international calls. This can be arranged through your hotel, and the company will provide delivery and pickup. Calls are charged to your credit card; rates vary.

🚩 In Bariloche **AAT Communicaciones** ✉ Moreno 107 ☎ 2944/437883. **Locutorio Quaglia** ✉ Quaglia 220 📠 2944/426128. **Mas** ✉ Moreno 724, in front of the hospital ☎ 2944/428414. **Telecentro Melipal** ✉ Pioneros 4400 ☎ 2944/520111.

🚩 In Puerto Madryn **El Rayo Azul** ✉ 28 de Julio 64 ☎ 2965/458964. **Telecentro Telecom** ✉ 25 de Mayo 157.

🚩 In San Martín **Abolengo** ✉ Av. San Martín 806 ☎ 972/27732.

🚩 In Trelew **Arnet** ✉ San Martín and Mitre. **Locutorio del Centro** ✉ Av. 25 de Mayo 219.

🚩 In Ushuaia **Nido de Condores** ✉ Gobernador Campos and 9 de Julio ☎ 2920/437753.

🚩 In Viedma **Telecentro Patagonia 1** ✉ Buenos Aires and Mitre ☎ 2920/420539.

TOURS

If you want a comprehensive tour of Patagonia, including the Parque Nacional los Glaciares, Lago Argentino, Trelew, and Bariloche, contact Gador Viajes in Buenos Aires, Causana Viajes in Puerto Madryn, or any of the tour operators listed below. Carlos and Carol de Passera of Causana Viajes have 17 years of experience leading custom and special-interest trips—focusing, for example, on archaeology, birding, botany, natural history, or whale-watching—for American and Canadian adventure travel companies. Gador Viajes has ecovolunteer trips, wildlife and horseback adventures, and general tours. Provincial tourist offices in Buenos Aires and local tourist offices throughout Patagonia are well-stocked with brochures, and staff are knowledgeable and helpful.

🚩 Tour Information **Causana Viajes** ✉ Moreno 390, Puerto Madryn ☎ 2965/455044 📠 2965/452769 🌐 www.causana.com.ar. **Gador Viajes** ✉ Av. Santa Fe 1339, Buenos

Aires ☎ 11/4811-8498 or 4813-8696 🖷 11/4815-6888 ⊕ www.gadorviajes.com.ar ✉ Gob. Moyano 1082, El Calafate ☎ 2902/491143.

BARILOCHE, EL BOLSÓN, ESQUEL & SAN MARTÍN DE LOS ANDES

The English-speaking owners of Alunco, a very professional travel office specializing in trips in and around Bariloche, are third-generation Barilocheans, expert skiers, and outdoors enthusiasts who have explored the remotest corners of the northern lake district. The main focus of Catedral Turismo is the lake crossing from Bariloche to Chile. Cumbres Patagonia leads easy to advanced adventure tours including horseback-riding, rafting, and mountain biking excursions.

San Martín de los Andes's El Refugio and Tiempo Patagonico both run horseback riding, river rafting, mountain biking, lake, and land excursions in and around San Martín and to Lanín Volcano.

Guided fishing, rafting, and horseback riding trips from El Bolsón and excursions to Lago Puelo National Park can be arranged by Patagonia Adventures and Quen Quen Turismo.

Plan Mundo organizes fishing trips in Los Alerces National Park for about $1,200. The package includes round-trip airfare between Buenos Aires and Esquel, airport transfer on both ends, three nights with breakfast and dinner in the Hostería Futalaufquen in Esquel, and three full days of fishing, including launch, guide, permit, meals, and equipment. For organized white-water rafting trips to the Río Corcovado, near the Chilean border, contact Leo Tours.

🚩 **Alunco** ✉ Moreno 187, fl. 1, Bariloche ☎ 2944/422283 🖷 2944/422782. **Catedral Turismo S.A.** ✉ Palacios 263, Bariloche ☎ 2944/425444 🖷 2944/426215. **Correntoso Travel** ✉ Av. Arrayanes 21, Villa La Angostura ☎ 2944/494803. **Cumbres Patagonia** ✉ Villegas 222, Bariloche ☎ 2944/423283. **El Refugio** ✉ Colonel Perez 1124, San Martín ☎🖷 2972/425140. **Patagonia Adventures** ✉ Pablo Hube 418, El Bolsón ☎ 2944/492513. **Tiempo Patagonico** ✉ Av. San Martín 950, San Martín ☎🖷 2972/427113 or 2972/427114 ⊕ www.tiempopatagonico.com.

EL CALAFATE, EL CHALTÉN & RÍO GALLEGOS

In El Calafate, most hotels arrange excursions to Moreno and Upsala glaciers. Hielo y Aventura specializes in glacier tours with "minitrekking" (walking on the glacier with crampons). Upsala Explorer combines a day at an estancia and a boat trip to Upsala Glacier. Horseback riding can be arranged by Gustavo Holzman or through the tourist office. Alberto del Castillo, owner of El Calafate's E.V.T. Fitzroy Expeditions, has English-speaking guides and organizes both glacier and mountain treks.

Interlagos Turismo arranges tours between Río Gallegos and El Calafate and to the glaciers. Tur Aiké Turismo organizes tours in and around Río Gallagos. In El Calafate, Cal Tur, Hielo y Aventura, and Upsala Explorer run local tours.

🚩 **Fitzroy Expeditions** ✉ Av. San Martín, El Chaltén ☎ 2962/493017 🖷 2962/49136. **Gador Viajes** ✉ Gob. Moyano 1082, El Calafate ☎ 2962/491143. **Gustavo Holzman** ✉ J. A. Roca 2035, El Calafate ☎ 2902/491203. **Hielo y Aventura** ✉ Av. Libertador 935, El Calafate ☎ 2902/492205. **Interlagos Turismo** ✉ Fagnano 35, Río Gallegos ☎ 2966/422614 ✉ Av. Libertador 1175, El Calafate ☎ 2902/491175 🖷 2902/491241. **Tur Aiké Turismo** ✉ Zapiola 63, Río Gallegos ☎ 2902/422436. **Upsala Explorer** ✉ 9 de Julio 69, El Calafate ☎ 2902/491034 🖷 2902/491292 ⊕ www.upsalaexplorer.ccom.ar.

PENÍNSULA VALDÉS, SARMIENTO & VIEDMA

Aiké Tour, Cuyun Co Turismo, and Factor Patagonia arrange all-day tours of the Península Valdés; reserve ahead, especially if you want an English-speaking guide. These companies also organize tours to Punta Tombo, Gaiman, the Dique Ameghino, and Camarones. Jorge Schmid specializes in whale-watching tours; his boat has ample covered space in case it rains. Zonotrikia leads treks through paleontological sites in the area.

Jose Luís Breitman arranges tours of Viedma, Carmen de Patagones, and nearby beaches and parks, including Balneario El Condor and La Lobería.

Aonik'Enk de Patagonia gives tours of Sarmiento, the Bosque Petrificado, and other nearby destinations; it also rents four-wheel-drive vehicles.
🚶 **Aiké Tour** Av. Julio Roca 353, Puerto Madryn ☎2965/450720. **Aonik'Enk de Patagonia** ⊠ Av. Rawson 1190, Comodoro Rivadavía ☎☎ 0297/446–6768 or 0297/446–1363. **Cuyun Co Turismo** ⊠ Julio A. Roca 165, Puerto Madryn ☎ 2965/454950 or 2965/451845 🖷 2965/452065 ⊕ www.cuyunco.com.ar. **Factor Patagonia** ⊠25 de Mayo, Puerto Madryn, ☎2965/454990 or 2965/454991. **Jorge Schmid** ⊠Av. Julio A. Roca, Puerto Pirámides ☎ 2965/495112 or 2965/495029. **Jose Luís Breitman** ☎ 2920/1560–5196. **Zonotrikia** ⊠Av. Roca 536, Puerto Madryn ☎2965/451427 or 2965/455888 🖷2965/451108.

TIERRA DEL
FUEGO In Ushuaia and the Tierra del Fuego, All Patagonia, Canal Fun and Nature, Tiempo Libre, and Tolkar all offer a wide variety of adventurous treks through the Parque Nacional Tierra del Fuego and around the Canal Beagle. Tolkeyén Patagonia and Rumbo Sur organize tours of the Canal Beagle and bus trips that give an overview of the national park. All Patagonia organizes bus trips to Lago Escondido and other spots in the area. Sailing out to sea usually means contact with wide-eyed seals, sea elephants, and sea lions sunning on the rocks. All Patagonia and Rumbo Sur do sea excursions as well as trips to Antarctica. To charter a sailboat, head to Club Naútico, where locals gather to talk about fishing.
🚶 **All Patagonia** ⊠Juana Fadul 26, Ushuaia ☎ 2901/433622 or 2901/430725 🖷 2901/430707 ⊕ www.allpatagonia.net. **Canal Fun and Nature** ⊠ Rivadavía 82, Ushuaia ☎ 2901/437395 ⊕ www.canalfun.com. **Club Naútico** ⊠ Maipú 1210, Ushuaia ☎ No phone. **Rumbo Sur** ⊠Av. San Martín 342, Ushuaia ☎2901/422441 or 2901/421139 🖷2901/430699. **Tiempo Libre** ⊠25 de Mayo 260, Ushuaia ☎2901/431374 🖷2901/421017. **Tolkar** ⊠ Roca 157, Ushuaia ☎ 2901/431408 or 2901/431412. **Tolkeyén Patagonia** ⊠ Maipú 237, Ushuaia ☎ 2901/437073 or 2901/434341 🖷 2901/430532.

TRAIN TRAVEL
Direct train service between Buenos Aires and Bariloche is not an option. Trains do, however, make a 20-hour haul from Bariloche to Viedma, leaving twice a week. For information, contact Servicios Ferroviarios Patagónicos.
🚶 **Servicios Ferroviarios Patagónicos** ⊠ In the Bariloche train terminal ☎ 2944/23172 in Bariloche; 2920/422130 in Viedma.

TRANSPORTATION AROUND PATAGONIA
Traveling the length of Patagonia is a formidable task, especially if you're short on time. To put its size in perspective, Patagonia is 1,930 km (1,200 mi) long, a bit more than the distance from New York City to Miami. Driving on RN40 from Bariloche south to Río Gallegos appeals to Argentines and adventurous foreigners who have the time (two weeks).

Some towns, such as Puerto Deseado, have no air service whatsoever and infrequent and inconvenient bus service. Most likely you'll find yourself taking a mishmash of planes and buses.

VISITOR INFORMATION
Neuquén, Chubut, Río Negro, Santa Cruz, and Tierra del Fuego all have provincial tourism offices in their capital cities and in Buenos Aires. Local tourist offices (Direcciónes de Turismo) are very helpful, easy to find, and usually open every day and into the evening.
🚶 Provincial Tourist Offices **Casa de La Provincia de Chubut** ⊠Sarmiento 1172, Buenos Aires ☎ 11/4432–8815. **Casa de la Provincia del Neuquén** ⊠ Gral. Juan Perón 685,

Buenos Aires ☎ 11/4327-2454. **Casa de la Provincia de Río Negro** ⊠ Tucumán 1916, Buenos Aires ☎ 11/4371-7066. **Provincial Tourism Unit of Chubut** ⊠ Av. 9 de Julio 280, Rawson, 9103 ☎ 2965/481113. **Subsecretaría de Turismo Santa Cruz** ⊠ Av. Roca 863, Río Gallegos ☎🖷 2966/422702 ✍ tur@spse.com.ar ⊠ Suipacha 1120, Buenos Aires ☎🖷 11/4325-3098. **Tierra del Fuego Tourism Institute** ⊠ Av. Maipú 505, Ushuaia ☎ 2901/421423. **Secretaría de Turísmo de la Provincia de Río Negro** ⊠ Gallardo 121, Viedma ☎ 2920/422150.

🚩 Local Tourist Offices **Bariloche** ⊠ Civic Center ☎ 2944/423022 or 2944/43122 🖷 2944/426784. **Comodoro Rivadavía** ⊠ Av. Rivadavía 430 ☎ 0297/446-2376. **El Bolsón** ⊠ Plaza Pagano and Av. San Martín ☎ 2944/492604. **El Calafate** ⊠ Terminal de Omnibus, Julio A. Roca 1004 ☎🖷 2902/491090. **Esquel** ⊠ Sarmiento and Alvear ☎🖷 2945/451927. **Gaiman** ⊠ Belgrano 234 ☎ 2965/491152. **Junín de los Andes** ⊠ Padre Milanesia 590 ☎🖷 2972/491160. **Puerto Deseado** ⊠ San Martín 1120 ☎ 0297/487-1157. **Puerto Madryn** ⊠ Av. Roca 223 ☎ 2965/453504 or 2965/452148. **Río Gallegos** ⊠ Av. Roca 863 ☎ 2966/438725 🖷 2966/422702 ⊕ www.scru.gov.ar. **San Martín de los Andes** ⊠ San Martín and Rosas ☎ 2972/427347. **Sarmiento** ⊠ Av. Reg. de Infanteria 25 ☎ 0297/489-8220. **Trelew** ⊠ Mitre 387 ☎🖷 2965/420139. **Trevelín** ⊠ Plaza de la Fontana ☎ 2945/480120. **Ushuaia** ⊠ Av. San Martín 674 ☎ 2901/432000 or 0800/333-1476. **Viedma** ⊠ On the Costanera between 7 de Marzo and Urquiza ☎ 2920/427171 or 2920/422287. **Villa la Angostura** ⊠ Siete Lagos and Los Arrayanes ☎🖷 2944/494124. **Villa Traful** ⊠ In center of town ☎ 2944/479020.

UNDERSTANDING
ARGENTINA

A LAND OF SUPERLATIVES

FROM THE DENSE TROPICAL JUNGLES in the North to the frozen landscape of Antarctica in the South, from the snowy peaks of the Andes in the West, across high plains, the Pampas, and Patagonia to the Atlantic coast, Argentina is a land of exceptional geographic diversity. It's also a land of superlatives. The highest mountain in the western hemisphere, Aconcagua (22,834 feet) towers above the crest of the Andes. Ushuaia, on the Beagle Channel in Tierra del Fuego, prides itself on being the world's southernmost city. The continental ice cap spreads over 21,756 square km (8,400 square mi) in southern Patagonia, descending into glaciers that crash in gigantic chunks from 150-foot walls into the lakes and streams of the Parque Nacional los Glaciares. In the northeast, on the border with Brazil and Paraguay, the Cataratas del Iguazú spill over a horseshoe-shape ledge into an explosion of 275 waterfalls, varying in height from 140 to 300 feet.

World-famous Argentine beef is raised in the Pampas, the grasslands that cover hundreds of miles in the heart of the country. The topsoil of this alluvial plain is said to be 6 feet deep, producing grass year-round, so rich that cattle don't need to be corn fed. The Northwest and the Cuyo possess an astounding diversity of geography, from barren *alteplano* (high plains) to multihued mountains, deserts, deep gorges, valleys, rivers, and lakes. Along the south Atlantic coast on the Península Valdés, countless species of marine life cavort on land and in the sea. In January, sea lions breed in rookeries, followed by killer whales, sperm whales, and elephant seals; and from September to March thousands of dignified little Magellanic penguins waddle back and forth on "penguin highways" from the sea to land in Punta Tombo.

Although Buenos Aires is now the major economic and cultural capital of Argentina, the country's history actually began in the Northwest. Five centuries before Columbus sailed to America, the Aymara people of Tiahuanaco were traveling from their capital at Lake Titicaca in Bolivia across the barren plains of La Puna down to the fertile valleys of northern Argentina. They came in search of food they could not grow on their high Andean plateau and brought back exotic fruits and feathers from the subtropical lowlands.

By the mid-1400s, the Incas were following the same route from Cusco, Peru, intent upon conquering the indigenous inhabitants of northern Argentina and Chile. Although the Incas never gained complete control over the region, they did establish agricultural communities in Catamarca, Tucumán, and as far south as San Juan and Mendoza. Remnants of these ancient civilizations can still be found along the Royal Road of the Incas from Bolivia southward across the Puna into San Salvador de Jujuy, Salta, Catamarca, and San Miguel de Tucumán, and over the Andes between Mendoza, San Juan, and Chile.

Argentina's first Spanish settlers landed on the banks of the Río de la Plata in 1536. But five years of attacks by the local population convinced them to flee north to the friendlier city of Asunción in Paraguay or to sail back to Spain, leaving their horses and cattle behind to thrive on the fertile plains and ultimately become part of Argentina's great resources. At about the same time, Spanish conquerors from the Viceroyalty of Peru and Alto Peru (present-day Bolivia) were venturing south to Argentina along the now established trade route, searching for silver and gold. The first permanent settlements in Argentina, beginning with Santiago del Estero in 1551, were all founded in the Northwest before the end of the 16th century. Trade routes from central Chile crossed the Andes to Argentina (in order to avoid the Atacama Desert) and went north to Peru, where Spanish vessels waited in the port at Lima to carry goods between Spain and the New World. In 1620, the region of Río de la Plata was officially incorporated into the Viceroyalty of Peru and later, in 1776, with present-day Bolivia, Paraguay, and Uruguay, was declared the Viceroyalty of Río de la Plata.

In 1806 and 1807, the British made two unsuccessful attempts to capture Buenos Aires and the Spanish crown, and the next year, Napoléon invaded Spain and sent King Ferdinand VII to prison in France. The residents of Argentina, emboldened, began to question Spanish leadership and its economic and military benefits. On May 25, 1810, at the Cabildo (Town Hall) in Buenos Aires, the Spanish viceroyalty was deposed by a revolutionary junta. Political chaos ensued, and it wasn't until July 1816 that independence was officially declared by a national congress in the city of Tucumán. Spanish Royalists persisted in attacking from their stronghold in Bolivia, and for 16 years, blood continued to spill on the battlefields of northwestern Argentina. It took General José de San Martín's brilliant and daring expedition in January 1817, across the Andes from Mendoza to Chile with 16,000 men and 10,000 horses, to finally liberate Argentina, Chile, and Peru from Spanish rule forever. With their newly won freedom and no experience in governing, local army generals took control, and for the next 40 years, the Unitarists (those who wanted free trade with Europe, immigration, education, and a central government) fought a civil war with the Federalists (wealthy ranchers who advocated provincial government and territorial rights). The latter were represented by *caudillos* (provincial dictators)—the most infamous of them being Juan Manuel de Rosas, who ruled Argentina from 1835 to 1852.

Rosas was overthrown by José de Urquiza in 1852. Under Urquiza's leadership this country of warring states finally became a nation, with the signing of the constitution (modeled after that of the United States) in May 1853. But all was not easy: Buenos Aires Province didn't accept the constitution and refused to join the federation until 1861. And the strife continued: in 1861 General Bartolomé Mitre overthrew the government and was elected president the next year. Throughout this period and during the enlightened presidency of Domingo Sarmiento (1868–74), thousands of immigrants arrived in Buenos Aires. Meanwhile, across the Pampas and vast reaches of Patagonia, the tenacious Mapuche and nomadic Tehuelche were engaged in a battle with the National Army, led by General Julio Roca, in the infamous Conquest of the Desert (1879–83). Almost the entire native population of Argentina had succumbed to

battle or disease by this point, leaving a few to work on ranches or live on reservations. Europeans began moving in, fencing in the wide-open ranges, and the British built railroads to transport beef, hides, leather, wool, and wheat to Buenos Aires for export.

* * *

I N THE EARLY 1900S, newly developed refrigeration made possible the export of agricultural products to Europe and the rest of the world. By the 1930s, Argentina was the eighth-richest country in the world, and Buenos Aires the major South American port on the Atlantic coast. European investors and wealthy immigrants employed Europe's finest architects and city planners to design and build their city. Today, when you walk the wide avenues and narrow cobblestone streets, look up at the art deco, art nouveau, Gothic, and stately Parisian-style facades to understand why Buenos Aires is referred to as the "Paris of South America."

By 1940, however, Argentina's prosperity was not trickling down to the masses of immigrants working in the industrial sector; nor was it benefiting the rural population. Juan Perón, having grown up on an *estancia* (ranch) where his father worked, was aware of the inequalities between the wealthy upper-class landowners (many of them British) and the rest of the country. Perón and his future wife, Eva, knew how to capitalize on the country's social unrest and its need for a strong, sympathetic leader. Together, they took up the cause of the disenfranchised *descamisados* (literally, shirtless ones) and rode to the presidency on the backs of Argentina's labor force. The adoration of the working class was rewarded by labor reform, job security, pensions, and child labor laws. When Eva Perón died of cancer in 1952, a severe drought, plummeting grain prices in Europe, and a soaring foreign trade deficit brought Argentina's economy to the brink of ruin. Perón was overthrown in 1955. Demagogue, facist, labor reformer, union leader, political genius, power-crazed, crook, dictator—Perón and "Evita" will be loved, hated, and discussed by Argentines forever.

In 1973, a repressive and fumbling military government brought Perón back from exile in Spain. He was elected president;

named his wife, Isabel, vice president; and then died in 1974, leaving her at the helm of a sinking ship. Her ineptitude got her ousted in 1976 and brought a military junta back to power. Military terrorists the likes of José López Rega, General Jorge Videla, Admiral Eduardo Emilio Massera, and General Leopoldo Galtieri launched what is known as the "Dirty War" against the perceived danger of left-wing workers, nuns, priests, intellectuals, and even whole families. Thousands were jailed, tortured, raped, "disappeared," and murdered.

In 1982 General Galtieri invaded the British-held Islas Malvinas (Falkland Islands), pitting an ill-prepared army against an enraged Great Britain. Argentina's military defeat was ultimately its victory: with it, the lies and fabrications of a ruthless military regime were finally exposed to a disbelieving (at first) country and to the world. The military government was replaced by Raúl Alfonsín, who began the process of restoring democracy. Under powerful opposition from the military and a populace frustrated by catapulting inflation, Alfonsín lost in 1989 to an enigmatic governor from La Rioja Province, Carlos Menem. Although a member of the majority Peronista party, Menem began the tricky task of privatizing state-owned companies and pegging the peso to the dollar with some success. In late 1999, however, Menem lost to Fernando de la Rua, the mayor of Buenos Aires.

Though de la Rua attempted to improve the economy through reforms and managed to purge the army and central intelligence of the last few "Dirty War" suspects, what he'll probably be remembered for is four years of recession and rising unemployment, which finally culminated in frequent protests and strikes, many of them violent. The mounting chaos doubled when the government tried a last ditch effort to stabilize the situation by restricting bank withdrawals; the crisis hit its peak in December of 2001 when 27 people were killed in violent protests over a few days. De la Rua resigned and after a series of interim presidents—five in two weeks to be exact—Eduardo Duhalde took office. Duhalde's first move was to unpeg the peso from the dollar. This move, though unpopular—the peso immediately dropped in value by more than 50%—succeeded in securing additional help from the International Monetary Fund.

By mid-2002 the economy had stabilized somewhat, though the peso was still devalued and unemployment remained high. In May of 2003, elections were held, and Néstor Carlos Kirchner, a governor of the Santa Cruz province in Patagonia, won in a runoff election held after Carlos Menem withdrew from the race.

Though economic and political issues continue to trouble Argentina, things are beginning to look up. The spirit of the Argentine people is a practical yet jubilent one, a spirit that can remember the repressive regimes of the past while rejoicing in the freedom of the present. And though the face of the country may change as it tries to rid itself of the cycle of bureaucracy, corruption, and coups, its superlative core—fascinating landscape, cosmopolitan cities, distinctive customs, heavenly food and wine—stays the same, waiting to be discovered and revered.

VOCABULARY

Words and Phrases

	English	Spanish	Pronunciation
Basics			
	Yes/no	Sí/no	see/no
	Please	Por favor	pore fah-**vore**
	May I?	¿Me permite?	may pair-**mee**-tay
	Thank you (very much)	(Muchas) gracias	(**moo**-chas) **grah**-see-as
	You're welcome	De nada	day **nah**-dah
	Excuse me	Con permiso	con pair-**mee**-so
	Pardon me	¿Perdón?	pair-**dohn**
	Could you tell me?	¿Podría decirme?	po-dree-ah deh-**seer**-meh
	I'm sorry	Lo siento	lo see-**en**-to
	Good morning!	¡Buenos días!	**bway**-nohs **dee**-ahs
	Good afternoon!	¡Buenas tardes!	**bway**-nahs **tar**-dess
	Good evening!	¡Buenas noches!	**bway**-nahs **no**-chess
	Goodbye!	¡Adiós!/¡Hasta luego!	ah-dee-**ohss**/ah-stah-**lwe**-go
	Mr./Mrs.	Señor/Señora	sen-**yor**/sen-**yohr**-ah
	Miss	Señorita	sen-yo-**ree**-tah
	Pleased to meet you	Mucho gusto	**moo**-cho **goose**-to
	How are you?	¿Cómo está usted?	**ko**-mo es-**tah** oo-**sted**
	Very well, thank you.	Muy bien, gracias.	**moo**-ee bee-**en**, **grah**-see-as
	And you?	¿Y usted?	ee oos-**ted**
	Hello (on the telephone)	Diga	**dee**-gah

Numbers

	1	un, uno	oon, **oo**-no
	2	dos	dos
	3	tres	tress
	4	cuatro	**kwah**-tro
	5	cinco	**sink**-oh
	6	seis	saice
	7	siete	see-**et**-eh
	8	ocho	**o**-cho
	9	nueve	new-**eh**-vey
	10	diez	dee-**es**
	11	once	**ohn**-seh

12	doce	**doh**-seh
13	trece	**treh**-seh
14	catorce	ka-**tohr**-seh
15	quince	**keen**-seh
16	dieciséis	dee-**es**-ee-**saice**
17	diecisiete	dee-**es**-ee-see-**et**-eh
18	dieciocho	dee-**es**-ee-**o**-cho
19	diecinueve	**dee-es**-ee-new-**ev**-ah
20	veinte	**vain**-teh
21	veinte y uno/ veintiuno	**vain**-te-oo-**noh**
30	treinta	**train**-tah
32	treinta y dos	train-tay-**dohs**
40	cuarenta	kwah-**ren**-tah
43	cuarenta y tres	kwah-**ren**-tay-**tress**
50	cincuenta	seen-**kwen**-tah
54	cincuenta y cuatro	seen-**kwen**-tay **kwah**-tro
60	sesenta	sess-**en**-tah
65	sesenta y cinco	sess-**en**-tay **seen**-ko
70	setenta	set-**en**-tah
76	setenta y seis	set-**en**-tay **saice**
80	ochenta	oh-**chen**-tah
87	ochenta y siete	oh-**chen**-tay see-**yet**-eh
90	noventa	no-**ven**-tah
98	noventa y ocho	no-**ven**-tah-**o**-choh
100	cien	see-**en**
101	ciento uno	see-**en**-toh **oo**-noh
200	doscientos	doh-see-**en**-tohss
500	quinientos	keen-**yen**-tohss
700	setecientos	set-eh-see-**en**-tohss
900	novecientos	no-veh-see-**en**-tohss
1,000	mil	meel
2,000	dos mil	dohs meel
1,000,000	un millón	oon meel-**yohn**

Colors

black	negro	**neh**-groh
blue	azul	ah-**sool**
brown	café	kah-**feh**
green	verde	**ver**-deh
pink	rosa	**ro**-sah
purple	morado	mo-**rah**-doh
orange	naranja	na-**rahn**-hah

red	rojo	**roh**-hoh
white	blanco	**blahn**-koh
yellow	amarillo	ah-mah-**ree**-yoh

Days of the Week

Sunday	domingo	doe-**meen**-goh
Monday	lunes	**loo**-ness
Tuesday	martes	**mahr**-tess
Wednesday	miércoles	me-**air**-koh-less
Thursday	jueves	hoo-**ev**-ess
Friday	viernes	vee-**air**-ness
Saturday	sábado	**sah**-bah-doh

Months

January	enero	eh-**neh**-roh
February	febrero	feh-**breh**-roh
March	marzo	**mahr**-soh
April	abril	ah-**breel**
May	mayo	**my**-oh
June	junio	**hoo**-nee-oh
July	julio	**hoo**-lee-yoh
August	agosto	ah-**ghost**-toh
September	septiembre	sep-tee-**em**-breh
October	octubre	oak-**too**-breh
November	noviembre	no-vee-**em**-breh
December	diciembre	dee-see-**em**-breh

Useful Phrases

Do you speak English?	¿Habla usted inglés?	**ah**-blah oos-**ted** in-**glehs**
I don't speak Spanish	No hablo español	no **ah**-bloh es-pahn-**yol**
I don't understand (you)	No entiendo	no en-tee-**en**-doh
I understand (you)	Entiendo	en-tee-**en**-doh
I don't know	No sé	no seh
I am American/ British	Soy americano (americana)/ inglés(a)	soy ah-meh-ree-**kah**-no (ah-meh-ree-**kah**-nah)/ in-**glehs** (ah)
What's your name?	¿Cómo se llama usted?	koh-mo seh **yah**-mah oos-**ted**
My name is . . .	Me llamo . . .	may **yah**-moh
What time is it?	¿Qué hora es?	keh **o**-rah es
It is one, two, three . . . o'clock.	Es la una. . . . Son las dos, tres	es la **oo**-nah/sohn lahs dohs, tress
Yes, please/ No, thank you	Sí, por favor/ No, gracias	**see** pohr fah-**vor**/ no **grah**-see-us

How?	¿Cómo?	**koh**-mo
When?	¿Cuándo?	**kwahn**-doh
This/Next week	Esta semana/la semana que entra	**es**-teh seh-**mah**-nah/lah seh-**mah**-nah keh **en**-trah
This/Next month	Este mes/el próximo mes	**es**-teh mehs/el **proke**-see-mo mehs
This/Next year	Este año/el año que viene	**es**-teh **ahn**-yo/el **ahn**-yo keh vee-**yen**-ay
Yesterday/today/tomorrow	Ayer/hoy/mañana	ah-**yehr**/oy/mahn-**yah**-nah
This morning/afternoon	Esta mañana/tarde	**es**-tah mahn-**yah**-nah/**tar**-deh
Tonight	Esta noche	**es**-tah **no**-cheh
What?	¿Qué?	keh
What is it?	¿Qué es esto?	keh es **es**-toh
Why?	¿Por qué?	pore **keh**
Who?	¿Quién?	kee-**yen**
Where is . . . ?	¿Dónde está . . . ?	**dohn**-deh es-**tah**
the train station?	la estación del tren?	la es-tah-see-**on** del **train**
the subway station?	la estación del Tren subterráneo?	la es-ta-see-**on** del trehn soob-tair-**ron**-a-o
the bus stop?	la parada del autobús?	la pah-**rah**-dah del oh-toh-**boos**
the post office?	la oficina de correos?	la oh-fee-**see**-nah deh koh-**reh**-os
the bank?	el banco?	el **bahn**-koh
the hotel?	el hotel?	el oh-**tel**
the store?	la tienda?	la tee-**en**-dah
the cashier?	la caja?	la **kah**-hah
the museum?	el museo?	el moo-**seh**-oh
the hospital?	el hospital?	el ohss-pee-**tal**
the elevator?	el ascensor?	el ah-**sen**-sohr
the bathroom?	el baño?	el **bahn**-yoh
Here/there	Aquí/allá	ah-**key**/ah-**yah**
Open/closed	Abierto/cerrado	ah-bee-**er**-toh/ser-**ah**-doh
Left/right	Izquierda/derecha	iss-key-**er**-dah/dare-**eh**-chah
Straight ahead	Derecho	dare-**eh**-choh
Is it near/far?	¿Está cerca/lejos?	es-**tah sehr**-kah/**leh**-hoss
I'd like . . .	Quisiera . . .	kee-see-**ehr**-ah
a room	un cuarto/una habitación	oon **kwahr**-toh/**oo**-nah ah-bee-tah-see-**on**
the key	la llave	lah **yah**-veh
a newspaper	un periódico	oon pehr-ee-**oh**-dee-koh
a stamp	un sello de correo	oon **seh**-yo deh koh-**reh**-oh

I'd like to buy . . .	Quisiera comprar . . .	kee-see-**ehr**-ah kohm-**prahr**
cigarettes	cigarrillos	ce-ga-**ree**-yohs
matches	cerillos	ser-**ee**-ohs
a dictionary	un diccionario	oon deek-see-oh-**nah**-ree-oh
soap	jabón	hah-**bohn**
sunglasses	gafas de sol	**ga**-fahs deh sohl
suntan lotion	loción bronceadora	loh-see-**ohn** brohn-seh-ah-**do**-rah
a map	un mapa	oon **mah**-pah
a magazine	una revista	**oon**-ah reh-**veess**-tah
paper	papel	pah-**pel**
envelopes	sobres	**so**-brehs
a postcard	una tarjeta postal	**oon**-ah tar-**het**-ah post-**ahl**
How much is it?	¿Cuánto cuesta?	**kwahn**-toh **kwes**-tah
It's expensive/ cheap	Está caro/barato	es-**tah kah**-roh/ bah-**rah**-toh
A little/a lot	Un poquito/ mucho	oon poh-**kee**-toh/ **moo**-choh
More/less	Más/menos	mahss/**men**-ohss
Enough/ toomuch/ too little	Suficiente/ demasiado/ muy poco	soo-fee-see-**en**-teh/ deh-mah-see-**ah**-doh/ **moo**-ee poh-koh
Telephone	Teléfono	tel-**ef**-oh-no
Telegram	Telegrama	teh-leh-**grah**-mah
I am ill	Estoy enfermo(a)	es-**toy** en-**fehr**-moh(mah)
Please call a doctor	Por favor llame a un medico	pohr fah-**vor ya**-meh ah oon **med**-ee-koh
Help!	¡Auxilio! ¡Ayuda! ¡Socorro!	owk-**see**-lee-oh/ ah-**yoo**-dah/ soh-**kohr**-roh
Fire!	¡Incendio!	en-**sen**-dee-oo
Caution!/Look out!	¡Cuidado!	kwee-**dah**-doh

On the Road

Avenue	Avenida	ah-ven-**ee**-dah
Broad, tree-lined boulevard	Bulevar	boo-leh-**var**
Fertile plain	Vega	**veh**-gah
Highway	Carretera	car-reh-**ter**-ah
Mountain pass, Street	Puerto Calle	poo-**ehr**-toh **cah**-yeh
Waterfront promenade	Rambla	**rahm**-blah
Wharf	Embarcadero	em-bar-cah-**deh**-ro

In Town

Cathedral	Catedral	cah-teh-**dral**
Church	Templo/Iglesia	**tem**-plo/ee-**glehs**-see-ah
City hall	Casa de gobierno	kah-sah deh go-bee-**ehr**-no

Door, gate	Puerta portón	poo-**ehr**-tah por-**ton**
Entrance/exit	Entrada/salida	en-**trah**-dah/sah-**lee**-dah
Inn, rustic bar, or restaurant	Taverna	tah-**vehr**-nah
Main square	Plaza principal	plah-thah prin-see-**pahl**
Market	Mercado	mer-**kah**-doh
Neighborhood	Barrio	**bahr**-ree-o
Traffic circle	Glorieta	glor-ee-**eh**-tah
Wine cellar, wine bar, or wine shop	Bodega	boh-**deh**-gah

Dining Out

A bottle of . . .	Una botella de . . .	**oo**-nah bo-**teh**-yah deh
A cup of . . .	Una taza de . . .	**oo**-nah **tah**-thah deh
A glass of . . .	Un vaso de . . .	oon **vah**-so deh
Ashtray	Un cenicero	oon sen-ee-**seh**-roh
Bill/check	La cuenta	lah **kwen**-tah
Bread	El pan	el pahn
Breakfast	El desayuno	el deh-sah-**yoon**-oh
Butter	La mantequilla	lah man-teh-**key**-yah
Cheers!	¡Salud!	sah-**lood**
Cocktail	Un aperitivo	oon ah-pehr-ee-**tee**-voh
Dinner	La cena	lah **seh**-nah
Dish	Un plato	oon **plah**-toh
Menu of the day	Menú del día	meh-**noo** del **dee**-ah
Enjoy!	¡Buen provecho!	bwehn pro-**veh**-cho
Fixed-price menu	Menú fijo o turistico	meh-**noo** **fee**-hoh oh too-**ree**-stee-coh
Fork	El tenedor	el ten-eh-**dor**
Is the tip included?	¿Está incluida la propina?	es-**tah** in-cloo-**ee**-dah lah pro-**pee**-nah
Knife	El cuchillo	el koo-**chee**-yo
Large portion of savory snacks	Raciónes	rah-see-**oh**-nehs
Lunch	La comida	lah koh-**mee**-dah
Menu	La carta, el menú	lah **cart**-ah, el meh-**noo**
Napkin	La servilleta	lah sehr-vee-**yet**-ah
Pepper	La pimienta	lah pee-me-**en**-tah
Please give me	Por favor déme	pore fah-**vor** **deh**-meh
Salt	La sal	lah sahl
Savory snacks	Tapas	**tah**-pahs
Spoon	Una cuchara	**oo**-nah koo-**chah**-rah
Sugar	El azúcar	el ah-**thu**-kar
Waiter!/Waitress!	¡Por favor Señor/ Señorita!	pohr fah-**vor** sen-**yor**/ sen-yor-**ee**-tah

MENU GUIDE

With so much meat on the menu, you'll need to know how to order it: *jugoso* (juicy) means medium rare, *vuelta y vuelta* (flipped back and forth) means rare, and *vivo por adentro* (alive inside) is barely warm in the middle. Argentines like their meat *bien cocido* (well cooked).

aceite de olivo: olive oil

alfajores: cookies

arroz: rice

bife de lomo: filet mignon

bife de chorizo: like a New York steak, but double the size

budín de pan: Argentine version of bread pudding

cabrito: roasted kid

cafecito: espresso

café con leche: coffee with milk

centolla: giant crab

chimichurri: a sauce of oil, garlic, and salt

chinchulines: tripe

chorizos: thick, spicy pork-and-beef sausages

churros: baton-shaped donuts for dipping in hot chocolate

ciervo: deer

civito: kid

cordero: lamb

cortado: coffee "cut" with a drop of milk

dulce de leche: a sweet caramel sauce served on pancakes, in pastries, on cookies, and on ice cream

empanadas: meat pies

ensalada de fruta: fruit salad (sometimes fresh, sometimes canned)

estofado: beef stew

facturas: small pastries

huevos: eggs

humitas: steamed cornhusks wrapped around corn meal and cheese

jamón: ham

lechón: roasted suckling pig

lengua: tongue

licuado: milk shake

locro: local stew, usually made with hard corn cooked slowly with meat and vegetables

lomo: pork

medialuna: croissant

mejillones: mussels

merluza: hake

milanesa: breaded meat cutlet, usually veal

milanesa a la neopolitana: a breaded veal cutlet with melted mozzarella cheese and tomato sauce

mollejas: sweetbreads

morcillas: blood sausages

pejerrey: a kind of mackerel

pollo: chicken

provoleta: grilled provolone cheese sprinkled with olive oil and oregano

puchero: meat and vegetables in a broth
queso: cheese
salchichas: long, thin sausages
sambayon: an alcohol-infused custard ice cream
tamales: ground corn baked with potatoes and meat and tied up in a corn husk
tenedor libre: all-you-can-eat meat and salad bar
tinto: red wine
trucha: trout

INDEX

NOTES

NOTES

NOTES

NOTES

FODOR'S KEY TO THE GUIDES

America's guidebook leader publishes guides for every kind of traveler. Check out our many series and find your perfect match.

FODOR'S GOLD GUIDES

America's favorite travel-guide series offers the most detailed insider reviews of hotels, restaurants, and attractions in all price ranges, plus great background information, smart tips, and useful maps.

COMPASS AMERICAN GUIDES

Stunning guides from top local writers and photographers, with gorgeous photos, literary excerpts, and colorful anecdotes. A must-have for culture mavens, history buffs, and new residents.

FODOR'S CITYPACKS

Concise city coverage in a guide plus a foldout map. The right choice for urban travelers who want everything under one cover.

FODOR'S EXPLORING GUIDES

Hundreds of color photos bring your destination to life. Lively stories lend insight into the culture, history, and people.

FODOR'S TRAVEL HISTORIC AMERICA

For travelers who want to experience history firsthand, this series gives in-depth coverage of historic sights, plus nearby restaurants and hotels. Themes include the Thirteen Colonies, the Old West, and the Lewis and Clark Trail.

FODOR'S POCKET GUIDES

For travelers who need only the essentials. The best of Fodor's in pocket-size packages for just $9.95.

FODOR'S FLASHMAPS

Every resident's map guide, with dozens of easy-to-follow maps of public transit, restaurants, shopping, museums, and more.

FODOR'S CITYGUIDES

Sourcebooks for living in the city: thousands of in-the-know listings for restaurants, shops, sports, nightlife, and other city resources.

FODOR'S AROUND THE CITY WITH KIDS

Up to 68 great ideas for family days, recommended by resident parents. Perfect for exploring in your own backyard or on the road.

FODOR'S HOW TO GUIDES

Get tips from the pros on planning the perfect trip. Learn how to pack, fly hassle-free, plan a honeymoon or cruise, stay healthy on the road, and travel with your baby.

FODOR'S LANGUAGES FOR TRAVELERS

Practice the local language before you hit the road. Available in phrase books, cassette sets, and CD sets.

KAREN BROWN'S GUIDES

Engaging guides—many with easy-to-follow inn-to-inn itineraries—to the most charming inns and B&Bs in the U.S.A. and Europe.

OTHER GREAT TITLES FROM FODOR'S

Baseball Vacations, The Complete Guide to the National Parks, Family Vacations, Golf Digest's Places to Play, Great American Drives of the East, Great American Drives of the West, Great American Vacations, Healthy Escapes, National Parks of the West, Skiing USA.

At bookstores everywhere.   www.fodors.com/books